FAITH:
JEWISH PERSPECTIVES

Emunot: Jewish Philosophy and Kabbalah

Series Editor:
Dov Schwartz (Bar-Ilan University)

EDITORIAL BOARD
Ada Rapoport-Albert (University College, London)
Gad Freudenthal (C.N.R.S, Paris)
Gideon Freudenthal (Tel Aviv University)
Moshe Idel (Hebrew University, Jerusalem)
Raphael Jospe (Bar-Ilan University)
Ephraim Kanarfogel (Yeshiva University)
Menachem Kellner (Haifa University)
Daniel Lasker (Ben-Gurion University, Beer Sheva)

FAITH: JEWISH PERSPECTIVES

Edited by AVI SAGI
and DOV SCHWARTZ
Assistant Editor:
YAKIR ENGLANDER

Boston
2014

Supported by: The Continental Fund,
The Program for Hermeneutics and Cultural Studies,
Bar-Ilan University, Israel.

Library of Congress Cataloging-in-Publication Data:
A catalog record for this title is available from the Library of Congress.

Copyright © 2013 Academic Studies Press
All rights reserved

ISBN 978-1-61811-282-8 (hardback)
ISBN 978-1-61811-283-5 (electronic)
ISBN 978-1-61811-304-7 (paperback)

Cover design by Ivan Grave

Published by Academic Studies Press in 2013, paperback 2014.

28 Montfern Avenue
Brighton, MA 02135, USA
press@academicstudiespress.com
www.academicstudiespress.com

In memory of Tal Zvi Kurzweil,
beloved son of Yaffa and David,
murdered in the flower of his youth
when studying Torah in Atzmona
24 Adar 5762

Contents

Avi Sagi and Dov Schwartz
    Introduction. 8

1. Conceptual Analysis

Avi Sagi
    Faith as Temptation 12

Eliezer Goldman
    On Non-Illusory Faith 123

David Shatz
    On Undermining the Beliefs of Others:
    Religion and The Ethics of Persuasion 137

Tamar Ross
    Religious Belief in a Postmodern Age 188

Gili Zivan
    Faith in the Face of Bereavement and Loss:
    Coping with the Question of Evil in the World 241

2. Kabbalah and Hasidism

Lawrence Kaplan
    Faith, Rebellion, and Heresy
    in the Writings of Rabbi Azriel of Gerona. 278

Ron Margolin
    On the Essence of Faith in Hasidism:
    An Historical-Theoretical Perspective 302

Dov Schwartz
    "Beyond Reason", on Faith in the Philosophy of Chabad 367

Zvi Mark
    Faith and Song in the Poetry of Zelda: on the Mystical
    Elements in Zelda's Ars Poetica and their Hasidic Origins 384

3. Persons and Ideas

Dorit Lemberger
   "My desire for the living God hath constrained me":
   Belief as Unfulfilled Desire in the Writings of Rabbi
   Judah Halevi 418

Isaac Hershkowitz
   The Strengthening of Faith in Orthodox Discourse:
   A Reevaluation of Models of Faith 457

Shraga Bar On
   Hillel Zeitlin in Search of God:
   An Analysis of Zeitlin's Meditation 'The Thirst'. 478

Tzahi Weiss
   A Metamorphosis in the Perception
   of God in Bialik's Poetry 500

Dov Schwartz
   Dialogue and Faith: *The Lonely Man of Faith* 513

Ronny Miron
   Unity and Fragmentation of the Self in Leibowitz's Idea
   of Faith and their Repercussions: A Critical Perspective 545

Index 584

Introduction
Avi Sagi and Dov Schwartz

The concept of "faith" has undergone fundamental changes in the course of time, and many different layers of meaning have been poured into it. In the biblical period, for instance, the term denoted mainly that individuals trusted in and relied on God. In medieval rationalist literature, faith was perceived as an epistemic concept, which reflected a kind of knowledge or lack of knowledge about God. Faith was examined vis-à-vis the concept of knowledge. Mystical traditions fluctuated between a perception of faith as a kind of knowledge (about the structure of the *sefiroth*, for instance), and an experiential outlook indifferent to epistemic attainments. Later, in the modern period, faith acquired open and intricate meanings. This process accelerated in the postmodern era, which questioned the very possibility of justifying truth claims about the world, and all the more so about God.

Given this reversal, the focus of faith shifted from the epistemic relationship between the individual and the object of faith (God or the world) to the individual's internal relationship, within the self. Against this background, we can understand Paul Tillich's statement: "Faith is the state of being ultimately concerned: the dynamics of faith are the dynamics of man's ultimate concern."[1] Faith, then, is a kind of disposition that places the individual in a particular relationship with himself. In this context, faith is perceived as the organizing principle of the "self" and God appears as part of the subject's inner world, meaningful only within this inner relationship. God loses metaphysic transcendent significance and becomes a component of the person's "language game."

Other approaches retain a notion of faith as referring to the human relationship with an external object, except that this relationship is no longer epistemic but a priori, a fundamental assumption through which the believer perceives the world and relates to the divine. Faith does not add knowledge and, instead, is a primary factor. An important question in modern philosophy touches on the basis of this primary experience: is it

---

[1] Paul Tillich, *Dynamics of Faith* (New York: Harper and Row, 1957), 3.

a voluntary action or do believers find themselves within the experience of faith against their will? If so, faith is a given. A further question, which concerns phenomenologists and philosophers of religion, is whether faith can be understood through other means (psychological, epistemic, and so forth), or whether it is only comprehensible from the inside, that is, from within the religious world. Yet another layer of the meaning of faith deals with the question of whether a subjective experience of faith is fundamentally communicative, meaning that it includes intelligible and transmittable universal elements, or whether it is a private experience that we can point to or talk about through indirect means (poetic, lyrical, and so forth), but never fully decipher.

The Jewish discourse on faith developed through a conscious and unconscious dialogue with the surrounding world. It is an impressive fact that the first systematic philosophical treatise written in the Middle Ages is *The Book of Beliefs and Opinions* by R. Saadia Gaon. Scholars have long considered the motivations behind the writing of this book. Unquestionably, Saadia was writing in reaction to the surroundings, as evident by his recourse in the introduction to a metaphor of the Jew as sinking in the water of doubts. These doubts, rather than an inner rift, denote a threat from Moslem or Karaite theology. *The Book of Beliefs and Opinions* strives to demonstrate that Judaism is also involved in a systematic discussion of faith and of questions that follow from it. Though the concept of faith *per se* is interpreted through terms in use in other theological traditions (Mutazilites, Karaites), it soon came to be perceived as reflecting an inner debate within Judaism. Maimonides' concept of faith conveys the internalization of the dialogue with the outside world. Following Moslem philosophy, Maimonides defines belief as the correspondence between reality and the concept's representation in the mind (*Guide of the Perplexed* I:50). Maimonides assumes that outside tradition embodies the inner content of the Torah. In the twentieth century, the many meanings of faith permeate the thought of R. Abraham Yitzhak Kook, whereas R. Joseph B. Soloveitchik shifted the concept of faith to the inner realm of personal existence, according to views prevalent in religious existentialism.

This book presents various manifestations of the concept of faith in Judaism as a tradition engaged in a dialogue with the outside world. The studies presented here obviously do not encompass the entire spectrum of meanings that faith assumes in Jewish discourse, but they do present the main outline, reflecting various junctions and turns in Jewish thought over the ages. This book, then, is an opening and an invitation to an ongoing conversation with faith.

We are grateful to all the participants in this volume for their contribution and for their cooperation. Special thanks to our assistants, Liat Lavi and Yakir Englander. Without them, we might not have been able to bring this project to its conclusion.

May 2012

1
CONCEPTUAL ANALYSIS

Faith as Temptation*

Avi Sagi

> Love needs a lock, so that it might spread only as needed.
> —Judah Aryeh Leib Alter, *Sefat Emet*[1]

> However intense, passion should not exceed its limits, and all acts should be performed properly.
> —Martin Buber, *Or ha-Ganuz*[2]

> It is perfectly obvious that a man who devotes his entire life to kites does not lack a germ of madness. The only question here is one of interpretation. Some call it a "germ of madness," others speak of a "holy spark." At times it is hard to distinguish one from the other. But if you truly love someone or something, give it all you have and all you are, and forget about the rest…
> —Romain Gary, *Les Cerfs-volants*[3]

I. Introduction

In different religious traditions, faith and temptation appear as antithetical. Believers are the ones who succeed in overcoming temptations that lead them outside the path of faith, whereas the tempted ones are those who fail and choose sin. The central place that religious discourse devotes to the temptations of the evil inclination points to the fear of it and to the perception of faith as its proper remedy. Faith is what will protect human beings from the evil inclination and lead them safely to redemption and salvation. This approach is articulated clearly in Talmudic literature:

---

* Many thanks are owed to Batya Stein, who translated this article and was also a critical reader. Her insightful comments, her superb translation, and her commitment helped to develop the final version. I would also like to thank my colleague and assistant Yakir Englander for his valuable help in the preparation of this article.
[1] Judah Aryeh Leib Alter, *Sefat Emet*, vol. 1 (Jerusalem: 1971), 72 (Hebrew).
[2] Martin Buber, *Or ha-Ganuz* (Jerusalem: WZO, 1971), 102 (Hebrew).
[3] Romain Gary, *Les Cerfs-volants* (Paris: Gallimard, 1980), 17.

> The Holy One, blessed be He, spoke unto Israel: "My children! I created the evil inclination, but I [also] created the Torah. If you devote yourselves to the Torah, you will not be delivered into its hand, for it is said: "If thou doest well, shalt thou not be accepted?" (Genesis 4: 7). But if you do not devote yourselves to the Torah, you shall be delivered into its hand, for it is written, "sin crouches at the door." Furthermore, the most important concern of the evil inclination is you, for it is said, "and to thee shall be his desire." But if you will, you can rule over it, for it is said, "yet thou mayst rule over him."[4]

In their prayers, believers turn to God asking to be saved from temptation. The Talmud (TB Berakhot 60b) reads:

> On going to bed, one says ... May it be your will, O Lord, my God, to make me lie down in peace, and grant me a share in your law and accustom me to comply with the commandments. Do not accustom me to transgression and bring me not to sin, or to iniquity, or to a test, or to contempt. And let the good inclination have sway over me and let not the evil inclination have sway over me.

As Jacob Licht noted,[5] this Talmudic text does not specify the nature of the test, but the context clarifies that believers view it as an incitement to transgression and as the evil inclination. The test, then, is a form of temptation to sin that the supplicant asks God's help in avoiding.[6] In light of this widespread belief, the possibility that faith itself will be thought of as a temptation to commit the sin that is its opposite appears fundamentally unfounded.

---

[4] TB Kiddushin 30b. For further discussion of the relationship between the evil inclination and the Torah in rabbinic literature, see Ephraim E. Urbach, *The Sages: Their Concepts and Beliefs*, trans. Israel Abrahams (Jerusalem: Magnes Press, 1975), 471-483.

[5] See Jacob Licht, *"Testing" in the Hebrew Scriptures and in Judaism of the Second Temple Period* (Jerusalem: Magnes Press, 1973), 91-92 (Hebrew).

[6] Licht claims that the identification of the test with temptation to sin is a rabbinic innovation (ibid., 87-88). This view of the test is widespread in the New Testament. See, for instance, Matthew 6: 13; 26: 41; James 1: 13-14. Elsewhere in his book (p. 14, note 3), Licht offers an hypothesis on the grounds for the turnabout that Christianity effected in the perception of the test—from the biblical view of it as a kind of hard and oppressive event, to one that identifies it with temptation. This account obviously does not explain why no such turnabout occurred in rabbinic literature as well.

In religious world views as well, the widespread approach is that what appears as a manifestation of faith is sometimes merely a delusion, disguising personal interest as faith. Abraham Joshua Heschel sensitively describes this situation as follows:

> Religious thinking, believing, feeling are among the most deceptive activities of the human spirit. We often assume it is God we believe in, but in reality, it may be a symbol of personal interests that we dwell upon. We may assume that we feel drawn to God.... We may assume it is God we care for, but it may be our own ego we are concerned with. To examine our religious existence is, therefore, a task to be performed constantly.[7]

According to this view, attempts to tease out faith from narrow, tempting, and misleading human contexts face many obstacles. Faith itself, however, is "pure." Faith and a life of faith have no dimension of temptation or deception.[8] To be precise: from a secular perspective that questions faith altogether, the view that faith is a temptation is perfectly plausible. The secular hero is the autonomous person who navigates reality as the exclusive sovereign and bears absolute responsibility for it. Faith and religion could be perceived as a kind of weakness and, in Camus' terms, an "escape,"[9] that is, a renunciation of consciousness, freedom, and responsibility in order to find consolation and peace in the bosom of religion.[10]

Both radical secularism and religiosity assume a complex association between temptation and faith, but differ concerning their actual relationship. Whereas radical secularism assumes that faith is a temptation

---

[7] Abraham Joshua Heschel, *God in Search of Man: A Philosophy of Judaism* (New York: Farrar, Straus and Giroux, 1983), 9. See also idem, *A Passion for Truth* (Woodstock, VT: Jewish Lights, 1995), 129.

[8] R. Judah Loew b. Bezalel (Maharal), *Derekh Hayyim, on M. Avot* (Jerusalem: 1971), Part III: 1, 109-110.

[9] See Albert Camus, *The Myth of Sisyphus*, trans. Justin O'Brien (Harmondsworth: Penguin Books, 1975), 35. For an extensive discussion of faith and religion in Camus' thought, see Avi Sagi, *Albert Camus and the Philosophy of the Absurd*, trans. Batya Stein (Amsterdam-New York: Rodopi, 2002).

[10] On this question see, for instance, Immanuel Kant, "An Answer to the Question: What is Enlightenment?" in *What is Enlightenment? Eighteenth-Century Answers and Twentieth-Century Questions*, ed. James Schmidt (Berkeley, CA: University of California Press, 1996), 59-60.

that emerges when confronting the anxiety of existence, the religious stance claims that temptation crouches outside the door of religion. This analysis, then, apparently allows for the option of faith appearing as a temptation in a secular context but not in a religious one. Contrary to this commonly held view, my thesis here is that faith may appear as a temptation *within* religious life. The analysis of this phenomenon will shed light on the phenomenon of faith in general and on Jewish faith in particular.

My basic assumption here distinguishes between *the temptation of faith* and *faith as temptation*. Psychological and sociological theories offer various answers to the question: what is the power of faith to tempt? Why are people attracted to and captivated by religious faith? The temptation of faith is part of the relationship between faith and life contexts external to religion, when faith emerges as a solution to problems emerging in these contexts. By contrast, faith as a temptation is a phenomenon within the core of religious existence.

Despite this sharp distinction between "the temptation of faith" and "faith as temptation," the relationships between them are not at all simple. The "temptation of faith" is based on human needs such as the demand for absolute authority, for divine rather than human order. Within a religious life-context, these needs could be translated into a stance called here "faith as temptation." If a person needs authority, if a person is unable to confront the anxiety of human freedom and finds refuge in religion, these needs could lead to a religious position that, from my perspective here, could be called "temptation." The temptation of faith, then, could lead to faith as temptation.

Freud points to the connection between these two phenomena. He assumes that the temptation of faith rests on the needs satisfied by religion: "it gives them [human beings] information about the origin and coming into existence in the universe, it assures them of its protection and of ultimate happiness in the ups and downs of life and it directs their thoughts and actions by precepts which it lays down with its whole authority."[11] According to Freud, religiosity is a displacement of the parents-children relationship:

---

[11] Sigmund Freud, "The Question of a *Weltanschauung*," in *The Complete Introductory Lectures on Psychoanalysis*, trans. James Strachey (New York: W. W. Norton, 1966), 625.

Their parents' prohibitions and demands persist within them as a moral conscience. With the help of this same system of rewards and punishments, God rules the world of men. The amount of protection and happy satisfaction assigned to an individual depends on the fulfillment of the ethical demands; his love of God and his consciousness of being loved by God are the foundations of the security with which he is armed against the dangers of the external world and of his human environment.[12]

For Freud, then, the temptation that generates faith also determines its nature. Camus may have followed him when formulating the following statement, which ties together the temptation of faith and faith as a temptation: "They [religious existentialist thinkers] embrace the God that consumes them. It is through humility that hope enters in."[13]

Although not absolutely separate, however, these two phenomena are not necessarily connected either, and for two reasons—one analytical and one theoretical-methodological. Analytically, the phenomenon of faith as temptation could originate in a religious stance that does not draw on the same needs that generated the temptation of faith. In a view of religion such as that offered by Kierkegaard and Leibowitz, religion is not a response to distress, at least not in these thinkers' own consciousnesses.[14] Quite the contrary, it is religion that creates anxiety and crisis as fundamental components of religiosity.[15] Kierkegaard, as shown below, explicitly develops the thesis of faith as temptation.

From a theoretical-methodological perspective, Clifford Geertz justly rejects distress theories as a basis for explaining cultural phenomena: "The link between the causes of ideology and its effects seems adventitious because the connecting element—the autonomous process of symbolic formulation—is passed over in virtual silence."[16]

---

[12] Freud, "The Question of a *Weltanschauung*," 628.//
[13] Camus, *The Myth of Sisyphus*, 121.
[14] I stress this because Leibowitz's radical religious version could serve to meet psychological needs, even though it might contradict his conscious religious approach.
[15] For an analysis and a comparison between them see Avi Sagi, "The 'Akedah'—A Comparative Study of Kierkegaard and Leibowitz," *Daat* 23 (1989): 121-134 (Hebrew).
[16] Clifford Geertz, *The Interpretation of Cultures: Selected Essays* (New York: Basic Books, 1973), 207.

The reduction of a cultural phenomenon, including all its psychological or sociological causes, fails to explain the full meaning of a cultural system and of the mutual relationships between symbolic systems. Analyzing the phenomenon of faith as temptation by reducing it to the temptation of faith is therefore misleading.

From a religious perspective, the idea that the state of faith is a state of temptation seems paradoxical. But the citation from *Sefat Emet* in the epigraph hints at a religious phenomenon in need of clarification: over-religiosity or, in the term I seek to coin here, faith as temptation. Given that this idea is at the very core of the discussion that follows, only an initial and provisional account of it is warranted at this stage.

The idea of faith as temptation means that basic foundations of faith could, as such, lead individuals to develop a stance perceived as negative from a religious perspective. People who embark on a voyage of faith begin as believers and adopt religious dispositions. Eventually, however, these dispositions create a state of temptation, ostensibly requiring believers to overcome them. But such a step seems impossible, since overcoming the basic dispositions of faith means renouncing faith itself. The believer's paradoxical aim, then, is to renounce the temptation but not the dispositions that enable it.

Clarifying the idea of faith as temptation, at least at this preliminary stage, requires noting its differences with the standard struggle of religion against idolatry. Even if we acknowledge that idolatry is a constant temptation, the struggle against it is entirely different from the struggle with faith as temptation. In the struggle against idolatry, religion tries to draw a distinction between the God that merits worship and the gods or divine images whose worship is forbidden. This struggle, then, focuses on the object of religious worship, whereas faith as temptation touches on the act of faith or, more specifically, on the disposition of the believer.

The problem posed by idolatry is thus basically different from the problem posed by faith as temptation. In the former, faith is expected to formulate in clear, cognitive, and rational terms the distinction between true and false objects of worship. Once this distinction has been drawn, the focus of religious worship on a false object is no longer part of faith. By contrast, faith as temptation is not based on a cognitive mistake but is part of authentic religious life, an outgrowth of the believer's basic religious stance. Faith can protect believers from sliding into idolatry—

if believers study their religious faith carefully, they can be sure they will not be misled. By contrast, religion cannot provide protection from faith as temptation, since temptation is inherent in the religious experience.

The final conclusion warranted by this idea is that faith cannot be exhausted through an unreflective, uncritical disposition. The analysis, critique, and reinterpretation of the religious disposition to some extent imply the renunciation of the temptation option, but this renunciation becomes impossible without the adoption of a critical stance. In Dostoevsky's formulation: "If you found out that you believed in God, you'd believe in Him, but since you still don't know, you don't believe yet."[17] Consciousness, and thus obviously critical consciousness, is not merely an additional and unnecessary stage of faith but indeed its constitutive foundation.

How should this riddle be understood? What does it mean that faith has a critical and reflective dimension? Do (or can) religious traditions in general, and Jewish tradition in particular, endorse a view of faith as temptation? Does this idea describe the religious experience, or is this a stipulative idea that seeks to reconfigure the religious field from an extra-religious perspective? To deal with these questions and explicate the idea

---

[17] Fedor Dostoevsky, *The Possessed*, trans. Andrew R. MacAndrew (New York: New American Library, 1962), 225. Nikolay Vsyevolodovitch hurls this sentence at Kirylov, who throws it back at him: "If he believes in God, he doesn't believe he believes, and if he doesn't believe, he doesn't believe that he doesn't" (634). Kirylov thus claims that Nikolay has been beguiled and captivated by the idea he believes in, which causes him to lose his capacity for reflection. When he believes in an idea, then, he does not take a critical stance—he believes that he believes. Contrary to the blame that had been tossed at him, Kirylov strives to make faith, or lack of faith, a voluntary reflective gesture: "I must affirm my disbelief" (636). This thesis is repeated by the demon, who is the alter-ego of Ivan Karamazov: "What's the good of believing against your will? Besides, proofs are no help to believing, especially material proofs. Thomas believed, not because he saw Christ risen, but because he wanted to believe, before he saw" (*The Brothers Karamazov*, trans. Marc Slonim [New York: Vintage Books, 1955], 774). This view of faith thus assumes two concepts of faith: faith in God and faith in faith. Faith is thus a reflective will to believe in God; that is, the will that faith in God should guide human beings. This analysis points to the closeness between Dostoevsky's perception of the will and that of Harry Frankfurt. See Harry G. Frankfurt, "Freedom of the Will and the Concept of a Person," *The Journal of Philosophy* 68 (1971): 5-20.

of faith as temptation more fully, I turn to the analysis of several relevant issues in religious literature through a series of texts from religious tradition in general and Jewish tradition in particular. These texts do not exhaust the full range of sources, and other texts could easily be found that present antithetical views on the topics discussed. Nevertheless, the texts I discuss are important; they show awareness of the problematic of faith in dimensions relevant to the theme of faith as temptation. The question of what can be concluded from these sources about tradition *per se* is postponed to Section V. In the following sections, I examine texts that present variations on the idea of faith as temptation.

II. Religious Practice as a Temptation

In a conversation between the protagonists of Herman Hesse's *Narcissus and Goldmund*, Narcissus says to his friend: "We know what is good, it is written in the Commandments. But God is not contained only in the Commandments, you know; they are only an infinitesimal part of Him. A man may abide by the Commandments and be far from God."[18]

Hesse claims that closeness to God is not necessarily synonymous with religious practice. This claim would appear particularly relevant to Christianity, which places faith rather than practice at the center of religious existence. Even observant individuals, then, can be far removed from God if they are not in the desirable state of faith.

A similar stance, however, is also found in Jewish literature, which presents an even more radical approach, stating that religious practice itself could be a temptation. The key question will be: is this the temptation of the evil inclination or is this faith as temptation?

1. Religious Practice, the Temptation of the Evil Inclination, and Error

In *Tsava'at ha-Ribash* [The Will of R. Israel Ba'al Shem-Tov], we read:

> There are two kinds of men—one who is absolutely evil, who knows who his master is and intends to rebel against him, and

---

[18] Herman Hesse, *Narcissus and Goldmund*, trans. Ursule Molinaro (New York: Bantam Books, 1971), 31.

> another who has been blinded by the evil inclination and perceives himself as absolutely righteous, and appears so to others. Yet, although he studies ceaselessly, prays, and practices self-denial, his effort is pointless because he does not unite with the Creator, may He be blessed, and having proper faith means uniting with God at all times. This person does not understand the essence of worship, which is to study, to pray, and to perform the commandment for its own sake.[19]

According to this text, the evil inclination appears in two forms. In the first, its manifestation is clear, transparent, and revealed in acts against faith; in the second, it acts within faith, and through its practices. According to the Ba'al Shem-Tov, this concretization of the evil inclination through religious practice is actually more dangerous to the believer:

> He who is absolutely wicked may be healed when he awakens to repentance, returns to God with all his heart, and begs to be shown the path of light. The second [the one who belongs to the category of the manifestation of the evil inclination within faith], however, cannot repent because he fails to discern the glory and the work of the Creator and is righteous in his own eyes, so how could he repent?[20]

Repentance is possible only when people understand their circumstances. But when the evil inclination is manifest *within* religious practice, the individual develops a false consciousness that precludes repentance and self-correction. The Ba'al Shem-Tov then argues that the more typical manifestation of the evil inclination occurs within religious practice and is meant to deceive. This deceit overtakes human existence: "It also deceives him in that, when he becomes ill, he prays to God to be healed through the merit of the Torah and the commandments he had observed, and does not know he is mentioning his transgressions, since all is the temptation of the evil inclination."[21]

---

[19] Israel b. Eliezer (Besht), *Tsava'at ha-Ribash* (Kfar Habad: Otsar ha-Hasidim, 1975), 12, #74. See also p. 21, #117.
[20] Ibid.
[21] Ibid.

Religious practice could thus be a trap ensnaring the person lacking faith.[22] This approach resonates in the work of André Gide. Reviewing his life as a believer, old M. La Pérouse confesses:

> When I was young, I led a very austere life; I used to congratulate myself on my force of character every time I refused a solicitation in the street. I didn't understand that when I thought I was freeing myself, in reality I was becoming more and more the slave of my own pride. Every one of these triumphs over myself was another turn of the key in the door of my prison.[23]

As shown in Section III: 2 below, M. La Pérouse ascribes this phenomenon to God, who tempts humans to view their pride in their own achievements as a virtue. In this sense, the trend outlined by the Ba'al Shem-Tov is entirely different and better fitted to Jewish tradition: temptation originates in us, not in God.

Rivka Shatz Uffenheimer[24] points to an extreme quietist trend in hasidic literature that views halakhic practice as an external manifestation of the innermost core and as a negative expression of worship. Action is located in the external, interpersonal space and is thus marked by personal interest and will. She illustrates this idea with a statement by R. Hayyim Haykl of Amdur, who says: "Whoever performs an act, [does so] out of self-aggrandizement, for because he wishes to aggrandize himself he performs the act, while nobody knows when it stays within his thoughts [alone]. We thus find that the act comes about because of self-aggrandizement."[25]

---

[22] Cf. also R. Israel Lipkin (Salanter), *Or Israel* (Vilnius: 1900), 39-40 (Hebrew), who points to the phenomenon of false consciousness: "The sickness, the passion, and the error of the soul are its downfall. A passion blazes and desire burns to purify this defiled creature called impure, impure ... whenever man strives to follow truth and make innocence his beacon ... until he is shamed into replacing deceit with truth and disguising crime as justice." Similarly, R. Yehiel Mikhl of Zlotschov writes: "As the evil inclination wishes to incite man to sin, so does it wish to incite him to be overly righteous" (Buber, *Or ha-Ganuz*, 149).

[23] André Gide, *The Counterfeiters*, trans. Dorothy Bussy (New York: Alfred A Knopf, 1957), 109.

[24] See Rivka Schatz-Uffenheimer, *Hasidism as Mysticism: Quietistic Elements in Eighteenth Century Hasidic Thought*, trans. Jonathan Chipman (Jerusalem: Magnes Press, 1993), ch. 8.

[25] Ibid., 119.

According to this approach, the essence of religiosity is in an inner union with God, which intense activity actually prevents. Religious *conjunctio* is the state of annihilating the will and obliterating the ego.[26]

A prominent difference between the Ba'al Shem-Tov and R. Hayyim Haykl of Amdur concerns the issue of faith as temptation. The text of the Ba'al Shem-Tov does not embody the idea of faith as temptation, since temptation for him lies in detachment from faith rather than within religious practice as such, and only becomes possible through the pre-faith disposition of a person who "does not know the essence of worship." One who holds that faith is equated solely with practice, then, could fall into the trap of the evil inclination. Practice only makes sense if it embodies the proper religious disposition, one that is woven into the proper relationship between individuals and their God. In this text, therefore, it is not faith that appears as the basis of temptation. The source of temptation is non-faith, or more precisely, the development of a false consciousness that identifies faith with religious practice.

By contrast, R. Hayyim Haykl of Amdur offers an antinomian notion whereby practice as such, including religious practice—meaning observance of the commandments—*is* the temptation, since it is external action "without inner spiritual justification."[27] This formulation appears to epitomize the idea of faith as temptation.

And yet, even these radical statements do not denote the idea of faith as temptation. In a quietist spiritual approach of this type, faith is concretized in an inner spiritual experience rather than in practice. Thus, even in this view, the temptation of practice is the temptation of the evil inclination. The recognition that religious practice, and Torah study in particular, does not release us from the shackles of the evil inclination appears in the writings of R. Avraham b. Yehuda Leib. He contrasts the statement in TB Kiddushin at the opening of this discussion with that in TB Berakhot 5a:

> R. Levi bar Hamma says in the name of R. Simeon b. Lakish: A man should always stir up the good inclination against the evil inclination .... If he prevails over it, good! If not, let him occupy himself with Torah .... If he prevails over it, good! If not, let him remind himself of the day of death.

---

[26] Ibid., ch. 2.
[27] Ibid., 120.

Given the statement in TB Kiddushin that the Torah protects us from the evil inclination, R. Avraham finds it difficult to understand the view in TB Berakhot: "And when he is occupied with the Torah, why does he need anything else, when the Torah is a full and complete remedy?"[28] He answers this question as follows:

> And we should say so [that the Torah saves and protects] of one who engages in it for its own sake, as it says in TB Shabbat 88b, "to those who go to the right hand thereof it is a medicine of life; to those who go to the left hand thereof it is a deadly poison" that will not rescue them from the evil inclination.... On that, it was said, "If he does not prevail over it with the Torah," it is because he is not occupied with the Torah for its own sake, so he should recite the *Shema*, and if he does not prevail, let him remind himself of the day of death. What he means is that there are two ways of [being occupied with Torah] "not for its own sake": one is if he does it to vex his friend, and the other is if he does it for self-aggrandizement. On which it was said that, in order for him not to study in order to vex his friend, he should recite the *Shema*, which hints at the unity of God and the unity of the people of Israel. And in order not to boast of his erudition, he should remember the day of his death so as to be chastened and humiliated.[29]

According to this approach, religious practice in general and observance in particular attain the religious goal of human amendment only if the person develops appropriate dispositions before studying Torah and, should he fail to do so, after studying. What actually determines that he is engaged in the worship of God are these dispositions rather than religious practice *per se*.[30]

Furthermore, Torah study alone is no guarantee against error; indeed, Torah study could be woven into an error that turns people away from faith. R. Ouzziel offers a lucid formulation of this view:

> The radiance and splendor of the Torah will not be found in a vague soul holding nothing of its own, in impervious empty matter, in

---

[28] He relates here to the beginning of the passage from TB Kiddushin.
[29] "Ahavat Eitan," in *Ein Yaakov*, ed. Jacob b. Solomon ibn Habib, TB Kiddushin 30b, s.v. "*ve-samtem*."
[30] See also R. Asher Weiss, *Minhat Asher: Lessons and Conversations on Genesis* (Jerusalem: Minhat Asher Institute, 2004), 531 (Hebrew). See also Heschel, *A Passion for Truth*, 11.

an amorphous mass.... The Torah will be found in one who prepares and girds himself, who trains his feeling ... and mind and thought to understand it and penetrate its depth.... Delivering the Torah into the hands of stubborn, unbending people, allowing people who lack self-understanding and common sense to be teachers is not only unhelpful but can also be damaging.... In the hands of corrupt people who hold evil and trivial ideas, the Torah becomes pernicious to them.... "The words of the Torah have the power of life and death. Thus Raba said: to those who go to the right hand thereof it is a medicine of life; to those who go to the left hand thereof it is a deadly poison" (TB Shabbat 88b).[31]

R. Ouzziel argues that the meaning of the Torah is not immediately apparent; human beings expose its significance but, without a previous suitable disposition unconditioned by the Torah, this meaning is not properly disclosed. Indeed, in the absence of such dispositions, the Torah becomes harmful, an obstacle as it were. In his view, this is the meaning of M. Avot 1:1, "Moses *received* the Torah from Sinai." The emphasis on reception is meant to underscore

> that the receiver was the cause of the act of giving and, without him, that act would never have occurred.... What was received becomes the property of Moses and of all who follow him, until they deliver it to one they consider worthy of receiving and exceptionally preserving this unique treasure so that it should not become extinct nor change form.... And as the Torah will not be found among people who are wrong in their opinions and beliefs, nor will there be Torah and ethics in those who are corrupt ... which is why, before receiving the Torah, we must prepare ourselves and be ready to receive it.[32]

In sum, religious practice as such is no guarantee against the temptation of the evil inclination or against improper use of the Torah. Only a fitting religious disposition ensures proper religious practice.[33] The warranted conclusion is that, barring the appropriate religious disposition, religious practice too can be an expression of error or of the evil inclination's temptation rather than a temptation of faith.

---

[31] Ben-Zion Meir Hai Ouzziel, *Drashot Ouzziel on Avot* (Jerusalem: 1991), 3-4 (Hebrew).
[32] Ibid., 4-6.
[33] Except for the radical stance of R. Hayyim Haykl of Amdor.

2. Religious Devotion:
The Temptation of the Evil Inclination
and Faith as Temptation

Consider another text that presents a more complex view of what appears to be faith as temptation. R. Zvi Elimelech Shapira relates the story of a man devotedly committed to observing what appears to him as a commandment. Although this devotion is a religious requirement, it could be revealed as a temptation. How, then, should we distinguish devotion from temptation? R. Zvi Elimelech answers as follows:

> The sign of whether this is indeed a commandment or a deception of the evil inclination is whether the person feels a much greater passion to observe other commandments too. If he feels so concerning matters that are definitely commandments, such as ritual fringes, phylacteries, and Torah—good. But if he feels that he does not yearn as much for these other commandments, he will clearly understand that the passion he imagines he feels for this matter that he considers a commandment is a temptation of the evil inclination to entrap him.... And when he discerns the truth, he will choose it and depart (even) from the commandment he had imagined, since he will understand that his passion had been tainted.[34]

R. Zvi Elimelech understands that there are strong similarities between religious devotion and a passion that is entirely personal. In both cases, individuals are ready to invest all their powers in order to realize the object of their passion or their devotion. The distinction between these two situations cannot be based on the individual's subjective stance but on the status ascribed to the object. Subjective passion grants its object special status, since all it wishes is to consummate its desire for it.[35] By contrast, religious devotion ascribes equal weight to all objects of obligation. This attitude situates the personal disposition as a religious dispo-

---

[34] Zvi Elimelech Shapira, *Sefer Agra de-Kalah: On the Pentateuch* (Brooklyn, NY: Emet, 1993), 519 (Hebrew). For a similar approach, see Schatz-Uffenheimer, *Hasidism as Mysticism*, 126, in the story about R. Meshullam Feibush of Zbarazh.

[35] *Cf.* Martin Luther: "For what is not commanded—and is concerned for self rather than for the commands of God—that is surely the devil himself" (Martin Luther, "An Open Letter to the Christian Nobility," trans. C. M. Jacobs, in *Works of Martin Luther*, vol. 2 [Philadelphia: Muhlenberg Press, 1943], 131).

sition; granting equal weight to the entire range of obligations implies that a commandment is different from an object of personal passion.

R. Zvi Elimelech is clearly aware of the religious restraint evident in this attitude and its apparent contrast with the disposition of the pious, who strive to transcend the restraint that characterizes the religious stance. Further on in his discussion, R. Zvi Elimelech relates to a passage in TB Sukkah 52b, stating that the remedy to the evil inclination is "the house of study": 'If you encounter this scoundrel, drag him to the house of study." R. Zvi Elimelech notes in this regard that the house of study is not a remedy for the godly and pious:

> David said on this matter, "Preserve my soul for I am godly" [Psalms 86:2]. But dragging it to the house of study will make no difference to the evil inclination, for it will say, "You are godly, so act beyond the letter of the law." This could perhaps be a slightly elaborate interpretation, but the wise man will nevertheless note that one will encounter the temptation of the evil inclination more than once. (Ibid., 520)

In situations of special religious devotion, only God can help us avoid entrapment in the snare of religious temptation.

The epitome of a religious piety that is a temptation of faith is, according to R. Zvi Elimelech, the sin of Korah and his companions. Korah "took it upon himself, following the counsel of the evil inclination, that he is a son to Yitshar, the son of Kehat, the son of Levi, who were greatly pious men and, in his view, he must necessarily follow them and behave piously" (ibid.). Datan and Aviram behaved similarly:

> They too assumed it was logical that, since they were the children of Reuben, a penitent who began with penitence, one should behave piously and not be satisfied with merely a middle course.... That is why they assumed it was logical to follow their ancestors, behave piously, and pursue the commandments. (Ibid.)

This approach does not view Korah and his congregation as an ordinary sect of sinners intent on rebelling against faith and religion. Their sin stems from their consciousness of religious piety, which leads them to transcend the bounds of the religious framework.

The sin of Korah and his congregation is thus seemingly the paradigm of the temptation of faith, since the source of their passion is the temptation of religious devotion. On further scrutiny, however, this is not a clear case of temptation of faith either, since R. Zvi Elimelech's starting assumption is that the disposition of extreme passion for one commandment is a "deception of the evil inclination" (ibid., 519). The situation that R. Zvi Elimelech is describing is one of false consciousness, where the true motivation for action does not fit its conscious manifestation; only the conscious expression of the action is religious, not its motivation. Thus, the thesis of R. Zvi Elimelech resembles that found in *Tsava'at ha-Ribash*.

Other texts offer a clearer expression of faith as a temptation that grows from religious devotion. R. Nahman of Bratslav, revealing deep religious sensitivity, writes:

> On the matter of drawing close to God as well, the evil inclination is very great (meaning that, at times, excessive enthusiasm comes from the evil inclination...). Therefore, when giving the Torah, God warned Moses (Exodus 19: 21), "Go down, charge the people, lest they break through to the Lord to gaze," because the children of Israel were then standing at a high rung, and had to be warned about the evil inclination to be found when drawn close to God.[36]

R. Mordechai Yosef Leiner uses similar terms for the sin of Aaron's sons, Nadav and Avihu, describing it as an uncontrolled yearning for closeness to God:

> "After the death of the two sons of Aaron..., Speak unto Aaron thy brother that he come not at all times..." [Leviticus 16:1]. At all times means whenever you wish, that is, after you have seen that the holiness of Nadav and Avihu did not save them from sin when approaching God because, in their depth, love was greater than fear. God therefore warned him he should not imagine he could shield himself from this, and he should be more careful than they had been. He should always be aware of this feeling and know that human beings always need God's help. "Thus shall Aaron come" means that he will come on the very same matter that had concerned Nadav and Avihu, because they came in holiness and purity and great care, and only "with a young bullock for a sin

---

[36] R. Nahman of Bratslav, *Sefer Likkutei Moharan* (Benei Berak: 1972), 39a, #72 (Hebrew).

> offering," and so forth.[37] That is why God warns the High Priest not to come [to the holy place] at all times—that is, he is warned not to come at times of great love and joy but only restrainedly, in fear and respect.[38]

R. Leiner points to the danger inherent in the religious phenomenon—the yearning for divine closeness, which evolves within faith, may eliminate the gap between the human and the divine. But this intimacy, to which the religious soul is driven, is a religious sin.

How, then, do we protect ourselves from the temptation of faith to achieve this closeness? According to R. Leiner, by developing a disposition of fear that restrains and confines human beings within the borders of their existence. This confinement, *"tsimtsum"* in his terms, ensures that the barrier between the divine and the human will not be crossed. And yet, deeply aware of the sweeping power of the religious yearning for closeness, R. Leiner claims that the disposition of fear is insufficient, and "human beings always need God's help." Only God can help believers abstain from realizing their religious yearning.

R. Naftali Zvi Yehuda Berlin (*Ha-Netsiv*) also confronts the religious problematic of the yearning for God's closeness and its restraint, and he too relies on the story of Nadav and Avihu to present his view. R. Berlin finds the biblical formulation puzzling: "And Nadav and Avihu, the sons of Aaron, took each of them his censer, and put fire in it ... and offered strange fire before the Lord, which he commanded them not" (Leviticus 10:1):

> "Strange fire before the Lord, which he commanded them not" is an imprecise formulation. Since offering a strange fire had been forbidden, why say "which he commanded them not," implying they had been careless about it?... And in an interpretation ... they were driven by the fire of their passionate love for God, and the Torah says that the love of God is precious to God, but not in this way, which he commanded not.[39]

R. Berlin is well aware that the love of God is a worthy religious yearning, but forbidden when unrestrained; it is a religious temptation that should

---

[37] Mordechai Yosef Leiner, *Sefer Mei Hashiloah*, vol. 1 (Benei Berak: 1995), 114 (Hebrew).

[38] Mordechai Yosef Leiner, *Sefer Mei Hashiloah*, vol. 2 (Benei Berak: 1990), 80 (Hebrew).

[39] R. Zvi Yehuda Berlin (*Ha-Netsiv*), *Ha'amek Davar*, Leviticus, *ad locum*.

be curbed. In a kind of hidden controversy with R. Leiner, R. Berlin holds that, instead of relying on a change of the religious disposition to restrain the religious yearning, Halakhah should be used for this purpose.

R. Berlin's approach is not a local, episodic interpretation but the expression of a widely accepted religious conception evident in several sources. In his view, the sin of the two hundred and fifty "princes of the assembly" who joined Korah,[40] reflects a similar religious yearning:

> You must understand that the two hundred and fifty people were indeed leaders of Israel in every regard, including their fear of God. And their exclusion from the priesthood, precluding their love and their union with God, burnt as a fire within them, not because they sought power and false honor but because they wished to be sanctified and reach this rung through their worship. They too knew that Moses spoke the truth of God's word and should not be questioned. They merely searched God's will in their hearts and were willing to die for the sake of their love of God, for love is strong as death ... although they knew they would not be forgiven and Moses' words would surely be fulfilled. And that is why they are "sinners against their lives" (Numbers 17: 3), in that they sought to give up their lives only to reach the rungs of love and piety, contrary to God's will.[41]

Religious yearning can lead people to the border of the abyss, up to a readiness to give up their lives. According to R. Berlin, the only way to religious self-restraint is rigorous adherence to the halakhic norm, which restricts us and sets us within limited human reality.

R. Berlin assumes that juxtaposing the commandment of the fringes and the Korah story is meant to point to the remedy for religious passion: "And for this reason, this matter [the Korah story] is juxtaposed to the commandment of the fringes, because the pious were warned with a thread of blue lest, in their piety, they should depart from God's commandments.... And the two hundred and fifty who refused to do so, deserved their lot."[42]

Elsewhere, R. Berlin offers a typological distinction between two types of believers: "One, whose life follows the course of the many, earns

---
[40] See Numbers 16.
[41] Berlin, *Ha'amek Davar*, Numbers 16:1.
[42] Ibid.

a living and simply observes each commandment in its time. The other retreats to worship God in seclusion and immerses in the love of God."[43]

R. Berlin emphasizes that even one who yearns for divine closeness and goes so far as to retreat from the world must restrain the religious experience and mediate it through the halakhic system:

> And one who has reached the rung of loving God and encountering the *Shekhinah*, if he needs to observe the commandment of hospitality he must interrupt this union with the divine and attend to the commandment, as did Abraham. And all the more so if the commandment happens to be an obligation to God, which cannot be observed by others.[44]

R. Berlin's formulations are at times harsh, viewing unrestrained religious passion as an expression of the evil inclination rather than as a temptation of faith:

> Unless it follows the divine will, and although it seeks the love of God in holiness, this passion too is merely an attempt of the evil inclination to delude and mislead the leaders of the people of Israel. And Moses explained they should all share one fear and one counsel in the service of God. If you heed the way of the Torah, you will all follow one way and one counsel, but not so if we seek the love of God outside the path of the Torah. Each one will then have his own Torah, congregations will worship separately, and that is against God's will and God's honor.[45]

---

[43] Ibid., Numbers 15:39.
[44] Ibid.
[45] Ibid., Leviticus 9:6. See also the exegesis of R. Samuel b. Meir (Rashbam) on "All things have I seen in the days of my vanity" (Ecclesiastes 7:15): "I have set my mind to consider several matters in the affairs of the world during my vain life. For you may have a righteous man in the world who is too righteous and he perishes because of his great righteousness; for example a certain righteous man who is killed because of a minor commandment, for he does not want to expound with regard to himself 'he shall live by them but not die by them.'" Samuel b. Meir, *The Commentary of R. Samuel b. Meir (Rashbam) on Qohelet*, ed. and trans. Sara Japhet and Robert B. Salters (Jerusalem and Leiden: Magnes Press and Brill, 1985), 158. In this text, Rashbam is scathing in his criticism of *Kiddush ha-Shem* at the time of the Crusades. See Simha Goldin, *The Ways of Jewish Martyrdom*, trans. Yigal Levin and C. Michael Copeland (Turnhout: Brepols, 2008), 231-232.

One cannot but notice here the hidden controversy between R. Berlin and Hasidism, which in his view had placed excessive emphasis on the personal religious disposition at the expense of the halakhic norm. In this sense, R. Berlin continues R. Hayyim of Volozhin's controversy with Hasidism, which I discuss in the next section. Against the background of this hidden controversy, the difference between R. Berlin and R. Leiner emerges even more sharply. R. Leiner had argued that, despite the fear of being swept away by religious enthusiasm, the combination of divine help and a refined religious disposition can structure and regulate the religious experience. For R. Berlin, by contrast, only Halakhah can be the mechanism restraining the religious experience.

Yeshayahu Leibowitz appears to follow R. Berlin's approach. Though extremely impressed by R. Berlin's characterization of the danger lurking in religious temptation, the conclusions that Leibowitz drew from it actually point to his closeness to R. Leiner's view: "In other words, the intention to worship God could become destructive if the person does not intend to fulfill the obligation incumbent on him and instead finds ways to satisfy his own feelings and impulses, even if these feelings and impulses are ostensibly pure."[46]

For R. Berlin, the appropriate way of contending with the temptation of faith is Halakhah. This solution should purportedly have been the one endorsed by Leibowitz, who ascribes to Halakhah a constitutive role in Jewish religion. In this passage, however, Leibowitz claims that halakhic observance is not a barrier against religious temptation; only the right religious intention in the fulfillment of the religious obligation ensures the purity of the religious act. Believers, then, cannot be sure of their proper religious existence without the suitable religious intention.

Although Leibowitz held that this was R. Berlin's view, the difference between them is entirely clear: Leibowitz adopts the construct proposed by R. Leiner. Both of them hold that the way to cope with the temptation of faith lies in the religious disposition, with R. Leiner pointing to the disposition of fear and Leibowitz to the purity of religious intention. Both seek the answer in the realm of subjective experience. Fear and the acknowledgement of the obligation are indeed extremely similar: both these mechanisms result in the restriction of autonomy and in

---

[46] Yeshayahu Leibowitz, *Seven Years of Discourses on the Weekly Torah Reading* (Jerusalem: Keter, 2000), 468-472 (Hebrew).

subordination to the transcendent. For R. Leiner, locating the defense mechanism within the subjective realm continues the hasidic tradition that views this realm as the scene of the human drama. But how should one understand Leibowitz's position? Why was Halakhah alone not sufficient for him? Leibowitz's strong emphasis on purity of intention follows both from his reliance on the Kantian legacy and from his adoption of the Protestant-Lutheran construct that viewed faith *per se* as an expression of religiosity.[47]

R. Pinhas of Polotsk, a disciple of the Gaon of Vilna, formulated a unique approach. In his controversial treatise attacking Hasidism, *Rosh ha-Giv'ah*, he points to the deep affinity between the religious disposition of devotion and that of passion:

> A true Hasid is a reckless person who forgoes himself, his honor, his life, his wealth, and all his assets for the honor of God. There is also one who will forgo his life, his honor, and his wealth for the sake of victory or for some compelling passion. He does not care if people talk about him, or slander him, of if he is a conversation topic and becomes a subject of loathing and contempt, since he has dispensed with himself. Since true Hasidism depends on recklessness, we will not know how to distinguish the truly reckless from the true Hasid.

The identical subjective stance in states of passion and states of faith necessitates a cognitive principle that will enable distinctions between them. The interesting point in R. Pinhas' responsum is that he does not adopt Halakhah as the basis for this distinction, and suggests instead a principle found within the disposition itself:

> And here, my son, is a proven test so that you may understand what he forgoes—does he forgo his own honor or does he forgo the honor of the world, viewing all others as animals and moving among people as if he were in an animal pen, without feeling any shame and thus preserving his honor?... The true Hasid forgoes his own honor and does not forgo the honor of any person in the world.[48]

---

[47] See Avi Sagi, "The Political Realm—Between the Divine and the Demonic: The Political Theology of Yeshayahu Leibowitz," in *The Jewish-Israeli Voyage: Culture and Identity* (Jerusalem: Shalom Hartman Institute, 2006), 29-56 (Hebrew).

[48] R. Pinhas of Polotsk, *Rosh ha-Giv'ah* (Jerusalem: 1898), 7b-8a (Hebrew).

The test of faith, then, is self-restraint. The believer dispenses with himself but never applies this attitude to other people; self-effacement is not accompanied by an affront to the honor of others. Authentic religiosity reflects a person's inner self-consciousness and does not project onto the attitude towards the other. The believer, then, moves in two ways: self-transcendence as a negation of the self through absolute devotion to God, and restraint of this transcendence and its restriction to the relationship with God. Extending this attitude to the relationship with others implies that this transcendence does not have only one intentional object—God.[49] This religious disposition is unique because it focuses only on God, even though its foundations could lead the believer to deny, or fail to honor, the other. Indeed, our test as believers is to limit this disposition solely to the one religious object—God.

The self-restraint of the religious stance leaves individuals in the only realm wherein they are supposed to realize themselves as believers—the human realm. In truth, going beyond the human border is a kind of hubris, where the individual strives to be a god and loses consciousness of any distance between the human and the divine. Absolute devotion to God, coupled with a self-restraint concretized in an attitude of respect for the other, preserves the distance between the human and the divine. This approach, then, emphasizes the call for the only worthy form of religiosity, one that does not transcend the proper social norms.[50]

To emphasize the uniqueness of R. Pinhas' stance, I will compare it with that of St. John of the Cross (1542-1591), the great Spanish poet and mystic. St. John too stresses that the test of religious progress is in the attitude to the other. One who has not yet progressed and is at the "childish" stage of spirituality is often occupied with extremist additions of external religious expressions, contrary to "the poverty of spirit

---

[49] *Cf.* Maimonides, *The Code of Maimonides, The Book of Seasons*, Laws of Repose on a Festival 6:18. This source notes that even a commandment that obliges us to enjoy food and drink, if one does not give "anything to eat and drink to the poor and the bitter in soul—his meal is not a rejoicing in a divine commandment, but a rejoicing in his own stomach." I am grateful to David Kurzweil for directing me to this source.

[50] For a different analysis of R. Pinhas' view, see Yoav Elstein, *The Ecstatic Story in Hasidic Literature* (Ramat-Gan: Bar-Ilan University Press, 1998), 127-132 (Hebrew).

which concerns itself with nothing but the substance of devotion."[51] People whose faith is complete and sincere, whose heart is pure,

> do not attach themselves to visible instruments.... They are not interested in knowing more than is necessary to do good works. They set their eyes on God alone, on being right with him. This is their passion! With abundant generosity, they give away all they have. Whether spiritual or temporal possessions, these souls are happy to learn how to live without them, for love of their God and charity to their neighbor.[52]

One clear difference is evident: R. Pinhas sees respect for the other as the test of religiosity, since the other's honor has religious value. For St. John, however, generosity to the other follows precisely from the fact that nothing in the world has any value and, therefore, people can be generous. This difference rests on their respective attitude to the world: St. John emphasizes the Christian stance that seeks release from the world and all that is in it, whereas R. Pinhas emphasizes the Jewish religious obligation to establish the connection with God within the world and through other people, while preserving the distance between the human and the divine.

In sum, religious devotion may become a religious temptation if the borders between the divine and the human are breached, if the gap between heaven and earth turns into intimate closeness as a result of human action. Simone Weil, among the most profound of twentieth-century believers, formulates the problem of the believer yearning for God: "To love purely is to consent to distance, it is to adore the distance between ourselves and that which we love."[53] Rainer Maria Rilke offers a similar formulation of this idea: "But once the realization is accepted that even between the *closest* human beings infinite distances continue to exist, a wonderful living side by side can grow up, if they succeed in loving the distance between them which makes it possible for each to see the other whole and against a wide sky!"[54] Faith as temptation urges

---

[51] St. John of the Cross, *Dark Night of the Soul*, trans. Mirabai Starr (London: Rider, 2002), 43.
[52] Ibid.
[53] Simone Weil, *Gravity and Grace* (London: Routledge and Kegan Paul, 1972), 58.
[54] *Letters of Rainer Maria Rilke 1892-1910*, trans. Jane Bannard Greene and M. D. Herter Norton (New York: W. W. Norton, 1945), 57-58. Thanks to Batya Stein, who referred me to this source.

us to bridge the distance, thus harming the structure of faith that rests on loving but respecting the distance from the remote God.

3. Communion with God as the Temptation of the Evil Inclination

Religious practice—Torah study and observance—could be a temptation of the evil inclination, as noted, unless accompanied by a suitable religious stance. Against this view that, as noted, was formulated by the Ba'al Shem-Tov and his hasidic followers,[55] R. Hayyim of Volozhin presented a contrary position, stating that making religious communion (*devekut*) a crucial value is a temptation of the evil inclination.[56] R. Hayyim's view is particularly interesting in the present context because he presents it through a unique analysis of the temptation of the evil inclination.

R. Hayyim holds that the hasidic approach exalting communion over study and practice is clearly a temptation of the evil inclination:

> Be extremely careful, lest your evil inclination misleadingly tells you that the crux of everything is to spend your life cleansing your thought so that it is constantly united with your Creator, that you should never allow the purity of your thought to leave you, and that all should be for the sake of Heaven, as it [the evil inclination] tells you that the sole essence of the Torah and the commandments is profound intention and genuine *devekut*.... Search and you will understand that its only concern is to conceal its wickedness behind signs of purity.[57]

R. Hayyim of Volozhin points to the potential implications of this approach: missing observance of the commandments in due time because the required mental preparation is lacking, or even renouncing their

---

[55] See Immanuel Etkes, *The Gaon of Vilna: The Man and his Image*, trans. Jeffrey M. Green (Berkeley, CA: University of California Press, 2002), 153-159.

[56] On the structural similarity between the two approaches, see Norman Lamm, *The Study of Torah Lishmah in the Works of Rabbi Hayyim of Volozhin and His Contemporaries* (Jerusalem: Mosad Harav Kook, 1989), 16-17.

[57] R. Hayyim of Volozhin, *Nefesh Ha-Hayyim* (Vilnius: 1874), ch. 4, 36 (Hebrew). See also R. Hayyim's commentary on M. Avot, *Ruah ha-Hayyim* (Jerusalem: 1993), 26-28, 66-67 (Hebrew).

observance altogether because of the view that religious communion is the essence of religious life. In this light: "What is the difference between that and someone who blows the *shofar* with deep intention on the first night of Passover instead of performing the commandment of eating *matsah ka-zayit*?"[58]

In pointing to the negative halakhic implications of an attitude exalting religious experience over practice, R. Hayyim backs his view with a description of the psychological unfolding of this attitude. He argues that in the religious world too, the temptation of the evil inclination posing as a religious stance plays a decisive role. The objects of temptation appear, rather than in their transparent form, cloaked in a deceitful religious cover. The danger crouching at the believer's door, then, is entrapment by false objects of temptation, whose positive appearance belies their negative essence. How does this misleading appearance take place? R. Hayyim answers as follows:

> And our sages have already said (TB Sukkah 52a), "the greater the man, the greater his evil inclination." In its cunning, the evil inclination changes and adapts according to every person's interest and to the rank he has attained in his Torah study and in his worship. If the evil inclination sees that the person will not agree to relinquish his standing and transgress, be it slightly or seriously, he will appear in the shape of a good man so as to blind his reason, drop its poison, and mislead him to do so in the very mode and at the level that this person is used to. It will then show him a way that, at first glance, will appear as the advice of the good inclination ... and the person will fall into its trap as a bird hurries to the snare, without too much scrutiny and without knowing he is risking death.[59]

The psychology of the believer presented by R. Hayyim assumes that the distinction between good and evil is not objective and cannot be separated from the person's psychological dispositions. The temptation to evil is not exclusively determined by the object of the temptation but also, and mainly, by the person's existential conditions. Believers are not easily tempted by the familiar temptations marked as evil; the temptations they face are *within* the religious modes of existence.

---

[58] R. Hayyim of Volozhin, *Nefesh Ha-Hayyim*, 36b.
[59] Ibid., 36. See also *Ruah ha-Hayyim*, 144-145.

This psychological description rests on a "phenomenological" distinction between the inclination to do good and the inclination and temptation to do evil; the inclination to do good is transparent, whereas the inclination to do evil is turbid:

> The good inclination ... always advises a person to do only true good, but the evil inclination does not remain in its designated place ... to incite to open sin and transgression. At times, it skips from place to place ... and appears to man as a good inclination that will lead him to greater holiness, without him realizing that evil hides within it.[60]

The conclusion warranted by this approach is that religious life entails a risk, not due to exaggerated religious demands but due to a blurring of the correct religious stance that is misguided by the evil inclination. Religious life as such is therefore open to the possibility of temptation destroying it from within. How, then, can a person draw a distinction between the temptation of the evil inclination and the correct religious stance? If the distinction is entirely subjective, this question becomes a persistent threat to a religious life, which becomes one of uncertainty.

In some approaches (particularly Protestant ones), religious life entails a basic uncertainty concerning the very meaning of religiosity, as shown below. The approach of R. Hayyim of Volozhin, however, is entirely different. In his view, the religious disposition and the religious demand are clear and established by Halakhah. Deviation from Halakhah, therefore, is indeed the temptation of the evil inclination, even if it appears as a religious position.

The interesting point is that neither the Ba'al Shem-Tov and his followers nor R. Hayyim make a similar assumption concerning religious life—religious life does not ensure absolute protection from temptation. It may provide answers to extra-religious temptations or to transgressions, but is unable to prevent a temptation present in the religious realm from sneaking into religious life. According to the Ba'al Shem-Tov, it will sneak into religious practice and study, and according to R. Hayyim, it will appear instead in religious devotion.

Leibowitz, whose thought in many ways continues the Volozhin tradition that placed Halakhah at its center, has recurrently pointed to the

---

[60] R. Hayyim of Volozhin, *Nefesh Ha-Hayyim*, 36, gloss.

temptation of the evil inclination crouching at the door of faith and to the mechanism enabling us to contend with it:

> The faith which is expressed in the practical *mitzvot*, in the worship of God, is not something which is meant to give expression or release to man's emotions, but its importance lies in the fact that the person has accepted upon himself what, in the post-Biblical tradition, is known as the Yoke of the Kingdom of Heaven and the Yoke of the Torah and *Mitzvot*. Faith is expressed in the acts which man does due to his awareness of his obligation to do them, and not because of an internal urge—even when he intends to worship God, but derives satisfaction for himself by this worship. That is illicit fire. And those that did this, the first priests after Aaron, and did it in the sanctuary, were punished as if they had committed idolatry.
>
> This is a very important lesson for all generations: not to transform the worship of God into a means to release the tensions of one's inner urges, which the person dresses up, possibly sincerely, as the worship of God.[61]

Leibowitz, who, as noted, made Halakhah the center of Jewish existence, was forced to recognize that, although faith is practical, halakhic practice is not the way to contend with temptation because practice can itself become a temptation. In his view, then, the only way to contend with temptation is the right religious disposition, namely, true faith. This approach exposes the profound Protestant facet concealed in the thought of Leibowitz, who like Luther held that faith is the only way to redemption.

4. Preferring the Ritual as a Temptation

Temptation is possible even when religious practice follows the rules. Part of the Temple worship was the removal of the ashes. That is, the priest would remove the cinders from the altar, put them in the fire shovel, and place them to the east of the ramp (M. Tamid 1:4). The time for removing the ashes was "at cockcrow or about that time, either before or after" (M. Yoma 1:4). The Mishnah tells that "originally, whosoever decided to remove [the ashes from] the altar, did so" (M. Yoma 2:1). That

---

[61] Yeshayahu Leibowitz, *Notes and Remarks on the Weekly Parashah*, trans. Samuel Himmelstein (New York: Chemed, 1990), 106.

is, any priest from the family assigned to work in the Temple on that day could remove the ashes from the altar. The Talmud (TB Yoma 22a) explains that, unlike other tasks, this one was not assigned by lot because it was meant to be performed at dawn and required rising early. The fear was that, if the task were assigned by lot, many priests would not want to give up sleeping at that hour. That is why they determined that any priest who wished to remove the ashes could do so, and early risers would perform the task. The Mishnah (Yoma 2:1) presents the way of assigning the task when many are interested in removing the cinders: "If they were many, they would run and mount the ramp [of the altar] and he that came first within four cubits obtained the privilege." In other words: the first that entered the first four cubits of the ramp removed the ashes.

This commandment, then, is one that is performed voluntarily, and this reality created a serious mishap, which the Tosefta[62] describes as follows:

> Two arrived there at the same time, running up the ramp. One pushed the other [M. Yoma 2:2] within four cubits[63] [of the altar]. The other took a knife and stabbed him in the heart. R. Tsadok came, stood on the steps of the porch,[64] and said, "Hear me house of Israel, our brethren! Lo, Scripture says, 'If ... one be found slain ... then thy elders and thy judges shall come out and they shall measure ...' (Deuteronomy 21:1-2). So come let us measure for what area it is appropriate to bring the calf, for the sanctuary or for the courts!"[65] All moaned after his speech. And afterwards, the child's father came to them and said, "Our brethren! I am your atonement. His [my][66] son is still writhing, so the knife has not yet been made unclean." This teaches you that the uncleanness of a knife is harder for the Israelites than murder. And so it

---

[62] Tosefta, Mo'ed, Kippurim 1:12.
[63] "Meaning he pushed him when he was first within the four cubits." Saul Lieberman, *Tosefta ki-Fshutah*, vol. 4 (Newark: Rabinowitz Institute, 1962), 735 (Hebrew).
[64] In the Hebrew Ish-Shalom edition of the *Sifrei* 62 b, the text reads *"ma'a lot ha-ulam."* See variant version in Lieberman, *Tosefta ki-Fshutah*, vol. 4, 735.
[65] TB Yoma 23b explains that this is merely a metaphor meant to evoke mourning, since the killer here is known and the ritual does not apply in this situation.
[66] See *Sifrei*, Ish Shalom edition., and variant versions in Lieberman, *Tosefta ki-Fshutah*.

says, "Manasseh shed very much innocent blood, till he had filled Jerusalem from one end to another" (II Kings 21:16). Hence, they have said, "Because of the sin of murder, the *Shekhinah* rose up and the Temple was made unclean."

According to this Tosefta passage, a voluntary commandment ultimately led to murder. The murder, however, and the strong condemnation of R. Tsadok, do not change the judgment of the flawed halakhic norms. Quite the contrary: the father of the murdered victim is more concerned with the purity of the knife than with his son's murder. The *tanna* indicates his condemnation when he notes: "the uncleanness of a knife is harder for the Israelites than murder." Is this critique aimed at the people of Israel as a whole or only at the priests? It appears to depend on the version, since the phrase "for the Israelites" appears in only some of the sources.[67] In other sources, the censure targets only the priests; they alone are responsible for the *Shekhinah* leaving and for the uncleanness of the Temple. But if the critique targets all the Israelites, the priests' behavior poses a more general problem.

Regardless of the version, one conclusion is clear from this Tosefta passage: whether the murder is committed for its own sake or out of an impulse and a desire to perform a commandment is irrelevant. The comparison between the priests' behavior and Manasseh's acts is the clearest proof that the Tosefta draws no distinction between the motives—even observing a commandment cannot be a justification for murder.

The Tosefta thus assumes that even one performing a ritual act as a priest in the Temple cannot relinquish the values meant to guide him in his religious activity. Even if the ritual act is performed out of religious passion and absolute commitment to God, human beings are expected to be critical and responsible creatures.

R. Berlin formulates these insights in direct reference to the destruction of the Second Temple. In his view, the verse "He is the Rock, his work is perfect ... just and right is He,"[68] is meant to

> justify God's decision to destroy the Second Temple, for this was a stubborn and crooked generation. And we explained that

---

[67] See Lieberman, *Tosefta ki-Fshutah*, vol. 4, 735.
[68] Deuteronomy 32:4.

they were righteous and pious, and they studied the Torah, but they were not honest. Hence, because of their groundless hatred for one another, they suspected that those they saw behaving contrary to their views in their fear of God were Sadducees and heretics, and they even came to bloodshed.... And this was the justification, because God is just and does not tolerate righteous men of this kind. Men should be honest and not take a crooked path even if for the sake of Heaven, since this causes the destruction of Creation and the devastation of human settlement.[69]

According to R. Berlin, an act can be performed for the sake of Heaven and still be immensely destructive if it violates the very foundations of human life. R. Berlin is thus aware that religious consciousness can cause people to disconnect from the broader constitutive contexts of their lives and lead them to absolute devotion to the worship of God as they understand it. Religious life can thus make a person endorse extreme and negative positions. In his view, absolute devotion to God is indeed negative if it involves renouncing basic values. R. Berlin thus returns to the fundamental principle that appeared in the Tosefta, whereby passion for and absolute devotion to God cannot release a person from comprehensive normative criticism. The worship of God must be founded in a range of life contexts, which also include moral, political, and halakhic aspects, not outside them or in denial of them.

Are extreme religious voluntarism, devotion, and absolute passion for God as described in the Tosefta story or in the passage by R. Berlin the temptation of faith or the temptation of the evil inclination? According to R. Berlin, the answer is complex: he does not deny the possibility that the state of faith may lead to negative radicalism. Although God does not "tolerate" this type of righteousness, the very need to struggle against it shows that it is a temptation of faith itself or, at least, that it appears as such. For R. Berlin, as noted, although religious devotion is to be celebrated, it could lead a person to transgress the limits appropriate to a human creature. Even believers must remain within their human borders.

By contrast, the Tosefta clarifies that this is not a temptation of faith; bloodshed in the observance of a commandment can only be a temptation of the evil inclination that leads one to wish to be the first to fulfill

---

[69] R. Berlin, *Ha'amek Davar*, the opening of Genesis.

this commandment. The commandment thus becomes an object one competes for rather than a religious act, a means for attaining another end that, at times, could lead to bloodshed. Sensitivity to the possibility that a religious act could be a temptation guided by personal interest is evident in the act of zealotry, which is discussed in the next section.

5. Religious Zealotry: Faith, Temptation, or Error?

One of the most interesting situations in both religious and halakhic terms is zealotry. Halakhah defines an act of zealotry as a reaction to a transgression in which the court cannot intervene, and a person inspired by a spirit of zealous devotion acts in its place. The Mishnah reads: "One who cohabits with a heathen woman, is punished by zealots" (M. Sanhedrin 9:6). A public display of cohabitation with a pagan woman is punished by zealots. Who are these zealots? Rashi says: "Fair men overtaken by a spirit of zealotry for God punish him when they see the act. His death, however, will not be cause for action by the court."[70]

The act of zealotry is a special act, for which only the zealot is responsible. If he turns to the court and asks for their permission, he is no longer a zealot. The Talmud states: "R. Hisda said: If the zealot comes to take counsel, we do not instruct him to do so" (TB Sanhedrin 82a).[71] Moreover, if the person that the zealot is threatening pursues him back and kills him, the zealot's killer is not condemned to death. The Talmud formulates this approach in connection with the biblical story of Pinhas,[72] who kills Zimri and the Aramean woman: "Had Zimri turned upon Pinhas and slain him, he would not have been executed, since Pinhas was a pursuer" (TB Sanhedrin 82a).

---

[70] TB Sanhedrin 81b, Rashi, s.v. "*kana'in pog'in bo*."
[71] Post-Talmudic halakhic literature includes a dispute as to the precise meaning of the phrase "*ein morin lo*" ["we do not instruct him to do so"]. Some hold that this is not a commandment but a voluntary act and, therefore, he is told that this act is a discretionary choice. Others argue that it means he is neither instructed to perform the act nor hindered from doing so. For an analysis of this dispute and its sources, see R. Shaul Israeli, *Sefer Amud ha-Yemini* (Jerusalem: Eretz Hemdah, 1992), 160 (Hebrew). On the relationship between the Palestinian Talmud and the Babylonian Talmud in post-Talmudic literature, see ibid., 160-162.
[72] See Numbers 25:1-16.

The view of the zealot in the Palestinian Talmud is extremely complex. Concerning the ruling in the Mishnah, "one who cohabits with a heathen woman, is punished by zealots," it says:

> It was taught: Without the sages' approval, and Pinhas acted without the sages' approval. R. Judah bar Pazi said: "They wanted to excommunicate him, had not the Holy Spirit rested upon him and said: 'And he shall have it, and his seed after him, the covenant of an everlasting priesthood, and so forth.'"[73]

The attitude of this source toward Pinhas, who serves as the paradigm of the zealot, is indeed complex and raises questions: how is it possible that his act was performed without the consent of the court, and perhaps even against their wishes, but is nevertheless praised in the Bible, and the Talmud even claims that the Holy Spirit comes to his defense? How could an act that is not normative, and possibly even despicable, be so highly praised?

R. Shaul Israeli analyzes the Mishnah wording—"one who cohabits with a heathen woman, is punished by zealots"—and notes that it enables several conclusions. First, the secondary instruction applies only to one who has already been defined as a zealot: "This is not a law for the community of Israel but for individuals."[74] Second: the expression "is punished by zealots" does not denote an obligation but "a kind of statement of fact about how zealots behave" (ibid.). According to R. Israeli, this linguistic analysis furthers the understanding of the zealotry phenomenon and of the special attitude towards it:

> It therefore appears that this is not truly a general law, or a guideline to every Jew who sees this event, or indeed an instruction at all, since we are told, "we do not instruct him to do so." Rather, it means that the court is neither obliged to issue a sentence of capital punishment for this transgression, nor to react as it happens. This law is only meant to apply to special individuals with a passionate devotion for God in their hearts, who feel the revulsion evoked by this act and the unfortunate consequences that follow it … so much so that the enormity of the pain does not

---

[73] PT Sanhedrin 9:7. My punctuation here differs from that assumed in the *Penei Moshe* commentary *ad locum*, whose interpretation seeks to reconcile the PT version with other Talmudic sources.

[74] Israeli, *Sefer Amud ha-Yemini*, 166.

> allow them to contain their feelings and they explode in anger to hurt the perpetrator of this abomination. And yet, were the law to forbid him to do this, he would surely restrain himself with supreme heroism to prevent the shedding of blood. It is regarding such men that Halakhah says they are under no obligation to make an effort to overcome their feelings, and they are allowed to express them and harm the perpetrator of this defilement. (Ibid.)

In this description, zealotry is not an act dictated by Halakhah but an expression of the believer's deep religious feeling. The act of zealotry is an initiative of the believer allowed by Halakhah as a religious expression, but not as a general halakhic expression. Hence, the court does not issue instructions to engage in acts of zealotry. With wonderful sensitivity, R. Israeli proceeds to state:

> Halakhah does not prescribe this act, it only approves it. If he is not driven to act because he is internally seething at the sight of profanation, then this act is indeed forbidden because he is as a murderer, since this is not a capital offense. Hence, had he not acted pushed by an inner impulse but only following Mosaic law, this act would be truly contrary to Halakhah, since Halakhah is not meant to awaken one into action but only to strengthen one who is ready to act upon his own inner feelings. (Ibid.)

R. Israeli points out that this analysis clarifies why the rule on this matter is not general, since a person must truly be a zealot *ab initio* so that Halakhah may approve the act *ex post factum*. And for this very reason, "we do not instruct him to do so" because, "if he is not moved to do so by himself, the instruction is indeed to refrain from it" (ibid.).

This complex analysis enables R. Israeli to describe the zealous moment as one involving a special dimension of inner decision. People should consider and examine themselves to see whether this is indeed an act of zealotry or perhaps one driven by personal motives:

> Even after this law has been issued, not everyone who wishes to call himself a "zealot" can actually do so. This matter requires great consideration and a detailed analysis of his feelings and motivations, lest he be actually influenced by his knowledge of Halakhah and, only because of it, be moved to harm the perpetrator. All the more so if other side-issues of revenge or personal rancor are involved ... this act, which goes beyond any context of orderly law, should be avoided. (Ibid.)

The reflection, or more precisely, the introspection required from those perceiving themselves as zealots, is meant to help them clarify to themselves the true motivation of their zealotry. R. Israeli points to two possibilities: one involves the zealot's personal feeling toward the other—if the act of zealotry is driven by a personal motive, it is absolutely forbidden. In this case, zealotry is indeed the temptation of the evil inclination, personal motives in halakhic garb, and the agent's consciousness is thus a false consciousness.

The second possible motive is that the act of zealotry follows from the halakhic ethos. This act would thus appear to be a typical instance of a temptation of faith, since the zealot is driven to act by Halakhah. Halakhah impels him to oppose with all his powers the profanation entailed by the forbidden act. Yet, a deeper analysis shows that even one driven to zealous action by the halakhic ethos is not driven by the temptation of faith but by his evil inclination. Had this zealot genuinely been driven by Halakhah, he would easily have discovered his mistake; as far as Halakhah is concerned, only the court is authorized to act, to punish, and to kill within a halakhically defined context. The very act of zealotry is non-halakhic since it is a personal initiative. One who wishes to ascribe responsibility for this act to Halakhah is acting out of false consciousness. This consciousness is not based on the temptation of personal inclinations but on an epistemic mistake: ignorance of Halakhah.

In sum, only a zealous act that follows from genuine religious feelings is a worthy act of zealotry. The decision on the type of motivation is a matter for the agent, not for the outside institutional system, which can approve the act *ex post factum* but cannot impose it as a halakhic obligation. Zealotry is thus a moment where individuals must examine their motivations but, whatever these might be, the act of zealotry is not a suitable instance of the temptation of faith.

The fact that temptation crouches at the door of religious practice raises the question: is religious practice the typical location for faith as temptation? The assumption that faith as temptation will not easily be found in religious practice seems well grounded, since religious practice organizes life systematically through enacted laws. The motivation to observe religious practice in a particular way or to disregard it lies in the person's concrete being, in the person's understanding or ignorance of it. Precisely the legal, ordered, and structured character of practice, however, is what considerably restrains the possibility that practice will, as such, create a religious temptation opposed to religiosity itself. Locating situations where faith is a temptation opposed to religiosity requires finding situations where the basic dispositions of faith are at work. Dispositions such as obedience or absolute devotion to God could lead to a deviation from the development of religiosity within the normative order.

III. Revelation and Faith as a Temptation

The more precise venue for locating faith as temptation relates to God's revelation. The believer responds to God's revelation with dispositions typical of faith that, as noted, may create a temptation to deviate from faith.

1. The Binding of Isaac: A Temptation of the Evil Inclination or a Temptation of Faith

The binding of Isaac has consistently been perceived as a setting where religious dispositions are fully disclosed. The analysis that follows focuses on two trends in the analysis of the binding or, more precisely, in the analysis of Abraham's religious dispositions in this event. According to one trend, the story of Abraham is one of confronting the temptation of error and of the evil inclination; according to the other, the story of Abraham is a classic story of faith as temptation.

I begin with an analysis of the first trend.

a) Confronting the Temptation of the Evil Inclination

The Midrash literature dealing with the binding of Isaac includes the following passage:

> When they were on their way, Satan appeared to Abraham disguised as an old man and said to him: "Was I not there when Satan told you, 'Take your only son whom you love and sacrifice him'"... Said Abraham, "It was not Satan but the Lord himself who told me."[75]

---

[75] Adolf Jellink, ed., *Bet ha-Midrash*, vol. 1 (Jerusalem: Bamberger and Wahrman, 1938), 36 (Hebrew).

According to this midrash, Abraham faces the possibility that the command that appears to him as God's is actually Satan's. Abraham, then, who acts out of profound religious devotion, is not worshipping God but Satan. Abraham decides that the voice he has heard is God's but, even so, the story's initial assumption is that God's command strongly resembles Satan's temptation, since, barring such resemblance, the story would lack the element that turns it into a story of faith. Were God's "voice" entirely different from Satan's "voice," what would be so special about Abraham's choice to obey? Why, this is God's command! Theologically, the midrash deals with the question of identifying God's voice. But religiously, it points to the extreme closeness between the disposition of divine worship and the disposition of giving in to temptation.

Samuel Hugo Bergman ties this midrash to Kierkegaard's interpretation of the binding, discussed below, and writes:

> The danger is that man will substitute the voice of Satan for the voice of God, for who can assure Abraham that God himself is demanding the sacrifice of his son?... Satan was attempting to mislead Abraham into thinking that it was not God's word he had heard but Satan's. This is the same dialectic that Kierkegaard had observed.[76]

This tradition, beginning with an ancient midrash and culminating in Bergman's thought, became deeply entrenched in philosophical thought, particularly because this was the common interpretation of Kierkegaard's stance in *Fear and Trembling*.[77] Sartre, who as an existentialist sought to found human action on individual decisions, uses the example of the binding to illustrate this situation and offers the following generalization: "If an angel appears to me, what is the proof that it is an angel? Or, if I hear voices, who can prove they are from heaven and

---

[76] Shmuel Hugo Bergman, *Dialogical Philosophy: From Kierkegaard to Buber*, trans. Arnold A. Gerstein (Albany, NY: SUNY Press, 1991), 84.

[77] Søren Kierkegaard, *Fear and Trembling: Repetition*, trans. Howard V. Hong and Edna H. Hong (Princeton, NJ: Princeton University Press, 1990). I reject this interpretation of Kierkegaard. See Avi Sagi, "Kierkegaard and Buber on the Dilemma of Abraham in the *Akedah*," *Iyyun* 37 (1988): 248-262 (Hebrew). See also Avi Sagi, *Kierkegaard, Religion, and Existence: The Voyage of the Self*, trans. Batya Stein (Amsterdam-Atlanta, GA: Rodopi, 2000), 122-135.

not from hell, or from my own subconsciousness or some pathological condition?"[78]

Similarly, Buber writes: "Where, therefore, the 'suspension' of the ethical is concerned, the question of questions which takes precedence over every other is: Are you really addressed by the Absolute or by one of his apes?"[79]

In this view, then, Abraham confronts the possibility of temptation by the evil inclination, which seeks to challenge God's command. This challenge, which emerges as an inner voice, is meant to divert Abraham from the path of devotion and religious commitment. The problem in the story of the binding, then, according to this view, is not the temptation of faith but the temptation of the evil inclination or of Satan.

b) The Binding as an Erroneous Understanding of God's Word

Another option in the context of this trend is that Abraham misunderstood God's word, and God never commanded Isaac's sacrifice. The source of this view is in Talmudic literature. On the verse, "which I commanded not, nor spoke it, neither came it into my mind" (Jeremiah 19:5), the Talmud says in TB Ta'anit 4a: "'Which I commanded not'—this refers to the sacrifice of the son of Mesha, the king of Moab...; 'nor spoke it'—this refers to the daughter of Jephtah; 'neither came it into my mind'—this refers to the sacrifice of Isaac, the son of Abraham."

In other words, even if God did say what the Bible claims, God never intended what Abraham understood from his words. So how to settle the contradiction between God's intention and God's word? The Midrash complements the TB Ta'anit story:

> The Holy One, blessed be He, said to him: Abraham, "My covenant I will not profane, I will not alter that which has gone out of my lips" (Psalms 89:35). When I told you "Take now thy son," I did not say slaughter him but take him up. Whom thou lovest, I said.

---

[78] Jean-Paul Sartre, *Existentialism and Humanism*, trans. Philip Mairet (London: Eyre Methuen, 1980), 31. Sartre's interpretation influenced Jean Wahl, *Philosophies of Existence: An Introduction to the Basic Thought of Kierkegaard, Heidegger, Jaspers, Marcel, Sartre*, trans. F. M. Lory (London: Routledge and Kegan Paul, 1969), 58.

[79] Martin Buber, *Eclipse of God: Studies in the Relation between Religion and Philosophy* (Atlantic Highlands, NJ: Humanities Press, 1979), 118-119.

You have taken him up and fulfilled my command, and now take him down.[80]

Abraham, then, was mistaken in his understanding of the word of God, who had never intended Isaac to be sacrificed. The philosophical literature explained the possibility of the mistake on either an epistemic or an ethical basis. Epistemically, the source of the mistake stems from the fact that the hearing of God's word is subjective: people think they have heard the word of God, but they cannot be sure, raising the possibility that they have heard the voice of Satan. Ethically, the large gap between the command and the ethical norm raises suspicions as to whether this is indeed the word of God. Kant joined these two factors and claimed: "Even though something is represented as commanded by God, through a direct manifestation of Him, yet, if it flatly contradicts morality, it cannot, despite all appearances, be of God (for example, were a father ordered to kill his son who is, so far as he knows, perfectly innocent)."[81] Kant then claims that, since revelation is transmitted through "men and has been interpreted by them, and even did it appear to have come to them through God Himself (like the command delivered to Abraham to slaughter his own son like a sheep), it is at least possible that in this instance a mistake has prevailed."[82]

Abraham's misunderstanding is indeed a sign of his religious devotion but, according to this analysis, this is a religious devotion that God does not care for. The gap between God's command and human understanding, then, is a kind of opportunity through which the temptation of faith could emerge. Abraham understood that God demands Isaac from him, and as a believer committed to God with absolute devotion and compliance, he acted according to his understanding. But God never intended the meaning that Abraham ascribed to his command.

R. Leiner suggests an illuminating formulation of this approach:

> Indeed, Abraham did not have an explicit command from God to slaughter his son, and that is why it is not written "JHWH did test Abraham" but "the Lord did test Abraham," that is, God spoke to

---

[80] Genesis Rabbah 56b.
[81] Immanuel Kant, *Religion Within the Limits of Reason Alone*, trans. Theodore M. Greene and Hoyt H. Hudson (New York: Harper and Row, 1960), 81-82.
[82] Ibid., 175.

> him through an unilluminated mirror (*Zohar*, Genesis 120b) .... Hence, this test is not named after Isaac, because Isaac believed Abraham, who said this is God's order and not really a test. Only Abraham was tested, since he had not been told explicitly, and had he been involved as a father with a son he would have pitied him, because it was indeed God's will that he should not slaughter him and the test was only a mirror to Abraham. As for what he had said in his prayer for Sodom "Behold now, I...who am but dust and ashes" (Genesis 18: 27), dust points to an act that is not thought through and requires amendment, since from dust something may grow, while ashes is something that has been lost, God forbid, and had he slaughtered him no amendment would have been possible.[83]

R. Leiner does not accept the view that the speaker could have been Satan; the binding is neither the temptation of the evil inclination nor of Satan, and the voice that Abraham has heard is indeed God's voice. But Abraham could not be sure of what God required from him, since God's revelation to him was "through an unilluminated mirror."[84]

Moreover, although Abraham had strong reasons that should have prevented him from sacrificing Isaac, he nevertheless decided to do so:

> The binding is a test of Abraham's faith in God because, although God had told him "so shall thy seed be" [Genesis 15: 5] and "my covenant will I establish with Isaac" [Genesis 17: 21], now that he is told "offer him there for a burnt offering" [Genesis 22: 2], he still believed in the initial words as he had before, and this is a faith that the human mind fails to grasp.[85]
>
> The essence of this test is that the explicit prohibition of murder was clear to him, all the more so to slaughter his son.[86]

Abraham's test, then is two-fold: he has strong religious reasons for rejecting the divine command, and he is not at all sure that these are God's words. His test, then, lies precisely in the uncertainty of the divine

---

[83] Leiner, *Mei ha-Shiloah*, vol. 1, 29.
[84] For further analysis of R. Leiner's approach, see Jerome I. Gellman, *The Fear, the Trembling, and the Fire: Kierkegaard and Hasidic Masters on the Binding of Isaac* (Lanham, MD: University Press of America, 1994), 24-28.
[85] Leiner, *Mei ha-Shiloah*, vol. 1, 29.
[86] Leiner, *Mei ha-Shiloah*, vol. 2, 19.

demand. This situation tests the believer's genuine being and basic dispositions. In a situation of uncertainty, Abraham could easily have extricated himself from what seems a divine command. He could have protested against this questionable demand, but he did not, thereby revealing his basic existentialist religious being—his absolute devotion to God: "Abraham wanted to do God's will ... even though this test was in an unilluminated mirror ... that is, one without clarity, and only in his core did he aim at God's will, even without divine help."[87]

This devotion could have led him to a loss, if he had indeed misunderstood God's words. But that is precisely the required religious devotion: a readiness to act upon a religious calling, even if this action could result in loss. Faith means a readiness to risk loss. This faith, writes R. Leiner, is one "the human mind fails to grasp," since the religious disposition is a readiness to act in situations that contradict human perceptions and interests. Faith is not revealed in situations of certainty but precisely in situations of uncertainty, danger, and loss. This was Abraham's reality, and that is why he was called "God-fearing."

This view of the event is extremely problematic, both religiously and theologically.[88] First, it erodes human certainty concerning the immediacy of the relationship with God—if Abraham did not really understand God's words, how can we be sure that other prophets did? In Abrabanel's formulation: "If the prophets erred in the understanding of their prophecies, serious doubts might be cast on the law of religion and on the ways of prophecy."[89] This question is particularly serious regarding Abraham who, according to the biblical story, acted following the words of God that he had heard. Second, could God not have formulated his request so as to preclude such a dreadful mistake by Abraham, who almost murdered his son because of it? Third, is it justified to test the faith of one person—Abraham—by turning another person—Isaac—into a means for performing the test? Finally, is it proper that the believer's disposition should be a readiness to risk loss?! Does faith imply the possibility of an absolute subversion of existence, an existence that God created and affirmed?

---

[87] Ibid., 20.
[88] See Avi Sagi and Daniel Statman, *Religion and Morality*, trans. Batya Stein (Amsterdam-Atlanta, GA: Rodopi, 1995), 126-130.
[89] Yitzhak Abrabanel, *Commentary on the Bible*, Genesis 22, #14.

These and other serious questions point to the difficulty and indeed the daring of this description of the binding in the context of religious life. Whatever the answers to them may be, this interpretation claims that the idea of faith as temptation does appear in the story of the binding, since Abraham acts out of his disposition as a believer. His being as a believer is revealed through his mistake or his misunderstanding of God's word. And yet, this is only the temptation of faith, since God is ultimately not interested in the realization of this religious disposition. In R. Leiner's words, had Abraham killed Isaac, "no amendment would have been possible" and he would have been lost forever.

Can there be a temptation of faith founded on a suitable understanding of God's command? Can the temptation of faith grow out of the religious context of life without somehow impairing this context? The answer is included in the discussion of the second trend in the interpretation of the binding story.

c) The Binding as a Moment of Temptation: R. Kook and Martin Buber

Martin Buber and R. Abraham Yitzhak Kook fully clarify this approach. Buber opens his analysis by presenting the true religious foundation of *molech* worship:

> The service of *molech* demonizes an actual and characteristic essential demand of JHWH. The demand, posed by the nature of JHWH Himself as the unconditional king of existence, for unconditioned surrender, for that "with all your heart, with all your soul, with all your might," finds its ritual response in the use of the *s'mikha* [the laying of hands on the ritual offering] which we scarcely meet with outside Israel.... It is the gesture of identification: You there are now (functionally) I.... The intention of self-presentation ... is accordingly in Israel the genuine basis of the sacrificial cult: man feels guilty before God.[90]

The believer's basic disposition is absolute devotion to God, up to a readiness for self-sacrifice. This religious disposition is not unique to the Jewish believer, and is also present in its demonic manifestation in the *molech* worship. The temptation of faith thus crouches at the door

---

[90] Martin Buber, *Kingship of God*, trans. Richard Scheiman (New York: Harper Torchbooks, 1967), 114-115.

of the religious disposition as such: the demonic quality is not a mistake or a temptation of the evil inclination, but a possibility based on the believer's actual religious stance.

This temptation of faith is the temptation that Abraham succumbed to or resisted. He resisted it in the sense that his readiness to sacrifice Isaac expressed the perfection of religious stance; he succumbed to it in the sense that it was only God's intervention that prevented this act. God teaches Abraham to distinguish faith from the temptation of faith:

> ... [T]he narrative of the child-sacrifice commanded by JHWH. The "son," the "only one," he "whom one loves" (Genesis 22: 2) is that creature which the loving man, which presents it as himself, simply was not able to offer with lesser reality of intention. Indeed, the essential action is even more final than if one had only to offer his own body. Therefore, JHWH demands of Abraham just this. And what happens must happen in utmost seriousness until the intention has attained its complete actuality. Only then does the compromise come; but then it must come. In actuality nothing but the intention was demanded, but the intention could only then become actual if the deed itself was demanded in utmost seriousness.[91]

The temptation of faith in this description is a course that believers must go through in order to extricate themselves from it. They must go through its full length, since only this readiness will reveal whether they have the proper religious dispositions. Once the process has been completed, however, they must amend their dispositions and adapt them to God's demand, which is no different from the moral demand. This obligation is not an external limitation imposed on the religious disposition, but its perfect manifestation.[92]

In this view, the temptation of faith is created by the fact that the religious stance could itself lead to the demonic. A religious stance does not, in and of itself, guarantee release from the possibility of demonic existence—it actually enables it. The believer's voyage to faith begins with a religious disposition that creates the temptation of faith and ends with the refinement and amendment of this disposition so that the temptation of faith ceases to represent a seduction.

---

[91] Ibid., 116.
[92] Buber, *Eclipse of God*, 118.

... the crucial religious experiences of man do not take place in a sphere in which creative energy operates without contradiction, but in a sphere in which evil and good, despair and hope, the power of destruction and the power of rebirth, dwell side by side. The divine force which man actually encounters in life does not hover above the demonic, but penetrates it.[93]

R. Kook too saw the binding of Isaac as a kind of voyage of liberation from the temptation of faith. Like Buber, R. Kook held that idolatry has a genuine religious basis, except that it should be emended. The starting point of the binding test is the imperfect state of Abraham, who is still bound to the temptation of faith from which he will be liberated at the end of the voyage:

> The deep craving for idolatry was so crucial to the savage that it overrode parental compassion and turned cruelty to sons and daughters in the worship of the *molech* into a habit, dimly reflecting the deep human understanding that all that is pleasant and loved is as nothing next to the divine. When the divine illumination needed to appear in all its purity, it was revealed at the height of its passion in the test of the binding. The test of the binding showed that the passion and the craving for the divine need not dimly apprehend the divine in despicable guises such as those of idolatry, where the spark of divine good is altogether lost. Instead, it can also be apprehended purely ... and we need not expand on how much it sheds light on all human ways, how much it amends social life and what a firm basis it creates for human moods ... all this is well known. But the passion of addiction should not be missing from the attachment to the divine in its illuminated version. This is the achievement of the binding test, which became the natural law forever and ever: even the subtle tie to the idea superior to any sensorial notion enters the heart. Were it not so, humanity would stand between a turbid, savage feeling that pulsates strongly in its tie to the divine, and a cold, filtered spirit lacking the quality of deep life.[94]

The test in this passage is not that of an individual, of Abraham. The binding is a paradigmatic test charged with imparting the suitable

---

[93] Ibid., 21.
[94] R. Abraham Yitzhak Hacohen Kook, *Iggerot ha-Rayha*, vol. 2 (Jerusalem: Mosad Harav Kook, 1962), 43 (Hebrew).

religious consciousness, which combines limitless religious devotion and commitment to a broad range of social and cultural values. Abraham's voyage in the binding is the voyage of every believer:

> The source of holiness in the idolatrous evil inclination is the enormous desire for closeness to God. Ignorance and the lack of a moral spark are great hindrances that hide the divine light from man, and if his natural passion is strong, it will burst through in the shape of idolatry.[95]

Through the test of the binding, God pointed to the ideal of a general religious law—"natural law" in R. Kook's terminology—which infuses life with deep religious feeling. Temptation, then, is a moment in the life of believers which they need to transcend. The Torah redeems us from the demonic religious yearning: "There is no true redemption from the evil inclination of idolatry except through the greatness of the Torah" (ibid.).

Elsewhere, R. Kook describes genuine fear of God, which reconciles a religious stance with moral commitment:

> Fear of God must not thrust aside man's natural morality, because then it is not pure fear of God.... If fear of God is described as a quality without whose influence life could be good and lead to useful results to the individual and to the collective, and with whose influence these benefits dwindle, such a fear of God is unacceptable.[96]

In sum, R. Kook and Buber view the temptation of faith as a state that follows from faith itself, from the believer's basic dispositions. The prominent difference between this approach and the one presented in the previous section lies in the question: when does the temptation of faith emerge? According to the previous section, the temptation of faith emerges in situations of error and misunderstanding—when God's command is unclear, the temptation of faith comes forth as a

---

[95] R. Abraham Yitzhak Hacohen Kook, *Shmonah Kvatsim*, vol. 2 (Jerusalem: n. p., 1999), *Kovets* 4, 149, #56 (Hebrew); see also idem, *Orot ha-Emunah*, ed. Moshe Gurevitz (Jerusalem, n. p., 1998), 107-108.

[96] R. Abraham Yitzhak Hacohen Kook, *Orot ha-Koddesh* (Jerusalem: Mosad Harav Kook, 1962), 27, #43.

reflection of the believer's being. According to the current approach, the temptation of faith is indeed based on the believer's being, but occurs as part of a dialectical process that believers must undergo in order to refine and repair their faith. The key question in this view is whether a single event such as the binding suffices to release all believers from the temptation of faith, or whether each believer must travel this road in order to repair his faith from temptation. Both Buber and R. Kook hold that the story of the binding is paradigmatic because it situates the correct approach to faith that should guide believers confronting the temptation of faith.

d) The Temptation of Faith as an Element of Faith: Kierkegaard's Position

Sartre and Bergman, as noted, argued that Kierkegaard describes the dilemma confronting Abraham as related to the question of whether he had heard the voice of God or the voice of Satan, an interpretation I have rejected.[97] Kierkegaard recurrently emphasizes that Abraham had an immediate connection to God, and a person involved in that type of relationship with God has no doubts about having heard God's word.[98] In *Fear and Trembling*, too, Kierkegaard emphasizes that Abraham's fear is rooted in his need to decide whether to obey the divine command, which stands against morality: "The ethical expression for what Abraham did is that he meant to murder Isaac; the religious expression is that he meant to sacrifice Isaac—but precisely in this contradiction is the anxiety that can make a person sleepless, and yet without that anxiety Abraham is not who he is."[99] The contradiction is thus between the self-evident religious obligation and the moral obligation, which is also self-evident. Kierkegaard then claims that this contradiction is precisely what makes Abraham what he is—a knight of faith. Fear, rather than any biographical characteristic, is a description of the believer's being, as the believer lives with the uncertainty as to what precisely is required from him. This perception of a contradiction between morality and religion as the foundation of the religious stance implies that morality, as

---

[97] Sagi, *Kierkegaard, Religion, and Existence*, 127-135.
[98] Ibid., 127.
[99] Kierkegaard, *Fear and Trembling: Repetition*, 30.

such, has religious meaning: for if God's command alone represents the religious obligation, then Abraham's hesitations attest to his failure as a believer rather than to his believer-being.[100]

What, then, describes God's command from a religious perspective? According to Kierkegaard, God's command creates what he calls the possibility of the "spiritual trial" (*anfaegtelse*).[101] The spiritual trial is constituted by the basic uncertainty typical of religious existence. According to Kierkegaard, this trial is the hallmark of religious life, and removing it would deny religious life any authenticity.[102] The spiritual trial is patently different from the temptation of the evil inclination. The evil inclination seduces us to act contrary to the ethical, to surrender to human weakness. By contrast, in the spiritual trial we are tempted to go beyond the permitted norm.[103] The spiritual trial is a kind of religious daring whose legitimacy is not entirely clear. The religious act may be a form of insolence against God's demand that the person not deviate from the accepted norm. Kierkegaard formulated the distinction between the temptation of the evil inclination and the spiritual trial as follows: "Spiritual trial belongs to the inwardness of religion, and inwardness belongs to religiousness. Spiritual trial belongs to the individual's absolute relation to the absolute *telos*. What temptation [*Fristelse*] is outwardly, spiritual trial is inwardly."[104]

Elsewhere, Kierkegaard clarifies these vague sentences in his journal. In his view, the spiritual trial appears at the heart of religious life, since the purpose of this life is to shape an absolute attitude toward God, which leads human beings to religious daring and risk-taking: "As soon as the relation to an absolute *telos* is omitted and allowed to exhaust itself into relative ends, spiritual trial ceases."[105] As soon as religious

---

[100] I discuss this issue at length in Avi Sagi, "The Suspension of the Ethical and the Religious Meaning of Ethics in Kierkegaard's Thought," *International Journal for the Philosophy of Religion* 32 (1992): 83-103. See also Sagi, "The 'Akedah'—A Comparative Study," 121-134.
[101] On this concept, see Sagi, *Kierkegaard, Religion, and Existence*, 156-171.
[102] Ibid., 157.
[103] Ibid.
[104] Søren Kierkegaard, *Concluding Unscientific Postscript to Philosophical Fragments*, trans. Howard V. Hong and Edna H. Hong, vol. 2 (Princeton, NJ: Princeton University Press, 1992), 92.
[105] Ibid., vol. 1, 458.

life loses its unique character, as expressed in absolute compliance and devotion, the phenomenon of the spiritual trial is no longer valid. Temptation is the challenge facing the moral person and leading the individual to breach the norm. In the moral realm, temptation plays a role similar to what the spiritual trial plays in religiosity: in both cases, the problem is deviation from the norm. As a sensitive thinker, however, Kierkegaard emphasizes the difference between these two phenomena: "In temptation, it is the lower that tempts; in spiritual trial it is the higher."[106]

It is precisely in these terms that Kierkegaard describes Abraham's test in *Fear and Trembling*. Kierkegaard draws a contrast between Abraham, the knight of faith, and the tragic hero, such as Agamemnon or Jephtah. The latter renounce the ethical and deviate from moral norms, but this deviation has no greater purpose:

> The knight of faith, however, is kept in a state of sleeplessness, for he is constantly being tested [*proves*], and at every moment there is the possibility of his returning penitently to the universal, and this possibility may be a spiritual trial [*anfaegtelse*] as well as the truth. He cannot get any information on that from any man, for in that case he is outside the paradox.[107]

Consequently, even if God's command is unclear, the decision about compliance is for human beings to make. Should Abraham sacrifice Isaac, or should he perhaps struggle against this demand? Abraham will not find the answer to this question anywhere outside himself; he will have to confront the question of what is truly requested of him: is the spiritual trial an ethical duty, a form of religious brazenness that he should reject by meekly obeying God, or is this God's demand from him? According to this approach, the temptation of faith is not a moment in the voyage of faith; it creates faith itself.

Kierkegaard's approach seems to resemble R. Leiner's. Both assume that, in the binding, Abraham faces uncertainty, and this uncertainty turns him into what he is—a knight of faith.[108] But the most prominent

---

[106] Ibid., 459.
[107] Kierkegaard, *Fear and Trembling: Repetition*, 78.
[108] This is Gellman's understanding. See *The Fear, the Trembling, and the Fire*.

difference between them is that, according to R. Leiner, the source of the religious uncertainty is the misunderstanding of God's command. Abraham is a knight of faith because he does not fully understand what God has commanded him to do. Kierkegaard, however, holds that Abraham knows very well what God has *commanded* him to do, but is not sure about what God truly *wants*. God may very possibly want him to act against the command and abide by his moral views and values.

In Kierkegaard's view, the uncertainty typical of a life of faith is not a random event to be found only when human beings do not understand God's command. Quite the contrary: uncertainty is always there because God's command and God's will do not necessarily overlap. God's command is a kind of religious temptation that one must resist.

Kierkegaard does see Abraham's trial as the unique test of someone who has heard God's word, but he also holds that ordinary people who have not heard God's word and have not witnessed divine revelation face the constitutive dilemma of faith as uncertainty, a dilemma that has the temptation of faith at its center: "Ordinarily, we human beings do not have an immediate relationship to God." This basic situation determines the character of the human relationship with God, and Kierkegaard therefore proceeds to state:

> His will is proclaimed to us *in abstracto* in his Word ... but I ... am not told: In these concrete circumstances, you are to do this and this, No, every single individual must, so to speak, translate God's commands *in concreto*. One way this takes place is with the aid of the *understanding*.[109]

In the lives of believers who are not witnesses to a divine revelation that will guide them in their relevant obligation, it is their duty to determine what God requires from them in their own specific circumstances. Each one acts according to his or her own knowledge and judgment. We have no other way of trying to determine God's will for us. The fact that we exercise our epistemic faculties means that identifying God's will is something that takes place within and outside of our concrete existence,

---

[109] This passage is cited from Kierkegaard's journal (*JP*, X^5 A 95 n.d., 1853, § 4479, emphasis in original) and discussed in Sagi, *Kierkegaard, Religion, and Existence*, 128.

which confronts God's word as manifest in Scripture. And Kierkegaard indeed writes: "But the more specific understanding—and what is thus broadly articulated in his Word is realized first of all in action on the part of the individual through a more particular understanding of his whole concretion—the more particular understanding I have in and through myself."[110]

The fact that God's word is revealed through human action imposes a heavy responsibility on us because, on the one hand, we could replace God's will with ours and thereby ease our task;[111] on the other, someone who genuinely desires to fulfill God's will faces the dilemma of the temptation of faith: how far can one dare within the religious realm; is not a human decision as such a kind of brazenness? Kierkegaard argues that, contrary to the person who has witnessed revelation, the ordinary religious person confronts a dual dialectic: the conflict with people and the problem of the relationship with God—"do I have the right to venture so far out" (ibid.). In this approach, then, the hesitations of faith clearly establish faith itself: the temptation of faith rests on the existential disposition toward God.

In sum, for Kierkegaard the temptation of faith is constituted entirely by the religious disposition. It is not God's action that creates temptation, but the fact that faith is a concern of the believing person and is constituted within the person's concrete being. As believers, individuals encounter the problematic of forbidden and allowed, religiously desirable and undesirable.

By contrast, for Buber and R. Kook, the temptation of faith unfolds through God's action. Yet God appears as tempter not in order to trip us up but in order to educate us to overcome temptation. In truth, divine temptation is a corrective response to the believer's basic disposition. Believers are ready to sacrifice their existence and their values, invoking their devotion and their obedience to God. God sets temptation in motion in order to enable our liberation from the negative conception of the religious disposition. Does God indeed promote religious temptation to allow for the religious trial that will test the believer? This is the subject of the next section.

---

[110] The journal passage (*JP*, X^5 A 13 n.d., 1852, § 1273) is cited in ibid., 129.
[111] Ibid.

2. The Temptation of Faith as a Divine Action: God as Tempter

Can God appear as a tempter? In approaches critical of the religious disposition as such, this option is indeed possible. This possibility finds one of its deepest literary expressions in *The Counterfeiters*. Old M. La Pérouse, as noted in Section II.1, angrily affirms that his success in overcoming the temptation to transgress had heightened his self-pride. Yet, he blames God rather than himself for it and, after claiming that every triumph is another turn of the key in the lock of his prison, he proceeds to argue:

> That's what I meant just now by saying that God had fooled me. He made me take my pride for virtue. He was laughing at me. It amuses him. I think he plays with us as a cat does with a mouse. He sends us temptations which he knows we shan't be able to resist; but when we do resist he revenges himself still worse.[112]

M. La Pérouse goes even further. After the "suicide" of his grandson Boris, who was pushed into the act by his friends, he again reflects on the relationship between the divine and the demonic. Edouard cites him as follows in his journal:

> "Have you noticed that in this world God always keeps silent? It's only the devil who speaks. Or at least, at least ..." he went on, "... however carefully we listen, it's only the devil we can succeed in hearing...
> "No, no!" he cried, confusedly; "the devil and God are one and the same; they work together. We try to believe that everything bad on earth comes from the devil, but it's because, if we didn't, we should never find strength to forgive God. He plays with us like a cat, tormenting a mouse ... and then afterwards he wants us to be grateful to him as well. Grateful for what? For what?..."
> "Do you know the most horrible thing of all that he has done?... Sacrificed his own son to save us. His son! His son!... Cruelty! That's the principal attribute of God."[113]

In this hard and profound passage, Gide points to the element that makes God resemble Satan—the sacrifice of Jesus in order to redeem human

---

[112] Gide, *The Counterfeiters*, 110.
[113] Ibid., 371-372.

beings. Christianity in general and Protestantism in particular, as shown below, emphasize religious temptation. In Judaism, by contrast, God does not ostensibly appear as tempter. But is this schematic description indeed accurate? Consider the following passage in Deuteronomy 13: 2-4:

> If there arise among you a prophet, or a dreamer of dreams, and he give thee a sign or a wonder, and the sign or the wonder come to pass, of which he spoke to thee, saying, Let us go after other gods, which thou hast not known, and let us serve them; thou shalt not hearken to the words of that prophet or that dreamer of dreams: for the Lord your God puts you to the proof, to know whether you love the Lord your God with all your heart and with all your soul.

In a literal reading, God tries the people of Israel by tempting them to transgress the very obligation to worship him. The purpose of the trial/temptation is to assess the measure of the people's love and devotion: should they deviate from their faith, their love for God will prove not to be absolute, but should they adhere to him, that will be proof of the absolute nature of the people of Israel's relationship with their God. The temptation is thus a kind of test that God requires the people to pass:

> "For the Lord your God puts you to the proof and so forth": God requires of you—as a test of your complete commitment and faithfulness—that even this temptation, supported by a sign or a wonder, shall not undermine your commitment and faithfulness.[114]

---

[114] *The Hirsch Chumash*, translation and commentary by R. Samson Raphael Hirsch, English translation by Daniel Haberman (Jerusalem-New York: Feldheim-Judaica Press, 2009), Deuteronomy 13:4. Licht, *"Testing" in the Hebrew Scriptures*, draws a sharp distinction between test and temptation as, in his view, does the Bible. Equating between them was the initiative of the rabbis on the one hand, and of the New Testament on the other. He therefore assumes that this story does not refer to temptation: "To be precise, we will find that this is neither a torture nor a temptation but a demand to persist in divine worship despite everything; God tries the people in the confusion that He causes them, a confusion that is both emotional and intellectual" (p. 16). Licht's claim is unnecessary and rests on a specific view of temptation, whereby temptation is related to a kind of sin that involves pleasure. If one renounces the pleasure dimension, however, a test can be equated with temptation whenever it involves a sin. In this reading, the test in this story too is obviously a kind of temptation, since responding to such a prophet would be a sin.

Jewish sages throughout the ages have felt uneasy with this reading of the text, since the classic trial is that of Abraham, where God himself demands absolute devotion and loyalty. By contrast, the current test is indeed a temptation that human beings should reject. But if God is the tempter—how can believers resist this temptation? One trend in the exegetical literature indeed held that the prophet discussed here is a false prophet,[115] but this interpretation is not free of problems either. The Torah attests: "for the Lord your God puts you to the proof,"[116] meaning that even if this prophet is not actually a true prophet, by failing to prevent his action God becomes an "accomplice." God's inaction, then, is a purposeful act, as the Torah shows according to R. Yitzhak Arama: "The Holy One, blessed be He, could have eliminated that sign and wonder so as to show it up as deceitful and, if He did not, it was in order to purify the people and know 'whether you love the Lord your God' and so forth."[117] But even according to this exegesis, God is still allowing human beings to be at the risk of temptation. How should this religious reality be understood? The answer to this question is particularly interesting, since it served in a way as an opportunity for redrawing the character of faith and of religious commitment. Maimonides offers an impressive expression of the confrontation with this problem, and many other thinkers followed in his wake. Maimonides assumes that the purpose of this test is to set up a religious paradigm:

> Know that the aim and meaning of all the *trials* mentioned in the *Torah* is to let people know what they ought to do or what they must believe. Accordingly the notion of a *trial* consists as it were in a certain act being done, the purpose being not the accomplishment of that particular act, but the latter's being a model to be imitated and followed.[118]

---

[115] This is Maimonides' stance in *The Guide of the Perplexed*, trans. Shlomo Pines (Chicago: University of Chicago Press, 1963), III:24, 497, and in Laws of the Foundation of the Torah 8:3. See the exegeses *ad locum* of Gersonides, Ibn Ezra, Abrabanel, and Yitzhak Arama (*Akedat Yitzhak*, Deuteronomy [1974], 52b); R. Moses Hayyim Luzzato, "Derekh Ha-Shem," in *Yalkut Yedi'ot ha-Emet*, vol. 1 (no publisher or date), Part 3, ch. 4, 138-139, and more.
[116] See Abrabanel *ad locum*, and also R. Akiva in TB Sanhedrin 90a.
[117] Arama, *Akedat Yitzhak*, 52b. See also Rashi *ad locum*.
[118] Maimonides, *Guide*, III:24, 498 (emphasis in original).

Resting on this assumption, Maimonides outlines in *Laws of the Foundations of the Torah* (8:2) the nature of faith in the Torah and in Moses. This faith rests, rather than on wonders, on every single Jew's direct experience of the Sinai epiphany. Faith in the Torah is the basis for testing the prophet:

> Hence, one may conclude with regard to every prophet after Moses, that we do not believe in such a prophet because of the signs he shows, as much as to say that only if he shows a sign, we shall pay heed to him in all that he says, but we believe in him, because of the charge laid down by Moses in the Torah that if a prophet gives a sign "he shall listen to him"; just as the Lawgiver directed that a cause is to be decided on the evidence of two witnesses even if we have no certainty as to whether they are testifying to the truth or to a falsehood. Similarly, it is our duty to listen to the prophet though we do not know if the sign he shows is genuine or has been performed with the aid of sorcery and by secret arts.[119]

Faith in the prophet is thus one of the institutions of the Torah. It derives its authority from a Torah command rather than from the epistemological truth of the prophecy. The believer is required to cling to this faith rather than yield to the temptation of misleading manifestations of prophecy.

According to this approach, then, believers are not required to renounce their rational-critical discretion even when faced with what appears to be a divine revelation. Indeed, believers must consistently exercise this discretion, which organizes the hierarchical order of their religious commitment. Therefore, wherever the "divine" revelation contradicts their religious commitment, believers must reject it and assume it to be misleading.[120] The irrationality of the prophet's words is thus the decisive testimony against the truth of the revelation, as suggested in the following commentary on the Deuteronomy verse:

> And He commanded that we should not listen to the words of the prophet, nor to his signs and wonders. Because the first lesson is

---

[119] *Mishneh Torah, The Book of Knowledge*, trans. Moses Hyamson (Jerusalem: Boys Town, 1962), 44a

[120] See also Menachem Krakovski, *Avodat ha-Melekh* (Jerusalem: Mosad Harav Kook, 1971) and Maimonides, *Code*, Laws of the Foundations of the Torah, 8:3.

> that one who gives a sign or a wonder denying the existence of God, may He be blessed, or His wisdom, or His grace and His goodness to His creatures, is surely engaging in self-contradiction. As is well known, one who negates one of the Creator's perfections negates all of them.... How, then, will he be able to bring evidence that he is an emissary of the omnipotent God when he himself negates his sender? Hence, when the prophet speaks God's word and gives a sign and wonder, his words must fit everything we have understood so far through the power of the intellect given by the Creator and, if they do not, he is a false prophet.[121]

When facing this prophet, then, we are tested not only on our absolute devotion to God but also on the nature of this devotion: unless it includes a measure of criticism, it could mislead us and cause us to stumble. In these circumstances, God indeed tempts us to sin. But if the believers start from a basically critical religious disposition, meaning that they examine religious phenomena such as prophecy according to the critical-rational criteria based on their religious commitment, the responsibility for their religious stance is contingent solely on them. Believers of this kind will not be tempted and will show the proper religious devotion.

Paul Tillich describes the distinction between demonic passion and religious ecstasy with great religious sensitivity. His views are discussed at length below, but the following statement is relevant at this point: "While demonic possession destroys the rational structure of the mind, divine ecstasy preserves and elevates it, although transcending it. Demonic possession destroys the ethical and logical principles of reason; divine ecstasy affirms them."[122] The prophet-inciter pairing confirms Tillich's distinction. It assumes that the believer is tested precisely on this matter: Does the believer's initial dispositional commitment to God include all the components of faith—commitment to the Torah and a constant critique of religious manifestations? Or is the believer perhaps enthralled by the religious manifestation as such, and led by religious devotion to the edge of the religious abyss?

---

[121] *Bi'ur ad locum. Cf.* also Ibn Ezra *ad locum*: "Because even if the sign and wonder come, he should not be believed because this contradicts reason."
[122] Paul Tillich, *Systematic Theology*, vol. 1 (Chicago: University of Chicago Press, 1967), 114.

In Deuteronomy, the initiative to the temptation is human: "If there arise among you a prophet... and he give thee a sign or a wonder."[123] This formulation confirms that the divine temptation is evident in God's very avoidance of interference with the human initiative of one considered a prophet. But in II Samuel 24:1, God is involved in direct temptation: "And again the anger of the Lord burnt against Israel, and he incited David against them, saying, Go, number Israel and Judah."[124]

In this story, God engages in tempting (literally: "he incited"[125]) David to commit a forbidden action—counting the people of Israel.[126] And yet, David assumes the responsibility and acknowledges his sin: "And David said to God, I have sinned greatly, because I have done this thing: but now, I pray thee, take away the iniquity of thy servant; for I have done very foolishly."[127]

Even if tempted by God, then, David is still responsible. He cannot give up his freedom and his responsibility by casting blame on the tempting God. This reading of the text evokes religious and moral problems: how can this direct act of temptation be ascribed to God? And if God is a tempter, why should blame be cast on David? Furthermore, according to the story, David accepts the blame and asks God for forgiveness—but if this was God's initiative, why does David see himself as a sinner? R. Levi b. Gershon writes in his exegesis on the Book of Samuel:

> Know that we should understand from this that God does not incite David to count them. Were it so, no blame could be cast on David for this, so how did then God inflict on him this divine punishment? What is said is that this incitement is ascribed to God generally, since He is the cause of all that happens.

Contrary to the ascription of the temptation to God in the Book of Samuel, however, in I Chronicles 21:1 the story is corrected and the temptation is ascribed to Satan: "And Satan stood up against Israel and provoked David to number Israel." The responsibility imposed on David,

---

[123] See also Nahmanides *ad locum*.
[124] Thanks to Dov Schwartz, who pointed out to me the importance of this text for the current discussion.
[125] See I Chronicles 21:1, *Metsudat Zion*, on temptation.
[126] See Exodus 30:12.
[127] I Chronicles 21:8.

as well as his feeling of guilt, is due to his having succumbed to Satan's temptation. Despite this correction, the key question is how to understand the text in the Book of Samuel which explicitly identifies God as the tempter.

The Talmud confronts this question in TB Berakhot 62b, and turns these two stories into two parts of one story. The text turns the reader's attention to David's question to Saul, where he ascribes Saul's incitement against him to God. The verses in I Samuel 26:18-19 read: "And he said, Why does my Lord thus pursue after his servant? For what have I done? Or what evil is in my hand? Now therefore I pray thee.... If the Lord has stirred thee up against me...." The Talmud assumes that David's statement is the key to the connection between these two stories:

> R. Eleazar said: "The Holy One, blessed be He, said to David: 'You call me an inciter. Behold, I will make thee stumble over something that even school-children know, as it is written, 'When thou dost take the sum of the children of Israel after their number, then shall they give every man a ransom for his soul to the Lord' [Exodus 30: 12]. Forthwith, 'Satan stood up against Israel' [I Chronicles 21:1) and it is further written, 'He incited David against them saying, Go, number Israel' [II Samuel 24:1]. And when he [David] did number them, he took no ransom from them and it is written: 'So the Lord sent a pestilence upon Israel from the morning even to the time appointed' [II Samuel 24:15]."[128]

According to R. Eleazar, the story in Chronicles reports what really happened: Satan tempted David, not God. But the question then is: How did God allow Satan's temptation? And if God did allow it, why was David punished? R. Eleazar's answer is that God allowed it as a punishment for David construing God as inciter and tempter.

On closer scrutiny, this Talmudic discourse is revealed as assuming that God is not a tempter; only Satan or the evil inclination tempts humans, who can overcome this temptation. Yielding to temptation, then, is solely a human responsibility. According to this interpretation, however, how should we understand that the Book of Samuel ascribes David's incitement to God? The Talmudic narrator does not answer this question, but post-Talmudic literature offers several answers. One

---

[128] TB Berakhot 62b.

argues that even if the tempter is Satan or the evil inclination, the temptation is ascribed to God because God refrained from helping David to overcome it. In his commentary *Ets Yosef*, R. Hanokh Zondel writes:

> The crux of the matter—God did not create the evil inclination to incite man. Quite the contrary, the Holy One, blessed be He, helps to save man from the incitement of the evil inclination, and evil is ascribed to the man who chooses to be attracted to it and who is vexed by God drawing attention to the good. Because man is free to refuse the good and to choose evil.... And as for what the Holy One, blessed be He, said, "you called me an inciter," as if it were from me that Saul was incited by the evil inclination ... that is why God said "Behold, I will make thee stumble"... When divine help was withdrawn from David, he was incited by the evil inclination.[129]

In this interpretation, the temptation story has two protagonists: Satan, who initiates it, and God, who refrains from preventing it. Because of this abstention, the temptation in the Book of Samuel is ascribed to God, though God is neither the initiator nor the tempter.

R. Shmuel Eidels (MaHaRSHA) offers another reading. In his view, God is not one of the protagonists in this story, and the story in the Book of Samuel reflects David's false consciousness: "'He incited'—God was the inciter according to David, as he said, 'If the Lord has stirred thee up against me.'"[130] The relationship between the story in Chronicles and the story in the Book of Samuel is like the relationship between the actual event—reported in the Chronicles story—and the inner, conscious event reported in the Book of Samuel. According to this interpretation, the distinction between the divine and the demonic is not self-evident. David was wrong and ascribed Satan's action to God. God is not present in the full transparency of his being, and mistakes are therefore possible.

And yet, MaHaRSHA too understands that the Talmudic story about the actual event poses a theological problem and, therefore, holds that this event is the result of David's erroneous behavior: "As for them calling the Holy One, blessed be He, an inciter, it was God's wrath that let

---

[129] Ein Yosef, in *Ein Yaakov*, TB Berakhot 62b, s. v. *"mesit karita li."*
[130] R. Samuel Eidels (MaHaRSHA) on TB Berakhot 62b, s. v. *"va-ya'amod."*

Satan incite David to count them without a ransom in order to mislead him" (ibid.). David's mistake, then, is not simply the result of a human epistemological limitation that results in his inability to distinguish the divine from the demonic, but of the sin that blinds his understanding.

The structuring of the Talmudic narrative and its interpretations suggest that, rather than God being the tempter, temptation originates in the sinner's acts. Emerging from this intergenerational discourse is a deep reluctance to ascribe an act of temptation to God and the imposition of responsibility entirely on human beings—they are free to choose between good and evil and should not ascribe the source of evil to God.

Other biblical sources, however, do ascribe the temptation to God, in tempting his prophets. The verse in Ezekiel 14:9 reads: "And if the prophet is enticed to utter a prophecy, I the Lord have enticed that prophet, and I will stretch out my hand against him and destroy him from among my people Israel." Similarly, I Kings 22:20-21 reads: "And the Lord said, 'Who will entice Ahab into attacking Ramot Gilead and going to his death there?' And one said on this manner, and another said on that manner."

In both these texts, God appears as the enticer causing the seduced to stumble. In the opening of his commentary on Kings, R. David Kimchi (RaDaK) indeed raises anew the reluctance to ascribe an act of temptation to God: "These words are a great embarrassment to one who understands them literally." In his view, both in Kings and in Ezekiel the reference is to false prophets. The temptation, then, is not meant to hamper the prophet but to administer the punishment deserved by a sinner. In the wake of this exegesis, Spinoza wrote:

> God never deceives the good, nor His chosen, but (according to the ancient proverb [I Samuel 24:14], and as appears in the history of Abigail and her speech) [I Samuel 25], God uses the good as instruments of goodness, and the wicked as means to execute His wrath. This may be seen from the case of Micaiah above quoted;[131] for although God had determined to deceive Ahab, through prophets, He made use of lying prophets; to the good prophet He revealed the truth, and did not forbid his proclaiming it.[132]

---

[131] Referring to the story in I Kings quoted above.
[132] Benedict de Spinoza, *Tractatus Thelogico-Politicus*, trans R. H. M. Elwes (London and New York: George Routledge and Sons, 1905), 28-29.

According to this interpretation, God neither tempts nor hinders his believers—he acts as a tempter only to the wicked. The key question is: Does this traditional exegesis, as summed up by Spinoza, fit the meaning of the text? Indeed, RaDaK himself noted that his own interpretation (and Spinoza's in his wake) fails to fit the literal meaning. But even if we assume it to be consistent with the biblical text, we cannot ignore the existence of an alternative interpretation. The story in the Book of Kings appears in a parallel version in II Chronicles 18:4-5:

> And Jehoshafat said to the king of Israel: Inquire, I pray thee, of the word of the Lord to day. Therefore the king of Israel gathered together prophets, four hundred men, and said to them, Shall we go to Ramot-Gilead to battle, or shall I forbear? And they said, Go up, for God will deliver it into the king's hand.

In an exegesis ascribed to Rashi, relating these verses to the story in the Book of Kings, they are interpreted as follows:

> "Inquire, I pray thee, of the word of the Lord to day"—and not of the word of the Baal prophets whom you trust. "Therefore the king of Israel gathered together prophets, four hundred men"—who were all true prophets, because he did what Jehoshafat had asked him, as he proves in the contiguous verse (ch. 20):[133] "And there came forth a spirit and stood before the Lord and said, I will persuade him" up to "I will go out and I will be a lying spirit in the mouth of all his prophets," telling them to tell Ahab "Go up; for the Lord shall deliver it into the hand of the king," so it follows that they were God's prophets who would only prophesy the word of God. *Had they been false prophets, temptation would not apply to them,*[134] and they would only prophesy whatever they imagined. Moreover, Jehoshafat again said: "Is there not here a prophet of the Lord and so forth."[135] I surely know they are God's prophets, except that I learned in my father's household that no two prophets ever speak the same words in the same ways, and all here say, go up and you will succeed.[136]

---

[133] Referring to the story in I Kings.
[134] My emphasis.
[135] II Chronicles 18:6.
[136] Rashi on I Kings 22:20.

Faith as Temptation

In this interpretation, the true prophets are actually the ones who might be tempted by God; by contrast, the false prophets do not need any temptation to prophesy deceit. Temptation is thus a phenomenon inherent in faith rather than external to it. Advocates of this approach must still contend with the question: How could God hamper his believers? Can God's prophets and believers reject the divine word? This text offers no answer to these questions, but Rashi's exegesis of Ezekiel is an initial attempt to confront this problem: "'And if the prophet is enticed,' and did not speak the truth, 'I the Lord have enticed,' I have allowed him to choose. Hence, we should say he is allowed to choose deceit."[137]

The assumption underlying this approach is that the prophet is not an entirely "passive entity," a medium devoid of any concrete being. Even a person found in the unique religious situation of prophecy does not cease to be a specific human creature. The mode of communication between God and human beings depends on both sides, a notion that Heschel formulates as follows:

> The prophet is not a passive recipient, a recording instrument, affected from without without participation of heart and will, nor is he a person who acquires his vision by his own strength and labor. The prophet's personality is rather a unity of inspiration and experience, invasion and response. ...
>
> Even in the moment of the event he is, we are told, an active partner in the event. His response to what is disclosed to him turns revelation into a dialogue. In a sense, prophecy consists of a revelation of God and a *co-revelation of man*.[138]

To someone turning to God with a negative disposition, God's word will also appear negatively. God's word, then, is not an autonomous event constituted by the prophetic vision and detached from any human context. Not only is human autonomy not dismissed, but the religious relationship between human beings and God is actually founded on it.

This implicit assumption is clearly exposed in another source—the commentary of R. Nissim Gaon on the story about the oven of Akhnai (TB Bava Metsia 59a-b). A classic question that persistently troubled rabbinic sages was: assuming that R. Joshua is right and "Torah is not in

---

[137] Rashi on Ezekiel 14:9.
[138] Heschel, *God in Search of Man*, 259-260. Emphasis in the original.

Heaven," what is the meaning of a heavenly voice stating that Halakhah follows R. Eliezer? R. Nissim gives two answers to this question, and the second is cited below:

> The intent is to test the sages and see whether the voice will lead them to change their views, as it is said, "for the Lord your God puts you to the proof" [Deuteronomy 13: 4], thereby pointing to the power of their convictions. And R. Joshua said, "It is not in Heaven," because God's Torah is complete and has already been given to us at Sinai, and He has advised us that nothing will be changed in it, and no contradictions or doubts remain in our Torah that would require a sign from Heaven.[139]

R. Nissim's answer explicates the role of divine temptation in the divine-human discourse in new terms. Prima facie, the heavenly voice is a direct and immediate expression of the divine demand, so how can a person resist it?! The Talmud provides a formal answer: the Torah is not in Heaven and the divine legislator has no right to interfere in the halakhic discourse. This formal answer, however, does not satisfy R. Nissim, since the religious question remains open: what is God's role in the halakhic discourse? From a theological-religious perspective, we cannot assume that God would not accept the rules of his own system. R. Nissim therefore argues that God's action is a kind of temptation that should be rejected. Halakhically, then, compliance and obedience are religious dispositions that should be rejected. They are a kind of temptation of faith against which the believer must struggle.

This approach, as noted, rests on the centrality of human autonomy in religious life, which requires a restrained religious disposition as dictated by Halakhah. In the opening to his book *Man'ulei ha-Talmud*, R. Nissim proclaims that rational moral duties bind human beings without a divine positive command: "All the commandments that depend on reason and on the understanding of the heart are incumbent on all from the day that God created human beings on earth, on them and on their descendants forever and ever."[140]

---

[139] *Shitah Mekubetset*, TB Bava Metzia 59b, s.v. "*ve-zeh leshono ha-R. Nissim Gaon z"l.*"
[140] R. Nissim Gaon, *Sefer ha-Mafteah le-Man'ulei ha-Talmud* (Vienna, 1847), 1:2. For a discussion of R. Nissim Gaon's position see Avi Sagi, *Judaism: Between Religion and Morality* (Tel Aviv: Hakibbutz Hameuhad, 1998), 119 (Hebrew).

These statements, like R. Nissim's view on the temptation of faith, rest on the fundamental meaning of halakhic practice. This practice does not unfold in a cultural vacuum: rather than an exercise in the detachment of human beings from the surrounding world, it is founded on the deepest and most elementary foundations of human existence. Halakhic practice is meant to refine, amend, and regulate human reality, not to negate it altogether. Halakhah assumes that human beings, as autonomous creatures endowed with consciousness and with independent judgment, are partners of God in the shaping of reality. Negating human autonomy by making unconditional obedience to God a religious ideal is thus a kind of religious temptation that must be rejected because it subverts the meaning of religious life itself. Addressing God's word as temptation is thus meant to push human beings back into their existence as autonomous creatures, and shape their religious disposition from that starting point.

Human beings are responsible for their disposition vis-à-vis God's word as well, as the following midrash excels in conveying:[141]

> You find that when the Holy One, blessed be He, said to him [to Moses]: "Go, get thee down, for thy people ... have become corrupt" [Exodus 32: 7], he still held on to the tablets and would not believe that Israel had sinned. He said, "Unless I see it, I do not believe it," as it is said, "And it came to pass, as soon as he came near to the camp..." [Exodus 32: 19), that he did not break them until he saw with his own eyes. Woe to them who give testimony on what they have not seen! Could it be that Moses did not believe the Holy One, blessed be He, who said, "thy people ... have become corrupt"? [Not so], but Moses thereby taught Israel a lesson—even one who hears something from the most trustworthy source must not accept the testimony and act upon it unless he has seen it.[142]

Even vis-à-vis God, human beings should not renounce their own discretion, judgment, and critical faculties. This, then, is the religious disposition required from believers, not self-disparagement or uncritical compliance.

---

[141] I am grateful to Menachem Fisch for the reference to this midrash as well as for the analysis that follows.
[142] *Midrash Rabbah*, Exodus, 46:1.

The importance of this analysis becomes clear given that protection from the temptation of faith might be attained through extra-halakhic values, which is precisely the view of theologian Arthur Green. As a theologian contending with his own concrete being, Green writes:

> In my own religious life, I have come to recognize the need for *submission* to God as a part of religious devotion.... I believe there is no room for God ... in our lives until we have overcome our own willfulness. To thus submit, to "negate your will before God's will," is essential to accepting the covenant as I have described it.[143]

What is the mechanism that Green offers for confronting the temptation of faith? He argues that only religious values, outside Halakhah, will supply this kind of protection:

> Here, the non-Orthodoxy of my theology is critical to my religious life. Because I know of the human role in the origin of the commandments, and because I know that all human creations are fallible, I never hand myself over entirely to them.... Out of my love for our ancestors and the divine spirit that dwelt within them, I choose to live in faithfulness to the religious discipline they created. I will do so wherever this discipline does not bring me into conflict with more deeply held religious principles: awareness ... recognizing all humans as bearers of the divine image, and the seven Noahide commandments as I understand them.[144]

The conclusion that emerges from Green's view is that only the non-halakhic believer endorses a critical religious position. A believer committed to Halakhah as the word of God is thus doomed to live in error and temptation.

This conclusion is incompatible with the rich Jewish literature discussed in this article, and expresses no more than Green's negation of the halakhic world of faith. This world is outlined in negative colors, presented as the antithesis of the religious world that Green believes in, but in fact it is not. The halakhic world of faith, which is aware of the possibility of temptation, makes the individual responsible for contending with

---

[143] Arthur Green, *Seek My Face, Speak My Name: A Contemporary Jewish Theology* (Northvale, NJ: Jason Aronson, 1992), 132-133 (emphasis in original).
[144] Ibid.

temptation, even when the tempter is actually God. The means are not the negation of Halakhah but the values and dispositions of Halakhah *per se*, which guide individuals to be critical even of what appears to them as a religious demand. Religious critique, then, is not an extra-religious, "non-Orthodox" stance but indeed an "Orthodox" halakhic stance.

Commenting on a halakhic passage, R. Judah Aryeh Leib of Gur recognizes a critical religious position as the height of religious perfection. His thesis states that, in certain circumstances, temptation is an affirmation of religious perfection and conveys God's confidence in the ability of the exemplary believer to resist it. Temptation is a reward, as it were, which God grants this kind of believer in recognition of the power of his faith. This view of temptation represents a radical turnabout in the meaning of religious temptation—from a kind of danger to be avoided into a kind of reward for religious perfection.

To understand R. Judah Aryeh Leib's position, it is necessary to present the full context of the discussion in which he participates, a context seemingly distant from the current subject. TB Yoma 86b reads: "How is one proved a repentant sinner?— R. Judah said: As, for instance, if he has an opportunity to repeat his original transgression, and he keeps away from it. R. Judah indicated: With the same woman, at the same time, in the same place." In the post-Talmudic literature, R. Judah's view evoked many questions, mainly concerning the relationship between the inner process of repentance and the external event of the opportunity to transgress. R. Moshe Sofer formulated these questions as follows:

> This is surprising—one who transgressed prohibitions of adultery and of other incestuous relationships punishable by death ... will atone by standing in the same place and so forth, no longer a sinner?... Moreover, one who has committed one transgression and one who has sinned ten times, both receive the same answer?[145]

The conclusion emerging from the Talmudic quotation is that repentance depends on the recurrence of the opportunity to sin. And yet, R. Judah Aryeh Leib asks: "This formulation is not clear ... if he has no option of transgressing again, can he not repent?"[146] In his answer to these questions, R. Sofer assumes that the act of repentance is an inner

---

[145] *Hiddushei Hatam Sofer* on TB Yoma *ad locum*.
[146] Alter, *Sefat Emet*, TB Yoma *ad locum*.

change, and the test that R. Judah proposes is only an epistemological mechanism allowing us to ensure that this inner event has occurred:

> The truth is indeed so. After he has ... desisted from his sin, and when he is fully determined never to repeat it, has shown remorse and pondered his original act, he is then as fit as any other Jew and trustworthy regarding the very thing on which he had transgressed.... But how will it be known that he has fully repented and forever abandoned this sin and that we should think of him as a repentant sinner?... The rabbis said that when he stands at the same time in the same place and with the same woman and does not sin, we shall know he has fully repented and has definitely left sin behind.[147]

R. Sofer rightfully notes that his analysis is compatible with Maimonides' ruling. In Laws of Repentance 2:2, Maimonides states: "It consists in this, that the sinner abandon his sin, remove it from his thoughts, and resolve in his heart never to repeat it... that he regret the past." Repentance is thus an inner event: the sinner changes his attitude toward sin by changing his disposition. In the previous law, Maimonides had formulated the epistemological principle attesting to the inner event: "What is perfect repentance? It is so when an opportunity presents itself for repeating an offence once committed, and the offender, while able to commit the offence nevertheless refrains from doing so, because he is penitent and not out of fear or failure of vigor."

This distinction between the inner event and the epistemological principle also explicates the change between R. Judah and Maimonides. The Talmudic passage states: "If the object which caused his original transgression comes before him on two occasions, and he keeps away from it"—that is, the event must take place more than once to justify the occurrence of repentance. Maimonides, by contrast, adopts the version of R. Yitzhak Alfasi (RYF): "How is one proved a repentant sinner? If one can do wrong but refrains from it."[148] Indeed, if the gist of repentance is the inner event rather than passing the test of an external event, once is enough. In R. Yosef Engel's formulation:

> Why two occasions regarding this matter? Twice applies in case of a presumption, and presumption does not apply here because

---

[147] *Hiddushei Hatam Sofer* on TB Yoma *ad locum*.
[148] See also *Dikdukei Soferim*, TB Yoma *ad locum*.

the whole matter of repentance is before the One who probes the heart and mind, may He be blessed, and He knows if repentance is genuine ... and if it is not, even refraining from it twice will not help.[149]

This insight is strengthened even further by the wording of the Talmudic passage stating: "as, for instance, if he has an opportunity to repeat his original transgression." The external event, then, is only an instance of repentance, but does not constitute repentance as such. Maimonides, too, who omitted the terms "for instance" in the first law, preserved the distinction between the internal and external events through the two terms he uses: in the first law he relates to "perfect repentance," and in the second he deals with the definition of repentance—"What is perfect repentance?"

This entire discussion was before R. Judah Aryeh Leib. He too understood that repentance is internal and unconditioned by an external contingent event. His textual sensitivity, however, leads him to reject the possibility of understanding the Talmudic passage in Yoma as describing a hypothetical situation: "And it is not plausible to understand this as saying that this person has repented so thoroughly that, had he had an opportunity [to repeat his transgression], he would not have done so."[150] This interpretation leaves open the question of how this external contingent event will be made to happen. R. Judah Aryeh Leib provides a surprising answer:

> Perhaps it means that one who has truly repented is given the opportunity to transgress in what he has avoided, so that he may know that his repentance has been accepted. Why would he need a first and a second time? Indeed, according to the version of *Dikdukei Soferim* and of Asheri, "when he had an opportunity to transgress and refrained." And this is how it should be.

According to this interpretation, the possibility of an external sin is ensured through divine intervention—he is "given the opportunity." Furthermore, the actual repetition of the possibility of sin is an affirmation to the individual of the nature of his or her repentance. Tempting

---

[149] R. Yosef Engel, *Giliyonei ha-Shas* (Vienna: 1924), TB Yoma *ad locum*.
[150] Alter, *Sefat Emet*, TB Yoma *ad locum*.

people could lead them to do wrong and, if God is the tempter, responsibility for the transgression will supposedly be assigned to God. R. Judah Aryeh Leib does not relate to this possibility nor does he assume, as noted, that even if God is the tempter the responsibility is ultimately human. Rather, the divine temptation attests to the repenter's exemplary religious merit.

This view recurs in the approach of R. Shakh when faced with the theological problem posed by the success of Zionism, a secular movement he considers destructive to Jewish existence. In his view, this success is a test and, in the formulation used here, a "temptation" believers must confront. Their success as believers becomes manifest in their refusal to endorse the Zionist outlook: "All this comes from the Holy One, blessed be He, to test the people of Israel, to see if they have deviated from the path he has traced for us."[151]

In sum, divine temptation is not a phenomenon that threatens religions "from outside" but a manifestation of religious perfection. The borders between the divine and the demonic are not clear-cut and absolute. Rather, the demonic crouching at the door to hinder us is inherent within the religious domain. This topic is at the focus of the next section.

IV. Faith as Temptation, the Temptation of the Evil Inclination and the Demonic

The texts I have discussed point to the similarities between the temptation of the evil inclination and a religiosity that materializes as temptation, so that the distinction between them may at times require subtle analysis. What appears to be the temptation of faith emerges, on closer scrutiny, as a temptation of the evil inclination. The history of religions points to many confrontations with the problem of the closeness between the demonic and the divine.

One frequently stated suggestion for distinguishing between them is to focus on the object of passion. Even in situations where the evil inclination materializes in the religiously demonic, it can be distinguished from a proper religious stance by focusing on the object of religious passion. The basic assumption of this stance is that the meaning of divine

---

[151] R. Eliezer Schakh, *Letters and Papers*, vol. 1-2 (Benei Berak: n. p., 1988-1998), 28 (Hebrew). See also vol. 6, 88.

worship cannot be discussed in isolation and without relating to the nature of the God that is the object of this worship: "Worship is an intentional type of activity or consciousness with a defined object—God. We can reasonably expect that the nature of this object will shape the nature of worship and the consciousness of worshippers toward it."[152] R. Ouzziel offers a clear formulation of this stance:

> When man creates his god in his own image as an arbitrary product of his imagination—how will he sanctify himself, how will he gain release from the wildness and coarseness inherent in his nature, and what spirit will cover him other than the impurity, the lust, the revenge, and the greed considered as permitted to him or as offerings bringing sweet savor to his idols? Have not all priests done this when enfolding themselves in the wrap of religiosity and for the sake of religiosity when, for the sake of their idolatry, they have plundered, ransacked, and killed, cruelly and savagely sacrificing the souls of pure innocents?! And all for what? To bring a sweet-savored offering to their god, who is of flesh in human image, who has suffered the pains of men and their torments, who has eaten and drank like men, fought, offended, hid, and denied himself like men, and who wishes to see the wicked game that men play with one another when they deny and kill the weak openly and by law.[153]

This text shows the author's profound controversy with Christianity. In his view, the glorification of human pain and human suffering found in Christianity originates in the perception of the Christian God. Christian religiosity took the form it did not because this is the nature of religiosity in general, but because the object of Christian faith is Jesus.

Albert Camus voiced a similar critique of Christian religiosity, holding that Christianity bears a large measure of responsibility for the flaws of human reality:

> For as long as the Western World has been Christian, the Gospels have been the interpreter between heaven and earth. Each time a solitary cry of rebellion was uttered,[154] the answer came in the form of an even more terrible suffering. In that Christ had suffered, and had suffered voluntarily, suffering was no longer unjust

---

[152] Sagi and Statman, *Religion and Morality*, 155.
[153] Ouzziel, *Derashot Ouzziel*, 5.
[154] Camus is referring here to rebellion against injustice.

> and all pain was necessary.... Only the sacrifice of an innocent God could justify the endless and universal torture of innocence. Only the most abject suffering by God could assuage man's agony.[155]

According to this view, what determines the nature of religiosity is the object of the religion rather than the believer's basic disposition. This statement is hard to deny—if religiosity has an object, the nature of the object will obviously determine the nature of religiosity, and if the object is demonic, so is the nature of the "divine" worship. The image of the god, therefore, could restrain the temptation of the evil inclination, even one materializing as a temptation of faith. Alternatively, the image of the god could intensify the materialization of the demonic temptation of faith and the temptation of the evil inclination itself.

And yet, even if we assume that the image of God plays a decisive role in curbing the temptation of the evil inclination or of demonic faith, we cannot but be impressed by the fact that religious literature includes texts pointing to the centrality of the dispositional element preceding the object of divine worship. According to these texts, the meaning of the object and the extent of its relevance to life are conditioned by this initial disposition. The texts discussed here so far recurrently emphasize that the believers' initial disposition is what will purportedly protect them from the temptation of faith, which may be initiated by God, and from that of the evil inclination. R. Ouzziel, who defended a thesis about the crucial role of the object of divine worship, was the one who, as noted, stressed the importance of the believer's disposition.

Only in light of the assumption about the centrality and primacy of the religious disposition vis-à-vis the religious object can we understand the duty of self-confrontation, through which individuals will develop the critical faculty that will ultimately lead them in the right course. The believers' confrontation covers three adjacent realms: the temptation of the evil inclination, the temptation of faith, and faith itself. More precisely: the religious struggle of believers for their faith covers what is seemingly outside faith—the evil inclination—and what might trip them up within faith itself—faith as temptation.

---

[155] Albert Camus, *The Rebel: An Essay on Man in Revolt*, trans. Anthony Bower (New York: Alfred A. Knopf, 1956), 34. For a detailed analysis of Camus' stance, see Sagi, *Albert Camus*, ch. 13.

Psychologically, the evil inclination and the temptation of faith resemble one another: both, and even faith itself, are constituted by a passion for the object. Individuals are sometimes carried away by this passion to the point of feeling worthless vis-à-vis the object of their passion.[156] This closeness between the mental states generated an approach that sought to create a spiritual process wherein the intensity of passion is corrected, refined, and realized anew within religious life.

At the start of the discussion, I cited the passage in TB Kiddushin stating that the Torah acts as a spice of the evil inclination, through which we overcome its temptation. But R. Abraham Hayyim of Zlotschov, a disciple of the Maggid of Mezeritch, writes:

> But the Rabbi ... my teacher Dov Ber ... commented on Kiddushin 30: "I have created the evil inclination and I have created a spice for it." The simile, however, does not resemble the referent—you spice meat, but the core is the meat rather than the spice, and here, he [the Maggid] said that the Torah is a spice and said that, indeed, the evil inclination is the core. A person, then, must worship with the passion ensuing from the evil inclination, and the Torah is the guide, truly as a spice.[157]

This daring text holds that the mental power concealed in the evil inclination is of great value in the worship of God.[158] R. Nahman of Bratslav writes in similar terms:

> A man who still has an evil inclination enjoys a great advantage because he can then worship Him, may He be blessed, precisely with the evil inclination. That is, take all the passion and the fervor and put them into the worship of God, pray and supplicate with the fervor and the passion of the heart, and so forth. And

---

[156] Weil notes: "Every creature which attains perfect obedience constitutes a special, unique, irreplaceable form of the presence, knowledge and operation of God in the world" (*Gravity and Grace*, 43).

[157] *Orah Hayyim*, Genesis 13: 2. The quote follows Mendel Piekarz, *Between Ideology and Reality: Humility, Ayin, Self-Negation and Devekuth in Hasidic Thought* (Jerusalem: Bialik Institute, 1994), 287 (Hebrew). See also the discussion in Mendel Piekarz, *The Beginning of Hasidism: Ideological Trends in Derush and Musar Literature* (Jerusalem: Bialik Institute, 1978), ch. 5 (Hebrew).

[158] For a bold development of this approach, see Tsadok Hacohen of Lublin, *Tsidkat ha-Tsaddik* (Jerusalem: 1968), 35 (44); 62 (102); 82-83 (133); 210-211 (249).

> if a person does not have an evil inclination, his worship is definitely not complete. And what is crucial is to restrain and contain the fervor at the time of passion and introduce it at the time of prayer and worship.... Even a man who is not altogether virtuous may occasionally pray with passion, and this also comes from the fervor of his evil inclination, although he is not rewarded for it. But for one who wishes to behave virtuously, having an evil inclination is a great advantage.[159]

Subjectively, then, the passion and the fervor of the evil inclination are identical to that of religiosity, and indeed foster it. The lack of instinctive passion mars the believer's religious stance. The atrophy of desire, writes Simone Weil, is the atrophy of the desire for the absolute, for the divine:

> Desire is evil and illusory, yet without desire we should not seek for that which is truly absolute, truly boundless.[160] We have to have experienced it. Misery of those beings from whom fatigue takes away that supplementary energy which is the source of desire.
> Misery also of those who are blinded by desire.[161]

The difference between the temptation of the evil inclination and that of faith lies in the object of passion. The closeness between the two mental situations—instinct and faith—could result in the blurring of the borders between them, which concretizes in faith as temptation. This state draws on the energy and the enthusiasm of instinctive desire without any constraint by God, who at times appears as the tempting element, or even by any other inner religious element, such as the halakhic norm.

A striking expression of the tension in the religious experience that extends between the divine and the demonic appears in the work of two thinkers—R. Nahman of Bratslav and R. Kook. R. Nahman writes:

> There are two types of daring [*he'azah*]. There is a daring of holiness, and we cannot receive the Torah except through it. As our rabbis said (Avot 2), "the shy man will not learn." And as our rabbis said (TB Betsah 25b), "Why was the Torah given to Israel? Because they are strong [*azim*]." And also (Avot 5), "be strong as the leopard." And that is why the Torah is called strength, as is

---

[159] R. Nahman of Bratslav, *Likkutei Moharan*, Tanina, #49.
[160] Weil refers to God through these terms.
[161] Weil, *Gravity and Grace*, 133.

written (Psalms 29) "The Lord gives strength to his people" ... because you cannot come to the Torah unless through the strength of holiness. And against it is the strength of the *sitra ahra*, from which come other laws, which are theirs.[162]

The extreme closeness between these two dispositions allows for their blurring, and R. Nahman therefore holds that only the *tsaddik* can distinguish between them:

> Through the strength that the *tsaddik* sees in each one as he really is, whether it is the strength of holiness or the opposite, through that he knows whether someone's prayer is fit or not. Because prayer too is strength, because you cannot pray before Him, may He be blessed, except through strength.[163]

R. Kook too, in one of his most personal texts, writes:

> And I will listen and hear, from the depths of my soul, from the feeling within my heart, God's voice calling. And I will fear greatly—have I stooped so low that I have become a false prophet, since God has sent me but God's word has not been revealed to me? And I will hear the voice of my soul sighing....[164]

This tortured personal confession presents R. Kook as one experiencing revelation but without this revelation bearing any religious certainty. This revelation could be God's but, no less so, it could also be demonic. The subjective experience *per se* cannot provide the answer to the question of revelation.[165] Indeed, R. Kook recovers immediately afterward and the rest of the text is an ode to prophecy, but the beginning expresses the hesitation and the uncertainty of the religious experience. No wonder, then, that this text was censored by David Hacohen, who appropriated R. Kook's *oeuvre* to himself. In *Orot ha-Koddesh*, therefore, an ellipsis replaces this opening.[166] This gap between the original reli-

---

[162] R. Nahman of Bratslav, *Likkutei Moharan, Tanina*, #30.
[163] Ibid.
[164] R. Kook, *Shemonah Kvatsim*, vol. 2, Kovets 4, 137, #17.
[165] See also Yaakov Moshe Harlap, *Mei Marom*, vol. 1 (Jerusalem: Bet Zevul, 1972), 61-63.
[166] See R. Kook, *Orot ha-Koddesh*, vol. 1, 157, #138.

gious experience and the attempt to conceal it is a clear expression of the religious difficulty of contending with the possibility of temptation that appears within the religious experience itself. But it is the unique experience reported by the man of faith, R. Kook, that points to the closeness between the demonic and the divine, a closeness constitutive of the religious disposition as such.

Paul Tillich traced this closeness between the demonic and the divine when he pointed out that the distinction between them grows from within the sphere of holiness itself: "The demonic is the Holy (or the sacred) with a minus sign before it, the sacred antidivine."[167] Tillich is aware of his analysis' implications for the religious realm—holiness itself becomes dialectical, meaning that its initial manifestation does not separate the divine from the demonic and they appear in it undifferentiated.[168] Religious consciousness is what discerns the demonic, and consequently identifies holiness with the divine.[169] In this view, the demonic is not equated with the secular but poses a challenge to the divine itself and, more precisely, offers what Tillich calls "a divine alternative."[170]

---

[167] Paul Tillich, *What is Religion* (New York: Harper and Row, 1969), 85. See also idem, *Dynamics of Faith* (New York: Harper and Row, 1957), 14-15.

[168] On this point, Tillich's analysis fits that of Rudolf Otto, *The Idea of the Holy: An Inquiry into the Non-Rational Factor in the Idea of the Divine and its Relation to the Rational*, trans. John W. Harvey (Oxford: Oxford University Press, 1958). Otto recurrently emphasizes the complex manifestation of the demonic and the divine. Clear traces of this ontological tradition appear often in kabbalistic literature. See, for instance, Isaiah Tishby, *The Doctrine of Evil and Kelippah in Lurianic Kabbalism* (Jerusalem: Akademon, 1979) (Hebrew).

[169] Tillich, *What is Religion*, 87.

[170] See Tillich, *Systematic Theology*, vol. 3, 102. The Gaon of Vilna suggests a similar outline of the religious field and says in *Seder Olam*: "Until now, prophets had prophesied in the holy spirit; henceforth, pay attention and heed the words of sages." *Seder Olam* (Jerusalem: 1987), ch. 30, 213. The Gaon comments: "'Until now, prophets'—means that once they have killed the evil inclination, prophecy is abolished" (ibid., #13). Like Tillich, the Gaon outlines the realm of holiness as one including both the demonic and the divine. Yet, one prominent difference between them is that, according to Tillich, the relationship between the divine and the demonic is dialectical and synchronistic. By contrast, the Gaon's position is far more radical: the demonic precedes and conditions the manifestation of the divine. I am grateful to David Kurzweil, who directed my attention to this text by the Gaon of Vilna.

Tillich holds that this basic demonic residue originates in ancestral myths that viewed demons as "divine-anti-divine beings."[171] But even after the removal of these demonic beings from religious history and culture, the demonic foundation remained. He argues that "the claim of something finite to infinity or to divine greatness is the characteristic of the demonic" (ibid.), and points out that demonization processes take place in all religions as a matter of routine.[172] Tillich's innovation is in the shift of the demonic realm from referring to an object "out there" to the act of consciousness itself; the act of consciousness constitutes the demonic. The distinction between the divine and the demonic thus shifts from the realm of objects to the realm of the subjective, hence the closeness of the demonic to the divine.

In this approach, the relationship between the divine and the temptation of the demonic inclination emerges in different terms. Usually, the evil inclination is perceived as an external threat to faith. Ethical literature in all its forms traces a linear progression, and the threat is invariably "outside." If we persist in the effort to amend our ways and attain self-control, we can be sure of overcoming the external threat. This approach assumes a dichotomy between holiness and temptation. R. David b. Yehoshua Maimoni offers a typical formulation of this view: "Should the pious man take this course, that is, [overcome temptation and] develop the proper disposition, he will reach the highest rung of happiness."[173] Progress is linear, even if fraught with obstacles.

---

[171] Ibid.

[172] Tillich claims that religion too can become demonic: "The demonic is a negative absolute. It is the elevation of something relative and ambiguous ... to absoluteness.... In the case of religion, the deification of the relative and the ambiguous means that a particular religion claims to be identical with the religious Absolute and rejects judgment against itself. This leads, internally, to demonic suppression of doubt, criticism, and honest search for truth within the particular religion itself; and it leads, externally, to the most demonic and destructive of all wars, religious wars. Such evils are unavoidable if a particular manifestation of the holy is identified with the holy itself." Paul Tillich, *My Search for Absolutes* (New York: Simon and Schuster, 1967), 132-133. Tillich offers a view of religious pluralism resembling those of Samuel Hugo Bergman and David Hartman. For an analysis of this pluralism and its limitations, see Avi Sagi, *A Challenge: Returning to Tradition* (Jerusalem: Shalom Hartman Institute, 2003), 349-355 (Hebrew).

[173] See David b. Yehoshua Maimoni, *Moreh ha-Prishut ve-Madrikh ha-Peshitut* (Jerusalem: 1987), 59.

Another impressive expression of this approach appears in two classic Christian texts, which guide the believer's progress. In *The Dark Night of the Soul*, St. John of the Cross describes the soul's "spiritual journey."[174] His basic assumption is that the believer seeking to be close to God must confront temptations. Confrontation with temptation is not merely a random event but a central component of the soul's path to God: "After all, if, through trials and temptations, a soul is not tempted and tried, if she is not tested and proved, how can her senses be quickened with wisdom?"[175]

The Dark Night of the Soul is an account of the soul whose initial state is that of imperfection. In this initial state, religious practice is not meant to serve God, but human beings:

> And so the soul [of the beginner] at first finds her bliss in spending long periods—sometimes whole nights—deep in prayer. Penances are her pleasures. Fasting makes her happy. Participating in rituals and discussing divine things consoles her.
>
> Even though she may tend earnestly to her spiritual practice, the beginner notices that she is spiritually weak and imperfect. This is because she is still motivated to engage in spiritual practices because of the comforts and pleasures they yield.[176]

The way to confront these temptations is through a process of acquaintance with the sins involved in the transformation of religious practice into a means of self-satisfaction. In the process of acquaintance, together with God's intervention, the soul undergoes refinement processes that ultimately lead to its union with God.[177] St. John therefore sees a linear process proceeding from a starting point pervaded by temptation toward the proper religious position—*conjunctio* and *unio mystica*. As the soul proceeds in its spiritual journey, it is gradually liberated from temptation.

Thomas à Kempis offers a more complex position. Contrary to St. John, who holds that progress is gradual and linear, à Kempis holds that so long as we live we are exposed to temptation:

---

[174] St. John of the Cross, *The Dark Night of the Soul*, 51.
[175] Ibid., 85.
[176] Ibid., 36.
[177] Ibid., 37-41.

> So long as we live in this world, we cannot remain without trial and temptation.... We must therefore be on guard against temptation and watchful in prayer, that the Devil finds no means of deceiving us; for he never rests, but prowls around seeking whom he may devour. No one is so perfect and holy that he is never tempted, and we can never be secure from temptation....
>
> Some people undergo their heaviest temptations at the beginning of their conversion; some towards the end of their course; others are greatly troubled all their lives...
>
> We must not despair, therefore, when we are tempted, but earnestly pray God to grant us his help in every need. For, as Saint Paul says, "With the temptation, God will provide a way to overcome it, that we may be able to bear it." ... In all these trials, our progress is tested; in them great merit may be secured, and our virtue become evident.[178]

Thomas à Kempis is clearly aware of the traps and temptations lurking in the believer's path, and the depth of temptation equals that of religious progress. Yet he too offers a typical approach whereby temptation is invariably outside religion and faith and poses a threat to them.

Heschel returns to the classic religious dichotomy between good and evil, between the divine and the demonic: "The choice today is ... between faith and horror, between the kingdom of Heaven or the rule of Satan."[179] In other words, a sharp distinction separates good from evil and the divine from the demonic, even if this distinction is realized in human life in the course of an existential struggle.

By contrast, the approach I have presented here indicates that temptation and the demonic are usually found within the realm of religious life. The demonic as well as the divine trace the borders of the religious field. Hence, religious progress is never linear but always dialectic, moving in the space extending between faith and faith as temptation, which is the concretization of the demonic in religious life.

---

[178] Thomas À Kempis, *The Imitation of Christ*, trans. Leo Shirley-Price (Harmondsworth, Middlesex: Penguin Books, 1952), 40-42.

[179] A. Elhananai, Pinchas H. Peli and Carl Stern, *Five Conversations with Abraham Joshua Heschel* (Jerusalem: Abraham Joshua Heschel Institute, 1975), 59 (Hebrew). Contrary to this schematic view, elsewhere Heschel offers a more complex approach, which returns to the Lutheran view that man is by nature either a God worshipper or a Satan worshipper. See Heschel, *God in Search of Man*, 260.

Clearly, then, faith is a kind of absolute self-concern,[180] where we confront the wholeness of our existence and the various options of our relationship with the divine absolute. Not only are human creatures the bearers of a relationship of faith but they are actually the ones who create it, through the relationship with their God.

V. Faith and Faith as Temptation: Initial Phenomenological Reflections

This extensive analysis enables a proposal for an initial outline of a phenomenological analysis of faith. The temptation of faith is a suitable perspective for an identification of faith itself because, on the one hand, it is within the possibilities of faith, and on the other, it marks its borders.

The limitation of the proposed phenomenological analysis is that it cannot rely on any datum beyond the texts I have presented. In this sense, the proposed phenomenology is merely the phenomenology of a given range of texts and, therefore, of one specific religious context. This phenomenology cannot rule out the option of another phenomenological analysis, based on a different set of texts. Indeed, texts may certainly be found in Jewish religious tradition—for instance, in kabbalistic or hasidic literature—presenting a religious stance different from that found in the texts discussed above. In truth, the texts presented were chosen on the basis of a preliminary understanding that they represent a particular religious view.

I will confine myself to the minimalistic claim that my proposal is only one possible phenomenology of religious life. Even this stance, however, is extremely valuable because it offers a coherent presentation of one view of faith. Furthermore, my hypothesis is that the set of texts I discussed reflects, at the very least, a tradition central to religion in general and to Judaism in particular. If this hypothesis is correct, the value of the phenomenology extends beyond the fragmented datum underlying it—a specific set of texts. Be that as it may, the proposed phenomenology is a challenge that religious tradition poses at least implicitly.

The texts discussed above point to the proximity prevalent among three mental states: the temptation of the evil inclination; faith; and faith as temptation. This proximity requires believers to develop a critical-reflective sensitivity through which they learn to distinguish and

---

[180] See Tillich, *Dynamics of Faith*, 1-8.

identify their own basic disposition. Self-criticism enables believers to identify the challenge facing them: the temptation of the evil inclination or faith as temptation. Identification alone obviously does not ensure that individuals can overcome these temptations, but it does place them in a position different from the one they had occupied prior to the stage of critical reflection.

The confrontation with the temptation of the evil inclination is essentially different from the confrontation with faith as temptation. The evil inclination is perceived as a threat to faith, as an element that incites believers to deviate from their path. By contrast, faith as a temptation rests on the religious dispositions; it is they that provide a platform for the temptation that undermines faith.

The fact that believers may be forced to confront the temptations of the evil inclination, however, means that faith is grounded in the totality of their being. Believers do not detach themselves from their real modes of existence; faith is not within a protected fortress removed from actual, extra-religious fields of life. Rather, faith is constituted within concrete human existence in all its manifestations and, for this reason, believers cannot be released from extra-religious temptations: the evil inclination on the one hand, or the mistakes derived from the proneness of human consciousness to error on the other. This phenomenological claim is reaffirmed in the textual sensitivity to the mutual interpenetration of modes of existence and to the possibility of the evil inclination misleading believers by appearing in the guise of the religious disposition.

The challenge of faith as temptation is supposedly free from the nonreligious context of life, since the source of temptation is within the religious disposition. On further scrutiny, however, this claim proves incorrect. The mental reality of faith as temptation is only possible if faith is a potential mental characterization of human reality. Since faith is a human mode of existence, it could well lead to a stance that is opposed to the religious demand. Were faith, as Leibowitz claimed, identical to the religious demand,[181] the only challenge confronting believers would concern their

---

[181] See Sagi, "The 'Akedah'—A Comparative Study." Leibowitz, as noted, acknowledged that the religious life context is conditioned by a disposition— the right intention. This disposition is located outside religious practice even though it is precisely what determines practice, the very core of religious life, as divine worship.

readiness to comply with this demand. But given that faith is also a mental characteristic of a possible human reality, believers are also supposed to confront the implications of these religious dispositions. Dispositions such as boundless obedience or a sense of worthlessness before God could result in positions opposed to the religious demand. At that point, they are a temptation of faith, compelling a response from the believer.

A deeper analysis reveals faith as constituted by two poles. According to the phenomenological tradition, these are the noetic pole, that is, the subjective act of faith, and the noematic pole, that is the objective content of faith. Whereas the noetic pole denotes the believers' immanent being in all its manifestations, the noematic pole denotes the transcendent dimension of the act or the disposition of faith, toward which believers develop their own dispositions. Faith as temptation shows that the distinction between the two poles is not absolute, since the disposition of believers is constituted not only by their internal mental state but also by their transcendent demand— the religious obligation or the image of God. But this obligation or the image of God do not constitute the mental state and disposition of the believer all by themselves. Recognition of the transcendent obligation as a religious obligation, as well as its concrete interpretation, is influenced by the religious disposition itself. Similarly, the image of God is also constituted by the religious disposition.

Faith, then, is constituted as a permanent tension between "inside" and "outside." The relationship between faith and the temptation of faith is a precise reflection of the tension between the poles. In phenomenological terms, the analysis I suggested shows that faith is an intentional act constituting a relationship between the agent—the believer—and his object—God or the contents of faith. This horizontal analysis, however, still leaves open the question about the precise relationship between the noetic and noematic aspects. Is faith a synergic manifestation mediated by the two dimensions, the noetic and noematic, or does one of them have precedence?

Religious intuition appears to lead to the conclusion that the noematic dimension precedes and constitutes the noetic one, and the situation of faith is determined by the actual religious demand, without which no situation of faith is conceivable. The situation of faith is a kind of responsiveness to transcendence, whether this transcendence is concretized in a divine presence or in specific religious demands.

Emmanuel Levinas deals at length with this perception of the presence of the transcendent in our world. In his view, transcendence is concretized above all in the other, coercing and imposing itself. The subject does not constitute the transcendent: "The subject as hostage has been neither the experience nor the proof of the Infinite, but the witnessing of the Infinite … a witnessing that no disclosure has preceded."[182] This witnessing or responsibility does not derive from the subject's freedom of consciousness but rather the opposite—it coerces the subject and thus precedes the subject's freedom.[183] In sentences full of religious pathos, Levinas formulates the religious meaning of this approach:

> This is a Saying bearing witness to the other of the Infinite, which tears me open as it awakens me in the Saying.... Saying is thus a way of signifying prior to any experience. It is pure witnessing: the truth of the martyr that depends upon no disclosure, even if this were a "religious" experience; this is an obedience preceding the hearing of the order. A pure witnessing that bears witness not to a previous experience but to the Infinite, it is inaccessible to the unity of apperception, it is nonappearing, and it is disproportionate to the present. It could not encompass the Infinite; it could not comprehend it. The Infinite concerns me and encircles me.... Here I am [*me voici*]. A marvelous accusative: here I am under your gaze, obliged to you, your servant. In the name of God! Without thematization! The sentence in which God comes to be involved in words is not "I believe in God." The religious discourse prior to all religious discourse is not dialogue. It is the "here I am," said to the neighbor to whom I am given over.[184]

An analysis of the religious space in Levinas' approach, a space concretized in the relationship with the other, exceeds the scope of this paper.[185] For my current purpose, what matters is Levinas' statement that it is transcendence that breaks into existence and imposes immanence rather the opposite. Levinas thereby offers a philosophy that goes beyond the

---

[182] Emanuel Levinas, *Of God Who Comes to Mind*, trans. Bettina Bergo (Stanford, CA: Stanford University Press, 1998), 73.
[183] Ibid.
[184] Ibid., 74-75.
[185] On this question, see Ze'ev Levy, *Otherness and Responsibility: A Study of Emmanuel Levinas' Philosophy* (Jerusalem: Magnes Press, 1997), particularly ch. 5 (Hebrew).

classic phenomenological path, which assumes the primacy of a subject who makes the transcendent present within its own consciousness.

Beyond its deep religious and moral pathos, however, Levinas' approach is hard to defend, given that any statement about the transcendent is made by consciousness and within its bounds. Even the statement that the transcendent imposes itself on the subject, that the subject is merely a witness to it and not its constitutive element, is made by consciousness, and hence within its bounds. A claim from within consciousness about what is beyond consciousness returns us to the epistemological absurd that empiricists such as Berkeley and Hume had already pointed out: it is impossible for consciousness to make claims about what is beyond it, and it is impossible to claim that what is found within it is "there," as an external imposition. Epistemologically, any determination about transcendence must be stated and decided within the borders of immanence. This conclusion fits the phenomenological approach whereby the noetic act logically precedes and conditions the object, given that every object, as such, is ultimately constituted by the subject's action. Every object transcends the subject since, as an object, it is found "there," outside the subject. But its characterization as an object in all its manifestations is conditioned by the subject, allowing Husserl to claim that the object's transcendence is immanent.

From a phenomenological perspective, at this point we are indeed facing what Jean-Luc Marion called the "paradox of phenomenology."[186] This paradox rests on the fact that phenomenology is "originary"; it sets up the project and the method but "it has no other ambition than to lose this initiative as quickly and completely as possible."[187] The act is not intended to take over and constitute the datum but to allow it to reveal itself through modes of givenness that appear already before the investigating consciousness. Hence, "the methodological beginning here establishes only the conditions for its own disappearance in the original manifestation of what shows *itself*."[188] From this perspective, immanence is the place within and from which transcendence is revealed; that is, transcendence is immanent.

---

[186] Jean-Luc Marion, *Being Given: Toward a Phenomenology of Givenness*, trans. Jeffrey L. Kosky (Stanford: Stanford University Press, 2002), 9.
[187] Ibid.
[188] Ibid.

This phenomenological outline is easy to understand regarding every object that preserves an element of transcendence. By its very nature as object, its transcendence is immanent. The challenge to the phenomenologist is that religion does not speak of immanent transcendence but of absolute transcendence. Immanent transcendence has indirect expressions—the manifestation before us, the experience we go through.[189] But what is the experience of absolute transcendence? Phenomenologically, the denial of the act in the epistemological process is what allows the datum to reveal itself—is there a kind of phenomenological negation that enables the revelation of absolute transcendence? In religious terms, Levinas' intuitions regarding transcendence answer the believer's yearnings; phenomenologically, however, these intuitions are unacceptable. Is there a phenomenological way of preserving religious intuitions within the phenomenological outline?

As a starting point in attempting to answer this question, note that the paradox of religious life is that the religious demand or the relationship with God are reconstituted by the believer's religious disposition; the autonomous aspect overrides the heteronomous aspect of religious life.[190] The statement that a particular demand or a specific presence is a "temptation" rather than a compulsory manifestation is ultimately a decision of the believer. Thus, even if the beginning of the religious experience and of religious life is in the immanent acceptance of the transcendent, its distinctive end—the full emergence of religiosity—occurs in absolute terms within the realm of the immanent. The location of the absolute transcendent within the immanent implies a recognition of the precedence of the immanent as the element shaping the attitude to the transcendent.

This phenomenological analysis compels a new characterization of the believer's attitude to God. The identification of faith and its distinction from the temptation of faith even in situations where God is perceived as tempter implies that the attitude to the transcendent (God) is contingent

---

[189] Ibid., 25, 39-45.
[190] On this question, see Eliezer Goldman, *Expositions and Inquiries: Jewish Thought in Past and Present*, ed. Avi Sagi and Daniel Statman (Jerusalem: Magnes Press, 1996), 236 (Hebrew). *Cf.* Felix Weltch, *Gnade und Freiheit: Untersuchungen zum Problem des schoepferischen Willens in Religion und Ethik* (Muenchen: K. Wolff, 1920), 7.

on the immanent (the believer). Believers shape their attitude to God, they interpret God's word and, ultimately, determine God's standing in human reality. The transcendent, then, is contingent on the immanent.

Immanent transcendence, however, does not fit the attitude to a God perceived as absolutely transcendent: God is in no way contingent on human beings. Quite the contrary, the believer assumes that humans are contingent on God. How can the immanent presence of what is considered absolutely transcendent be possible? If God is essentially different from every worldly object, how can one describe the believers' phenomenological attitude to God?

Indeed, the question of the relationship between the characterization of God as transcendent and the perception of the believer that relates to God as immanent is the fundamental question of religious existence. Phenomenologically, the immanent expression of God's absolute transcendence is reflected in the reversal of the conscious trend in the believer's disposition. In the course of constituting the attitude to God, which emphasizes the precedence of the noetic over the noematic, the immanent over the transcendent, a conscious reversal occurs and the believer expresses the standing of the transcendent in the immanent through the restriction of the immanent element. This restriction can be expressed in various ways, ranging from a transition from activity to passivity up to casting doubt or absolutely negating the subject. Passivity places the individual in a posture of attention and openness, which is indeed the one that fits the attitude to the transcendent.[191] Attention and openness do not negate immanence. Quite the contrary: this is the active passivity of individuals opening themselves up to the transcendent. In more radical cases, however, believers negate their actual conscious stance and express the transcendent in their world through self-negation. This negation too is an immanent action of the believer, but its purpose is precisely the elimination of immanence. Whereas openness and attention do not deny immanence, self-negation denies it absolutely.

Marion, as noted, emphasized that engagement in active phenomenology is meant to lead to self-negation, which becomes manifest in the datum revealing itself. If the attitude to the absolutely transcendent is phenomenological, this negation should be permanent. Only self-negation—"I ... who am but dust and ashes" (Genesis 18: 27)—can

---

[191] On this issue, see the profound analysis of Weil, *Gravity and Grace*, 169-176.

express the moment of transcendent exposure. This negation is concretized in the attitude to halakhic norms as a constant nullification of the immanence that constitutes the basis for their fixation as transcendent. Religious life is therefore based on two contradictory movements of immanent faith that coexist synchronistically: the primary and positive one constitutes and mediates the transcendent object and its modes of revelation; the secondary and negative is directed toward the positive act of faith and turns the act of constitution into solely an act of revelation, and the transcendence into an imposed presence.

This dual movement of faith is the decisive moment of shaping the relationship between immanence and transcendence. This is the dangerous moment of religious life. Its danger is concretized in the situation where the two movements—the positive and the negative—split and separate from one another. If the positive movement takes over, then God and the religious contents are no more than the constitution of consciousness as such, and the absolute transcendent disappears from religious life altogether. If the negative movement takes over, then faith stops being a human disposition and the transcendent comes to dominate life, turning the gesture of faith into an objective content without bearers who mediate it through their consciousness. According to this analysis, Levinas detaches the negative act of faith from the positive one, intensifies it, and denies it any content as an act of faith.

This tension in the relationship between the immanent and the transcendent mediated by two antithetical acts of faith is the moment when faith as temptation appears. Faith as temptation seeks expression for the transcendent within immanence through absolute self-negation. Temptation thus emerges whenever a trend develops seeking to split and separate the two movements that constitute faith.

VI. Faith as Temptation and Religious Life

The proposed phenomenological analysis clarifies why faith as temptation is an option within faith, since it rests on the fundamental tension within religious life: the will to have the transcendent God in all his otherness present within immanence. Yet, the statement that this mode is a temptation rather than a suitable representation of faith means that making the transcendent present within immanence requires the affirmation of immanence, that is, the affirmation of human existence in all its fullness. From what source would believers draw support for re-embracing human existence? How will they resist the temptation to self-negation when facing God's absolute transcendence?

In *Halakhic Man*, R. Soloveitchik deals with this question directly. In his view, Halakhah is the mechanism that repeatedly affirms reality,[192] since the halakhic system is geared to the regulation and amendment of reality, not to its negation. If Halakhah is a concretization of God's word, then the realization of God's will in the world takes place through the affirmation of the world. The religious experience, as Eliezer Goldman clarified, contains a deep element of negation: the recognition of human reality as finite, ephemeral, and contingent. The culmination of that experience is self-negation.[193] Yet, the very fact that God turns to human beings and to human reality is an affirmation of reality:

> The divine revelation in the Torah and the commandments, which creates the religious norm for Judaism, is a radical innovation.... It does not follow from human culture, as its radical heteronomy attests. But it addresses human culture, it is intended for it, and it thereby confers religious meaning on it.[194]

The ability to preserve the tension between self-negation and the affirmation of reality is the believer's constant test. R. Yaakov Yehiel Weinberg offers an illuminating account of this complex relationship:

> Faith and denial are not always antithetical: at times faith is merely denial, a man's denial of his body, the denial of his self, giving up on himself....[195] Serene and uncritical faith attests only to internal emptiness and lack of thought. Self-negation when facing impressions stronger than his mental readiness takes away the personal vigor from his own self. He is progressively swept away, gradually captivated by the abundance outside, which affects his senses. His will is smashed and broken and he cannot rebel and protest—he believes because he is impotent to deny.

---

[192] See Joseph B. Soloveitchik, *Halakhic Man*, trans. Lawrence Kaplan (Philadelphia: Jewish Publication Society of America, 1983), 39-63.
[193] See Goldman, *Expositions and Inquiries*, 311-312.
[194] Ibid., 313.
[195] Ellipsis in original.

> This is an unworthy faith, merely the absence of heresy.... The way of creative religious faith, one worthy of its name, is uproar and tumult, it springs from a plethora of moral might and power. Such faith is not a mental psychological state but rather the vibrant expression of mental activeness aspiring to create and conquer. Rather than submissive and compliant, it orders and decides, it binds and coerces.... Such a believer both subjugates and submits.[196]

Self-glorification, together with humility and submission, are constitutive of the faith experience or at least of Jewish faith. Clear indications of this dialectical tension are already found in Scripture. Abraham, critical of and struggling with God—"Shall not the judge of all the earth do right?!" (Genesis 18:25)—is the very one who later says: "I have taken upon me to speak to the Lord, who am but dust and ashes." This approach, combining dependence with responsibility and self-respect,[197] recurs in the prophetic literature: "Right wouldst thou be, O Lord, if I were to contend with thee: yet I will reason these points of justice with thee: Why does the way of the wicked prosper? Why are all they happy that deal very treacherously?" (Jeremiah 12:1). Divine justice does not preclude the prophet's attempt to judge God. Indeed, divine justice provides the prophet with a basis for taking a strong stand and demanding answers to his questions: "The prophet said, I knew, O God, that you are righteous on the matter I mean to fight with you about, but I will contend with you, as if saying, I will nevertheless argue in order to know the reason and the cause, not because I doubt you are righteous in your judgment."[198] Self respect, then, is not the antithesis of a religious stance; quite the contrary, it rests upon it.

In this sense, the halakhic project appears intended to reshape the dialectic between submission and selfhood. Contrary to Leibowitz's one-dimensional description of Halakhah as meant for self-negation

---

[196] R. Yehiel Yaakov Weinberg, *Chapters* (Jerusalem, 2003), 178 (Hebrew).
[197] For further analysis of the story of Abraham in Sodom, see Menachem Fisch, "'And they shall keep the way of the Lord, to do justice and judgment': Faith, Knowledge, and the Obligatory Nature of Jewish Religion," in *Yeshayahu Leibowitz: His World and Philosophy*, ed. Avi Sagi (Jerusalem: Keter, 1995), 110-112 (Hebrew).
[198] *Metsudat David*, Jeremiah *ad locum*.

vis-à-vis the religious demand, Halakhah directs individuals to realize themselves as self-respecting creatures and to restrain the self-negation impulse. This perception of the religious project rests on the actual standing of halakhic man in the world and on the normative structure established by Halakhah. Halakhic man is required to be a rational agent exercising autonomous discretion, even vis-à-vis the divine voice—"it is not in Heaven."[199] Furthermore, the halakhic system is shaped as a normative complex that organizes human life through its affirmation. Halakhah is the regulation of existence, not its negation.

The height of the trend affirming immanence and the view of human reality as a place where the transcendent will be made present through human activity in the real world is expressed in the idea of the "sanctification of the name," which is a constitutive element of halakhic tradition. Samuel Hugo Bergman analyzes this idea in depth. He opens his discussion with the verse: "And you shall keep my commandments, and do them: I am the Lord. Neither shall you profane my holy name; I will be hallowed among the children of Israel: I am the Lord who makes you holy" (Leviticus 22:31-32). Bergman then challenges this statement: "How can that be? If God is holy in himself, what does it mean to say that God is hallowed through human beings?"[200] Yet, he claims, this question is based on a misunderstanding of Jewish religiosity:

> In the Western and current conception, God and man are each fixed in their eternal immutability, and the world and man are separate and different from God. The Jewish view also divides and separates God from the world, but unites and links the fate of God and the fate of the world one to the other, until we find that not only does the world depend on God but also that the fate of God ... depends on the world.... In European thought, the relationship between God and the world is static, whereas in the conception of Judaism this relationship is dynamic. In that thought, God is a self-contained entity, He is one, holy, and so forth. Judaism perceives God from the perspective of man, as the source of human life and as his purpose and mission.... God is a mission for man, which he is bound to realize.... God created the world, but man

---

[199] For an extensive analysis of this approach in Halakhah, see Avi Sagi, *The Open Canon: On the Meaning of Halakhic Discourse*, trans. Batya Stein (London: Continuum, 2007); idem, *Judaism: Between Religion and Morality*.

[200] Samuel Hugo Bergman, *On the Path* (Tel Aviv: Am Oved, 1976), 183 (Hebrew).

is sustained through his union with the divine. He draws down the divine to his own world. Every person performing a moral act, like a fair and righteous judge, becomes a partner to the Holy One, blessed be He, in the act of creation ... and as man renews God's act of creation through his moral action, so does he reduce God's greatness through his transgressions.[201]

Bergman holds that the complex human relationship with God is the key to an understanding of what is meant by the "hallowing of the name." Prima facie, this is a paradoxical concept: "If there is a God, how does he depend on us and how can his very being be tied and linked to our actions? Can a creature work upon its creator in return? How can we, as human beings, hallow the name??"[202] The claim that the transcendent is itself constituted by the immanent is an inconceivable assumption.[203] And yet, argues Bergman, God is not an object found "there" in the world, between other objects. For us, God is what we do. We must make room for God in our lives so that we may become aware of the divine presence, and this is what is meant by the sanctification of the name:

> The Jew asks: How is He God for me as well? And he answers: When God becomes in your life an act that you do. Because you have been a witness to the reality of God in your life, God will become a reality in your world. Hence, on the verse in Isaiah (43:10): "You are my witnesses, says the Lord.... I am he, before me there was no God formed, neither shall there be after me" we read in *Pesikta de-R. Kahana* (102:2): "R. Simeon b. Yohai says, 'If you are my witnesses, I am the first and after me there will not be, and if you are not my witnesses, as it were, I am not God'".... This, then, is the dual and unique nature of God—he is found and he is also a task.[204]

---

[201] Ibid., 183-185.
[202] Ibid.
[203] Ibid. These approaches have mistakenly been attributed to Kierkegaard. See my critique in Sagi, *Kierkegaard, Religion, and Existence*, 143-145.
[204] Bergman, *On the Path*, 185-186. Menachem Mendel of Kotsk offers a similar formulation: "'Where does God dwell?' The Rebbe of Kotsk surprised several scholars who were his guests with this question. They laughed at him. 'What is the rebbe saying? The whole earth is full of his glory!' The rebbe answered the question himself: 'God dwells wherever he is allowed to enter.'" Buber, *Or ha-Ganuz*, 433.

This approach, which Bergman considers unique to Judaism, is also found in other religions. Luther had already noted the centrality of the religious disposition in the worship of God:

> To have a god therefore is nothing else but to believe in him and trust him from the heart. As I have often said, it is nothing but the trust and faith of the heart which makes god, whether true or false. When faith and trust are right then is thy god right, and contrariwise, when trust is false and wrong then the right god is not.[205]

The nature of the object—God—is materialized in the religious disposition. True faith relates to God whereas the object of the false faith is not god. In Luther's view, the human being is by nature a god-worshipper[206] and the nature of the object—whether God or Satan—is clarified through the act of faith. Lutheranism holds that God is a transcendent entity and therefore not present in the world but, precisely on these grounds, human beings play a decisive role—the religious subjective disposition bears the burden of the divine "presence" in the world. Hence, only the true faith that believers themselves foster and develop represents true worship.[207]

Kierkegaard, who was influenced by Lutheran tradition, presented a similar religious approach. At its core is the recognition that the

---

[205] This text is from Luther's work, *Catechismus Major*, as cited in Harald Hoffding, *The Philosophy of Religion* (London: McMillan, 1931), 121.

[206] See John Dillenberger, ed., *Martin Luther: Selections from His Writings* (Garden City, NY: Doubleday, 1961), 188-190. See also the *Selichot* (penitence) prayers for the eve of the new year: "All his life man serves two masters, doing the will of his Maker, and following his own inclination; well for him if all times he clings to his Creator, for then he is a servant free from his master" *The Authorized Selichot for the Whole Year*, trans R. Abraham Rosenfeld, 4th edition (London, 1969). Thanks to David Kurzweil who directed me to this text.

[207] A similar view appears in *The Zohar*, which assumes that the basic human disposition is to seek conjunction, but the nature of this conjunction, whether it will be with God or with Satan, depends on human behavior: "When one follows the path of truth ... he draws supernal holiness upon the son he engenders.... But when he follows the left side ... he draws an impure spirit upon the son who issues from him into the world, who is thereby defiled by the impurity of that side." *The Zohar*, trans. Daniel C. Matt, vol. 1 (Stanford, CA: Stanford University Press, 2004), 54a. See also vol. 3, 53b.

existence of God in the world and for human beings is contingent upon them. In a passage in his journal, Kierkegaard succinctly formulates this stance:

> Immanently (in the imaginative medium of abstraction) God does not exist or is not present—only for the existing person is God present, i.e., he can be present in faith … if an existing person does not have faith, then [for him] God neither *is* nor is God *present*, although understood eternally God nevertheless eternally is.[208]

The human creature, then, is the bearer of the relationship with God. This relationship is constituted by the subjective turn to God, a turn that will shape the individual's religious disposition. This basic religious fact substantiates the possibility of religious temptation, which I have called here "faith as temptation." Only an uncritical, unreflective believer is rescued from this titanic struggle of faith. But the religious price of such a stance is a slide into faith as temptation, which ultimately leads to the absolute takeover of the transcendent by the immanent—the human disposition. Paradoxically, the innocent believer actually subjugates the object of faith to his own being, since he founds the relationship to the object according to his own dispositions; he leads a religious way of life of his own, not necessarily fitting the divine will. By contrast, the critical believer who appears to rule the transcendent is the one who constantly criticizes the immanent religious dispositions. This believer recurrently asks himself whether he lives as a believer or perhaps as a captive of the temptation of faith. This constant tension attests to the limitation of immanence and to the turn to transcendence; this tension is the deep expression of the attention to the transcendent entity and of the openness toward it. The critique of faith, as a concrete mode of existence, is an expression of the human ability to overcome our immanent modes of givenness and genuinely turn to God. Consequently, critical-reflective believers are the ones doing their utmost to fulfill God's will, to confine their being to its concrete borders, and, within them, to respond to their God.

---

[208] This text is quoted from Kierkegaard's journals (JP, VII¹ A 139 n. d., 1846, § 1347) in Sagi, *Kierkegaard, Religion, and Existence*, 143.

VII. Theological Aspects of Faith as Temptation

The discussion has so far centered on faith as temptation through an analysis of the believer's disposition. But faith has an object—God, perceived by believers not merely as the object of their faith but also as an acting substance whose actions give rise to the possibility that God is indeed the tempter. In this light, a theological question emerges: How should the possibility of temptation be understood? The entry of the demonic into the religious realm?

In response to this question, I will retrace the course that Thomas Mann suggests in *Doctor Faustus*.[209] Relying on classic theological traditions, Mann argues that the possibility of sin and temptation is anchored in the concept of a "complete creation," which is embodied in two components: human freedom and the concept of the good.

The starting point of this approach is that a world where human freedom exists is more complete than one without it.[210] "Denying from the created being the free will to turn away from God … would have been an incomplete creation," so that God "preferred to expose men and angels to sin rather than withhold freedom from them."[211]

Since God gave human beings freedom to choose, the possibility of sin is inherent in human nature:

> …evil, the Evil One himself—was a necessary emanation and inevitable accompaniment of the Holy Existence of God, so that vice did not consist in itself but got its satisfaction from the defilement of virtue, without which it would have been rootless; in other words, it consisted in the enjoyment of freedom, the possibility of sinning, which was inherent in the act of creation itself.[212]

From this perspective, faith or fear of God cannot rest on the absolute renunciation of freedom, since renouncing freedom means renouncing

---

[209] Thomas Mann, *Doctor Faustus: The Life of the German Composer Adrian Leverkühn as Told by a Friend*, trans. H. T. Lowe-Porter (New York: Alfred A. Knopf, 1948).
[210] For further analysis of this idea see Avi Sagi, *Jewish Religion after Theology*, trans. Batya Stein (Boston: Academic Studies Press, 2009), 195-196.
[211] Mann, *Doctor Faustus*, 101.
[212] Ibid., 100.

the completeness inherent in creation. The fear of God rests on this freedom itself or, in Mann's terms:

> Freedom was the opposite of inborn sinlessness, freedom meant the choice of keeping faith with God.... Freedom is a very great thing, the condition of creation, that which prevented God making us proof against falling away from Him. Freedom is the freedom to sin, and piety consists in making no use of it out of love for God, who had to give it.[213] (Ibid.)

Mann did not proceed to the obvious next step: human freedom is concretized not only in the confrontation with the evil outside the religious realm. It must contend with all evil, including that within religion that, as noted, is not shielded from it. The sin in the freedom to sin is found not only outside the religious realm. Faith as temptation embodies the freedom to sin within religious life.

The second idea that Mann discusses is the dependence of good on evil. In a programmatic passage, Mann returns to one of theodicy's classic theses:

> Of course the dialectic association of evil with goodness and holiness.... Evil contributed to the wholeness of the universe, without it the universe would not have been complete, therefore God permitted it, for He was consummate and must therefore will the consummate—not in the sense of the consummately good but in the sense of All-sidedness and reciprocal enlargement of life. Evil was far more evil if good existed; good was far more good if evil existed; yes, perhaps—one might disagree about this—evil would not be evil at all if not for the good, good not good at all if not for the evil.[214]

At the basis of this theology is the idea that good and evil are intensified through the dialectic contrast between them. Without evil, the good would not be discovered. This view rests on several considerations. The first is analytical and assumes that the good is meaningless without its negation—evil. Mann knows that this is not a simple claim and that it can be challenged. Thus, for instance, Plato did not hold that the idea of

---

[213] Ibid.
[214] Ibid., 103.

the good has a negative denotation as well, such as the negation of evil. For Plato, the good is in no way conditioned by evil; it denotes a kind of wholeness and fullness that is not contingent on anything else.[215]

The second consideration is psychological and assumes that the intensification of the good depends on the existence of evil. Faced with evil, its amendment by the good becomes more urgent. Evil is a kind of awakening, inspiring power that can be channeled, refined, and mobilized for the sake of the good. This idea, which is discussed below, recurs in the history of religious philosophy, both Jewish and Christian, and is at the heart of the Freudian insight about the evolvement of human culture.[216] Mann formulated this insight as follows: "What sphere of human endeavour, even the most unalloyed, the most dignified and benevolent, would be entirely inaccessible to the influence of the powers of the underworld, yes, one must add, quite independent of the need of fruitful contact with them?"[217] Mann holds that the religious realm is one that distinctly exposes the penetration of the good into the evil and the demonic. The divine is exposed as criticism and reason, while passion originates in the demonic: "It comes but from the devil, the true master and giver of such rapture."[218] Passion is the cornerstone of religious life, but its source and its horizon are unconditioned and even transcend the borders of this life.

Freedom and evil, which constitute the foundation of a perfect existence and a perfect world, turn religious life itself into a constant arena of conflict demarcated by the demonic and the divine: "holiness was unthinkable without temptation, it measured itself against the frightfulness of the temptation, against a man's sin-potential."[219]

In sum, theologically, the temptation to sin and faith as temptation express the perfection of creation and of the Creator, who created a world with human freedom and the demonic. Human life is the arena of the permanent struggle between the demonic and the divine, which

---

[215] For an extensive and profound analysis of this issue, see Arthur A. Lovejoy, *The Great Chain of Being: A Study of the History of an Idea* (Cambridge, MA: Harvard University Press, 1950), ch. 2.

[216] For a critical analysis of Freud's view, see Herbert Marcuse, *Eros and Civilization: A Philosophical Inquiry into Freud* (London: Sphere Books, 1969).

[217] Mann, *Doctor Faustus*, 9.

[218] Ibid., 237.

[219] Ibid., 105.

is decided by human freedom. The fear of God, then, is not outside the realm of freedom and human reflection but rather the opposite—it relies on it.

VIII. Reflection, Simplicity, and Faith

The critical discourse leads to the conclusion that it is improper for faith to express a kind of immediate and primary experience. This conclusion appears problematic given the religious intuitions on the pursuit of religious simplicity. A critical-reflective stance cannot, on its face, comply with the biblical demand: ""Walk before me and be *tamim*" (Genesis 17:1) "You must be *tamim* before the Lord your God" (Deuteronomy 18:13).[220] What, then, is the relationship between these intuitions and the religious demand on the one hand, and this conclusion on the other? This is a particularly complicated question because, even though I did present what is religiously "proper," I also relied on the phenomenology of religious life. The question, therefore, is whether the phenomenology proposed here is indeed compatible with the experience of religious life: does this article offer a plausible explanation of religious life, given the tension between simple faith and criticism?

These questions allow us to reconsider the quality of the faith experience. A person may indeed have an immediate experience of faith. My claim, however, is that simple, immediate faith cannot be a constant experience woven into our standard experiential web but only a momentary random event. Indeed, an even more radical claim can be substantiated, stating that the simple immediate occurrence is not part of our real experience but merely an imagined concept, because the simple experience is a creation of consciousness. Consciousness creates it by relating to it through the mind and through language. If this argument is correct, the claim that religious life rests on primary, immediate experience cannot be verified through the concrete experience of our life.

Romanticism had emphasized primary simplicity. Hegel, however, pointed out the crucial role of language and consciousness in the

---

[220] The Hebrew word *tamim* is polysemic and includes denotations of perfection, innocence, immediacy, and simplicity—all relevant to the discussion that follows.

negation of this experience: "since the universal is the true [content] of sense-certainty and language expresses this true [content] alone, it is just not possible for us ever to say, or express in words, a sensuous being that we *mean*."[221] By nature, language is universal and communicative whereas the primary simple experience is unique and therefore uncommunicative. Our consciousness is shaped by language and by placing the experience in the subject-object relationship. The experience of primary simplicity, which cannot become an object, is thus not a real experience for us as conscious creatures.

Kierkegaard too, who struggled to preserve the personal unique experience, was sensitive to the Hegelian critique and noted in one of his early writings:

> Cannot the consciousness, then, remain in immediacy? This is a foolish question, because if it could, there would be no consciousness at all. But how, then, is immediacy canceled? By mediacy, which cancels immediacy by pre-suppositioning it. What, then, is immediacy? It is reality itself. What is mediacy? It is the word. How does the one cancel the other? By giving expression to it, for that which is given expression is always presupposed.[222]

Contrary to Hegel, Kierkegaard continued to strive for simplicity, except that it was no longer primary but rather post-reflective—"second immediacy" or "supreme immediacy." According to Kierkegaard, this is the believer's goal: "No doubt, immediacy can be attained again ... only ethically: immediacy itself becomes the task—you shall attain it.... Ethics or, better, the ethical, is the turning point and from there the movement is into the dogmatic."[223] The conclusion warranted by this

---

[221] Georg W. F. Hegel, *Phenomenology of Spirit*, trans. A. V. Miller (Oxford: Clarendon Press, 1977), 60 (emphasis in original).

[222] Søren Kierkegaard, *Johannes Climacus, or De Omnibus Dubitandum Est: A Narrative*, ed. and trans. Howard V. Hong and Edna H. Hong (Princeton: Princeton University Press, 1985), 167-168.

[223] This text is quoted from Kierkegaard's journals (JP, X1 A 360, n.d. 1849, § 972) in Sagi, *Kierkegaard, Religion, and Existence*, 79. For an extensive discussion, see ibid., ch. 5. The notion of second immediacy was developed later by Peter West. On this notion, see also Ernst Simon, *Are We Still Jews* (Tel-Aviv: Sifriat Po'alim, 1983), 135-169 (Hebrew).

analysis is that immediate faith is not an element that consciousness finds; at most, it is an analytical datum or an imagined concept within language, and consciousness has nothing to say about it.

Faith, moreover, is not an autonomous and autarchic experience but part of complex conceptual systems that, in their totality, shape a religious world view. The experience of a Jewish believer, for instance, is interpreted and organized within the horizons of Jewish faith as a whole, which usually comprise a belief in God's revelation at Sinai and in historical events, a belief in divine providence, and so forth. Similarly, the faith of a Christian believer is part of a series of Christian dogmas, at the center of which is the belief in Jesus as a divine incarnation. Every one of the various faiths also includes a spectrum of values it adopts and others it rejects. If faith is part of a general world view, then Hoffding was correct when he claimed "that no religion can be constructed on the basis of immediate experience."[224]

Henceforth, the key question is whether this understanding percolates down to the real religious experience, at least as reflected in the texts. Unquestionably, some texts intensify the simple, immediate experience and fixate it as the foundation of faith. But the problematic entailed by the ascription of exaggerated religious value to simplicity is also evident in texts that enhance its value. In *Netivot Olam*, R. Loew devoted a special chapter to *temimut*,[225] defining it and exalting its religious value. R. Loew seeks to draw a contrast between honesty and *temimut*: "One who is honest in his reason and his wisdom seeks to do what is honest, and the *tamim* is one who takes the right path by himself, without any reflection, just goes guilelessly on his way."[226]

According to this description, the quality of *temimut* denotes the non-reflective, natural mode of existence, which is contrasted with the honesty that denotes a conscious intellectual decision—"whose mind directly makes the choice." R. Loew is aware that both these qualities are desirable, and at times prevail in the same person. And yet, he ascribes higher religious value to the quality of *temimut*: "Because one possessing the quality of *temimut*, one who preserves this quality and

---

[224] Hoffding, *The Philosophy of Religion*, 95.
[225] R. Judah Loew b. Bezalel (MaHaRaL), *Netivot Olam*, vol. 2 (Jerusalem: n. p., 1971), 205-208.
[226] Ibid., 205.

refrains from smart wiles, will never stray from the Holy One, blessed be He."[227]

With great sensitivity, R. Loew highlights the gap between one whose religious stance is primary, natural, and non-reflective, and one whose religious position reflects a rational decision that, by nature, is removed from its object. This view, then, purportedly supports the non-reflective simplicity that results in the self merging with its object.[228] A closer reading of R. Loew's view of simplicity, however, makes this hierarchical relationship between *temimut* and reflectiveness appear questionable. First, R. Loew contests Maimonides' view on Adam's sin in *The Guide of the Perplexed* I:2. Contrary to Maimonides, he holds that Adam's sin diminished human life: "Because this wisdom[229] is a ploy that started from *temimut* and brought death ... so you should learn from this that *temimut* is life. As long as Adam was *tamim*, he lived and was not doomed to die, and because of the deceitful serpent, he was doomed to die for this."[230]

Like many romantics after him, R. Loew sees in *temimut* the foundation of life and in rational consciousness the foundation of death. But R. Loew does admit that, after sinning, Adam acquired a rational consciousness that eliminated *temimut* and brought death to the world. *Temimut*, then, has disappeared from real human history. Second, precisely when R. Loew seeks to exalt *temimut*, he hints at its inhuman character. R. Loew cites talmudic sources (TB Bekhorot 44b; TB Hullin 5b) praising people who compare themselves to animals. In his view, such people are the ones who realize the quality of *temimut*.[231] In another source, however, R. Loew emphasizes the distinction between human beings and beasts. The human being is an entity that is fundamentally potential and, in that sense, resembles the earth, which represents a potential for growth. R. Loew therefore claims: "Because man [Adam] has not realized his perfection, he is like the earth (*ha-adamah*) ... and therefore, being called Adam after *adamah* is fit ... and the beast (*behemah*) is named

---

[227] Ibid., 206.
[228] *Cf.* R. Loew's view on penitence as self-sacrifice. See *Netiv ha-Teshuvah*, 150.
[229] Referring to the wisdom acquired after Adam's sin—knowledge of good and evil.
[230] Loew, *Netivot Olam, Netiv ha-Temimut*, 206.
[231] Ibid., 208.

after *bah* [in it] *mah* [what], meaning that the whole of the beast is what is [already] in it [without any potential for growth]."[232]

This source clearly notes that characterizing human beings as animals is not a form of praise. Instead, it devalues the human creature, whose essence is precisely that it is not a fully realized "natural entity" but must instead work and shape itself: "Because man was not created whole. Rather, he was created in order to realize his wholeness and will never be entirely realized in the world but will always labor to realize his final wholeness, and this is his ultimate perfection."[233]

We could assume that R. Loew is inconsistent—at times, he views primary-animal natural *temimut* as a valuable quality, and at times, he negates it. But another view is possible if we adopt the principle of charitable interpretation, claiming that natural *temimut* is not the primary datum but a supreme goal that one should strive for, and that the journey to attain it lasts throughout life. Taking into account R. Loew's stance regarding Adam's sin, the voyage toward *temimut* is the eternal human journey to amend the damages of Adam's sin.

R. Loew's view of faith lends support to this interpretation. He holds that faith demands everything from us, "because he who believes in Him, may He be blessed, must do so with all his might. Faith requires power and strength ... because this is what faith is, to stand by one's faith with power and strength and never to stray from it."[234]

The juxtaposition of this text and R. Loew's view on *temimut* yields an interesting result. R. Loew, as noted, had claimed that *temimut* ensures closeness to God: "Because one possessing the quality of *temimut* ... will never stray from the Holy One, blessed be He." If faith implies a persistent effort to cling to God, it is not easily compatible with the quality of *temimut*. If *temimut* is indeed the basic element of religious life, the emerging result is paradoxical: the disposition of faith is antithetical to the disposition of *temimut*, the basis of religious life. The only way

---

[232] R. Judah Loew b. Bezalel (MaHaRaL), *Tif'eret Israel* (Jerusalem: n. p., 1970) ch. 3, 12-13. On this distinction in the writings of scholars from Ashkenaz and Poland, see Jacob Elbaum, *Repentance and Self-Flagellation in the Writings of the Sages of Germany and Poland 1348-1648* (Jerusalem: Magnes Press, 1993), 120, note 8 (Hebrew).

[233] Loew, *Tif'eret Israel*, 13.

[234] Loew, *Netivot Olam*, vol. 1, *Netiv ha-Emunah*, 206.

out of this entanglement is to argue that *temimut* is the sublime goal of religious life rather than its starting point.

A seemingly perfect expression of the view that exalts primary *temimut* appears in a story of R. Nahman of Bratslav known as "*Ma'aseh be-Hakham ve-Tam*."[235] The protagonist is indeed the *tam*, living a life of faith without reflection or guile, contrary to the clever man who sinks into heresy and is ultimately redeemed only because of the innocent believer.

But this view of *temimut* is in my view too schematic. The *tam* is not a person who lacks consciousness. Rather, he has a conscious position toward reality as a whole: he chooses to accept it as is despite his awareness of the gap between his concrete existence and the surrounding circumstances. His simple garb, the coat, and his food, the bread, are charged with a conscious baggage that allows him to see in them what they are not. The *tam*, the story's protagonist, is definitely not one who lacks the ability to think and reflect; he draws a distinction between his own stance and the other's and consciously endorses his own. In this sense, the *tam* of the story is the antithesis of a *tamim* living at an immediate level of existence. He actually shapes an ideal of life where *temimut* consists in the endorsement of reality and the renunciation of skepticism. Even if we do not accept this interpretation of the *tam*, Yosef Weiss rightly notes:

> R. Nahman's strong opposition to the "mediating" faith of philosophy in favor of the simple faith of ordinary people does not follow from the simple faith he favors but from a highly dialectic state of faith. Searching for parallels in the history of religion is unnecessary, since this state tends to emerge whenever faith is no longer possible unless in its dialectic form. The concept of faith that emerged from our analysis is not a return to the point of immediacy.[236]

But a conscious-reflective position need not be associated with skepticism. A person may conduct a reflective life without stumbling into a

---

[235] R. Nahman of Bratslav, *Sefer Sippurei Ma'asiyot* (New York: 1949), 49-69; Pinhas Sadeh, ed., *Rabbi Nahman of Bratslav: Tikkun ha-Lev* (Jerusalem: Schocken, 1981), 38-48 (Hebrew). The title as quoted is taken from Sadeh.

[236] Joseph G. Weiss, *Studies in Bratslav Hasidism* (Jerusalem: Bialik Institute, 1974), 145, 157 (Hebrew). But see also Mendel Piekarz, *Studies in Bratslav Hasidism* (Jerusalem: Bialik Institute, 1972), 22-23 (Hebrew).

skeptical stance, and in that case, reflection does not lead one beyond concrete life but to its conscious endorsement.[237]

R. Nathan, who writes the preface to the stories, subtly formulates the lesson to be drawn from it:

> Let us pay some attention to the story of the clever one and the *tam*. There you will see some explanation of the intention in that story, which is that the main goal is to choose the path of *temimut*, without any guile at all. And pay careful attention to every word and you will find wonderful hints on strengthening the paths of *temimut*, which is the essence of the good in this world and all the more so in the world to come.[238]

R. Nathan understood that religious *temimut* is not a primary datum but a religious challenge to be met. This approach continues that of R. Nahman of Bratslav himself, who recurrently emphasized that religious simplicity is a goal one should strive for rather than a given. As Mark sums up: "The abandonment of one's rational mind becomes then a kind of spiritual exercise and the suspension of one's rational mind becomes a desired state of religious consciousness."[239] Religious *temimut* is contrasted with rational skeptical inquiry rather than with religious reflection:[240]

> When a person follows his mind and his knowledge, he might stumble into many mistakes and fallacies and suffer grave calamities, God forbid. And some have brought great harm, like those famous wicked men who have misled the world, all because of their knowledge and their mind. The essence of Judaism is only to walk on the path of *temimut* and simplicity, without any guile at all.[241]
>
> Because some scholars say that the main purpose and the world to come is [to be found] only [in] knowing everything as is… and that is the purpose and the world to come for them, where the knower, the knowing, and the known become one…

---

[237] See Weiss, *Studies*, 145, 157.
[238] R. Nahman of Bratslav, *Sefer Sippurei Ma'asiyot*, 10.
[239] Mark, *Mysticism and Madness*, 17-18.
[240] Arthur Green, *Tormented Master: A Life of Rabbi Nahman of Bratslav* (Alabama: University of Alabama Press, 1979), 289-292.
[241] R. Nahman of Bratslav, *Likkutei Moharan, Tanina*, #12.

> And in their wrong view, the essence of attaining this purpose is through inquiry and through their sciences. But the truth is that, for us, the essence of attaining this purpose is only through faith and observance of the practical commandments, through the worship of God according to the Torah simply and guilelessly... and it is truly a strict prohibition to be a scholar, God forbid, and to study the books of their sciences, God forbid.[242]

According to R. Nahman, contrary to philosophy, which should indeed be ruled out, religious reflection as constant self-criticism is a condition of faith. Faith is not a given; it is attained with great effort, involving ceaseless cleansing of the dross and temptations that accompany it.[243] The dross and temptations include philosophical study and exaggerated religious piety. Both are antithetical to the required religious *temimut*:

> The essence of taking on the yoke of Heaven is to abandon and reject all our elaborate ideas and walk in the path of *temimut* and simplicity because only the Holy Torah is the true wisdom and every other wisdom is nothing by comparison.... People should dismiss all their elaborate notions and worship God, may He be blessed, with simplicity and *temimut*.... When a man follows his reason and his knowledge, he can fall prey to many mistakes and traps.... Neither should one inquire much into God's worship nor adhere to excessively strict practices, because all these are muddles and illusions from Satan to deter one from the service of God, and the Holy One, blessed be He, does not and so forth,[244] and as our sages, may they be blessed, have said, "The Torah was not given to the ministering angels." All these ideas, when one thinks too much about His worship (which is called *übertrachtn*) lead one away from it. The greatest wisdom of all is not to be wise at all. Only to be *tam* and simply straight ... though one should also be cautious about *temimut*, to avoid being a fool.[245]

Temimut is not a primary datum in this text either, nor is it identical with a view that is uncritical and unmediated by consciousness. We do not find ourselves within faith, but must struggle with ourselves

---

[242] Ibid., #19; see also #44.
[243] See, for instance, ibid., #22, #25, #30, #72, and more.
[244] The missing end of this saying is "does not belittle his creatures."
[245] R. Nahman of Bratslav, *Likkutei Etsot* (Jerusalem, 1977), 118 a-b.

to achieve it. This struggle is conducted at two levels: cognitive and conative. At the cognitive level, critical reflection could turn its glance from the person's inner struggle with faith to faith itself. Faith becomes the object of alienated philosophical speculation, as one would inquire into any object of study. At the conative level, the problem is the opposite: our religious inclination could lead us to religious extremism. The temptation of faith could lead one to forget that the Torah was given to human beings as they are, not to the "ministering angels." In R. Nahman's view, religious extremism is a kind of inquiry: "neither should one inquire much into God's worship nor pursue excessively strict practices." This inquiry, however, differs from theoretical speculation, since it is basically a superfluous examination of ourselves as believers that radically stretches the limits of our will. The person is no longer satisfied with worshipping God or with halakhic religious practice, and seeks to examine the religious practice itself by setting new and extreme practical goals. In R. Nahman's terms, such a person "thinks too much about His worship."

R. Nahman does not support respectable religious conduct. Indeed, he resolutely states: "At times, one should do things that appear mad in order to do His will, may He be blessed," but this behavior is not frequent and, furthermore, is only justified when it clearly reflects God's will.[246] Religious extremism as a guideline to religious life is not God's will and, in religious terms, represents religious temptation, when the true tempter is not God or the religious standing but "illusions from Satan."

In sum, religious *temimut* is complex. It demands thought and constant self-criticism—"if you do not prepare your heart, you cannot attain faith."[247] Simplicity (*prostkeit*), meaning a way of life where one is "really a simple person ... who behaves in simple ways and does not discover anything and engages in ordinary talk,"[248] may occasionally characterize the *tsaddik*. R. Nahman begins the cited passage as follows: "The *tsaddik* is sometimes a really simple person (what is called *prostik*)."

---

[246] Ibid., 118a. On madness in the thought of R. Nahman, see Mark, *Mysticism and Madness*, particularly 247-282.
[247] R. Nahman of Bratslav, *Sefer ha-Midot*, ed. Zvi Kenig (Benei Berak: Friedman, 1970), 37.
[248] R. Nahman of Bratslav, *Likkutei Moharan, Tanina*, #78.

This behavior of the *tsaddik* has religious goals, but is not itself the goal of religious life. Thus, even for a religious hero such as R. Nahman, who at least in some of his writings[249] exalts simplicity and *temimut*, this *temimut* is far from the original one. In his view, a life of faith is impossible without struggle and constant self-criticism, wherein individuals must constantly confront their very disposition as believers.

The distinction between primary and secondary *temimut* recurs in the thought of R. Kook, who distinguishes "natural faith" (which he equates with primary *temimut*) from "simple faith" (which he equates with secondary *temimut*). Concerning natural, primary faith, R. Kook writes:

> Natural faith, with its natural vigor and with the freshness of courage, is to be replanted in the field blessed by God in the giving of the Torah, where it becomes a Torah faith. There, with all its strength and fortitude, it refines itself and rises, ascending higher and higher in purity and cleanliness.....[250] Natural religiosity, which in its fundamental inner quality includes a ferment of idolatrous defilement, affects man with its fantasies and its inclinations in an undifferentiated mixture of darkness and light. Only when it comes to legislate duties and morality is it separated from evil.[251]

Like his predecessors, R. Kook identifies the problematic quality of primary *temimut*: it does have the passion of faith, but this passion is by nature uncritical and, to become valuable, it must undergo refinement and criticism. According to R. Kook, only the normative religious-moral system provides the mechanism for a proper development of the original sense of religiosity.

Having gone through this process, it is then mature to reach the stage of secondary *temimut*, where it renounces the reflectivity that elevated it to this experience: "It is through simple divine faith, containing no limitation or human guile, that the supreme light and the inner glow of a more perfect life is revealed—'Walk before me and be *tamim*.'"[252] The citation of the Genesis verse that commands Abraham concerning the

---

[249] Green, *Tormented Master*, Excursus I.
[250] R. Abraham Kook, *Orot ha-Emunah*, 105.
[251] Ibid., 107.
[252] Ibid., 105. The reference is to Genesis 17:1.

proper disposition enables the reader to trace the course of Abraham's faith, according to R. Kook:

> The conventional view is that Abraham inquired and examined until he understood the correct particulars about the Creator. In other words, light will not come into the world only from natural faith.... In every natural content, nebulous dross will necessarily be blended, and mixed within its vagueness will be the results that should be spread like refined gold. After pure reason refines and distils the power of natural faith that stands strong, it is ready to become God's preserve.[253]

Temimut in Abraham, then, is not a primary uncritical spontaneity. Indeed, his *temimut* is a return to spontaneity after critical reflection.

R. Kook's interpretation of the Genesis verse, "Walk before me and be *tamim*," is a fascinating new perspective in biblical commentary, since most Jewish and Christian exegetes explain the term "*tamim*" without relating it in any way to the problematic of simple faith, be it first or secondary *temimut*. According to this tradition, *temimut* is a kind of religious perfection that is required from the believer.[254] Bahya ibn Pakuda explained it as follows:

> You should know that the aim and value of the duties of the heart is the balance between outside and inside[255]—they should be equal in their service of God, may He be exalted and magnified,

---

[253] Ibid., 121.

[254] In the Latin translation of the Genesis verse, "*tamim*" is rendered as *perfectus*. See *Biblia Sacra*, vol. 1 (Stuttgart: Wuerttembergische Bibelanstalt, 1969), 260. See also *The Septuagint Version of the Old Testament*, trans. Lancelot Charles Lee Brenton (London: Bagster, 1879), 256. The equation of simplicity with perfection appears already in early Jewish sources. See, for instance, the Onkelos translation of Genesis 6:9; 17:1; Deuteronomy 18:13, and more; *Pesikta Rabbati*, ed. Meir Ish Shalom (Vienna, 1880), 195. In many sources, perfection is ascribed to the body, resembling the kind of perfection required in battle. Hence, physical perfection is equated with circumcision. See, for instance, M. Nedarim 3: 11; *Midrash Rabbah Leviticus*, ed. Mordecai Margulies (New York: JTS, 1993), Kedoshim 581-582; *Midrash Rabbah Numbers*, Naso 12:8. See also Rashi on Genesis 17:1: "Since as long as you have your foreskin, you are a cripple." Rashi relies here on TB Nedarim 32a and also on *Genesis Rabbah* 46:4.

[255] In the original Hebrew, "*izun niglenu u-matspunenu*," meaning that the outside [*niglenu*] should be identical to the inside [*matspunenu*].

so that the heart, the tongue, and the organs attest equally to their service of God, and each one of them verifies and confirms the other and does not oppose it or contradict it. This is what Scripture calls *tamim*, as it is written, "Thou shalt be *tamim* with the Lord thy God"[256] ... and Scripture says of one whose outside is opposed to his inside "and his heart was not perfect with the Lord his God" [257].... And it is well known that if one contradicts himself or gives himself the lie in word or deed, his honesty is not to be trusted and people will feel ill at ease about his truthfulness. So too, should our outside contradict our inside, and our ideas our words, and the movements of our limbs our conscience, the service we render to our Creator, may he be exalted and elevated, will not be perfect.[258]

Following Bahya ibn Pakuda, Bahya b. Asher writes: "'Thou shalt be *tamim*'—perfect, without additions or subtractions, as it is written 'The Torah of the Lord is *temimah*' [Psalms 19:8]... and know that we call '*tamim*' one whose inside is like his outside, and speaks not with a forked tongue."[259]

According to this interpretation, *temimut* is a kind of general human perfection required from the believer. This perfection, which belongs in the category of required moral qualities, refers to what in modern terms is known as integrity or absolute sincerity. Clearly, this perfection does not point to a renunciation of criticism or reflectivity. Quite the opposite, it requires from believers a constant reflective effort in order to coordinate their inner and outer beings.

Another exegetical direction is already found in the Midrash on Psalms known as *Shoher Tov*. According to this approach, *temimut* means exclusive and absolute devotion to God:

> "Happy are those whose way is blameless" [*temimei derekh*] [Psalms 119:1]. As it is written, "He that walks uprightly [*be-tom*] walks surely" [but he that perverts his ways shall be found out] (Proverbs 10:9). He that walks uprightly will be told that the way

---

[256] Deuteronomy 18:13.
[257] I Kings 11:4.
[258] R. Bahya b. Joseph ibn Pakuda, *Duties of the Heart*, ed. Yosef Kappah (Jerusalem: 1973), 30 (Hebrew).
[259] Rabbenu Bahye, *Commentary on the Torah*, ed. Hayyim Dov Chavel (Jerusalem: 1977), Genesis 17:1 (Hebrew).

of the Holy One, blessed be He, is successful, but he who perverts his ways knows that the world will know about it....

Another explanation for "walks uprightly." It refers to Abraham, as it is said, "Walk before me and be *tamim*." What did the Holy One, blessed be He, say to him? "Get thee out of thy country, and from thy kindred" [Genesis 12:1]. And he did not answer the Holy One, blessed be He, "What is the difference between my remaining here and going to another city?" ... He did not delay and immediately did everything he was told.[260]

The words of the Talmudic saying resonate in this midrash: "'How do you know you should not consult Chaldeans [sorcerers]?' Because it is said 'You must be *tamim* before the Lord your God' [Deuteronomy 18:13]."[261] Similarly, Rashi notes in his commentary: "'You must be *tamim* before the Lord your God'—Walk with Him in *temimut* and trust what He has in store for you and do not inquire into the future. Instead, accept in *temimut* whatever comes upon you, and you will then be with Him and part of Him."[262] Nahmanides expanded on this approach:

> We have been commanded to be wholehearted with Him, as it is said, "You must be *tamim* before the Lord your God," and this commandment tells us to direct our hearts only to Him, and to believe that only He alone has made all, and that He is the one who knows the truth of the future, and that only from Him will we ask about what is to come, from his prophets or from his followers ... and this was the commandment issued to Abraham, when He came to make the covenant with him and give him offspring. He said: "Walk before me and be *tamim*." He [Abraham] was the foundation of faith and challenged the Chaldeans—they had attributed all the powers to the sun, the moon, and the stars while he saw that above them is a creator and a leader. And God commanded him to be *tamim* with Him, and not to believe in his heart that there is any truth but Him ... and be only for Him, may He be blessed.... And perhaps the rabbi [Maimonides] thought

---

[260] *Midrash on Psalms Shoher Tov*, ed. Shlomo Buber (New York: 1957), Psalm 119, p. 245 (Hebrew).
[261] TB Pesahim 113b.
[262] Rashi, Deuteronomy 18:13. See also *The Hirsch Chumash*, Genesis 17:1 and Deuteronomy 18:13; Baruch Halevi Epstein, *Tosefet Brakhah*, Deuteronomy (Tel Aviv: Moreshet, 1965), 147, and more. See also Abraham Karelitz, *Sefer Hazon Ish* (Jerusalem: 1954), ch. 2, 17-18 (Hebrew).

that to walk in the paths of Torah is a commandment encompassing all, as it is said, "Happy are those whose way is blameless, who walk in the Torah of the Lord" (Psalms 119:1), and that is why he did not enumerate it separately in his list.[263]

According to this approach, *temimut* is a distinct religious quality—exclusive devotion to God and absolute faith in his leadership. This is a broadly endorsed exegetical tradition.

Temimut is thus a kind of moral and religious perfection required from the individual and does not imply the negation of reflection and constant self-criticism. Quite the contrary, attaining religious and moral perfection entails a constant effort and ceaseless self-criticism. Believers must examine their own faith dispositions: are they indeed fully devoted to their God? Do they indeed trust their God unconditionally, or does their trust depend on future results? Are they truly worshipping their God rather than Satan? Can they be sure of the fit between their inner and outer selves? Only constant self-criticism may help individuals to be *temimim* with their God. If *temimut* does not rely on criticism and reflection, it may lead individuals to perdition in their relationship with God and within themselves. A hasidic source offers an illuminating insight on the critical faculty:

> "You must be *tamim* before the Lord your God," means even when you are studying Torah, of which it is said "The Torah of the Lord is perfect [*temimah*]" (Psalms 19). Since it is said "you must be *tamim*," then even when you are studying Torah you must be with the Lord your God, and you should not say that the Torah is in any event called the Torah of God. Be very mindful of this.[264]

Temimut as a kind of immediate experience may be a human and religious goal we long for, but which must remain unfulfilled. Childlike *temimut* may be an ideal worth yearning for, but childhood cannot

---

[263] Maimonides, *The Book of Commandments with Nahmanides' Glosses*, ed. Hayyim Dov Chavel (Jerusalem: 1981), commandment 8, 248. See also Nahmanides, *Commentary on the Torah*, trans. Charles B. Chavel (New York: Shiloh, 1976), Deuteronomy 18:13, and S. R. Driver, *A Critical and Exegetical Commentary on Deuteronomy*, 3rd edition (Edinburgh: Clark, 1973), 227.

[264] *Baal Shem-Tov al ha-Torah*, Part 2 (Jerusalem, n.d.), 218; see also *Likkutei Moharan*, #6.

return as it had been, because the human being is a being that thinks itself. Friedrich Schiller, who devoted a great deal of thought to this matter, notes:

> In the child, the *predisposition and determination* is represented, in us the *fulfillment,* which always remains infinitely far behind the former. Hence, the child is to us a vivid representation of the ideal, not indeed of the fulfilled, but of the commissioned, and it is therefore by no means the conception of its poverty and limits, it is quite to the contrary the conception of its pure and free force, its integrity, its infinity, which moves us. To the men of morality and feeling, a child will for that reason be a *sacred* object, an object namely, which through the greatness of an idea annihilates every greatness of experience.[265]

Schiller understood that, for the person living within a culture, the distance from primary naïveté is unbridgeable. Individuals stand as free creatures, armed with their consciousness and their self-awareness. This existence turns immediate and primary experiences into a memory or an ideal, but not into a way of life. Thinkers such as Kierkegaard, R. Nahman, or R. Kook, who each held at one or another stage of their thought that, at least in principle, we should return to the original immediacy, knew well that this is a paradoxical and possibly unattainable goal. In any event, it is an endless mission rather than a program for human life.

Christian and Jewish religious literature both include many sources praising the figure of the *tamim*, the simple person, lacking reflection and self-criticism. This idea appears already in medieval Jewish literature,[266]

---

[265] Friedrich Schiller, *On Naïve and Sentimental Poetry*, trans. William F. Wertz Jr. http://www.schillerinstitute.org/transl/Schiller_essays/naive_sentimental-1.html For a similar interpretation, see Friedrich Hölderlin, *Hyperion or The Hermit in Greece*, trans. Ross Benjamin (New York: Archipelago, 2008): "Peace of childhood! Heavenly peace! How often I stand still before you in loving contemplation and attempt to fathom you! But we have concepts only of what was once bad but has been made good; of childhood, of innocence we have no concepts" (14).

[266] See, for instance, *Sefer Hasidim* (Ms. Parma H 3280), ed. Yehuda Hacohen Wistinetsky (Frankfurt, 1924), #5 and #6 (Hebrew). See also Eli Yassif, *The Hebrew Folktale: History, Genre, Meaning*, trans. Jacqueline S. Teitelbaum (Bloomington, IN: Indiana University Press, 1999), 385-388; Gedalyah Nigal, *The Hasidic Tale*, trans. Edward Levin (Oxford: Littman Library for Jewish Civilization, 2008), 257-263.

and becomes widespread with the beginning of Hasidism, possibly supporting Gedalyah Nigal's view: "A beloved figure in Judaism, who appears in a favorable light in stories from long before the hasidic period, is that of the *tamim*, the simple and innocent person."[267] Indeed, in the story in *Sefer Hasidim*, the praise for the *tamim* is based on the talmudic statement: "for the Almighty sees into the heart"—For here, [it was] neither Torah nor deeds, but [his desire] to do good [that] God counted as a great deed, for the Almighty sees into the heart."

The presence of the "*tamim*" as a figure in religious literature, however, cannot substantiate the claim that this figure reflects an attainable or desirable religious goal. This figure, as it appears in Jewish narrative literature, does not describe the normative believer. Rather, the "*tamim*" is a marginal figure, an ignorant simpleton living on the margins of society. This marginality is both the strength and the weakness of this figure and of its literary representation. As a marginal figure that is opposed to society's predominant ethos, it constitutes a possibility that standard normative culture poses as a kind of self-criticism of its values, its beliefs, and its way of life, as is already prominent in *Sefer Hasidim*. The story about the *tamim* is cited as a critique of religious practice. The opening lines prefacing the story are: "Anything a man can do he should do, and anything he cannot do he should think of doing. Like the tale of a man who was a herdsman and did not know how to pray...."

These opening lines suggest that the story is meant to emphasize the importance of religious intention, even if it is not always compatible with practical halakhic demands. As a critique, however, which is personified through a marginal figure, it does not suggest a practical ideal meant to be realized. The marginality of the figure is clearly stressed—a herdsman. As Rivka Dvir-Goldberg justifiably notes: "In Jewish tradition, a herdsman could evoke negative associations," unlike a shepherd.[268] The marginality of this figure clarifies its role in the story: members of the normative culture are not required to abandon their cultural practices and strive for a non-normative way of life. In normative religious life, reflection and critical thought play a significant role. Against this back-

---

[267] Ibid., 257.
[268] Rivka Dvir-Goldberg, *The Tsaddik and the Palace of Leviathan: A Study of Hasidic Tales Told by Tsaddikim* (Tel Aviv: Hakibbutz Hameuchad, 2003), 32 (Hebrew).

ground, the *tamim*, simple person, is doomed to appear as only a marginal figure, whose role is to warn of and criticize the distortions found in the normative context.

True, the marginal figure sometimes occupies the full expanse of consciousness. It becomes more and more significant until it appears to embody the practical ideal. In these situations, however, the question is whether this is still the "traditional" *tamim* figure or rather, in the guise of the *tamim* figure it represents one who is in tension and contrast with normative religious life. *Temimut* and the *tamim* in the stories of R. Nahman of Bratslav do indeed trace this dialectical tension, of which he is very much aware. In his work, as noted, *temimut* is not a primary datum. The *tamim* is the archetype of a religious life attained only with great effort and as a lifetime goal, if at all.

R. Menachem Mendel of Kotsk, who sensed the religious tension typical of a life of faith, contrasted the gap between certain feelings, which preclude reflection when experienced, and the religious experience, where the negation of reflection is only a goal:

> Once upon a time, he asked a Hasid whether he had seen a wolf and he answered yes. The holy rabbi then asked him whether he had been afraid of the wolf and he answered yes. He then asked this Hasid whether he had remembered at the time of his fear that he had been afraid, and the Hasid answered that he could not remember whether he had felt fear because of his fear. The holy rabbi then said that this is what fear of Heaven should be—he should not feel that he is afraid of the Holy One, blessed be He, at the time of his fear.[269]

Fear or awe overtakes us, until subjectivity dissolves in the power of the experience. Concerning the fear of heaven, however, this is not the case. The first experience of awe does not collapse the self and consciousness. Quite the contrary—in its original manifestation, self-consciousness accompanies the experience. The person's goal is to turn the religious experience into one whose characteristics resemble natural fear. The very emphasis on "should be" highlights the gap between the two experiences. My claim is that this gap, rather than being incidental, rests precisely on the fundamental characteristics of faith as an experience

---

[269] Yoetz Kim Kaddish Rakatz, *Siah Sarafei Koddesh* (New York: n.d.), Part 1, 66.

constituted by individuals as conscious creatures who forge a conscious attitude to their God.

The preceding analysis can be summed up in the following statements: the faith constituted in the real, historical, cultural experience of the individual cannot be a return to the natural situation that preceded sin. Like every human disposition, it bears the tensions that characterize human life, and the confrontation with the "temptation of faith" and with "faith as temptation" is thus a situation typical of a sincere life of faith. The believer's renunciation of a ceaseless confrontation with the temptations of both faith and the evil inclination is a conscious renunciation of the ability to shape faith as a human disposition and, ultimately, a renunciation of faith itself. Temptation, then, is constitutive of a life of faith.

On Non-Illusory Faith*

Eliezer Goldman

1

Professor Samuel Hugo Bergman's comments, published in *De'ot* (July-August 1949, 3-6), can be a starting point for presenting non-illusory religiosity from an additional perspective. For this purpose, I will attempt to redefine this stance and distinguish it from views specific to Professor Yeshayahu Leibowitz that he outlines when presenting his basic positions, even if these positions are not necessarily cohesive.

The religious person's consciousness is usually sensitive to flaws in human reality. Even when contemplation of human reality does not as such emphasize these blemishes, the very contrast between this reality and the description of divine perfection must evoke thoughts about its flawed character. These failings—death, sin, instinctual drives, the flimsy foundations of human knowledge, the inevitable confusion between good and evil, the originality of human existence as such—are neither accidental nor historical. They are essential to humanity and cannot be eliminated, either naturally or through historical evolution. Seemingly, these failings cast doubt on the possibility of any real link between the human creature and its Creator. There are two religious approaches to this situation, which are diametrically opposed typologically. One is a religiosity of redemption, which Leibowitz calls "illusory religion," holding that religion offers human reality the chance of a transformation that liberates it from its flaws and enables actual closeness to the divine. The religious means adopted for this purpose in the course of human history have been extremely diverse, ranging from magic to contemplation. In its most developed forms, this religiosity aspires to freedom from the fetters of humanity simply by dismissing them. Religion, then, redeems human beings from the fundamental flaws of their reality.

---

* This article is a chapter in the book by Eliezer Goldman, *Expositions and Inquiries: Jewish Thought in Past and Present*, ed. Avi Sagi and Daniel Statman (Jerusalem: Magnes Press and Jacob Herzog Center for Jewish Studies, 1996), 361-371 (Hebrew). Thanks to Batya Stein who translated this article from Hebrew.

For non-illusory religion, by contrast, the essence of the religious position lies in the contrast between the Creator and the created reality and in the unbridgeable distance between the human and the divine. Human reality must be accepted as it is and without illusions of possible rescue from it, and it is within it that we must worship God, "for this is the whole man" (Ecclesiastes 12:13). This worship expresses the only possible link between us and God, without any false belief in its power to dismiss the basic conditions of created reality and to redeem us from its flaws. This approach also emphasizes the possibility of such a link as resulting from divine grace. In the Bible, for instance, the covenant invariably appears as grace. This grace, however, does not redeem human beings from their reality; quite the contrary, the attributes of compassion and grace are actually tied to this reality: "For He knows our frame; He remembers that we are dust" (Psalms 103:14).

A special meaning is attached to this redemption, one that non-illusory religion negates. It is entirely detached from the concept of biblical redemption, which does not refer to the basic conditions of human existence but rather to specific historical conditions of subjugation to foreign nations, at times also to evil rulers. But even the miraculous descriptions involving expectations of change in the fundamental order of the world do not deal with human redemption in the sense that we use this concept here. Hence, eschatological visions do not prove that Judaism is a religion of redemption, even though many elements in these visions (as well as elsewhere in our sources) do suggest that Jewish religion can be categorized as a "giving" religion. The classification of religions into "giving" and "demanding" appears to me unfounded in any event—what would prevent a demanding religion from being also a giving one? Although we can claim—in my view justifiably—that Jewish religion was fundamentally non-redemptive and that soteriological elements percolated into it only at a later stage, we nevertheless cannot claim that it never had any giving foundation. The fact that the greatest religious figures in Judaism have tended to negate the element of reward as a factor in religious motivation does not allow us to deny the important role that reward plays in our sources. How we relate to the element of reward is an important question in the theological interpretation of our sources, but our position on this question cannot enable conclusions about Judaism as a historical corpus. By contrast, the claim that the main approaches familiar to us from the Bible and from rabbinical commentaries are fundamentally non-illusory seems hard to contest.

One of the main channels for the penetration of illusory elements into Judaism was the ontological conception of reason in the *Philosophia Perennis* tradition, an approach whose renewal Bergman seeks and whose beginning Aristotle ascribed to Anaxagoras. Official Catholicism, not surprisingly, is deeply attached to this philosophy and has refused to this day to renounce it. This philosophy has enabled it to overcome the constant clashes between the biblical and the later Hellenistic elements from which Christianity too drew its typical concept of redemption. Its influence on Judaism is most prominently evident in Maimonides. Few have emphasized like him the element of "holiness" in the concept of the divine, and hence also the absolute distance between the divine and the human. In one regard, however, Maimonides acknowledged the continuity between the divine and the human: human wisdom is, in his view as well, an "overflow" of divine wisdom. This continuity is what enables Maimonides to reach mystical heights in the last chapters of the *Guide of the Perplexed*, which deal with the possibility of contemplative "conjunction" with God. It is hard to conceive a greater misunderstanding of Maimonides than the presentation of his rationalism as clashing with the possibility of the *conjunctio mystica* that he acknowledges. Indeed, ontological rationalism is precisely what enables him to introduce this possibility into Judaism, despite his identification with the biblical and rabbinic conception of the divine as "devouring fire."

The character of human wisdom, however, is not a religious but a philosophical issue. Only in light of our philosophical understanding of the character of wisdom will we be able to adopt a religious stance toward it. The view of reason as an ontological foundation that human reason partakes in has long been questioned. Many epistemological theories reject it, among them not only those known as positivist or pragmatic but even some of those known as idealist. In their view, what is called the "rational structure of the world" is merely the structure of our thinking tools, language, and consciousness, as well as our experiential tools. We discover order in the world because our understanding organizes it selectively. We ignore the elements of disorder if we do not need them in order to explain known kinds of order. What we call "reason" in theoretical terms is essentially technical: (1) The type of thought that first developed while attending to practical and technical tasks.

(2) The criterion of this form of thought is methodological—use of a scientific method.

True, many who tend to accept this denotation of knowledge are driven by an anti-religious motivation. They view this as part of an ideology that ascribes importance only to human values and to scientific knowledge and does not wish to acknowledge the relevance or "significance" of anything beyond this frame, which human beings feel they transcend. Such an epistemology, however, is also backed by weighty non-ideological arguments. For instance, the view that determining the use of a scientific method as a criterion of "knowledge" offers, for the first time, an answer that is not too obscure to Plato's classic problem: how to define (or more precisely, how to explicate) "knowledge." Many hold that, in our philosophical situation today, this is the only answer that more or less fits Plato's intention. Using the terms "knowledge" or "reason" in other ways will simply return us to the same tangle of associations from which only the isolation of our problem ensured some clarity in its understanding.

A religious person can deny ontological rationalism. But for a Jew whose religious approach is not fundamentally mystical—which is the type that fits most of us—adopting this position implies denying classic theology any option of introducing "illusory" elements into Judaism. This view of human rationalism precludes any perception of continuity between human and divine wisdom, at least insofar as theoretical wisdom is concerned. This option of transcending the human condition is also closed to us.

2

Wisdom and reason are usually discussed not only in reference to our theoretical pursuits but also in regard to our actions in the moral realm. Is the situation any different here?

I did not fully understand Leibowitz's claim that "morality as a value *per se* is a 'distinctively' atheistic category." In his view, much of our life is religiously indifferent and, in principle, the moral consideration could definitely appear as an independent, religiously indifferent "value." Any other conclusion would require us to argue that what is religiously indifferent is also morally indifferent—a claim that is simply inconceivable without further explanation. Moral philosophy, by contrast, would indeed appear to support the anti-illusory stance.

Is practical reason able to evade the technical character that, as noted, tends to be currently ascribed to theoretical reason? As long as practical reason deals with the adaptation of means to ends, or even with a concern for coherence when striving for aims—to avoid the pursuit of contradictory goals—it remains within the bounds of technique or technical thought. The situation does not change when we view our morality in deontological terms and seek ways of fulfilling or reconciling our obligations. In order for practical reason to rise above the technical level, it must be capable of offering us ends in themselves or categorical imperatives. The practical moral experience accumulated in the course of human history as well as the attempts to clarify the foundations of ethics increasingly show this to be impossible. Ends appear to us as ends in themselves only because, in the contexts in which we strive for them, we do not question them. As soon as our context broadens, or as soon as we are capable of examining ourselves in a slightly different perspective, the aim that had appeared self-evident requires justification too. As for categorical imperatives—even contemporary philosophers who speak of an intuition of duties acknowledge that this concept always refers to a duty at first glance, and that we have to be ready to discover the limitations of our duties when they come into mutual contradiction.

This claim would not surprise a religious person. A creature of contingent reality will have to be satisfied with contingent aims and duties. Indeed, what should have surprised religious individuals is the successful outcome of an attempt to reach an autonomous definition of an absolute imperative. The relationship between morality and religion is a rather complex question, but the success of the Kantian attempt would have evoked unbearable difficulties in trying to define this relationship. In a sense, Kantian morality could be described as an attempt to offer an alternative to illusory religion in the shape of an illusory morality, with individuals as citizens sharing equal rights with all creatures endowed with reason. Yet, as most philosophers today would probably agree, the attempt failed. From a non-illusory perspective, this is an additional instance of the total detachment of the absolute from human reality.

For non-illusory religiosity, the religious and the non-religious person do not differ in their evaluation of the technical character of the conditions of human existence. We cannot escape the technical character of this reality, including also all that we are used to calling "spiritual," insofar as the spiritual is equated with the rational. Spirituality is, at most, dissatisfaction with what is only technical. Its importance lies in its pushing human beings to increasingly broader and deeper perspectives, but it will never surpass technique. What is the conclusion? The secular person will argue that technique (in the broad sense of my use of this term here) is everything; the religious person will also be forced to admit that study and morality cannot raise him above the technical level as long as the pre-rational is still dependent on contingent biological existence.

Hence, the reality that human reason refers to will hold no value for the religious person as long as we lack assurance that the Creator, the only one whose reality is non-contingent, considers this reality valuable, as it were. Discovering the nature of knowledge and of morality will not bring religious people to deny religion, but will strengthen their tendency to deny humanism as a basis for their lives, without necessarily requiring them to deny a priori all the conclusions that were drawn also based on humanism. Religious individuals will be no less supportive of principles such as: "Did you think your blood was redder than ..." or "Whatever is hateful to you ..." or "whosoever destroys a single soul of Israel it is as if he had destroyed a complete world." They will not, however, rest these principles on such slogans as "the infinite value of the human being" or on the idea that the human being is an end in itself.

3

One significant difference between the illusory and non-illusory view is the attitude to the law and to what it represents. By nature, law is merely the tentative regulation of potentially conflicting actions. The law is always incomplete. Aristotle had already acknowledged that the law, which generally seeks to arrive at the best possible arrangement, cannot supply the best or fairest one in every single case. Maimonides accepted this view and, in the *Guide* III:34, he extends it also to Halakhah. The law is a classic example of the fundamentally pragmatic and incomplete means that we are forced to resort to in the organization of our lives. A typical trend of many utopias is, not by chance, the abolition of the law as a fixed institution with a technique of its own. In this sense, a utopia is a paradigm of different illusory approaches that, in one way or another, negate the law. This negation assumes two main forms. In one, the law is perceived as the incomplete realization of a morality that, as such, is complete and flawless. The law is a consequence of the attempt to realize in real conditions values that, in and by themselves, are ideal (in the two main senses of this word). The negation of the law follows from its being a "technification" of the spiritual ideal. Not in vain do supporters of this view often speak of the contrast between the letter and the spirit of the law. Only the letter of the law, in their view, is subject to randomness, whereas the spirit can be free and complete. In the other form, the law appears as a necessary evil that we must tolerate for as long as the human creature is in a state of "fall" or, in the term common today, in a state of "alienation." "Redemption," the rise from fall to grace, liberates the person from the necessary connection with the law. Thus, for instance, the appearance of the Christian redeemer liberates his believers from the authority of the Torah. In the ideologies prevalent in the Christian West over the last two centuries, which have also percolated into Jewish thought, we often find a mixture of these two viewpoints.

By contrast, in the anti-illusory approach, the law is a limitation imposed on the spirit due to the weakness of the flesh, and no spiritual morality is free from the law's limitations. The limitations of the law reflect not only the practical conditions for the realization of this principle but also the limitations of the human "spirit." I do not wish to imply thereby that the law is merely the realization of morality; the relationship between law and morality, like the relationship between religion and morality, is too complex to be condensed in such a simplistic formulation. Unquestionably, however, in the legal realm we do try to implement moral principles. The law, for instance, is the classic realm for the implementation of principles of justice. But the flaws of the law concerning justice also reflect, no less than flaws in the implementation tool, the ambiguity and the vagueness of the principles of justice per se. The tentativeness of our moral evaluations is no less than that characterizing the concrete implementation of the law. We could even claim that the concrete experience gained in the course of implementing the law is a condition for the clarification of the moral principles we seek to realize by means of the law.

The law is thus one of the cultural institutions that best reflects the actual human situation, with all its essential possibilities and limitations. Because it leaves no room for illusions, the law is not particularly popular among the pursuers of the illusion. By contrast, the anti-illusory approach perceives the law as paradigmatic of culture, including its technical and "spiritual" aspects.

4

Another realm where the anti-illusory position will play a significant role is in the conception of faith. In its original denotation, the word "faith," as we know, referred to a characteristic of one worth believing in, not to a characteristic of the believer. The Bible ascribes this attribute to God, referring to truth, honesty, and keeping promises. This is the attribute intended also by the prophet Habakkuk in the verse, "and the just shall live by his faith" (Habakkuk 2:4), as is made evident by the contrasting other half of the verse. In a later use, faith became the characteristic of the believing person. The word now symbolizes the typical feature of the pious person, the measure of trust.

The current widespread use of the word "faith" as pointing to agreement with abstract notions is a much later denotation. The importance of the concept of faith in the Middle Ages follows from the religious importance that was ascribed in this period to the "correct" attitude toward theoretical dogma. Today, too, faith in this denotation will have religious significance only insofar as we ascribe religious significance to a person's abstract views.

Most of the statements to which theologians had tended to ascribe dogmatic significance are in a category whose conceptual importance might appear questionable to a believer in a non-illusory religion, who tends to minimize the weight of theoretical assertions in religion. In these believers' view, even statements about the existence of God lack theoretical meaning because they relate to what is beyond human experience, although in a broader sense of the term "meaning" trust in God is what endows life with meaning. In this sense, they are not really revolutionaries, because the conclusions of classic theology point in the same direction. As contemporary theologians have recurrently emphasized, one about whose existence we may speak of in abstract terms is merely one existent among others, an object among the other objects in our consciousness. Anti-illusory faith, then, will be faith in the sense of trust.

In Judaism, this faith involves two stages, corresponding to what the rabbis called "accepting the yoke of the Kingdom of Heaven" and "accepting the yoke of the commandments." The first stage refers to the relationship with the divine and its unconditional reality, which is beyond the realm of human value and experience: a view of the world as created, and of the human standing before the Creator. At this stage, the believer may sense that, "The sense of the world must lie outside the world", that

"... If there is any value that does have value, it must lie outside the whole sphere of what happens and is the case. For all that happens and is the case is accidental."[1] He will tend to shift the words "If there" from the second to the first quotation. He does trust the value that is beyond any occurrence. Belief in a divine "reality," however, does not ensure meaning to the world. In Jewish terminology, this is not yet faith in the "Lord God of your fathers, the God of Abraham, Isaac, and Jacob." Had we stayed within the primeval track of the divinity, we would have found it impossible to connect it to our contingent reality. The conclusion warranted by this experience would certainly have been acosmic—the dismissal or nullification of human reality vis-à-vis the divinity.

The second stage of faith is tied to revelation, which offers the possibility of connecting with the Creator and of granting religious meaning to human life by subjecting it to God's worship: "And this shall be a token to thee, that I have sent thee. When thou hast brought the people out of Egypt, you shall serve God upon this mountain" (Exodus 3:12). This worship is actualized in the only context open to human action—that of the "technique" typical of God's existence. The worship of God through the commandments expresses, *inter alia*, the fact that human beings can worship God only within the conditions of human reality. The covenant is an expression of divine grace, which enables the worship of God from this reality. Without the covenant, this worship would be inconceivable (to preclude misunderstanding, it may be necessary to add that the two stages are neither chronological nor psychological, but rather stages in the structure of religious consciousness).

At this point, Leibowitz appears to follow the usual views on illusory approaches. The view that "Halakhah is based on faith but at the same time justifies faith" and that "Halakhah creates the faith that underlies it" might be a logical paradox only when we speak of faith in abstract terms, of a faith divorced from observance. From the perspective described here, however, observance (insofar as we have a religious act here rather than a traditional ritual) *is* itself faith. The deepest content of faith is a Jew's trust that one can worship God by observing his Torah. It is on this belief that Jews cast their hope. Without this trust, their whole lives so far lose all sense and meaning. It is thus neither an exaggeration nor a paradox

---

[1] Ludwig Wittgenstein, *Tractatus Logico-Philosophicus*, trans. D. F. Pears & B. F. McGinnes, 2nd edition (London: Routledge & Kegan Paul, 1961), 6.41.

to claim that the Torah and the commandments are not the institutions of Jewish faith but its main content. If a paradox is involved here, it lies at a deeper level, touching on the very possibility of worshipping God.

5

This approach is diametrically opposed to the sentimental illusion making prayer the most distinct expression of primeval religious experience, given that this experience is conceived of as an "I" and "Thou" encounter. Here, the primeval, pre-Torah religious experience is the total negation of the "I"-"Thou" relationship. We meet divine holiness in the "devouring fire," precluding access. The Bible describes an important religious personality who negates the possibility of prayer—Job. Job's religious approach emerges through the primeval experience that is described with great sincerity—it is Job's hallmark to speak the truth. It is not by chance that Job was not familiar with the concept of the commandment, as evident from the absence of any hint of this concept even where we could have expected it. Only one who has been told "Get thee" (Genesis 12:1) prays, because only acceptance of the commandment justifies turning to the Creator as "Thou."

And still Leibowitz's attempt to make the value of prayer hinge on its mechanical element is unsustainable. It contradicts the content of prayer and the halakhic requirement of intention in prayer. The problematic that could lead to an approach of this kind follows not only from Leibowitz's singular view of Providence, but is also linked to certain aspects in the view of the Jewish divinity that are hard to reconcile with prayer as such. The rabbis were right when they claimed that prayer had been set by the patriarchs. Had it not been for their example, the legitimacy of prayer could have appeared dubious precisely because it is impossible to restrict it to the mechanical meaning that might be ascribed, for instance, to sacrifices.

Once we have been compelled to a fixed request for needs, we may wonder what this means. Even Leibowitz's radical stance might bear emphasis on two points:

(1) The religious position tends to view reality as "creation" and what takes place within it as the work of God, blurring what from a religious perspective is the obvious and less important element, since we encounter this creation in the shape of "nature."

(2) Our relationship with the Creator comes into being in our reality as it is, with all our human needs. Just as most of the commandments deal with everyday life, so does prayer.

The analysis so far has no bearing on the general risk that many see in the turning of the Torah into an empty shell. Endowing observance of the commandment with religious meaning depends on one condition—that it be performed for its own sake, because it is God's command. A distinction is required between this condition and the halakhic technical question of whether the commandments require intention; whether the obligation has been fulfilled when the person has observed the commandment for the sake of another goal; or whether he has to perform the action again (R. Nissim Gaon sums up this matter clearly in his discussion in TB Rosh Hashanah 28b). A distinction is also necessary between this condition and the requirement of intention in the sense of spiritual concentration concerning observance of the commandment. Performing the commandment for its own sake is possible even without intention in this sense. We perform many activities in our lives whose intention is reasonably clear even though we do not intend to do them. Intention is specific to prayer.

6

Readers of the preceding analysis will certainly find fault with the use of the terms "illusory" and "non-illusory" regarding the typology that concerns me here. More than they describe or characterize, these terms in a way convey evaluations of these two types of religiosity. Some will rightfully claim that even one who identifies unequivocally with one of these views should not use terms that imply a form of praise or censure and, at most, one might state that a certain type of religiosity appears to reflect and foster illusions. From Bergman's philosophical perspective, there is no room for viewing the religiosity of the last few chapters of the *Guide of the Perplexed* as illusory. Nor can it be said to an authentically mystical idea (as opposed to someone playing around with mystical terminology) that loyalty to the contents of his experience involves fostering an illusion. At most, I might say to him that I do not see this content as valid for others, and that one who is not a partner to the experience is allowed to relate to it as merely a psychological phenomenon, obviously without detracting from the respect we might feel for someone who undergoes such an experience. But this is also said about the faith of my non-believing friends.

I have remained loyal to Leibowitz's terminology because, at the conclusion of my remarks here, I must direct attention to the illusions fostered by those who typologically belong to the category of halakhic religion, illusions that ascribe redeeming effectiveness to the Torah itself. I will note the character of these illusions in a way that will also allow us to address in passing the relations of autonomy and dependence between culture and religion.

A religious approach of the type that has been called here "non-illusory" includes a radical critique of every culture as such. On the one hand, it denies any pretension to reach out, through human culture, to what is beyond it. At the same time, as a religious position, it is not satisfied within the closed circle of the human. For human beings, meaning is invariably connected to a cultural domain: language, art, science, and so forth. But in our religious position, we address what is beyond all frames. This position, as a human fact, can be expressed in cultural frames—in the science of psychology, in poetry, in music—but its content does not belong to the culture, nor is it adopted from the perspective of a cultural context. If the human attempt to refer to the divine can be described and even expressed with the tools of human culture, it is not possible to do this concerning what we relate to.

By contrast, a revelation in teaching Torah and commandments points to the possibility of worshipping God in ways that belong to human life and thus also to various cultural domains, though without thereby implying the religious validation of culture in its nature as an activity of the human spirit. Indeed, typical of Halakhah are limitations on freedom of action. These limitations, needless to say, apply not only to our organizational activities but also to our "spiritual" ones, such as, for instance, those in the aesthetic domain. We tend to be vague about this because of the unfounded belief bequeathed by religious liberalism that religion will not negate whatever is spiritually valuable. But examples of such negation are almost necessary in order to convey religion's qualms about culture. The implication is not that the Torah and the commandments are an alternative to culture. They are not a magic tool for solving human problems. Study of Torah and observance of the commandments do not redeem us from the essential problems of existence or liberate us from the need to deal in autonomous ways with problems arising in various places at various times. Halakhah does touch on more situations than is assumed by many who are not experts in it, but the modern ideology stating that for every human question there is a ready halakhic answer would have astonished earlier halakhic authorities. According to this ideology, many medieval Jewish practices would have had to be revoked.

Psychologically, however, the most dangerous illusion is the one conveyed by the vanity of those who think that their course is assured in all its details, that they have an unequivocal answer to everything, and that only lack of faith is the source of all confusion. Uncertainty is a fundamental condition of human existence. It accompanies us wherever we turn—in our abstract knowledge, in our moral choices—in the fundamental assumptions and in the details. Faith does not change this situation. Believers adopt a clear stance concerning the various possibilities: they tie their lives, their attitudes to the world and to reality, and their criteria of importance and of "success" to their religious position. Adopting an absolute stance, however, has nothing to do with certainty. Pious people who cast their lot with God are no longer open to other options. But trust is not identical with certainty as we understand this concept in a theoretical or moral context. The motivation that brings believers to their stance may persuade others, but this is not necessary when they themselves examine the alternatives to their faith as hypothetical possibilities that will support it. Equating faith and trust with certainty leads believers to a false understanding of their religious position.

The uncertainty of every human act, however, touches not only on the basic position. The faith expressed in Halakhah must come to terms with uncertainty concerning Halakhah itself. From the moment we received the written and oral Torah, our position resembles that of people abiding by an ordinary legal system insofar as the actual implementation and decisions according to it are concerned. Decisions concerning the Halakhah that applies in a particular case are human decisions made by the relevant authority according to the static and dynamic norms (in Kelsen's sense) found in the sources and in their discretion. But not only regarding concrete provisions: the formulation of halakhic rules is often a generalization from details found in the sources through logical inference and discretion. We all know that the sources are not unequivocal. Even more clear is that discretion is not uniform. Lay persons may heed the authorities' instructions, but the authorities themselves are forced to exercise discretion. A normal situation is one in which we observe halakhic instructions in a particular way while unsure that this is the "intention of the Torah." Reliance on the dynamic norms generally used in halakhic rulings (even if we assume that these are clear-cut and unequivocal) only confirms the basic claim that the implementation of Halakhah follows principles that also include human considerations, with all the potential mistakes involved. Hence, although its autonomous validity is absolutely unquestionable, the concrete manifestations of Halakhah still cannot escape the characteristics of a cultural creation.

Fundamentally, these remarks are banal and not too original. Nevertheless, there are ideologies that seek to blur these fundamental facts by relying on absurd harmonistic assumptions or by making the authority of the sages synonymous with the authority of the prophets. The recent interpretation of the notion of unshakeable trust in the rabbis' wisdom and knowledge (emunat hakhamim) is not only a naivety that can be dismissed with a forgiving smile; it leads to a distortion of fundamental views in Judaism, among them the fence the rabbis sought to erect between wisdom and prophecy.

If I have repeated here what are basically Leibowitz's ideas with different emphases and with some caveats, it is mainly because I hold that there is no room to approach the position described as if it were an idiosyncratic stance. Nor do I see here any basis for a claim of schizophrenia, apparently deriving from the view that positivist anthropology is absolutely incompatible with a religious stance. Fundamentally, the question is the location of the main division line between the technical and the spiritual or between the human and the divine. My comments above are only the outline of a view, and the systematic structure still requires clarification, particularly through a more detailed examination of how it might integrate the contents of our sources. Among those who are not used to protecting themselves from foreign ideas by hurling insults and abuse, my position deserves at least a discussion that will shed light on differences and enable criticism.

On Undermining the Beliefs of Others: Religion and the Ethics of Persuasion

David Shatz

When, if ever, may adherents of a religion proselytize—that is, try to persuade members of another religion, or unaffiliated theists, or secularists, to join their religion? When may members of one denomination of a religion try to persuade members of another denomination to accept some of their tenets?[1] Is it ethical for Jews-for-Jesus to try to convince traditional Jews to believe in the divinity and messiahship of Jesus? Is it morally proper for an atheist, or someone who denies some other central tenet of a religion, to try to talk believers in those tenets out of their beliefs?

Contemplating questions like these confronts us with a paradox. On the one hand, people sometimes take offense at proselytizing efforts, whether these are efforts at proselytizing to a religion or at proselytizing away from it. Such offense is taken even when the proselytizers present evidence and philosophical arguments as opposed to merely warning their targets of an impending hell.[2] The message of the offended seems to be, "Leave me [or them] alone." In a *U.S. News*/PBS poll in 2002, 71 percent of those polled, including 70 percent of Christians, said that Christians should be tolerant of people of other faiths and leave them alone.[3] Some university campuses in America have anti-proselytizing

---

[1] Among Christians this is sometimes called "sheep-stealing."
[2] Which is not to say that the threat of hell is not a good reason to embrace a religion. But it is prudential reason rather than an evidential one.
[3] See Jeffrey L. Sheler, et al, "Faith in America," *U.S. News & World Report* (May 6, 2002): 40.

policies.⁴ Thus there seems to be a genuine animus toward using persuasion to win religionists. Reciprocally, at the same time, religious people often view atheistic tracts as not only false but distasteful, and perhaps even morally wrong to produce.

Yet here lies our paradox. Debate and argumentation seem essential to any liberal democracy, as does freedom of expression. It seems almost ludicrous to contemplate a free society in which people do not express their beliefs *and* argue for them. What would politics be like, or science, or spectator sports? Decrying attempts to "convert" someone to a particular view on such matters seems laughable. Shouldn't a democratic society welcome and encourage rational debate, both advocacy for religion and advocacy against it? Furthermore, shouldn't citizens be *interested* in acquiring the truth, which would necessitate others helping them find the truth? Initially, therefore, it is hard to see why arguing for *anything* should be deemed morally problematic—let alone when that "anything" is something so important to life as the truth or falsehood of religious beliefs.⁵ Yet, as one protagonist put it in connection with Georgetown University's anti-proselytizing policies, "People talk about all kinds of other stuff—politics, sports, all kinds of contentious things. Then someone brings up Jesus and suddenly...."⁶

Thus, the question of whether efforts at persuasion are justified and ethical seems to rear its head specifically and perhaps even uniquely

---

⁴ Some countries have anti-proselytizing laws, Israel among them. Israel has considered more sweeping laws than are currently in its penal code; see, for example, http://oknesset.org/bill/4063/ ; http://www.oknesset.org/bill/3231/. While concern about Christian missionizing in a Jewish state is only natural, Israel has even considered bills that govern *dati-hiloni* proselytizing (in either direction) in the case of minors: see http://oknesset.org/bill/4962/ as well as: The Knesset Private Members Bill p\18 (2003; 7435503), p\1086 (2003; 13766603) . My thanks to Liat Lavi for these references.

⁵ Although arguing for a position with the aim of convincing someone involves giving reasons, one might give reasons without trying to persuade. (My thanks to Daniel Rynhold for pointing this out.) I can give reasons to a Gentile neighbor why I observe Shabbat, or study philosophy, but that is not persuading him to do so and not even *trying* to persuade him.

⁶ http://www.washingtonpost.com/wp-dyn/content/article/2007/07/20/AR2007072002030_2.html. When I use the word "paradox" to describe the situation, I am of course using it in the colloquial sense of "seeming inconsistency" or "perplexing situation," not the philosopher's technical sense.

when the topic is religion.⁷ If sermons are not objectionable, why should other religious persuasion efforts be?⁸ Opposition to proselytizing might even be accused of intolerance—and has been.⁹

This disconnect between attitudes to religious and anti-religious persuasion¹⁰ on the one hand, and the democratic ethos on the other, ideally should be examined on two planes—the psychological and the normative. Speaking psychologically, we might explain the offense that some people take by reference to their simply not liking it when, in a struggle to win souls, their ideological adversaries spread their own views and win devotees. (Jews typically will not care if Catholics proselytize Protestants, if their success or failure will not affect Judaism.) We expect, in fact, that how people react to religious persuasion (or dissuasion) will depend upon whose ox is being gored—the party trying to persuade or the party being addressed.¹¹ Notice, however, that this split

---

⁷ As Yitzchak Blau reminded me, the question of differential or discriminatory treatment of religion arises in other contexts too. Consider, for example, the common argument, "You think Judaism (or Christianity, or Buddhism...) is true only because you were raised that way." These arguments are not used as frequently to discredit belief in political, scientific, or medical views, even though they could be raised against them. (Many professionals, whether in the liberal arts or medicine or law, often follow their mentors' views.) Another example of differential treatment of religion is the demand for "sufficient evidence" (see my later discussion of Clifford). See Peter van Inwagen, "It Is Wrong Anywhere, Everywhere, and for Anyone to Believe Anything on Insufficient Evidence," in *Philosophy and Faith*, ed. David Shatz (New York: McGraw-Hill, 2001), 433-442. Finally, liberal political theory often seeks to exclude religious reasons from debates in the public square, an exclusion that critics argue lacks a compelling rationale for distinguishing religious reasons from others.

It is interesting that a religious commitment is often called a "persuasion," as in "monotheists of all persuasions."
⁸ John Stuart Mill himself did not oppose religious proselytizing *per se*, though he of course profoundly deplored how it was practiced. See Mill, *On Liberty* (Chicago: Henry Regnery, 1955).
⁹ See Elmer Thiessen, *The Ethics of Evangelism: A Philosophical Defense of Proselytizing and Persuasion* (Downers Grove, IL: InterVarsity Press, 2011), passim (e.g., 223).
¹⁰ Occasionally I will use the term "religious persuasion" to include both pro and con argumentation.
¹¹ See, in a related vein, Mill, 77-78.

reaction does not arise, at least not in theory, in politics and science—leaving us with our paradox intact at the psychological level.[12]

No doubt, as well, the use of coercive, deceptive, sophistic and manipulative tactics by religious proselytizers (including cultish brainwashing), makes their enterprise morally distasteful to people.[13] There are also legitimate concerns about proselytizers' honesty, openness, respect for others, and simply demeanor.[14] A major figure in Jewish-Christian dialogue who is, however, a vociferous opponent of proselytizing in dialogue, has said of proselytizers, "They inevitably come across as men and women who are so self-righteous that they feel no compunction in denigrating other faiths and their cultures...," so that "Those of us who have been exposed to these efforts ... have been deeply resentful of the arrogance of those who proselytize."[15] But the question persists: why worry about these matters only in the case of religion, and not in science and politics? Academic conferences are hardly arrogance-free, and hardly always paradigms of civility.

More importantly, it is wrong to *conflate* persuasion and coercion, or persuasion and deception/manipulation, as if *all* cases of persuasion exemplified unsavory methods. Likewise, notwithstanding the words quoted earlier, "inevitably come across," it is a contingent and changeable fact that proselytizers display vices like arrogance. It is wrong to tar an entire practice based on the deplorable conduct of some or even many practitioners, and descents down slippery slopes to coercion and manipulation may be avoidable. Let there be no mistake: Reservations and concerns about coercion and so forth are of vital, undeniable moral

---

[12] In practice there are efforts to stifle certain political and scientific speech, but relatively few put forth *theoretical statements* that those political or scientific views should not be aired or argued for in a liberal democracy.

[13] It is not clear that, as a matter of psychology, someone can change a person's beliefs by threats or force, as opposed to changing what the person professes or *verbally* affirms. I need not take a position on this question. In any event, deceptive and manipulative argument could be viewed as a form of persuasion, albeit involving bad reasoning and unethical tactics.

[14] To use terms that Yoel Finkelman used in an email to describe real-life challenges in education.

[15] David Novak, "Proselytism in Judaism," in *Sharing the Book: Religious Perspectives on the Rights and Wrongs of Proselytizing*, ed. John Witte Jr. and Richard C. Martin (Maryknoll: Orbis Books 1999), 43.

importance when dealing with praxis, with implementing a policy of religious persuasion in the real world. And they may, ultimately, justify treating religion differentially. But unless we simply give up on preventing coercion, deception, manipulation, and arrogant conduct, we should not conflate issues of implementation with issues of principle, and we must figure out principles before we deal with praxis.[16]

And so, what about at the level of principle? There is something deeper that can motivate opposition to religious persuasion beyond abhorring what ideological adversaries are saying and beyond contemplating how proselytizers could or often do behave and beyond worrying about the possibility of people resorting to coercion and manipulation. (Which is not to say that those who oppose religious persuasion consciously articulate that deeper justification to themselves.) Implicated in the ethics of persuasion and proselytizing are basic questions regarding the value of truth as opposed to other goods, skepticism about our ability to arrive at truth, epistemological pluralism, the right to privacy in religious belief, and the need to preserve individual and group identity. It is these questions that must be considered here. I will not provide a full-dress, comprehensive defense of any particular position on the issue. In fact, at points I will raise questions but not answer them. I do want to explain the positions, however, to understand what might be behind attempts to limit persuasion *specifically* in the religious sphere, and to argue that these objections to persuasion are often reasonable and deserve serious discussion, even though they sometimes are *un*reasonable or unresolved in my thinking and in need of further examination.

The ethics of persuasion addresses primarily the following questions:

- Are there good reasons to persuade others to believe that which you believe?
- Are you *obligated* to try to persuade others to believe that which you believe?
- Are there circumstances in which you are not *permitted* to persuade others of what you believe—that is, in which you are obligated *not* to persuade?

---

[16] The in principle/in practice slide is alleged often in Elmer Thiessen's criticisms of anti-proselytizing arguments. See Thiessen, *The Ethics of Evangelism*.

While philosophers have written much on "the ethics of belief," they have written little on the ethics of persuasion, even in the context of religious belief.[17] I am trying to fill this gap.

I. Preliminaries

Here are a few matters to keep in mind. These preliminaries are somewhat lengthy, but they are important and I beg the reader's indulgence.

First, in its ordinary usage, "persuading," like "remembering," is what philosophers call a success verb. That is to say, if I persuade you, then by definition I have succeeded in an effort—you have come around to my position. Nonetheless, I will not be using "persuade" in this way, but rather, for the sake of avoiding clumsy sentences, will use it as synonymous with "*try to* persuade."[18]

Second, we should distinguish targeted persuasion from general persuasion.[19] Targeted persuasion zeroes in on a specific individual or group by means of direct communication addressed to that individual or group specifically—oral presentations, letters, brochures and flyers in mailboxes, buttonholing, the placing of leaflets in shuls, the mailing

---

[17] The available literature is mostly on the use of persuasion in journalism, advertising, marketing, and education, and predominantly is not philosophical in character. This is Thiessen's judgment in his survey of literature in *The Ethics of Evangelism*, 238-53. Thiessen's book is a major exception to the rule and the author states that his is the first book-length philosophical treatment of the subject (ix). See also the more confined discussion in Jay Newman, *Foundations of Religious Tolerance* (Buffalo, NY: Prometheus Books, 1982), which Thiessen criticizes in several places. For rich essays about different religions' attitudes to proselytizing, see Witte and Martin, eds., *Sharing the Book*.

Because I grapple with the topic as a philosopher, my discussion will be abstract, and I leave real-life challenges, complexities, and dilemmas in specific contexts like education somewhat on the sidelines. That is not, of course, to belittle their importance.

[18] Compare: The word "refute," which originally was a success verb meaning to show false, has come to mean "rebut," that is, reply to, which does not imply success in argumentation.

[19] See also Solomon Schimmel, *The Tenacity of Unreasonable Belief: Fundamentalism and the Fear of Truth* (New York: Oxford University Press, 2008), 227-228.

of books. Non-targeted or general persuasion is exemplified by writing academic or trade books that contain arguments.[20] No precise line can be drawn between targeted and general persuasion, but many cases are clearly one rather than the other. General persuasion would seem less objectionable than the targeted type. There is a difference between Richard Dawkins dropping translations of his atheistic books on Meah Shearim, and his publishing the books in the first place and letting consumers decide whether to obtain them. Professional philosophers carry on vigorous pro-con debates in academic journals and books, and occasionally scientists and others join in such non-targeted persuasion. This does not seem problematic. One reason that targeted persuasion is worse is that targeting might annoy and inconvenience the target, and in that respect religion may be no different from other areas: people who badger other people with "truths" are a nuisance, no matter whether they are putting forth conspiracy theories, quack science, or even sound history and sound science. At the same time, there may lie something deeper than annoyance.

Third, we should distinguish, at least initially, between talking people out of their prior beliefs, persuading those who have pondered the matter but suspended belief, and persuading those who have not thought about the question being raised by the persuader. Among those who have not yet formed beliefs about a given subject matter, some (like Judah Halevi's Khazar) might actively seek truth—they "invite" persuasion attempts. I will be dealing with cases of the first kind (talking people out of prior beliefs), but the varied cases of fence-sitters/agnostics are not as straightforward as they might look, inasmuch as some people object to religious proselytizing even toward the hitherto agnostic.

Fourth, we should distinguish not-persuading from an activity well known to scholars of Talmud, medieval Jewish philosophy, and Kabbalah, and recently illuminated by Moshe Halbertal: concealment

---

[20] A book criticizing a particular group is not necessarily designed to persuade them to give up their views, but rather to convince others not to follow them and to block people belonging to the group from performing certain functions in which, if the criticisms are sound, their participation is not appropriate. Any expatriates or defectors won by the arguments are simply an additional dividend. The intention might make a moral difference.

and esotericism.²¹ Certainly some people who choose not to persuade are also concealers who want to hide what they regard as truths, and/or want to hide truths about themselves—that is, about what they believe. They may fear that revealing what they believe will cost them a job or a *shiddukh* for their children, and so they conceal their belief even if they genuinely believe that Judaism teaches what they believe and they believe it for that very reason. So often not persuading others is just a consequence of wanting to conceal. Nonetheless, the concealer does not want the other party to so much as hear what the concealer thinks is the truth about a subject matter; but when X chooses not to persuade Y, it often is the case that X doesn't mind if Y hears the truth—indeed, may wish that Y knew the truth—and also doesn't mind if Y knows that X believes such-and-such. X may clearly announce what he or she believes, but elects not to try to persuade Y. Perhaps X decides that the benefits of trying to persuade are not worth its costs, or that benefits cannot be realized, or that the dispute with Y has reached rock bottom, a point of disagreement that simply cannot be resolved, making further debate a waste of time. Or X feels that his or her truth is incommunicable.²²

---

²¹ Moshe Halbertal, *Concealment and Revelation: Esotericism in Jewish Thought and Its Philosophical Implications* (Princeton: Princeton University Press, 2007). For Maimonides, spreading the truth to a broad audience may not just endanger the philosopher, as Leo Strauss stressed, but it can cause confusion (people may think that the philosophy they learn necessitates abandoning religion [commentary to *Hagigah* 2:1]). More centrally, Maimonides believed that unless people believe in divine emotions, frequent direct divine intervention, and other "noble fictions" (to use Plato's phrase, popularized by Leo Strauss), obedience to Halakhah will be weakened. Halbertal paraphrases Maimonides succinctly: "Society would collapse under conditions of epistemic transparency" (50). Concealment can also be justified, Halbertal explains, by reference to the unknowability of ultimate truth and by the fact that concealment enables the integration of Torah with the wider culture by positing a deeper meaning to texts. In addition to recognizing the power of naive belief to produce obedience, Maimonides proposes in his introduction to his commentary on the Mishnah the interesting argument that if all people were philosophers, humanity would be wiped out within a short time—for no one would be available to plow and reap and thresh and grind and cook.

²² Partly because of the contemporary stress on equality (see Halbertal, 140-141), the esotericist tradition's idea that hiding religious truth is justified at

A fifth, final, and very important clarification relates to an ambiguity in the phrase "giving another person reasons." We normally think of persuading as a matter of showing evidence and drawing logical inferences from the evidence. This is because we normally think, in the words of the British mathematician and philosopher William Kingdon Clifford in his celebrated 1877 essay "The Ethics of Belief," that "It is wrong, anywhere, everywhere, and for anyone, to base his belief upon insufficient evidence." In other words, everyone has a duty to withhold belief in a claim unless they have sufficient evidence in its support.

Clifford designed his principle to undermine religion. It seemed to pithily capture the philosophic method used through the centuries, and did not seem to have any real competitors as an epistemic practice and a criterion for justified belief. But times have changed. Clifford's thesis resonates poorly, to say the least, in a post-modern world, a world in which pluralism, multiculturalism, relativism, skepticism and epistemological Balkanization rule the day. Indeed, "objective" principles like Clifford's are perceived as precisely what has been wrong with philosophy for centuries upon centuries, an utterly wrongheaded approach to forming beliefs. Even many analytic philosophers nowadays maintain that the "sufficient evidence" condition is too stringent. They note that adopting the condition would lead to our saying of many intuitively justified beliefs that they are not justified, from belief in an external world to beliefs about politics and philosophy (the mind-body problem, for example). We could not live were we to follow Clifford. Philosophers today often argue, instead, that certain beliefs—including religious

---

first strikes modern readers as bizarre. From the point of view of a religionist today, however, the advance of science, by leaving little room for the God-of-the gaps, undeniably has eroded many people's faith, even if in truth some traditional authoritative figures teach that God plays a limited role in the world's affairs. Disseminating a view that limits divine providence may not be a good idea, then, especially when educating children. Bear in mind, too, that some individuals believe that the results of certain social scientific inquiries (e.g., into certain differences between groups) should not be disseminated, or that such inquiries should be held to a higher standard of evidence, or that the inquiries not be undertaken at all. The notion of secret truth—"forbidden knowledge"—has not disappeared entirely in modern society. See Roger Shattuck, *Forbidden Knowledge: From Prometheus to Pornography* (New York: St. Martins' Press, 1996).

beliefs—are "properly basic" (or foundational) and need no evidence to justify them; or that fideism, belief on pure faith, is a rationally defensible option; or, following William James, that beliefs, including religious beliefs, may be justified by pragmatic considerations, such as the fact they yield happiness, security, group solidarity, and a sense of meaning.[23] On the Jewish side, R. Abraham Yitzhak Kook's writings even suggest that certain beliefs are obligatory because they are necessary components of national identity, so long as they are not harmful to human welfare; and R. Kook proposed choosing between rival metaphysical outlooks—say, theism vs. pantheism—on the basis of which is more life-affirming and optimistic.[24] R. Joseph B. Soloveitchik declares that "the act of cognition [is] a concomitant of a valuing act that occurs under certain practical and teleological aspects.... In sum, approval or disapproval precede any cognitive act. The reason is the

---

[23] It is difficult to see how philosophers who consider their religious beliefs "basic" could ever provide someone else with reasons for adopting their beliefs—this, by the very nature of basicality. One way, however, is to persuade the prospective proselyte that she suffers from some prejudice or flaw that prevents her from grasping certain truths.

For a survey and assessment of alternatives to the "sufficient evidence" requirement, see my introduction to the readings on "Is There a Place for Faith?" in *Philosophy and Faith*, ed. Shatz, 424-428. See also my "The Overexamined Life Is Not Worth Living," in my *Jewish Thought in Dialogue: Essays on Thinkers, Theologies, and Moral Theories* (Boston: Academic Studies Press, 2009), 387-412. Clifford's essay, "The Ethics of Belief," is reprinted in most anthologies in philosophy of religion, along with William James' opposing pragmatic view in "The Will to Believe" (1896). Against Clifford, see especially Van Inwagen, "'It Is Wrong Anywhere, Everywhere, and for Anyone to Believe Anything on Insufficient Evidence." Finally, for responses to the phenomenon of peer disagreement, see Richard Feldman and Ted A. Warfield, eds., *Disagreement* (New York: Oxford University Press, 2010).

[24] For these points, see, respectively, Shalom Carmy, "Dialectic, Doubters and a Self-Erasing Letter: Rav Kook and the Ethics of Belief, " in *Rabbi Abraham Isaac Kook and Jewish Spirituality*, ed. Lawrence J. Kaplan and David Shatz (New York: New York University Press, 1994), 205-236; and Tamar Ross, "The Cognitive Value of Religious Truth-Statements: Rabbi A. I. Kook and Postmodernism," in *Hazon Nahum: Studies in Jewish Law, Thought, and History Presented to Dr. Norman Lamm on the Occasion of His Seventieth Birthday*, ed. Yaakov Elman and Jeffrey S. Gurock (New York: The Michael Scharf Publication Trust of the Yeshiva University Press, 1997), 479-528.

instrument of the will, and the theoretical act is subordinated to the volitional."²⁵

Although I recognize that, within a religious standpoint, it is important to persevere in a life of faith even when sacrifice is demanded and even when one is surrounded by evil and hardship—a point generally ignored by proponents of pragmatic justification—in what follows I will suppose that *in certain cases* a Jamesian, i. e. pragmatic, approach to epistemic justification is a viable candidate.²⁶ "You'll be happy and secure, your life will be infused with meaning" will count as persuading (again, it is really *trying* to persuade).²⁷ I will generally avoid making a commitment on the question of how to circumscribe the cases where pragmatic justification is legitimate, but at points I will have to raise it.²⁸

---

[25] *The Halakhic Mind* (New York: Seth Press, 1986), 109, n. 15. Daniel Rynhold shows that this passage relates to R. Soloveitchik's perspectivist view. See Rynhold, "Perspectivism and the Absolute: Soloveitchik's Epistemological Pluralism," *Revue Internationale de Philosophie* (forthcoming).

[26] However, for an attack on pragmatic approaches that is rooted in the need for sacrifice and the experience of crisis, see Joseph B. Soloveitchik, *Halakhic Man*, trans. Lawrence Kaplan (Philadelphia: Jewish Publication Society, 1983), 139-143, note 4. Soloveitchik even insisted that suffering is integral to religious life. There is tension between this view and the quotation from *The Halakhic Mind*, but that can be removed if the quotation is referring to benefits other than happiness. In *The Lonely Man of Faith* (New York: Doubleday, 1992), 98-99 (starred note), Soloveitchik allows that religion brings happiness, and cites the Bible as proof, although religion has non-pragmatic elements as well. See also Reuven Ziegler, *Majesty and Humility: The Thought of Rabbi Joseph B. Soloveitchik* (Boston: Maimonides School; New York: OU Press; and Jerusalem: Urim Publications, 2012), 163, including the additional references he cites.

[27] If one could justifiably believe something on pragmatic grounds, the question of whether a person can be coerced into holding a specific belief is reopened, insofar as the threat presents a pragmatic inducement to believe. But in cases of coercion, the pragmatic advantages do not arise from the content of the belief but from the way it is induced. So cases of coercion are not cases of pragmatic justification as far as my goals in this essay are concerned. Readers who find the above qualifications and distinctions arbitrary are welcome to differ and to modulate the forthcoming arguments accordingly.

[28] James, for his part, demarcated the "certain cases" in which pragmatic justification is acceptable (or rather necessary) as cases where (a) the evidence does not support one belief over another—in terms of evidence, there is a stalemate that is unresolvable; and (b) the option that presents itself is "genuine"—i.e., living, momentous, and forced (terms that I will not bother to define here).

II. Why Persuade?

So: should people seek to persuade others, and if so why?

There can be many *motives* for trying to convince others. Recently, psychologists Hugo Mercier and Dan Sperber have developed an unsettling theory, according to which the aim of reasoning is to persuade, and the aim of persuading is to win. "Skilled arguers are not after the truth but after arguments supporting their views."[29] Putting this theory aside, other, though perhaps related, motives may include: needing like-minded people in order to feel good about myself and my identity; wanting to make everyone in my image; feeling powerful; fearing a bruised ego over being contradicted; boosting self-esteem; and escaping loneliness.[30] Religious extremists want "groupthink" to the point of wanting to kill anyone who does not think like them, and (not to make too close a comparison, of course), academics sometimes threaten with ostracism colleagues who dissent from their favored positions because they loathe being contradicted. These motives are of great psychological interest, but blatantly unpersuasive at the moral level. When we say things like "I can't remain silent" or that we "feel impelled" to convince people to come around to our views, are there good reasons for this feeling of normative pressure, an ethical burden? There are at least two main answers.

The most obvious moral argument for persuading invokes the duty of benevolence: "If I believe something to be true, then I have a moral obligation to try to persuade those around me to accept my position."[31] After all, truth is indisputably good, and, as Mill put it, "the truth of an opinion is part of its utility."[32] Furthermore, you might be obligated to *seek* the truth, which strengthens *my* obligation to bring you around

---

[29] See Hugo Mercier and Dan Sperber, "Why Do Humans Reason: Arguments for an Argumentative Theory," *Behavioral and Brain Sciences* 34 (2011): 57-111, which includes responses to the article and an authors' response. The quote is from the abstract on p. 57. Sperber and Mercier claim that their view is supported by the prevalence of human irrationality, as in the case of confirmation bias (bias toward one's antecedently held views).

[30] Proselytizing efforts increase the self-confidence of sects. See the classic work by Leon Festinger, Stanley Schacter, and Henry W. Riecken, *When Prophecy Fails* (Minnesota: University of Minnesota Press, 1956), 25ff.

[31] Thiessen, 149.

[32] *On Liberty*, 32.

to believing it.³³ (As Halbertal explains, the Enlightenment sought to "uproot ignorance and enlighten the furthest corners of the earth with the light of knowledge."³⁴) Now there are epistemic goods besides truth, like rationality, i.e., being able to ground your belief in reasons.³⁵ Hence, even if you already believe what I take to be the truth, and need no convincing of the truth itself, I might place a high value on your being rational, on your having good reasons for what you believe; so I want you to have adequate justification for your belief, and therefore I supply you with reasons for believing what you believe already. (This is really reinforcement rather than persuasion. In this instance, preaching to the choir does serve a purpose.) I also might feel it important to strengthen my community's beliefs by giving its members good reasons for holding these beliefs. Persuading also reflects a belief that all should have access to the truth—a version of belief in equality.³⁶

The goods I want to share with you may be not epistemic but rather pragmatic. I have security, happiness, and meaning because I believe a certain way; I want you to have security and happiness, so I try to persuade you.³⁷ I believe that your endorsing my way of thinking will bring you to the afterlife, so I supply you with the truths you need to get there. I think you will be harmed by holding certain beliefs or by forming beliefs a certain way, so I protect you through persuasion. Martin

---

[33] Despite the frequent invocations in philosophical literature of "the obligation to seek truth," there is no assurance that, if there is such an obligation, it is an ethical one—it could be of an epistemological type, governed by a special ethics of belief. Moreover, Yitzchak Blau wrote to me: "Do I have to read Nietzsche or Ayn Rand in my pursuit of truth if I am concerned that I may become more selfish as a result? Do I have to endlessly read communist ideologues and see if I am convinced? Perhaps we do not engage in a dialogue because we are comfortable with and firm in our commitments and see no reason to try to shake them up."

[34] Halbertal, 141.

[35] See John Kvanvig, *The Value of Knowledge and the Pursuit of Understanding* (Cambridge: Cambridge University Press, 2003). Cf. the review essay by Michael R. DePaul and Stephen R. Grimm, *Philosophy and Phenomenological Research* 74, 2 (2007): 498-514.

[36] See Halbertal, *Concealment and Revelation*, 140-41. Halbertal contrasts the Enlightenment's belief that all people are capable of accessing the truth with esotericist concealment, and sees the advent of the Enlightenment as a reason why esotericism rarely arises in modern Jewish thought.

[37] See also Thiessen, 149.

Marty argues that "in an age characterized by insecure identities, the proselytizer does a favor" by helping the proselytizee feel secure.[38] We can proscribe coercion, deception, and manipulation because they are immoral means to these goals. But in the absence of these unethical practices, benevolent persuasion, it seems, is a duty.

In some cases it's not that by persuading people of what I see as the truth I'm increasing the good possessed by this or that individual, but rather that I am increasing the good of a social unit. I might think it is important for society that people hold correct scientific beliefs; that people be Republicans; and that people not hold fundamentalist beliefs that menace society. I might think that religion provides not just a philosophical grounding for ethics, but a psychological one; persuading people to be religious thus produces for the many the good of morality. Contrarily, in propagating "The New Atheism," Richard Dawkins, Christopher Hitchens, and others combine scientific critiques of religion with citations of terrible moral consequences they see in religion, consequences typified by the Crusades and by 9/11 but that they find also in the Bible itself.[39] Atheism, they believe, is a bulwark against violence and, even though convincing theists to become atheists dissolves their group's identity, religion must be combatted.[40] Think what you will of the Dawkins-Hitchens argument (both have trouble explaining atrocities perpetrated by secular regimes; moreover, religion serves many great social causes, as evidenced by statistics on charitable giving, social services, etc.[41]), their position is clear: persuading people of the

---

[38] Marty, "Introduction," in *Sharing the Book*, 6-7.
[39] Dawkins, *The God Delusion* (Boston and New York: Houghton-Mifflin, 2006); Hitchens, *God Is Not Great: How Religion Poisons Everything* (New York: Twelve, 2007). See also the autobiographical essays by atheist philosophers in Louise M. Antony, ed., *Philosophers without Gods: Meditations on Atheism and the Secular Life* (New York: Oxford University Press, 2007). Many of these essays cite moral objections to religion.
[40] I am reminded of a biting email that made the rounds after 9/11, in which the author reported on a new strategy for defeating al Qaeda—sending a group of atheist philosophers to convince al Qaeda members that there is no God. Cf. Shalom Carmy, "Is Religion a Primary Cause of War?: An Essay in Understanding and Self-Examination," *The Torah u-Madda Journal* 11 (2002-03): 35-49.
[41] See, for example, Arthur C. Brooks, "Religious Faith and Charitable Giving," http://www.hoover.org/publications/policy-review/article/6577 (accessed July 13, 2011). Religious people give more even to *non-religious* causes. Terry

truth of atheism protects society and is therefore morally required. All of the above are variants of the benevolence argument, with a strong pragmatic component as well. It needs only to be added that people should *want* to acquire goods for themselves, be they epistemic goods or pragmatic ones.

A different set of arguments for persuasion is rooted in what is loosely called liberalism. In *On Liberty*, Part II, John Stuart Mill stressed the value of disagreement and of enabling, in Oliver Wendell Holmes' later famous phrase, a marketplace of ideas. Modifying Mill for our purposes, the point is not that I want to benefit you by sharing a truth with you, but rather that in the process of trying to persuade you, that is, in giving you my reasons for believing certain things, I am also forcing myself to articulate my reasons *to myself*. I am opening myself, healthily, to the prospect of your undermining those reasons and convincing me of *your* view. (Anyone who has benefited from a critical referee report in a peer review process, or has been persuaded of another viewpoint in some other context, will appreciate this argument.) Further, again drawing on a point Mill makes, even when you fail to persuade me that I'm wrong and that my reasons are unconvincing, making myself vulnerable to criticism of my reasons for belief will enable me to firm up my reasons and prevent the belief from becoming a dead dogma. Finally, by presenting my reasoning to you I open up the possibility that you will persuade me that you possess part of the truth about the matter at hand, making my own view more nuanced and balanced. Collectively, the Millian arguments just raised are simply variants of that author's celebrated set of arguments for free speech, open debate and tolerance. When, as is the case nowadays, television shows devoted to analyses of the news have as guest pundits only people on one or the other side of an issue (only Republicans, or only Democrats, for example), and magazines and other publications publish only articles on one side of the political spectrum, some of the benefits of practicing persuasion are lost. Other goods can

---

Eagleton has written of Dawkins: "The countless millions who have devoted their lives to the selfless service of others in the name of Christ or Allah or the Buddha are simply wiped from human history—and this by a self-appointed crusader against bigotry." See Eagleton, *Reasons, Faith, and Revolution: Reflections on the God Debate* (New Haven and London: Yale University Press, 2009), 97.

be preserved, however: rationality, for example (again, providing people with good reasons for what they believe already), which prevents beliefs from hardening into dead dogmas.[42] Furthermore, by persuading, I encourage others with my opinion to do the same, which by both the benevolence argument and the liberalism argument increases utility further. Perhaps surprisingly, then, liberalism could provide a rationale for proselytizing.[43]

The benevolence argument focuses on the gain for you; the liberalism argument focuses on the gain for both me and you. Both arguments proffer reasons not only to persuade, but to open oneself up to persuasion. Taken together, therefore, the arguments suggest that seeking to persuade another may benefit you, may benefit society, and may benefit me, particularly but not only if you resist and counter-argue when presented with my arguments. A culture of persuasion seems like a good aspiration. If particular targets don't want to be bothered being persuaded, that may be a good reason for would-be persuaders to hold their tongues, but such potential targets, it might be said, can be faulted for their insufficient attention to the quest for truth.

There are three other arguments for mandating persuasion, two identified by Martin Marty in discussing pro-religious proselytizing. One is that "A person or community certifies its own authenticity and depth of commitment by instinctively wanting to share it."[44] A second is that "groups not firm or dedicated and ambitious enough to proselytize will continue progressively to wane and may well disappear. Those that are most aggressive, make most demands, and are most sure of their product, will prosper."[45] The latter claim need not be viewed as a simple appeal to the self-interest of political survival, but rather might be born out of a sense of an obligation to keep a community going, particularly when that community is convinced that it is right and just and does good. (It is striking that, despite the dangers that a policy of not proselytizing poses to their self-preservation, adherents of Judaism generally

---

[42] See also David Lewis, "Academic Appointments: Why Ignore the Advantage of Being Right?" in *Morality, Responsibility and the University*, ed. Steven M. Cahn (Lanham, MD: Rowman & Littlefield, 1990), 231-242.

[43] Indeed, Thiessen bases his call for proselytizing on liberal principles. See especially chap. 6.

[44] Marty, "Introduction," 13.

[45] Ibid., 13-14.

do not actively seek Gentile converts, although they do engage in *kiruv* [outreach] toward other Jews.[46]) There are other arguments: for example, equality demands sharing positions and reasons, and autonomy demands that all evidence be imparted (just as discussions of informed consent in medicine often state that disclosing information promotes autonomy).[47] These arguments deserve mention, and hints of them will return to our discussion later, but to keep matters manageable, they will figure only marginally in what follows.

The case for not only permitting but mandating persuasion seems so strong that readers might be wondering what grounds could possibly be adduced for opposing persuasion. (In fact, one even wonders whether the fact that persuaders can be nuisances justifies people in not wanting to listen.) That question will only be intensified by the arguments in the next section.

III. Assessment of the Pro-Persuasion

Differences Between the Arguments

The two arguments we examined—the benevolence argument and the liberal one—do not co-exist easily. The benevolence argument assumes that I am right—that I have epistemic confidence; if not what Mill called "an assumption of infallibility,"[48] then at least an assumption of being right. The liberal argument, by contrast, presupposes humility— I'm not certain of what the truth is. So someone who uses the first argument can't use the second, and vice-versa. One response to this tension, advanced by Mill,[49] is to use the second argument (the marketplace one) to set up the first (benevolence). That is, *once* I have settled my belief system by interacting in a process of debate and persuasion, then—but *only* then—am I entitled to be confident about my view.

---

[46] The transliteration should be *keiruv* or *keruv*, but *kiruv* has become the almost universal spelling.
[47] The democratization of scholarship that is evident today in blogs and print media—where nonexperts criticize experts without humbly questioning their own credentials for doing so—seems to me almost a logical extension of the Enlightenment's leveling effect, identified by Halbertal.
[48] *On Liberty*, 25.
[49] Ibid., 25-29.

Once I have that confidence, I should benevolently spread my beliefs.[50] But at what point can a person really say that his or her opinion has withstood rational debate and now can be used for benevolent reasons? Is there really some chronological marker? (By Mill's own admission, no.) And is it wise to wait for the outcome of debate? Mustn't someone whose beliefs have not been subject to rational debate act on what he or she tentatively believes at a given time? Acting includes persuading based on the views one regards as correct at that time, whether or not they have been tested in the marketplace, and that is the impetus for benevolent sharing.[51] Thus the benevolence and liberalism arguments not only presuppose contrasting epistemic stances but are somewhat inconsistent.

Another difference between the arguments—at least prima facie—has to with whether to encourage a *policy* of persuasion. Presumably, if you and I both use persuasion, then by my lights, those people you successfully convert, or whose (by my lights) false beliefs you reinforce, are worse off than before, contrary to the benevolence principle. You might even win over a member of my own group. Given that, the wisdom of my advocating persuasion as a policy would depend on whether I can win adherents better than you can. If I cannot, then by advocating a policy of persuasion I will be making people worse off rather than better off. If you will use tactics of manipulation or you control the media, you are likely to win even if logically your case is weaker. So the benevolence argument may actually end up dissuading persuasion, on the grounds that implementing a policy of persuasion might lower utility as calculated by someone with a particular view. Thus, someone who is pro-Israel might shun a debate with someone who is anti-Israel even though he or she thinks logic supports the pro-Israel position—for he or she might feel the audience will be taken in by the other side's

---

[50] See David Lewis, "Mill and Milquetoast," *Australasian Journal of Philosophy* 67 (1989): 160.

[51] Cf. Mill, 26-27: "Judgment is given to men that they make use of it. Because it may be used erroneously, are men to be told that they ought not use it at all?" And: "If we were never to act on our opinions because the opinions may be wrong, we should leave our interests uncared for, and all our duties unperformed.... We may and must move on our opinion to be true for the guidance of our conduct." Utilitarianism requires some such doctrine, because calculations about consequences are often complex and uncertain.

tactics, heightening its popularity. The liberal argument seems different in this regard—it does not yield an objection to persuasion as a policy, because whoever wins over the marketplace has won legitimately. This reasoning can be questioned as it often has been, since, *inter alia*, certain groups might control the media. But if we grant the reasoning, the liberal argument would automatically justify a policy of persuasion, or so it appears.

The Benevolence Argument: Assessment

Having noted the tension between the arguments, let us turn to them individually and in particular to potential weaknesses. First, benevolence.

   a) One objection is that in its strong form—"persuasion is an obligation" (and not merely permitted)—the benevolence argument does not grapple with the incredulously posed, rhetorical question, "Am I really obligated to persuade you of *all* my beliefs on important subjects?"[52]

   But a persuader need not forego the pursuit of other goals or be benevolent all day long. One can legitimately have non-moral goals (e.g., athletic achievement) as well as moral ones other than persuasion.[53] And there can be a division of labor among different persuaders.[54]

---

[52] One correspondent wrote to me, not speaking specifically of religion: "The very idea that one is obliged, all things considered, to 'straighten people out' sounds to me like a busybody's idea of moral obligation. Is the thought really that one should go about one's daily life buttonholing people and stamping out any mistaken thoughts they might have? I've certainly met people occasionally who seemed to think that this was their mission in life. Yuk! The suggestion that anyone should be like that is appalling. The idea that we should all be like that is outrageous." See also Gil Student, "The Enlightened Man's Burden," http://torahmusings.com/2011/06/the-enlightened-mans-burden/, which discusses "the obsessive enlightener" who objects "to every truth he encounters."

[53] See the celebrated argument in Susan Wolf, "Moral Saints," *The Journal of Philosophy* 79, 8 (August 1982): 419-439. Wolf's argument need not be accepted to the hilt in order for someone to accept what I say in the text.

[54] At bottom, the objection just considered may really be an objection to the claim that there is a duty of persuasion, rather than to the benevolence argument *per se*. But it is easily discussed in the context of the benevolence argument.

b) The benevolence argument has a strongly paternalistic flavor, and exudes a feeling of *noblesse oblige* and moral burden. For this reason some will be put off by it—by what they perceive as smugness, condescension, and feelings of superiority. Alternatively, they might find the posture of benevolence disingenuous, for one does not particularly get a sense of benevolence from writers like Dawkins and Hitchens, but rather perceives a destructive attitude. By the same token, theistic tirades against atheism might feel destructive in intent. There is frequently a suspicion that ethically unattractive psychological forces lie behind efforts of persuasion but masquerade as benevolence, though I believe that many proselytizers do sincerely try to help people by proselytizing. So, fairly or unfairly, advocates of the benevolence argument for persuading are caught betwixt and between. Either their self-projection as benevolent feels paternalistic and smug, or it seems disingenuous. For this reason, many people will reject the benevolence argument.

Yet these points do not *really* show that the argument is wrong, but only that people will be put off by it. Moreover, the *motives* of the "benefactor" do not change the fact that he or she is bestowing a good. So we do not have here an effective objection to the benevolence argument.

c) Another challenge to the benevolence argument is that it proves too much. It might, objectionably, justify suppression, because in the judgment of X, Y's view is dangerous to society, and even if it is not dangerous, society is badly served by false beliefs. (The liberal argument disagrees.) Someone might counter here with an argument from skepticism: X has no right to assume that he or she is correct. But that response would undercut the benevolence argument altogether, since the benevolence argument starts from a position of epistemic confidence which is strong enough to justify changing others' opinions. And again, although certainty is not attainable, people do and must act on their opinions, especially but not only when they perceive a danger. Scientists must act on their best theories despite risks; grant evaluators and peer reviewers must judge in light of their best assessments, again at times taking the risk of being wrong and thereby creating harm or preventing good. Given their offices and positions, they can *in effect* suppress views without using legal interference. So why can't a person who perceives a danger, even if it's just the danger of falsehood, try to take action and suppress the other's belief? If no answer is forthcoming, the benevolence argument is severely threatened since it supports what seems like a repugnant conclusion.

It could be replied that those who would justify suppression on utilitarian grounds violate the principle of universalizability. They would have to allow others to suppress too—which they wouldn't want. The Golden Rule should reign. There is, though, an interesting and controversial response to the universalizability/reciprocity objection, to wit, that the objector's use of the universalizability principle is flawed; the *reductio ad absurdum* does not really yield the absurd. After all, the proselytizer perceives a relevant difference between himself and the other: his views are right, the other's are wrong.[55] Consider: If we spread reasons for respecting innocent life, must we say that al Qaeda must be allowed to spread its philosophy? If a government assassinates another country's leader, is it logically committed to the moral permissibility of a reciprocal assassination of its leader, when it believes the other leader is a serious danger but its own is not? So, too, one might say, *kiruv* workers do not have to sanction what we might facetiously call *rihuk* activities, nor vice versa, in order to regard their own efforts as justified.[56]

Assessment of this response would prove somewhat complex. It may therefore be simplest for the advocate of a benevolence argument to proffer an additional principle that every person has a *right* not to have his or her opinion suppressed, a right that remains even if suppression would yield greater utility by the lights of the would-be suppressor. How to block creating rights in the other cases (e.g. al Qaeda) must

---

[55] I thank Aaron Segal for making this point.
[56] What about a *neutral* observer? Prima facie he or she should say that if one side may persuade, so may the other. But, to be exact here (as Aaron Segal commented to me), if the observer thinks one side is right but doesn't have an opinion about *which* side is right, only one side *really* is right in persuading (according to the logic presented in the text).

be explored, but it is a familiar problem for liberal societies.[57] Alternatively, perhaps someone who is pondering whether to be benevolent should assign *great* risk to the possibility that he or she is wrong and on that grounds not suppress. This may still allow for too much suppression, so the rights answer seems superior; but Mill-like concerns over the risks of being wrong are worth noting.

d) Suppose we ask, parallel to the case of suppression, whether those who persuade for their cause on the grounds of benevolence would be willing to allow others to persuade for *their* cause on the same grounds.[58] The presumed answer of an objector is no, they would not be willing; if we then apply the universalizability principle, it follows that people should not persuade.[59] But this objection fails immediately if in fact people who seek to persuade are fine with others persuading for their cause on the same grounds. And I believe that to be the case, within limits.[60]

However, we should examine religious persuasion closely, because a case might be made that religious persuaders on the

---

[57] Such right-ascriptions are commonplace in discussions of free speech. Mill, however, allowed people to induce others to change their life styles by tactics that include not only persuasion but also social opprobrium and ostracism. Using these tactics is not really *fully* tolerating another lifestyle or set of beliefs. To tolerate them fully would be to adopt a total *laissez faire* policy.

[58] Or, for that matter, on any other grounds—see the next note. (One side might not even like the other side *stating* its views, but I will present the issue in terms of persuasion.)

[59] This is not really an objection to the benevolence argument *per se*, but rather to the practice of persuasion, whatever reasons are offered on its behalf. Nevertheless I include it here under assessments of the benevolence argument (rather than later under objections to persuasion), because the discussion of universalizability relates so closely to item (c). Of course the idea that nobody should persuade anybody seems massively counterintuitive, but it will gain some support from pluralism, as we will see later.

[60] The idea behind saying that a persuader is fine with others persuading for their cause only "within limits" is of course that if the opposition voices claims that menace society, the persuader may believe that he or she can persuade but the others can't. Prima facie this violates universalizability. However I think that this case merely illustrates the problems I raised earlier about an across-the-board universalizability argument.

various sides are not "fine" with others proselytizing for their cause. Neither *kiruv* nor *rihuk* advocates (the objector will say) are likely to harbor such feelings of reciprocity.[61] Similarly, adherents of a particular religion may believe that only they can proselytize, while adherents of another religion may not. And as a general matter, adherents of a view don't want adherents of competing views to extend what by *their* (the others') lights is benevolence. Given all that, religious and anti-religious persuasion, it might be claimed, violate universalizability. This objection from universalizability has indeed been raised against pro-religious proselytization,[62] but consistency dictates that it be extended to the "con" side, even though those who oppose pro-religious proselytization on grounds of universalizability allow themselves (inconsistently) to persuade on behalf of atheism.[63]

Now, even if we set aside our earlier reservations against applying universalizability, the objection at hand would not apply across the board. Some religious proselytizers may indeed believe that *every* religion may proselytize, and may say (admittedly this is not as likely) the analogous thing about secularists. (If they endorse liberalism they certainly will say this.) Such people do not violate the universalizability principle.[64] Lastly, supplementing the benevolence argument by rights principles will serve to permit persuasion across the board.

Let us review these four criticisms of the benevolence argument. Objections (a) and (b) failed rather clearly; objection (c)—that the benevolence argument licenses suppression—fails if universalizability can be correctly applied to rule out suppression (a claim on which I have cast doubt, but which may nonetheless be true), or if advocates of benevolence find another, non-utilitarian principle that will prevent suppression, e.g. rights-ascriptions, or if they can show that there is *great* risk in suppression; (d) fails for those cases where persuaders for one side are

---

[61] Here and elsewhere, I borrow the useful term "kiruv" from Jewish discourse even though I am talking about adherents of any religion, not only Judaism.
[62] See Newman, *Foundations of Religious Tolerance*. Cf. Thiessen's critique of Newman in Thiessen 125-127.
[63] See Thiessen, 125.
[64] Ibid., 125-126.

fine with the other side persuading.⁶⁵ The benevolence argument therefore will remain standing if certain details pan out (e.g., the rights thesis), and with it there will remain in place the notion that persuasion is justified and maybe obligatory. The question of *mah nishtannah*—why is religious persuasion treated differently?—returns with increased force.

The Liberalism Argument: Assessment

There is something that Mill did not consider in his utilitarian argument for free speech and tolerance but which has been pointed out by David Lewis.⁶⁶ Mill's assessment of utilities studiously avoids assessing the content of opposing beliefs. But why should we calculate utilities based on a stance of neutrality? We now go down a familiar road. For someone who is convinced of the truth of his or her belief, the liberal calculation is simply wrong—in point of fact, tolerance is worse than suppression. Willard Van Orman Quine, rarely a participant in political philosophy or philosophy of religion, puts the point succinctly: "If someone firmly believes that eternal salvation and damnation hinge on embracing his particular religion, he would be callous indeed to sit tolerantly back and watch others go to hell."⁶⁷ To phrase it differently, it seems inconsistent

---

⁶⁵ Again, (d) is an objection to persuasion, not to the benevolence argument *per se*. The same may hold for (a), but, as I said in an earlier note, in (a) the idiom of benevolence makes both the objection and the reply clearest.

⁶⁶ Lewis, "Mill and Milquetoast." See also Craig Duncan, "The Persecutor's Wager," *Philosophical Review* 116, 1 (January 2007): 1-50. Lewis and Willard van Orman Quine (soon to be quoted) are two of the most prominent analytic philosophers of the twentieth century.

⁶⁷ Quine, *Quiddities: An Intermittently Philosophical Dictionary* (Cambridge, MA: Harvard University Press, 1987), 208. More elaborately, Alan Montefiore writes (he does not accept the argument, though).

> If, however, one believes, or is committed to the belief, that everyone's best hope of virtue and/or salvation (however exactly *they* may be understood) must depend on the doctrinal nature of their religious commitment, one is bound to find a prima facie difficulty in the way of according equal respect to the commitments of those whose doctrines or practices one believes to be in some way mistaken. If I believe that my tradition provides the only true account of the nature of God and of what He requires from His creatures, it would be strange indeed if I did not also believe that it was of vital importance to others that they should come

for a religious person to insist on freedom, as many liberal theologians do, rather than to focus on the consequences of heresy and religious errors.[68] The point can be generalized from the case of religious belief to any instance in which the holder of a belief also believes that others will be worse off if they hold the opposite belief. To take Lewis's argument one step further, Mill's thesis that open and free discussion leads to the emergence of truth would be dismissed by a religionist on empirical grounds, because debate over the past few centuries has weakened belief in *his* truth. Open debate has produced atheism, he will say. From the religionist's point of view, too many wrong views have gained wide acceptance as a result of the liberal ethos. Thus that ethos, says the religionist, reduces utility, and a proper calculation of utility—so Lewis asserts—would license suppression. (After presenting this argument for suppression to discredit Mill's reasoning, Lewis puts forth his own utilitarian defense of toleration.[69])

Liberals are likely, in response, to once again invoke an argument from skepticism or an argument from reciprocity: X has no right to assume that she is correct and Y incorrect, and also if X allows herself

---

to accept that account. ("Ecumenical Movements and Truth," *Midwest Studies in Philosophy* 21 [Notre Dame: University of Notre Dame Press, 1997]: 150. See also 145-146. Montefiore, it must be noted, resists the argument.)

Montefiore states that if I hold a belief about the chemical composition of the atmosphere, I might not feel that anyone is better or worse off for accepting or rejecting it, or for ignoring the matter entirely. But, "it would be a strange sort of religion," continues Montefiore, "which left it open to its adherents to regard its central doctrines as having a purely cognitive significance, and knowledge of what it claimed to be its truths as valuable only for the satisfaction of a certain type of intellectual curiosity." (Since people do persuade in science—one of my starting points!—the comment about the importance of a belief that has "purely cognitive significance" should be understood as referring to importance in the eyes of humanity at large, as opposed to science specialists, who *will* be "better or worse off." But since scientists also want the populace to be scientifically literate, I am not sure Montefiore's concession is appropriate.)

[68] See Lewis, "Mill and Milquetoast," 160.
[69] He suggests the model of a treaty. Both sides desist from persuasion lest they go to war and lose. At one point Lewis notes that his treaty theory would also preclude proselytizing (166, note 13); by "proselytizing" he means persuasion, and not specifically religious persuasion.

to proselytize, X must allow Y to do the same. And the challenger may reply to the fallibility objection (as Lewis in fact does) just as before: that although certainty is not attainable, people do and must act on their opinions when they perceive a danger, by Mill's own admission. Likewise it may be argued that the universalizability argument is flawed, for reasons already given. This leaves an appeal to rights as the liberal's main recourse.[70]

These reflections leave advocates of the liberalism argument for persuasion with problems. Like advocates of the benevolence argument, they need to supplement their utilitarian reasoning with principles about rights not to have one's views suppressed.[71]

Objections to Persuasion

We have seen and assessed the case for persuasion; it has emerged strong. But however good the pro-arguments are, problems confront the pro-persuasion position, beyond those noted already. The most obvious challenge arises when we consider trends like pluralism, relativism, perspectivism, and postmodernism. These promote the idea that each belief system is, in Wittgenstein's phrase, "in order as it is."[72] Persuasion thus seems unnecessary and inappropriate.[73] Abraham Unger makes the point this way:

> Philosophically then, we are living in a period that presumes a confidence in the authenticity of one's own cultural context, obviating the need to negotiate one's particularistic convictions.....

---

[70] Lewis's argument may have a psychological correlate. It could well be that some religious people and some atheists who try to win adherents by persuasion would, if they really had their druthers and did not live in a society enamored of tolerance, favor suppression. Living in a society that espouses tolerance, they must use persuasion rather than suppression. But perhaps deep down they think that if persuasion is allowed, so should suppression be.

[71] The famed comedian Groucho Marx said, "These are my principles. If you don't like them—I have others." This, I suggest, is a near-perfect statement of how philosophers often deal with objections.

[72] Wittgenstein, *Philosophical Investigations* 1:98 (in a different context).

[73] As others have noted, to be a pluralist is not to *tolerate*: I tolerate a belief when I think it's false; when I think it's equal in "truth-hood" to mine, I am not tolerating it, because I am not even contradicting it.

> Our age is one of multiple global identities not necessarily in competition with one another, but rather ideally co-existing in their happily independent and authentic cultural lives based on their own self-understood communally transmitted truths.....[74]

Conversion efforts, as Martin Marty puts it, "violate at least the implicit rules of the pluralist game."[75] So pluralism, along with relativism, perspectivism, and post-modernism, discourages an ethic that mandates persuasion.[76]

Many will dismiss this objection by dismissing pluralism, relativism, perspectivism, and postmodernism. This rejection would invoke matters like (i) the self-defeating character of the views (e.g., is the thesis of relativism itself true only relatively?); (ii) the fact that pluralists themselves maintain strong views, including strong opposition to others' views, contrary to their stated approach; and (iii) the fact that what one believes becomes, on the cited views, a matter of indifference—why should I care what I believe? (*A fortiori*, it has been said, pluralism cannot explain the mandate in Judaism to martyr one's self rather than perform certain acts [e.g., *avoda zarah*][77]) There are more matters for pluralists to address, such as (iv) explaining the role of argumentation and polemics in their framework. These are well-known problems, and I doubt that pluralists are without resources here.[78] In terms of our issue, however, the more basic challenge is that the wielder of the pluralist argument would never dream of applying it to eliminate persuasion in science, politics, history, or philosophy.[79] Why is religion singled out for special adverse treatment?

The arguments for persuasion are strong, a common argument against it—pluralism—is weak, and in any event unhelpful in dissolving

---

[74] Abraham Unger, "A Modern Orthodox Approach to Interfaith Dialogue," *Conversations* 8 (Autumn 2010/5771): 138.
[75] Marty, "Introduction," 2. As mentioned earlier, however, Marty suggests at one point that precisely because people confront so many choices of beliefs, the proselytizer does them a favor by leading them to accept one rather than remain overwhelmed.
[76] See also Thiessen, 62-71.
[77] See also Meir Soloveichik, "Of (Religious) Fences and Neighbors," *Commentary* 123:3 (2007): 38-43.
[78] See, for example, Rynhold, "Perspectivism and the Absolute."
[79] Thiessen too presents this challenge.

our paradox. So we are back to the question: why are religious people barred from an enterprise that in other disciplines and settings is deemed not only permissible but desirable?

IV. Limits on Persuasion: Proselytizing and Privacy

It is natural to suppose that our search for reasons against religious proselytizing can be facilitated by an examination of Jewish attitudes toward proselytizing. For, despite some historical fluctuations in these attitudes,[80] predominantly Judaism does not seek to proselytize. Certainly there is no doctrine of mission as there is in Christianity—and in fact Jewish law discourages prospective converts.[81] Indeed, Judaism's attitude to other religions is largely live-and-let-live,[82] except where those religions threaten the welfare of society. In Michael Broyde's words, Judaism emphasizes inreach—"the process by which Jews make Jews into better Jews"—but not outreach.[83]

---

[80] See Robert Goldenberg, *The Nations That Know Thee Not: Ancient Jewish Attitudes Toward Other Religions* (New York: New York University Press, 1998). An instructive summary of rabbinic thinking appears on p. 93: "Overall, the [ancient] rabbinic corpus presents a wide variety of attitudes toward the value of proselytism.... These diverse opinions cannot be homogenized into a single 'normative' rabbinic view." Goldenberg's statement may be extended to later periods. See also David Novak, "Proselytism in Judaism," in Witte and Martin, eds., *Sharing the Book*, 17–44, and David Berger, "Reflections on Conversion and Proselytizing in Judaism and Christianity," in idem, *Persecution, Polemic, and Dialogue: Essays in Jewish-Christian Relations* (Boston: Academic Studies Press, 2010), 367–377, esp. 368. On Gentile adoption of Jewish practices and active proselytizing by Jews during part of the ancient period, see Marc Hirschman, "Rabbinic Universalism in the Second and Third Centuries," *Harvard Theological Review* 93 (2000): 101–115.

[81] This opposition is based principally on *Yevamot* 47a. It is ironic how much controversy and tension the issue of conversion standards has generated today, thrusting into the public eye a phenomenon that theoretically is minor in Judaism.

[82] Some of the arguments used in this section appear also in my "Morality, Liberalism, and Interfaith Dialogue," in *New Perspectives on Jewish-Christian Relations*, eds. Elisheva Carlebach and Jacob J. Schacter (Leiden: Brill, 2011), 491-519.

[83] Broyde, "Proselytism and Jewish Law: Inreach, Outreach, and the Jewish Tradition," in Witte and Martin, eds., *Sharing the Book*, 45-60. The quoted words are from p. 45.

There would seem to be a variety of reasons for the restrained attitude among Jews toward proselytizing Gentiles, but these reasons do not automatically extend to such activities in general—i.e., to Gentiles doing proselytizing. For example, the rabbis teach that righteous non-Jews have a path to salvation (i.e., the world-to-come) without joining the Jewish people. In a famous letter to Johann Kaspar Lavater, Moses Mendelssohn exclaims: "Convert a Confucius or a Solon? What for?... It seems to me that anyone who leads men to virtue in this life cannot be damned in the next."[84] If indeed righteous non-Jews enter the world-to-come, that neutralizes the benevolence argument for proselytizing, since the good of salvation can be achieved without Judaism; conversion is superfluous.[85] So the benevolence argument could not be cited as grounds for *Jews* to proselytize. This leaves unanswered, however, why, if we use the benevolence argument, the many Christians who believe that there is no salvation outside the church should not proselytize others.[86] Moreover, even by the lights of a Jewish proselytizer, proselytizing will convey *truth*, which could be valued independently of salvation, so the Jewish reluctance to proselytize is not yet fully explained. Additionally, salvation and truth aside, religion is so bound up with basic questions of how to live and find meaning that, by the lights of each interlocutor, convincing the other will benefit that person in the here and now. So again we face the question: why not proselytize?

---

[84] See Mendelssohn's letter to Lavater in *Disputation and Dialogue*, ed. Talmage, 268-269. The Talmudic support for Mendelssohn, "The righteous among the gentiles have a share in the world to come," is found in *Tosefta Sanhedrin* 13:2 and *Sanhedrin* 105a, albeit along with a contrary view. Maimonides (Laws of Kings 8:11) restricted the scope of the statement, asserting that non-Jews who observe Noahide laws attain *olam ha-ba* only if they observe those laws because God commanded them, via Moses, to do so. If they arrive at the laws by reason, they have no share in the world-to-come. This upset Mendelssohn. See Eugene Korn, "Gentiles, the World to Come, and Judaism: The Odyssey of a Rabbinic Text," *Modern Judaism* 14, 3 (October 1994): 265-287. Menachem Kellner, *Maimonides' Confrontation with Mysticism* (Oxford: Littman Library, 2006), 241-250, interprets the passage from Laws of Kings 8:11 in a way that negates the commonly adopted understanding.

[85] See also: Berger, "Reflections," 368.

[86] I must note that the doctrine that there is no salvation outside the Church now meets with significant dissent.

David Berger presents other possible explanations of the Jewish reluctance to proselytize: the sheer danger of trying to convert Gentiles (especially in the Middle Ages); the improbability of succeeding; a wish that Gentiles be damned; and a desire to retain the uniqueness of Jews as a people.[87] These, too, do not extend to deter proselytizing efforts by non-Jews. To my mind, it is not clear whether the mostly philosophical—indeed, modern philosophical—reasons that will be given here for not proselytizing impacted classical Jewish attitudes to proselytizing. (Again, we must distinguish outreach from inreach, an enterprise in which Orthodox Jews have been especially aggressive.)[88]

The Jewish reluctance to proselytize is often shared by Christians in the specific context of interfaith dialogue. (The force of arguments against proselytizing, of course, is directed mostly at Christian mission.) Consider, to start, the view expressed by Sallie B. King:

---

[87] See Berger, "Reflections," 369-370. Martin Marty points out that "Jews realize that not to proselytize keeps this diaspora small" and "makes their very future precarious." See Marty, "Introduction," 10.

[88] Do Jews have an obligation to persuade the world to observe Noahide laws? Despite the prominence given in our time to the notion that Jews must engage in *tikkun olam* (improvement of the world through fighting for ideals like social justice, which prima facie includes persuasion), by and large Jewish thinkers, such as R. Samson Raphael Hirsch, have held that the obligation of Jews, if any, to influence the world to observe Noahide laws—to become "a light unto the nations"—may be fulfilled by their serving as ethical and spiritual paragons (a passive form of *tikkun olam*). That would exclude persuasion of the nations from the list of Jewish *obligations*. An exception is the late Lubavitcher Rebbe, R. Menachem Mendel Schneerson. For more on this topic, see See J. David Bleich, "*Tikkun Olam*: Jewish Obligations to Non-Jewish Society" and Michael J. Broyde, "The Obligation of Jews to Seek Observance of Noahide Laws by Gentiles: A Theoretical Review," both in *Tikkun Olam: Social Responsibility in Jewish Thought and Law*, ed. David Shatz, Chaim I. Waxman, and Nathan J. Diament (Northvale, NJ: Jason Aronson, 1997), 61-102 and 103-43 respectively. Cf. Jacob J. Schacter, "*Tikkun Olam*: Defining the Jewish Obligation," in *Rav Chesed: Essays in Honor of Rabbi Dr. Haskel Lookstein*, ed. Raphael Madoff, vol. 2 (Jersey City, NJ: Ktav, 2009), 183-204. R. Joseph B. Soloveitchik in "Confrontation," *Tradition* 6:2 (1964): 5-29, is the primary Orthodox advocate of the view that Jews must actively join the quest for social justice. A well-known portrait of persuasion is Maimonides' depiction of Abraham as persuading the world to accept monotheism. See *Hilkhot Avodah Zarah* 1:1.

> It is forbidden to enter dialogue with the intention or desire of converting one's dialogue partner. People participating in dialogue don't want to be converted; they want to belong to the religion they already belong to. If people discover that their dialogue partner's purpose is to convert them, they will stop attending. Dialogue is fundamentally incompatible with mission....[89]

Thus, too, does Novak write that "disavowal of proselytizing has been the indispensable precondition of Jewish-Christian dialogue."[90] Some writers, in fact, see dialogue precisely as a *substitute* for proselytizing, an alternative to it, implying, like King, that dialogue and proselytizing are mutually exclusive.[91] King seems to contradict herself with her next statement: "One should enter the dialogue without preconceptions of where the dialogue will lead. Dialogue is a process of discovery."[92] But let us stay with the first quotation. (Note that whereas proselytizing normally conveys seeking to convert another wholesale to one's religion, in our context it includes "conversion" to even a single central or quasi-central proposition or ritual practice.)

The position advocated by King and Novak can be described as "no concealment of yourself, no persuasion of the other." But why is proselytizing, whether it is an attempt to convert someone to an entire religion or only to specific beliefs or practices, wrong in the context of interfaith dialogue, one of whose oft-stated purposes is that each participant will learn *from* the others and not merely *about* the other?[93]

---

[89] Sallie B. King, "Interreligious Dialogue," in *The Oxford Handbook of Religious Diversity* (New York: Oxford University Press, 2011), 106.

[90] See David Novak, *Jewish-Christian Dialogue: A Jewish Justification* (New York: Oxford University Press, 1989), 129. Novak's reasoning is cited in the text accompanying note 15.

[91] See, for example, Harold Coward, *Pluralism in the World Religions: A Short Introduction* (Oxford: Oneworld, 2000). Cf. Thiessen, 216-219, and Pope John Paul II's 1991 encyclical letter, "*Redemptio Missios*: On the Permanent Validity of the Church's Missionary Mandate."

[92] King, 106.

[93] For a fuller examination of this argument see Shatz, "Morality, Liberalism, and Interfaith Dialogue." On the distinction between "about the other" and "from the other," see Tsvi Blanchard, "Is There A Moral Imperative to Engage in Interfaith Dialogue?" in *What Do We Want The Other to Teach About Us?*, ed. David L. Coppola (Fairfield, CT: Center for Christian-Jewish Understanding of Sacred Heart University Press, 2006), 13-28.

Opposition to proselytizing is even more surprising when we consider the earlier argument that benevolence dictates persuasion. After all, there are high stakes in "getting it right" when it comes to credo. Yet the intuition that proselytizing is wrong seems for many (myself included) strong. What might override the imperative of benevolence and justify the intuition?

Several ideas suggest themselves. Most are unconvincing or limited in their force.

1) Proselytizing will produce rancor in a dialogue even if *per se* proselytizing is justified. This is especially so in Jewish-Christian dialogue, because the Jewish participants carry the baggage of history, of forced conversions, anguish, and horrific slaughter.

    Reply: This argument does not explain why *in principle* proselytizing should be disallowed during dialogue. Furthermore, by the argument's logic, proselytizing would not be wrong when the dialogue is between two religions that have amicable relations. Some believe that the current state of Jewish-Christian relations is amicable, yet still disapprove of proselytizing.[94]

2) Strategically, it's not wise to proselytize because if you do, the other side will *de facto* feel free to proselytize toward your group. And you won't like it.

    Reply: This objection to dialogue has limited scope. It implies that if you won't mind being proselytized, it won't be imprudent for you to proselytize. And why *should* you mind being proselytized, if you can learn from the other?[95]

3) Applying Kantian principles, if you would not like to be proselytized, then ethically speaking you can't proselytize either. Do unto others as you would have them do unto you.

    Reply: This does not answer the question of why an open-minded person would not want to be proselytized if a rational argument is produced contrary to his or her views. Maybe such

---

[94] See Eugene B. Korn, "Rabbi Soloveitchik on Interfaith Dialogue," http://www.bc.edu/dam/files/research_sites/cjl/texts/center/conferences/soloveitchik/index.html, and cf. the response by David Berger, "Revisiting 'Confrontation' After Forty Years: A Response to Rabbi Eugene Korn," repr. in *Persecution, Polemics and Dialogue*, 385-391.

[95] See also Thiessen, 125.

people should open themselves to refutation. Also, the Kantian argument allows someone to proselytize if he or she won't mind being proselytized in return. Finally, we have seen that this argument overlooks the importance of the content of beliefs, that is, each advocate's thinking himself or herself to be right, and therefore relevantly different from the other. Arguably, therefore, the objection accords reciprocity arguments more weight than they deserve.[96]

4) Proselytizing violates freedom. Marty, paraphrasing this sort of argument without necessarily endorsing it, speaks about "the freedom to be alone and to choose one's own opinion, belief, creed, or party without intrusion...."[97]

Reply: It is difficult to see why being proselytized compromises freedom, except in cases where the proselytizing tactics are coercive and manipulative. On the contrary: If a religionist is enjoined from considering other religions, that constricts his or her freedom. Why can't someone exercise freedom by freely waiving the right not to be proselytized? Finally, why wouldn't persuading you to abandon a scientific theory violate your freedom to choose without intrusion? Why only religious belief?[98]

5) People have an obligation to uphold their traditions. By proselytizing, you make it difficult for them to fulfill their obligations.

Reply: It is questionable whether all the people who employ this argument to ban proselytizing are ready to say that someone who abandons his or religious tradition for a secular belief system and lifestyle, or who converts, is guilty of a moral offense. Nonetheless the argument *per se* has force, and we will discuss it later when examining the value of group identity.

6) Religious beliefs are private.

This last notion—privacy—seems to me critical but obscure. Moshe Halbertal sees it as connected to individuality. Privacy, he says, "protects

---

[96] Yitzchak Blau pointed out, however, that Jewish opposition to proselytizing could reflect opposition to the very notion that only Christians are saved.
[97] Marty, "Introduction," 2. A freedom argument also appears in Soloveitchik, "Confrontation," 23.
[98] I discuss waiving a right not to be proselytized in a religious context in "Morality, Liberalism, and Interfaith Dialogue," 514-515.

the very ability of a person to define himself as an individual."[99] Privacy can be taken to preclude proselytizing, and is so taken by R. Joseph B. Soloveitchik, who opposed Jewish participation in dialogues about theological doctrines even while advocating dialogue on social and ethical issues. R. Soloveitchik seems to have thought that, because religion is private, religions must be sealed off from criticism and from aggressive—or even mild—dissuasion with regard to theological principles.[100] Even R. Abraham Joshua Heschel, who argues for dialogue on the grounds that no one religion has all the truth, tells us that:

> Faith and the power of insight and devotion can only grow in privacy. Exposing one's inner life may engender the danger of desecration, distortion and confusion. Syncretism is a perpetual possibility. Moreover, at a time of paucity of faith, interfaith may become a substitute for faith, suppressing authenticity for the sake of compromise.[101]

The argument we must consider, then, is that proselytizing violates privacy. But what does the word mean, and can it really ground an objection to proselytizing? Why would religious belief be any more "private"

---

[99] Halbertal, *Concealment and Revelation*, 142. Some theologians say that just as God has both a hidden and a revealed aspect, so too does the human being.

[100] See "Confrontation." Cf. Soloveitchik, *Community, Covenant and Commitment: Selected Letters and Communications* (New York: Toras HoRav Foundation, 2005), 247-65, esp. 259-65. Note that by the very logic by which R. Soloveitchik opposes proselytizing, it seems also that Jews *should* seek to talk Christian clerics out of one salient element in their religion: missionizing, since missionizing violates moral principles. Indeed, "Confrontation" does precisely that "talking."

David Hartman proposes that in Soloveitchik's opinion, theological dialogue is not wrong across the board. Rather, in Soloveitchik's view as understood by Hartman, only those who can appreciate their uniqueness and their distance from the other can enter into communication and dialogue. See Hartman, *Love and Terror in the God Encounter: The Theological Legacy of Rabbi Joseph B. Soloveitchik*, volume 1 (Woodstock, VT: Jewish Lights, 2001), 150-151. In light of the Heschel quotation that follows, Hartman's approach would seem to view Heschel and Soloveitchik as taking much the same position. (In Hartman's view, Soloveitchik, in "Confrontation," conceals his true position.)

[101] Heschel "No Religion is an Island," in *Disputation and Dialogue*, ed. Talmage, 350. He continues: "Both communication and separation are necessary."

than beliefs about quantum physics or American history, which are debated vigorously?

Ironically, one reply to this question draws upon liberal philosophy.[102] Although their position enjoys less support than it once did, some liberal thinkers oppose allowing "religious reasons" to enter into the discourse of the public square because, *inter alia*, those reasons are "private," i.e., not accessible to universal reason.[103] A position based on religious beliefs is, on this view, *ipso facto* not part of "public" morality. It seems to me that this position also dictates not seeking to talk people out of their religious beliefs—regardless of whether the talker is a secularist, a member of another religion, or what-have-you. After all, the beliefs, or some of them, are not amenable to evaluation by public reason.

We come, then, to the following thought about what makes religious beliefs private: religious beliefs (or some of them) are not supportable by reasons, and may not be possible to defeat by reasons. Rather, they are a matter of faith, of existential choice. If so, people can't be rationally persuaded to believe. Nor can they be rationally dissuaded from believing. Reasons in the case of religion are relevant to an extent, perhaps

---

[102] "Ironically" because liberalism is often viewed as an opponent of religion, while in our context we are trying to see whether religion should be protected from dissuaders.

[103] A related claim (or complaint) is that religious reasons are not refutable. Considering the obstinacy of politicians who never budge from their positions, this objection seems odd. For arguments for and against introducing religious considerations into public debate, see Paul J. Weithman, ed., *Religion and Contemporary Liberalism* (Notre Dame, IN: Note Dame University Press, 1997). For discussions set in a Jewish context, see Martin P. Golding, Liberal Theory and Jewish Citizenship," in *Tikkun Olam: Social Responsibility in Jewish Thought and Law*, ed. David Shatz, Chaim I. Waxman, and Nathan Diament (Northvale, NJ: Jason Aronson, 1997), 201-214, and, in the same volume, Marc D. Stern, "Jews and Public Morality," 159-200. These articles of course need to be updated to cover literature that has appeared since their publication.

Admittedly, the issue about using religion in the public square is about using specific moral beliefs of a religion, not about arguing that God exists or that the religion is true. At most, though, making this distinction undermines the connection I draw between privacy in the context of proselytizing and privacy in the context of offering reasons in the public square. It does not undermine the construal of privacy now under discussion.

even a large extent—but not a *large enough* extent, as they are in science and philosophy.[104]

There are several problems with this argument, or rather limitations to it. One is that people are sometimes persuaded to be religious by hearing or reading other people's opinions and arguments, e.g. the fine-tuning argument for God's existence (a version of the argument for design rooted in modern science). People also sometimes leave religion because of the problem of evil or attacks on the historicity and/or ethical character of the Hebrew or Christian Bible. So reasons (evidence) have relevance to many religious people. And it is certainly the case that there are arguments for and against particular religions or particular denominations that use premises shared by the interlocutors, which makes persuasion possible. Of course, certain people's beliefs might not be malleable in these ways—and in such cases the privacy doctrine under discussion will apply. Thus, for example, Soloveitchik's largely fideistic approach can ground a privacy argument *for him*. Nonetheless, privacy does not extend across the board to all believers, and ostensibly, a privacy argument, in the present sense of privacy, cannot readily militate against proselytizing someone whose religious commitment is evidence-based.

One attractive response is that even when a religious commitment is evidence-based, and *to that extent* public, a part of it is not public. David Berger puts it this way:

> Thus, as much as theological propositions can be conveyed, as much as even religious emotions can be partially expressed, that which ultimately commits a person to God or a faith community to its particular relationship with God remains essentially private, leaving not only a lonely man of faith but a lonely people of faith—a nation that dwells alone.[105]

It may be difficult to apply this description to every single case of religious belief. But the resistance of religious beliefs to evidence even when there is a rational component to the faith suggests, indeed, that more is involved than reasons. The situation seems different in the sciences and

---

[104] Soloveitchik believes that faith requires fusing diverse aspects of the human personality. See *The Lonely Man of Faith*, 99. About pragmatic reasons, see the end of section I above and note 26.

[105] Berger, "Revisiting 'Confrontation' After Forty Years: A Response to Eugene Korn," 388.

politics, even though it must be granted that in those domains, too, the basis for beliefs might not be purely evidential and people sometimes or often cling to their antecedent beliefs in the face of contrary evidence. There is at least a difference of degree between religion and these other cases. (Soloveitchik maintains that subjectivity is inexhaustible, and this thesis, too, appears to apply more forcefully to religion than to science or politics.[106])

Does a repudiation of proselytizing on the grounds of privacy (construed in the way we have just suggested) make interreligious polemics a wasted and irrational exercise? In fact, we can pose the question more strongly: did not R. Soloveitchik himself polemicize against Christianity by castigating its rejection of law, its focus on the next world to the disparagement of this one, and its fixation on a single emotion (love) rather than the gamut of emotional life?[107] How can his use of polemics be reconciled with the picture of isolated private systems that emerges in "Confrontation"?[108] The problem is not only the Rav's; it affects *anyone* who justifies opposition to proselytizing by invoking privacy and at the same time believes his or her religion to be superior and has arguments for that claim.

The answer may be that Soloveitchik, in these polemics, is explaining the internal coherence of Judaism and articulating its worldview on many matters, showing how its ideas coalesce and fit together. He of course knows that, as a result of his explanations, many others too will find these ideas worthy of appreciation and embrace. But with regard to ultimate commitment, after outlining the position that the Jewish religion will not become universal at the end of days and that pious Gentiles can achieve the world-to-come, Soloveitchik writes:

> This tolerant philosophy of transcendental universalism does not exclude the specific awareness of the Jews of the supremacy of their faith over all others.... Religious tolerance asserts itself in

---

[106] See especially *The Halakhic Mind*, 73. Even in the fideist case, we should distinguish targeted from general persuasion: seeking to win over someone from another religion personally, versus addressing an audience impersonally by writing a book or an article.

[107] Most of these themes appear frequently in his writings. On the last, less familiar theme, see "A Theory of Emotions," in *Out of the Whirlwind*, 183.

[108] Not to mention the cognitive pluralism and at least seeming relativism of *The Halakhic Mind*. See Rynhold, "Philosophical Foundations," esp. 119, n. 57.

> the knowledge of the existence of a variety and plurality of God-experiences and in the recognition that each individual is entitled to evaluate his great unique performance as the most redeeming and uplifting one. Tolerance has never demanded of the religious personage to eliminate the sense of axiological centrality from his feelings.[109]

This passage requires explication, but it is at the least consistent with the idea that the religious individual cannot provide a full set of reasons for his feeling of "axiological centrality."

My discussion has been at points indecisive, but I have isolated one sense in which religious commitment may be deemed private (it is not based on reasons) and tried to discern the impact of this sense upon the scope of the privacy argument against religious proselytizing. I have also called attention to the challenge of understanding the role of polemical arguments within a private commitment.[110] Daniel Rynhold, however (in correspondence), noted that some people embrace another understanding of privacy. Religion is private, in this conception, in the sense that it often has no social consequences. Now, it is certainly not the case that religion is private in the sense that it has *no* impact on public matters. On the contrary, religious adherents seek to shape public policy, whether the subject is the teaching of evolution in schools, abortion, gay marriage, or stem cell research. When it does so, religion becomes public and fair game for persuasion—just as science is. But when it does not,

---

[109] Soloveitchik, *Community, Covenant and Commitment*, ed. Helfgot, 21–22. See also "Confrontation," 19. Consider, too, the interesting comment about arguing against Conservative and Reform Judaism (pointed out to me by Rynhold): "My approach is not to speak negatively about other movements but rather to praise my own wares. I have never fought against another group in Jewry" (*Community, Covenant, and Commitment*, 223). Yitzchak Blau pointed out to me that whereas works like *Halakhic Man* and *U-Vikkashtem mi-Sham*, which are addressed to Jews, contain anti-Christian polemics, *The Lonely Man of Faith*, which was delivered to a Catholic audience, does not.

[110] Elsewhere, in *The Halakhic Mind*, R. Soloveitchik advocates a general cognitive pluralism, which, one could argue, entails that polemicizing in religion is no more problematic than doing so in science, politics, etc. We are then back in our original paradox (why is religion treated differently). See *The Halakhic Mind* (New York: Seth Press, 1986) and the analysis by Rynhold in "Perspectivism and the Absolute." For my purposes, there is no reason to assume a general cognitive pluralism.

religion is fairly regarded as a private matter and should be protected from persuasion.[111]

Does this sense of privacy yield a good reason for not proselytizing? Clearly, there is a certain pointlessness and at times inappropriateness in persuading people to give up or adopt beliefs that make no practical difference. But quite apart from the fact that religion often does have a practical import, don't people seek to persuade others about matters in philosophy, history, and math that have no practical import? Both the benevolence and liberalism arguments presented earlier regard truth as valuable in itself (as was meaning, security, salvation, etc.). So even if lack

---

[111] There are analogies *within* religious groups to this form of private vs. public. A Modern Orthodox Jew may not care whether his ultra-Orthodox neighbor believes the world is less than six thousand years old, but does care if the neighbor also announces that it is prohibited or perhaps heresy for a Jew to believe in evolution. For that Modern Orthodox Jew, if a *haredi* authority declares it heresy to believe in evolution, that *is* of practical import, since it affects how the supposed heretic is treated by others in the community; and the Modern Orthodox Jew will want to combat the charge. Furthermore, Judaism is a culture of authority, and one source of evidence for and against particular positions is *ma'aseh rav*—how this or that rabbi behaved, even in the absence of an explicit declaration. Therefore, if a *haredi* Jew denies that in his youth R. Eliyahu Dessler read *Uncle Tom's Cabin*, but (as is the case), the evidence strongly suggests he did, the false denial does have practical import *for Judaism*, for it may be used to keep intact *haredi* polemics against reading secular literature. Likewise, if the *rosh yeshivah* of a famous *haredi* yeshivah in America attended a Yom Ha-Atzma'ut celebration in the 1950s (which he did), that has implications for ideology and practice. Tactically it is profitable for anti-Zionists to delete the rabbi's attendance from the annals of history, but Modern Orthodox Jews are justified in persuading *haredim* and their own ideological group that the record has been altered. This is because the truth has implications for practice—it legitimizes attending *Yom Ha-atzma'ut* celebrations. So, too, with censorship and doctoring of texts—they have practical import for Orthodox Jews. On Rynhold's suggestion, persuasion (here, of an intra-Orthodox nature), is in place in all these cases I have borrowed the examples of falsifications of history by the Orthodox right from Jacob J. Schacter, "Facing the Truths of History," *The Torah u-Madda Journal* 8 (1998-1999): 200-276; see also his "Haskalah, Secular Studies, and the Closing of the Yeshiva in Volozhin," *The Torah u-Madda Journal* 2 (1990): 76-133. Cf. my "Nothing But the Truth?: The Uses of History in Modern Orthodox Polemics," forthcoming in *Jewish Thought and Jewish Faith*, ed. Daniel Lasker, to be published by the Goldstein-Goren International Center for Jewish Thought at Ben-Gurion University.

of practical import seals off religion from persuasion, it does not seal off other areas where disputes lack practical import—restoring our puzzle.

A third way to justify a rejection of proselytizing was proposed by Aaron Segal (in correspondence). What makes religious belief private or intimate is that it involves not just belief but a *relationship* (with God). People often prefer staying reticent about their innermost feelings in a relationship, and others ought not to try to talk them out of those relationships; in fact, perhaps others ought not to discuss them at all with the people who are in the relationship. We often wonder, "How could B ever marry A? What did she see in him?" But we know it is improper to ask B that question.

True, there are instances in which it is proper to talk someone out of a relationship, such as the case of an abusive family member or a deceitful or dangerous friend. Nonetheless, and despite Richard Dawkins' notorious remark that teaching religion is a form of child abuse, an atheist or member of another religion usually will have a hard time persuading a believer that a relationship with God (as that believer conceives it) is abusive or harmful. Segal's suggestion covers many cases and, I think, fares well as an explication of privacy.

In sum, then, the animus against proselytizing in the case of religion can stem from two sources: (1) Views like pluralism, relativism, perspectivism, and postmodernism, which maintain that each religion is in order as is, and (2) the privacy of religious commitment. Privacy can refer to (i) the absence of reasons for religious belief; (ii) its lack of social impact; or (iii) the fact that religion involves the feeling of relationship. I have argued that pluralism and cognate views cannot justify distinguishing between religion and other areas as regards the propriety of persuasion. The privacy argument has merit, however, albeit not in all cases. The absence-of-reasons understanding of privacy works best when the potential proselytizee believes in some measure on faith. Lack of social impact may play a role in the notion of privacy, but if that is a critical factor we would still have a puzzle; religion would still be treated differently from other areas that have no social impact. The suggestion about relationship works well but would not apply if belief in a relationship with God is thought by an atheist or an adherent of another religion to be harmful.[112]

---

[112] An extreme example is killers who kill because the inner voice of God told them to.

The privacy argument applies more in one direction than another. It explains why adherents of one religion should not try to proselytize adherents of another, and why atheists should not try to proselytize theists; but prima facie it does not explain why religious people should not try to proselytize secularists. One could reply, however: if religious reasons are private in either the absence-of-reasons or relationship senses, how *could* they persuade the non-religious? Thus the privacy argument, it could be claimed, in truth applies both ways—nobody can persuade in religious matters, neither religionist nor secularist. Like numerous other matters in this paper, I leave this one open for further discussion.[113]

IV. Persuasion and Group Identity

There is another source of the animus against proselytizing. This can roughly be described as the obligation to respect traditions and personal as well as group identity.

In cataloguing reasons for opposition to pro-religious proselytizing, Martin Marty writes:

> The fabric of social relations is gossamer, easily pulled at and torn. Bombarded from all sides by advertisers, public relations experts, strangers, and seducers, people have few psychic defenses that will help them keep to boundaries and uphold traditions. The proselytizer violates boundaries and disrupts traditions.... Be caught off guard, and, whether or not one succumbs, there is a challenge to personal and social identity.[114]

In the spirit of this concern, suppose we address the following question to the non-religious who seek to persuade the religious: isn't there

---

[113] One question I have not resolved fully is the following. If religious reasons can't be used to persuade in the public square because they are private in the sense of lacking rational backing, couldn't the same be said about moral argumentation in cases where moral disagreements trace to opposing rock-bottom ethical intuitions, between which rational argument will not adjudicate? Yet, to rule moral argumentation out of bounds in the public square would be a virtual *reductio ad absurdum* of the privacy theory regarding participation in public discourse. Perhaps the answer, or part of an answer, is that in the case of *religious* arguments for moral positions, "rock bottom" comes very early in the discussion.

[114] Marty, "Introduction," 2.

something distasteful and wrong about intruding on happy, well adjusted people, and undermining their collective memory, the web that holds the community together, a core part of both the individual's and the group's identity, by showing that their beliefs are not true to the facts? What justifies "hocking a chinik" about the (presumed) falsity of those beliefs, and trying to persuade their holders? Why is it important that people "get it right"? Shouldn't the non-religious just tolerate? Now, we could ask the same question about what justifies a religious person in persuading a secularist to adopt religion. One could argue that secularism lies at the core of many secularists' identity. For there are people (e.g., many scientists) for whom a naturalistic outlook is so much their comprehensive worldview that it is part of their personal and professional (and hence group) identity; the same may be said of, say, secular humanists, or those who abhor religion at a deep level. Religious people might *still* feel that somehow, "it ain't the same"—secular identity and religious identity differ in strength and perhaps even in kind. We don't have to evaluate this response, though there may be something to it; focusing on the case of anti-religious persuasion (i.e., attacks on religion) will suffice to bring out key points that can then be applied in reverse as is deemed appropriate.

In carrying through this discussion we must *bracket* the question of whether the target group's beliefs are true or false. That is, I am asking what the situation should look like to someone who, *rightly or wrongly*, finds those beliefs false. What moral constraints should govern the person's decisions about how much of his or her opinion to voice, and how much of his or her reasoning to publicize? My claim is that even from the point of view of someone who takes a religion or form of religion as false—*even* from his or her point of view—there is still a moral issue about affecting individual or group identity. As Liat Lavi commented,[115] there is a difference between trying to change your mind, and trying to win your soul.

Regarding individual identity, religion is often viewed as lying at the very center of a person's identity, and so "Failure to maintain the belief threatens the very identity of the individual so addressed."[116] One could

---

[115] In correspondence.
[116] Carmy, "Dialectic, Doubters, and a Self-Erasing Letter," 215. In context, Carmy is speaking not of persuasion but of a self-regarding obligation to preserve one's identity.

construe this fact as an aspect of the privacy theme, as Halbertal does in a quotation I adduced in the previous section, but it does not have to be understood this way, and it does not matter for my purposes whether it is. Shalom Carmy suggested[117] that because persuasion may undermine identity, we have not only an issue of undermining a person's identity but (at least in targeted persuasion) an issue of belittling the person. This result is both harsh at the personal level and inimical to social cooperation. These claims might not apply to everyone, however, in that some or many people who believe in God and attend prayer services do not have religion at the core of their being, and some may be wavering so that their religious identity is not strong. In such instances, persuasion will not destroy personal identity. So the argument about undermining personal identity has its limits, and becomes progressively less forceful as we assume weaker and weaker levels of the prospective persuadee's commitment.

What about impairing *group* identity?[118] Many writers maintain that there are societal advantages to group "memory."[119] Moreover,

---

[117] In correspondence.

[118] The group identity objection to persuasion would be strongest when the persuasion involves a book targeted at the group. Banning the publishing of books across the board seems counterintuitive, so I would apply the argument to targeted persuasion of *some* kind, without being sure of *what* kind. See also n. 20 for potential distinctions.

[119] In "Nothing But the Truth?," I say more on this theme. For a small sampling of pertinent works, see Ernst Renan, "What Is a Nation?" (1882) in *Nation and Narration*, ed. Hori K. Babhah (London: Routledge, 1990); William Galston, "Civic Education in the Liberal State," in *Philosophers on Education: Historical Perspectives*, ed. Amelie Rorty (London: Routledge, 1998); Jon A. Levisohn, "Patriotism and Parochialism: Why Teach American Jewish History, and How?," *Journal of Jewish Education* 70, 3 (2005): 2-15; David Lowenthal, *The Heritage Crusade and The Spoils of History* (Cambridge: Cambridge University Press, 1998) (published in 1997 as *Possessed by the Past: The Heritage Crusade and the Spoils of History* [London, 1997]); and idem., "Fabricating Heritage," *History and Memory* 10:1 (1998): 5-24. Lucy Dawidowicz, in *What Is the Use of Jewish History?*, ed. Neal Kozodoy (New York: Schocken, 1992),19, argues that the answer to Y. L. Peretz's question, "And what is the use of history?," is "as an instrument for Jewish survival." If we accept this thesis, however, then, one may argue, insofar as there may be good survival strategies that do not require historical truth, accurate history may not be the best way to go.

groups may be *obligated* to "remember." The most obvious bearers of such an obligation are historians, journalists, and others whose *professional* obligation is to chronicle and interpret, to depict and understand the past accurately. In a postscript to a later edition of his celebrated book *Zakhor*, Yosef Hayyim Yerushalmi, notwithstanding his valuing of a sort of memory that *contrasts* with academic historiography, states that historians have a "moral imperative," "now, more urgent than ever," to battle "the agents of oblivion, the shredders of documents, the assassins of memory, the revisers of encyclopedias, the conspirators of silence."[120] But it is not only professional historians who have an obligation of memory; and others who have this duty do not and need not seek to fulfill it with the tools of the academic historian.[121] Avishai Margalit writes; "The responsibility over a shared memory is on each and every one in a community of memory to see to it that the memory will be kept."[122] Salient among the memories that must be preserved are memories of past injustices (e.g. genocide, slavery), memories of heroic, self-sacrificial, and benevolent acts,[123] and, most important for the religious case, memories of "from whence we came."[124] To be sure,

---

[120] Yosef Hayyim Yerushalmi, *Zakhor: Jewish History and Jewish Memory* (Seattle and London: University of Washington Press, 1996), 116. Here Yerushalmi is rebutting those who interpret *Zakhor* "as a rejection on my part of the historical enterprise *per se*, or as a nostalgia for premodern modes of historical cognition."

[121] In considering the epistemic duties of non-professionals, we should bear in mind that standards of proof are relative to context. Thus, standards used in peer reviewed history journals and books are not the standards that need to be applied in everyday life. In fact, even a professional historian may form beliefs about everyday subject matters without meeting the professional standard. In any event, we will shortly be considering the possibility that memories need not be accurate to fulfill a duty of group memory (when we are not dealing with academic historiography).

[122] Margalit, *The Ethics of Memory* (Cambridge, MA: Harvard University Press, 2002), 58.

[123] See Jeffrey Blustein, *The Moral Demands of Memory* (New York: Cambridge University Press, 2008), 217. In what follows, I am heavily indebted to Blustein's excellent discussion in chapter four, esp. 211-229.

[124] As Margalit and Blustein note, obligations to remember may at times be mitigated by temporal distance and by the insignificance of the past events, but while its precise scope may be debated and its grounds require elaboration, we may proceed on the assumption that there is such an obligation on each community member.

in an age of religious individualism, in which people adopt idiosyncratic belief systems, pasting together elements of different religions, many people with religious beliefs do not belong to a definite group. But many others do, and that makes the discussion of group identity still pertinent.

Indeed, people have a duty to remember not only as a general human duty, but also as members of particular groups who have what are called "thick" relations analogous to those between family members. Someone who leaves the group might be haunted by feelings of betrayal.[125] Moreover, collective memory "shapes a community's sense of its own identity, draws the community's members together around a shared understanding of their past and its contributions to the present, and is capable of inspiring and motivating collective action."[126] Therefore, the imperative to remember is justified "by its relationship to the good of the collective it sustains."[127] Memories can have symbolic meaning and resonance, even if the memories are not accurate. Jeffrey Blustein explains:

> Ethical imperatives justified in this way are neither restricted to, nor chiefly concerned with, accurate representations of the past. There are many ways in which acts and practices of collective remembrance can sustain collective life even though they do not aim for and do not satisfy the criteria of historical accuracy. Their obligatoriness derives not from the demand for fidelity to the past but rather from the good of sustaining a particular valuable form of human relationship..... Ethical oughts, therefore, encompass memorial acts that are significant for the identity of groups, and fulfilling them is an integral part of a group's having a collective identity worth sustaining.[128]

---

[125] The word "betrayal" was suggested by Aaron Segal. As seen in the previous section, he makes the further point that in the case of religion, leaving would not just betray the group, but would betray a being, God. This is an intriguing additional argument and resembles what Walter Wurzburger would call a moral Pascalian argument: believe in God because otherwise, if God exists, you betray Him and default on moral obligations.

[126] Blustein, 222.

[127] Ibid., 224.

[128] Ibid., 228.

While insisting that memories must be accurate in certain contexts, Blustein also writes: "We make room for ethical obligations [=particularistic or thick obligations] if we recognize that collective memory is not merely a recorder, preserver and transmitter of historical truths, but has other social functions that do not track truth."[129] Sometimes of course the immoral character of a group makes preserving the group immoral—the Mafia and Al Qaeda promptly illustrate this point. Likewise, we would not encourage patriotism in a nation that does not merit loyalty between members. Needless to say, this condition opens floodgates, since many groups think the others are immoral. The issues here seem to be similar to those implicated in suppression, which we discussed above.

How do these reflections on the obligation to remember bear on the question of whether it is appropriate to talk groups out of their commitments? The answer is that, apart from the general thesis that it is wrong to harm group identities, there is something incongruous about asserting that a group has an obligation to retain certain memories and relationships while also giving others permission to prevent the group from fulfilling this obligation. To talk the group's members out of their beliefs is to preclude their dispatching their obligation to the group. How much more so is it incongruous to affirm an *obligation* to talk the group out of its beliefs.

Now, the view that there is an obligation to remain in a group is not self-evidently cogent. If one must retain the memories of his or her group, does it follow that it is immoral to switch groups and participate in the *other* group's memories? (In the case of religious groups, is it wrong to convert?) We are torn here between yes and no. On the one side, it can be argued: "While a member of the group, he or she must retain its memories. And leaving the group may be reprehensible by the group's standards. But he or she has violated *only* her group's standards, not the other group's standards and not a supposed general moral obligation to remain in the group." The other way to look at it is that abandoning a tradition is wrong by some universal ethical standard.

Not surprisingly, Nietzsche sees no problem in leaving a religion as long as the person is self-aware:

---

[129] Ibid.

> He who wants to desert a party or a religion believes it is incumbent upon him to refute it. But this is a very arrogant notion. All that is needed is that he should be clear as to the nature of the bonds that formerly tied him to this party or religion and to the fact that they no longer do so; that he should understand what kind of outlook impelled him to them and that it now impels him elsewhere. We did not attach ourself to this party or religion on *strictly rational grounds*: we ought not to *affect* to have done so when we leave it.[130]

Yet, even though we recognize that family bonds are not dictated by "strictly rational" grounds, many of us would not agree with Nietzsche were the issue one of leaving one's family; that is, many of us will think that one cannot simply pick up and leave family on non-rational (e.g., emotional) grounds.[131] Our disagreement might extend to cases of other thick relations, like friendships. Likewise, Nietzsche does not give credit to other moral reasons, like a duty of loyalty and the wrong of diminishing the good a group can produce. And he gives no credence to the notion that the group itself has the ethical "power" to impose a binding norm that makes it wrong to leave the group. But even if X has no duty to remain in a group and therefore Y has no duty not to interfere with X *based on the premise that X has a duty to remain in the group*, the general idea that it is wrong to undermine group identity may be correct, and intuitively is (so long as forbearing carries no moral cost, as it would in the case of a criminal or fanatic group). Interestingly, in one respect Nietzsche's argument supports privacy, in one sense of the term, for he does not require rational justifications for our attachments.[132]

Solomon Schimmel is aware of the *prima facie* immorality of destroying individual and group identity, but he bids readers to consider the potential negative ethical impact of (certain) religious beliefs. They lead, he thinks, to hatred of the other, coercion, violence, discrimination,

---

[130] Nietzsche, "The Wanderer and his Shadow," in *Human, All Too Human*, trans. R. J. Hollingdale (Cambridge: Cambridge University Press, 1991), §82. Daniel Rynhold called my attention to this quotation in another context.

[131] Of course if we bear in mind Nietzsche's views on ethics, the matter becomes more complicated.

[132] This was pointed out by Daniel Rynhold.

and the like.[133] Schimmel concedes, however, that, since *kiruv* specialists draw up their own cost-benefit analysis, his approach validates *kiruv* no less than *rihuk*. The decision whether to interfere with group identity depends upon an all-things-considered judgment by the critic as to which course is best. (To his credit, Schimmel supplies a long list of benefits on behalf of the view he criticizes, and notes costs generated by the view he favors.) Furthermore, Schimmel notes, some Scriptural fundamentalists "live in an isolated enclave and do not seek to influence nonfundamentalists, as in the case, for example, with some ultra-Orthodox hasidic sects, Christian snake handlers, and some Muslim communities." He argues that it is harder to justify undermining the beliefs of such fundamentalists than to justify undermining the beliefs of those fundamentalists who interact with the larger society in harmful ways. He is even willing to say that it is wrong to try to raise the consciousness of women in these insular groups if they are happy in their faith and content in their role and lifestyle. But he then argues

---

[133] Schimmel, *The Tenacity of Unreasonable Belief*, 221-228. While his focus is Orthodox Jews, including the Modern Orthodox, Schimmel also criticizes the beliefs of fundamentalist Moslems and Christians. Superficially, the objection Schimmel raises is like one that the feminist writer Susan Okin levels against an article by Moshe Halbertal and Avishai Margalit, "Liberalism and the Right to Culture," *Social Research* 61 (1994): 491-510. Halbertal and Margalit maintain that in a liberal society, those who are part of an illiberal culture have a right to that culture, and merit government support, even if the culture "flouts the rights of an individual in a liberal society." They reference in particular *haredi* society. Okin argues against them, first, on the grounds that students in *haredi* schools are taught almost no secular subjects, and, second, that women are mistreated (Okin, "Feminism and Multiculturalism," *Ethics* 108, 4 [July 1998]: 670-674).But Schimmel is not doing anything so radical as asking government not to support such cultures. He is arguing only that it is all right, even obligatory, to argue against such cultures. This accords with Mill's distinction (in *On Liberty*) between using government coercion of behavior and using persuasion. See also Jan Feldman, *Lubavitchers As Citizens: A Paradox of Liberal Democracy* (Ithaca, NY: Cornell University Press, 2003), and the review by Peter Berkowitz, "Lubavitchers and Liberals," http://www.hoover.org/publications/policy-review/article/6660. Further literature and arguments on the topic are found in A. Yehuda Warburg, "The Practice of Gender Separation on Buses in the Ultra-Orthodox Community in Israel: A View from the Liberal Cathedral," *Tradition* 44, 1 (Spring 2011): 19-29.

that some fundamentalist beliefs must be rooted out for the sake of their children:

> The critic feels that it is his ethical right, and maybe even his duty, to try to undermine the belief system of the parents in order to protect the present and future children of the fundamentalists from the negative consequences of the fundamentalist belief system, as long as he does not engage in illegal behavior to accomplish this goal.[134]

This is obviously the analogue to Dawkins' condemnation of teaching religion to children as child abuse.[135] We are being told that the attack on religion is being written for the sake of the children. Some readers harbor skepticism about this explanation.[136] But what about the argument itself, viz., that children will be (or least may be) corrupted?

In this connection it is important to note, as Schimmel does, a consideration in favor of an isolationist approach: the alternative culture has many drawbacks and dangers. I would note as well that ultra-Orthodox Jews run many social services, particularly in the area of medical care (e.g., *bikkur holim* and physician referral services). Religious beliefs surely heighten concern about human welfare. And certainly most Orthodox Jews are not militants. That, too, must figure in a cost-benefit analysis.[137] Further, whatever the merits of Schimmel's argument as regards the ultra-Orthodox, it does not in my estimation affect *Modern Orthodoxy*, which accepts the values of "democracy, rationality, freedom of thought and expression, the rich cultural and intellectual repository of Western civilization, and the opportunity to contribute to the allevia-

---

[134] Schimmel, 225.
[135] See *The God Delusion*, 366-367.
[136] Additionally, it may seem naive to think that an academic book will change the minds of fundamentalists, since they won't even read the book. But we should not underestimate the number that will and the number that will be influenced.
[137] As I finalize this paper, the horrendous behavior of ultra-Orthodox groups in Beit Shemesh toward women and schoolgirls they consider inappropriately dressed has become a subject of much conversation in the media. So has the relegation of women to the backs of buses by ultra-Orthodox men, along with other incidents.

tion of human suffering by devoting your energies to more productive pursuits than the preoccupations of ... fundamentalist religion."[138] Thus it seems wrong to destroy that group's identity by arguing against their central religious doctrines.[139] On the contrary, the bonds between that group's members may be worthy of being preserved even by the critic's standards.

To reiterate, I am bracketing the question of the truth or falsity of the individual's or group's belief. I am asking only what a non-believer should maintain about the morality of talking the individual or group out of its beliefs. And again to reiterate, although I do not think the identity argument applies to secularists to the same extent as it applies to religious believers, nevertheless, if secularists and secular groups have secularism as part of their individual and group identities, they will want to extend the arguments given here.

V. Concluding Remarks

In this paper I have put forth more questions than theses. Ironically, given my topic, my aim has not primarily been to persuade readers about when persuasion is right and when it is wrong. Rather, I have tried to shed light on certain aspects of the morality of persuasion by providing a framework and a close analysis, particularly with respect to pro-religious proselytizing on the one hand and undermining religious beliefs on the other. Questions that we broached and in some instances left open include: how one can distinguish targeted from general persuasion, how one weighs truth versus other goods (happiness, security, meaning), when do reciprocity/universalizability arguments apply, how one prevents arguments for persuasion from morphing into arguments for suppression, what privacy means in the religious sphere and why it might be thought to pertain uniquely there, whether religious beliefs have rational grounds, when it is wrong to hurt personal and group identity, whether secularists have identity in the same degree as do religious groups, and whether it is moral to leave a group and especially a tradition when they serve a good.

---

[138] Ibid, 226.
[139] The book does this, however.

It has been said that a conclusion is where you are when you are too tired to keep thinking.[140] In that spirit, I leave these questions open for further reflection. Their remaining in limbo suggests that the paradox with which I began retains some of its force, even though that force has been attenuated. I hope I have persuaded readers about the theses for which I have argued, and that those matters which I have left as questions will breed fruitful lines of inquiry, as will, no doubt, the prodigious number of practical challenges to creating an ethics of persuasion, even when general principles are clear and agreed upon.[141]

---

[140] Attributed to the comedian Steven Wright.
[141] I thank Shalom Carmy, Yoel Finkelman, Daniel Rynhold and Aaron Segal for their comments on an earlier draft; David Berger, Warren Zev Harvey, and Hilary Kornblith for helpful discussion of some relevant issues; and Liat Lavi for her observations and her careful editorial work.

Religious Belief in a Postmodern Age

Tamar Ross

Introduction

An increasing number of Halakhah-abiding Jews are admitting to a disturbing sense of cognitive dissonance between several of their most deeply held convictions and the official directives of religious belief.[1] More significantly, such confessions are not made—as often used to be the case—in a spirit of apology and guilt regarding some regrettable psychological lapse on their part which prevents them from fulfilling their clear-cut religious obligations. Rather, their complaints take a more assertive form of appeal to the spiritual leaders of the generation, faulting them for their inability to adjust the substance and form of Judaism to the changing reality and spiritual condition of the community of believers.

The major thrust of this attack is directed against some of the practical prescriptions of Halakhah (e.g., discriminatory attitudes to women and non-Jews, seemingly irrelevant laws of *Shemitah*). This is to be expected; it is only natural that stress stemming from disparity between the existential state of the believer and the formal prescriptions of faith would appear first and foremost on the level of practice. However, even when reasonable halakhic proposals are offered in order to resolve difficulties in the practical realm, such responses obviously cannot suffice. As with any religious system imposing practical demands on the believer, the halakhic way of life must also attend to preserving the persuasive force of its creedal grounding, in order to ensure continued survival of

---

[1] Anyone following the drift of Orthodox Jewish blogs on the internet will find fascinating testimonies to this effect, alongside determined battles to stem the tide. For some samples, see the range of related topics appearing on the forums of Hirhurim, Not the Godol Hador, Hasidic Rebel, Mar Gavriel, Orthoprax, Dov Bear, Mis-nagid, and Frum Kiruv Maniac, and the volatile discussions that these provoke. A variation on these themes appears in Hebrew language blogs, such as *Atzor, Kan Hoshvim,* and *Behadrei Haredim*.

its praxis. Any weakening of arguments that link the authority of the Halakhah with infallible doctrinal claims would appear to lead to an ultimate breakdown of the Halakhah itself. As Judaic scholar Martin Jaffee has aptly phrased it, "Jewish practice without grounding in the divine has no more compelling a claim to the religious attention of Jews than the Code of Hammurabi."[2] In other words, adjustment of the legal system that is unaccompanied by an equally thoughtful reconstruction of its connection to the divine will most likely prove to be a hermeneutic failure. In the last resort, any project seeking to restore religious viability to Jewish tradition in the face of intellectually compelling counter-claims that cannot be simply attributed to the *yetzer ha-ra* (the evil urge) and weakness of the will requires a comprehensive interpretive method that can be consistently applied to both the theological and the practical level. Given the contemporary state of Western thought and culture with which Jewish thought and practice is inextricably engaged, I would like to suggest that the key to such a project nowadays involves focusing on the *nature and significance* of religious belief, rather than on the details of its content.

The Problems of Literalism

As with all ancient religions whose canonic texts were written many generations ago, Judaism has been exposed over the course of time to various pressures to move away from literalist understandings of some of those texts and their subsequent rabbinical interpretations. In light of new scientific discoveries, changes in the human condition, and the inevitable repercussions of these upon our moral understanding, more and more statements of Jewish tradition appear wanting for this or that reason when interpreted literally. Beyond the perennial problem of evil that has always plagued the minds of those committed to the notion of a just and omnipotent God, much discussion was already devoted in Hellenistic and medieval times to the challenge of rationalism as represented by Platonic/Aristotelian physics and metaphysics. The difficulties

---

[2] Martin S. Jaffee, "'Halakhah as Primordial Tradition': A Gadamerian Dialogue with Early Rabbinic Memory and Jurisprudence," in *Interpreting Judaism in a Postmodern Age*, ed. Steven Kepnes (New York: New York University Press, 1996), 108-109.

raised by this world-view focused mainly upon philosophical and theological questions: can we say that God is angry and jealous, possessed of a strong hand, speaks and reacts in time? Nearly two thousand years later, in the early modern period, we find that the critique of biblical narrative moved on to the natural sciences: Does the earth have four corners? Was the world created in six days? Is it really only five thousand years old? Next in line were questions of factual accuracy raised by the social sciences and the humanities: archeology, history, linguistics and textual analysis: Can various reports of the past offered by the Torah and its traditional interpretation stand up to empirical scrutiny? Did specific people and cities mentioned in it actually exist as described in the tradition? Is it possible to attribute the literary genesis of the Torah to only a single source? In similar fashion, moral questions regarding various localized issues have plagued religious believers since Temple times: did God actually intend that we pay an eye for an eye in damages? More recently such criticism has reached more pervasive levels of the most penetrating sort. Aided and abetted by postmodern sensibilities, this manner of thinking now poses challenges to the very foundations of religion itself: is it at all possible to assert any absolute, metaphysical, and universal claim that is free of bias and the ubiquitous traces of cultural relativism?

The Allegoric or Symbolic Response of Conservative Apologetics[3]

Originally, the method most commonly employed by defenders of the faith in responding to such challenges was to distinguish in some manner between the content of religious statements and their literary form

---

[3] It's difficult to avoid the temptation of succumbing to theological jargon because of the convenient shorthand it supplies. This inevitably brings on trouble because of the lack of terminological uniformity in the professional literature. The division between pre-liberal, liberal, and post-liberal which will appear in what follows relies upon the terms adopted by George Lindbeck and the theological circle surrounding him. See, for example, his *The Nature of Doctrine: Religion and Theology in a Postliberal Age* (Philadelphia: Westminster Press, 1984), 112-113. In note 1 of his book Lindbeck offers an explanation (to my mind, only partial) for preferring this term over the more common division between various stages of modernism. For further explanations behind this terminology and reservations mainly regarding the label of "post-modernism," see: Peter Ochs,

of expression.[4] This involved adopting metaphoric, allegoric, or symbolic understandings of problematic norms or propositions in order to align them more closely with attitudes or opinions developed independently via sources external to the religious system.

However, as the gap between the believer's understanding and the plain meaning of religious doctrine and narrative continued to grow, even the extra slack granted by occasional non-literalist readings was not always capable of grounding their credibility. The steadily increasing disparity between the simple meaning of religious statements and descriptions of reality and our ability to accept these at face value has encouraged contemporary theology to veer away from the tendency to view religious and scientific discourse as rival systems competing for the same stakes on a common field. Efforts at defending the supremacy of religious belief, on the strength of its purported ability to render a more faithful and accurate description of the cosmos, the origins of being, and the nature of human existence and history, have begun to appear in the eyes of many as futile, pathetic, and even absurd. As a result, contemporary theology has begun cultivating a new interest in the meaning of religious language *per se*. Due to the breakdown of belief in the cognitive value of a major portion of religious doctrine and narrative, the understanding is developing that figurative approaches to religious language are not the only method of maintaining the legitimacy of its claims. Any further validation of such claims must be based on the recognition that religious truth statements are far more complicated than ordinary everyday propositions, and serve various functions that interact in a multitude of ways.

In the wake of this understanding, philosophers and religious adherents of a more reflective bent have felt the need to articulate the relationship between these functions in a manner that would more

---

"A Rabbinic Pragmatism," in *Theology and Dialogue: Essays in Conversation with George Lindbeck*, ed. Bruce Marshall (Notre Dame: University of Notre Dame Press, 1990), 217-218; and mainly: Kathryn Tanner, *Theories of Culture: A New Agenda for Theology* (Minneapolis: Fortress Press, 1997), 138-144.

[4] A classical expression of this method as a solution in principle to problems of this sort was phrased by Maimonides in Guide II:25 in the context of his discussion of the contradiction between the traditional concept of creation ex nihilo and Aristotle's notion of the eternity of matter, when Maimonides argues that "the gates of interpretation are never sealed."

accurately reflect the complexities involved. In this connection, instead of asking whether a religious proposition is literally true, many present-day theologians prefer to ask: what is the purpose and function of religious discourse; what is it meant to accomplish? Because certain obstacles to verification are indigenous to a system that blithely moves between the natural world and metaphysics (how on earth are we to examine whether "His glory fills the world"?) such theologians strive to understand religious statements as something other than propositions representing any manner of correspondence to an objective state of affairs ("the way things are") and its description.

The Expressivist/Experiential Response of Liberal Theology[5]

One alternative to a more conservative approach to problematic religious statements that can no longer be taken as descriptions of reality even in a figurative sense understands the function of such statements as a pointer to, or expression of, the internal existential experience of the believer. In this liberal view, religious narrative and doctrine come to introduce us to a metaphysical dimension of human experience (e.g., awe, reverence and a sense of the holy, moral duty, order and creativity in the world, dependence and trust in the Creator) that is not given to effective expression in ordinary language, or—at the very least—to open us out to its very possibility by providing a cognitive framework for

---

[5] Even the term "expressivism," when equated with liberalism (see note 3 above), can be understood in various ways. In my use of this term I again follow the path of post-liberalists such as Lindbeck. See Lindbeck, ibid., 34-35; John E. Thiel, *Nonfoundationalism* (Minneapolis: Fortress Press 1994), 52-54, taking it to refer only to the expression or exposure of a subjective experience of the divine dimension rather than to the description of an external state of affairs. However, I do not understood expressivism as necessarily denying the cognitive import of the religious statement, which according to Avi Sagi, for example, is a second implication of this term. Sagi distinguishes on the basis of this second consideration between the expressivist position, which he understands as necessarily non-ontological, and a realist position, which contends that the object of the religious statement has ontological force, but is capable of being expressed only in religious praxis (see his article "Religious Exclusivism, the Dilemma of Hume and the Basis of Inter-religious Pluralism," *Iyyun* 45 [1996]: 436-438) (Hebrew).

understanding reality as such.⁶ Thus, for example, religious depictions of God's "book-keeping" activities on the inevitable "day of judgment" following death come to convey an understanding of the momentous nature of human behavior in the long run.

The expressivist/experiential understanding of the meaning of religious truth statements, which had already been assumed by some religious theoreticians in the nineteenth century,⁷ was re-appropriated and further embellished in the first half of the twentieth century as an outgrowth of and opposition to the new philosophic school known as "logical positivism." Philosophers attached to this liberal school of thought claimed that "truth" is a label that can only be applied to statements providing factual information that is given to examination, verification or refutation on the basis of sense experience.⁸ This argument encouraged defenders of the faith to argue that in order for a statement to qualify as religious it must relate to precisely those aspects of religion that the positivists reject—namely, the personal, subjective, non-cognitive, emotional, and intuitive. Thus, religious statements were as a rule understood by liberalist theologians as relating only to those rock-bottom premises of existence and eternal truths about God and humanity that demand lifelong loyalty and absolute commitment.⁹

According to this approach (which has been identified as "existentialist" since the late 1940's) there is no need to prove the scientific veracity of the biblical story of creation by understanding it as a symbolic

---

⁶ For various formulations of this approach, see Paul Tillich, "Truth and Verification," 100-103; "The Actuality of God," 235-252, in *Systematic Theology*, vol. 1 (Chicago: University of Chicago Press, 1951); idem, "Symbols of Faith," 47-62, in *The Dynamics of Faith* (New York: Harper&Row, 2001), 47-62; E.D. Klemke, "Are Religious Statements Meaningful?," *Journal of Religion* vol. 40 (1960): 27-39.

⁷ Such as the German philosopher, Friedrich Schliermacher. See F.D.E. Schleiermacher, *The Christian Faith*, English translation of the second German edition, ed. H.R. Mackintosh and J.S. Stewart (Edinburgh: T.& T. Clark, 1928); paperback edition (New York: Harper and Row, 1963).

⁸ For a statement of this argument, see Alfred Ayer, "Critique of Ethics and Philosophy," in *Language, Truth and Logic* (New York: Dover Publications, 1935), 102-120; "The Self and the Common World," ibid., 120-133.

⁹ See Kai Nielsen, *An Introduction to the Philosophy of Religion* (New York: St. Martin's Press 1982), Chapter 1: "Perplexities about Religion," 2.

rendition of the big bang theory.[10] There is also no need to establish the sanctity of the Torah by seeking external evidence for the historical accuracy of the traditional account of revelation at Sinai. Religious truth statements may indeed be regarded as false or nonsensical if we insist upon understanding them as literal or even figurative representations of an objective reality. But such statements can be validated when understood as guides to, or expression of, a level of meaning extending beyond the empiric descriptions of science. This is not to say that religious statements, even when taken as symbolic expression of a higher level of meaning,[11] need not answer to external criteria. Such criteria, however, relate more to the inner life of the believer than to the external conditions of reality. Hence the validity of religious truth claims is verified experientially, over the course of an entire lifetime, and in an investigative manner far less precisely defined than that of the logical positivist, who mistakenly relates to science and religion as competing forces warring over the same goods.[12]

One method of distinguishing between pre-liberal and liberal apologetics for religious truth statements might be to adopt the well-known distinction between "belief that" and "belief in"—i.e., between propositional and non-propositional statements.[13] The former type of statement asserts facts, while the latter indicates attitudes, dispositions, and values, such as trust, awe, love, fear, loyalty and commitment. This dual view of truth, which confirms the irrelevance of religious verification on a factual level, bears a certain affinity to the earlier thought of the Austrian born philosopher Ludwig Wittgenstein, whose seminal

---

[10] After the fashion of Nathan Aviezer, *In the Beginning: Biblical Creation and Science* (Hoboken, NJ: Ktav, 1990) and Gerald Schroeder, *Genesis and the Big Bang:The Discovery of Harmony Between Modern Science and the Bible* (New York: Bantam Books, 1990).

[11] As suggested by Tillich (note 6 above).

[12] For a discussion of the relative advantages and disadvantages of this argument, see Paul Edwards, "Professor Tillich's Confusions," *Mind* LXXIV, No. 294 (1965): 192-214. For further amplification and sources on this topic, see Nancy K. Frankenberry and Hans H. Penner, eds., *Language, Truth, and Religious Belief: Studies in Twentieth-Century Theory and Method in Religion* (Atlanta: Scholars Press, 1999), 11-13; 130.

[13] See H.H. Price, "Belief 'In' and Belief 'That,'" in *The Philosophy of Religion*, ed. Basil Mitchell (Oxford: Oxford University Press, 1971), 143-167.

insights regarding language and its uses—and the implications of these insights for questions of metaphysics, evidence, and belief—have had a decisive influence on the way that many theologians in the latter half of the twentieth century reconceived their task.

The primary meaning of language for Wittgenstein in this first period of his thought involved the implication of a logical structure which is mirrored in speech as a replica or "picture" of the structure of the external reality (or "fact") which is being described. Thus, for example, the sentence "Snow is white" has meaning and therefore can be verified or falsified by pointing to the external reality (i.e., the fact) that snow is white. As metaphysics (as well as aesthetics and morality), by contrast, does not deal with empiric data, any cognitive statements made in these realms have no meaning in the above sense and are therefore "nonsense." Although the logical positivists of the Vienna Circle pounced upon this observation as support of their total rejection of religion and metaphysics at large, Wittgenstein thought nothing of the kind, but was convinced that these areas—though not capable of ordinary linguistic expression—were of great importance in the life of man. This led to the Wittgenstinian understanding of religious statements as relating to the mystic realm of the ineffable, a realm best expressed by silence.[14] Religious existentialists, in opposition to Wittgenstein, nevertheless continued to speak religiously and metaphysically and simply allowed for two sorts of truths: empirical and scientific on the one hand, and existentialist on the other.

It has been observed, with some measure of justice,[15] that the dichotomy between the two types of statements is less clear-cut than would appear on surface. Attitudes can imply propositions and be understood as such; stating that I believe "in" God normally entails the assertion "that" He exists. Alternatively, the proposition "that" God is good or all-powerful might similarly involve attitudes of trust, love or fear. On this more nuanced account, the difference between "belief that" and "belief in" is merely that the latter extends beyond science, supplementing

---

[14] Wittgenstein, *Tractatus Logico-Philosophicus,* trans. D.F. Pearce and B.F. McGuinness (London: Routledge & Kegan Paul, 1971), proposition 7, p. 151.

[15] See Moshe Halbertal, "What is Faith? A Study of the Concept of Faith," in *Al ha-Emunah: Iyyunim Bemusag Ha-emunah U-bitoldotehah Ba-masoret Ha-Yehudit,* ed. Moshe Halbertal, David Kurzweil, and Avi Sagi (Jerusalem: Keter, 2005), 13-14.

empiric descriptions of reality with cognitive propositions of another sort. Science describes our physical reality; religion reveals its inner meaning. Thus the battle between the two cannot be resolved by relieving religion of all propositional claims. Instead, the believer might view the rival claims of physics and metaphysics as disparate but complementary perspectives on human experience.

The Rise of Constructivism

Alongside the notion of complementary truths, however, the "theological positivism" of liberals who insisted upon the validity of existential truths gradually paved the way for another understanding of religious statements that rejected the duality of "facts" and "values" altogether. On this view, the test of *all* religious propositions is not the extent of their correspondence to *any* existing reality but rather the function that they fulfill in the life of the believer.

The constructivist approach to religious truth (variously known as pragmatism, functionalism, or instrumentalism) exhibits no interest in positivist distinctions between propositions relating to the physical/empirical reality and those referring to matters that are metaphysical or existential in character. As opposed to conservative apologists (who still strive to find and defend the meaning of religious doctrine and narrative with reference to an external reality) or liberal expressivists (who justify the persistence of questionable religious truth claims by relegating them to a more spiritual and subjective realm), constructivists locate the import and significance of such claims in what they engender rather than in what they convey.

Classical Pragmatism

The notorious suggestion put forward by the seventeenth-century French religious thinker, mathematician, and physicist Blaise Pascal, and subsequently known as Pascal's Wager,[16] might be regarded as an unwitting first step in this direction. Pascal personally was a firm religious believer in the traditional sense and undoubtedly formulated his

---

[16] William James, "The Will to Believe," in *The Will to Believe and Other Essays in Popular Philosophy & Human Immortality* (New York: Dover, 1956), 5-6.

wager as a last-ditch weapon against the unconvinced. This led him, however, to propose that although God is infinitely incomprehensible and not provable by human reason, given the relative weight of the stakes involved (expectation of infinite bliss versus the finite loss involved in devoting temporary life on earth to one cause), assertion of religious belief even in the face of doubt is well worth the gamble and therefore the most prudent choice. While the substance of belief referred to in Pascal's proposal relates to an objective reality, the considerations of the doubter for asserting its truth are a matter of pragmatic self-interest rather than cognitive persuasion.

In his influential essay, "The Will to Believe," William James—the pioneering American psychologist and philosopher who subsequently came to be regarded as one of the chief proponents of classical pragmatism—states that Pascal's wager deserves to be rejected as vile opportunism were it not for the fact that sometimes "faith in a fact can help create the fact."[17] In the case of some truths (and religious truths figure prominently in this category), it is only a faith in their possibility and the willingness to act upon it which holds any hope for their realization.[18] On James' understanding, truths of this sort are by nature those that cannot be decided on purely intellectual grounds, yet it is precisely such truths that evoke in us the greatest passion and bear the potential for the most momentous consequences in our lives. Because not only the *effect* of such belief (as Pascal suggests), but even its very *discovery*, is contingent upon the decision and behavior of the believer, the will to religious belief can be justified on grounds more honorable than the soulless calculations of the hardened skeptic.

The notion that religious truth is a matter of will might appear on the surface as unintelligible. Despite James' caveat that he is dealing with religion only in a very broad and generic sense, and not with its varying accidental features,[19] the "will to believe" policy is obviously an inadequate guide to religious truth when such truth refers to the concept of a theistic external God who stands over and above the universe. In this case, the argument that any act of will on our part can affect reality and establish His existence seems to make no sense. But James' contention

---

[17] James, ibid., 25.
[18] James, ibid., 5-11.
[19] James, ibid., 25.

could hold water when the object of our religious belief is less fixed and circumscribed—a kind of "divine dimension" of an immanent nature that inheres in all of reality and flows with its changing conditions.[20] While James, like Pascal, does not give up on the notion of objective truth,[21] his understanding of the nature of that truth is looser in the sense that some of its elements are established, at least in part, only by our openness to interaction with them.

As implied by James himself in his caveat, the "will to believe" solution, like Pascal's wager, can only be of limited value for the contemporary religious adherent. So long as the leap of faith applies to broad metaphysical claims linked to a dynamic vision of truth, appeal to the pragmatic benefits of religious belief may suffice as an incentive for overriding doubt. However, it would appear that once religious doctrine and narrative get more specific, the skeptic would find difficulty in willing a belief in the details of a historical, biological, or cosmological account that fails to tally with the testimony of scientific investigation. The same may be said even regarding the existential/expressivist approach of religious liberalism. Understanding biblical narratives as figurative expression of the existential state of man can only extend so far. Noah's flood, for example, may bear a moral message regarding the relationship between man and God, but can sundry details and contradictory information regarding Noah's progeny and mistaken chronological calculations regarding their generational duration be explained away in quite the same fashion?

Neo-pragmatic Non-foundationalism

A resurgence of pragmatism in the late twentieth century offers a new, more radical, and thorough-going approach to these issues. This approach, identified by various labels[22] but perhaps best described as non-foundationalism—i.e., the view that there is no firm "foundation" that serves as the basis for our knowledge, no "raw chunks of reality"

---

[20] A similar suggestion has been made by Ludwig F. Schlecht, "Re-reading 'The Will to Believe,'" *Religious Studies* 33 (1997): 217-225.

[21] James, ibid., 17.

[22] Some of the rival labels are: linguistic pragmatism, non-realism, neo-pragmatic holism. As a movement, this approach is also identified with post-modern religion, religion without ontology, or religion after metaphysics.

to which our notions of truth correspond—continues the functional thrust of classical pragmatism in its appreciation of the link between practice and philosophy (or human behavior and truth), while aiming to avoid the remnants of realism still lingering in the pragmatic approach of James and his contemporaries. This newer approach, as we shall see later, seeks to do away with the distinction between realism and non-realism altogether, by making a move which has come to be known as "the linguistic turn" in theology.

Neo-pragmatists taking the linguistic turn focus greater attention on the relations between language and context than on the interplay between experience and nature when establishing the meaning and worth of religious beliefs. They are also far more emphatic than their pragmatist fore-runners in their rejection of the distinction between faith and scientific method, adopting the view that the truths of science, as well as those of religion, do not correspond to a reality beyond them; both do not refer to "the way things are." No language simply refers to or describes an objective or neutral state of affairs. The meaning of all language is relational—forever changing in accordance with the practical necessities of its particular setting. As a result, neo-pragmatists in principle deny the very possibility of a single universal truth and meaning as metaphysically conceived, in principle. Thus religion is freed of all ontological claims; its validity is not measured by its degree of accuracy in representing objective or subjective realities as in pre-liberal or liberal apologetics, or by its use*fulness* (i.e., expediency) for discovering these as in classical pragmatism, but by its *use*.

This new focus of theology on language also largely reflects the influence of the later thought of Wittgenstein, alongside absorption of some more recent trends that have arisen in Continental postmodern philosophy. As opposed to his earlier view of what gives meaning to language, Wittgenstein's later writings reflect the understanding that language does not serve the same purpose in all contexts; there are many kinds of things that can be said. For example, if I say: "The house is on fire," this may be a descriptive statement in one set of circumstances, a practical joke in another, and a call to action in a third. Given this insight, Wittgenstein gave up his earlier theory about meaning. He no longer viewed language as mirroring reality in its logical structure, but rather as functioning in a particular way in accordance with the relevant activity of its speakers in their manner of interaction with their surroundings.

To illustrate the diversity of discourse, Wittgenstein in his later philosophy introduced the concepts of "language games" and "forms of life." The different functions or substructures of language comprise different "language games," each doing a particular job, conveying certain meanings to those who participate in its particular discourse. Justification is internal to the activity or "form of life" concerned. Applying this insight to religious truth statements, Wittgenstinians—like the neo-pragmatists—do not ask what such statements convey, but ask rather what their function is in the activities of the speaker. On this basis, instead of being "nonsense" and something about which we are enjoined to be silent, religion—as well as aesthetics and morality—can now legitimately be spoken of, since the use of language in each of these spheres serves its own legitimate function.

Religious Reductionism and the Specter of Relativism

While it is not logically necessary and certainly was not Wittgenstein's intention, a common consequence of the neo-pragmatism that comes close to his view in its religious application is a type of reductionism that is typified by the tendency to avoid the appeal to metaphysics altogether. At the heart of this approach lies the idea that individuals and/or societies have certain biological, socio/political, psychological, and even moral/spiritual needs that must be addressed. This permits a more philosophical use of the ideas of certain sociologists, who maintain that religious beliefs provide an answer to these needs, granting social and cultural stability, preserving law and order, reducing anxiety, and offering meaning to human existence.[23] Hence, all religions are "true" to the extent that they succeed in providing for the needs of the individual and society, without claiming any more profound form of correspondence to the state of affairs of "the world as it is." The natural by-product of such reductionism appears to be relativism and selectivity, for if religion does not make any metaphysical claims at all, but functions simply as a response to psychological or social needs, then (so many conclude)

---

[23] Emil Durkheim, *The Elementary Forms of the Religious Life* (Glencoe: Free Press 1954); Melford Spiro, "Religion: Problems of Definition and Explanation," in *Anthropological Approaches to the Study of Religion*, ed. Michael Banton (London: Tavistock Publications, 1966), 85-122.

religious beliefs are anchored at the very most in what is "objectivity for us." The very appeal to transcendence which is made by tradition as the basis for all the other beliefs is itself measured in accordance with its functional value. When such rhetoric impedes the ability of religion to respond to new needs, it too becomes a relative matter.

This attitude has raised the ire and contempt of hard-core traditionalists who regard such a position as not only misguided but downright immoral, transforming religious belief into no more than a glorified metaphor for sanctifying self-serving interests.[24] To this the neo-pragmatist might retort that once one has taken the linguistic turn, there is no turning back. Nevertheless, the question remains: is there still room in the world of the neo-pragmatist for a system of belief that relates somehow to metaphysics and to absolute standards, while at the same time taking seriously the radical nature of the postmodern sensibility and its revolutionary insights regarding the determining influence of context on the meaning of language, and the implications of this insight for the ontological status of religious truth claims and their justification? Does the approach of non-foundationalism mandate that all forms of what many Continental philosophers (following Heidegger) have called "onto-theology" be left behind? And if so, can such a view foster the long-term commitment and conviction typically characterizing the lives of those for whom such symbols bear deep religious meaning? Indeed, it would seem that maneuvering between the Scylla of the cognitive dissonance raised by various religious truth claims when understood foundationally and the Charybdis of neo-pragmatic relativism is no easy task.

---

[24] Critiques of postmodernism and the linguistic turn are rampant among Christian evangelists. See, for example, Gary E. Gilley's five-part series on post-modernism published on the internet: http://www.svchapel.org/Resources/Articles/read_articles.asp?id=42. For somewhat milder variations on this theme on the part of Jewish traditionalists, see Meir Rott, "Judaism Between the Straits of Modernism and Post-modernism," in Be-darkhei Shalom: Iyyinim Be-hagut Yehudit Mugashim Le-Shalom Rosenberg, ed. Binyamin Ish-Shalom (Jerusalem: Bet Morasha, 2007), 33-49, and Barukh Cahana's account of nascent opposition to postmodernist trends in the writings of Yosef Kelner, Michael Abraham, Shalom Rosenberg, and Yosef Kelner, in "In Which Direction is the Wind Blowing? Religious Thought and Postmodernism," Akdamot 20 (2008): 14-18 (Hebrew).

The Cultural/Linguistic Response of Post-liberalism

Attempts to negotiate the linguistic turn in metaphysics have thus far largely been based upon the theological sensibilities of various individuals rather than representing full-blown movements or schools of thought. Moreover, most of these interpretive projects still reflect the contours of debate set by logical positivism, expressivist liberalism, and classical pragmatism. As such, their primary concern is to defend religion against the threat of empiricism and the need for verification, rather than to establish a modus vivendi with some of the more worrisome conclusions (e.g., relativism, the flight from ontology, and a concomitantly insufficient basis for true religious devotion) that might be thought to be implied by a non-foundationalist view.[25] In this sense,

---

[25] One example of this limited response to non-foundationalism is the line of thought developed by Reformed Epistemology—so named because several of its most active proponents, such as Alvin Plantinga, Nicholas Waltersdorff, and William Alston are Protestant philosophers in the Calvinist or Reformed tradition. Although Calvinists are noted for favoring Old Testament legalism and this-worldly politics of social justice rather than other-worldly spiritualism in a manner that is firmly fundamentalist, the "Reformed" label is a word-play on double meanings, as members of this camp also attempt to use analytic philosophy in order to reform current epistemology in a manner that pays attention to the fact that philosophy has moved away from the foundationalist premises of Bacon and Descartes. Nevertheless, a certain remnant of the old modernism is reinstated by introducing a notion of "basic beliefs." Such commonsense gut feelings, such as the theistic belief in God, may not be foundational and provable, but are nevertheless as "real" and ontologically respectable as conclusions drawn on the basis of sense experience. The only difference lies in their method of justification: theistic belief is justified not by deduction, but because it serves as the necessary condition for ways of life and world views that would be meaningless without it.

Another method of establishing some form of middle ground between foundationalism and total relativism is that of critical realists such as John Hick, who still posits the reality of a higher metaphysical being but denies our ability to fully know its character. As he states: "None of the descriptive terms that apply within the realm of human experience can apply literally to the unexperienceable reality that underlies that realm." John Hick, *An Interpretation of Religion: Human Responses to the Transcendent* (New Haven/London: Yale University Press, 1989), 350. Thus religious concepts and metaphysical statements must be understood as imaginative human creations which embody

it might be preferable to examine the more highly developed response of a somewhat loose alliance of theologians, most of whom were either trained or taught at Yale Divinity School. This group of theologians—known as post-liberals, and best represented in the work of Hans Frei and George Lindbeck—are influenced by the thought of Wittgenstein in his later period, in developing a cultural-linguistic approach to religion which combines, at one and the same time, elements that are radically post-modern with others that are radically traditional.[26]

Affinities with Radical Post-modernism

On the one hand, the cultural-linguistic approach appears committed to the latest insights of post-modern philosophy, rejecting the idea that religion must correspond to some predefined foundational truth, which exists "out there." As in Wittgenstein's later understanding of the incommensurability of truth statements as stemming from their participation in disparate "language games," this approach likewise maintains that the meaning of religious truth claims, like that of all other truth claims, is subject to their own unique framework. Any such framework provides its own distinctive conceptual meta-scheme for filtering and organizing its particular content. Hence the purpose of religious discourse is not substantive (referring to a *particular* truth, objectifying a *particular* state of being, responding to a *particular* need), but rather constitutive or regulative—offering us a cultural-linguistic universe of discourse, within which to live the life of faith. Religious discourse does not merely lead to the truths that it articulates; it is also what in actual effect enables their formulation. Rather than teaching us to distinguish between truth and falsehood, religion provides us with

---

our claims about the world and the way we represent it. Nevertheless, such creations may mediate the divine reality to us, so that their truth or untruth consists of the appropriateness or inappropriateness of the practical dispositions which they tend to evoke. Although we will never arrive at a final ultimate reality, we can and should aim at that form of truth which produces the most appropriate results, relating to it as absolute, but also to realize the limitations of what we are aiming for and to recognize it for what it is.

[26] For various formulations of this approach, see George Lindbeck, ibid.; John Thiel, ibid.; Katherine Tanner, ibid.; *Theology and Dialogue: Essays in Conversation with George Lindbeck*, ibid.

the way of life, cultural context, or world view which allows us to address such questions.

The process of converting an unbeliever into a believer on this view resembles the teaching of a language, not because religion itself is a language, but because it functions as one,[27] in helping us internalize views and acquire skills which have already been formulated and developed by others. When we acquire the knack for its conceptual syntax, we begin to intuitively know how to use its symbols in a manner that suits its internal logic. Sometimes explicit formulations of the beliefs and opinions of our particular religion guide us in the learning process, but their ultimate significance should by no means be invariably reduced to their literal import. The final product of the religious learning process is not meant to be an authoritative list of religious dogmas or an ideal moral system, but rather implied or suggestive directives as to how to think about God and conduct one's life in accordance with these thoughts. In a best-case scenario, such directives become second nature and fulfill an essential role in fashioning the life of the believer.

Thanks to this more subtle and oblique understanding of the manner in which religious truth claims function, it would seem that the cultural-linguistic approach is even more liberated than expressivism or classical pragmatism in the extent to which it is capable of divorcing the meaning of religious statements from the manner in which they are formulated. The total rejection, on the part of post-liberals, of the impulse to defend pre-modern statements of religion by recasting them in a modernist mold is testimony to this freedom.

Affinities with Radical Traditionalism

Despite their rejection of the notion of foundational truth, however, post-liberals appear almost reactionary and fundamentalist in their absolute commitment to abide by the constitutive guidelines of their

---

[27] Thiel, 94; Lindbeck, 17-18; 33-34; David Kelsey, "Church Discourse and the Public Realm," *Theology and Dialogue*, ibid., 7-35. This approach is also associated with the views of anthropologists such as Clifford Geertz, whose seminal essay "Religion as a Cultural System," in *Anthropological Approaches to the Study of Religion,* ed. Michael Banton (London: Routledge, 1966) has exerted great influence upon many and continues to be cited admiringly to the present day.

religious tradition and to submit to their internal authority.[28] According to the cultural-linguistic view of post-liberalism, acceptance of a religious scheme means agreeing to speak in a very specific way. It involves a willingness to behave according to the rules established by the religious tradition for conducting its activities, rather than conveying impressions or making claims with regard to any natural, metaphysical, or moral reality that bears an independent existence outside of this framework. In contrast with factual, allegoric-symbolic expressive or functional statements, all of which require verification in terms of some form of external criteria in order to be regarded as true, the cultural-linguistic approach is self-referential. Since the deepest urge of religious discourse according to this approach is not to report *about* reality, but rather to fashion and direct it in accordance with the guidelines unique to this discourse, the frame of reference and criterion of validity for its statements is derived internally. The propositions that are created in accordance with the regulative models of this discourse are measured only from within and by the system itself, and are not translated into other terms.

For this reason it is perhaps no coincidence that when George Lindbeck writes about the manner in which he sets out to explain his own post-liberal thesis regarding the function of religious language, he comments:[29]

> The case developed in this book, it should be noted, is circular rather than linear. Its persuasiveness, if any, does not depend on moving step by step in a demonstrative sequence, but on the illuminating power of the whole. It may be that if light dawns, it will be over the whole landscape simultaneously.

According to this understanding of the constitutive role of religious truth statements, theological coherence is preserved by members of

---

[28] This more moderate aspect in their position is what causes them apparently to distance themselves from the label of "postmodernism." See Tanner, ibid., 76. Common to the two streams is the non-foundationalist assumption, but post-liberals distance themselves from other aspects of post-modernism, rejecting, for example, the notion of the total fluidity of religious statements, which stems from a lack of fixedness of any ground rules in the interpretive enterprise.

[29] Lindbeck, ibid., 11.

the faith only in their ability to continue conducting their religious discourse and behavior in accordance with the principles deriving from its unique paradigms. These paradigms establish the basic grammar of the religious tradition. So long as a particular statement is made in accordance with the conceptual framework of these paradigms and the logical principles that flow from them, it maintains continuity even when its meaning is understood or experienced in a new way.[30] If—and only if—the very same principles or concepts that guided the formulation of the original paradigms serve in the construction of the newer formulations may such formulations be regarded as expressing the same truth and be considered religiously valid. Thus, paradoxically, rejection of the traditional rhetoric of appeal to an objective context-free truth,[31] even when conducted from a post-liberal position that denies the very possibility of speaking in the name of a neutral "God's eye view," would be regarded as a violation of the ground rules of religious discourse.

This is not to say that the illuminations of Enlightenment rationalism and modernity hold no interest for the post-liberal, but rather that even such insights and their degree of relevance for religious belief are understood from within the religious framework, and via the prism of prior religious loyalties.[32] When the post-liberal applies such discoveries to metaphysical claims to transcendence, he may feel himself utterly free to adopt the understanding of the liberal existential/expressivist that such talk represents the attempt to describe an experience that is not given to ordinary factual description. Alternatively, he might claim,

---

[30] For expression of a similar (but not totally identical) approach in the thought of R. Kook, see what he has to say in *Orot ha-Emunah* (Brooklyn: Langsham Associates, 1985), 25, regarding the relationship between the "explicit expression" (*ma-amar ha-mivtaee*) of "all the generalities and particularities of religious belief," and "their inner essence, which is the main thing desired in faith," and also his comments regarding "the necessary beliefs of Maimonides," where he establishes that "it is impossible that a person should uproot the images of these beliefs from his heart, and not uproot with them the higher truths, which are the basis of ultimate truth," but nevertheless then adds: "and after all this, in every generation, new changes are made with regard to the relationship to these necessary beliefs, but the inner truth always remains steadfast." Ibid., 48-49.

[31] Such as relating to the Torah as the perfect expression of God's eternal will.

[32] Lindbeck, ibid., 130-131.

after the manner of the pragmatists, that such talk comes to induce feelings of absolute commitment to those norms which religion posits, and to preserve the stability of the community of believers and instill in them confidence in their traditional way of life. But despite such similarities, these understandings do not release the post-liberal from his primary obligation to refer to the original mythic or metaphysical language of tradition as the ultimate grounding of his religious belief, with all that this implies. Rather than truth being its objective, the original language of tradition determines the definition of what a religious truth is by setting up a cultural framework that allows us to live out these truths in practice, assisted by the dogmas, myths, rituals, and attitudes that naturally flow from the paradigms it engenders. Justification is internal to the activity or "form of life" concerned and takes place in a web-like manner, where means justify ends and vice versa.

Since the true mission of religious language does not lie in the beliefs and opinions that it expresses but rather in the form of life that it engenders, its virtue exists less in its philosophical or moral appropriateness than in its suggestiveness and intimations. The significance of its paradigms is not necessarily connected with the visual or mental images that they arouse, but rather in the multitude of echoes and net of associations that they engender, in the long-term moods, dispositional attitudes, and movements of the mind. The beliefs to be distilled from such paradigms are not to be equated with direct factual claims or positions that are politically correct in and of themselves. Religious beliefs are rather to be understood as tools that we adopt in fashioning our spiritual mien, in developing a sense for discovering the best ways of expanding their underlying images to new areas of application and to new patterns of behavior.

The Convoluted Functioning of Religious Language

If the meaning of religious language is only loosely directed but never exhausted by the initial import of its paradigms as they were originally phrased, then the manner in which religious discourse functions is far more oblique than might be understood from its critics. Relating seriously to the basic images of religion does not mean accepting them as dogma in a church catechism sense or even expecting them to exhibit perfect coherence or consistency. On the contrary, the power of a cultural-linguistic approach to religion lies in the fact that it is capable of absorbing and combining various and even opposing points of view. Since the manner in which religious statements influence us according to this approach is not always straightforward, transparent, and predictable, understanding their effect upon us could lead to conclusions that appear convoluted or even paradoxical.[33] In order to create a certain mindset or mood, the cultural linguistic approach is sometimes forced to adopt a ritual language of myth and drama bearing messages that on the face of it are very far removed from the declared moral purpose of the religious life, or from commitment to truth in the usual sense of this term. Exclusionary particularism in the context of religious worship may conceivably be the shortest road to universalism.[34] Delusions of grandeur may be required to achieve ultimate humility. Demonization of the other may be the grammar necessary, under certain circumstances, for developing a healthy sense of self. Because the basic paradigms of religious belief are capable of absorbing new influences and continuing to flourish through these, the spiritual reality constructed by any given religious statement may emerge in larger context as far removed from or even completely contradictory to its apparent purpose when viewed on its own.

While the relative merit of basic religious paradigms is not measured in accordance with the degree of their correspondence to some neutral form of rationality or even in terms of their appropriateness as ideal standards for human behavior, their vitality and survival power as opposed to those of other possible models is nevertheless no arbitrary matter. Their value lies in virtues that are unique precisely to these models, in their ability to engender distinctive ways of being and experience

---

[33] For application of this thought to rabbinic Judaism, see Howard Wettstein, "Theological Impressionism," *Judaism* 49 (2000): 131-152; idem, "Doctrine," *Faith and Philosophy* 14:4 (1997): 423-443. For application of this approach to interfaith dialogue, see: Tamar Ross, "Reflections on the Possibilities of Interfaith Communication in our Day," *Edah Internet Journal* 1:1 (2000).

[34] This insight, which is offered in the writings of Rabbi Judah Ha-Levi as an excuse for the lowly condition of the Jewish people in his time, is a principal motif in the teachings of R. Kook, who employs it more affirmatively: not as an apologetic for Jewish suffering, but as justification for Jewish exclusionism. See, for example, *Orot* (Jerusalem: Mosad Harav Kook, 1969), section 15, 32-34.

which would otherwise be lost.³⁵ For this reason compensating for whatever philosophical shortcomings or pernicious moral effects such paradigms may expose in time is not accomplished by replacing them, but rather by allowing them to absorb new corrective contexts. In this manner the original paradigms are constantly enhanced and refined by developments emerging authentically from within.

It is particularly instructive to see how this combination of radical post-modernism and reactionary traditionalism plays out in the way that post-liberals approach canonical texts. Hans Frei criticizes the often pernicious effect that modern Protestant historical-critical scholarship has had on the understanding and reading of the Bible. This "great reversal" turned the Bible into an odd repository of (questionable) historical facts and religious ideas. Interpretation became "a matter of fitting the biblical story into another world with another story rather than incorporating that world into the biblical story."³⁶ As a result, the meaning of the Bible was decipherable only to an academic elite employing highly artificial methods of harmonization in order to fabricate "solutions" not to be found in scripture at all. What was lost, according to Frei, in the often over-accommodating apologetics of liberal theology was the traditional reading of the Bible as a "realistic narrative," resulting in what he refers to in the title of his book: *The Eclipse of Biblical Narrative*. On the other hand, the cultural-linguistic approach rejects the notion of biblical inerrancy (i.e., that Scripture is completely accurate in all matters of history and science). Even in matters of faith and practice, the rational-

---

[35] Thus we may understand certain expressions of appreciation that are found in the writings of R. Zadok Hacohen and R. Kook for pagan motifs as a necessary preamble to the religious fervor of monotheism. See, for example, R. Kook's commentary to the Haggada in *Olat Riyah* 2 (Jerusalem: Mosad Harav Kook, 1985), 261, and R. Zadok, *Resisei Layla* (Bnei Brak: Yahadut, 1967), par. 13; *Sihot Malakhei ha-Sharet* (Bnei Brak: Yahadut 1963), 32:b; *Divrei Sofrim* (Bnei Brak: Yahadut, 1963), 21:a. Another application of this understanding of the indirect influence of religious rituals appears in Maharal's understanding of the importance of petitionary prayers, whose aim is ostensibly to turn to God so that he will answer our wishes, but in practice their importance is in their declarative character—i.e., in displaying and demonstrating man's dependence on God in the very act of turning to Him. See *Netivot Olam*, 1 (London: L. Honig & Sons, 1961), "Netiv Ha-avodah," chapter 3, *simman* 6.

[36] Hans Frei, *The Eclipse of Biblical Narrative* (New Haven: Yale University Press, 1974), 130.

ity and relevance or "truth" of religious tradition is maintained not by appeal to external evidence, but rather by skillfully using its internal grammar to provide an intelligible interpretation on its own terms.[37]

Thus, for example, if the Bible describes God in an impressionistic manner, and adopts grossly anthropomorphic images, understanding these primary images literally could be regarded as unacceptable from a religious point of view. But when such images function as basic formative principles and not as direct references, they are capable of absorbing corrective influences that stem from an utterly different way of thinking, and drawing upon the benefits of philosophical inquiry without forfeiting their original form. And this is what did indeed transpire when Jewish tradition was forced to face the infiltration of Greek philosophy via the channels of Islamic theology and assimilate ways of thinking that were geared towards describing God in more abstract terms. The Bible also speaks of a God that is not necessarily omniscient, omnipotent, and invariably just, forcing those who cling to its imagery to face the developing moral sensibilities of the community of believers. Here too, when such images operate on a primary foundational level, their privileged status does not prevent them from absorbing further conceptual refinement. Sometimes the new adaptations faithfully reflect original understandings of these basic images, but sometimes they work against them, allowing the images to exert their influence in a more complex and oblique manner upon our daily lives. The final product is not some perfect, theoretical, and comprehensive formula, but rather a variegated potpourri of motifs—some functioning alongside others in obvious tension. Nevertheless, the sum total of these motifs leads us to a state of the soul and a practical way of knowing that appears worthy and natural in our eyes.

Problematic Aspects of Post-liberalism

In a sense, the cultural-linguistic approach to religious truths can be taken as the apologetic of all apologetics, a type of meta-solution broad enough to cover even the most general and all-pervasive critique regarding the "truth" of religious belief. In an age when the abyss between the

---

[37] Lindbeck, ibid., 79-84.

literal meaning of religious statements and the ability of the community of believers to accept them at face value steadily increases, post-liberals can justifiably view their intra-textual approach as a more effective guarantee for the continued validity of such statements than the liberal or classical pragmatic attempts to understand them in terms of their compliance with any external standard. In rejecting the modernist foundational notion that truth is only what can be empirically verified and redefining it as a community-based activity that embodies the ongoing history of its interpretive tradition, cultural-linguists dissolve the inerrancy debate by rendering it a non-issue. In this they claim to come closer to the pre-modern manner of relating to biblical texts, according to which truth is what is spiritually transformative. Such a view makes a place for the empirically verifiable and the historical but insists that the factual in this sense neither exhausts the meaning of religious truth nor constitutes its essence. A narrative account which is inaccurate in some of its details or even a total fabrication could still be adopted by a community and be revealed as the word of God from within the form of life that it supports. The Rabbinic injunction[38] that individual members of each and every generation must see themselves "as if" they personally had been delivered from Egypt, using this as the basis for existentially re-enacting the renewal of the covenant, illustrates this point.

Despite the appeal that such an approach to religious language holds for traditionalists, however, it is not problem-free. One of the problems arises out of a sense that the cultural-linguistic approach does not go far enough in addressing practical problems emerging from the contemporary believer's sense of cognitive dissonance on a moral plane. The other arises out of a feeling that its pragmatic thrust extends too far on the level of theory, thereby weakening the believer's sense of conviction and commitment on the psychological plane. Within the limited framework of our discussion I would like to address these two difficulties in the following two sections of this paper, in order to point to the type of philosophical work that lies ahead for those who nevertheless regard the cultural-linguistic approach as a path that bears theological promise. Thereafter, in the concluding sections, I would also like examine the extent to which traditional Jewish thought might have something unique to contribute to this effort.

---

[38] BT *Pesahim* 116b.

The Practical Danger
of Morally Questionable Expressions

One anthropological difficulty arising from a cultural-linguistic approach to religious language relates to the negative effect that some of its problematic images may still exert on the community of believers on a subconscious level. Despite the advantage of post-liberalism in its appreciation of the non-cognitive import of religious discourse and its convoluted method of operation, people with a highly developed moral sense will note that there still remain some areas of life in which the residual effect of the literal meaning of language, even when functioning on a constitutive level, is capable of wielding pernicious influence on human behavior. Thus, for example, feminists are likely to argue, with respect to the example brought above regarding the nature of God's imagery, that the disadvantages of corporeal descriptions of God cannot be compared to the shortcomings of describing God in exclusively male terms. Continued use of language referring to God's strong hand can be tolerated even when this allows vaguely anthropomorphic images to remain in the mind of a believer untrained in philosophical thinking, as such language need not bear negative consequences on his relations to others. But this may not hold true regarding the prophetic images of Hosea, according to which God's relationship to the nation of Israel is similar to how an abusive husband relates to his adulterous wife.[39] In this case, critics sensitive to feminist concerns will point to the demeaning effect that such language could have on men's attitudes to women on a hidden level, fortifying a lack of appreciation and respect.

At this stage, however, it would be well to reiterate that even according to the post-liberal approach, fidelity to the language of religious tradition still leaves room for creativity in the effort to overcome dissonances stemming from rival sensibilities. Such creativity does not lie in adjusting the language of authoritative texts and traditions to outside experience, but rather in exploring ways in which such experience can be absorbed by this language itself. A religious system bearing the legacy of its past cannot—according to the post-liberal approach—eradicate

---

[39] See Naomi Graetz, "God is to Israel as Husband is to Wife: The Metaphoric Battering of Hosea's Wife," in *Unlocking the Garden: A Feminist Look at the Bible, Midrash and God* (Piscatawy, NJ: Gorgias Press, 2005), 69-86.

its previous history and start constructing a "clean" religious culture, appropriate for all times, from scratch. It must take into account prior identities and make full use of the potential of interpretive approaches in overcoming anomalies. The continued ability of any given tradition to arrange the experience of the believers in accordance with its cultural-linguistic world is the true test of its worth.

The Halakhic Corrective

Viewed from a Jewish perspective, it would seem that the most effective solution to moral dissonances lies in the corrective influence of *haaramot* (legal fictions).[40] When *poskim* (halakhic decisors) provoked by surrounding cultural circumstances can draw support from the interpretive tradition and prevailing communal sensibilities, their rulings often serve as a moderating influence in cases where literal understanding of religious statements could lead to morally disastrous results. Thus, for example, when confronting norms that are clearly discriminatory or inhumane in their prescriptions for relating to members of other faiths, secularists, or other "Others" (such as *ben sorer u-moreh*, the rebellious son), *poskim* are likely to introduce creative halakhic tactics in order to interpret such prescriptions as dictates that must be deferred until some unidentifiable eschatological period when the true faith will finally achieve the requisite conditions of sovereignty, moral deservedness, etc. In other instances, *poskim* might enlist the even more decisive argument of *nishtanu ha-teva'im* (circumstances have changed). This halakhic corrective does more than just allow the community of believers to avoid carrying out a morally questionable demand in practice; relegating the law to dead letter status can influence unconscious attitudinal stances as well. An example of this is the halakhic justification that R. Abraham Yitzhak Kook brings for ignoring the *mitzva* of *Tokheha* (the injunction to reprimand sinners) with regard to heretics of our day (the fact that the authoritative powers of the Jewish nation are

---

[40] Yoske Ahitov has on various occasions expressed his awareness of the corrective function of halakhic *haaramot* and the creative use of halakhic principles as a means of bridging with new moral sensibilities. See, for example, ibid, chapter 17: "Halit'ehu le-rasha ve-yamut," 231-249. See also Rabbi Israel Rosen, "On Haaramot as Halakhic Policy," *Akdamot* 11 (1992): 113-123.

not currently functioning at optimal strength),[41] and the basis he finds for this in the testimony of the Jerusalem Talmud regarding R. Simeon Bar Yohai, which states that "he rejoiced over the temporary suspension of the laws of Israel, because 'we are not wise enough to judge.'"[42] The neutralizing of the biblical injunction for destroying the seed of Amalek down to its last descendant on the strength of the argument that "since the time of Sanherib the nations of the world have been commingled" (thereby rendering Amalekites indistinguishable) is another case in point.[43] Sometimes even the enlisting of vague meta-halakhic principles—such as the obligation to avoid inflicting harm to Gentiles *mishum darkhei eivah* (so as not to behave in a manner that arouses hatred), or due to the obligation of avoiding *hillul Hashem* (desecration of God's name), which on the surface appear to be the by-products of purely pragmatic considerations—are in actual fact the product of moral sensibilities seeking to revise traditional norms without overturning the system entirely.[44]

If we adopt a cultural-linguistic (rather than an ontological/moral) standard for assessing the appropriateness of our religious language not only in terms of our relationship to God but even on an interpersonal level, this allows us to continue to employ the vocabulary of tradition even when its language and imagery might fall short of what we would consider worthy in terms of dogma or practice. The overall atmosphere created by these traditional images, when supplemented by our professed philosophical insights, the moral intuitions that have accrued to these, and the specific behavior patterns emerging as a result, produces a distinct way of life with its own unique values and satisfactions.

---

[41] *Iggerot ha-Reayah* I (Jerusalem: Mosad Harav Kook, 1985), 20.

[42] JT, *Sanhedrin* (Venice: Bomberg, 1523), chapter 1, halakha 1, p. 18, column 1. The reference brought in *Iggerot ha-Reayah* (above n. 40) is mistaken.

[43] For examples of halakhic use of this escape, see Avi Sagi, *Yahadut: Bein Dat u-Musar* (Tel Aviv: Hakibbutz Hameuchad, 1998), chapter 10: "The Punishment of Amalek: The Methods of Jewish Tradition for Struggling with the Problem and the Status of Morality in the Jewish Tradition," 219.

[44] For an example of such pesika in connection with Jewish-Gentile relations, see Rabbi Isser Yehuda Unterman, "'Ways of Peace' and Their Definition," *Kol Torah* (Nissan 1966), and Michael Farbowitz, "The Responsibility of the Jewish Physician in Jewish Law," *The Pharos* (Spring 1994): 28-33.

The Psychological Difficulty of Heightened Contingency Awareness

A knottier problem raised by the cultural linguistic approach relates to the psychological implications involved for the believer, when such an approach is adopted consciously and deliberately as a response to the loss of innocence. Even if we accept the premise that when speaking of matters of faith we must at some stage turn to non-representational modes of expression that do not purport to simply state "the facts of the matter," much of the emotional fervor characterizing theological debates regarding this issue stems from the question of to what extent can the move from a propositional to a constructivist mode be tolerated or condoned? Does it stop at the point of non-literal interpretations of God's mighty arm, His creation of the world in six days and resting on the seventh, His fashioning of Adam from the dust of the earth and Eve from his side (or rib), the hearing of His voice at Sinai? We often tend to ignore the fact that what is really at stake in such debates is not the question of what degree of objective difficulty posed by historical or philosophical insights compels fine-tuning of the religious framework; what really concerns us is where exactly the key to our ultimate commitment lies.

Applying a cultural-linguistc approach in order to speak descriptively and after-the-fact regarding the function of our religious language (such as when we understand how the male images of God work upon us in our prayers in a manner that is quite removed from their surface meaning) is one thing. But adopting this approach deliberately and in advance, as a general panacea for overcoming the possible unacceptability of any religious model when understood literally and realistically, is quite another. Speaking reflectively about our religious belief in a manner that can only be justified pragmatically, by examining the nature of its practical influence on our lives, implies openness to the possibility of various levels of commitment to this belief, as the grip of its picture upon us can no longer be complete. Such levels of commitment could range from the contention that *x* is not necessarily so, to the contention that *x* is bad, or even that the world would be better off without *x* entirely.[45]

---

[45] Ian Hacking, *The Social Construction of What?* (Cambridge, MA: Harvard University Press, 2000), 19-21.

Although a cultural linguistic framework typically functions as a type of Kantian a-priori-like scheme, the moment we accept the possibility that *any* religious statement parading as truth is capable of being understood as simply a construct, all that such an a priori scheme amounts to is a system of acquired skills that could have been otherwise.

It is certainly reasonable to suppose that every religious system must pose certain barriers against divorcing its statements from any possible ontological claims, if it is to support the talk of ultimate values and the long-term commitment to them that are the bread and butter of the religious life. The fact that the primary myths of all religions present themselves as historical accounts, imposing an aura of objectivity, surely has something to do with their staying power. It also has something to teach us regarding a universal human need to ground our religious commitments on firmer territory than a self-sufficient language game that bears no overlap with our common-sense view of reality. Whether or not our truth formulations are only "words all the way down" (as Richard Rorty, the non-foundationalist par excellence, would have it),[46] or at the very most "objectivity for us" (in accordance with Hilary Putnam's milder version of non-foundationalism, which allows for a limited intersubjective notion of realism),[47] there is no denying that we naturally assume that there *is* "a way things are" and that our religious beliefs in some way relate truly to an external state of affairs. Negating any form of attunement between our religious way of life and this assumed reality would render our religious loyalties arid indeed.

As neo-Wittgensteinian Christian theologian D.Z. Phillips has persuasively argued, language game theory alone cannot suffice as explanation for the persistence of the religious truth claims: "The point of religious beliefs, why people *should* cherish them in the way they do, cannot be shown simply by *distinguishing between* religious beliefs and other features of human existence."[48] Despite the fact that different language-games do indeed serve different purposes and do not make up

---

[46] Richard Rorty, *Consequences of Pragmatism* (Minneapolis: University of Minnesota Press, 1982), xxxv.
[47] Hilary Putnam, *Representation and Reality* (Cambridge, MA: MIT Press, 1988), 109.
[48] D.Z. Phillips, "Religious Beliefs and Language Games," in *The Philosophy of Religion*, ed. Basil Mitchell (London: Oxford University Press, 1971), 132.

one big game, language itself forms a family of relationships between its various activities, so that the meaning and force of religious beliefs depend in part on the relation of these beliefs with other features of human existence. If religious beliefs were grounded in an isolated language game, intelligible only from within its own terms, Phillips asks, how could we explain any of the characteristic difficulties connected with religious beliefs? Why should tragedy, for example, constitute a difficulty or trial of faith?[49] Approaching religious belief as an esoteric activity cut off from everything which is not formally religious, and without taking into account its relation to other modes of life, would amount to no more than conforming to "a neat set of rules that could not be distinguished from sham worship ... a charming game which provides a welcome contrast to the daily routine, but which has no relevance to anything outside the doors of the church. In fact, this is what religious practices often do become for those for whom they have lost their meaning: a charming game which provides a welcome contrast to the daily routine, but which has no relevance to anything outside the doors of the church."[50] The whole point of religion is the bearing that this activity has on other features in the life of the worshiper.[51] Religion must take these features seriously in order to assume the critical importance that it does in our lives.

It is precisely because of the importance of everyday "realist" assumptions in cementing religious commitment that so much effort is expended by religious conservatives in cordoning off some religious beliefs as off-bounds to demythologizing or re-interpretation. Because the notion of "truth" and religious commitment are so intimately connected in the human psyche, critical scrutiny of beliefs that appear indispensable to the system is sometimes held back by upholding the remote possibility that future investigation will overturn current impressions. When scientific discoveries or deeply felt moral intuitions render even such eventualities incredible, religious adherents may resort to deliberate bifurcation, conducting themselves in accordance with reason in the laboratory and in their everyday lives while preserving professions of faith in the synagogue and in formal allegiance to what are regarded

---

[49] Ibid., 135-136.
[50] Ibid., 134-135.
[51] Ibid., 134.

by current halakhic consensus as unavoidable halakhic constraints.[52] Irrespective of the difficulty some may have in granting legitimacy or persuasive value to such policies, it would be fair to say that a religious world-view lacking any claims of attunement to a reality beyond its self-contained universe of discourse will never match traditional belief in its ability to preserve the intensity of feeling generated by its models and paradigms and to transmit the passion of its message to future generations.

Commonalities with the Simple Believer

So long as we remain on the level of second-order theology (i.e., engaged in the attempt to substantiate the particular path of a particular religion on its own terms) the self-aware cultural-linguist can nonetheless travel hand in hand with the naive realist for a very long way in preserving the psychological force of his religious commitments. For all practical purposes, the two will not differ radically on this level in the mix of pragmatism and realist rhetoric that they may adopt in order to defend the claims upon which such commitments rest.

Ordinarily, believers of both camps assume the accepted doctrines of their faith unreflectively, simply allowing the concrete experience of their everyday lives to be constituted and shaped by the truth claims

---

[52] Such a position could explain Maimonides' anomalous position in demanding belief in the thirteen principles of faith. Given his rationalist view that belief is synonymous with knowing, one might ask how anyone can be commanded to intellectually affirm what he does not know to be true. If, however, we understand the obligation to believe as the obligation to protect those premises necessary for grounding a way of life which holds promise of leading us to eventual intellectual acceptance of these, such a position could make sense even for a rationalist. Maimonides' distinction between "necessary beliefs" (*l'tiqadat*) and "true opinions" (*ara' sahiha*) provides further defense of formal compliance with doctrine. See *Guide of the Perplexed* III: 28. Given these precedents, we would do well to rid ourselves once and for all of the misnomer of Orthopraxy, often invoked in a pejorative sense in order to dismiss halakhically conformist behavior that is not grounded on acceptance of dogma in its literal sense. Any behavior externally conforming to that which is historically and sociologically identified with traditional halakhic practice indicates some form of belief or justification, though it may not tally with the naive objectivism of strict correspondence theory.

of their religious traditions. Under such circumstances they employ these claims quite naturally as the grammar to be used when speaking about their ultimate values, without dwelling overmuch on their creedal content. Intuitively they will have mastered the skill of stating their belief in a manner that does not overstep the context and regulative purpose for which the statement was meant. Thus, believers will sense that talk of God's love is more appropriate than talk of God's wrath when conversing with others about their infirmity. Or, that it is better to draw initially on a religious repertory of lament rather than songs of praise for God when confronted with grave injustice and its perpetrators.[53] In each of these instances there are no objective criteria for determining the appropriateness of the response. The final determiner is the pragmatic need to highlight the unacceptability of injustice in God's eyes.

Even when inability to reconcile a religious truth claim with reason presents a more formidable or intransigent obstacle to its acceptance, the self-aware post-liberal no less than the rank and file believer will feel compelled to subject these claims and doctrines to a more deliberate process of examination that will remove such complaints. Although conveying reasonable import is not the main function of religious truth claims, a strong sense that they are *unreasonable* may well render them ineffective in accomplishing the regulative function for which they *are* meant: to compose the "picture" that stands behind the religious form of life.[54] In the case of descriptive statements open to critical scientific investigation (such as the age of the universe, the splitting of the Red Sea, the chronology of biblical accounts), the sophisticated cultural-linguist will find the task of relating such statements to a presumed reality relatively easy, as there already exists a long history of naturalistic

---

[53] Tanner, ibid., 81.

[54] This sensibility informs James Barr's sharp critique of Christian theologian and biblical scholar Brevard Child's intra-textual and pan-theological approach to understanding scriptures. Barr rejects the dichotomy between theology and the history of religion and insists that biblical interpretation must maintain holistic coherence with ordinary common sense. On this view, understanding the Bible even within a religious context mandates proper attention to historical critical method and to theology as it was thought or believed in the time of the Bible itself. See James Barr, *The Concept of Biblical Theology* (Minneapolis: Fortress Press, 1999), chapters 23 and 24.

or allegorical interpretations within the religious tradition itself upon which he can draw. Although his attachment to the tradition will not rise or fall on the results of this enterprise, he may well regard such efforts at reconciling reason with faith as part and parcel of the religious language game itself.

Dealing with mythic explanations of descriptive statements that border on the historic is also relatively unproblematic. We may have no way of knowing whether or not the Red Sea did indeed split, whether the ancient Hebrews really did undergo some revelatory experience at Sinai, or whether someday there actually will appear a Messiah who will inaugurate a new epoch in the history of mankind. Nonetheless, as we have already noted, in the eyes of a constructivist the "truth" of these accounts and their justification is not inferred from close testing of their accuracy. It is embodied in the spiritual attitudes which they engender, in the ways of reacting to and meeting situations which they inspire. Hence, even when such explanations assume the existence of metaphysical forces or an occurrence of historic events not liable to scrutiny, the self-aware cultural-linguist will find no problem in employing traditional religious vocabulary grounded on "realist" epistemological assumptions, and in justifying this practice in pragmatic terms.

In the event that the difficulty posed to religious belief stems from statements that are even farther removed from rational demonstration or confirmable human experience, more innovative theological solutions are often brought into the fray. God's justice, despite the Holocaust, may be explained as reflecting a new development in the covenantal relationship with the nation of Israel, in which divine responsibility is abdicated in the interests of greater equality between the partners. God's transcendence, despite dogmatic assertions that every word of the Torah was transmitted from Heaven by direct dictation, may be defended by blurring distinctions between divine speech and natural historic process. Here too, a religious constructivist will find little difficulty in appropriating the speculative interpretive adjustments that such creative efforts entail. Once again, his only difference with the ordinary believer will be his awareness of the fact that the basis for these adjustments stems from internal rather than ontological considerations, allowing him to view his attempts at reconciling religious truth claims with a hypothetical objective "reality" as part and parcel of the religious language game itself. Because of this, his theology may be offered tentatively as a plausible, but not necessarily exclusive, model for explaining the anomalies of religious propositions. Even when identifying passionately with this model, he will always entertain the background possibility that it may eventually be replaced by another more illuminating picture, and can therefore co-exist with other explanations.[55] Indeed, in this sense, the cultural linguist is arguably better equipped for preserving his religious commitment than is the less reflective believer who is still operating with naive ontological pretensions. Precisely because of his ability to view the appeal to a hypothetical metaphysical reality as a reality-producing construct open to revision, he may be more capable of tolerating the fragility of his theological explanations, recognizing them for the temporary stopgaps that they are.

But can the same be said for the manner in which such a believer relates to the totalizing claims of religion that purport to extend beyond the confines of the religious language-game itself, knowing full well that such a pragmatic and contextual manner of relating can be justified only from within the particular vocabulary of a specific religious tradition? What meaning can statements attesting to the certainty of attunement of one's religious belief to an absolute reality transcending language and the expression of human desires, values, and visions possibly hold for the self-aware cultural linguist consciously adopting a position of non-foundationalism? In other words, can we speak, from within a context, of a reality that is free of context? And if not, are we left with anything more than a feeble motive for ultimate religious commitment?

Philosopher Jeffrey Stout's wry characterization of the position he identifies as "skeptical realism" (i.e., questioning whether words refer

---

[55] Expression of both the necessity and the fragility of theology can be found in the following statement: "An honest religious thinker is like a tightrope walker. He almost looks as though he were walking on nothing but air. His support is the slenderest imaginable. And yet it really is possible to walk on it." Ludwig Wittgenstein, *Culture and Value*, translated by Peter Winch (Oxford: Basil Blackwell, 1980), 76. Similar ideas abound in R. Kook's writings. See, for example, his defense of Maimonides' incorporation of Aristotelian ideas in his theology in *Maamarei Ha-reayah* 1 (Jerusalem: Golda Katz Foundation, 1980), 105-112.

to any pre-defined objective reality) aptly illustrates the dilemma of a die-hard constructivist at this stage of religious belief:

> The skeptical realist is more like someone who wants to be his own father and then has the nature of that desire brought to light in therapy. He might be unhappy, perhaps even hard to console, upon realizing that he will never be his own father, but it's hard to see how he could have good reason for wallowing in the disappointment of such an incoherent desire. What fuels the unhappiness, it seems safe to suppose, is still half-thinking that maybe the desire does make sense.[56]

At this point, it would appear that even a cultural-linguistic approach to balancing the tension between cognitive dissonance and religious loyalty has reached the limits of its power. Non-foundationalism may serve to override localized intellectual and moral objections faced by the contemporary religious adherent, but can such a view—side-stepping, as it does, the question of the referential nature of religious symbols altogether—nurture true religious passion?

The Philosophical Quest for Metaphysical Solutions

The inherent inability of a cultural-linguistic approach to provide a patent "objectivity" that is at any point transcendentally guaranteed leads all who struggle with this question from the psychological to the philosophical problem: Given the premise that true religious commitment is tied to *some* sense of divine transcendence, can we know or experience a God that is by definition beyond definition and beyond our grasp?[57]

---

[56] Jeffrey Stout, *Ethics after Babel: The Languages of Morals and their Discontents* (Boston: Beacon Press, 1988), 254.

[57] On the surface, this difficulty might appear no different than that which Maimonides sought to resolve with his negative theology. See *Guide of the Perplexed* I:50-59 Maimonides, however, still believed in the objectivity of material existence, so that God could be defined—albeit by negation—as against this firm foundation. For the non-foundationalist, however, all knowledge is context-related, even our knowledge of material objects. There may be a "way that things are," but this "way" is always relative in its manner of definition.

Responses of Nascent Jewish Post-liberalism

Until fairly recently, the effort at adapting non-foundationalist views to a theological context was conducted almost exclusively from within the ranks of Christianity. In terms of awareness of the inherent inescapability of subjectivism with reference to metaphysics, traditionalist Jewish theology has not advanced much beyond Maimonides' theory of negative attributes, and in general lags far behind the more sophisticated developments in Christian theology over the past hundred years. In the last few decades, however, some attention to the postmodern dilemma has appeared in the writings of Reform theologian Eugene Borowitz,[58] and more recently in a few articles by leading thinkers of the Conservative movement.[59] Perhaps more significant are hints of similar tendencies that have begun to emerge in the writings of several modern Orthodox expositors of Judaism, as members of this rendition of Judaism would seem on the surface to be more greatly invested in a highly constrictive metaphysical core. The initial spadework in locating such tendencies (best characterized as "metaphysical minimalism"),[60] as well as in providing an in-depth analysis of their salient features, figures prominently in various articles authored by Israeli philosopher Avi Sagi[61] and in a

---

[58] See his *Renewing the Covenant: A Theology for the Postmodern Jew* (Philadelphia: The Jewish Publication Society, 1991).

[59] See, for example, the contributions of Neil Gilman and Gordon Tucker to the discussion of "Contemporary Philosophic Quests for God," *Conservative Judaism* 11:2 (1999): 59-96.

[60] See Yoske Ahitov, "Thoughts on the Secret of the Appeal of Fundamentalism," in *Al Gvul-ha-Temurah: Iyun be-Mashmauyot Yehudiyot be-Yameinu* (Jerusalem: Dept. of Education—The Branch for Torah Culture, 1995), chapter 4, 57.

[61] See Avi Sagi, "Religion without Metaphysics? Between Leibowitz and Wittgenstein," *Mahshavot* 67 (1995): 6-17 (Hebrew); "The Holy Canon and its meaning in the thought of Leibowitz and Soloveitchik: A Chapter in the Ways of Struggling with Modernity," *B.D.D.* 1 (1995): 49-62; "Religious Commitment in a Secularized World: Introductory Chapters to the Thought of Eliezer Goldman," *Daat* 36 (1996): 69-88 (Hebrew); "Leibowitz the Person as against his Thought: Philosophical Thought and its Possibilities," *Daat* 38 (1997): 131-143 (Hebrew); "Judaism as Interpretation: Studies in the Thought of Goldman," *Daat* 41 (1998): 57-75 (Hebrew); "David Hartman: Modernist Jewish Thought—Introductory chapters," in *Mehuyavut Yeudit Mithadeshet: al Olamo ve-Haguto shel David Hartman*, vol. 1, eds. Avi Sagi and Tzvi Zohar (Tel Aviv: Machon Shalom Hartman/Hakibbutz Hameuchad, 2001), 445-493.

recently-published book on the confrontation between Orthodoxy and postmodernism written by Gili Zivan, [62] based on a doctorate written under Sagi's mentorship. In a sense, the very singling out of a common denominator of nascent postmodernism in the thought of R. Joseph B. Soloveitchik and Professors Yeshayahu Leibowitz, David Hartman and Eliezer Goldman contributes its share in advancing this trend. Although every one of these thinkers would no doubt disassociate himself from the postmodernist label,[63] scholarly research often engenders its own dynamic, contributing its fair share in shaping the developments it purports to observe. The hidden assumption fueling such research is quite likely a hope that such developments bear the potential for transporting Orthodox Judaism to new theological territory, redeeming it from a certain stultification of thought in which it has been mired for some time, and infusing it with a dose of much-needed vitality.

The four above-mentioned thinkers are, admittedly, not all cut from the same cloth. Various and even contradictory positions regarding to the ontological status of religious truth statements can be gleaned from their writings. These differences in their philosophical approach to the possibility of attunement with a metaphysical reality beyond language also lead to differences between them in their understandings of the motivation for lasting religious commitment, most of which suffer from paradox or a type of circular reasoning.

R. Soloveitchik vacillates inconsistently between relating to religious statements as the faithful description of an existing ontological reality and adopting an expressionist-experiential approach which rejects any attempt to prove the validity of such statements on the strength of

---

[62] Gili Zivan, *Dat le-lo Ashlaya Nokhach Olam Post-Moderni: Iyyun be-Haggutam shel Soloveitchik, Leibowitx, Goldman, ve-Hartman* (Tel Aviv: Machon Shalom Hartman/Hakibbutz Hameuchad, 2005). See also her articles "The Religious Experience according to Rabbi Soloveitchik," in *Emuna b'Zemanim MIshtanim: al Mishnato shel Harav Yoseph Dov Soloveithcik*, ed. Avi Sagi (Jerusalem: Dept. of Torah Education and Culture in the Diaspora and Mercaz Yaakov Herzog, 1997), 219-248; "Orthodox Thought in the Face of Postmodernism," in *Yahadut Pnim va-Hutz: Dialog bein olamot*, eds. Avi Sagi, Dudi Shwartz, and Yedidya Stern (Jerusalem: Magnes, 2000); "Pluralistic Religious Thought: Consideration of the Thought of Eliezer Goldman," *Daat* 41 (1998): 75-96 (Hebrew).

[63] See Zivan's correspondence with Goldman regarding his personal stance in this matter, in the appendix to her book (above, note 61), 295-297.

external evidence and prefers instead to relate them to the existential experience of man.[64] Despite this existentialist strain in his thought, however, Soloveitchik does not completely refrain from basing religious commitment on claims of correspondence between religious truths and an objective ontology. While subjective and unmediated certainty provides—to his mind—the basic starting point for the inner experience of the believer,[65] when this experience is subsequently transposed and formulated in accordance with the given a priori categories of Halakhah, he regards the end result as a reliable guide to an existing metaphysical reality which these ideal categories are meant to realize.[66]

Yeshayahu Leibowitz assumes the position of a "theological positivist" even more emphatically, adopting an absolute distinction between expression of facts and expression of values, and contending that there is no way to empirically test a "religious fact."[67] In the type of interpretation that he chooses to grant such "facts" when stripping them of their literal meanings, he comes fairly close to understanding them as having a constitutive role, but nevertheless falls short of adopting a truly post-liberal position. This is because his reservations regarding a literal understanding of religious propositions do not stem from a full-fledged non-foundationalism, but rather from a Maimonidean-like objection

---

[64] For textual sources in the writing of Rabbi Soloveitchik and a discussion of his ambivalence in this matter, see David Shatz, "Science and the Religious Mindset in the Thought of Rabbi Soloveitchik," in *Emunah b'Zemanim Mishtanim: al Mishnato shel Harav Yoseph Dov Soloveitchik*, ibid., 307-344; Avi Sagi, "Rabbi Soloveitchik: Jewish Thought in the Face of Modernity," ibid., especially 461-483.

[65] "U-bikashtem mi-sham," *Ish hahalakhah: galui venistar* (Dept. of Torah Education and Culture for the Golah, 1979), 127-137.

[66] See, for example, Joseph Dov Halevi Soloveitchik, "Halakhic Man," in *Ish ha-Halakha: Galui veNistar* (Jerusalem: Dept. of Religious Culture and Education for the Diaspora of the International Zionist Federation, 1979), 56-59.

[67] For textual sources and a discussion of Yeshayahu Leibowitz's position on this matter, see Avi Sagi, "Leibowitz: Jewish Thought in the Face of Modernity," in *Yeshayahu Leibowitz: His World and Thought* (Jerusalem: Keter, 1995) 162-175 (Hebrew); "Religion Without Metaphysics? Between Leibowitz and Wittgenstein," *Mahshavot* 67 (1995): 6-17 (Hebrew); "Leibowitz: The Man as Against His thought: Philosophical Thought and its Possibilities," *Daat* 38 (1997): 131-143 (Hebrew); Avi Sagi, "Yeshayahu Leibowitz: A Breakthrough in Jewish Philosophy: Religion Without Metaphysics," *Religious Studies* 33 (1997): 203-216.

to applying human categories to an absolutely transcendent God. Since for him any knowledge of a metaphysical reality is beyond our reach, Leibowitz refuses to base the choice to lead a religious way of life on any contentions regarding the nature of God or on empiric observations regarding the beneficial influence of such worship upon the natural world or human experience. Such a move, according to him, would reduce religious ritual to a self-serving activity (*avoda shelo lishmah*), and fall under the forbidden category of idolatry.[68] Instead, he predicates religious commitment entirely on the voluntary decision of the believer. In his eyes, the only legitimate basis for religious commitment ("worship for its own sake", or *avoda lishmah*) is a willingness on the part of the believer to submit to the authority of revelation as a binding divine norm.[69] This willingness can only be explained paradoxically in a circular manner, self-justifying in and of itself.

David Hartman (in his later writings, at any rate) concurs with Leibowitz in rejecting the attempt to discover traces of divine immanence in creation and history. He nevertheless comes far closer to a relativist approach in his readiness to be selective in the religious statements he is prepared to adopt, at times explicitly justifying such selectivity on considerations that are centered on man and not on God.[70] As opposed to Leibowitz's sharp distinction between theocentric worship and practices designed to fulfill human needs, Hartman's religious commitment

---

[68] Yeshayahu Leibowitz, "Belief, Religion and Science," in *Yahadut, Am Yehudi u-Medinat Yisrael* (Tel Aviv: Shocken, 1976), 343.

[69] See for example, Yeshayahu Leibowitz, "The Reading of *Shema*," in *Judaism, Human Values, and the Jewish State*, trans. and ed. Eliezer Goldman, et al (Cambridge, MA/London: Harvard University Press, 1995), 37-38; "Religious Praxis: The Meaning of Halakhah," ibid, 4-5; "On History and Miracles," *Emunah, Historiyah v-Arakhim* (Jerusalem: Akademon, 1982), 169.

[70] See, for example, his justification for preferring the covenantal image over the Akeda image as a model for imitation in religious worship, which is based on the importance of autonomous thinking, David Hartman, *A Living Covenant:The Innovative Spirit in Traditional Judaism* (New York: The Free Press, 1985), and especially chapter 2,: "Assertion Versus Submission: The Tension Within Judaism," 42-59, and chapter 10, "Two Competing Covenantal Paradigms," 229-255. See also Ehud Luz's critique of this aspect of Hartman's thought: "Zionism, History and Demythologization," in *Mehuyavut Datit Mehudeshet: al Olamo ve-Haguto shel David Hartman*, vol. 1, ed. Avi Sagi and Zvi Zohar (Tel Aviv: Hakibbutz Hameuchad, 2001), 341-342.

appears to draw largely upon the capacity of religion to respond to our spiritual interests. At any rate, he sharply dissents from Leibowitz's meticulous concern for *lishmah* behavior that grants no religious legitimacy to the moral insights of man.[71] Because Hartman's tendency is to view the major significance of religious systems in their functional aspect, and to evaluate their beliefs and practices in anthropocentric terms, something of the palpable reality of God, as well as of the obligatory nature of *mitzvot* transmitted in His name, becomes dissipated in the process.[72]

Eliezer Goldman is the only one of the four who comes close to formulating a comprehensive and systematic view of religion reminiscent of post-liberal Christians. His theology, like that of Leibowitz, is still driven at least in part by denial of man's ability to know God in and through the world, but it also stems from a greater awareness of man's inability to overcome the social conditioning of knowledge altogether. Perhaps because of this, he is also the only one of the four thinkers who directly confronts questions regarding the meaning of religious truth statements and grapples openly and explicitly with the resulting question of religious commitment.[73] Considering man's inability to arrive at absolute and unconditioned truths, is it still possible to base the demands of religion on that feeling of total commitment which has always been the marked characteristic of piety in the past, and to preserve the normative quality of propositions of faith?

While Goldman re-iterates Leibowitz's views regarding the unbridgeable chasm between man and a transcendent God, and like him resists grounding religious obligation on claims drawing upon empiric evidence, he nevertheless relegates a certain role to human experience

---

[71] See Avi Sagi, "David Hartman: Modernist Jewish Thought—Introductory Chapters," in *Mehuyavut Yehudit Mithadeshet*, vol. I, ibid., 471-472.

[72] For a discussion of the degree of realism of God in Hartman's religious conception, see Avi Sagi, ibid., 460-471. The truth is that Hartman himself offers a similar critique of the secularization of religion in the view of Mordechai Kaplan. See: David Hartman, *Conflicting Visions: Spiritual Possibilities of Modern Israel* (New York: Schocken, 1990), 184-206.

[73] For an exhaustive account of Goldman's views regarding this issue, see Avi Sagi, "Religious Commitment in a Secularized World: Introductory Chapters to the Thought of Eliezer Goldman," *Daat* 36 (1996): 69-86 (Hebrew); idem, "Judaism as Interpretation: Studies in the Thought of Goldman," *Daat* 41 (1998): 47-57 (Hebrew).

in the religious life in a manner that testifies to some measure of attunement to metaphysical certainty. This attunement is implied firstly in the right of the believer to be selective in the interpretation that he chooses to grant to the hallowed formulations of tradition, even though he has no right to detract from their formal status as canonical and binding.[74] Secondly, Goldman sees in the very observance of *mitzvot* expression of man's belief that in the performance of such acts he is indeed worshipping God.[75] What this means, in effect, is that the *experience* of God's presence itself, and not merely the decision to seek it, is created from within and by means of religious practice, thereby reinforcing the conviction that we are indeed capable of engaging with an existing metaphysical reality. The validity of the religious statement stands in direct proportion to the ability of the community of believers to find experiential value in its religious practice, while constantly refraining from inappropriate metaphysical conclusions.

Goldman's argument is reminiscent of the loose correspondence with reality intimated in the "will to believe" recommended by William James, according to which the very openness to the possibility of certain hypotheses enables their realization, except that it appears to be based more on formal logic than on experiential conviction. It is even more similar to the view of contemporary philosopher Edward Henderson,[76] who concedes that religious belief may be a conscious choice, out of a state of uncertainty, to adopt the religious perspective and to live a way of life that will deepen our subjective conviction of its certainty,[77] but insists that such belief nevertheless necessarily affirms God's reality. This is because every religious statement is in and of itself a communicative act that is directed to a particular object, and therefore necessarily referential.

Do these formal solutions offer sufficient escape, for both Jews and Christians, from the great divide created by non-foundationalism between religious belief and ontology? Do they suggest a breakthrough

---

[74] E. Goldman, *Mehkarim ve-Iyunim: Hagut Yehudit be-avar uba-hoveh* (Jerusalem: Magnes 1997), "Scientific statements and religious statements," 344.
[75] Ibid., "On Faith without Illusions." chapters 4-5, 366-368.
[76] Edward Henderson, "Theistic Reductionism and the Practice of Worship," *International Journal for Philosophy of Religion* X, no. 1 (1979): 25-40.
[77] Ibid., 39-40.

experientially powerful enough for overcoming the skeptic non-foundationalist's sense of entrapment in the limitations of his finite perceptions and the social conditioning of knowledge, a barrier that even Goldman believes that we cannot really avoid?

The Contribution of Modern Jewish Mysticism

At this stage it is worth noting that modern rationalists or postmodern skeptics living on the outskirts of the religious heartland are not the only ones to have confronted the issue of God's ontological status in a non-foundationalist scheme. Amongst twentieth-century Christian theologians, the most influential effort in this direction is that of the neo-Wittgensteinian theologian D.Z. Phillips, who adopts a distinctly para-ontological (or rather "beyond ontological") position in refusing to relate to God as another "being among beings." As he declares: [78]

> Coming to see that there is a God is not like coming to see that an additional being exists.... Coming to see that there is a God involves seeing a new meaning in one's life, and being given a new understanding. The Hebrew-Christian conception of God is not a conception of a being among beings. Kierkegaard emphasized the point when he said bluntly, "God does not exist. He is eternal."

This leads Phillips to describe the significance of prayer as bringing the believer to a new understanding, existential rather than intellectual, of himself and his situation in the world, rather than deriving from it external proof for the *existence* of God as a metaphysical object.[79]

---

[78] D.Z. Phillips, "Religious Belief and Philosophical Enquiry," in *Faith and Philosophical Enquiry* (London: Routledge and Kegan Paul, 1970), 68-69.

[79] Idem, *The Concept of Prayer* (Oxford: Blackwell/New York: Seabury, 1981), 61-62. A similar neo-Wittgenstinian attempt at responding to the threat of non-foundationalism is represented in the thought of Norman Malcolm, who like Phillips appeals to more popular, experiential understandings of religion in rejecting talk of God's *existence* as unintelligible, whereas the idea of belief in God is entailed in "some religious action, some commitment, or if not, at least a bad conscience." Norman Malcolm, "The Groundlessness of Belief," in *Reason and Religion*, ed. Stuart C. Brown, (Ithaca/London: Cornell University Press, 1977), 155.

According to this, the dispute between the believer and the disbeliever is not over a *matter of fact*; religious truth statements must be understood in the context from which they derive their meaning rather than through the type of philosophical reflection on reality appropriate to propositional assertions. Indeed, it is this position of so-called "theological reductionism" that prompts Henderson's critique of Phillips, which contends that there is no way to separate between religious belief and ontological statements by escaping to Wittgenstinian theories of "language games." However, I believe that describing Phillips' position as "theological reductionism" is in fact a misnomer; it should not be equated with the more radical rejection of metaphysics that stems at times from postmodern theology, and is more closely aligned with Continental "deconstructionism" and the work of the American post-analytic philosopher, Richard Rorty.[80] Appreciation of the inappropriateness of Henderson's description leads me to suggest that perhaps the alleged "flight from metaphysics" attributed to modern Continental thought and post-analytic philosophy may have been overdone; there may be room even in a constructivist position for a metaphysics that refers to something *beyond* the linguistic scheme. Unpacking Phillips' formulation into other terms may bring us closer to such an understanding.

Although the use of internal symbolism and esoteric terminology has contributed to a lack of familiarity with their writings, it would be helpful in this connection to direct our attention to a veritable treasure of highly sophisticated thought pertinent to the philosophical issue of "reality" raised by non-foundationalism which has been produced by a group of traditional Jewish thinkers who—unlike Goldman and his colleagues—are far removed from contemporary Western trends. I refer here to an important body of literature which represents an eighteenth-century offshoot of Lurianic Kabbalah and develops a

---

[80] Some samples of this more radical rejection of metaphysics may be found in assorted contributions to several recent anthologies of postmodern theology. See, for example, Nancy K. Frankenberry and Hans H. Penner, eds., *Language, Truth, and Religious Belief* (n. 12 above); Nancy K. Frankenberry, ed., *Radical Interpretation in Religion* (Cambridge: Cambridge University Press, 2002); Mark A. Wrathall, ed., *Religion after Metaphysics* (Cambridge: Cambridge University Press, 2003); Kevin J. Vanhoozer, ed., *The Cambridge Companion to Postmodern Theology* (Cambridge: Cambridge University Press, 2003).

theological scheme capable of illuminating the concept of God which Phillips perhaps has in mind, in what has come to be known as "the allegorical interpretation of the doctrine of *tsimtsum*."

According to the original Lurianic image, the existence of a created world was first made possible by an act of withdrawal on the part of *Einsof* (the Infinite One) from the central point of His monolithic unity, contracting into Himself in order to make room within his absolute para-existence for a mode of being other than Himself. While this image (which provides an archetypal paradigm for the process of birth) is always accompanied by pious caveats of *kivyakhol* ("as it were"), even a metaphor must be a metaphor for *some*thing. For this reason later kabbalists found difficulty in ignoring the more-than-a-whiff of heresy that the crudely anthropomorphic character of this image evokes, enabling talk of a divine being that develops in time ("before" *tsimtsum* and "after"), occupies space ("more" or "less"), and allows for the existence of other non-divine entities alongside the absolute and total nature of its infinite existence. Their solution to the problem forms the basis of a *panentheistic* worldview embraced by both Hasidim and Mitnaggedim, traces of which can be found in almost all of the offshoots of these two movements which are active in traditional Judaism to the present day. The main idea promoted by these later interpreters of Lurianic teachings is that the original image of divine contraction in order to make space for a finite world should not be understood literally, as an actual physical displacement and creation of a void, but as a metaphoric withdrawal. The act of *tsimtsum*, then, refers merely to a hiding or a concealment of God's all-pervasive presence in order to enable the establishment of a realm of appearance, thus affording the illusion of a boundary between subject and object, Creator and created being, and the possibility of particularization and individuation of consciousness.

It is certainly important to note that, unlike in the case of non-foundationalists, the sense of contingency leading to the allegorical interpretation of the doctrine of *tsimtsum* does not relate to doubts regarding the validity of the religious truth claim. The ontological problem worrying the latter-day Kabbalists was not, "Can we speak of an absolute metaphysical being (i.e., what we call 'God')?" For them, the problem was rather: "How can we possibly conceive of the existence of a finite entity that is not God (i.e., what we call 'the world')?"—a question which in their view arose due to the necessarily limited manner in which the absolute existence of God was reflected in the mind of the believer. Nevertheless, I believe that theologians sometimes have the very important task of mediating between mysticism and empiricism, and that the non-foundational post-liberal may have something valuable to learn from the various theological positions that were developed in response to the latter-day Kabbalist understanding of the limits of human perception and the possible forms of engagement between religious belief and metaphysics.

One consequence of the allegorical understanding of *tsimtsum* is the recognition that God's reality must be spoken of in terms of at least two differing perspectives: (a) how we, as perceiving creatures, see God's relationship to the world from *our* point of view—*mitzidenu*; (b) how we, as perceiving creatures, imagine that God relates to the world from *His* point of view—*mitzido*. Talk of God on the first level is certainly not a faithful representation of "what is," and could be more accurately regarded as parallel to the neo-pragmatic notion of a religious construct or model for organizing reality from our point of view. As for the second level: stretching our imaginations beyond ourselves, we understand that from God's point of view there is no divine transcendence—only the monolithic undifferentiated unity beyond *tsimtsum*. Nevertheless, such talk of God *mitzido* is also not a pure reflection of the way things are, because in conceptualizing God's reality in his terms, as it were, we must still begin our formulation *mitzidenu*—referring to him as distinct from the world, even as we come paradoxically to deny this distinction. But over and above these two levels of perception is an absolute unity which is ultimately all that there is, and which, as such, defies definition; even the attribute "God" as applied here would be inadequate, as this would imply comparison with something else. At this stage, the distinctions between object and subject, ontology and perception (or reality and its linguistic expression), are superfluous and equally meaningless, for all these are one and the same.

While all the Kabbalists adopting the allegorical interpretation of the doctrine of *tsimtsum* are united regarding the nature of the latter two stages, they do maintain important differences of opinion regarding the nature of the first stage, which is the most critical one in practical terms, as it defines the parameters of religious worship. These differences, which fueled bitter ideological differences between Hasidim and Mitnaggedim in the eighteenth and nineteenth centuries (and to a lesser extent to this day), can be broadly divided into three different streams.[81] A major hasidic approach, as explicated by R. Shneur Zalman of Lyadi (RSZ), posits that although the world from our point of view is suffused with God's light, and were it not for this emanation of the divine presence at every moment the world as a separate entity would cease to exist, in our perception this distorted reflection of God's infinite unity is qualitatively different than God as He is in Himself, suggesting total transcendence. Mitnaggedic ideology, on the other hand, as explicated by R. Hayyim of Volozhin (RH), the chief disciple of the Gaon of Vilna, suggests that while God's emanation in this world is so far removed from its source that it *appears* qualitatively different, in truth we should regard this difference even from our point of view as merely a quantitative difference of degree.[82] Moreover, the intellectual study of Torah and formal observance of Halakhah provide an onto-

---

[81] For further detail regarding these three possibilities, see Tamar Ross, "Two Interpretations of the Doctrine of Tzimtzum: R. Hayim of Volozhin and R. Shneur Zalman of Liadi," in *Mehkerei Yerushalayim be-Mahshevet Yisrael* 2 (Jerusalem: Hebrew University, 1981), 153-169; "The Place of Tzimtzum in the Thought of Harav Kook," in *Mehkarim be-Hagut Yehudit*, ed. Sarah Heller-Wilenski and Moshe Idel (Jerusalem: Magnes, 1989), 159-172; "Some Reflections on Torah Lishmah by Norman Lamm," *Jewish Action* (Winter 1989-90): 81-85.

[82] A source of much confusion is the fact that while R. Shneur Zalman of Lyadi and R. Hayyim of Volozhin both make use of the Zoharic distinction between *ohr sovev* and *ohr memale*—both of which emanate from *Ein sof*—in order to designate the two stages of *mitzido* and *mitzidenu*, the two authors use them in opposing ways. I.e., according to RSZ, the term *sovev* comes to describe reality from God's point of view (Stage 2) and the term *memale* refers to reality as we see it (Stage 1). R. Hayyim uses these terms in reverse order. To add to the confusion, their understanding of the meaning of these terms is not completely identical. If we equate the term *sovev* quite simply with the term "transcendence," the conclusion might easily be drawn that RH and RSZ have a genuine difference of opinion as to the nature of Stage 2 as well, and that what RH regards as God's perception in this stage could be equated with what RSZ regards as our perception in Stage 1 and vice versa. In truth, however, even though RSZ uses the term *sovev* and RH *memale*, both mean to indicate an ontological state whereby worldly existence is annihilated. In this sense, RSZ's only difference with RH is the former's contention that stage 2 is a state that is *perceptually* inaccessible as well.

logical bond with the God that is beyond *tsimtsum* even while operating within this-worldly perceptions.

It is perhaps precisely because of the perceptual inaccessibility of stage two according to RSZ that his theology encourages the yearning to achieve a more spiritualized ideal—*bittul ha-yesh* (self-annihilation)—as a state of mind to be realized even *mitzidenu*. In piercing the veil of illusion leading to our false perception of God's transcendence, we must strive to draw the *ahdut shava* (undifferentiated unity) that lays beyond *tsimtsum* into the cosmic reality of this world, abolishing the dichotomy of spirit and matter, miracle and nature. The hasidic suggestion that our common-sense perception of God's transcendence bears no correspondence to the way things are, and that it therefore deserves to be broken down and stripped of its illusory authority and appeal, betrays some unexpected affinity with the logical positivist's rejection of religion as "nonsense."[83]

Mitnaggedic realism, on the other hand, urges compliance with the given reality as it is perceived on our part, understanding that this perception represents the limits of our epistemological ability. Such a position suggests that since the limited nature of our religious beliefs is an unavoidable element of our conceptual baggage, our job is to make do with it as best as we can, without entertaining overly-spiritualist ambitions. As R. Eliyahu Dessler (a prominent twentieth-century exponent of the Musar movement) has notably phrased it, in the context of his emphasis on our inability to perceive the absolute nature of divine existence (or, in his language, *geder ein od milvado*):

> It is very difficult for man to admit this in his heart of hearts. He imagines that he has the ability to grasp the truth in an absolute manner, and will not be ready to believe that after all his efforts he will not manage to arrive at more than a relative truth; a truth that relates to his situation as a created being. Only with this recognition can man avoid the confusion of the various definitions and imagined contradictions, and base his faith on firm foundations.

---

[83] As Scottish philosopher David Hume aptly phrased it: "... how do you *mystics*, who maintain the absolute incomprehensibility of the Deity, differ from skeptics or atheists, who assert that the first cause of all is unknown and unintelligible?" See David Hume, *Dialogues Concerning Natural Religion*, Part IV.

> What is the value of a relative perception? Its value lies in the fact that it is relative to us, in accordance with our situation in this world, the world of free will and worship, and therefore only this is the truth for us.[84]

R. Dessler's pragmatic attitude to human perceptual limitations bears some resemblance to some of the more conservative attempts to reconcile the linguistic turn in metaphysics with normative religion.[85] This approach differs from the first in that it favors making peace with religious beliefs as formulated from within the limits of our partial perception, encouraging the believer to go back, for all practical purposes, to redefining metaphysics in a Platonic-Aristotelian rather than in a Kantian fashion. This involves abandoning the Kantian distinction between the "thing in itself" and the "phenomenal world," and rejecting the hope for achieving a vantage point beyond this-worldly limitations. Instead of attempting to examine reality as it is, all that we are obligated to do is relate to the world as it is perceived by us, seeking to understand it in the most satisfactory and coherent manner possible. The recognition that this perspective is not all that there is must of necessity be relegated to the back burner.

A third approach to the allegorical interpretation of *tsimtsum*, that of R. Kook, combines elements of both the hasidic and the mitnaggedic responses, suggesting that even when working within the bounds of human perception and affirming our existence as created beings living in a fragmented reality, we can reconstruct a credible facsimile of the undifferentiated and infinite Reality beyond, and even regard this activity as an enhancement of the divine—at least from our point of view.[86] This is to be accomplished by relating more and more elements of our world to the divine without obliterating their unique particularity.

R. Kook's approach allows us to reclaim the importance of metaphysics in a spirit of critical realism. We now understand our metaphysical

---

[84] *Michtav Me-Eliyahu* III, 256-257 (my translation).
[85] As explicated above, note 25.
[86] This same view of metaphysics may be reflected in the paradoxical attitude of the Vilna Gaon, who regarded R. Isaac Luria's ideas, and particularly the doctrine of *tsimtsum*, as innovations bearing the status of allegory, but an allegory that should nevertheless be taken literally (*mashal kipeshuto*) and treated as holy.

propositions as relating to truths which in principle seek to describe everything in an absolute manner, or, in other words, as statements which purport to constitute ultimate truth. Although we never achieve this in practice, the metaphysical basis of any truth claim achieves greater and greater force the more areas of experience are interpreted in its light, thus demonstrating the degree of its growing identity with that infinite reality with which we strive to connect. Although R. Kook's position retains ironic awareness of the disparity between the facsimile of infinity that we create and the original, he—like William James—finds support for the attunement of this view of our earthly reality to a metaphysical one in the concrete results engendered by adopting the partial religious expression, intensifying the spiritual and even the physical power of the believer.[87] The practical success of the religious vision in energizing vital life forces confirms its privileged access to some intelligible structures of reality that reflect an ontology of right relationships of beings to one another.

All three of the above approaches share some common ground with several of the modern attitudes to religious belief discussed thus far that have nothing to do with mysticism. The difference between these responses and other more philosophical approaches that posit epistemological modesty with regard to metaphysics is in their multi-layered approach. Taken on its own, stage one of each approach clearly does not have the power to revive the vitality of religious commitment. Even R. Hayyim of Volozhin, in explicating the approach that is most interested in making peace with human perceptual limitations as they stand, recommends relating to our awareness of the other higher level of *mitzido* by considering it embers of fire that should ignite our religious enthusiasm from afar, while at the same time recognizing that getting too close

---

[87] For further amplification regarding R. Kook's relationship to non-foundationalism, see Tamar Ross, "The Cognitive Value of Religious Truth Statements: Rabbi A.I. Kook and Postmodernism," in *Hazon Nahum: Jubilee Volume in Honor of Norman Lamm* (New York: Yeshiva University Press, 1997), 479-527. For an example of the practical implications of faith on the abilities of the believer, see Tamar Ross, "Immortality, Natural Law, and the Role of Human Perception in the Writings of Rav Kook," in *Rabbi Abraham Isaac Kook and Jewish Spirituality*, ed. David Shatz and Lawrence Kaplan (New-York: New York University Press, 1995), 237-257.

to the source of fire would subject us to the danger of being consumed by its heat.[88]

Another critical point to be made is that these three levels of perception are not unconnected. Even the mitnaggedic position, which prescribes sufficing with the illusory cosmic reality that constitutes our point of view, views the study of Torah and performance of mitzvot as capable of bonding us ontologically (if not perceptually) with that entity that is beyond words. The other two approaches strive even further to attain some perceived sense of metaphysical attachment (*devekut*), dissolving the dichotomy between the phenomenal world and the thing as it is in itself, physics and metaphysics, outside and inside, part and whole, subject and object.

When R. Kook writes, "We do not speak or even think of the source of sources, but in the very fact that we do not deny it, it already all lives and exists eternally,"[89] he means to say that our very contingent reaction testifies to the existence of a more perfect and complete foundation which engenders it. Even if this infinite reality beyond *tsimtsum* is never to be perceived, and "its definition amounts to spiritual idolatry … and even the divine itself and the name of God is a definition,"[90] the use of religious language, despite its limitations, is legitimate not only because we have no better choice, but because from the point of view of the whole, the partial expression is indeed contained within it, and from the point of view of the part, every partial expression adds to the whole and enhances it.[91] Even if the source of sources "is not revealed except in *Shekhinah* (i.e., in a limited revelation of God's presence), what of it?" asks R. Kook, reminding us of the Kabbalistic teaching that the name *Ani* (the individualized self and also a reference to *Shekhinah*, the lowest sefirotic emanation) and *Ayin* (Nothingness and also a reference to the transcendence and imperceptibility of the highest expression of the divine) are composed of the same Hebrew letters, indicating their evident spiritual connection.[92]

---

[88] *Nefesh Ha-hayyim* (Bnei Brak: Yissachar Rubin, 1989), part 3, chapter 1, 147-148.
[89] *Iggerot Ha-Reayah* I (Jerusalem: Mosad Harav Kook, 1985), 48.
[90] *Orot* (Jerusalem: Mosad Harav Kook, 1985), 124.
[91] For further exposition of this theological position, see Tamar Ross, "R. Kook's Concept of God," parts 1-2, *Daat* 8 (1982): 109-128, and *Daat* 9 (1982): 39-70 (Hebrew).
[92] *Iggerot Ha-Reayah* I, 48.

What may appear to lay eyes here as abstruse metaphysical gymnastics is actually a serious attempt to overcome a tension even more extremely stated than in classical Kabbalah, between two conflicting religious sensibilities (pantheism and theism), by developing a very intricate and finely tuned conceptual scheme that will allow these two incompatible bedfellows to somehow lie peacefully together. For our purposes, however, the various theological constructs emerging from this effort can also point the way to a fruitful form of religious negotiation in a postmodern age. Such constructs accommodate the understanding that postmodern theology is not simply a matter of exchanging one philosophical master for another in striving to correlate religious belief with postmodern interests and concerns rather than modern ones. Finding a middle way between pretensions to absolute and objective truths and denial of truth altogether is not its only concern. Doing theology under the conditions of post-modernity also means that philosophy is no longer the exclusive determiner in setting the agenda for this type of activity. This is because postmodernism involves not only a new epistemology and understanding of language, it also involves a different mindset and way of experiencing our everyday world and its relationship to another dimension that lies beyond it—one that is closer to mysticism than to philosophy. Rather than being satisfied with the vision of a fragmented and atomized universe, the path of postmodernism leads to viewing reality in holistic terms, as composed of various inter-related parts. In a passage that R. Kook wrote with amazing prescience almost a century ago, he indicates that this new holistic sensibility applies not only to our latest scientific models of reality (the examples he offers relate to innovative conceptions in the realms of anthropology, cosmology, and biology), but also to our understanding of greater connectivity between the world and God.[93]

In Conclusion

For a few rare intellectuals, grappling with the theoretical issues raised in this essay is a crucial element and direct expression of their yearning for the divine, and in this sense their unique method of worship.

---

[93] Abraham I. Kook, *Orot Ha-kodesh* 2 (Jerusalem: Mosad Harav Kook, 1985), 538-545.

However, I fully realize that philosophy and theology are not everyone's preference, and certainly do not mean to imply that the wave of the future for all religious believers involves delving into language theory or the intricacies of Kabbalistic thought. But I do believe that traditionalists confronting the radical implications of contemporary scientific and moral insights, and seeking to incorporate these into their religious way of life without forfeiting its credibility or normative force, will intuitively gravitate towards some of the more promising implications that the postmodern sensibility holds for traditional Jewish belief when informed by a mystic sensibility. The sympathy of so-called "secularists" for more fluid forms of New Age spirituality and the rise of "HaBaKookism" (an amalgam of more individualized anti-establishment modes of religiosity gleaned from the writings of Habad, Bratslav, and R. Kook) amongst some segments of religious youth in Israel are testimony to this trend.[94]

Postmodern language theory can redeem modern Orthodoxy from its counter-productive attachment to naive objectivism. The epistemological modesty of non-foundationalism can help religious adherents move away from overly rigid definitions of doctrine and allow them to return to the pre-modern function of religion as providing a valuable universe of discourse and a compelling way of life. It can extricate them from a mindless and stultifying triumphalism and encourage the willingness to refine religious convictions by listening carefully to other points of view. Initial recognition of this promise has been articulated by the late Shagar (R. Shimon Gerson Rosenberg), an unconventional religious Zionist *rosh yeshiva* in Israel, whose recently published collection of lectures, *Kelim Shevurim*[95] contains two essays suggesting—as implied by

---

[94] For further documentation of the awakened twentieth-century Jewish interest in Kabbalah and New Age spirituality, see Yehonatan Garb, *"Yehidei ha-Segulot Yihyu la-Adarim": Iyyunim be-Kabbalat ha-Meah ha-Esrim* (Jerusalem: Hartman/Carmel, 2005).

[95] *Kelim Shevurim: Torah ve-Tziyonut-Datit be-Sevivah Postmodernit*, ed. Odeyah Tzurieli (Efrat: Yeshivat Siach Yitzhak, 2004). A similar position is taken by Daniel Shalit—see his *Sefer ha-Kanyon* (Kedumim: Bet-El Publishers 2005). See also Cahana, "In Which Direction is the Wind Blowing?" (n. 24 above, 24-26, 30-31) for a discussion of these two appropriations of postmodernism in the service of religion. (See also my corrections to Cahana's account of my position [ibid, 15, 27-30] in *Akdamot* 21).

the title—that the deconstructive features of postmodernism embody the paradigmatic kabbalistic image of the primordial breaking of the vessels of the original *sefirot*, following upon the act of *tsimtsum*: every constructive effort must be preceded by a nihilistic act. Deconstruction is a necessary preamble, paving the way to a higher *tikkun*, and to the rebuilding of a redeemed world.[96] But (as Shagar would have been the first to admit), if this unexpected expression of enchantment with postmodernism is to fulfill its promise, it must also be fortified by the discipline of immersion in the rich legacy of tradition and the rigorous cultural-linguistic construct that it provides for formulating our religious beliefs. At the same time, this construct will remain a lifeless shell if unaccompanied by the background spark of fundamental metaphysical conviction that has always ignited the long-standing devotion and passion marking our identity as creatures of faith.

---

[96] Shagar, ibid., 23-26, 122.

Faith in the Face of Bereavement and Loss: Coping with the Question of Evil in the World

Gili Zivan

This essay has been written on the assumption that many believers today feel a growing discomfort regarding the methods proposed by Jewish tradition for dealing with evil, suffering, and affliction in our world. These believers are not satisfied, in contrast to previous generations, with the classic answers to the question of "Why?" that arises naturally with the arrival of the news of an awful disaster, an unexpected death, or the outbreak of an incurable disease.

Fundamental trust in a good and beneficent God leads the believer to the question that religious philosophy calls "the question of theodicy," namely, the question of the justice of God's deeds. The ancient question, "Why does the way of the wicked prosper?" (Jeremiah 12:1), or "How is it possible that the righteous should suffer and the wicked should prosper?," gives no rest to the believer, who struggles all his life to discern a good and just divine order in the world. The assumption that the goodness of God cannot allow wrongs and torments to befall the innocent has produced many responses, with the underlying basis common to all of them being the assumption that suffering, torments, and evil are only apparent; one who adopts a deeper, more penetrating perspective—if you will, a more sublime and divine viewpoint—will be able to solve the problem of theodicy and be freed from the distress that human reality confronts him with, and so restore a beneficent order to the world and divine justice to God.

It seems that many believers today, including those who are not professional philosophers, feel that they can no longer "live with" the justifications that have been offered in the past for God's deeds—justifications that are in general metaphysical and try to prove that evil in the world is only apparent, and that really, from God's perspective, this is not the way things are. Jewish tradition has offered several different responses to the question, "Why do the righteous suffer?"[1] For example, sources speak of a hidden sin, the retribution for which comes due only now; of trials through which God is testing his chosen ones; of a descent for the purpose of ascent; of suffering in this world and happiness in the world to come; of the one saint who atones for the entire community, etc.[2]

Over against this classic faith position, I wish to present those believers who are aware of the limits of human understanding and the unbridgeable gap between the divine and the human.[3] These figures have difficulty continuing to accept responses such as those mentioned. They regard them as "speculative philosophical thought" or "empty casuistry," as R. Joseph B. Soloveitchik terms them, and they identify with his frank words in his essay, "On Mental Health,"[4] in which he admits that he for one cannot continue to use answers of this kind when he in his capacity as a community rabbi comes to console mourners:

> I can state with all candor that I personally have not been too successful in my attempts to spell out this metaphysic in terms meaningful to the distraught individual who floats aimlessly in

---

[1] This formulation of the problem of theodicy is found in the midrash collection *Tanna d'Bei Eliahu Zuta*. See, for example, ch. 6.

[2] See, for example, the discussion in the Babylonian Talmud, Berakhot 5a-b; Kiddushin 40b; Hullin 142a; or Song of Songs Rabba, parasha 35. Philosophical commentary throughout the generations has for the most part continued along these lines of thought.

[3] See Avi Sagi, "Criticism of Theodicy: From Metaphysics to Actuality," in *The Challenge of the Return to Tradition* (Tel-Aviv: The Shalom Hartman Institute, The Faculty of Law, Bar-Ilan University, Hakibbutz Hameuchad, 2003), 409 (Hebrew).

[4] The lecture "Mental Health and Halakha: Judaism in the Perspective of Halakha" was given by R. Soloveitchik on December 6, 1961, in the framework of a conference on religion and mental health that was sponsored by the National Institute for Mental Health, in the USA. The essay was translated into Hebrew under the title, "On Mental Health," and published in a collection of essays by Rabbi J. D. Soloveitchik, *Adam v'Olamo* (Jerusalem: Eliner, 1998), 249-278. In 1999, the essay was published in English by Rabbi Zigler, D. Shatz, and J.B. Wollosky, under the title, "A Halakhic Approach to Suffering," *The Torah U-Madda Journal* 8 (1999): 3-24.

all-encompassing blackness, like a withered leaf on a dark autumnal night tossed by wind and rain. I tried but failed, I think, miserably, like the friends of Job.[5]

A religious sensibility that aims to be satisfied with human reality and does not believe in man's ability to exit from humanity and finitude will try to avoid as much as possible giving religious-metaphysical explanations to natural events. Such a sensibility will see in answers of the classical type the fruit of despair and the sin of human pride that is expressed in the presumption that we can know God's will and plan. At the very least, such answers are an unsatisfying answer to a loved one's sufferings, or to the nagging question "Why him/her (and not someone else)?" that accompanies the painful longings for someone who is no longer with us.

The question of the meaning of suffering, and the question of theodicy that usually accompanies it, constitute a kind of "litmus test" for the believer who is trying to avoid metaphysical explanations. This is because the deep human need for an all-inclusive explanation, metaphysical or theological, gets stronger in the face of enduring pain and incomprehensible suffering. As David Hartman writes, "Others would find life unbearably chaotic if they could not believe that suffering, tragedy, and death were part of God's plan for the world."[6] Yeshayahu Leibowitz explains the suffering of Job in a similar manner: "Job's own suffering is no longer the main thrust of his complaint, but rather his inability to understand the meaning of this suffering."[7] If we cannot depend upon a metaphysical explanation, or on "a deeper level" (as Isaiah Berlin expresses it), a level on which "the true order" exists, we are faced with pointless and meaningless suffering that is difficult to bear.

Clifford Geertz[8] lists three situations in which human beings tend to discover a strong need for an all-encompassing picture. In these three areas, "chaos," as he puts it, is particularly threatening: 1) when man

---

[5] Soloveitchik, "On Mental Health," 13 (English edition); 263 (Hebrew edition).
[6] David Hartman, *A Living Covenant* (New-York: Free Press, 1985), 202.
[7] Yeshayahu Leibowitz, *Faith, History and Values* (Jerusalem: Akademon, 1982), 22 (Hebrew).
[8] Clifford Geertz, *The Interpretation of Cultures* (New York: Basic Books, 1973), 100.

reaches the limits of his analytic capacities; that is, when we experience an ongoing, powerful experience of what Geertz calls "an embarrassment of understanding"; 2) when man reaches the limits of his powers of endurance; i.e., when we experience a sustained and powerful experience of uninterpretable suffering; 3) when man reaches the limits of his moral insight and senses a feeling of intractable ethical paradox ("the suffering of the righteous"). We have before us therefore a triple challenge that faces every religion and with which every religion must try to cope.

If so, the main difficulty with which the religious thinker must contend in coming to deal with the question of suffering and evil is not the pain or sadness that suffering brings with it, but rather with the fact that it is incomprehensible, uninterpretable, and therefore also unjust. As Geertz says,

> As a religious problem, the problem of suffering is, paradoxically, not how to avoid suffering but how to suffer, how to make of physical pain, personal loss, worldly defeat, or the helpless contemplation of others' agony something bearable, supportable—something, as we say, sufferable.[9]

As mentioned, in monotheistic religions in which God is conceived of as the source of everything, including equally the source of both evil and good, the question of theodicy comes up unavoidably in this context. Not only does physical or psychological pain seek its meaning in an all-encompassing and inclusive explanation, but indeed the question of "the suffering of the righteous" intensifies the suffering of the believer. The problem of suffering and the problem of evil, says Geertz, come together into one problem: the problem of interpretability:

> ... the dumb senselessness of intense or inexorable pain, and the enigmatic unaccountability of gross iniquity all raise the uncomfortable suspicion that perhaps the world, and hence man's life in the world, has no genuine order at all—no empirical regularity, no emotional form, no moral coherence.[10]

---

[9] Ibid., 104.
[10] Ibid., 108. See also 106.

David Hartman continues this line of thought. In his discussion of "The Yemen Letter," by Maimonides, Hartman points out Maimonides' sensitivity to the distress of the suffering community, and according to him, this sensitivity is what led Maimonides to locate the immediate experience of the suffering of the community that is set within a broad context as part of a "comprehensive plan," or part of a deep drama that encompasses the whole of human history." In his words,

> One of the characteristics of suffering, which makes it intolerable, is its arbitrariness. Sometimes suffering is connected not only to physical afflictions, but also to insane fear, which derives from the sense the sufferer has that his fate is subject to blind, irrational forces. It is possible to endure this imposing dimension of fear connected to suffering, if the sufferer is convinced that at the bottom of things there exists a meaningful purpose that gives meaning and order to his world.[11]

Religion tries to respond to this existential distress in different ways. One way is, as mentioned, the integration of specific suffering into a transcendent theological explanation, as part of a religious, metaphysical, "meta-narrative," in which suffering receives meaning.[12] In this metaphysical explanation, for the most part we sketch a theory that can

---

[11] David Hartman, *Leadership in Times of Crisis: On the Letters of Maimonides* (Tel-Aviv: Hakibbutz Hameuchad, 1989), 98 (Hebrew).

[12] The orientation that struggles for a transcendental meaning, and tries to find a justification for the suffering of the righteous, has been expressed by thinkers throughout the history of the Jewish tradition. Among contemporary scholars, Eliezer Schweid has given comprehensive expression to this, claiming in his book, *To Say that God is Just: The Righteousness of God in Jewish Thought from the Period of the Bible to Spinoza* (Bat Yam: Tag, 1994) (Hebrew), that the question of the righteousness of God is the foundational question upon which the whole of Jewish tradition from the Bible to contemporary times turns. Yehuda Liebes criticizes Schweid precisely with regard to this issue ("Need a Justification for God be Sought?", *HaAretz*, Musaf Tarbut ve-Sifrut, Erev Rosh Hashanah, 1995) [Hebrew]. In his view, the motive for Schweid's reading the traditional texts in the above-mentioned manner lies in the trauma of the Shoah. The question of theodicy in and of itself is missing from many sources, and furthermore, the God pictured in various biblical, midrashic, and kabbalistic sources is a totalistic personality, who demands complete devotion that needs no justification (I am grateful to Yoske Achituv, who called my attention to Liebes' critique).

include the existence of suffering. On the one hand it can affirm, "or at least accept the fact that ignorance, pain and injustice are unavoidable elements of human existence, but at the same time, on the other hand, it can deny that this irrationality characterizes the world as a whole."[13]

The question of meaning in the religious and philosophical sense returns in all its power after the Shoah. In the formulation of Emmanuel Levinas: "What is the meaning of the suffering of the innocent? Does it not bear witness to a world without God, a universe in which man is the sole standard for good and evil? The simplest answer, the most widespread, will be the choice of atheism."[14]

Isaiah Berlin in many places in his books also insists upon the powerful human need for a transcendent explanation, and he sees in it one of the central motives for the development of metaphysical and teleological theories that provide order and rationality on the level of the "whole":

> For the teleological thinker all apparent disorder, inexplicable disaster, gratuitous suffering, unintelligible concatenations or random event, are due not to mature of things but to our failure to discover their purpose. Everything that seems useless, discordant, mean, ugly, vicious, distorted, is needed, if we but knew it, for the harmony of the whole which only the Creator of the world, or the world itself (if it could become wholly aware of itself and its goals) can know.[15]

In light of these remarks, I wish to explore now the positions of several twentieth-century Jewish thinkers—R. Joseph B. Soloveitchik, Emmanuel Levinas, Yeshayahu Leibowitz, Eliezer Goldman, and David Hartman—who offer a different way of coping with this issue, in contrast to the traditional way. What interpretation do they propose, and does suffering have any meaning at all? Who can (or needs to, or is permitted to) give meaning to human suffering, and what is the place of metaphysical assumptions in this context? What is the meaning of religious faith for those thinkers who negate the direct connection between

---

[13] Hartman, *Leadership in Times of Crisis*, 108.
[14] Emmanuel Levinas, "To Love the Torah More than God," in Zvi Kolitz, *Yosl Rakover Talks to God* (Tel-Aviv: Ministry of Defense, 2000), 68-69.
[15] Isaiah Berlin, *Four Essays on Liberty* (New-York: Oxford Uni. Press, 1969), 55.

God and man, and who refuse to formulate relationships of cause and effect between the deeds of human beings and the response of God?

I will supplement the words of these thinkers with the testimony, personal and extremely moving in its powerful honesty, of Professor Ariel Rozen-Zvi—"a believer without illusions"[16]—who adds his own interpretation to the sufferings that befell him a few months before his death from cancer.

1. Rabbi Joseph B. Soloveitchik

Let us begin our study with the thought of R. Soloveitchik, who devoted two essays to coping with the meaning of suffering, on both the level of individual life and that of the national-collective: "Kol Dodi Dofek"[17] and "On Mental Health." Soloveitchik's point of departure is the recognition of the existence of suffering in the world. He does not try to obscure the reality of evil in the world by giving it a metaphysical meaning that would shed a new light on human experience:

> Judaism, with its realistic approach to human beings and their place within reality, understands that evil cannot be obscured and hidden.... Evil is a fact that is not to be denied. Evil exists. Suffering exists, and there are terrible mortal afflictions in the world. Anyone who wants to deceive himself by turning a blind eye to the rent in human experience ... is nothing other than a fool misled by hallucinations.[18]

---

[16] The expression "a believer without illusions" is my paraphrase of a concept that Professor Eliezer Goldman coined in his essay "On Faith Without Illusion," op. cit., *Researches and Examinations*, ed. Avi Sagi and Dani Statman (Jerusalem and Ein Zurim: Magnes, 1997), 361-371 (Hebrew). In this essay, Goldman develops a systematic distinction between two types of religious faith—"illusory faith" and "faith without illusion." Goldman developed this concept following the words of Yeshayahu Leibowitz in various contexts, for example, Y. Leibowitz, *Judaism, the Jewish People and the State of Israel* (Jerusalem and Tel-Aviv: Schocken Publishing House, 1979), 24 (Hebrew). For an analysis of these two kinds of faith, see Sagi, "Criticism of Theodicy," 409-412.

[17] The lecture, "Kol Dodi Dofek," was given on Israel Independence Day 1957 and published in 1965 in the collection *Man of Faith* (Jerusalem: Mossad Harav Kook, 1975), 67 (Hebrew). This will be referred to in the rest of this chapter as "Kol Dodi Dofek."

[18] "Kol Dodi Dofek," 67.

Since "it is impossible to overcome the monstrosity of evil through speculative philosophical thought,"[19] human beings must abandon these barren theoretical attempts, and try to derive the utmost from the disaster. A person must ask himself not why sufferings have come upon him, but rather what they obligate him to do, "because it is a crime for the sufferer to condemn his pains to oblivion and to be left without meaning and purpose."[20] The question of evil changes from a question directed towards God to an existential challenge placed before the believer, and he is required to translate his suffering into practical norms. In Soloveitchik's words,

> I am asking a simple question: What should the sufferer do to live with his suffering? On this level, the emphasis is shifted from the dimensions of cause and purpose ... to the practical dimension. The problem is now formulated in the language of simple Jewish law, and turns in a roundabout way into a day-to-day task. The real question is, What do sufferings obligate man to do? ... We do not wonder about the mysterious ways of God, rather we ponder the way upon which human beings should walk when afflictions befall him or her. We ask not for the cause of evil and not for its purpose, but rather for its correction and its sublimation; how should a person **behave** in a time of trouble? What should a person **do**, and so not collapse in his suffering?[21]

The question of cause and purpose that demands a religious-metaphysical explanation is thus exchanged for a practical question, and the religious meaning of human suffering is shifted from the theological level to the human, to the interpretation and activity of the believer.

These initial and general remarks receive a sharper and clearer formulation four years later, in the essay "On Mental Health."[22] Not only is there no place within the practical-realistic *Halakha* that Soloveitchik

---

[19] Ibid.
[20] Ibid., 69.
[21] Ibid., 68. Emphasis here and below is mine.
[22] See above, note 4. For an analysis of this essay, see Avi Sagi, "Rabbi Soloveitchik, Jewish Thought in Modern Form," in his *Faith in Changing Times: On the Thought of Rabbi J. D. Soloveitchik* (Jerusalem and Ein Zurim: Eliner Books and Yaacov Herzog Center, 1996), 461-500 (Hebrew). For a specific discussion of Soloveitchik's ways of dealing with the meaning of evil in the world, see in particular 484-485, and see too Sagi, "Criticism of Theodicy," 424-429.

offers for the illusion that metaphysical solutions provide, but according to his view, it is possible to cope with evil only by means of human deeds, by struggling against evil.

In this essay, Soloveitchik distinguishes between "thematic *Halakha*" and "topical *Halakha*."[23] Thematic *Halakha* strives to provide metaphysical answers, and thus tries to dispel the reality of evil by means of "the metaphysics of evil" and the idealization of death. By contrast, topical *Halakha* expresses the connection of the *Halakha* to the concrete realities of time and place. In concrete human reality, the acknowledgement of evil is essential. However, Soloveitchik goes on to claim, this recognition does not mean surrender and acclimation to suffering, but rather functions as a means of struggling with it. And so he writes,

> The topical Halakhah could not accept the thematic metaphysic which tends to gloss over the absurdity of evil, and it did not engage in the building of a magnificent philosophical facade to shut out the ugly sights of an inadequate existence. Realism and individualism, ineradicably ingrained in the very essence of the topical Halakhah, prevented it from casting off the burden of the awareness of evil. [...] The topical Halakhah is an open-eyed, tough observer of things and events and, instead of indulging in a speculative metaphysic, acknowledged boldly both the reality of evil and its irrationality, its absurdity. [...] In short, the practical Halakhah did not and could not evolve a metaphysic of suffering. It simply refused. It was not eager to find the rational of evil and to convert the negation into an affirmation. [...] The topical Halakhah has evolved an *ethic* of suffering instead of a *metaphysic* of suffering. [...] The metaphysic seeks to justify evil or deny its reality. The ethic of suffering seeks the transformation of an alien *factum* which one encounters into an *actus* in which one engages, the succumbing to an overwhelming force into an experience impregnated with directedness and sense.[24]

According to Soloveitchik, halakhic ethics is based upon several claims. First, "Evil indeed exists and it is unacceptable.... The world in which we live is not free of shortcomings and defects, and as a result of them, there is an eternal tear between human interests and the fixed natural

---

[23] The concept of "topical *Halakha*" is derived from the Greek word for "place"—*topos*—and it expresses the way of life of the believer embodied in concrete, earthly commandments.

[24] Soloveitchik, "A Halakhic Approach to Suffering," 13-15.

order. In other words, the reality of evil is not to be doubted." Secondly, "it is forbidden to acquiesce with evil or to make one's peace with it." Therefore, the *Halakha* demands that human beings **"actively oppose evil,** using all the means that God placed at their disposal."[25]

In this essay, Soloveitchik does not make do with the answer that reconciles itself to suffering and gives the experience of suffering human meaning; rather he emphasizes the active religious imperative "to actively oppose evil." In contrast to Camus,[26] he does not conceive of active opposition to evil as anti-religious. The opposite is the case: the struggle against evil is conceived of by Soloveitchik as a religious challenge, as a *mitzva*. This struggle does not need to spring from the assumption that the world in which evil exists is not God's world. Such a claim is among the metaphysical claims that do not contribute to coping with evil and suffering in the world. The only possible way of coping is the practical, which works to find the necessary serum for the cure, for diminishing the number of work accidents and road accidents by finding technological solutions, etc. Soloveitchik affirms the approach that sympathizes with the *Halakha* of medicine and doctors and determines:

> To the Halakhah, it was obvious, apodictic, simple. "*Ve-rappo yerappe*, he shall surely be healed," says the Torah (Ex. 21:19). From here we learn that the physician should cure and heal (*Berakot* 60a). Man should actively interfere with evil. Man is summoned by God to combat evil, to fight evil, and to try to eliminate it as much as possible.[27]

Apparently, Soloveitchik identifies with existentialist approaches that reject the metaphysical ways of dealing with the question of evil, and is

---

[25] Ibid.

[26] Sagi has already noted in a number of places the closeness and distance between R. Soloveitchik's approach to suffering and that of Albert Camus. See Sagi, "Criticism of Theodicy," 428-429. It seems that the position attributed to doctor Rieux in the book *The Plague*, which does not rely on religious faith, is very close to that which Soloveitchik presents. This position, which is expressed in an uncompromising struggle against sickness and suffering, sees in attempts to give suffering a theological-metaphysical explanation a dangerous position that leads to submission and passivity, which characterizes Father Paneloux. See Albert Camus, *The Plague*, trans. Stuart Gilbert (New York: Modern Library College Editions, 1948), 116-118; 196-197.

[27] Soloveitchik, "A Halakhic Approach to Suffering," 15.

committed to ways of coping that come about through active struggle against suffering and the personal meaning that the individual gives to it. However, a closer look shows that this is not exactly so.

First, it should be noted that Soloveitchik is not consistent in what he says about "topical *Halakha*" in relation to historical events. If in his discussion on the suffering individual Soloveitchik tries to renounce any metaphysical theory, his discussion of national events in "Kol Dodi Dofek" (1957) differs from his declarations in his 1961 essay, "On Mental Health." It seems that when he discusses the meaning of the establishment of the State of Israel, in the 1957 essay he shifts the discussion from the normative level to that of the metaphysical, and tries to discover the word of God and His will in historical national events. The decision of the United Nations on the division of the Land of Israel, the victory of the small Israeli army over the forces of the Arab states, etc.—all these, in his view, are "knockings of the beloved" (God) on the door of "the Shulamit" (the community of Israel). He calls to diaspora Jews to respond to the beckoning of the lover and immigrate to Israel, and not miss the metaphysical meaning of historical events. The Shoah too is interpreted in various places in traditional metaphysical terms. Although it cannot be explained, still it is termed a period of "the hiding of the face" of God, in contrast to the establishment of the State of Israel, which reflects the return of God to historical providence.[28] In the transition from the level of the individual to the national level, Soloveitchik returns to speak in metaphysical terms, and points to the processes of Divine Providence in history.

Secondly, even his words about the meaning of evil for the individual are not consistent in relation to metaphysical explanations. Although in a discussion of the halakhic meaning of evil in "Kol Dodi Dofek"

---

[28] See "Kol Dodi Dofek," 77-87. Elsewhere he writes, "The Shoah is a phenomenon of 'hiding the face.' We cannot explain the Holocaust but we can, at least, classify it theologically, characterize it, even if we have no answer to the question 'why?' The unbounded horrors represented the *tohuvavohu* anarchy of the pre-*yetzirah* state. This is how the world appears when God's moderating surveillance is suspended. The State of Israel, however, reflects God's return to active providence, the termination of *Hester Panim* [Hiding the Face]." Avraham Beit-Din, ed., *Reflections of the Rav* (Jerusalem: W.Z.O. Torah Education Department, 1979), 37. Hebrew edition (Jerusalem: W.Z.O. Torha Education Department, 1974), 37.

Soloveitchik asks, "What is the sufferer to do in order to live with his suffering?," still it seems that in his response he returns to the accepted metaphysical linguistic formulas that describe suffering as purposeful:

> The halakhic response to this question is very simple. Afflictions come in order to elevate man, to purify his spirit and consecrate it, to clear his mind . . . to refine his soul and to expand the horizon of his life. The general principle of the matter of suffering – its role is to repair that which is flawed in the human personality.[29]

Admittedly, it is possible to read this passage too as one that gives human meaning to suffering, without presuming to know God's intention, but it seems to me that the formula, "Afflictions come in order to ...," or "the role of suffering is to repair ...," does not mesh well with such an attempt, and I agree with Avi Sagi, who points out, "Although the question is phrased in practical terms, the answer is given in metaphysical-teleological terms."[30] Soloveitchik's previous programmatic statement, which tries to shift the discussion from the level of causation and teleology to the practical level, is not fully realized.

In Soloveitchik's words, the classical assumption is that "somewhere" the formula exists that explains, that gives meaning to suffering and evil, but that "man's ability to understand is always limited and handicapped, and he only sees isolated segments.... It is impossible for him to penetrate the furnace of evil."[31] If we were able, so to speak, to look at the world from the viewpoint of God, we would understand the meaning of suffering and afflictions and be able to justify the ways of God. But what is the meaning of this statement? And can human beings ever depart from their partial, narrow point of view, and adopt for themselves the "viewpoint of God"?

Statements like these, which express Soloveitchik's attempt not to lose completely the classical formulation of the problem of evil, are found also in "On Mental Health." Further study of this essay shows that in spite of Soloveitchik's personal difficulties as a modern person in

---

[29] "Kol Dodi Dofek," 68.
[30] Avi Sagi, "Judaism as Interpretation: Studies in the Thought of Goldman," *Daat* 41 (1998): 62 (Hebrew).
[31] "Kol Dodi Dofek," 67.

internalizing the thematic *Halakha*, he does not reject it entirely, and he adheres to Jewish tradition and its statements mentioned above despite his criticism.

Furthermore, in spite of the rigorous distinction between the orientation that seeks to provide a metaphysical explanation for evil ("the thematic *Halakha*") and the orientation embodied in the practical *Halakha*, which acknowledges the reality of evil and conducts a sober struggle against it with the human tools available to it (the "topical *Halakha*"), the metaphysical aspect still does not disappear from the latter. Soloveitchik does not absolutely abandon the reliance on eschatological redemption, and so he claims in relation to the topical *Halakha*:

> The third proposition is faith.[32] If man loses a battle in a war, the topical Halakhah has always believed, based on an eschatological vision, that at some future date, some distant date, evil be overcome, evil will disappear; "*Bila ha-mavet lanezah u-mahah Hashem dim'ah me'al kol panim*," "He will swallow up death for ever, and the Lord God will wipe off the tears from all faces" (Isa. 25:8) Yes, it is long war; it is a long struggle.[33]

How are we to understand these words? How is the third argument brought here to be integrated with the first two arguments that we presented above? Is not the faith in eschatological consolation at the eradication of evil by God likely to weaken the power to struggle against

---

[32] The first two arguments in relation to "the topical *halakha*" are those presented above: 1) the argument with regard to the existence of evil, and 2) the argument with regard to the religious obligation to fight against it. The third argument is as stated here, eschatological faith, and the fourth argument is that "If man loses a battle from time to time and evil triumphs over him, he must bear defeat with dignity and humility" ("A Halakhic Approach to Suffering,' 16). The intention is not that man must reconcile himself to his suffering with stoic acceptance, but rather that he must bear it with dignity. The ability to endure evil with dignity derives according to Soloveitchik from the special halakhic dialectic that educates man to subdue and adapt, to win and lose, as a movement internal to the experience of the *Halakha*. See ibid, 16-17; and my essay, "The Religious Experience according to Rabbi Soloveitchik," in Sagi, *Faith in Changing Times*, 219-248.

[33] "A Halakhic Approach to Suffering," 16.

actual evil? Of course, it is possible to see in this argument a general faith in a better future, a faith that is so weak and indistinct that in practice it is not likely to influence the life of the believer and the way he or she conducts it. But if so, why does Soloveitchik mention it? Perhaps in order to preserve the conventional linguistic idiom of the religious world? Or perhaps in order to offer a general consolation in a place where all hope has run out? It is possible that the process of preferring the language of the topical *Halakha*, necessary to the ethics of suffering, over the language of the thematic *Halakha*, necessary to the metaphysics of suffering, was so revolutionary that in an intuitive way he had to restrain the dramatic transfer of responsibility "from God to man" and restore to its traditional place the pristine faith in a future world in which all is good.

To summarize: Soloveitchik's coping with the meaning of evil exposes two simultaneous voices: an initial, primary voice explicitly renounces the traditional form of thinking, which relies upon metaphysical-theological assumptions, and provides a new way of coping with afflictions and evil by means of personal and social, halakhic and scientific action; and a secondary voice that returns in several places to make use of traditional formulations justifying the ways of God, formulations that seek to provide a religious-metaphysical explanation for events, or that hint at an eschatological cure in the end of days.

2. David Hartman

David Hartman, a student of R. Soloveitchik, criticizes the conception of his teacher at precisely this point. He emphasizes over and over again his reservations with regard to Soloveitchik's approach, which despite his statements to the contrary has not freed itself completely from the religious-metaphysical approach:

> Although Maimonides and Soloveitchik evidently gave up hope of making sense of God's justice, their explanation of human history still operates within this model. While Soloveitchik does not suppose that we shall ever achieve a full rational comprehension of God's actions in history, he does believe that, in principle, were we able to look at the world from God's vantage point, we would understand how all of human suffering is

compatible with the belief in God as a loving Creator and just Lord of History. He suggests that we respond to suffering ... by becoming more sensitive, loving, and caring toward other human beings.... Nonetheless, believing in principle that events in history are the carriers of God's will, Soloveitchik looks forward to the eschatological moment of unity between nature and history.[34]

According to Hartman, thinkers who hold that natural and historical events must reflect a personal, just God are forced into dubious explanations by their desire to explain every event in human life according to a rational, all-encompassing paradigm. On the other hand, seeing suffering as a natural and necessary part of human life avoids the need to explain everything that happens as an expression of the judgment of God: against all attempts to maintain the righteousness of God by blurring it stands the position that recognizes the idea of the covenant between God and man. This covenant is expressed in the fulfillment of commandments by human beings, and it includes two components: man's commitment to the command of God, and his freedom and human responsibility. The believer does not seek to cancel out our human sense of justice; rather he chooses the covenant despite the fact that the world is not entirely comprehensible to him. This world is one that "proceeds according to its own rules," and therefore what happens in it is neutral from an ethical and religious perspective.[35]

> I therefore do not accept that all of history embodies an inscrutable form of divine justice ... it is "foolish" to imagine that one could be human and yet not be vulnerable to death and suffering. **Underserved suffering is a permanent possibility of life in this universe.** In "pursuing its normal course," the world functions according to its own **morally neutral pattern**. It is therefore an error to try to explain such a world *in toto* by means of

---

[34] Hartman, *A Living Covenant*, 267-268. It is important to note that the book in which this criticism of Soloveitchik appears was published before the publication of the essay "On Mental Health," in which Soloveitchik presents an almost complete analysis of metaphysical conceptions.

[35] For more on the principle of the covenant in the thought of Hartman, see Sagi, "Criticism of Theodicy," 432-433.

human ethical categories. Not everything that occurs in human history and nature expresses the moral judgment of a personal God. Nor does the covenant of *mitzvah* offer a worldview that enables everything that occurs in the world to be placed within a larger, rational moral scheme—not now and equally not in an eschatological future.[36]

A good number of the chapters of the book *A Living Covenant* are devoted to an examination of the various rabbinic responses to the question of evil and theodicy. Hartman sets before the reader the innovative ways that the sages proposed to cope with this issue. However, he argues, we do not see in rabbinic literature a comprehensive and radical revolution in relation to the biblical concept of reward and punishment, and yet new ways of coping with the question of suffering are already visible, which do not necessarily see in personal and national pain a sign of heavenly punishment. Hartman himself admits that these antimetaphysical conceptions, which are found in rabbinic literature and which were developed by Maimonides, constitute for him a convenient foundation on which to ground a concept based upon the principle, "the world pursues its own course." He develops this principle and sees in it a foundation for his own religious conception.[37] Therefore, he asserts, the believer who acknowledges his own finitude and the "way of the world" is not to see in the suffering that befalls him the punishing hand of God: "Suffering and human tragedy are not signs of divine rejection

---

[36] *A living Covenant* 268.

[37] The principle "the world pursues its own course" first appears in the Babylonian Talmud (Avodah Zarah 54b) in a *beraita* that raises questions about the ways God manages the world. For example, the question is asked there about a man who steals a measure of wheat and sows it in the ground—would it not be right for it not to sprout? And the Gemara answers, "but the world pursues its natural course, and as for the fools who act wrongly, they will have to render an account." The principle assumes that the laws of nature do not depend upon good and evil, on permitted and forbidden, but rather that they operate according to an internal regularity. The principle is adopted by Maimonides, who developed it in relation to God's providence in the world, and it reached a maximal development in the thought of Leibowitz, Goldman, and Hartman. See below for an analysis of Yeshayahu Leibowitz's position with regard to this principle.

or punishment."[38] Like Soloveitchik before him, who argued that "there is an eternal rupture between human interests and the fixed orders of nature," which results in the fact that "the reality of evil is undeniable," Hartman declares unequivocally that "As finitude is willed by God, death need not be viewed as punishment for sin."[39]

The personal link between human beings and God is not expressed, according to Hartman, in personal providence—a surveillance for reward or punishment according to a person's deeds; rather it is expressed by the acceptance of the yoke of the commandments, which expresses the commitment to the Sinai covenant. In his words, "God is present as personal reality through the hearing of *mitzvoth*."[40] On this basis, we understand that someone who says "Blessed be the True Judge" upon hearing evil tidings "does not imply that it should be possible to explain to the mourner why the death of a beloved parent or child was necessary to the divine plan and therefore ultimately rational and just.... Rather, the benediction can be seen as a means of affirming one's determination to continue to live by the covenant despite every disappointed expectation.... Not everything needs to be explicable, not even in principle, in order to live with faith in the covenant. The world pursuing its normal course is accepted as the world in which it is given us to live our short life, and in which we must decide either to live or not to live by the covenant of Torah."[41]

Hartman asks the believer not to look to faith for an ultimate explanation for suffering. The choice of a life of faith becomes stronger precisely because it does not provide a metaphysical meta-narrative that solves all puzzling questions of the sufferer. The believer must deal with a world in which everything is not understood, and within this world to serve God. It seems to me that Hartman would agree with this sentence attributed to Leibowitz: "It is also possible to arrive at a fear of heaven from a recognition that the world pursues its normal course."[42]

---

[38] Hartman, *A Living Covenant*, 17.
[39] Ibid., 259.
[40] Ibid., 17.
[41] Ibid., 268-269.
[42] Goldman says that he heard Leibowitz formulate this acknowledgement orally. See Goldman, "On Faith without Illusion," 249.

3. Yeshayahu Leibowitz

As is well-known, the Maimonidean conception of "the world pursues its normal course" was adopted to the utmost by Yeshayahu Leibowitz. Historical and natural phenomena do not hold ethical, religious, or any other kind of meaning in and of themselves. Therefore illnesses, natural disasters, accidents, deaths, and all other kinds of tragedy and suffering that befall human beings do not have religious meaning. Suffering, like good health, childbirth, and success, are part of natural reality, and therefore they are without any value and meaning.

To this basic Kantian distinction between what exists and what is valued must be added an important religious distinction that Leibowitz often emphasizes, namely his distinction between "religion for its own sake" and "religion not for its own sake." Faith, which expresses human beings' stance towards God, can be embodied in one of the following ways:

1) The first way reflects the human consciousness that sees itself as standing before God "on the basis of what he (i.e., man) knows or thinks he knows about God's relationship towards him."[43] It is expressed mainly in the believer's expectation of what he is supposed to receive from faith. This is faith "not for its own sake," and in such faith, man serves himself. According to this conception, faith liberates or redeems man from his tormented existence. In Leibowitz's view, this kind of faith embodies the conception of "God for the sake of man."

2) The second way reflects a conception in which the believer does not ask, "What does faith give me?"; rather, he asks, "What am I obligated to give to religion?"[44] According to this conception, at the center of religious faith stands the recognition of human obligation to God.

These two forms of religious faith express two different conceptions of reward and punishment: the first conception ("not for its own sake") nourishes a hope for reward as a consequence of serving God, and fears

---

[43] Yeshayahu Leibowitz, *Five Books of Faith* (Jerusalem: Keter Publishing House, 1995), 12 (Hebrew).
[44] Leibowitz, *Judaism*, 23.

a punishment that comes as a result of refraining from such service; the second conception ("for its own sake") sees a reward in the service of God itself, and punishment is man's being cut off from serving God. Those who maintain the latter position do not expect reward or punishment from God, and therefore they also do not try to interpret historical or natural events as punishment or recompense for the deeds of the individual or the community. This position, which does not acknowledge a direct cause and effect in relations between man and God, of course denies any validity to the traditional questions of the suffering of the righteous and the meaning of suffering.

Leibowitz sets up the two religious responses described above as dichotomous positions, and he confronts them in relation to various issues, as he does, for example, in connection with the faith of Job. Leibowitz sees the figure of Job at the beginning of the Book of Job as an archetype of the kind of faith that holds the first position, of one who suffers and searches for a metaphysical religious meaning to his suffering and cannot understand why God has punished him in his innocence. By contrast, the figure depicted at the end of the book represents a believer of the second kind, who serves God without expectation of reward:

> All his days Job believed in God according to the faith that was widespread among the multitude of believers, who believe in God and accept his service upon themselves as a result of his being a God for their benefit ... but now "the eye of Job has seen" a God whose divinity consists in his own essence, and the world as it actually is constitutes God's providence. This provident surveillance is embodied in natural reality itself; it is not intended to meet Job's needs.... Job understands that he must decide whether to accept belief in God and serve him in the world as it is ... simply because God is God.[45]

Leibowitz intends to see in Judaism a demand for a faith that is "the service of God for its own sake"—religion that does not set up divine reward or punishment as a motivation for serving God, but rather the opposite: the one who serves God "for its own sake" "commits himself

---

[45] Leibowitz, *Faith*, 23-24.

to serving God even though the Holy Blessed One is not revealed in history.... The one who believes in God is obligated to free his religious consciousness from any dependence upon historical events."[46]

Suffering, pain, and afflictions are the currency of the given human world, derived from the natural course of the world, and they do not point to the punishing or redeeming relationship of God to human beings. The individual who chooses to believe in God and to serve Him "in the world as it is," even in the presence of the death of his beloved child, in the presence of suffering and torments, is according to Leibowitz the paradigm of the believer. The test of faith is revealed precisely in moments of pain and disaster such as these.[47]

4. Eliezer Goldman

Professor Eliezer Goldman also deals with the question of the justice of God and the meaning of suffering and evil, although not directly but rather incidentally, as part of a discussion of the question of the meaning of the traditional concept of providence for the contemporary believer. Goldman knew the thought of Soloveitchik and Leibowitz well, and even published essays that dealt with their thought.[48] In his writings, he develops Leibowitz's argument (which Hartman also accepts, as I have shown above) that religious faith cannot supply a causal link between human deeds and God's response, and therefore he repudiates all discussion of theodicy as irrelevant to the contemporary believer.[49]

This argument raises questions about the understanding of traditional texts. The Bible, rabbinic literature, most of the literature of Jewish thought, and the prayerbook all offer completely different

---

[46] Ibid., 61.
[47] On Leibowitz's conception of suffering as a form of religious coping, see Sagi, "Criticism of Theodicy," 417-418.
[48] See, for example, Goldman, "On Faith without Illusion," 225-261. With regard to Leibowitz, it is important to indicate that Goldman sees in him a friend and meaningful dialogue partner in the field of religious thought. See the interview with Avi Sagi, "Religious Language in the Modern World," *Gilayon* (Av 5755): 11 (Hebrew).
[49] For an extended analysis of this topic, see Sagi "Criticism of Theodicy," 409-416.

understandings of relations between God and his faithful. The passage, "And if you obey" (Deuteronomy 11:13-22), which an observant Jew repeats daily in the morning and evening recital of the "Shema," clearly expresses the concept of reward and punishment, which completely contradicts the conception that Leibowitz, Goldman, and Hartman adopt with regard to the role of nature as an agent of God in recompensing human beings according to their deeds.

Goldman is indeed aware of this gap between the conception of faith that he articulates and traditional religious language, and he develops a radical interpretive approach to understanding religious language. According to him, religious language does not employ the language of cause and effect in the sense that the natural and social sciences do. Rather it is a language "of a different kind," a language of meaning. A religious statement does not make a factual claim about the world; rather it seeks to give religious meaning to a series of events. As Goldman says,

> The *halakha* commands us to relate to certain revelations of the natural world that surrounds us or to the historical circumstances in which we live, not only as they appear in reality, but also **from a different perspective**.[50]

To clarify his approach, Goldman explains the words of Maimonides in the *Mishneh Torah*, at the beginning of the Laws of Fasting (1, 3):

> It is a positive commandment from the Torah to cry out and blow trumpet blasts over afflictions that come upon the community ... and this matter is among the means of repentance ... but if they do not cry out and do not blow trumpet blasts, but rather say that this event befell us as a natural result of the world's course ... this is a cruel approach and causes people to adhere to their wicked ways.

In response, Goldman says that according to Maimonides' interpretation of the concept of providence, he means to say that we are commanded to see suffering as a **catalyst** for repentance.

---

[50] Goldman, "On Faith without Illusion," 356.

> We should see suffering as a **sign** that indicates our need to examine our deeds, to repent.... A Jew who experiences a tragedy must think about ... how he should connect the disaster to his own deeds. The tragedy is a catalyst to bring him to examine his deeds.... We are commanded to relate to events from a certain perspective. We do not have here a **replacement** for a causal conception, but rather **a completely different conception that is not causal and does not intend to compete with natural causality.**[51]

The religious meaning attributed by the *Halakha* to tragedy or joy does not therefore intend to describe the world "as it really is," and does not try to expose the hidden hand concealed behind historical events, but rather presents a religious world of meanings, in addition to the world of "natural causes." And so in the introduction to his book Goldman describes the idea that he develops in his essay "On Providence":

> In a lecture on providence, I raised the possibility that the meaning of a religious statement could be a signal to take a position. **Afflictions that befall someone must serve as motivation for repentance; joyful events obligate praise and thanksgiving. A religious statement is nothing other than a hidden normative demand.**[52]

It follows that rain that does not fall in its season, a tragedy that befalls one as a result of illness or disability, or the death of a relative are the result of natural laws that operate on their own account, as reflected in the saying, "the world pursues its natural course." But Jewish religious tradition has chosen not to leave these tragic events without normative meaning, and it has transformed them into catalysts for the religious and ethical development of the individual and the community. As formulated by Soloveitchik (who as mentioned shifts the question of cause and purpose [Why has this suffering come upon me?] to the issue of responsibility): "The real question is what does suffering obligate man to do." This is the task of turning fate (a blow that lands upon someone "innocent of wrongdoing" or a blessing that someone receives "through

---

[51] Ibid., 356-357.
[52] Ibid., 11.

no merit of his own") into destiny. This is the task of turning "living by force, confusion and silence—into living filled with free will, imagination and initiative."[53]

Goldman expands Soloveitchik's approach and turns it into a principled position that also shapes his interpretation of canonical texts. In his mind, religious statements, biblical or rabbinic, as descriptions of the evolution of this or that sequence of cause and effect, are nothing other than practical halakhic demands addressed to human beings that teach us how to respond to natural events and what meaning to attribute to them.

Maimonides, according to this interpretation, does not try to get human beings to see sufferings that befall them as punishments for a specific sin; rather, he tries not to let suffering "get lost." That is, he tries not to leave them bereft of normative meaning, but rather to derive from suffering the capacity of the individual and the community for repair and correction. Therefore, someone who does not turn suffering into a motive for self-correction and improvement loses the opportunity for positive change. In religious language, he or she loses the opportunity for repentance. In this light, Maimonides' words become clear where he summarizes this position and terms it "a cruel way" that causes people to adhere to their wicked ways.

This demand is formulated by Soloveitchik in the sharpest terms:

> Woe to a person if suffering does not bring him to a spiritual crisis, and his soul rather remains paralyzed and bereft of forgiveness! Woe to the sufferer if his soul does not become energized by the fire of suffering,… when pains wander in the space of the world like mute forces without purpose. A powerful indictment is brought against the person **who loses his suffering**.[54]

In order to understand the transformation that Goldman seeks to bring about in our understanding of the meaning of religious language, we must understand the distinction he makes between religious language and scientific language. In his essay "Religious Statements and Scientific Statements,"[55] Goldman insists on a principled, unbridgeable

---

[53] Soloveitchik, "Kol Dodi Dofek," 67.
[54] Ibid., 70.
[55] See Goldman, "On Faith without Illusion," 340-345.

gap between these two language games.[56] One of the characteristics of religious statements is that, unlike a scientific statement or a factual expression, a religious statement always remains incomprehensible in its literal sense. So for Goldman, the statement, "When God began to create the heavens and the earth," is patently incomprehensible. The subject of the sentence, God, cannot be understood on the basis of human thinking; the predicate, too, "began to create," attributed to God, we cannot understand, not only because of the fact that its verb "to create"—*bara'*—expresses creation "out of nothing," which is beyond human capacity, but also because neither could a different verb be understood by a reader, because it is attributed to an unknowable God. If so, what is the meaning of religious statements? Their meaning is not the usual theoretical meaning that we attribute to statements of this kind, but rather normative meaning that shows the believer how to respond in the presence of various events that befall him.[57]

Halakhic categories, reasons for the commandments, and statements of religious experience are no longer considered to reflect ontological or metaphysical truth; rather natural and historical events are given religious meaning by the *Halakha*.

In an essay on religious language, Rachel Shichor summarizes the religious concept of D.Z. Philips (a contemporary philosopher who writes

---

[56] The term "language game" is taken from Wittgenstein. See, for example, Ludwig Wittgenstein, *On Certainty* (Oxford: Basil Blackwell, 1969), section 65; Ludwig Wittgenstein, *Philosophical Investigations* (Oxford: Basil Blackwell, 1953), sections 23, 81-83. See also Gili Zivan, *Religion Without Illusion: Facing a Post-Modern World* (Tel-Aviv: The Shalom Hartman Institute, The Faculty of Law, Bar-Ilan University, Hakibbutz Hameuchad, 2005), 39-40 (Hebrew). This concept refers to various forms of thought and principles of organization that are characteristic of a culture, an organization, a profession, or any particular community (so for example, it is possible to talk about a language game in the world of science, of Western ethical discourse, of an Australian tribal culture, of Christian culture, etc.).

[57] One of the subjects where this interpretive revolution comes to expression is in the area of the reasons for the commandments. See Goldman (above, note 15), 257. In spite of Goldman's opposition to giving reasons for the *mitzvot*, he refuses to eliminate elements of religious language that discuss the reasons for the commandments, while at the same time seeking to convert their meaning. An interesting example of a transformation of this kind is found in Goldman's explanation of the reason Rabbi Meir offers for the laws of *niddah* (ibid., 315).

about religious language and faith in a critical and skeptical world) in words that capture perfectly Goldman's position:

> The substantial links between the language game of religion and the world are links of *values* rather than facts. In this light, religious faith is not grasped as an hypothesis that experience has the power to refute or substantiate as a fact in the world of facts, but rather it is grasped as an activity whose meaning is located first and foremost in itself, an activity that directs itself to the world not in order to draw from it a foundation and a justification, but rather in order to give its own meaning to the world.[58]

Goldman is well aware of the shift he has made with regard to the role of the reasons for the commandments and the place of various halakhic and religious concepts, as well as of the revolution implied in his approach.[59] As a believer-without-illusions who is not prepared to commit himself to "all-knowing" statements about God, his will and his plans, Goldman chooses to relinquish the support contained in an all-encompassing religious explanation, and suggests making do with an interpretation that does not try to reflect "the Divine Truth." And yet he does not dispense with the traditional religious language.

In this respect, Goldman joins Hartman, who claims that having religious faith means that even though not everything in our world is explainable, and even if pain and suffering do not receive a theological justification in Holy Scriptures, the individual decides to continue maintaining the religious way of life governed by Torah and *mitzvot*. The religious way of life and the texts woven into it indeed do give meaning to events, but they do not give them a transcendent explanation. They provide no answer to the question of "Why?"

---

[58] Rachel Shichor, "On the Problem of the Significations of Religious Language: On the Concept of Redemption and its Meaning in the Chasidism of Radzin," *Daat* 5 (1980): 54 (Hebrew).

[59] In an interview, Avi Sagi said, "I do not think that ordinary religious language expresses religious contents in an exactly correct way. A good example of my approach can be found in a lecture on Providence [...], I rejected the conventional conception of Providence, but I acknowledged the need to interpret it in a way that will give it religious meaning" (Sagi, "Religious Language in the Modern World," 16).

5. Emmanuel Levinas

As mentioned, the issue of faith in the face of suffering and loss became acute once the dimensions of the Shoah—the enormity of its destruction and the depth of its horror—were exposed. One of the first essays that raised discussion of this issue was a small booklet in the fifties, "Yosl Rakover Talks to God." Yosl Rakover, one of the last surviving fighters in the Warsaw Ghetto uprising, wrote his final words to God in Yiddish as the German tanks completed the destruction of the Warsaw Ghetto, sealed the paper in a glass bottle, hid it among the ruins, and then welcomed death.

From the moment this testimony was discovered it aroused great interest, and it was translated into many languages. It also provoked disagreements over its authenticity. In time it became clear that this booklet was not in fact an authentic historical artifact, and its author was really Tzvi Kolitz, who wrote the essay in Buenos Aires after the end of WWII, according to the information available to him at the time. Nevertheless, the literary and philosophical value of the work is not diminished by this fact.

In 1955, even before the book's true author was known, Radio France broadcast a piece by the French-Jewish philosopher Emmanuel Levinas, who described the work as "a text that is beautiful and also true, true as only a story can be." In an essay entitled, "To Love the Torah More than God," which relates to Kolitz's work, Levinas articulates his conception regarding ways that a Jewish believer copes with suffering.[60]

It is interesting to note that even though they did not know each other, Levinas' concept of faith is very close to the concept of the thinkers I have discussed above. It seems that Levinas continues the discussion that Soloveitchik and Leibowitz began, and "corresponds" with the ideas that Hartman developed much later, apparently without knowing it.[61]

---

[60] The piece that was broadcast on the radio was published in Kolitz, *Yosl Rakover Talks to God*. This collection of writings included the text written by Tzvi Kolitz in the name of Yosl Rakover (9-24), the controversy over the testimony's authenticity (25-66), and the essay by Levinas (67-73). The quote cited is found on page 67.

[61] As far as I am aware, Levinas did not know Leibowitz's views on the subject, since most of his writings had not yet been published at the time that Levinas

According to Levinas, one who sees in suffering and affliction evidence of "a world without God," as "Yosl Rakover" claims,[62] is responding to an image of God in the role of a kindergarten teacher, who gives out prizes and punishments to human beings. In his view, not only does this image raise great theological difficulties, but it leaves human beings locked in an "eternal childhood." Levinas determines that the simplistic and childish response to suffering that is derived from this position is "the choice of atheism," and he adds:

> This is also the most logical response of all those who have until now conceived of God as a kind of kindergarten divinity, who gives out prizes, imposes punishments or forgives mistakes, and out of her great goodness relates to human beings as perpetual children.[63]

To someone who has chosen, as a result of incomprehensible suffering, a "world bereft of God," he addresses the following question: "With what kind of narrow-horizoned demon, with what kind of strange wizard have you populated your heavens, you who declare today that these heavens are in fact empty?"[64]

Like Soloveitchik, Hartman, and Leibowitz, Levinas too seeks to produce a sober believer, one without illusions, and in his terms "a mature human being." The God of this mature believer "is revealed in the

---

gave his lecture on French radio, and those which had been published had not been translated into English. Neither did Levinas know the essay and lecture of Soloveitchik, which had not yet been published in 1955. Hartman's writings were published only at the beginning of the 90s, and so in spite of the great philosophical closeness between them, apparently Hartman did not know Levinas' essay, which was translated only recently from French. It seems to me that, as often happens in the history of thought, we find here the development of very similar ideas without the thinkers knowing each other. This is in truth unsurprising, since all the thinkers I mentioned have emerged from a similar philosophical background, aware of modern and post-modern thought that emphasizes the limits of human understanding, and were part of a world that relinquishes the presumption that we can see the world through the eyes of God.

[62] Levinas, "To Love the Torah More than God," 68.
[63] Ibid., 69.
[64] Ibid.

emptiness of the heavens of childhood."⁶⁵ The existential experience of the mature believer, who has abandoned the image of the kindergarten divinity, is a constant experience of "the hidden face of God," in the Talmudic language of Yosl Rakover. Levinas does not conceive of such hiddenness as an historical period in which God hides his face from his creatures and, as it were, abandons the world that he created. Rather, this is an expression of the mature faith of a human being who has chosen to believe in spite of having relinquished the conception of the God of childhood. This is a formulation that describes the change that has taken place in the consciousness of the believer, not in historical reality. In our world, many are the situations in which "the good cannot win," and this is a "situation of suffering."⁶⁶ The hiddenness of the face of God therefore is

> The moment when the righteous man cannot find any external aid, the moment when no institution can protect him, the moment when even the consolation of the divine presence within the religious feeling of childhood is withheld from him, **the moment when the individual can be victorious only within his own consciousness**, that is, only through suffering.⁶⁷

Hartman describes this maturation in a similar fashion: "in spite of the pain, the person decides to continue the life of covenant,"⁶⁸ and Soloveitchik too, as mentioned, insists upon the principle of the struggle against evil and suffering as part of the religious struggle of man, similar to Levinas' description: "a God who has relinquished any revelation that has within it the power to succor … calls for the full maturation of a human being that assumes complete responsibility."⁶⁹

However, how does a person express his or her faith in a God who is present and intimate? The answer that Levinas gives to this question is found in the practical sphere. Like the other thinkers we have seen, Levinas too diverts the discussion from theological questions to

---

[65] Ibid.
[66] Ibid., 70.
[67] Ibid., 69-70.
[68] Hartman, *A Living Covenant*, 293.
[69] Levinas, "To Love the Torah More than God," 70.

religious practice, and focuses on the connection between the believer and his God in the Torah and its commandments:

> The relationship between God and man is not expressed by an emotional union in the love of God that has been revealed in flesh and blood, but rather by a spiritual connection in the mediation of the Torah.... The trust in God that is not expressed in any earthly authority cannot be supported except by an interior proof and by the value that is in the Torah.[70]

The faith in God is expressed, therefore, not in beliefs of any kind in God or in the ways He runs the world, but rather in the realization of religious practice, i.e., in the fulfillment of the commandments of the Torah. God is revealed to the believer "not from the power of revelation," as in the idea of the Christian incarnation, but rather "from the power of the heavenly law," namely, in God's commands and *mitzvot*.

In order better to understand Levinas' argument regarding the position of the believer in the face of suffering, I want to clarify the debate that he held in the above-mentioned lecture with regard to Protestant concepts, which try to emphasize the mystery of God and His holiness, which neutralizes the human being. Levinas rejects the religious experience formulated by Rudolph Otto, who sees in the encounter with absolute holiness, with the numinous,[71] a standing in the presence of the infinite and the incomprehensible.[72] In the presence of this absolute holiness, "man comprehends himself as a complete nullity, without value, without holiness, that is, as impure,"[73] and therefore he cannot ask, and he has no right to ask, about the suffering in the world. In contrast to this conception, Levinas adopts the conception

---

[70] Ibid., 71.
[71] A term that Rudolph Otto coined, meaning a powerful religious experience that is characterized by the feeling of holiness derived from the very presence of God, and which precedes ethical or rational considerations. See Rudolph Otto, *The Idea of Holy*, trans. John W. Harvey (London, Oxford, New-York: Oxford University Press, 1976), 5-11.
[72] See ibid., 77-81. In these pages Otto discusses the question of theodicy.
[73] See Yosef ben Shlomo, "Afterword" of Hebrew translation, *The Holy: On the Irrational in the Idea of God and its Relation to Rationality* (Jerusalem: Carmel, 1999), 191.

of God that is embodied in the Torah and its commandments, a God who is reflected mainly in rational-legal discourse and not in mystical-theological discourse:

> God is perceptible not by virtue of embodiment but by virtue of the Torah; and His greatness is not in the mysteries of holiness. The Torah's magnificence does not arouse fear and trembling; it fills us with the most sublime thoughts.[74]

Unlike Otto, who describes God's response from the whirlwind to Job as a revelation of the mysterious, incomprehensible Holy, emphasizing the neutralization of man, and on that basis justifying God and dismissing the question of evil, Levinas emphasizes the stance of a believer who is confident and proud: "this man has matured by virtue of a faith whose origin is in the Torah, and he complains before God about His exaggerated greatness and His excessive demands."[75]

With regard to God's response from the whirlwind at the end of the Book of Job, Otto claims:

> We feel the **value** of the incomprehensible within a positive value that cannot be expressed in words.... It has nothing in common with our rational values. It remains sealed and hidden in mystery, but in such a way that is revealed to feeling, it at once **justifies** God and compensates Job completely and with serenity."[76]

If Otto's Job substitutes the demand for justice for submission in the presence of "the Wholly Other that cannot be endured, that mocks all our conceptions, and yet conquers and makes us tremble to the depths of the soul,"[77] the Job (or the Yosl Rakover) of Levinas stands before God "as a subject." The Protestant position is opposed, as mentioned, to the positions of Levinas and Hartman, who emphasize that despite the lack of clarity and incomprehensibility of suffering, the believer does not relinquish the feeling of injustice that accompanies him, nor his right to cast his protest at the heavens, even if this protest remains

---

[74] Levinas, "To Love the Torah More than God," 71.
[75] Ibid., 72.
[76] Otto, *The Idea of Holy*, 90.
[77] Ibid.

unanswered. In Hartman's words, the God who "subordinates Himself to human intelligence in the Study Hall," does not seek to nullify "our human sense of justice."[78]

Levinas formulates this position of the sufferer facing God as a dialectical, even paradoxical position: the demand of the believer for justice—and in the language of Yosl Rakover, "Don't stretch the rope too much"[79]—expresses the position of a man who refuses to yield, who takes his stand before God as an equal, who at the same time knows that he stands in the presence of the Incomprehensible, the Divine. The believer's right to come before God with a demand derives from the fact that the Divine, with his demands and his commandments, summons man to a partnership with him, one that expects man to take responsibility:

> God created a human being who is capable of responding, able to draw near to God as a creditor and not always as a debtor—isn't this really God's greatness? The creditor, after all, is someone who trusts the other, but he is also one who does not yield to the evasions of the debtor.... In what a powerful dialectic has the equality between God and man been embodied in the face of the disproportion between them!
> So it is clear that we have distanced ourselves from the warm and almost sensual unity with the Divine to the same extent that we have distanced ourselves from the arrogance of the atheist.[80]

The question of faith in God in the face of suffering and afflictions in the thought of Levinas takes a significant turn: from a theological question it becomes a question of the religious maturity of the believer, and a question of moral demand, whose meaning is ethical responsibility for the conduct of human history. The believer is not silenced by the awesome voice of God; he does not reconcile himself to the incomprehensibility into which he has been thrown. Rather he chooses an ethical response (like Soloveitchik's believer, who chooses the "topical *Halakha*"), chooses the Torah, on the basis of a proud stance in the presence of a consciousness of the hiddenness of God's face.

---

[78] Hartman, *A Living Covenant*, 292.
[79] Levinas, "To Love the Torah More than God," 72; see also 20-21.
[80] Ibid., 72-73.

The struggle of the believer for justice in the human world is, as expressed in the title of Levinas' essay, the struggle of someone who "loves the Torah" more than he loves God. He rises in protest against this divinity just as he yields to Him, because he senses God's personal presence in the divine command embodied in the Torah. He does not look for God in the world; he finds him in his Torah. "The divine speech is undefined and not fully expressed, it is precisely what a God who lives among us promises."[81]

Conclusion

The sober consciousness that the historical and natural world as we know it is bereft of a metaphysical order, and operates according to its own laws—"the world proceeds according to its own rules"—characterizes the thought of the thinkers I have discussed, and produces a different kind of religious faith than that which was widespread in the past and which is common in many sectors of the religious public today as well. Instead, these thinkers propose a faith without illusions, a faith that does not provide the believer with a religious metanarrative or a response to the question of "Why?" ("Why me?," "Why now?," "Why do I deserve this?," etc.) This is a faith that does not try to withhold from the believer the "philosophical dilemmas and psychological distress inherent within uncertainty."[82] It offers rather the opposite: the faith that these thinkers present is the faith of someone who chooses to "hold onto the divine covenant even when uncertainty, sufferings and tragedy remain in the realm of arbitrary possibilities in history."[83]

Faith is expressed in religious practice, in the believer's way of life, and not in metaphysical explanations given to events. It demands of the believer, in the words of Levinas, a relinquishing of the "kindergarten teacher God, who distributes rewards and imposes punishments or forgives mistakes, and in her great goodness, relates to human beings as perpetual children," as has been discussed.

---

[81] Ibid., 71.
[82] Geertz, *The Interpretation of Cultures*, 124.
[83] Hartman, *A Living Covenant*, 280.

In contrast to Leibowitz,[84] who makes do with only a negation of illusory faith and does not offer a positive religious alternative, Soloveitchik, Goldman, Hartman, and Levinas propose a religious faith that comes to terms with the presence of evil in the world and struggles against it. The believer who is suffering may attribute to evil various meanings, but in any case he does not see evil as part of the divine plan; rather it is, as Goldman says, "a signal that indicates the need to examine our deeds, to repent...."

It seems that in this matter Soloveitchik goes farthest in his practical and active approach to struggling against evil,[85] in spite of the fact that he does not, as I have shown, "purify" religious language in a systematic way of metaphysical elements. He calls for a struggle against evil by technological, moral, social, and other means, and not to accept it as

---

[84] With regard to the analysis of the positions of the thinkers discussed in this essay, I have chosen to present a division that is a little different from that presented by Sagi (see Sagi, "Criticism of Theodicy," 408-434), who speaks about the thought of Leibowitz, Goldman, Soloveitchik, and Hartman. Sagi suggests that we distinguish between two different streams: the first, which comes to expression in the thought of Leibowitz and Goldman, "presents a penetrating critique of the fundamental assumption of classical theodicy" (408); and the second, which is represented by Soloveitchik and Hartman, "presents a social, existential critique of this theodicy" (ibid.). Although I agree with the main points of Sagi's argument, I have chosen to emphasize other fundamental assumptions in the thought of the four thinkers. Among these thinkers, I have chosen to focus especially on two: Leibowitz, who more than the others presents a critique of the discourse of classical theodicy but does not offer a positive alternative for faith at a time of crisis. As opposed to this position, it seems to me that both Goldman (who in contrast to Leibowitz does not abandon the classical religious language, but rather transforms it into normative and not reflective language), and certainly Soloveitchik and Hartman, propose a positive alternative (one that is not metaphysical) for faith at a time of crisis. On the other side of the balance stands Soloveitchik, who proposes a practical, active alternative to the rejection of metaphysical thought. Hartman, even if he criticizes Soloveitchik for this, does not completely distance himself from metaphysical thought, though he does not go as far as his teacher regarding the imperative to fight evil actively.

[85] The position of Levinas, as I have already indicated, is close to Soloveitchik's position, which also calls for an active struggle against evil. However, Levinas does not relate to individual suffering insofar as it is inherent in the human condition, but rather to the suffering of the individual Jew insofar as he is part of the suffering of the historical Jewish people.

part of divine providence that visits human beings as punishment for sin. He proposes an "ethics of evil" as an alternative to a "metaphysics of evil." In his view, someone who believes that evil is the will of God will not fight against it:

> It simply couldn't assimilate this philosophy preached by Gandhi and then by Nehru, not to combat evil activity, not to fight evil the way Jacob engaged combat with his mysterious antagonist on a dark night, but simply resist evil passively.[86]

The believer musters the forces of his soul and intellect for the advancement of medicine, the widening of dangerous roads, social improvement, the prevention of crime, safety, the advancement of peace agreements between nations, etc. The *Halakha*, says Soloveitchik, "has idealized scientific intervention on behalf of man in his desperate struggle to control his environment in every area: in the ethical sphere, the physical…, the social, etc."[87] This is the faith of a man who has "matured," in the formulation of Levinas, a human being who has forged from within himself the sheltering "metaphysical blanket" and set out to struggle against human and natural evil, full of faith in God and in his own power, in spite of the fact that he will never find an answer to his metaphysical questions.

Epilogue

I would like to conclude these meditations concerning faith at a time of deep personal crisis with a passage from the diary of Professor Ariel Rozen-Tzvi, Z"L, writen in the final days of his struggle with the cancer which in the end overcame him. His words were published by his son, Yishai Rozen-Tzvi, in his eulogy for his father:

> When the disease was discovered in my body, I did not feel a need to respond with defiance towards heaven, "Why me?" This was a question that did not exist in the world of my religious conceptions. The combination of a recognition that "the world proceeds according to its own laws," together with a faith in an absolute

---

[86] Soloveitchik, "A Halakhic Approach to Suffering," 16.
[87] Ibid., 266.

divine power, did not allow such a question to be part of my theology....

I did not ask why God would afflict those who keep his commandments. If I were to ask such a question, I would be turning my back on my whole way of life, which when it carries on a perpetual dialogue with God does not make faith a hostage to successes. My faith does not accept an approach of give and take or of direct cause and effect in the world of faith....

I do not interpret the cells metastasizing in my body as an expression of reward and punishment. I do not accept a single-value or one-dimensional approach like this as part of my faith life. For this reason, I did not see a need for the bribery of vows and oaths or religious extremism. However, I saw in them a sign. Especially in the absence of bodily control, these cells signaled the need for greater control over one's life, of the need for doing the true things in life ... family, in-depth study, faith. These are the pillars that we must strengthen and build. This sign I turned into a covenant between me and the Creator of the world. Not conditions and not vows, but rather a renewed covenant, whose basis was the understanding that the distress that I was immersed in obliged a true examination of life and a perpetual personal accounting. The living presence of the rebellious cells became for me the living presence of God within me. This is perhaps a strange and megalomaniacal consciousness, to identify in a diseased cell a covenantal sign, but that was how I felt and how I feel to this day.[88]

Rozen-Tzvi's frank words reflect a religious faith of the type that the thinkers I have mentioned speak of—coping with afflictions and suffering not by searching for a metaphysical answer. Such faith does not look for a direct connection of cause and effect, and certainly not for a connection of sin and punishment. As he says: "My faith does not accept an approach of give-and-take or of direct cause and effect in the world of faith ... the cells rebelling in my body I do not interpret as an expression of reward and punishment." Suffering and cancer are part of the way the natural world operates. Therefore, he does not ask "Why have sufferings come upon me?" Rather, he asks "What do these sufferings show me?"

---

[88] Passages from the diary of Ariel Rozen Tzvi, Z"L, from the eulogy by Yishai Rozen Tzvi for his father, recorded in Menachem Mautner, Avi Sagi and Ronen Shamir, eds., *Multi-Culturalism in a Democratic Jewish State: A Memorial Volume for Ariel Rozen-Tzvi, Z"L* (Tel-Aviv: Ramot, 1998), 15-17 (Hebrew).

In his words, "I saw in them a sign.... These cells were a signal for the need for greater control over one's life, of the need to do the true things of life."

Rozen-Tzvi testifies about himself, about how suffering brought him to a renewed covenant with God. In a paradoxical fashion, from his pain grew ethical, social, and new religious comprehension, in consequence of which he renewed his covenant with his God. It was a covenant at whose foundation he discovered the understanding that the suffering in which he was immersed "obliged real examination of life and perpetual personal accounting." Sufferings bring human beings to examine their deeds, as the Talmud says, but not in the sense of a search for the reason or sin that caused the sufferings; rather they stimulate the formation of a new existential position, a kind of shaking up that summons the individual to examine the structures of his life, to examine his beliefs and to choose faith anew—despite the changed conditions.

KABBALAH AND HASIDISM

Faith, Rebellion, and Heresy in the Writings of Rabbi Azriel of Gerona

Lawrence Kaplan

The writings of the great thirteenth-century kabbalist R. Azriel of Gerona on faith (*emunah*), rebellion (*meri*), and heresy (*kefirah*) are widely considered to be among the most searching and profound of the many discussions of this issue that abound in Jewish thought. We therefore owe a debt of gratitude to the distinguished scholar of Kabbalah and Jewish ethics, Professor Mordecai Pachter, for providing us with a learned and thorough examination of R. Azriel on this issue.[1] Since my own reading of R. Azriel differs significantly from Pachter's, I wish to emphasize that it was precisely my study of Pachter's stimulating essay that first led me to formulate my own views on the subject.

R. Azriel discusses this issue in two treatises: *Sha'ar ha-Sho'el* or *The Explanation of the Ten Sefirot*[2] and *Derekh ha-Emunah ve-Derekh ha-Kefirah* (*The Way of Faith and the Way of Heresy*).[3] I will discuss each treatise separately, since I believe, contrary to Pachter, that R. Azriel's approach to this issue in *Sha'ar ha-Sho'el* differs fundamentally from his approach in *Derekh ha-Emunah ve-Derekh ha-Kefirah*. As I hope to show, R. Azriel's

---

[1] Mordechai Pachter, "The Root of Faith is the Root of Heresy," in *Roots of Faith and Devequt: Studies in the History of Kabbalistic Ideas* (Los Angeles: Cherub, 2004), 13-51. An earlier Hebrew version of this essay appeared in *Kabbalah* 4 (1999): 314-343, and was reprinted in *'Al Ha-Emunah*, ed. Moshe Halbertal, David Kurzweil, and Avi Sagi (Jerusalem: Keter, 2005), 280-293, 625-641.

[2] *Sha'ar ha-Sho'el* or *The Explanation of the Ten Sefirot* was published as a prolegomenon to Meir ibn Gabbai's *Sefer Derekh Emunah* (Warsaw: Meir Halter, 1890), 3-9; English translation in *The Early Kabbalah*, edited and introduced by Joseph Dan and texts translated by Ronald Keiner (New York: Paulist Press, 1986), 89-96. I have used Keiner's translation with some slight emendations.

[3] *Derekh ha-Emunah ve-Derekh ha-Kefirah*, ed. Gershom Scholem, in "*Seridim Hadashim mi-Kitvei R. Azriel mi-Gerona*," in *Sefer Zikkaron le-Asher Gulak ve-li-Shmu'el Klein*, ed. Simḥah Assaf and Scholem (Jerusalem: Hebrew University, 1942), 207.

approach in *Sha'ar ha-Sho'el* is rather conventional and, again contra Pachter, pretty much follows along lines set forth by R. Judah Halevi in the *Kuzari*. Only in *Derekh ha-Emunah ve-Derekh ha-Kefirah* does R. Azriel break with the Halevi model and present a truly original, innovative, and bold approach to this issue.

The key text in *Sha'ar ha- Sho'el* reads as follows.

> [Question] 2. If a questioner asks: Who can compel me to believe in *Eyn Sof*?
> *Answer*: Know that everything visible and perceivable to human contemplation is limited, and that everything that is limited is finite, and that everything that is finite is not undifferentiated. Therefore, that which is not limited is called *Eyn Sof* and is absolutely undifferentiated in a complete and changeless unity. And since He is without limit, then nothing truly exists outside Him. And since He is both exalted and hidden, He is the essence of all that is concealed and revealed. Thus, since He is hidden, He is both the root of faith and the root of rebellion. Concerning this it is written: "The righteous man shall live by his faith" (Habakkuk.2:4). Furthermore, the philosophers are in agreement with these statements that our perception of Him cannot be except by way of negative attribution.

Let us examine Pachter's analysis of this text.[4] Pachter begins by arguing that the text raises three difficulties:

> First, it is worded in an unusual way, since R. Azriel copied its conclusion ["He is both the root of faith and the root of rebellion"] word for word from R. Judah Halevi's *Kuzari*, as a commonly accepted figure of speech.[5] The very use of it in this context

---

[4] More recently, Sandra Valabregue-Perry in her exceptionally comprehensive and incisive study, "Concealed and Revealed: 'Ein Sof' in Theosophic Kabbalah" (Los Angeles: Cherub, 2010), 71-83 (Hebrew), subjects both questions 1 (71-78) and 2 (78-83) of *Sha'ar ha-Sho'el* to a very profound and extensive analysis. However, in accordance with the theme of her book, she focuses on R. Azriel's characterization of the *Eyn Sof*, while concerning the issues of faith and rebellion in question 2, she pretty much follows along the lines set down by Pachter.

[5] The phrase is first used by the *Haver* in *Kuzari* 1:77, picked up by the King in 1:78, and elaborated upon by the *Haver* in 1:79. I am using the English translation of Barry Kogan (to be published in the *Yale Judaica Series*). I would like to thank Prof. Kogan for making this translation available to me before publication.

is problematic.... But the problem increases in the light of the second difficulty—the logical validity of the argument—which turns out not to be self-evident, though it may seem so at first glance. R. Azriel himself found it necessary to back up the argument by quoting "The righteous man shall live by his faith," showing that logic is not the main thing: faith is. The third difficulty is linked to the second one: the argument indicates that faith and heresy[6] are in principle of equal value, since, coming from the same root, one is not preferable to the other. Therefore choosing between the two is a choice of faith, not of logic, as indicated by the above quotation. But if that is so, then the first in R. Azriel's series of arguments is no longer a valid and sufficient answer, and the whole logical structure is undermined.[7]

What is the meaning of Halevi's famous statement "the root of faith [is] the root of rebellion," and what is the significance of R. Azriel's reference to it? Pachter understands Halevi's statement thus:

In Halevi, the common root of faith and of [rebellion] lies in man, more precisely, in the way man understands the nature of reality. Accordingly, for everyone who understands that "The elements, the sun and the moon and the stars do have activities [that they perform] by way of warming and cooling, moistening and drying ... without wisdom being ascribed to them, but, on the contrary, [only] constrained action. As for giving form, assigning determinations, bringing forth things fully developed, and anything else that involves wisdom directed toward an end—they may be ascribed only to the One who is wise, powerful and capable.... [Therefore] divine and noble influences [appear] in this lowest of worlds when ... different kinds of matter have been properly disposed to receive them"—his insight and understanding will be the root of faith. By contrast, whoever thinks that wisdom, not only function, should be attributed to the forces of nature and that, therefore, this wisdom should be studied, and one should

---

[6] Pachter uses "heresy" to translate both *"meri"* and *"kefirah."* But this is to blur the difference between them. (Valabregue-Perry in her discussion of question 2 similarly uses *"meri"* and *"kefirah"* interchangeably.) Even if readers will disagree with the distinction I propose later on, the two terms should be translated differently to allow readers to arrive at their own conclusions. I have therefore from this point on substituted in brackets the word "rebellion" for "heresy" every time Pachter uses the latter word to refer to *"meri."*

[7] Pachter, *Roots of Faith and Devequt*, 18-19.

try "to modify things in order to receive that [influence] through ingenuity, reasoning, and conjecture".... —whoever understands reality this way will find it the root of [rebellion].... These distinctions show clearly that faith and [rebellion] are in the main the outcomes of human tendencies, meaning that their significance lies in the psychological or the epistemological plane. Hence their common root is only in man. He and he alone decides one way or the other.... The important thing is that in man and his decision lie the root of faith or the root of [rebellion].[8]

This explanation of Halevi is inexact. The contrast between the believer and the rebel is not that the believer understands that "giving form, assigning determinations, bringing forth things fully developed, and anything else that involves wisdom directed toward an end ... may be ascribed only to the One who is wise, powerful and capable," while the rebel thinks that "wisdom, not only function, should be attributed to the forces of nature." No. Both the believer and the rebel, as is clear from *Kuzari* 1:79, understand that "giving form, assigning determinations, bringing forth things fully developed, and anything else that involves wisdom directed toward an end ... may be ascribed only to the One who is wise, powerful and capable" and that "divine and noble influences [appear] in this lowest of worlds when ... different kinds of matter have been properly disposed to receive them." The rebel and believer differ "only" regarding how to prepare human beings so that they are "properly disposed to receive ... that divine influence." The believer understands that only by conforming to "consummate divine knowledge, thoroughly explained by God ... in accordance with its [specified] limits and conditions with pure intent" can one receive the divine influence. The rebel, by contrast, is "someone who has tried to modify things in order to receive that [influence] through ingenuity, reasoning, and conjecture...."

That said, Pachter's basic claim with regard to Halevi's position is unquestionable. For Halevi, indeed, "faith and [rebellion] are in the main the outcomes of human tendencies, meaning that their significance lies in the psychological or epistemological plane. Hence their common root is only in man. He and he alone decides one way or another.... In man and his decision lie the root of faith and [rebellion]." Indeed, our own

---

[8] Ibid., 19-20.

analysis of Halevi, if anything, only strengthens Pachter's point, since, as we have seen, the believer and the rebel respond in opposite ways to precisely the same fundamental reality, namely, that "divine and noble influences [appear] in this lowest of worlds [only] when ... different kinds of matter have been properly disposed to receive them," the believer relying upon divine communication in order to become "properly disposed," the rebel upon his own reasoning.

Pachter, however, goes on to argue:

> While R. Azriel uses a quotation from Judah Halevi, it does not necessarily mean that he agrees with him. The opposite turns out to be true. R. Azriel quotes Halevi's exact words, but gives them a different meaning.... R. Azriel asserts ... that the root of faith and of [rebellion] is not in man but in *Eyn Sof*. While he copied R. Judah Halevi's verbal formula, quoting literally from the *Kuzari*, he immediately transposes it from its human context into a divine one. In other words, he transplants the root of faith and of [rebellion] from the subject to the object, from the believer or the [rebel] to the object of his belief or [rebellion]. The transplant without doubt involves a dramatic innovation.[9]

As I have already indicated, while I believe Pachter's claim is valid with reference to R. Azriel's analysis of faith and heresy in *Derekh ha-Emunah ve-Derekh ha-Kefirah*, I do not believe it is valid with reference to his analysis of faith and rebellion in *Sha'ar ha-Sho'el*, where R. Azriel, as I will show, essentially operates within a Halevian framework. Consequently, his use of Halevi's figure of speech in this context is *not* problematic. But in order to establish this point let us leave to the side for the moment R. Azriel's use of Halevi and turn to the second and third difficulties raised by Pachter, both having to do with the logical validity of R. Azriel's argument.

But are these real difficulties? Only if we unquestioningly assume, as does Pachter, that the opening statement of R. Azriel's answer to question 2 is intended to be an argument based on logic. Thus, Pachter writes: "R. Azriel's opening argument is indeed in itself a complete and satisfactory answer, since it proves that it is logically necessary to

---

[9] Ibid., 19-20. Valabregue-Perry, *Concealed and Revealed*, 78, cites this statement of Pachter and appears to agree with it. Also see below, note 17.

assume the existence of *Eyn Sof*."¹⁰ And, in a footnote, ad loc., he adds that "R. Azriel's proof ... may be considered an anthropological proof of the existence of the *Eyn Sof*, and as such it closely resembles Descartes' first proof of the existence of God."¹¹ I would contend, however, that what we have here is not and is not intended to be a logical argument or proof at all. All R. Azriel is doing is presenting and describing the concept of the *Eyn Sof* as the exact opposite of everything visible and perceivable to human contemplation. There is no argument to be found here for his existence. As for the supposed comparison with "Descartes' first proof of the existence of God," the comparison begs the question in two ways. First, Pachter claims that "R. Azriel's writing [here] is so condensed as to require interpretation."¹² But this is the case only if we suppose that the opening statement is intended to present us with a logical argument or proof. Under such a supposition, since no such logical argument or proof is evident, "interpretation" is "required." But if the opening statement is not and is not intended to be a logical argument or proof at all, then it is clear and can stand on its own, dispensing with any need for "interpretation." Second, if the opening statement is intended to present us with a logical argument or proof, as Pachter believes, then some version of "Descartes' first proof of the existence of God" is as good a choice as any.¹³ But of course this begs the question of whether the opening statement is intended to be such a logical argument or proof.

Indeed, compare the opening statement of R Azriel's answer to Question 2 to the opening statements of his answers to Questions 1 and 3.

> 1. If a questioner asks: Who can compel me to believe that the world has a ruler (*manhig*)?
> *Answer*: Just as it is inconceivable that a ship be without its captain, so too it is impossible that the world be without a ruler. This ruler is infinite (*Eyn Sof*) in both His Glory and His Word....

---

¹⁰ Pachter, *Roots of Faith and Devequt*, 15-16.
¹¹ Ibid. 6, note 5.
¹² Ibid.
¹³ In truth, I believe that an objective comparison of R. Azriel's statement with Descartes' proof will indicate, contrary to Pachter's contention, that there is no "close resemblance" between the two, indeed no resemblance at all.

> 3. If a questioner persists: By what necessity do you arrive at the assertion that the *sefirot* exist? I rather say that they do not exist and that there is only *Eyn Sof*!
> *Answer*: *Eyn Sof* is perfection without any imperfection. If you propose that He has unlimited power and does not have finite power, then you ascribe imperfection to His perfection. And if you claim that the first limited being that is brought into existence from Him is this world—lacking in perfection—then you ascribe imperfection to the force that stems from Him.

In both cases we have a clear logical argument proceeding from premises to conclusions. Note the "Just" - "so too" structure of answer 1 and the "If" - "then" structure of answer 3. Indeed, if the readers will examine the answers to Questions 4-7, they will discern similar logical structures. By contrast, no such logical structure is to be found in the opening statement of Answer 2.[14]

The correct answer, then, to the second question "Who can compel me to believe in *Eyn Sof*?" is: "No one can compel you." That is, since the existence of the *Eyn Sof* is completely hidden and, furthermore, since there is no logical proof or argument for His existence, to believe in the existence of *Eyn Sof* is a matter of faith. Precisely the existence of the

---

[14] To be sure, there is a chain of logical inferences from a thing's being visible to its being limited, and from its being limited to its being finite, etc. Similarly there is a chain of logical inferences from the *Eyn Sof*'s not being limited to its not being finite, and from its not being finite to its being undifferentiated. Finally, we have the inference that "since He is without limit, then nothing truly exists outside Him." The point I am making is that there is *no* logical inference from the existence of that which is limited, finite, and differentiated to the existence of the *Eyn Sof*. The "Therefore" (*'im ken*) at the beginning of the second sentence of the answer refers to the inference that since the *Eyn Sof* is not limited it is not finite, which is precisely why it is called *Eyn Sof*. As for the concluding sentence in this answer, "Furthermore, the philosophers are in agreement with these statements that our perception of Him cannot be except by way of negative attribution," whatever its significance may be—and it appears to be an argument in favor of the meaningfulness of a negative conception of God—it is not a logical argument for the existence of the *Eyn Sof* Valabregue-Perry (p.81) understands this sentence differently. See my critical remarks below, note17. In any event, even she does not understand the sentence as a logical argument for the existence of the *Eyn Sof*.

Eyn Sof, the capstone or the foundation stone of the entire kabbalistic system, is not amenable to logical argument or proof. Indeed, "The righteous man shall live by his faith!"[15]

It follows directly from the immediately above that the second and third difficulties raised by Pachter regarding the "logical validity" of the argument lose their force.

To return, then, to R. Azriel's use of Halevi in *Sha'ar ha-Sho'el*: contrary to Pachter, R. Azriel does *not* transpose Halevi's statement "from its human context into a divine one," does not transplant "the root of faith and of [rebellion] from the subject to the object, from the believer or the [rebel] to the object of his belief or [rebellion]." The root of both faith and rebellion is not so much the *Eyn Sof*, but the hiddenness of the *Eyn Sof*. That is to say, R. Azriel's believer and rebel, in a manner similar to Halevi's believer and rebel, face precisely the same fundamental reality. While it is demonstrable that the world has a divine ruler (*manhig*), that ruler, as Pachter convincingly argues, is

---

[15] In his astute and penetrating examination of the esoteric Jewish tradition, *Concealment and Revelation: Esotericism in Jewish Thought and its Philosophical Implications* (Princeton and Oxford: Princeton University, 2007), on p.77, Moshe Halbertal correctly describes *Sha'ar ha-Sho'el* as "a systematic exposition, clearly philosophically Neo-Platonic, of the nature of the *sefirot*." He goes on to say, "According to Rabbi Azriel the *sefirot* may be deduced by reason alone, without reference to the sacred scriptures. At the outset of his work, the *sefirot* are presented as something that may be deduced by reason. Only subsequently does the discussion turn to the examination of the evidence for this doctrine in the Bible and in Talmudic literature." If my analysis is correct, Halbertal's point holds true only with reference to the doctrine of the *sefirot*. The existence of the *Eyn Sof* itself cannot "be deduced by reason alone," but is a matter of faith. In this connection, the following story was recounted to me by a very eminent and distinguished philosopher. While perhaps not strictly relevant, it may be of interest. In his youth, this philosopher had studied Talmud for several years with one of the greatest rabbinic scholars of the past century, and, indeed, was ordained by him. After his ordination he began to study philosophy in graduate school. His studies, however, raised doubts in his mind as to the rational basis of belief in the existence of God. He brought his doubts back to his teacher, who in addition to being a great rabbinic scholar had a very fine philosophical education. After the young man had related his doubts, his teacher replied, "Intellectually, it's 50/50. Of course, you have to have faith."

not the *Eyn Sof*.¹⁶ And precisely because God qua *Eyn Sof*, as opposed to God qua divine ruler, is unlimited, is absolutely undifferentiated in a complete and changeless unity, his existence is not demonstrable, is NOT visible and perceivable to human contemplation, but rather completely hidden. The person who possesses faith chooses to believe in the existence of the *Eyn Sof* despite his hiddenness, despite the fact that his existence is not demonstrable, despite the fact that he is not visible and perceivable to human contemplation. The rebel chooses not to believe in the existence of the *Eyn Sof*, whose existence is hidden, but only in the existence of that which is visible and perceivable to human contemplation, only in the existence of that whose existence is demonstrable, including, we hasten to add, God qua divine ruler.¹⁷ Contra Pachter, it is not the case "that faith and [rebellion] are in principle of equal value, since coming from the same root, one is not preferable to the other." But it is the case, as we have just seen, that faith is

---

[16] Pachter, *Roots of Faith and Devequt*, 1, note 3. Valabregue-Perry (p.73) accepts Pachter's distinction between the divine ruler (*manhig*) and the *Eyn Sof*, but (p. 76) argues that one should not make too sharp a distinction between them. See the following note.

[17] Valabregue-Perry (p. 80) in her discussion of R. Azriel's view regarding faith in the existence of the *Einsof*, remarks that since, for R. Azriel, the existence of the *Eyn Sof* is completely hidden, of necessity "faith begins in the place where all demonstration comes to an end." In this regard she comes close to my analysis. However, on p. 81, starting from the same premise of the hiddenness of the existence of the *Eyn Sof*, she argues that, for R. Azriel, the rebel is he who while acknowledging the existence of the *Eyn Sof* denies His presence in the world or denies that the world has a divine ruler. But that denial has already been dealt with in question 1. Moreover, since the question at hand is "Who can compel me to believe in *Eyn Sof*?," it makes more sense to assume, as I have argued, that the rebel, lacking faith, denies *Eyn Sof*'s existence altogether, precisely since His existence is indemonstrable. In this regard, the denial of the existence of the *Eyn Sof*, discussed in question 2, is described there as an act of rebellion, while the denial of the existence of a divine ruler, discussed in question 1, is described there as an act of perversity (*sherirut lev*), precisely since the existence of a divine ruler, as opposed to the existence of the *Eyn Sof*, is demonstrable. Given my understanding, as opposed to Valabregue-Perry's, of the nature of the rebel according to R. Azriel, I similarly cannot accept her reading (p. 81) of the concluding sentence of the answer to question 2: "Furthermore, the philosophers are in agreement with these statements that our perception of Him cannot be except by way of negative attribution."

not *logically* preferable to rebellion. Indeed, if it were, it would not be faith. Therefore, for R. Azriel in *Sha'ar ha-Sho'el* as for Halevi in the *Kuzari*, "faith and [rebellion] are in the main the outcomes of human tendencies, meaning that their significance lies in the psychological or epistemological plane. Hence their common root is only in man. He and he alone decides one way or another.... In man and his decision lie the root of faith and [rebellion]."

Perhaps we can carry this analogy between R. Azriel and Halevi one step further. We may tentatively suggest that for both R. Azriel and Halevi the source of the rebel's rebellion resides in his exclusive reliance upon reason. Halevi's rebel "tries to modify things in order to receive that [divine influence] through ingenuity, reasoning, and conjecture," rejecting the claim that one can receive the divine influence only on the basis of "consummate divine knowledge, thoroughly explained by God ... in accordance with its [specified] limits and conditions." In a similar manner, R. Azriel's rebel, while willing to accept the existence of a divine ruler, since the world's having a divine ruler is rationally demonstrable, refuses to believe in the existence of the *Eyn Sof*, since the existence of the *Eyn Sof* is not rationally demonstrable.

Let us now turn to *Derekh ha-Emunah ve-Derekh ha-Kefirah*, where, as I have already said, Rabbi Azriel does break with the Halevi model and presents a truly original, innovative, and bold approach to the issue of the relationship between faith and heresy. The key text reads as follows:

> If [someone] asks you: "How did He bring forth *yesh* from *'ayin*? Isn't there a great difference between *yesh* and *'ayin*?"—Answer him: He who brings forth *yesh* from *'ayin* is not lacking. The *yesh* is in the *'ayin* in the mode of *'ayin*, and the *'ayin* is in the *yesh*[18] in the mode of *yesh*. Concerning this they have said (*Sefer Yetzirah* 2:6): "He made *'eino* (His nothingness) into *yeshno* (His being)" and not "He made *yesh* from *'ayin*," to indicate that the *'ayin* is the *yesh* and the *yesh* is the *'ayin*. And the *'ayin* is called *'omen*. And the place of the attachment of the *yesh* as it begins to emerge from *'ayin* into existence is called faith (*emunah*), as it is written, "counsels from afar; faith [of] faithfulness" (*emunat 'omen*)

---

[18] "*Ve-ha-'ayin hu be-yesh.*" For this reading, see Pachter, *Roots of Faith and Devequt*, 21, n.19.

(Isaiah 25:11). For faith neither applies to the *yesh* that is seen and comprehended, nor to the *'ayin* that is neither seen nor comprehended, but only to the place of the adherence of *'ayin* and *yesh*.... The *yesh* is therefore nothing but the *'ayin*, and everything is one in the simplicity of Absolute Undifferentiation. And concerning the inquiry into this, it is said, "Neither make thyself over wise" (Ecclesiastes 7:16), since it is not in the power of our defective understanding to comprehend the perfection of this "beyond inquiry" (*heker*) which is one with *Eyn Sof*. And concerning this it is said, "Do not search into that which is hidden from you" (Ben Sira 3:19; cited in TB Haggigah 13a) .... And if someone should ask you whether the Creator, Blessed be He, is equal to All, reply to him that He is above all, and nothing is prior to Him, since He brought the *yesh* out of the *'ayin*, and He is [indeed] equal to All, since nothing exists outside him, neither in *yesh* nor in *'ayin*. And since the Creator is a principle equal to All, the way of faith and the way of heresy are equal in the place of the adherence of *'eino* and *yeshno*.[19]

As Pachter indicates, this passage has been much studied from many different angles, and a host of distinguished scholars of Kabbalah have cited and commented upon it.[20] Here we will focus first on R. Azriel's definition of faith, then seek to determine his view regarding heresy, and finally examine his concluding statement "And since the Creator is equal to All, the way of faith and the way of heresy ... are equal in the place of the adherence of *'eino* and *yeshno*."

It is clear that in this passage R. Azriel indeed transposes faith "from its human context into a divine one," since faith refers first and foremost to "the place of the attachment of the *yesh* as it begins to emerge from *'ayin* into existence." Here we can do no better than to cite Pachter's analysis:

---

[19] See above, note iii. The English translation is taken from Pachter, 21-23, with some modifications.

[20] See the references in Pachter, *Roots of Faith and Devequt*, 23, notes 27-29. More recently this passage has been examined by Valabregue-Perry, ibid,, 233-34; Michael Fishbane, *Sacred Attunement: A Jewish Theology* (Chicago and London: University of Chicago, 2008), 37-39; and Dov Elbaum, *Masʻa be-Hallal ha-Panui: Autobiographiyyah Ruhanit* (Tel Aviv: Am Oved, 2007), 78-79. As the latter two works' subtitles indicate, they are not works of strict scholarship, but rather of theological and spiritual reflection.

At the outset, one must emphasize that R. Azriel's primary and basic definition of faith grants it an ontic-metaphysical objective status that in essence does not depend on man. Nevertheless, he perceives faith as a human inclination ... [and] falls back on clearly epistemological categories, declaring that as one cannot relate the concept of faith to what is clear to us or understood by us [*yesh*. -LK], because an attitude of faith would be out of place here, so we cannot apply it to what we cannot see and is beyond our perception [*'ayin*. -LK], since by definition it is beyond the realm to which we can relate consciously. Clearly this explanation encapsulates the idea that faith is first and foremost a human way of relating.... This widely accepted concept of faith lies at the basis of R. Azriel's endeavor ... to define precisely the outer limit of human reason, which by nature and definition is beyond human grasp, although it is still possible for human beings to relate to it—in a relationship of faith. This is indeed the conclusion derived from the argument: faith as a human trait relates only to what is at the outer limit of understanding, where the *yesh* and the *'ayin*, i.e., the revealed and the concealed, or the comprehensible and the incomprehensible, touch one another....

Faith [then, for R. Azriel] is a human phenomenon that on the symbolic-mystical level reflects its root in the divine and so teaches us the nature of that root.... As a human trait and inclination, [faith] cannot apply except in "the place of the adherence of *'ayin* and *yesh*," which is the outer limit of what humans can apprehend. As such, this very point reflects the nature of its root in the upper realms: "the place of the attachment of the *yesh* as it begins to emerge from *'ayin* into existence." And precisely this is the primary and basic definition of faith, whose validity, according to R. Azriel, is proved to be self-evident....

Thus it is determined unambiguously that the real significance of faith is ontic-metaphysical, and faith in the psychological-epistemological sense is merely its reflection. One might argue that one is talking of two sides of the same coin, but if this were so, the two sides would not be of equal value. The ontic priority of faith with its hypostatic status in divinity shows that it is clearly independent of faith as a human phenomenon, which being a mere reflection of the first, is entirely dependent on it.... In this link between faith in the psychological-epistemological sense and the higher faith, the former draws strength from the latter, and its truth and validity thus become clear and obvious.[21]

---

[21] Pachter, *Roots of Faith and Devequt*, 24-26.

But if R. Azriel's conception of faith is clearly and powerfully set forth, his view of heresy is shrouded in darkness, while the passage's concluding statement juxtaposing faith and heresy—"And since the Creator is equal to All, the way of faith and the way of heresy are equal in the place of the adherence of *'eino* and *yeshno*"—strikes one as both provocative and obscure, perhaps provocative because of its obscurity. Moreover, it is obvious that these two issues—that is, R. Azriel's view as to the nature of heresy and the meaning of his concluding statement—are inextricably linked to one another.

What then, for R. Azriel, is the source of heresy, and what does he mean by heresy? Pachter suggests:

> It is ... reasonable to suppose that [R. Azriel] perceives heresy, as generally defined, like faith, as primarily a human inclination and tendency that as such reflects in a symbolic-mystical way an ontic-metaphysical essence. Furthermore, since heresy is only the obverse side of faith, one could assume that its ontic-metaphysical manifestation lies at the opposite pole from the ontic-metaphysical manifestation of faith. I might even dare to say that this pole is the place where being becomes non-being, that is, where being touches non-being. In any case, R. Azriel's words seem to allow the conclusion that he sees the ontic-metaphysical category, of which human heresy is simply the symbolic reflection, as lying at the bottom of the ladder of being.[22]

In a footnote, Pachter elaborates:

> The meaning of this term here is purely Neo-Platonic, i.e. it designates that which does not exist, namely both matter and evil.... In any case, non-being in this sense is the diametric opposite of what R. Azriel calls *'ayin* or *'efes* ..., which signifies all that it is above the *yesh*, in the sense of the infinite fullness of being that transcends the *yesh*. With that, it is not simply a coincidence that we have not found in all R. Azriel's writings any mention of non-being. Possibly he identified completely nihilistic heresy with non-being, so he did not discuss it at all..., just as he did not mention it. From this I tend to assume that heresy in its ontic-metaphysical status, as diametrically opposite from faith in its highest ontic-metaphysical status, is the lowest rung of the ladder of *yesh*....[23]

---

[22] Ibid., 27.
[23] Ibid., 27, note 38.

But this understanding of heresy and its source would appear to be contradicted by R. Azriel's concluding statement, "And since the Creator is equal to All, the way of faith and the way of heresy are equal in the place of the adherence of *'eino* and *yeshno*." Pachter formulates the difficulty thus:

> If this, then, is R. Azriel's view of heresy, does it not contradict his above statement that heresy is on a par with faith in the highest place on the scale of being?[24]

His response is as follows:

> Not necessarily. If we scrutinize R. Azriel's language, we find that "faith" and "heresy" are not used in the same sense as "the way of faith" and "the way of heresy." The former are likely to be perceived either ontic-metaphysically or psychologically-epistemologically, as their context indicates. This is not so in the latter case. These unequivocally and consistently indicate only the second meaning or sense. Thus, when R. Azriel declares, "The way of faith and the way of heresy are equal in the place of adherence of *'eino* and *yeshno*," he means that these mutually contradictory human approaches are equal at the upper boundary of existence, i.e. that the contradiction between them is annulled. This happens because faith at this point reaches its highest root, and is naturally strengthened, while heresy reaches its end point, becoming nothing. This appears to me the only correct understanding of R. Azriel's statement as to the equality of the two ways "in the place of the adherence of *'eino* and *yeshno*," since this point is the ontic-metaphysical embodiment of faith, which is at the basis of his whole discussion.[25]

Both Pachter's understanding of R. Azriel's view of heresy and his suggestion as to the meaning of R. Azriel's statement "The way of faith and the way of heresy are equal in the place of the adherence of *'eino* and *yeshno*" are very difficult to accept. First, granted that the "ontic-metaphysical essence" of heresy "lies at ... the place where being becomes non-being, that is, where being touches non-being,... at the [very] bottom of the ladder of being," we still have not clarified what heresy is "as

---

[24] Ibid., 27.
[25] Ibid., 27-28.

primarily ... a human inclination and tendency that as such reflects in a symbolic-mystical way [this] ontic-metaphysical essence."

Second, if indeed the "ontic-metaphysical essence" of heresy "lies at ... the place where being becomes non-being, that is, where being touches non-being," it is very strange that we should not find in R. Azriel's writings, as Pachter notes, "any mention of non-being."

Third, the distinction Pachter draws between "faith" and "heresy," on the one hand, and "the way of faith" and "the way of heresy," on the other, strikes me as forced and ad hoc.

Fourth, Pachter's claim that "when R. Azriel declares 'The way of faith and the way of heresy are equal in the place of the adherence of *'eino* and *yeshno*,' he means that these mutually contradictory human approaches are equal at the upper boundary of existence, i.e. that the contradiction between them is annulled. This happens because faith at this point reaches its highest root, and is naturally strengthened, while heresy reaches its end point, becoming nothing," strikes me as similarly forced and ad hoc. How can one say that "The way of faith and the way of heresy are equal in the place of the adherence of *'eino* and *yeshno*," if in that place only faith exists, and not heresy? As for Pachter's argument in favor of his reading, namely, that for R. Azriel "the place of the adherence of *'eino* and *yeshno*,... is the ontic-metaphysical embodiment of faith," we will turn to it very soon.[26]

---

[26] Elbaum, *Mas'a be-Hallal ha-Panui*, 78-79, understands R. Azriel's claim that "the way of faith and the way of heresy are equal in the place of the adherence of *'eino* and *yeshno*," to mean that "in the realm of the *'ayin* ... there are no distinctions and limitations. It is a light that is so strong that it appears to us as darkness. In this place there is no meaning to what is traditionally termed 'faith' and 'heresy'—all is equal there in its value and weight." But R. Azriel in this statement does not speak of the way of faith and the way of heresy being equal in the realm of *'ayin* as a whole, but only "in the place of the adherence of *'eino* and *yeshno*," that is, only at the border between the two. Moreover, Elbaum's view that "in this place there is no meaning to what is traditionally termed 'faith' and 'heresy'—all is equal there in its value and weight" strikes me as a projection of a typically modern religious sensibility, with all its doubts and struggles, back onto R. Azriel—which is perhaps not so surprising in a work whose subtitle is "A Spiritual Autobiography." Finally, Elbaum appears to understand R. Azriel to be asserting in this passage the principle of the coincidence or cancellation (*bittul*) of opposites. Just as R. Azriel in this passage supposedly cancels the opposition between *yesh* and

Finally, Pachter completely ignores the significance and relevance of R. Azriel's warning:

> And everything is one in the simplicity of Absolute Undifferentiation. And concerning the inquiry into this, it is said, "Neither make thyself over wise" (Ecclesiastes 7:16), since it is not in the power of our defective understanding to comprehend the perfection of this "beyond inquiry" (*heker*) which is one with *Eyn Sof*. And concerning this it is said, "Do not search into that which is hidden from you" (Ben Sira 3:19; cited in TB *Haggigah* 13a).

In light of these difficulties, an alternative approach is called for. Let us begin with R. Azriel's warning.

This warning, particularly in its use of citations from Eccl. 7:16 and Ben Sira 3:19 (via *Haggigah* 13a), calls to mind Maimonides' very similar warning in *Guide of the Perplexed* I:32:

> If, when engaged in the study of divine matters ... you aspire to apprehend things that are beyond your apprehension ... you will have joined *Elisha Aher* ... and will be overcome by imaginings and by an inclination toward things defective, evil, and wicked, this resulting from the intellect's being preoccupied and its sight extinguished.... In spite of this [apprehension's] sublimity, greatness, and what it has of perfection, if it is not made to stop at its proper limit ... it may be perverted into a defect.... This notion is ... referred to in Scripture in the dictum ... "Neither make thyself over wise; why shouldst thou destroy thyself?" (Ecclesiastes 7:16) ... The Sages too intended to express this notion in their dictum: "Do not search into that which is hidden from you" (Ben Sira 3:19; cited in TB *Haggigah* 13a). This means that you should let your intellect move about only in the domain of things that man is able to apprehend. For in regard to matters that it is not

---

'*ayin*, so he similarly, Elbaum claims, cancels the opposition between faith and heresy. However, as Valabregue-Perry (235-236) convincingly argues, the passage does not refer to the cancellation of the opposition between *yesh* and '*ayin*, but rather to their being joined together, to each being contained in the other. While, as I shall immediately argue, faith and heresy, for R. Azriel, are not contained in one another, they do touch each other "in the place of the adherence of '*eino* and *yeshno*."

in the nature of man to apprehend, it is very harmful to occupy oneself with them.[27]

That Maimonides here has heresy in mind is confirmed by his reference to *Elisha Aher*, who "cut the shoots."[28]

Maimonides and, so we would contend, R. Azriel following in his wake are thus both arguing that what leads to heresy is pushing beyond the limits, seeking to "apprehend ... matters that it is not in the nature of man to apprehend." Coming specifically to R. Azriel, then, the nothingness that is the "ontic-metaphysical category of which human heresy is simply the symbolic reflection," is, contra Pachter, *not* the nothingness "lying at the bottom of the ladder of being, the place where being becomes non-being" in the Neo-Platonic sense of non-being, but precisely that nothingness that "R. Azriel calls *'ayin* or *'efes* ... which signifies all that it is above the *yesh*, in the sense of the infinite fullness of being that transcends the *yesh*." Indeed, R. Azriel precisely in the context of a warning against inquiring into the divine *'ayin*, the divine nothingness, refers to it as "that which thought cannot apprehend" (*mah she-ein ha-mahshavah masseget*),[29] an almost exact echo of Maimonides' "matters that it is not in the nature of man to apprehend."

---

[27] The English translation is taken from Shlomo Pines' translation (Chicago and London: University of Chicago, 1962), 68-70, with some modifications. In particular, I have, unlike Pines, consistently translated *"hassagah"* as "apprehension" and *"le-hassig"* as "to apprehend," both in the interest of accuracy and to better bring out the comparison with R. Azriel.

[28] See the famous *beraita* in *Haggigah* 14a [citing *Tosefta Haggigah* 2:3-4]: "Four entered the *Pardes*. One gazed and died; one gazed and was stricken; one gazed and cut the shoots; one ascended in peace and descended in peace [other versions read: entered in peace and departed in peace]. Ben Azzai gazed and perished...; Ben Zoma gazed and was stricken...; Elisha gazed and cut the shoots...; R. Akiva ascended in peace and descended in peace [other versions read: entered in peace and departed in peace]...." The meaning of "cut the shoots" is obscure, but from the evidence in both the Babylonian and Palestinian Talmuds it clearly refers to some form of heresy. The exact nature of this heresy, however, has been and continues to be a matter of some debate among both commentators and scholars.

[29] *Commentary on the Aggadot of the Talmud*, ed. Isaiah Tishby (Jerusalem: Magnes Press, 1983), 104 (Hebrew): "It need not be said that one should not inquire into that which thought cannot apprehend."

But how can this be? Is not "the place of adherence of *'eino* and *yeshno*," precisely the point, as Pachter indicates, which is "the ontic-metaphysical embodiment of faith." This is indeed the case, but it must be stated more exactly. True, R. Azriel says that "faith ... applies ... only to the place of the adherence of *'eino* and *yeshno*," but more precisely he argues that faith refers to "the place of the attachment of the *yesh* as it begins to emerge from *'ayin* into existence." That is, if a person focuses on "the place of the adherence of *'eino* and *yeshno*" from the standpoint of "the *yesh* as it begins to emerge from *'ayin* into existence," that is, from the standpoint of "He made *'eino* (His nothingness) into *yeshno* (His being)," the standpoint of the outermost limits of the *yesh*, he is a believer and has attained true faith. But if that believer proceeds one infinitesimal step beyond, crosses the border, and focuses on "the place of the adherence of *'eino* and *yeshno*" from the standpoint of the *yesh* being transformed back into the *'ayin*, that is, from the standpoint of "He made *yeshno* (His being) into *'eino* (His nothingness)," the standpoint of the outermost limits of the *'ayin*, then one seeks to understand "that which thought cannot apprehend" (*mah she-ein ha-mahshavah masseget*) and from the sublime depths of faith falls into the terrifying abyss of heresy. And that is what R. Azriel means when he states that "the way of faith and the way of heresy are equal in the place of the adherence of *'eino* and *yeshno*"!

This understanding of R. Azriel's statement "the way of faith and the way of heresy ... are equal in the place of the adherence of *'eino* and *yeshno*" is confirmed by a parallel passage in his *Commentary on the Aggadot of the Talmud* regarding the dangers involved in contemplating the divine *'ayin*, a passage which, in turn, is a reworking of a passage from R. Ezra of Gerona's own somewhat earlier *Commentary on the Aggadot of the Talmud*.

> Thought cannot ascend higher than its source [the *sefirah* of Wisdom]. Whoever breaks through to contemplate that to which thought cannot extend or ascend will suffer one of two consequences. Because of his forcing his thought to apprehend and cleave to that which he cannot apprehend, his soul will ascend and be severed [from his body] and return to her root or he will confuse his mind and his intellect. And this is what the verse states "Neither make thyself over wise; why shouldst thou destroy thyself?" (Ecclesiastes 7:16) ... And concerning this they

[the Sages] taught "Do not search into that which is hidden from you, and do not inquire into that which is concealed from you." [Ben Sira 3:19; cited in TB *Haggigah* 13a][30]

It should be noted that the evil consequence of "his soul will ascend and be severed [from his body] and return to her root" reminds one of the fate of Ben Azzai, who "gazed and died," while the evil consequence of "he will confuse his mind and his intellect" reminds one of the fate of Ben Zoma who "gazed and was stricken."[31] Similarly, the citations from Ecclesiastes 7:16 and Ben Sira 3:19 (via *Haggigah* 13a), echoing, as we have seen, Maimonides, remind one of the fate of *Elisha Aher*, who "cut the shoots" and committed heresy. We may then say that the tragic fate of these three Sages, according to both R. Ezra and R. Azriel, resulted from their "break[ing] through to contemplate that to which thought cannot extend or ascend," namely, the divine *'ayin*. By contrast, it appears that the reason why R. Akiva succeeded in "ascend[ing] in peace and descend[ing] in peace" was precisely because his thought did not aspire "to ascend higher than its source," that is, the *sefirah* of Wisdom or *yesh* (and that is what the phrase "ascended in peace" means), or, to put it differently, he, unlike the three other Sages, did not gaze upon the divine *'ayin*.

Be this as it may, it is clear that Rabbis Ezra and Azriel, these two kabbalists of Gerona, would often warn against contemplating the divine *'ayin*, cite in support of the warning of Ecclesiastes 7:16 and Ben Sira 3:19 (via *Haggigah* 13a), and predict that all sorts of destructive consequences would result from disregarding it, including committing heresy.[32] The innovation of R. Azriel in *Derekh ha-Emunah ve-Derekh*

---

[30] Ibid, 39-40. See Tishby's notes, ad loc., for the differences in wording between R. Ezra and R. Azriel. See, as well, Moshe Idel's discussion of this passage in *Kabbalah: New Perspectives* (New Haven and London: Yale University, 1988), 47.

[31] Note Rashi's comment on "was stricken" (*nifga*): "went mad" (*nitrefah da'ato*).

[32] Daniel Matt, in his very rich and learned essay to which I am greatly indebted, "Ayin: The Concept of Nothingness in Jewish Mysticism," in *Essential Papers on Kabbalah*, ed. Lawrence Fine (New York and London: New York University, 1995), 82, argues that "[R.] Azriel is aware of a positive return [to the source, i.e., the *'ayin*], characteristic of Neo-Platonic mysticism." In so arguing, he is following, as we shall see immediately, in Scholem's footsteps. In my view, however, the texts both he and Scholem cite do not substantiate their point. On p. 80 Matt cites several texts from R. Azriel's *Sod ha-Tefillah* regarding restoring

ha-Kefirah would appear to be the following. While both R. Ezra and R. Azriel, as we have seen, maintain that "Thought cannot ascend higher than its source," that is, the *sefirah* of Wisdom or *yesh*, the new point made by R. Azriel in *Derekh ha-Emunah ve-Derekh ha-Kefirah* is that thought can ascend to the "outer limit" of Wisdom, to the very "place of the attachment of the *yesh* as it begins to emerge from *'ayin* into existence," and that that place is the place of faith. Conversely, while both

---

the individual words of prayer to nothingness. "You should know that one who prays ... must restore each word to its nothingness (*'afisato*)." Again, true prayer is one in which "we have directed (*hidrakhnu*) the words to the nothingness of the word (*'efes davar*)." But it is one thing to speak about the need to "restore each word to its nothingness" or to "have directed the words to the nothingness of the word," and quite another to insist that the mystic himself return to and contemplate the divine *'ayin*. Scholem, who published these texts in "*Seridim Hadashim*," 215-216, discusses them in his article "The Concept of Kavvanah in the Early Kabbalah," in *Studies in Jewish Thought*, ed. Alfred Jospe (Detroit: Wayne State University Press, 1981), 167-168 (originally published in *MGWJ* [1934]. He remarks: "Directing (*hadrakhah*) one's words ... towards the 'nothingness of the word,' which is the *fons et origo* of the divine Will to which the Kabbalist surrenders himself in prayer and with which he is imbued—this is the religious concern of prayer." But in none of these texts does R. Azriel speak of being imbued with the divine Will. On p. 177, note 35, the note appended to Scholem's immediately above claim about R. Azriel, Scholem refers the reader to a passage from R. Joseph ibn Gikitilla's *Sha'arei Orah*. There ibn Gikitilla states, "For a person must have the proper intention in his prayers and ascend from *sefirah* to *sefirah* and from will to will until he will reach in his heart the source of the supernal Will which is called *Eyn Sof.*" But Scholem—I would argue— is projecting this radical unitive view of ibn Gikitilla back onto R. Azriel without any warrant. Matt on p. 82 further cites another statement from R. Azriel's *Sod ha-Tefillah* about "one who ascends from the form of forms to the root of roots ... [i.e.], the root [that] extends through every form." But, as Tishby convincingly demonstrates in dealing with somewhat similar passages from R. Azriel's *Commentary on the Aggadot of the Talmud*, it is *Hokhmah* or *yesh* and not *Keter* or *'ayin* which is the root of all forms. See Tishby, 82, note 7 and (especially) p. 84, note 4 (taking issue with Scholem). Given this the passage from R. Azriel's *Commentary on the Sacrifices*, cited by Matt on p. 82, which speaks of the ascension of the priest's soul and "return to her root, whence she was taken" must again refer to *Hokhmah* and not *Keter*. It is surprising that Matt refers to Idel's discussion of this passage in *Kabbalah: New Perspectives*, p. 52, since Idel on pp. 46-47 appears to take for granted the view for which I have been arguing, namely that R. Azriel, under the influence of R. Ezra, believes that the soul cannot ascend higher than the *sefirah* of *Hokhmah*.

would often warn against contemplating the divine *'ayin*, the new point made by R. Azriel in *Derekh ha-Emunah ve-Derekh ha-Kefirah* is that one may not even contemplate the "outer limit" of the divine *'ayin*, that is, the place at which the divine *'ayin* adheres to the divine *yesh*, and that that place is the place of heresy. And the conclusion which follows from these two points is the most daring innovation of all: namely that these two places, the place of faith and the place of heresy, are in truth one and the same place, that one place which is the meeting point of the outer limits of both the divine *yesh* and the divine *'ayin*, that is "the place of the adherence of *'eino* and *yeshno*" seen from two different perspectives. Faith and heresy, thus, are both in existence at the border between *yesh*

Finally, Scholem, in his early article already referred to, "The Concept of Kavvanah in the Early Kabbalah," on 172-174, published an important manuscript, "Sha'ar ha-Kavvanah le-Mekubalim ha-Rishonim, z'l." This text propounds a radical type of *unio mystica* in which "the upper [divine] will clothes itself in his [the mystic's] will," and thereby the two wills are unified. In the text of the article Scholem surmises that "this piece was composed around 1280-1300, but I am unable to state by whom" (171). However, by 1962, Scholem in *Ursprung und Anfange der Kabbala* attributed the text to R. Azriel "to judge by the style as well as the thought." See *Origins of the Kabbalah*, ed. R.J. Werblowsky and trans. Allan Arkush (Philadelphia and Princeton: Jewish Publication Society and Princeton University, 1987), 416. Similarly, in a note appended in the mid-70s to the English version of his 1934 article, Scholem authoritatively states "I have come to recognize that R. Azriel is the indubitable author [of this text]." See p. 179, note 52a. Joseph Dan, however, in *The Heart and the Fountain: An Anthology of Jewish Mystical Experience* (Oxford and New York: Oxford University Press, 2002), 117, states: "Scholem suggested that the author [of "Sha'ar ha-Kavvanah le-Mekubalim ha-Rishonim, z'l"] may be R. Azriel ... but no conclusive proof of this attribution has been found. It is better to regard it as an anonymous text." I would go further than Dan. Scholem's attribution of this work to R. Azriel is of a piece with and no doubt influenced by his reading of R. Azriel's authentic works as expressing a radical view of *devekut*. But the different, complementary lines of argument put forward by Tishby, Idel, and myself indicate that such a reading is untenable. To state matters more strongly: given the evidence that R. Azriel followed R. Ezra in believing that the soul cannot ascend higher than the *sefirah* of *Hokhmah*, it is highly unlikely that he is the author of "Sha'ar ha-Kavvanah le-Mekubalim ha-Rishonim, z'l," with its espousal of a radical type of *unio mystica*. More recently, Valabregue-Perry, 148-149, follows Scholem in maintaining that this text was "apparently" ("kanireh") authored by R. Azriel. Like Scholem, however, she brings no arguments in support of this attribution.

and *'ayin*, but faith is always on the *yesh* side of the border, while heresy is always on the *'ayin* side of the border.

But how, it may be queried, can R. Azriel assert (according to my understanding) in *Derekh ha-Emunah ve-Derekh ha-Kefirah* that faith can ascend no higher than "the place of the attachment of the *yesh* as it begins to emerge from *'ayin* into existence," and that indeed if one focuses on "the place of the adherence of *'eino* and *yeshno*" from the standpoint of the *yesh* being transformed back into the *'ayin*, the standpoint of the outermost limits of the *'ayin*, one will fall into the abyss of heresy, when R. Azriel in *Sha'ar ha-Sho'el* asserts, as we have argued, that faith means faith in the existence of the *Eyn Sof* despite his hiddenness, despite the fact that his existence is not demonstrable, despite the fact that he is not visible and perceivable to human contemplation? The answer, I would suggest, is that R. Azriel in his two works is referring to two different types of faith. The type of faith of which R. Azriel speaks in *Sha'ar ha-Sho'el*—setting to the side the well-known but often debated distinction between "belief that" and "belief in"—is a propositional type of faith, a faith in the *existence* of the *Eyn Sof*. It is, so to speak, a faith from afar. By contrast, the type of faith of which R. Azriel speaks in *Derekh ha-Emunah ve-Derekh ha-Kefirah* is a contemplative type of faith, a faith of relationship. It is a faith where one contemplates and seeks to relate to "the place of the attachment of the *yesh* as it begins to emerge from *'ayin* into existence." It is a faith from up close, as it were.[33] And here, as we have seen, R Azriel's point is that if in this moment of contemplation, of relationship, one seeks to contemplate and relate to the divine "*'ayin* that is neither seen nor comprehended," then precisely because that divine "*'ayin* ... is neither seen nor comprehended," one will be left with (literally) nothing to contemplate and relate to and will lose his footing entirely. We may therefore understand R. Azriel's statement, "For faith neither applies to the *yesh* that is seen and comprehended, nor to

---

[33] On the issue of faith in general and, more specifically, the distinction between "belief that" and "belief in," see Shubert Spero, "Faith and its Justification," *Tradition* 13:1 (1971): 54-69 and Moshe Halbertal, "'Al Ma'aminim ve-Emunah," in *'Al Ha-Emunah*, ed. Moshe Halbertal, David Kurzweil, and Avi Sagi (Jerusalem: Keter, 2005), 11-38, 585-586. In light of my analysis, it would be worthwhile to reexamine Rabbi Nahman of Bratslav's views of faith and heresy, discussed by Pachter in "The Root of Faith is the Root of Heresy," 51-91. But to do this would take us much too far afield.

the *'ayin* that is neither seen nor comprehended, but only to the place of the adherence of *'ayin* and *yesh*" as follows: if one contemplates and relates to "the *yesh* that is seen and comprehended," that is not faith but knowledge. Conversely, if one seeks to contemplate and relate to "the *'ayin* that is neither seen nor comprehended," even the *'ayin* at the place of adherence to the *yesh*, one will end up not with faith but with heresy. Only the contemplation of, the seeking to relate to, the *yesh* at "the place of the adherence of *'ayin* and *yesh*," that is, the place where "the *yesh* … begins to emerge from *'ayin* into existence"—only that is faith.

In his recent book of constructive theology, *Sacred Attunement*, the distinguished scholar of Bible and Jewish thought, Michael Fishbane, after setting to the side R. Azriel's "mystical metaphysics," paraphrases his understanding of faith in *Derekh ha-Emunah ve-Derekh ha-Kefirah* thus:

> At the very borderline between the unknowable realm of Absolute Reality, the realm of the Naught, and all that might be humanly conceived or known by human minds, the realm of the Aught,… we have … some imaginable sense of aught grounded in naught; that is, a sense that the all-unfolding of reality and being of existence, whose source is God, is ultimately effaced in the depths of God's Godhood.… [For R. Azriel] the realm of *emunah* is … an ontological reality effectuated by God, [for] whatever we understand as Being is, ultimately, grounded in and faithful to God's most ultimate truth of all-sustaining steadfastness [*emunat 'omen*].… Human "faith" (*emunah*) should be understood not as some cognitive suspension of ordinary consciousness, but rather as the concern to attune oneself faithfully to the divine source where the seeds of all Being are sown and sustained-faithful to God's own truth. Theology would then have the task of cultivating this spiritual attunement so that a person might live in *emunah*—that is, living faithfulness to God's *yesh* (or Aught) such as it is and unfolds in worldly existence, where the human self may receive it and bend it to thoughtful and sustainable ends.[34]

---

[34] Fishbane, *Sacred Attunement*, 36-37. Fishbane, unfortunately, does not seek to determine what R. Azriel means by heresy. At one point in his discussion, however, he refers to "our sense of God where the Naught is the ultimate reality wherein all mindfulness is eclipsed" (p.37). If my understanding of R. Azriel is correct, it is exactly this ultimate reality, precisely because therein "all mindfulness is eclipsed," which is the place of heresy.

Returning from faith to its opposites, we can now also understand the difference between the rebellion discussed in *Sha'ar ha-Sho'el* and the heresy discussed in *Derekh ha-Emunah ve-Derekh ha-Kefirah*. The rebellion discussed in *Sha'ar ha-Sho'el* is a refusal. The rebel refuses to believe in the existence of the *Eyn Sof*, since the existence of the *Eyn Sof* is not rationally demonstrable. He relies exclusively upon his reason and refuses to go any further. The heresy discussed in *Derekh ha-Emunah ve-Derekh ha-Kefirah*, by contrast, results from the attempt to go beyond, to break through "the outer limit of what humans can apprehend," in which case one ends up apprehending nothing at all. To put it succinctly: the rebel does not go far enough; the heretic goes too far.

To conclude: as we saw, Pachter maintains:

> Thus, when R. Azriel declares "The way of faith and the way of heresy are equal in the place of the adherence of *'eino* and *yeshno*," he means that these mutually contradictory human approaches are equal at the upper boundary of existence, i.e. that the contradiction between them is annulled. This happens because faith at this point reaches its highest root, and is naturally strengthened, while heresy reaches its end point, becoming nothing.

In light of everything we have seen, I would maintain that exactly the opposite is the case. "The place of the adherence of *'eino* and *yeshno*," is precisely the place where the danger of heresy is *the greatest*. For if "the place of the adherence of *'eino* and *yeshno*" from the standpoint of "the attachment of the *yesh* as it begins to emerge from *'ayin* into existence" is the place of true faith, that *very same* "place of the adherence of *'eino* and *yeshno*" from the standpoint of the *yesh* being transformed back into the *'ayin* is the place of heresy.

Indeed, how appropriate are the great words of the Sages: Only a hair's breadth separates heaven from hell![35]

---

[35] Indeed, for Maimonides as well, as should be clear from *Guide of the Perplexed* I:32, only a hair's breadth separates R. Akiva from Elisha Aher; and, as should further be clear from *Guide of the Perplexed* I:21 (which refers to I:32), it is only an even thinner hair's breadth that separates *Elisha Aher* from Moses himself.

On the Essence of Faith in Hasidism: An Historical-Theoretical Perspective

Ron Margolin

Translated from the Hebrew by Orr Scharf

Scholars have often described Hasidism, founded in Ukraine during the second half of the eighteenth century by disciples of R. Israel Ba'al Shem Tov (also known as the Besht, 1700-1760),[1] as a direct offshoot of medieval Kabbalah. However, little scholarly attention has been devoted, particularly in the past fifty years, to the notion of faith in Hasidism. This was due, among other reasons, to the view that faith in Hasidism is identical with the faith in its antecedent Kabbalah and Musar literatures. A significant contribution to the consolidation of this view has been Yosef Weiss' influential article, "Mystical Hasidism and Hasidism of Faith."[2] In it, Weiss distinguishes between two major hasidic schools: mystical Hasidism, whose main proponent was R. Dov Ber, the Maggid of Mezeritch (1710-1772);[3] and Hasidism of faith, whose main proponent

---

[1] On the Besht, see Immanuel Etkes, *The Besht: Magician, Mystic, Leader* (Waltham: Brandeis University Press, 2005); Moshe Rosman, *Founder of Hassidism: A Quest for the Historical Baál Shem Tov* (Berkeley: University of California Press, 1996).

[2] The article "Mystical Hassidism and Hassidism of Faith" was first published in 1950. See Yosef Weiss, *Studies in Braslav Hassidism* (Jerusalem: Bialik Institute, 1974), 87-95 (Hebrew).

[3] On the life of the Maggid and his influence see Simon Dubnow, *History of Hassidism* (Tel Aviv: Dvir Publishing House, 1960), 76-87 (Hebrew); Immanuel Etkes, *The Beginning of the Hasidic Movement* (Tel Aviv: Ministry of Defense, 1998), 57-67 (Hebrew); Zeev Gries, *Conduct Literature (Regimen Vitae): Its History and Place in the Life of Beshtian Hasidim* (Jerusalem: Bialik Institute, 1990), 103-124; 292-308 (Hebrew).

was Rabbi Nahman of Bratslav (1772-1810).[4] Weiss's article is based on the assumption that there is an essential difference between the two schools: one is based on a pantheistic or quasi-pantheistic perception of divinity, which is impersonal in essence, and the other holds a personal or voluntaristic perception of God that is based on faith.[5] The hasidic preoccupation with faith was chiefly manifest in the teachings of R. Nahman of Bratslav, whereas the Maggid's disciples perceived the spiritual plane as a mystical-pantheistic realm that does not concern itself with such questions.[6]

The masters and followers of Hasidism were acquainted with the rich variety of Jewish sources produced throughout the ages up until their own time. Therefore, it is no wonder that their writings express diverse manifestations of Jewish faith inspired by these sources. As a relatively recent movement, which relies on *Musar* literature and an intense preoccupation with questions of faith, Hasidism's writings engage with a myriad of traditional aspects of faith in a world-creating God, including faith in individual providence and trust in God in the spirit of early pious figures found in Talmudic literature and in the moralistic, philosophical, and kabbalistic literatures of the Middle Ages. In this article I intend to focus on the aspects of hasidic faith that are unique to the disciples of the Besht, demonstrating how they underlie the very essence of all hasidic schools. Moreover, the dilemma of having to choose between faith in or denial of divine providence—experienced across Europe by

---

[4] On the life and teachings of R. Nahman of Bratslav, see R. Nathan Sternhertz, *Hayey Moharan*, (Jerusalem: Agudat Meshech Hanachal, 1985); for academic studies, see Arthur Green, *Tormented Master: The Life and Spiritual Quest of Rabbi Nahman of Bratzlav* (Alabama: University of Alabama Press, 1979); Mendel Piekarz, *Studies in Braslav Hasidism* (Jerusalem: Bialik Institute, 1995) (Hebrew); Weiss, *Studies in Braslav Hassidism*; Zvi Mark, *Mysticism and Madness: The Religious Thought of Rabbi Nahman of Bratzlav* (London: Continuum, 2009).

[5] Weiss, *Studies in Braslav Hassidism*, 89-90.

[6] Following Weiss, Rivka Shatz Uffenheimer (among others) focused in her book *Hasidism as Mysticism: Quietistic Elements in Eighteenth Century Hasidic Thought* (Princeton: Princeton University Press, 1993), on the world of the Maggid of Mezeritch and his disciples, without making any reference to the question of faith in their writings. Unlike her, I will present below numerous passages discussing the nature of faith in the world of the Maggid and his disciples.

Jews and non-Jews alike—is key to an understanding of Hasidism as a religious movement contending with the intellectual challenges of the Enlightenment. This aspect has escaped the attention of the majority of scholars of Hasidism. In what follows, I will focus on teachings and tales that reflect the spiritual world of the great hasidic masters. The sources span nearly a hundred and fifty years, beginning in the mid-eighteenth century with the Besht and ending in the late nineteenth century.[7] The challenges Hasidism has been facing since the late nineteenth century until our day, including massive desertion in the wake of the *Haskalah* movement in the mid-to-late nineteenth century and the destruction of hasidic communities and historical centers in the two world wars, call for an entirely separate discussion.

According to a popular story about R. Pinhas Shapira of Korets (1726-1791),[8] the considerable influence the Besht had over him followed from the advice he gave R. Pinhas for overcoming doubts of faith:

> Once it entered [R. Pinhas'] heart to say that Nature [rather than God] directs each and every thing [in the world] etc. And the Besht came into the town and went to [see R. Pinhas], and the Besht said: "Why was the war against the Amalekites more clamorous than any of the other nations over which triumph was facile?[9] [Because] the Amalekites' sin was that they considered all

---

[7] Contrary to the unilateral approach of Martin Buber and Gershom Scholem, who preferred to focus on a single genre of Hassidic literature—the former on tales and the latter on homiletics—I am convinced that integrating both of these important genres is essential for gaining a comprehensive understanding of the world of Hassidism.

[8] R. Pinhas of Korets died while journeying to the Land of Israel, where his disciple R. Ya'akov Shimshon, the rabbi of Shfitovka, is believed to have resided. On R. Pinhas of Korets see Abraham Joshua Heschel, "On the Life of Pinhas of Korets," in *ALEI AYIN: The Salman Schocken Jubilee Volume—Contributions on Biblical and Post-Biblical Hebrew Literature, Poetry and Belles-Lettres—Issued on the Occasion of His Seventieth Birthday by a Circle of His Friends* (Jerusalem: 1948-1952), 213-244 (Hebrew); Dubnow, *History of Hasidism*, 104-106; *Imrey Pinhas Hashalem: Otzar Torat HaRav HaKadosh Rabbi Pinhas MeKaritz ve Talmidav*, vol. 2 (Benei Brak: Yecheskel Shraga Frenkel, 2003), 441-490 (hereinafter, *Imrey Pinhas*).

[9] Based on the verses, "Whenever Moses held up his hand, Israel prevailed; and whenever he lowered his hand, Amalek prevailed ... his hands were steadfast until the going down of the sun" (Exodus 17:11-12).

miracles to be part of Nature"; and [R. Pinhas] understood that [the Besht] was directing these words at him. And he went to pray *minhah* and then came back to [the Besht]. [R. Pinhas told] And I said to [the Besht]: how is that explained? And he said to me: for we see that a prayer is recited, and that we pray and [we] are answered, and it is proved that there is a Creator and an Overseer, and [R. Pinhas] went and prayed over that and rid himself of these thoughts, this is what I heard clearly.[10]

According to the hasidic tradition, R. Pinhas met with the Besht twice, in meetings which turned the son of a Lithuanian rabbi into a disciple and friend of the progenitor of Hasidism. The following story, related by disciples of R. Raphael from Bershad, himself a loyal disciple of R. Pinhas of Korets, candidly presents the admired teacher as suffering from rationalistic doubts of faith. In a longer version of the story, appearing in three different manuscripts, the story begins with a more detailed opening:

> The following is a true story: in the days of the holy R. Pinhas of Korets, the sea flooded a city that lay on the seashore. And R. Pinhas had heard of the event, and erred to think: "There, this city lies on the seashore, hence the sea has flooded it, yet this did not happen to another city, and if this is so then nature is responsible for this event, Heaven forbid. And then he said: What am I doing [thinking these thoughts]? They weaken [my] faith! And he made up his mind to travel to see the Besht....[11]

The Hasidim of Bershad are known for their accurate factual accounts. Testimony to their rabbi's doubts of faith, which led him to see the Besht, reinforce the impression that the story is reliable. This motif of grappling with doubts about the traditional belief in the existence of individual providence that operates independently of the deterministic laws of nature is typical of the Bershad hasidic tradition. Years later, according to

---

[10] *Imrey Pinhas*, vol. 1, 355. An adaptation appears in Martin Buber's *Tales of the Hasidim: The Early Masters*, trans. Olga Marx (New York: Schocken Books, 1961), 60.

[11] According to *Kitvey Yad Rabbi Yehuda Lev me Kalmiya*, stored in the archives of the *Siftey Tzaddikim* Institute; and also *Kitvey Yad Rabbi Avraham Shlomo Goldenboim me Tzfat*, see *Imrey Pinhas*, vol. 1, note 25.

the tradition of Korets Hasidim, R. Pinhas gave encouragement to young students who were grappling with doubts similar to the ones attributed to him.[12] On the face of it, the fact that the Korets tradition attributes the successful dismissal of doubts of faith to the Besht does not necessarily authenticate this tale, because it is quite plausible that the hasidic authors ascribed it to the Besht irrespective of historical fact. However, in additional sources ascribed to other Besht disciples, which appear below, we find time and again references to the positive impact of the unique prayer technique the Besht taught for reinforcing the faith in individual providence. According to the above story, the Besht explained to R. Pinhas that the Amalekites' sin was that they doubted providential presence on earth. This aspect of providence entails, among other things, the plausibility of supernatural miracles, about which we learn

---

[12] This is related, for one, in *Imrey Pinhas*, ibid., vol. 2, section 152, p. 183, and see also ibid., section 154, p. 184:
> A rabbi who was his disciple [i.e., of R. Pinhas of Korets's disciple] came to have doubts about faith in the blessed Creator, thoughts of heresy, Heaven forbid, and strange scruples as to how is it possible that the blessed God knows human thoughts and stratagems. But as that rabbi was immersed in the Torah and the fear of God from his youth, he suffered grief and torments over this and traveled to see his holy rabbi R. Pinhas to learn the meaning of these doubts and to ask his rabbi that he alleviate his heart's torment. And as he approached the house of the holy rabbi, the holy rabbi saw him through the window and recognized in his mien from afar all of those false ideas. And when he entered [the rabbi's] house to be greeted, even before beginning to share his thoughts with the rabbi, at the moment of greeting the holy rabbi said to him "Is it possible for the blessed Holy One not to know if I know?" These were his holy words. And the rabbi immediately turned back and returned home at peace with his thoughts.

R. Pinhas "read the thoughts" of the young disciple. The spiritual potential inherent in thought is the secret of its divine essence, and therefore what allows one to read the thoughts of one's fellows is one's attachment to their spiritual nature through one's inherent spirituality. Religious doubts originate from the separation of the spiritual from the corporeal. The skeptic assumes that the physical world is unrelated and unconnected to the spiritual world; mind-reading undermines this view and uproots such heresy. Hence we learn that thought is divine and God inheres in thought itself. For further discussion of this issue see Ron Margolin, *The Human Temple* (Jerusalem: Magnes Press, 2005), 264-267.

that R. Pinhas was himself skeptical.[13] One could attribute these doubts to the influence of medieval philosophy on R. Pinhas, or more specifically the rationalist doubts that followed from his reading of Maimonides' *Guide of the Perplexed*, which according to his disciples the rabbi knew very well. Still, one must concede that such doubts of faith are not essentially different from the philosophical doubts concerning miracles raised, for instance, by Spinoza in his *Tractatus Theologico-Politicus*.[14] Indeed, in the latter part of the eighteenth century such doubts began to preoccupy growing numbers of Jewish literati, and not only those from the circle of Moses Mendelssohn in Germany. The unique case of Shlomo Maimon, described in his autobiography,[15] of the prodigy from Nesvizh, Lithuania, who left his home and joined Mendelssohn and the Berlin intellectual circles, is exceptionally extreme. At the same time, it would be improbable to assume that there were no other similar, if less extreme, cases among his East European contemporaries.

The implications of the development of scientific determinism had begun to seep slowly into the minds and hearts of curious and intelligent young people in the hasidic heartland of Eastern Europe, and certainly among those living in the northern areas that were more exposed to the German culture of eastern Prussia. The Besht's reply to R. Pinhas may strike us as a simplistic, traditional response: the fact that prayers are helpful proves that there is a providential Creator who responds to those who pray to him. If the Besht's conception of prayer was that naive

---

[13] In *Likutey Moharan*, Tanina (Jerusalem: Braslav Publishing House, 1968), section 19 (Hebrew), we find an identical interpretation of the sin of Amalek:
> For Amalek was a philosopher and a scholar and denied the principles of faith, as it is written "and he did not fear God" (Deuteronomy 25:18), that is, that he only acts according to reason, and is not God-fearing whatsoever; but the *tzadik*, when he learns these seven [principles of] wisdom, he sustains himself and remains unswerving by virtue of faith, as in the vitality "the righteous shall live by his faith" (Habakkuk 2:4) [...] and this is what Scripture means when saying of Moses that "his hands were steadfast" (Exodus 17:12), in the war against Amalek, for it was through faith that he weakened Amalek, that is, the abovementioned attachment to reasoning and scholarship.

[14] Benedictus de Spinoza, *Theological-Political Treatise*, trans. Michael Silverthrone & Jonathan Israel (Cambridge: Cambridge University Press, 2007), 81-96.

[15] Salomon Maimon, *The Autobiography of Salomon Maimon*, trans. J. Clark Murray (London: East and West Library, 1954).

and simple, this explanation of his reply would have sufficed. However, a more careful consideration of the Besht's conception of prayer will lead us to not take his words at face value.

Faith is Prayer is *Devekut:* The Doctrine of the Besht

R. Jacob Joseph Hacohen of Polonnoye (d. 1782),[16] the first hasidic author, often mentions teachings in the name of his rabbi and teacher the Besht pertaining to the bond between faith and prayer:

> These *tzadikim* are emissaries of the *Matronita* [queen][17] called prayer, as it is written "I am all prayer" (Psalms 109:4), and this should be read to mean faith, as [is well] known, but while [the queen] has many attributes, in this context the attribute of faith supersedes all others, because faith and *dvekut* are one, as it is written "and they believed in God and his servant Moses" (Exodus 14:31), as the Holy Spirit was upon them through the *dvekut* in Him, may He be blessed, as the Rabbis said,[18] "Then believed they His words; they sang His praises" (Psalms 106:12). And thus is the order of prayer, as it is written in the *Tur*, Orah Haim 39,[19] that the abstraction of corporeality and intensification of the mental powers are required when approaching the degree of prophecy, etc.[20]

In the world of Kabbalah, and especially in the *Zohar*, "faith" and "prayer" are epithets for the *Shekhinah* (also known as *Matronita*), the tenth *sefirah* connecting the supernal, divine realm with the lower, cor-

---

[16] On R. Jacob Joseph and his books, see, e.g., Dubnow, *History of Hassidism*, 93-101; Yaakov Yosef of Polonea, *Tzafnat Paánach* [*Nigeál Edition*] (Jerusalem: Institute for the Study of Hasidic Literature, 1989), 7-50.

[17] This is an idiom brought in the name of the Besht. See Ya'akov of Polonea, *Toldot Yaákov Yosef* (Jerusalem: Vegshel Publishing House, 1973; Korets, 1780), Parashat Vaéra 141; ibid. Parashat Shalach 507, etc.

[18] *Mekhilta of Rabbi Ishmael*, BeShalach; *Yalkut Shimoni*, I, 247, section 40.

[19] *Tur, Orah Haim*, Hilchot Tefila, section 98: "And this is what *hassidim* and men of deeds would do, they would go to be alone and direct their prayer until nearly reaching the point of abstracting corporeality and intensifying the spirit of their mind until they approached the degree of prophecy."

[20] Jacob Joseph of Polonnoye, *Ketonet Passim* [*Nigeál Edition*] (Jerusalem: Prie Ha'aretz Publishing House, 1985), Parashat Pinhas, 47b.

poreal one.²¹ The Besht and the early hasidic masters use this synonymy to denote their perception that faith is an intense form of devotion called *devekut* that is attained through prayer; hence, faith and prayer are one.

Throughout his *Toldot Ya'akov Yosef*, R. Jacob Joseph repeats the following formulation: "For it has been learned that faith is the clinging [*devekut*] of the soul to the blessed Holy One, as I have heard from my teacher when he taught the verse 'and they believed in God and in His servant Moses' (Exodus 14:31)."²² In light of this, I shall hold *devekut* in general, and prayer inspired by *devekut* as taught by the Besht in particular,²³ as a new key to understanding the notion of faith in Hasidism.²⁴

In one of the instances where R. Jacob Joseph mentions the Besht's equivocation of faith with *devekut*, he ties this formulation to *The Code of Maimonides (Mishneh Torah)*, Laws of the Foundations of the Torah 8.1, where Maimonides claims that the foundational element of Israel's faith is not the miracles that they witnessed during the exodus from Egypt, but rather the revelation at the Sinai covenant.²⁵ Therefore, according to

---

²¹ See Yosef Gikatilia, *Gates of Light*, trans. Avi Weinstein (San Francisco: Harper Collins, 1994), 163-164.

²² Ya'akov of Polonea, *Toldot Yaákov Yosef*, Parashat Ki Tavo, section Aleph; Parashat Shalach, 489; Parashat Tzav, sections Bet and Gimmel; Parashat Nasso, section Gimmel; Parashat Masaéy, section Aleph.

²³ See *Besht al HaTorah*, ed. Shimeon Menahem Mendel Gorbachov, vol. 1-2 (Jerusalem: 1962), Parashat Noah, *amud hatefilah*.

²⁴ In his article "'Dvekut' or Intimate Communion with God in Early Hassidism," Gershom Scholem established his argument that the uniqueness of Hasidism lies in its transformation of the value of *devekut*—based on the statement of R. Jacob of Polonnoye that "faith is *dvekut* of the soul in the blessed Holy One." Gershom Scholem, *The Messianic Idea in Judaism And Other Essays on Jewish Spirituality* (New York: Schocken Books, 1971), 208-209. According to Scholem, "The realization of *dvekut* as a social value ... could be done only at a high price, namely, by binding dvekut to the institution of Zaddikism, a connection wholly foreign to primitive Hasidism," 217. Scholem's claim that Hasidism had popularized Kabbalistic values by completely changing the status of *devekut* within the hierarchy of spiritual progress, is misleading, at least from the viewpoint of R. Jacob Joseph, on whom he based his claim, since R. Jacob Joseph insists repeatedly that *devekut* is a virtue that a select few possess.

²⁵ A great many teachings of R. Jacob Joseph of Polonnoye are influenced by his readings in Maimonides' writings and those of other medieval Jewish philosophers, as well as from readings in the various Kabbalistic sources which are essentially different from them, as he integrates them into a new thesis.

Maimonides, faith is founded on knowledge obtained through revelation. R. Jacob Joseph writes as follows:

> In the verse "I come unto thee in a thick cloud, that the people may hear when I speak with thee, and may also believe thee for ever" (Exodus 19:9), the doubts abounded, although they had already believed, as it is written "And the people believed" (Exodus 4:31). For Maimonides has also interpreted it this way (*Mishneh Torah*, Hilkhot Yesodei HaTorah 8.1). And also what is the meaning of "... and may also believe..."? And we think that this [passage] makes perfect sense: it is difficult [to explain] how did [God] say "I come unto thee in a thick cloud"; the thick cloud is a separating curtain, as He was forced to sojourn on a path and Moses could not arrive at the Tabernacle before the cloud was upon it. But this was not so, since [in the Tabernacle] speech was directed only at Moses and therefore it was possible [for God to speak to him directly], which was not possible at the giving of the Torah, as [God] had to reveal Himself to the entire nation. Therefore, He had to descend in a thick cloud which is [required by] the degree [of virtue] of the entire nation, for the people to hear [God] and for them to acknowledge His existence so they would connect with Him. And this was necessary for later, when Moses returned to his high degree [of virtue], and when [the people] connected with Him also, they also ascended with [Moses] by believing in Him forever, because as is well known faith is *dvekut*, and on this Scripture says "and [they] may also believe you for ever" (Exodus 19:9) and this is easy to understand.[26]

According to R. Jacob Joseph, the revelation at Sinai enabled the people to "see the thundering" (Exodus 20:14) and connect with God, that is, to experience *devekut* with God. Revelation is the foundation of faith in God and Moses his servant, and therefore the meaning of the verse "And they believed in ... Moses" (Exodus 14:31), is that they experienced *devekut* in God, they connected with him experientially and personally. Maimonides' analysis therefore becomes a paradigm for understanding the notion of "faith" as connection and *devekut*. This meaning of faith denies the speculative sense of the term, i.e., faith does not arise out of ignorance, but is rather based on a personal experience of connecting to

---

[26] Ya'akov of Polonea, *Toldot Yaákov Yosef*, Parashat Yitro, section Dalet. See also Parashat Tzav, section Gimmel: "Maimonides has commented that faith is the cleaving of 'face to face'" (*dvekut panim be panim*).

God. The Besht, according to R. Jacob Joseph, does not make do with adopting Maimonides' view on the experiential foundations of faith; he also insists that prayer emerging out of *devekut* can impact the corporeal world. Such a prayer attests—by virtue of its tangible impact—to God's sovereignty over the world, and as such it is a proclamation of faith. The worshipper's ability to bring about change by means of his prayers is explained by R. Jacob Joseph, in the name of the Besht, with kabbalistic teachings on the mystical power of the combination of letters:

> And apart from that we shall interpret what is meant by the prayer "the righteous [*tsaddik*] shall live by his faith" (Habakkuk 2:4); I have heard from my teacher that Nahmanides had pointed out a puzzle concerning the matter of prayer, and so has the commentator on Chapter 5 in [Tractate] Berachot *zichru* in the name of R. Hasday etc.,[27] as follows: [divine] judgment was transformed through prayer from worse to the better, and that a change in His will, may He be blessed, takes place, for if one prays for oneself then we must say that since one changes from worse to the better so too one's judgment changes from worse to the better. This is not the case if others pray for him, and [remains] a puzzle. And he explained: since prayer is aimed to mitigate the judgment of *Malkhut*, which is called *Din*, whose root is in *Bina*,[28] when one prays for one's friend in this manner then he ties together [that which is] on-high with the root [but] he is a different person, not the [one for whom the prayer is said], etc. And [the Besht] explained most clearly, that it has become known that the judgment is a drop in the uterus of *Malkhut* [and this drop] is the letters [of the alphabet], as said in the Talmud in [Tractate] Berachot, "Bezalel knew how to combine the letters by which the heavens and earth were created," etc,.[29] and surely the King Himself does not execute his judgments of others, but orders an emissary [to do that] with an ark of [letter] combinations that sounds the judgment [that God] issues regarding [the person being judged]. And the emissary may use the judgment's letters as acronyms to change the judgment's meaning. And here the *tzadik*, the Queen's emissary, who knows to moderate judgments at their root, to link the drop of *Malkhut* with *Bina* and change [the judgment] to a

---

[27] See *HaKotev le Ein Ya'akov*, Berachot 70a: "And the Rav Hasdai [Crescas] cites it in his *Or Hashem* as follows."
[28] See II *Zohar* 175b; ibid., III 65a.
[29] TB Berachot 55a.

different meaning [....] And the splendid [prayer] "the *tzadik* shall live by his faith," means that through prayer, faith and *dvekut*, the *tzadik* connects and links [the judgment] at its root, where as we know life is, and *Bina* is a synonym for The Living God[30] and hence "the *tzadik* shall live by his faith."[31]

Similar to the implication of the Kortes tradition, the words of R. Jacob Joseph indicate that the Besht believed that praying with *devekut* could impact the tangible world, and thus provide a counter-response to rationalist doubts in the vein of medieval philosophical literature. In his *Or Hashem*, R. Hasdai Crescas writes:

> The faith that depends on this mitzvah [prayer] is, that we should believe that the blessed God submits to the request of the praying man, who puts his trust in Him by following the truthful path in his heart [...] and we describe in our prayers the attributes of the blessed God using allegory and poetry, it would be appropriate for the *Kaddish* to contain passages confirming this. And the proclamation "to God out of all of the blessings, singing and praises," hints at the blessings that He, may He be blessed, rejects, for He is the one Who bestows them. And it is said that "singing and praises" hints at the attributes, which are described either with poetry or praises. And they said "His consolation" will indicate the beseechment by the needy, so that it should not be thought that He is moved by [our] prayer and is consoled by it, because this is not so. [God's attention to prayer] originates in His primordial will to submit to the prayer that is worthy of Him [...] and it has been said, that [this] has been gleaned also from the stories in the Torah. And the prayer of Moses for the people of Israel, and the prayer of Abraham for Sodom and Gomorra, and the prayer of Isaac for his wife, and acts [of miracle working] related in the Talmud, are based on the fact, that thanks to the prayer of the *tzadik* it may be that the Blessed God would submit to [the *tsaddik*'s] prayer even if he prays for his fellow.[32]

Crescas maintains that God himself, being infinite—or as he phrases it: in His being "without any end"—cannot be influenced by

---

[30] I *Zohar* 16a; ibid., II 68b.
[31] Jacob Joseph of Polonnoye, *Ketonet Passim*, 47a-b.
[32] R. Hasdai Crescas, *Or HaShem*, Shlomo Fischer Edition (Jerusalem: Sifrei Ramot, 1990), 372-375.

the content of any specific prayer. The possibility of effecting change through prayer lies in a "primordial will to submit to the prayer." That is, change is always present potentially, but nevertheless it does not prove divine susceptibility to change or influence. Crescas emphasizes that God can exert influence but cannot be influenced. The Besht's reply reveals a perception of divinity as aloof from the worshipper's sway, which at the same time allows the latter to be a divine emissary. Change may be effected as a result of the prayer of the *tsaddik* that ascends to the roots of the world-creating, divine letters. In connecting to the roots of these letters, and to the very core of *Einsof*, the *tsaddik* can change their combinations, since the combinations of letters represent the word of God, who creates worlds and destroys them. By means of the kabbalistic combinatory art of letters,[33] the Besht overcomes the rationalistic scruples concerning belief in prayer potential of effecting change, a problem that also preoccupied Jewish medieval philosophers. In this way he dispels the rationalistic doubts concerning the plausibility of intervention of the eternal and infinite divinity, triggered by the prayer of a single individual, in the futures of other humans who are completely oblivious to the fact that they are the subjects of that prayer. The Besht taught that praying with *devekut* is the answer to the doubts of faith, thanks to the power to change reality that is inherent to prayer.

To elaborate on our inquiry further, we must take a step deeper into the Besht's conception of prayer. One of its most important formulations is found in *Tzava'at HaRibash* (the will of the Besht), edited posthumously on the basis of his sayings:[34]

> Rabbi Israel Baál Shem Tov, May he be remembered in the World to Come, commented about the verse "make a porthole *tzohar* for the ark," (Genesis 6:16) that [this was in order for] the Word will

---

[33] See Shatz Uffenheimer, *Hasidism as Mysticism*, 169-173; Moshe Idel, *Hasidism: Between Ecstasy and Magic* (Albany: State University of New York Press, 1995), 149-170.

[34] Author of the *Book of Tanya* and founder of Chabad, R. Schneur Zalman of Lyadi wrote in *Iggeret HaKodesh*, section 25: "Understanding the words of wisdom written in the book called *Tzava'at HaRivash*, although it is not really his will and he did not [dictate] a will before he died, but it is a collection of his pure sayings, collected one by one."

be illuminated.[35] For in each letter there are worlds and souls and divinity. And they ascend and connect and unite with one another and with the Godhead. And then the letters unite and connect together and become a *teiva*, and unite truly in conjugating with the Godhead. And man must encompass in his soul each and every one of the aforementioned aspects, and then all the worlds unite as one, and ascend and unfathomable joy and pleasure abound. And this is [what is meant by the verse] "make it lower, second and third decks," (ibid.), that is, worlds and souls and divinity, [as God] has three worlds, etc. And one must listen carefully to what each word [*teiva*] says. For the *Shekhinah*, the realm of speech, speaks and has a *tzohar* [=both illumination and porthole] to come out clearly and please the Creator. And great faith in the above is required: that the *Shekhinah* is called complete faith [*emunat oman*] and without faith it would be called, Heaven forbid, *nirgan mafrid aluf* ("a whisperer separates close friends," Proverbs 16:28).[36]

*

In order for prayer to effect change in the combination of the letters that comprise the divine language governing worldly events, it must embody the entire range of meanings of the Hebrew root *tz.h.r.*: to illuminate and to open a porthole. According to the Maggid of Mezeritch, "Said R. Israel Ba'al Shem Tov, God said 'make a porthole for the ark' (Genesis 6:16) for it to illumine the ark."[37] While according to the grandson of the Besht, "My master and grandfather, may he rest in peace, has taught that 'ark' [*teiva*] implies word, which is [also] called *teiva*. And [as God] said 'make a porthole for the ark [*teiva*],' [the Besht] said 'so that you can illumine the word [*teiva*] that leaves your mouth.'"[38] An additional source

---

[35] The Besht is making a pun on the double meanings of *teiva*—ark and word—and the Hebrew root *tz.h.r*—porthole (*tzohar*) and daylight (*tzaharaim*). The literal meaning is made in the context of the ark's structure, and the Besht reads it as referring to the function of words in the supernal realm.

[36] "Tzava'at HaRibash," in *Tzava'ot ve Hanagot ha Besht ve Talmidav* (Benei Brak: Machshevet Publishing House, 1987), sections 79-81. For an identical teaching see also *Or Torah: Likutim me Divrey R. Dov Ber me Mezhirech* (Jerusalem: 1968), Parashat Noah, 14.

[37] Dov Ber of Mezeritch, *Or Ha Emet* [facsimile] (Benei Brak: Yahadut Publishing House, 1967), 1a.

[38] Moses Haim Ephraim of Sudylkow, *Degel Machaneh Efraim* (Jerusalem: Books Export Enterprises, 1963), Parashat Noah and Parashat Shelach.

comments on this issue as follows: "When praying one must invest all of oneself in uttering [the words], moving thus from one letter to the next until one forgets one's body, thinking that the letters join and connect with one another, and this is a great pleasure."[39] Praying with *devekut* requires, according to the Besht, tremendous concentration, or in the words of his *Will*: "One must hear the sound made by the utterance of each and every letter." This prayer possesses distinctive meditative features, as it deconstructs the literal meaning of its text, leading the worshipper to focus on the sound and shape of each and every letter.[40] According to the *Will*, in order to pray adequately, in a manner allowing the letters to embody the illuminative and open nature of the verb *tz.h.r.* and therefore ascend to the divinity, one must believe that the *Shekhinah*, identified in the opening of this teaching with the divinity, inheres even in the letters that comprise our spoken language. This belief is a condition for adequate prayer, whereby its words illuminate and are open to their divine essence. This conception is expressed in two formulations which are related in the name of the Besht, ubiquitous in early hasidic writings. The first pertains to letters, "for every letter holds worlds, souls and divinity," while the second describes the act of speech during prayer as a moment when "the *Shekhinah* speaks [in] the world of speech." We will now examine these formulations in greater depth.

I. For in Each and Every Letter There are Worlds, Souls, and Divinity

The first formulation found in the *Will* is found also in a missive of the Besht known as the "Epistle of the Ascent of the Soul."[41] This document is the only surviving text identified with the original authorship of the Besht; he had sought to send it with his disciple R. Jacob Joseph of Polonnoye to his brother-in-law, R. Gershon of Kutow, who had moved

---

[39] *Keter Shem Tov* (New York, 1987), part II, 217c.
[40] On contemplative prayer, see Shatz–Uffenheimer, *Hasidism as Mysticism*, 168-188.
[41] On "Epistle of the Ascent of the Soul," see *Shivehey ha Besht*, Mundshein Edition (Jerusalem: Published by Yehoshua Mundshein, 1980), 229-237; Moshe Idel, *Messianic Mystics* (New Haven: Yale University Press, 1998), 213-220. On the epistle of the Besht and the meaning of *yihud* in early Hasidism see Margolin, *The Human Temple*, 231-241, 338.

to live in the Land of Israel. As R. Jacob Joseph ended up not embarking on the journey, the epistle remained in his estate and was eventually published at the end of his *Ben Porat Yosef*:[42]

> But this I instruct you and may God help you on your way and let [these teachings] not escape [from you],[43] particularly in the Holy Land. In your prayer and study and each and every act of speech and utterance of your lips you shall direct to conjugate [on-high], for in each and every letter there are worlds and souls and divinity all rising and connecting and conjugating with one another, and then the letters connect and conjugate and become a word and truly unite with the divinity. And you shall bind your soul with each and every aspect of theirs [so that] all of the worlds unite as one and become a great joy and pleasure, far beyond your comprehension of the meager joy of corporeal brides and grooms; [this is] all the more so in this supernal sphere.[44]

A comparison of the epistle and the *Will* reveals that the encouragement of this form of intense faith is not found in the original epistle. This fact may imply that the *Will* reflects the perception of the Besht's students more than that of their master. The Besht instructs his brother-in-law to focus on the performance of every act of speech—be it for prayer, study, or everyday conversation—and on the esoteric meaning of each and every letter. During prayer and study, the Besht instructs the worshipper to merge his soul with the divinity found in each and every letter of the prayer text.[45]

Worlds are created with letters and therefore letters contain entire worlds; letters revive souls and therefore there are souls in them; letters contain the divinity for it is the divinity that revives worlds and souls. The divinity of the letters becomes united at the time of prayer with the

---

[42] Jacob Joseph of Polonnoye, *Ben Porat Yosef* (Korets: 1781).
[43] According to the verse "Let them not escape from your sight" (Proverbs 4:21).
[44] "Epistle of the Ascent of the Soul," ibid. The Korets version is almost identical with the version of the earlier manuscript presented in *Shivehey ha Besht*, 235-236.
[45] See Moshe Idel, "Universalization and Integration: Two Conceptions of Mystical Union in Jewish Mysticism," in *Mystical Union in Judaism, Christianity and Islam*, eds. Moshe Idel and Bernard McGinn (New York: Continuum, 1996), 27-57.

divinity inhering in the human soul, and that is the meaning of the term *yihud*, which literally means conjugation but is derived from the Hebrew root *y.h.d.*, with which *ehad* (one) and *ihud* (union or unification) share the same letters; in this context, *yihud* means spiritual unification with the divine, which generates much greater pleasure than the corporeal, sexual pleasure of conjugal unification. This manner of prayer and study appears in early hasidic writings as *dekhilu u-rekhimu*: prayer and study out of fear and love. By the power of this *yihud*, or unification, the letters keep connecting amongst themselves and create new combinations in the divine sphere—combinations that have the power to change corporeal reality.

Hasidic writings offer numerous explanations for this conception. Contrary to Weiss's claim, the hasidic school that he dubs "mystical and pantheistic faith," did not dismiss the belief in individual providence and in the power of prayer to change reality. Hasidism established creative bridges for overcoming the gap between the belief in an immanent divinity and the belief in a world-creating God who continues to oversee and direct his creation. First and foremost of these bridges is the conception of letter combination described above.

R. Pinhas of Korets opined that the Besht's formulation was inspired by the teachings of R. Isaac Luria (known as the ARI) in *Sha'ar Hayihudim*:

> And it is also found in the writings [of the ARI] and *Shc'ar Hayihudim*, that a single letter is a chariot [*merkabah*] to the Blessed Holy One and His *Shekhinah*, and all the worlds and souls depend upon a single letter. And it has been found that when a person speaks and believes that all of the worlds and the angels depend on a single letter and especially on the Blessed Holy One and the *Shekhinah*, thanks to this belief [that man] carries all of the created to the Creator, may His name be blessed, and even the nations of the world, all are carried. And anyone with the power to be carried finds sweet relief there, and whoever lacks vitality falls down. And this way we must pray even for the wicked from the nations of the world and this [is what we learn from] "reigned ... died" (see III *Zohar* 292a on Genesis 36) that were left without any vitality. And this is an important principle, because so long as one does not pray in this manner the Messiah will not come, and this will even lead to the resurrection of the dead [...]. And this is the important principle: that one knows with complete

certainty that each and every letter is a chariot to the *Shekhinah* and even to the Divine Throne.[46]

Through recognition of the divine element inhering in each letter comprising the words of speech, man becomes linked, indeed connected with and clinging [*middabek*] to the whole of divinity. R. Isaac Judah Safrin of Komarno, author of *Zohar Hai*, adds:

> And one must believe that one's every act of speech, contains these aspects [worlds, souls and divinity] as well as all existing entities, for the blessed God had created all creatures and the world through His power [of speech]. And He and the world are connected by means of souls that tie the entire world and its creatures to the God of truth, Who is one and incomparable."[47]

In prayer of this sort, the *yihud* with the letters exposes the immanent divinity, while the whole of reality ascends toward divinity by virtue of this observation. According to both R. Pinhas of Korets and R. Isaac Judah Safrin of Komarno, hasidic faith is the belief in an all-permeating divinity, particularly the letters comprising language. Prayer that is based on such belief becomes itself a declaration of faith in the concealment of the all-permeating divinity. On this R. Pinhas of Korets comments:

> All of my teachings concern the reinforcement of faith, [and] as I teach that the blessed Holy One inheres in any thing, in this way I bring closer the Messiah's [arrival]. Because faith is like legs, and the *Shekhinah*'s [presence] in this era is implied [in the verse] "her feet go down to death" (Proverbs 5:5), and when faith grows stronger death shall be gone forever and Messiah will come.[48]

---

[46] *Imrey Pinhas*, part I, 286. R. Isaac Judah Safrin of Komarno writes in his *Zohar Hai*: "It is explained in the writings of our teacher and rabbi the ARI, that the *Shekhinah* and the souls of angels ride on letters. The Besht had been taught by Achihu the Shilonite as follows: worlds, souls, divinity, are all one and the same." Isaac Judah Safrin of Komarno, *Zohar Hai* (Lemberg: M. Nick, 1878), Parashat Vayikhal, 161a.

[47] Isaac Judah Safrin of Komarno, *Netiv Mitzvotekha* (Jerusalem: Published by Abraham Mordechai Safrin, 1983), Netiv Emunah, path Gimmel, 14, pp. 27-28.

[48] *Imrey Pinhas*, 354, section 38.

Faith in early Hasidism was essentially the belief in an all-permeating divinity; it is a belief that the world's material composition—and indeed even the letters possess a material aspect—serve as the garment of a divine essence that enlivens all and permeates everything. In the writings of the Besht's disciples and their successors, his conception of the divinity that permeates reality as a whole, and the letters of the alphabet in particular, is posited as the essence of hasidic faith. R. Jacob Joseph explains the three aspects inhering in every letter as three degrees found also in man:

> And this is how one should understand the three decks in Noah's ark, "make it lower, second and third decks" (Genesis 6:16); in addition to interpreting the decks as symbolizing the three aspects in man, the days of youth, maturity and old age etc., we should also interpret the three degrees in man as symbolizing Noah's ark. Because we find matter, internal form and garment [external form] in the world, or [in a] city and state, and also in the individuality of man according to the secret of *a.sh.n.*[49]

In light of this, we may say that he perceives the "worlds" as the material aspect of every letter; the "souls" are the garment; and "divinity" their internal form.

According to R. Menahem Nahum of Chernobyl (1730-1797),[50] connecting to divinity through prayer that contemplates divinity is

---

[49] *Toldot Ya'akov Yosef*, Parashat Noah, section Aleph. The secret of *ayin-shin-nun* (acronym for *olam-shana-nefesh*) world-year-soul—is mentioned numerous times in the books of R. Jacob Joseph, and even in the writings of the Maggid of Mezeritch (e.g., *Maggid Devarav le Ya'akov* [Shatz Edition] [Jerusalem: Magnes Press, 1990], sections 64, 86, 194). That is, that which is found in the world is also found in the human soul and in human history. The origin of the triangle "world-year-soul" is *Sefer Yetzirah*, Chapter 4. It is defined by the Maggid of Mezeritch as follows: "*Olam* is the entire world; *Nefesh* is all the creatures; *Shanah* is time" (ibid., section 86).

[50] According to certain Hassidic traditions, R. Menahem Nahum met the Besht while still young in Mejibuz, and after the latter's death became one of the senior disciples of the Maggid of Mezeritch. On R. Menahem Nahum of Chernobyl see Dubnow, *History of Hassidism*, 199-203; Idel, *Messianic Mystics*, 221-334; Arthur Green, "Introduction" in *Menahem Nahum of Chernobyl: Upright Practices: The Light of the Eyes*, trans. and Introduction by Arthur Green, (New York: Paulist Press, 1982), 20-24.

conditioned upon the belief that this can be done. Similarly to R. Jacob Joseph, he interprets Jacob's dream in the spirit of the teachings of the Besht, and explains how the prayer that is contemplated with fear and awe (*dekhilu u-rekhimu*) makes it possible to overcome the evil he terms, following the kabbalistic tradition, *dinin* (demonic presence):

> It is only Israel's lack of the faith and mind, needed to bind this world to the world of the soul, that causes the world to fall constantly and to remain cut off from life. Then judgment comes to the world,[51] and it is only for the few righteous ones in each generation who serve God with mind and with love and fear that the world is allowed to exist and does not fall utterly [....] In messianic times (speedily and in our day, God willing!) there will be so much mind-awareness in the world that this world and its corporal self will indeed be purified and matter will be joined to form, the two worlds united. Then evil, excess, and dross will all fall to the side, [eventually] to be purified [....] The lessening of faith brings about a diminishing of mind.[52]

That is, according to R. Menahem Nahum, in order to reach the knowledge of the spiritual, divine essence inhering in materiality and in the letters of the Torah, one must believe in the spiritual, divine interiority of the visible material garment of divinity, i.e., corporeal reality. In other words: faith is the condition for knowledge.

II. The Shekhinah Speaks from His Mouth

The formulation "the *Shekhinah* speaks [in] the world of speech," found in the *Will*, is phrased somewhat differently but in the same context in the Maggid of Mezeritch's *Maggid Devarav Le Ya'akov*:

---

[51] R. Menahem Nahum explains on behalf of the Besht that evil is an outcome of the fall of the *dinin* from on-high down to earth: "The fact that a person has enemies below is only the result of some judgment *(dinin)* on him from above, mixed with evil impurities and then garbed in the sort of person in this world who would be appropriate to such a role. The best advice in this situation is not to challenge the enemy, but to go daily to the House of Study, into the innermost Torah, to a place of awareness. By studying and praying with love and fear you will arouse true *da'at*." Menahem Nahum of Chernobyl, *Upright Practices, The Light of the Eyes*, Parashat Vayetze, 218-219.

[52] Ibid., 221-224.

> Because when a man begins to pray, as soon as he recites "O Lord, open thou my lips," the *Shekhinah* assumes him as her garb and recites the prayer, and when he possesses the faith that the *Shekhinah* recites these prayers surely he will be overcome by dread and awe, and even the blessed Holy One so to speak contracts Himself and inheres in him as it is written "looking through the lattice" (Song of Songs 2:9), [that is] through the letters which are *hekhalot*.[53]

As in the *Will*, in the above passage from the Maggid's writings the worshipper is asked to believe that it is the *Shekhinah* that speaks the words of prayer coming out of his mouth. It is important to notice here that the *Shekhinah* is in fact the divine vitality that sustains speech. This is not the tenth *sefirah* known in the kabbalistic hierarchy of *sefirot* also as "faith." In hasidic teachings, the *Shekhinah* becomes a generic term for divinity and no longer refers to a single attribute in the complex Kabalistic divine system. The *Shekhinah* is faith, in the sense that it is the belief in the divine vitality that permeates everything, particularly the man whose prayer it facilitates.

The quotations attributed to the Besht and the version found in the writings of the Maggid (including the *Will*, whose authorship, as I have mentioned, is attributed to the circle of his disciples), call on all people to pray with *devekut* out of the belief that when we pray the *Shekhinah* speaks from within us.[54] This is not the case with the majority of other hasidic writings that discuss the concept of the *Shekhinah* that speaks from man's mouth. In later hasidic works, this notion, which is derived from a passage in the *Zohar* about Moses, applies only to a select few *tsaddikim*:

> "And I have put my words in your mouth, and hid you in the shadow of my hand, stretching out the heavens etc." (Isaiah 51:16.) Here the blessed Holy One places His holy words in the mouths of the *tzadik* so he may bestow mercy and grace upon the world and all of their needs, and though the *tzadik* speaks with his own mouth and tongue, still the ability to speak and speech itself are an ability of the blessed God Himself and are not, Heaven forbid, separate from Him whatsoever. And as it is written, Moses our

---

[53] *Maggid Devarav le Ya'akov*, 13.
[54] For example ibid., sections 2, 50, 173.

Teacher was leader to all prophets, as the *Shekhinah* would speak from his mouth. And [from the mouth of] each *tzadik* according to the degree of his virtue and *dvekut*. Therefore, due to the divine ability within him, the mouth [of the *tzadik*] has the ability to create new heavens and to lay foundations for the earth, and Rashi has commented "and to finish gathering [them]."[55]

In the version of the *Will* that is attributed to the authorship of the Besht, the notion of the *Shekhinah* speaking from the mouth of man does not apply to the specific contents of uttered speech, but to a more general conception similar to the "prayer of lips" that Shlomo Naeh describes in his study of free-flowing prayer.[56] It seems that this conception underlies the Besht's yearning to disseminate his approach, reflected in the story of his encounter with the Messiah upon the ascension of his soul, which he describes in the epistle to his brother-in-law (mentioned above). This conception assumed an additional dimension already in the early days of Hasidism, and throughout the hasidic corpus we find that it relates to the content of prayer, rather than to its praxis.[57] The *tsaddik*

---

[55] Yisrael of Koznitz, *Avodat Yisrael ha Shalem* (Levov: Published by Israel Zeev from New York, 1954), *likutim*, 91b.

[56] Naeh proposes to understand Rabbi Akiva's prayer described in TB Berakhot 31a, and the prayer of Rabbi Hanina ben Dossa, who said "if my prayer is fluent in my mouth I know that it is accepted" (Mishnah, Berakhot 5:5)—as passive prayer. According to Naeh, the more fluent the prayer, the less it is dependent upon the intentions and wants of the praying person. What Naeh calls "prayer of the lips," depended to a considerable degree on self-abandonment and contraction of rational intent and personal will, measures that increase the "fluency" of prayer (through a linguistic analysis of the root *sh.g.r*, including a comparison with Syriac and Arabic, Naeh has demonstrated that the verb should be understood as denoting flow or emergence, and in verbal contexts as denoting fluency and flow. The standard meaning of the root today—routine—is secondary and derives from the initial meaning). In free-flowing prayer, the speaker is not led by his active consciousness but by a higher power that partakes in the prayer and assists the praying person in uttering the words. Shlomo Naeh, "Borre Niv Sefatayim: A Study in the Phenomenology of Prayer according to Mishnah, Berakhot 4:3; 5:5," *Tarbitz* 63 (1994): 185-218 (Hebrew). The contraction of the praying person's will and self-consciousness, and his opening up to spontaneous verbalism, seems somewhat close to the phenomenon of prophesying.

[57] "And once I heard that the Maggid [either of Mezeritch or Zlotvshov] told us 'I certainly will teach you the preferable manner for speaking words of Torah:

that the passage compares to Moses gains a unique status, and his words are the words of God, just like the words of Moses, from whose mouth the *Shekhinah* had spoken.[58]

We find an explicit reference to this in the *Zohar*: "The *Shekhinah* speaks from the mouth of Moses."[59] This expression may be traced to R. Avraham Abulafia's biblical exegesis and prophetic kabbalistic writings.[60] Early hasidic writings explicitly state that "the prophecy of Moses originated from the fact that the *Shekhinah* itself spoke from his mouth with them."[61] R. Zadok Ha'cohen Rabinovitz from Lublin (1823-1900) elaborates on this issue:

> And Moses our Teacher had this ability that all his speech was the manifestation of his very vitality because he was privy to the knowledge of Him who puts together *Hokhma* and *Bina* which are father and mother [II *Zohar* 85a], which is the revelation of the covenant [that is manifested through] language. And this is why [Moses] is called Husband to the Queen of the Realm of the Mouth (*ba'alah dematronita demalkhut peh*) and has the power of

---

when one does not feel oneself at all, but the ear is hearing how the realm of speech [The realm of speech, *Olam ha Dibur*, is commonly used to denote the lowest *sefirah* of *Malkhut*, which is also the *sefirah* of the *Shekhinah*] speaks through one, and one does not speak on one's own accord; and immediately when one begins to hear one's own words he will stop. And how many times mine own eyes and not a stranger's have seen, that when one opened his mouth to speak words of Torah it seemed to all that the speaker is not in this world at all, and the *Shekhinah* was speaking from his throat." Ze'ev Wolf of Zhitomir, *Or ha Me'ir* (Warsaw: 1883), Chapter 1 p.2—Chapter 2 p.1.

[58] See Mendel Peikarz, *The Hassidic Leadership: Authority and the Faith of Tzadikim in the Mirror of Hasidic Literature* (Jerusalem: Bialik Institute, 1999), 21-22 (Hebrew).

[59] III *Zohar* 232a.

[60] On the emergence of this idea in rabbinic commentary on the verse "Moses spoke, and God answered him in thunder" (Exodus 19:19) and in the writings of R. Abraham Abulafia, see Moshe Idel, *Abraham Abulafia: An Ecstatic Kabbalist* (Lancaster: Labyrinthos, 2002), 80-81. Rashi's interpretation of Exodus 19:19 doubtless contributed significantly to this notion: "When Moses spoke and related the Commandments to the Israelites, for they did not hear [the commandments directly] from God save 'I am God ... You shall have no other gods before me' (Exodus 20:2-3), and the blessed Holy One was helping [Moses] by giving him the strength to make his voice louder and heard" (ibid.)

[61] *Ketonet Passim*, 70b.

> influence over the mouth, and that is why [he] said the following: that [Moses'] speech was the actual word of God [and the] *Shekhinah* speaks from his mouth, for he spoke by the power of his very vitality, that is, the letters of his soul; the way he spoke was the way his soul was combined at the time, that is, that all the vitality of his soul was concentrated in the speech that he spoke with all his might and it has been found that the letters of his soul became this very combination.[62]

The original conception of the Besht is identical with that of Rabbi Avraham Abulafia, who mentions in the above passage its underlying principle. This conception also echoes the "prayer of the lips" that Naeh describes. The conception of "the *Shekhinah* speaks from his mouth," which is applied mostly to the Torah teachings of the *tsaddikim*, is taken in its literal sense and derives directly from Rashi's commentary. The Besht perceives prophecy in light of Abulafia's prophetic Kabbalah, whereas the hasidic masters that came after him tended to perceive the *tsaddik* as a prophet in the biblical sense, as a person whose words are the words of the living God.[63]

Knowledge, Vision, and Faith in the World of the Besht According to the Parable of the Barriers

The saying brought in the name of the Besht that "faith is *devekut*" has two principal meanings. The first is instructive, a general directive for the believer to follow the verse "The whole earth is filled with His glory" (Isaiah 6:3)—that he ought to live a life of *devekut* and tie his thoughts to God by every means possible: through prayer, study, everyday speech, and all the matters of corporeal life:

> But it is most important to uphold both: to practice *derekh eretz* [good manners] and cleave [*davuk*] with one's heart unto Him, may He be blessed. And then would one possess both [aspects],

---

[62] R. Zadok Ha'cohen from Lublin, *Likutey Mamarim*, included in *Divrei Sofrim* (Benei Brak: Yahdut, 1973; Lublin, 1913), chapter 11.

[63] On this perception in the writings of R. Yosef Karo, see R. J. Zwi Werblowski, *Joseph Karo: Lawyer and Mystic* (Oxford: Oxford University Press, 1962), 257-286; see also Piekarz' discussions of this theme in his *Between Ideology and Reality* (Jerusalem: Bialik Institute, 1994), 82-103; 295-297 (Hebrew).

which is not the case when one practices *derekh eretz* and does business whereby one's heart is free to linger in idleness and to refrain from contemplating the Torah; and by that one's preoccupation [with idle thoughts] leads to forgetfulness, and "He who forgets one word of his study, is considered to have put his own soul at risk" [Avot 3:8]. And perhaps this is what is meant in the Talmud, Tractate Makkot (24a) "But it is Habakkuk who came and based them all on one [principle], as it is said, 'The righteous shall live by his faith,'" for faith is the *dvekut* in Him, may He be blessed, and by that one would lead a life that is the opposite of he who renders his heart to idleness and puts his soul at risk....[64]

The second meaning is definitional or descriptive, whereby the statement "faith is *dvekut*" is construed as a declaration that the *dvekut* practiced by the mind is the essence of faith. The impression one gains from the above teachings that are ascribed to the Besht is that for him faith is a term describing an internal, experiential state possessing a high degree of certainty. The belief that "No place is void of Him" is presented as a way of thinking that possesses the validity of certain and proved knowledge. From the Besht's perspective, the difference between faith and knowledge is very much blurred. Unlike many of his successors, who see an evolutional link between the belief in an all-permeating God and knowledge gained through experience about the relation between the divine and the material, the Besht does not make an essential distinction between faith and knowledge.

The Parable of the Barriers, which the Besht used to tell before the blowing of the *shofar* on Rosh Hashanah, reflects more than anything else his belief in the synonymy of faith in an all-permeating God with the verse "No place is void of Him":

> I have heard from my teacher may he be remembered in the world to come, a parable he told before to the blowing of the *shofar*: Once there was a wise and great king who made walls, towers and gates with trickery, and ordered [people] to walk through his gates and towers, and ordered to place in each and every gate the king's treasures; and some went over to the first gate and came back, and some [got through to the second gate and came back] etc., but his dear son tried very hard to get through to his father, the

---

[64] Ya'akov of Polonea, *Toldot Ya'akov Yosef*, Parashat Vayishlach, section Vav, p. 96.

king, and then he saw that there was no barrier separating him from his father for it was all trickery, and the lesson is clear....[65]

The expression "trickery," *ahizat eynayim*, appearing both at the beginning and the end of the parable is puzzling and surprising: did the Besht intend to claim that the world is no more than an illusion? In the early twentieth century, Solomon Schechter observed that the Parable of the Barriers is an expression of the hasidic conception of divine immanence. According to him, "We must not interpret the parable to mean that the Besht denied the reality or even the importance of the actual phenomenal world. The very contrary is the truth. The world is for him full of God, penetrated through and through by the divine, and therefore as real as God himself."[66] Unlike Zweifel and others who interpret the Parable of the Barriers as an expression of acosmical pantheism, Yosef Weiss claimed that it is characterized by a "psychological pantheism."[67] Weiss's argument is correct insofar as it refers to the epistemological conception that is unique to the Besht, succinctly encapsulated in the hasidic catchphrase "One is where one's thoughts are."[68] This conception, ascribed to the Besht, is found in the writings of the Maggid of Mezeritch in a form identical to those found in the writings of R. Jacob Joseph of Polonnoye and R. Moses Ephraim of Sudylkow.[69] The implication of the assumption that "One is where one's thoughts are," is that mental activity has actual impact on the external world. According to the Besht and his disciples, inner processes are not private illusions of the observer; they are real and take place within the mind, while at the same time affecting and shaping the reality that is external to it:

> And man wants to worship God and to cleave unto him adequately, but then his thoughts stray to other, worldly matters, and indeed

---

[65] Jacob Joseph of Polonnoye, *Ben Porat Yosef*, Parashat Miketz, 339-340; also ibid., *Derush le Shabbat Teshuvah*; Moses Haim Ephraim, *Degel Mahaneh Ephraim*, haftarat Tavoh, 257-258; Parashat VaYelekh, 264-265.

[66] Solomon Schechter, "The Chassidim," *Studies in Judaism* I (1915): 34.

[67] Joseph Weiss, "The Early Days of the Hassidic Way," in *Chapters in the Teachings of Hassidism and its History*, ed. Abraham Rubinstein (Jerusalem: The Zalman Shazar Center for Jewish History, 1977), 175 (Hebrew).

[68] On the meaning of this perception see Margolin, *The Human Temple*, 184-191.

[69] Ya'akov of Polonnoye, *Toldot Ya'akov Yosef*, Parashat Hayei Sarah, 69; Moses Haim Ephraim, *Degel Mahaneh Ephraim*, Bereishit, 4.

> *the things one's mind contemplate are where one is,* and indeed the earth is filled with His glory, and no place is void of Him. And anywhere man is, *dvekut* in the blessed Creator will be present in the place where he is, for no place is void of Him. But He is with his face hidden, which is as though [He faces us with His] rear side, which is the lowest degree [of His being]; and you must study this carefully, for you know that thought not possessed by the divine is by necessity possessed by a corporeal being.[70]

Gershom Scholem discerned that the *devekut* described in early hasidic writings is an intellectual-emotional experience. Though linked to intellectual effort, it also possesses a clear emotional character.[71] One who cleaves to divine presence in one's mind experiences and senses its reality. Reading the commentaries of the Besht's disciples and followers on the Parable of the Barriers, one finds that they too understood the parable as expressing faith that is a form of knowledge. R. Jacob Joseph of Polonnoye emphasizes in a commentary adduced to the parable that:

> Man knows that the blessed God fills the whole earth with His glory and any movement and thought emanates from Him, may He be blessed; and with this knowledge all workers of iniquity will be scattered etc. Hence, if all the angels and all the heavenly halls [*hekhalot*] were created so to speak from His bones, may He be blessed, like the grasshopper whose shield is part of its body, with this knowledge all workers of iniquity will be scattered, for with this knowledge there is no barrier or curtain separating man from Him, may He be blessed.[72]

The corporeal world strikes us as made up of material barriers separating us from the divine world, whichpurportedly lies behind a dividing curtain. This view, however, is erroneous. R. Pinhas of Korets even says that "The whole world is God himself, as it is written 'Like the grasshopper

---

[70] *Maggid Deverav le Ya'akov*, Section 142; see also ibid., beginning of section 62.
[71] "By the practice of *dvekut*, thought is transformed into emotion; it is, if I may be permitted to use the expression, de-intellectualized. In other words, the insight which is won by *dvekut* has no rational and intellectual content and, being of a most intimate and emotional character, cannot be translated into rational terms." Scholem, *The Messianic Idea in Judaism And Other Essays on Jewish Spirituality*, 218.
[72] Jacob Joseph of Polonnoye, *Ben Porat Yosef*, Parashat Miketz, 340.

whose shield is part of its body (Genesis Rabba 21:5).'"[73] R. Jacob Joseph makes an astute observation on the nature of these obstacles:

> And the moral is clear: that the great, brave and terrible King, the King of all Kings, the blessed Holy One, hides behind several barriers and walls of iron, as we find in the Babylonian Talmud "From the day on which the Temple was destroyed [the gates of prayer have been closed] (TB Berakhot 32b), and the barriers are idolatrous thoughts and the neglect of Torah and prayer, as we find in the *Zohar* (Nasso, 123a) "For the hidden good surrounds the darkness and the husks [as in] the parable of the king" etc. and see ibid. Indeed, men of wisdom know that all of the barriers and the iron wall and all of the garments and covers are also part of His very being, may He be blessed, for no place is void of Him. Therefore this [erection of barriers] is not for Him to hide behind, as I have commented elsewhere [on the verse] "Our Lieges[74] are strong" (Psalms 144:14): when one knows that the world's Liege is everywhere, one endures any strife etc., and read there.... [75]

In comments he adduced to another Besht parable about a king and his son,[76] R. Jacob Joseph explains that the king's son is the human soul.

---

[73] *Imrey Pinhas*, Part A, Section 13, 327.
[74] The verse reads in Hebrew "*alufeinu mesubalim*," which is customarily translated and interpreted as referring to the prosperity of oxen or cattle; here, however, R. Jacob Joseph makes a pun on the other meaning of *aluf*, which is champion or liege, in order to refer to the blessed Holy One.
[75] Jacob Joseph of Polonnoye, *Ben Porat Yosef, Derush le Shabbat Teshuvah*.
[76] But it seems to me, that a parable I heard from my teacher [illustrates the point]: Once there was a prince who was sent far away to a village of lesser men, and after staying there a while, he received a letter from his father, and [the prince] wished to express joy over [receiving] the letter, but feared that the villagers would mock him by saying, "Why is he so joyous over such a daily trifle." What did the prince do? He invited the villagers and bought them wine and other such inebriating liquors until they were merry with wine, and he had an opportunity to be very joyous over his father's [letter] [...] And the moral is clear: that the soul feels embarrassed to be joyous on Shabbat with the indulgences bestowed by her Father, King of all Kings, the blessed Holy One, through the *neshamah yetera* [enhanced soul] which is an epistle of greetings from the Father; due to the body which is like the villagers, the Torah has commanded to pleasure the body on Shabbat and on holy days, and then, when the body is merry with bodily joy the soul is free to be merry with the joy of *dvekut* in the King, the blessed Holy One, and this is sufficient. (*Toldot Ya'akov Yosef* (fn.17 above), Parashat Ki Tavoh, section Aleph.

Therefore, the divine soul that inheres in man is aware of its true source, and does not fear the obstacles that seem to separate it from its King Father. R. Moses Ephraim of Sudylkow, grandson of the Besht, makes similar observations in his commentary on a long version of the parable brought in his book:

> But he who knows that all of the things that hide the King's face are not covers, for the whole earth is full of His glory, and cries brokenhearted to his Father, the blessed Holy One, for he knows that He is a merciful King and in His grace He has created the entire world and wants His divinity recognized, and knows that his soul was actually extracted from Him, as it is said "and breathed into his nostrils a living soul" (Genesis 2:7).[77]

hasidic commentators on the parable are careful not to use the term "faith," opting for "knowledge" instead. The term "trickery" and the general atmosphere of the parable indicate that the king's son knows that the barriers are not genuine obstacles on his path to his father. In reference to this parable, Joseph Shechter wrote that these barriers are the inhibitions that prevent one from becoming closer to God, the primary inhibition being the lack of a powerful will. The parable's genius, according to Schechter, is that it points out that these inhibitions are illusory. Although in their teachings the Besht and his students devote considerable attention to the issue of struggles of faith, this parable reflects the understanding that these struggles are directed against nonexistent threats. Those perceiving the inhibitions as unreal trickery, in the same way that the Besht had perceived them, have strong faith.[78] In other words, for such a person, the belief in the presence of God is certain knowledge. The Besht's unique personality was likely characterized by such exceptional religious certainty, by the internal knowledge that "The whole earth is filled with His glory," and by the ability to see the divine clad with the material, independently of mediating beliefs. In the description of the death of Chabad founder R. Shneur Zalman of Lyadi, with which *Shivhei Harav* ends, it is told that the rabbi asked one of his famous grandchildren: "Do you see what [truly] takes place? And

---

[77] Moses Haim Ephraim, *Degel Mahaneh Ephraim*, Parashat Vayelekh.
[78] Yosef Schechter, *Readings in the Thought of our Times* (Tel Aviv: Yachdav Publishing House, 1977), 114-115 (Hebrew).

the grandchild wondered at the question, and his grandfather told him: Believe me, I do not see anything but the divine force that brings to life all things corporeal, otherwise I see nothing."[79] It seems that R. Shneur Zalman of Lyadi confided to his close followers such an unequivocal vision only on his deathbed, whereas the Besht lived for years with the certain knowledge that no barrier separated him from God. The intensity of this ongoing experience enabled the Besht to recruit his followers to the ranks of a spiritual revolution that flourished and inspired his disciples and their followers in the decades following his death.

Unlike the synonymy of faith and knowledge in the conception of the Besht, the writings of his disciple R. Dov Ber, the Maggid of Mezeritch already distinguish between "faith" and expressions of a certainty that is based on experience. Contrary to Weiss's claim that the Maggid was a mystic whose confidence in God's existence was superior to that of the Besht,[80] we find in several of the teachings of the former a distinction between "faith" and "knowledge," absent from the teachings of the Besht. I believe that this attests to the dominance of the speculative-rational aspect of his thought over the speculative-experiential one:

> The Rabbis have said: Israel provide for their Father in heaven, and every person need strongly believe that what he does down [on earth] gives great pleasure on-high. And [one] should not say "How is it possible for me to give great pleasure on-high;" rather, when performing the *mitzvoth* one should think that they give great pleasure on-high and that all the things one does will reach the realm of pleasure, where the breaking [of the vessels] never took place, according to the principle that wisdom shall enliven he who possesses it, [it] shall enliven he [who performs the *mitzvoth*].[81]

---

[79] Michael Levy Fromkin, *Shivhey ha Rav* (Laemberg: 1864), in Buber, *Tales of the Hasidim: Early Masters*, 271.

[80] Yosef Weiss, "The Early Days of the Hassidic Way," 122-181.

[81] *Maggid Devarav le Ya'akov*, 154. Compare very similar statements on ibid., 258, which begin as follows:

> Each and every man must wholly believe that everything he does—be it a *mitzvah*, Torah study, or prayer—will cause pleasure on-high. And he must not say in his heart, "How is it possible that I would cause pleasure on-high." On this it has been said, "and a whisperer separates close friends," (Proverbs 16:28), because such faith is called truthful faith [*emunat oman*].

The Maggid of Mezeritch presents kabbalistic ideas—employed by the Besht personally and practically—as principles of faith which have to be adopted and must guide one's actions:

> And if one does not believe wholeheartedly that one may have influence through his speech and attachment to the blessed God, then indeed he has no influence on-high whatsoever. And on this it has been said, "the hollow of his thigh" (Genesis 32:26), which means that [by so doing] he took faith away from him. And faith is of primary importance, because some men love and fear [God] but do not have influence on-high due to their lack of wholehearted faith. [82]

The absence of faith from the kabbalistic conceptions underlying the hasidic world constitutes, in the Maggid's view, a genuine obstacle preventing the actualization of their potential. We should therefore assume that the Maggid also defined as a necessary belief the founding notion of Hasidism—"The whole earth is filled with His glory"—which is discussed above at length. Weiss's distinction between "Hasidism of Mysticism" and "Hasidism of Faith" fails the test of correspondence with the textual sources. Even the Maggid of Mezeritch, whom Gershom Scholem crowned as "radical in a way that can only be described as mystical intoxication,"[83] spoke of the importance of faith in his theology. It is not my intention to dismiss completely Weiss' categorization of the various schools of Hasidism; however, in my view such categorization should be based on significant differences between the important hasidic schools, and construed as arising from disagreements between the early hasidic masters. An attempt to outline such a distinction will be made later on, in our discussion of the conscious development of existentialist faith in Hasidism.

The Belief in Individual Providence in Early Hasidism

Alongside the *devekut* rooted in the principle that "No place is void of Him," the early hasidic masters often discuss the traditional belief in individual providence: "Faith is the [utmost] principle. To believe that all

---

[82] Ibid., 237.
[83] Scholem, "'Dvekut' or Intimate Communication with God in Early Hassidism," 226.

of His acts and events, all emerge from Him may He be blessed, through individual providence."[84] Statements of this sort could easily be construed as loyal to the traditional religious beliefs concerning individual providence, which are not at all related to hasidic conceptions of divine presence. However reading two exemplars of early hasidic teachings on individual providence proves that this belief too was understood in early Hassidism as deriving from the conception of the all-permeating divinity and linked directly to it. The first example is from the writings of R. Menahem Nahum of Chernobyl:

> For it has been learned from *Sefer Yetzira* that the letters are called rocks with which worlds are constructed, for this is why Torah scholars are called builders busy with the construction of the world, as it is written "Read not *banayikh* [your children] but *bonayikh* [your builders]" (TB, Berakhot 64a). And with the utterance of these letters worlds are created, as it has been learned, by cleaving [*mitdabkim*] unto the interiority of the light of *Ein Sof* in the letters. Thus when one becomes grieved, Heaven forbid, the divine portion within one's self should cleave unto the letters, to the internality of the light that emanates within them; when praying or studying one should pray to the Creator [and] with God's help [read] truly into the letters [that] elevate this [trouble] on-high so that grief should be driven away from him. But this requires complete faith, for him to believe wholeheartedly in divine providence, that no other [god] exists but Him, and not rely, Heaven forbid, on chance or witchcraft, Heaven forbid; but only [believe] that the Creator, with God's help, oversees all his matters, big or small [....] And all events appear to Him in a single continuum, and he will believe completely in entrusting this [grief] with divine providence, which is called *sikra*. Because so long as one does not have faith one's prayer is not useful, nor is the prayer of others for his sake, for he does not truly believe in His providence, may He be blessed. As it is written in Psalms 145:18 "God is nigh ... to all who call upon Him in truth": truth [*emet*—spelled *aleph-mem-tav*] is the beginning [*aleph*—first letter of the aleph-bet] middle [*mem*—middle letter] and end [*tav*—last letter]; the beginning is the blessed God, Who is first [among beings] and His beginning has no beginning; the middle is the vitality of all worlds and beings, on-high and down-low; and He is the end, may He be blessed, for

---

[84] *Imrey Pinhas*, part I, p. 354, section 37.

His kingship ruleth All—even matters down-low such that there is no other [god] but Him.[85]

According to R. Menahem Nahum of Chernobyl, the call to connect with the divinity and cleave to it, because it actually lies behind the world's external camouflages or through them, and because the divinity hides, in particular, in the internality of the letters—is based on the belief in individual providence. The Maggid of Mezeritch claims that the active potential inherent in contemplative prayer depends on the very belief in the worshiper's ability to influence the supernal realms. Similarly, he claims that the belief in individual providence construed as the belief in the presence of the divine in each and every ingredient comprising our world is the infrastructure of the hasidic conception of *devekut*. In fact, the traditional belief in individual providence is equated in these teachings with the notion that "No place is void of Him." Individual providence is not measured with external, miraculous parameters; rather, it is what makes these parameters possible, because material reality is not only material. It exists by virtue of the divine element hidden within it:

> And [the Besht] has interpreted "*tzadik* shall live by his faith" (Habakkuk 2:4), [as meaning] that he who believes in individual providence of the blessed God, and knows that everything that befalls man comes from Him, be it matters big or small, all follows the law of the Master—the law of the heavenly kingdom [*Zohar, Pinchas* 227a]—and is the cause for his sins, and [the sinner] immediately regrets and becomes filled with terror and fear of God, and he is immediately absolved, because he is a believer who changes his ways and cleaves with his mind to the blessed God [...]. And this [divine aspect, *Sefirat Malkhut*] is called David [the letters *dalet-vav-dalet*], because *Ein Sof* that is called *Ein* [i.e. nothing] is the *dalet*, from which *vav* is drawn to the [second] *dalet*, ultimate baseness. It is all overseen by His individual providence. And when one does not believe that all is overseen by His individual providence, and only says "My power and the might of mine hand hath gotten me this" (Deuteronomy 8:17) he is called a heretic unto the blessed God.[86]

---

[85] R. Menahem Nahum of Chernobyl, *Meor Enaim (The Light of the Eyes)* (Jerusalem: Yeshivat Meor Enaim, 1975), 306–307 (Hebrew).
[86] Jacob Joseph of Polonnoye, *Ben Porat Yosef*, Parashat Vayishlah, 303–309.

With the homily on the meaning of the name "David," R. Jacob Joseph of Polonnoye explains in the name of the Besht the meaning of traditional belief in individual providence. On the face of it, the Besht also asserts that the core of this belief is that the blessed God is the source of everything. However, according to R. Jacob Joseph, *Einsof*, symbolized by the Hebrew letter *dalet* at the beginning of the name "David" (spelled in Hebrew with the consonants *dalet vav dalet*) is drawn and descends—an act symbolized by the letter *vav*— from the supernal realm to the earthly realm, symbolized by the second *dalet* at the end of the name. The earthly realm, the material world we live in, thus contains the hidden infinite divinity.

In observing the conceptual development in traditional faith that the Besht had instigated, we may easily discern the revolutionary aspects of his perception: rational skepticism tends to undermine the basic meaning of the belief in individual providence. The hardships of life, personal injustices, the triumph of the evil, and the failure of the just in everyday life have stirred, since biblical times, uneasiness and a profound need of a theodicy. The conception of individual providence arising from the teachings of the Besht, in fact, dissolves the weaknesses that underlie the belief in individual providence. The realization that the physical reality is the external garment of another reality, which is divine and infinite, and that every person, concurrently with his material composition, is also a spiritual, immaterial entity subsisting by the power of a divine vitality—means that this world and all human lives exist under the aegis of divine providence. Following this conception of individual providence, the Hasid is able to overcome the doubts arising from daily hardships and life's iniquities.

Indeed, individual providence is not measured by the degree of personal protection and care one enjoys throughout one's life; its main advantage is the sense of security with which it endows a person who connects his mind with the divine presence that sustains him, hence "One is where one's thoughts are." By contemplating the fact that one's existence is not merely external, and that it is made possible through the hidden divine principle which sustains it, one feels the taste of individual providence.

The expectation for miracles, the occurrence of unexpected changes and the belief in their existence, is characteristic of the hasidic way of life and is reflected in hundreds of miraculous tales. The miracle is perceived in the hasidic world as it has always been: as a confirmation of the existence of individual providence. And yet, a closer look reveals that the hasidic explanation of the plausibility of miracles is founded on the conception described above: since the entire world, and every individual within it, are the finite and material garb of an infinite spiritual reality, the strict constancy and regularity of material processes known as "the way of nature," are mere trickery, similarly to the conclusion of the Besht's Parable of the Barriers.

The second example is brought in the name of R. David Moses of Chortkov (1827-1903), the son of R. Israel from Ruzhyn, the Maggid of Mezeritch's great grandson.[87] His view reflects a profound integration that took place in the hasidic thought of the second half of the nineteenth century; the integration between the expectation for the occurrence of miracles, the belief in individual providence, and the Hassidic infrastructure of this belief discussed above:

> Once the holy R. David Moshe of Chortkov asked his followers about a venerable man in need of deliverance, wishing to know if that man had already been saved. And they told him that he had not yet been delivered as the cause for his strife required an act that is almost supernatural. And to that the holy rabbi replied with his holy words, that this man's faith must have not been wholehearted,[88] because it appears difficult to discern the natural from the supernatural, for natural and supernatural things both come from God, and hence there is no difference between the two. It would also appear that one should never ask for supernatural [deliverance], since one should not rely on miracles. And about such matters we have found many times even among the greatest of *tzadikim* requests for supernatural intervention. But indeed, during the creation of the worlds, the emanation of lights was so intense, without limits, that the world could not tolerate the lights and the breaking of the vessels [*shevirat hakelim*] was inevitable. Thus the *tzimtzum* [divine retraction] took place in a vessel of limited size, so that the world could absorb the lights, and this is what we call natural: the vessel of retraction of the

---

[87] See David Assaf, *The Regal Way: The Life and Times of Rabbi Israel of Ruzhin* (Stanford: Stanford University Press, 2002).

[88] Buber added here in his anthology: "When he saw that the hasidim did not understand him, he continued...." Martin Buber, *Tales of Hasidim: The Later Masters*, trans. Olga Marx (New York: Schocken Books, 1961), 77.

creation of the world to allow the absorption of the lights to a limited degree. And [the] vessel is man's preparation and [that] preparation is faith: we have found that nature is not perceived by every man and at any time equally; it has been found that those of greater faith also have a larger and broader vessel of retraction, and therefore for them the ways of nature extend to the limits of their extensive faith, for faith is a vessel within which [God] retracted Himself according to the ways of nature. And it is also plausible that a man was of little faith yesterday and thought a certain deliverance to be supernatural, and today his faith grew and expanded and therefore his vessel, which is natural, also grew and expanded and today [he sees] deliverance as very natural. And this is what we have found in the parting of the Red Sea, when Nahshon the son of Aminadav who jumped into the sea neck-deep "and uttered" only a soft and pleasant utterance and did not shout loudly.[89] He only said simply "Save me, O God! For the waters have come up to my neck" (Psalms 69:1), that is, that the sea was ahead of them and the Egyptians behind them, but Nahshon was not compelled to shout loudly, he only said simply "Save me, O God" because his faith in God was so great that it all seemed simple and natural even though the waters rose up to his neck. There is no obstacle preventing God from delivering, and this [fact] is natural. Therefore, [Nahshon] did not yell with excitement but only said simply "Save me, O God," and thus every man should have great faith, for nothing supernatural belongs to God, and anyhow everything He does is natural and can be easily delivered....[90]

---

[89] According to the midrash in Numbers Raba, 13:4:
R. Judah b. Ilai expounded: When Israel stood by the Red Sea, the tribes stood contending with each other, one saying, "I will go in first," and the other saying, "I will go in first." Thereupon Nahshon leapt into the waves of the sea and waded in. In allusion to him David said, "Save me, O God; For the waters have come up to my neck" (Psalms 69:2). Said the blessed Holy One to Moses: "My beloved is drowning in the sea and you stand praying!" "Speak unto the children of Israel, that they go forward." (Exodus 14:15). This explains "By Judah God is known." For this reason the blessed Holy One made great the name of Nahshon in Israel, inasmuch as he was privileged to be the first to present his offering; as it says, "and he that presented his offering the first day was Nahshon," etc. Thus we have explained, "His name is great in Israel."

[90] R. Israel Berger of Bucharest, *Esser Orot* (Pietrikov: 1907), 148-149. Appears in Buber, *Tales of Hasidim*, 76-77.

The world as a creation expresses the *tsimtsum* (contraction) of divine light in the spirit of the Lurianic doctrine of *tsimtsum*, allowing among other things the creation of man for serving as a vessel of the divine light within him. Faith functions as a vessel; that is, it enables man to grasp the divine essence through the natural reality of the world, which was also created from the divine contraction. Contrary to common belief, R. David Moses claims that it is precisely when faith is scant and contracted that salvation—i.e. the possibility that a sick man will be healed—is perceived as a supernatural, miraculous event. Whereas when faith is more profound it is like a large vessel capable of containing a more extensive divine meaning; and then salvation is perceived as part of divine nature. The true believer does not distinguish between that which obeys the natural order and that which does not, and views the entire material reality as a product of divine contraction; hence no distinction can be made between natural salvation and miraculous salvation, because everything is part of divine nature. The miracle is not an expression of individual providence in the sense of a divine interference with the deterministic laws of nature; that which appears to be a miracle to the partial believer is perceived by the true believer as the way of nature, because according to his faith, the existence of the material world is made possible by the contraction of the divine light to a *reshimo*—a mere impression. The whole world is a vessel that contains the contracted light, and faith serves man as a tool for the understanding of the divine reality which keeps nature under the eternal protection of providence.

The power of the Besht's unmediated knowledge that the whole of reality is trickery is weakened, and even *tsaddikim* of R. David Moses' generation fail to experience revelation. They overcome the intensity of divine concealment by the power of their belief in God's presence through *tsimtsum* (as we will see below). The homily on Nahshon the son of Aminadav reveals to us the essence of the believer's salvation according to Hasidism: the essence of this salvation is not an external event. Since according to the Besht all occurrences follow divine nature, and in light of the Lurianic doctrine as incorporated into the Besht's essentially Cordoverian view, salvation is the fruit of the divine *tsimtsum*:[91] true

---

[91] On the decline of the Kabbalah according to the school of the ARI in the eighteenth century, see Idel, *Hasidism: Between Ecstasy and Magic*, 33-44.

salvation lies in the way one thinks. Since "One is where one's thoughts are," when one believes—that is, when one thinks that ultimately no place is void of Him—then one experiences divine providence. R. David Moses turns the tale in the homily of Nahshon the son of Aminadav into the description of a Stoic prayer: Nahshon did not cry out to the heavens, but calmly called *"hoshi'a HaShem"* (save me, O God). In this act, he did not expect a miracle or an unnatural occurrence; rather, he expressed the belief that he himself is the source of salvation. In light of the foregoing, we may understand the added value of the hasidic trust in God, which at face value does not seem to offer any innovation.

Hasidic Faith and Trust in God

Hasidic writings abound with homilies and tales that may be categorized as belonging to the long line of stories and proverbs praising trust in God. This tradition begins in biblical verses; continues in Rabbinic tales; is particularly meaningful in the New Testament; and plays an important part in medieval Musar and homiletical literatures. This tradition considers the ability to refrain from worrying about the future to be the test that measures trust in God:

> On the verse "I will rain bread from heaven for you; and the people shall go out and gather a day's portion every day, that I may prove them, whether they will walk in my Torah or not" (Exodus 16:4), the holy Rabbi Menahem Mendel of Rymanov queried: will the Israelites be tried by the amount of manna they gather every day, as to whether they follow the blessed Torah or not? And how are these two matters related? But he explained that our holy Torah teaches man knowledge and righteous conduct, for if one asked the people, even the commons, if they believed that the blessed Holy One stands alone in the world, they would reply confidently why do you ask such [an obvious] question? For all of God's created knew that He is the world's only master. But if one asked that man if he trusts the blessed Creator to provide him all his needs, then he would reply feebly, "were I so lucky to reach this degree, but for now I have not yet reached that degree." And if their minds were sound they would know that their mouths would utter empty words if they said that they do not trust God, for faith and trust are glued together and match inseparably and are conjoined. For he who is a man of strong faith is also strongly

confident and he who does not trust God, Heaven forbid, his faith is very weak and slight and anyhow he does not engage in Torah study. And this is what Scripture says, "I will rain bread from heaven for you," that is, I have the ability to rain down on you all at once bread that will suffice for many days and yet I do not give this to you. For if the people will gather every day, that is, in order to instill in their hearts a measure of trust, though they will see [the bread] gathered today, they will not worry about tomorrow. And say "who knows if this will be tomorrow too,"—they will only put his trust in God Who provides the manna like the rain on the earth today, surely He will provide [it] also tomorrow, and then when trust will be instilled in their hearts will they also reach the truth of faith which is the foundation of the entire Torah, as it is written "all Your commandments are faithful," (Psalms 119:86) so that I may try them. This means that according to their measure of trust I will test them and see whether they follow my Torah or not; that is, if they trust me strongly enough that I will provide for them sufficiently, their awe and faith in me will also be complete and if their faith be complete, so will My Torah not escape their attention.[92]

R. Aharon Ratta, who passed away in 1947, was the leader of a hasidic court in Hungary who moved with his followers to Jerusalem in 1927-8, where he founded the ultra-Orthodox hasidic court of *Shomer Emunim*. His book by the same name abounds with rabbinic proverbs, passages from homiletic and moralistic literature, kabbalistic teachings (particularly concerning reincarnation), and quotes from hasidic sources about

---

[92] Gershon of Tarna, *Mevasser Tov, Torot R. Menahem Mendel of Rymanov* (Krakow, 1900), on Beshalah, 16-17. Published in abbreviated form in Buber, *Tales of Hasidim*, 131. A similar statement is brought in the name of R. Menahem Mendel of Kotsk:

And to the believer—confidence. It is written: "Even the darkness is not dark to thee" (Psalms 139:12)—when one believes that darkness emanates from the blessed Holy One it is dark no longer. In Kotsk the confident [believers] are appreciated, those who expose themselves to the whims of fate. "Feivel," the *Saraf* [R. Menahem Mendel of Kotsk] asks the usher, "What is the meaning [of the saying] 'The Torah was given only to those who ate the manna'?" Rabbi Feivel is silent. The *Saraf* answers for him: "To those who do not worry for tomorrow." (Appears in Yehudah Leib Levin, *Beit Kotzk: HaSaraf, Toldot Hayav shel ha Admor ha Gadol me Kotzk* [Benei Brak: Yahadut Publishing House, 1972], 86)

topics such as faith, individual providence, trust in God, etc.[93] In the section entitled *Sha'ar Habitachon* (gate of trust or confidence), he writes:

> And most important is to encourage one's heart to accept suffering with love, and to draw encouragement from the confidence that the blessed Holy One will help him, as we find in *Sefer Hatoldot [Ya'akov Yosef]* in the name of our rabbi the Besht, that in man's hour of sickness and sorrow, the inclination thrives to let go of his trust in his God and, Heaven forbid, to diminish that confidence, so that his final verdict [to end his life] is given,

---

[93] Aharon Ratta, *Shomer Emunim* (Jerusalem: Zokef Kfufim, 1961). The book was written in Jerusalem in 1942, that is, during the Holocaust, as the horrible news of the events in Europe reached the author. Explicit reference to this fact appears in the introduction to the 1959 edition, written by his son-in-law Rabbi Abraham Isaac Kahn. The most candid passages concerning faith in wake of the Holocaust are to be found in this book in an essay on individual providence, chapters 10-12; ibid., part I, 115-121. His impassioned words reflect his conviction that the Holocaust is the harbinger of the Messiah, and he calls on his disciples who remained in Europe to accept this fate with love:

> And you should know that now in our generation, that now is the purpose and consummation of all of the evaluations, *tikkunim* [rectification] and *gilgulim* [reincarnations], and thus it is by necessity that Holy Israel shall be taken through such purgatory of grief, and some, Heaven forbid, are killed, and some are slaughtered or burned, Heaven forbid, and some are buried alive, and some are taken captive, and some are beaten and tortured, and some are exiled, and some are hungry and thirsty, all according to the value of the *tikkun* their soul requires, and the holy *Shekhinah* stands next to each and every Israelite and weeps and wails over him, until God shall have mercy and look on the affliction of His people, and shall say 'enough' to the vicissitudes of Israel, that is, by necessity even if, Heaven forbid, Israel do not repent. (Ibid. 117a-b)

In a letter from the same period, published by Ratta's son-in-law in the 1959 edition, the author of the *Shomer Emunim* writes:

> And know that the blessed Holy One shall not forsake His people, Heaven forbid, for we have received [the tradition that] when the time comes that, Heaven forbid, [our people] will believe that our existence has lost its meaning, then on that day the Savior of Israel shall be seen and sprout, and now is the time to accept with love each his share, and not abnegate and doubt, Heaven forbid, our God, blessed be He and blessed be His name, for then [one] is torn away from both worlds, Heaven forbid, and in any event the nations of the world can only take our body and torture it, and what is the body if not an odious drop, but our soul they cannot touch. (Ibid., 118b)

Heaven forbid.⁹⁴ That is why one must find much encouragement at such hour of sorrow and distress, Heaven forbid, and to ask the good God not to take away from him the confidence, so that he should encourage himself [....] And they also wrote there in the name of the Besht⁹⁵ that if, Heaven forbid, man is in any kind of distress, Heaven forbid, it is a virtue not to pray at all about his woes at that time, but to only encourage his heart with God and with his confidence in God, and then "Israel shall be saved by God (Isaiah 45:17)."⁹⁶

At the end of his book, R. Aharon Ratta provides references to the Hassidic sources on which he relies. Therefore his advice to refrain from praying for relief specifically in times of need originates from the unique hasidic contribution to the traditional conception of "trust in God." Early hasidic writings generally resent prayer that addresses specific requests (*tfilat bakashah*), due to their being perceived as prayers that fulfill base wants, prayers that turn God into the provider of personal needs.⁹⁷ To reinforce his position, R. Aharon Ratta quotes R. Pinhas of Korets:

---

⁹⁴ "I have heard from my teacher that when it is wished that punishment be unleashed on he who deserved it, then his confidence [in God] is undermined; therefore it is fitting to pray before Him, may He be blessed, to reinforce the confidence in Him, etc." Ya'akov of Polonea, *Toldot Ya'akov Yosef*, on Mishpatim, sections Dalet and Heh—*uvaze yuvan ness*.

⁹⁵ "It is found in the holy books and in [sayings] attributed to the holy Besht, may he rest in peace, that when the verdict [*din*] presides one shall not pray [for the retraction of the verdict] but in thought alone, so that he will not, Heaven forbid, criticize [God]." Yehoshua of Osterova, *Sefer Toldot Adam* (Jerusalem: mgm"h, 1997), on Vayigash, 49.

⁹⁶ Aharon Ratta, *Shomer Emunim*, part I, 106.

⁹⁷ When one needs asking something of the blessed Creator, one should think of one's soul as an organ of the *Shekhinah*, so to speak, as a drop from the sea. And one should ask from the *Shekhinah* that one thing that she lacks, and he will have the faith that indeed he is acting [on a] higher [plane] than the *Shekhinah*. Only if he be adequately cleaved unto the *Shekhinah* the abundance shall be drawn to him as well. Like the joyous man who taps with his hand even though he does not intend to, because the joy spreads in that organ, the same is in this matter, which is so to speak an organ of the *Shekhinah*, the plenty shall be drawn to him also. (*Maggid Devarav le Ya'akov*, 51-52.)
Since a request for personal needs is inappropriate, it should be directed as a request that answers a need of the *Shekhinah* itself and then from the drawing

It is written in *Midrash Pinchas* letter 157: I heard from R. Pinhas that when, Heaven forbid, some hardship befalls a man, and he is very stricken, there is no recourse but to believe in divine eternal mercy. He should not take any action [or] apply any remedy whatsoever but only trust [God], and not even pray to the blessed Holy One, and not go to ritual immersion, etc., only have trust as I have said.[98]

Though this is seemingly yet another traditional praise of the trust in God, from the broader context of R. Pinhas's writings on the trust in God it emerges that they rely on the hasidic belief in the all-permeating divine void: "Livelihood is God Himself, and when one truly puts one's trust in God, one becomes void; this is faith, through which the *Shekhinah* ascends and all falls into its right place. And also when one believes that all is from the Him may He be blessed, there is no evil, only good."[99] R. Pinhas of Korets's statement that livelihood *is* the blessed Holy One, i.e., that everything we have comes from God, means more than what its literal meaning may imply. Fully understood, this passage expresses the belief in the mental connection with the all-permeating divine void. Evil is canceled out by living according to the thought that everything that exists comes from the divine source.

Faith as *Hamshakhah* and the Faith of the *Tsaddikim*

Moshe Idel discusses at length the meaning of the kabbalistic-hasidic notion of *hamshakhah* (drawing-down of divine forces), and its manifestations in prayer, Torah study, and the hasidic doctrine of the *tsaddik*.[100] In what follows, I would like to emphasize the aspect of faith in the doctrine of *hamshakhah*, and its importance to the development of the belief in the *tsaddik* in Hasidism. The Maggid of Mezeritch insisted

---

of general plenty that follows as a result, and following from the teachings of the Besht discussed in the same context above, the specific request will be met. On the growing doubts concerning straightforward prayer in early Hasidism see Shatz Uffenheimer, *Hasidism as Mysticism*, 144-167.

[98] See note 91 above.
[99] *Imrey Pinhas*, part I, section 125, p.441. Also see ibid., section 151, p.446.
[100] Idel, *Hasidism: Between Ecstasy and Magic*, 147-208.

that in addition to the doctrines of ongoing divine emanation, derived from obeying the commandments with the form of *devekut* described above—faith in and of itself may also generate changes and draw into the world an abundance of vitality.

> In the verse "And if you say, 'What shall we eat in the seventh year, if we may not sow or gather in our crop?' I will command My blessing upon you in the sixth year" (Leviticus 25:20-21), and we must ask why it is written "And if you say," as it makes redundant [the rejoinder] "I will command my blessing." We should say that it is known that when Israel are devoted to the Torah and God's commandments they sustain the abundance in all of the realms, and there is one more thing that Israel may [do to] sustain [the abundance] and that is through faith, as the Rabbis have said "Israel came out of Egypt thanks to their faith." And it is said of Abraham, "And he believed in God and He reckoned it to him as righteousness," (Genesis 15:6) for to begin with [Abraham] was not of wholehearted faith as he said "for I continue childless" (Genesis 15:2), later he believed with wholehearted faith. And it is said in the *Zohar*, "what is Truth and what is Faith,"[101] and we must understand the reason why [faith] is called thus[102] and why through faith one can bring about great abundance [....]
>
> Only he who can bring this about through the above *tikkun*, he who has faith in the blessed God because he knows the truth of "the whole earth is full of his glory" (Isaiah 6:3) and His enduring abundance, may He be blessed, everywhere. We have found that within faith truth is instilled, and it is the cause of its operation; we have found that faith has become the vessel for the truth...[103]

R. Yehiel Michal, the Maggid of Zlotshov (1726-1786),[104] in his homily on the verse "And Noah went in, and his sons, and his wife, and his sons' wives with him, into the ark, because of the waters of the flood"

---

[101] *Zohar* (Raya Meheimana), Numbers 230a.
[102] *Emunah* is derived from the Hebrew root *a.m.n.* which means belief, trust, loyalty, or honesty.
[103] *Maggid Devarav le Ya'akov*, 244-245.
[104] On him see Dubnow, *History of Hassidism*, 188-191; Mor Altshuler, *The Messianic Secret of Hassidism* (Leiden: Brill, 2006), 67-80.

(Genesis 7:7), extrapolates that faith itself has a drawing power, or *hamshakhah*:

> And Rashi has commented: "Even Noah was among those of little faith, for he believed and then did not believe that the Flood would come, until the waters pressed him," end quote. And it is very strange to suspect Noah, who was a *tzadik*, of having little faith in the blessed God, Heaven forbid. And to me it seems that the term "faith" means here two things. The first is literal, i.e. to believe that something will turn out in a certain way. Also, faith [*emunah*] should be used as it appears in the verse "He had brought up [*vayehi ommen*] Hadas'sah," (Esther 2:7) which denotes continuity and growth, for faith possesses this power of sustaining and drawing something from its source. That is, by believing in the blessed God and having full confidence in Him in relation to a certain thing, that thing is drawn and brought [into existence] in full form. And hence Noah the *tzadik* certainly wholly believed in everything that the blessed God had told him, with all his heart and soul and innocently as always was his good custom. But in this context [of the Flood], he feared to believe with wholehearted faith, for then he might end up being the cause for the Flood, that is, the wholeness of his faith would draw the Flood into existence. And he did not know what to think and what to do. And that is why Rashi commented [on the verse] that he was of little faith as he believed and then did not believe. That is, he was truly a believer, only he feared to wholly believe that the blessed God would bring about the Flood because perhaps he would be the cause for it, as I have said above. Until the waters pressed him....[105]

In fact, the Maggid of Zlotshov speaks of the primeval fear of thoughts' power of actualizing in reality. This fear was translated by Karl Marx in the nineteenth century into the epistemological principle in which thought can fulfill itself. Hasidism, for which the epistemological interiorization that "One is where one's thoughts are" became central, developed great sensitivity to the power of thoughts. In the same way that Marx argued, based on his observations on human thought processes, that mental insights may generate social revolutions, the

---

[105] *Ohev Israel le R. Avraham Yehoshua Heschel me Afta* (Jerusalem: ha-Mosad le-hotsa'at sifre Musar ve-Ḥasidut, 1962), 6-7. See also Buber, *Tales of the Hasidim*, 152-153.

early Hassidic masters claimed that the belief in the presence of God in the world could draw, *lehamshikh*, abundance to this world. In fact, this is identical to the claim of the Maggid of Mezeritch, that faith is a vessel containing truth: faith contains reality. Faith itself creates a religious experience that is underlain by sensing divine presence in the world. This way it generates in man an internal revolution so powerful that it can, at times, change his life altogether. This conception is one of the important keys to understanding the doctrine of the *tsaddik* in Hasidism.

The following tale relates an event involving the Besht and R. David Leikis, one of his close associates. It offers a vivid illustration of the feeling shared by the early Hasidism that faith in and of itself can impact reality, and that their belief in the power of their masters brings about changes in the world by means of the power of *hamshakhah*.

> The holy righteous R. David Leikis who was father-in-law of the righteous R. Mordechay [Motl] of Chernobyl whose virtue will protect us and all of Israel. Rabbi Motl married a second wife who was the daughter of R. David Leikis. And once when R. David Leikis came to Chernobyl, and a messenger announced in advance that [R. Leikis] is ready to arrive on a set date. And prior to the hour of his arrival the righteous R. Motl traveled to meet him and give him great honor as was his due. And prior to his departure his disciples walked toward [R. Leikis] both in his honor and in honor of their rabbi. And they walked earlier an hour or two, so they may stand and attend the meeting. And after they walked about a mile they saw [R. Leikis'] cart traveling. They stood and walked no further. And when the righteous R. David Leikis saw them he asked them who they were and whence they came? And they said: 'We are disciples of the righteous R. Motl of Chernobyl.' And he said to them: 'Do you have faith in your rabbi?' And they were silent, for who will say that he truly has faith? And [R. Leikis] said: 'I will tell you what faith is. There we were, disciples of the Besht, when we were by the Ba'al Shem Tov, once on the holy Sabbath we had the third banquet. And the banquet lasted a few hours into the night. Then we said the food benediction and stood there to pray *ma'ariv*. And then we did *havdalah* and sat down immediately for the *melaveh malka* banquet. And we were all poor and paupers and had not even a penny on weekdays let alone on the Sabbath. And yet after the *melaveh malka* banquet the holy Besht whose virtue will protect us, told me thus: "David, give me [money] for a honey

drink." And though I knew I had nothing of the sort, because the rabbi had said to me 'give me for the drink' I could not ignore him and put my hand into my pocket and pulled out one gold coin and paid for the drink. This is faith! Faith is *hamshakhah*!'[106]

Mendel Peikarz's monograph *The Hassidic Leadership* studies the authority and faith of the *tsaddikim* in hasidic literature.[107] In his introduction, Peikarz makes a distinction between the "faith of the sages," which is praised extensively in the pre-hasidic homiletic and *Musar* literatures, in works such as R. Elijah Vidas's *Reshit Hokhmah* and R. Isaiah Horowitz's *Shnei Luchot Habrit*;[108] and the "hasidic faith in *tsaddikim*." In Peikarz's opinion, a further distinction should be made between the belief in the *tsaddik* in the first two generations of Hasidism and the one that developed in light of R. Elimelech of Lyzhansk's *Noam Elimelech*.[109] Peikarz argues that in the eyes of the Hassidic public, "their leaders were perceived among many as so-called representatives of divine providence on earth if not even more than that," yet, in his opinion, "it must be remembered that the teachings of the Hassidic masters on nothingness and being, *devekut*, the extension of corporeality and other matters, were not what had conquered the souls and minds of the Jewish masses, since Hassidism is a social-religious movement under whose wings many entered in order to find spiritual solace, calm their personal and existential confusion, and particularly to find relief from their lives' travails."[110] We may accept this sociological-psychological explanation, at best, for understanding the perspective of the hasidic public; but for prodigies such as R. Jacob Joseph of Polonnoye, R. Pinhas of Korets, R. Shneur Zalman of Lyadi, or R. Levi Isaac of Berdichev, such an explanation obviously borders on

---

[106] Ya'akov Sofer, *Sippurey Ya'akov* [Nige'al Edition] (Jerusalem: Carmel Publishing House, 1994), 96-97. A similar parallel text is to be found in Yshayahu Wolf Tzikernik, *Sippurey Hasidut Chernobyl* (Nige'al Edition) (Jerusalem: Carmel Publishing House, 1984), 56. In this version the story ends with all those present thinking that the Besht directed his request to them in asking for a penny to buy a drink, and each of them finding the coin in his pocket. See also the story version in Buber, *Tales of the Hasidim*, 55-56.

[107] Piekarz, *The Hassidic Leadership*, 15-59, and especially 35-41.

[108] R. Eliyahu Di Widash, *Resheet Hokhmah* (Jerusalem: Or Hamusar, 1984); R. Yeshaya Horowitz, *Sheney Lukhot ha Berit* (ShLA) (Amsterdam: 1698).

[109] Elimelekh Melizhnsk, *Noam Elimelekh* (New York: Agudat Hasidei Kalib, 1973).

[110] Piekarz, *The Hassidic Leadership*, 31.

the scandalous. From the viewpoint of the founders of Hasidism, the phenomenon of *tsaddikim* can only find its explanation in conceptual notions formulated in homilies on biblical verses, Rabbinic sayings, and medieval writings of thinkers and kabbalists.

The story of the Besht and R. David Leikes shows that the discussion of belief in the *tsaddikim* is inseparable from the discussion of hasidic religious beliefs discussed above. The power of the belief in the *tsaddik*'s ability to bring about *hamshakhah* runs parallel to the power of the *devekut* of the *tsaddik* to bring about change and *hamshakhah* in the world.

> First let us explain the [commentary in the] *Mekhilta* (BeShalach) [on the verse] "And they believed in God and in Moses his servant" (Exodus 14:31); if they believed in Moses then they did all the more so in God, and why does [Scripture] add [that they believed] "in Moses"? To teach you that all those who believe in the Shepherd of Israel actually believe in Him Who said may the world come into existence.'[...]
>
> Hence we wish to say that we should be puzzled by this [commentary of the] *Mekhilta*, as it is said simply that if they believed in Moses they did so all the more in relation to God. This [verse] is certainly good for emphasizing what [Scripture] wishes to say [...] for if it would have only said "And they believed in Moses," there was room to err and think that, Heaven forbid, they believed that Moses is the true source of all the miracles that he worked, both in the Exodus from Egypt and in the parting of the Red Sea, and that he had not done these things in the name of the blessed God, and that they were executed collaboratively [by God and Moses]. Therefore [Scripture] had to explain precisely that [Israel] believed in God and in Moses His servant, that [Moses] acted in the name of the blessed God as his loyal servant, and the core of their faith in God was that He had acted and worked all of those miracles for them, and Moses is only His servant, his agent working those miracles. And we should say that the intention of the *Mekhilta* was in truth to inquire how both statements have the same meaning, that they believed in Moses, and believed all the more so in God [....] Indeed, in this passage the inquirer has found reason to inquire why should [Scripture] say at all [that they believed] "in Moses"? What does it seek to teach us through the fact that they believed in Moses too? [...] that the community leader should, in God's name, direct the people in corporeal and spiritual matters alike, not only at work and with words of reproach and morals, but also through contemplation, that he connect himself with the

blessed God, and then seek to connect himself with the people of his generation and to help them ascend and cleave unto Him; and if they also cleave unto the leaders of their generation, then the leaders of the generation would be able to hold their hand out and help them ascend etc. Therefore it is made clear that all those who believe in the Shepherd of Israel attain the belief that they should love Him and cleave unto Him, as it is said in *Reshit Hokhmah* [*Sha'ar Ahava* 12] and see ibid. And the issues of faith and trust [in God] and love are all interconnected, and see ibid. And that is why it is said that those who believe in the Shepherd of Israel actually believe in Him, for the former is an intermediary stage for the latter. And that is why [Scripture] says "And they believed in God," that is, by virtue of their faith in Moses and their cleaving unto him, from there they ascended to the faith in Him, and it is easy to understand.[111]

In this passage we may find an explanation for fundamental questions concerning the faith of the *tsaddik* in Hasidism: the *tsaddik* is an emissary and the faith in him is derived from the scriptural description of Israel's faith in Moses.[112] The faith of the *tsaddik* is *devekut* in the sense described earlier, and faith *in* the *tsaddik* serves as a middle-ground and mediator between the Hasid and God by means of *devekut*. The hassid's *devekut* in the *tsaddik* allows him to climb on the *tsaddik*'s shoulders like a ladder, so that he too can partake of the *tsaddik*'s *devekut* in God—*devekut* is made possible by the emotional and mental processes described in the first part of this article. The *tsaddik*'s leadership is different than that of other religious figures—the *maggid* and *mochiach* (moralist)—who rest content with moral admonition. The core of the *tsaddik*'s activity is his mental *devekut*—i.e., the cleaving of the mind unto God. A community of enthusiastic followers of the *tsaddik* increases his power and turns him into a *Shaliach Tzibur*—leader of communal prayer—in the deepest sense of the term. The community's faith in the *tsaddik*, and that of the *tsaddik* in God, is what enables the *tsaddik* to draw upon his followers the divine abundance that he draws by means of his *devekut*. The drawing of divine abundance that depends on the *tsaddik*'s faith, on the one hand, and on the faith of the Hasidim in their master, on the other hand, turns the *tsaddik* into a miracle worker. One of the earliest

---

[111] Ya'akov of Polonea, *Toldot Ya'akov Yosef*, on Eqev, end of section Aleph.
[112] See above, "Angels are the agents of the Queen," as discussed in note 17.

examples of an account of a hasidic leader as a miracle worker is the following story:

> [R. Raphael of Breshod] said: the first *tzadikim*, "Torah was their craft";[113] this means that when they said a certain thing their utterance became reality, like in the lifetime of the late rabbi [R. Pinhas of Korets] the rains had ceased, and once on Sabbath eve after *kiddush* said the late rabbi, it is written "I will give you your rains in their season,"[114] (Leviticus 26:4) and Rashi had read [their season] to mean on Sabbath eves, because we find in the Talmud that "No rain falls unless the sins of Israel have been forgiven,"[115] and we also find in the Talmud that "he who keeps the Sabbath, be he an idolater, is forgiven." [116] Therefore rains fall on the Sabbath, and immediately after he finished saying that the rain began to pour down.[117]

R. Pinhas of Korets does not seem to make any direct reference to the figures of Honi Hame'agel and R. Hanina ben Dosa, the famous tannaitic miracle workers. And yet, the story told about the Hassidic master by his disciple attests that in the eyes of his followers R. Pinhas was perceived as capable of bringing down the rain by the power of speech, similarly to the stories of rain-making by these *Hasidim haRishonim* (the pious men of earlier generations). This story doubtless belongs to the model of hasidic tales that demonstrate the *tsaddik*'s fulfillment of R. Abahu's commentary on 2 Samuel 23:1-3: "Said R. Abbahu, 'What does this [verse] mean:' 'The God of Israel said, The Rock of Israel spoke to me [to David].' [By this God meant to say] 'I rule over man; who rules over Me? [It is] the *tzadik*: for I make a decree and he [may] annul it.'"[118] In other words, the blessed Holy One issues a decree which the *tsaddik* is able to overturn.

From a hasidic perspective, R. Abahu's commentary in praise of the great power of *teshuva*—repentance—provides a framework for

---

[113] TB Shabbat 11a.
[114] Leviticus 26:4.
[115] TB Ta'anit 7b.
[116] "He who observes the Sabbath according to its laws, even if he practices idolatry like the generation of Enosh, is forgiven." TB Shabbat 118b.
[117] *Imrey Pinhas*, 200, section 44.
[118] TB Mo'ed Katan 16b.

instilling faith in *tsaddikim*. David, symbolizing the *tsaddikim*, is not merely a ruler governing by virtue of his fear of God; he has the power to change divine decrees. In the hasidic mind, the homilies on David that are related to the stories of the miraculous powers of Honi Hame'agel and Hanina ben Dosa pave the way to the world of the hasidic *tsaddikim*, who are perceived as also possessing the capacity to affect divine will by means of their *devekut*.

As the hasidic movement swelled in the nineteenth century, the vulgarization of the belief in *tsaddikim* became not only a major target for criticism by well-known members of the Jewish Enlightenment (such as Yosef Perl, author of *Megalle Temirin*[119]), but also the subject of criticism from within the hasidic movement itself. Piekarz discussed extensively how the later hasidic *tsaddikim* felt that their predecessors, who had to endure the harsh criticism of the Gaon of Vilna and his circle, had been worthier of the faith in them than the much-admired current leadership.[120] In R. David Moses of Chortkov's discussion of his father's opinion about this issue,[121] an additional aspect of the faith in *tsaddikim* is discussed which had already surfaced in the writings of the early hasidic masters:

> Once [R. David Moshe of Chortkov] spoke of faith and quoted his father, the Rizhiner [Rabbi Yisrael Friedman of Ruzhin], who said that because in the lifetime of the Besht and the Maggid there were great and holy *tzadikim* that the world[122] refused to believe in and fiercely opposed, the world's punishment was to believe in walking sticks.[123] And the holy R. David of Chortkov said that this was seemingly a puzzle: how could one say that the impor-

---

[119] [Perl Yosef], *Megalleh Tmirin* (Vienna: A. Strauss, 1819) (Perl did not use his name as the book's author, instead using the pseudonym Ovadia ben Petahyah). On this book see S. Werses, "Studies in the Structure of *Megalle Temirin* and *Bochen Zaddiq*," *Tarbitz* 31 (1962): 377-411 (Hebrew).

[120] Piekarz, *The Hassidic Leadership*, 60-77.

[121] On the preoccupation of R. Israel of Rozhin with the inferiority of the *tsaddikim* of his own generation compared to the founders of Hasidism, see Assaf, *The Regal Way*, 244-255.

[122] Meaning the Jewish community at large.

[123] In the nineteenth century, Hassidic *tsaddikim* used to have fancy walking canes. R. Israel of Rozhin comments sarcastically that the majority of them have nothing to boast other than their canes.

tant task of instilling fit faith in *tzadikim* amongst the crowds, Heaven forbid, has become believing in wood and sticks. But in truth, faith is always a lofty virtue. This is similar to the owner of an expensive gold watch that suddenly stops working. Usually, he would try to rattle this watch even though he knows full well that it will not go back to function properly, but [this way] he at least prevents the cogs and wheels from rusting beyond repair. And it is the same with Israel in relation to the vessel of faith that is a precious virtue and thanks to which they were delivered. Hence, even he who at present is not fortunate enough to be attached to a true *tzadik*, in order to prevent all of his vessels of faith from becoming impaired and rusty, the blessed Holy One in His grace still leads that man to use the vessels of his faith from time to time for the sake of [a *tzadik*] who does not merit true faith; but since the believer thinks that [this person] is also a *tzadik*, he accustoms himself to [practice] faith. Therefore, when God will induce the earth to become filled with divine knowledge, then [the believers in false *tzadikim*] will know how to use the vessels of their faith, which they had not lost. In truth the vessel of faith is of utmost importance and without it faith is useless. Therefore, the great *tzadikim* acted to instill faith in the world and when [the inhabitants of the world] become fortunate to acquire [divine] knowledge they will use the faith in God and in true *tzadikim* ...[124]

R. David Moses' consideration of religious belief as a vessel for awareness of divine presence in the world of *tsimtsum* we live in[125] was also his view in relation to the faith in the *tsaddikim*. R. Moses is aware both of the decline in the status of the *tsaddik* within the hasidic establishment already in his father's lifetime (and all the more so in his own day), as well as of the dissolution of religious faith in the second half of the nineteenth century. This crisis, common to both Christians and Jews, is perceived by R. Moses as an incurable loss for the human spirit, which runs the risk of reaching a point in the future where it will not be able to evolve through religious faith. He finds consolation in the argument that even an unworthy subject of faith such as the illusory power of a false *tsaddik* keeps faith alive, by preparing the spirit for worthier faith in the future. R. David Moses hoped for a future of renewed faith in worthy spiritual leaders, perhaps even to the point of reviving the faith

---

[124] R. Israel Berger, *Esser Orot*, 149.
[125] See above.

is based on *devekut* of early Hasidism. Meanwhile, nineteenth-century hasidic belief in the *tsaddikim* is, in many cases, a mere tool for spiritual practice of faith and the retention of the very ability to believe.

Existentialist Belief in Hassidism: Rabbi Nahman of Bratslav and the Disciples of Rabbi Simha Bunem of Przysucha

As mentioned earlier, in his studies of Bratslav Hasidism, Yosef Weiss argues that R. Nahman of Bratslav is the foremost representative of the Hasidism of faith, as opposed to the mystical Hasidism, whose foremost representative is, according to Weiss, the Maggid of Mezeritch. In some of R. Nahman's teachings and recorded conversations, a clear distinction is indeed made between "faith" and "knowledge," which early Hassidism had sought to blur: "That which the mind understands has no relation to faith, and the core of faith lies where the mind cannot proceed, and one cannot fathom with one's mind. This is where faith is required."[126] Both R. Nahman and his disciple R. Nathan Sternherz (1780-1845), who was R. Nahman's scribe and the architect of Bratslav Hasidism,[127] considered the early proponents of Jewish Enlightenment, *Haskalah*, to be men of the scientific heresy which they called "*Mehakrim*" (literally: men of scientific research), or rationalists (because of their resemblance to medieval Jewish thinkers), and the biggest threat to Jewish faith in a world-creating and providential God.[128] Without a doubt, the cause of challenging the *Maskilim* (members of Jewish Enlightenment) lay at the heart of R. Nathan's project:

> And indeed faith is a very powerful matter and one's life is greatly reinforced by faith. Because when one has faith, even if, Heaven forbid, woes befall him, then he is able to console himself and

---

[126] *Likutey Moharan*, vol. II, torah 8, section 7.
[127] For his biography, see *Yemey Moharanat* (Jerusalem: Agudat Meshech Hanachal, 1982).
[128] Haim Lieberman, "R. Nahman ve Maskiley Uman," in the above, *Ohel Rachel*, Part III (New York: 1984), 310-328; Piekarz, *Studies in Braslav Hasidism*, 21-55; Green, *Tormented Master*; Ron Margolin, *Religion and its Denial in Braslav Hassidic Thought According to the Book "Likutei Halakhot" by Rabbi Nathan Sternherz* (M.A. Thesis, Haifa University, 1992) (Hebrew).

revive himself. For the blessed God will have mercy upon him and improve his future, and the sufferings will be to his benefit and atonement; and ultimately the blessed God will ameliorate his condition either in this world or in the world to come. But the *mehaker* [who is] deprived of faith, when woe befalls him he has no one to turn to and no way to sustain and console himself. The learned will understand this effortlessly and will glean the message of my teachings, because it is not possible to explain it all in writing. And the rule [to be learned] is that most importantly faith requires no further investigations, and thanks to this, one will have strength in this world and in the world to come and that which he has shall never be shaken.[129]

In his article "The *Qushiyah* in Rabbi Nahman's Teachings," Weiss describes the existential nature of Bratslavic faith:

Clearly, the traditional notion of faith does not capture the content of faith as it appears in the writings of R. Nahman of Bratslav. Faith in Bratslavian thought is not intellectual by nature ... [R. Nahman's] faith is not an intellectual consequence or fact, it is an intellectual paradox. Therefore faith does not belong to the realm of reason, but to the realm of being, the realm of man's existence. It is man's existence within the contradiction that he must overcome with his faith. That is: faith is the overcoming of reason's tyranny through the law of contradiction. This overcoming as an existential act takes the notion of faith beyond any definition that supports truth, of "matching the internal image within the soul with the reality that is external to the soul." An analysis of the notion of faith reveals the existentialist content of this faith: it does not support truth, but it rather sustains itself by overcoming rational truth.[130]

Weiss' description is reinforced by passages in R. Nathan's *Likutey Halachot*, influenced by R. Nahman's *Likutey Moharan* (I 64 Section 2): "And therefore Israel are called *Ivrim* (Hebrews), because through their faith they believe that the blessed God is God of the *Ivrim*, as said above, they violate [*ovrim*] all of the sciences, and the things unscientific, that is the other [form of] heresy, as said above."

---

[129] *Sihot HaRan* (Jerusalem: Hasidei Braslav, 1961), conversation 32.
[130] Weiss, *Studies in Braslav Hassidism*, 142-143.

For when one has complete faith in His providence, may He be blessed, which is manifested in *ratzo vashov*;[131] and which is manifested in the universality of the [notion] that the end [of a process] derives [from its] beginning, as I have said above; through these [realizations] one earns a good end as in [the verse] "there is a good end for the man of peace" (Psalms 37:37). For with wholehearted faith one may skip and jump over all of the pitfalls, incitement, temptations, procrastinations and feebleness of mind with which the evil inclination and its forces seek to ensnare him, as though he still has no hope (yet). For through faith one passes and skips over them all, because one believes that the blessed God is first and last, God of the first and of the last [generations]. [132]

Indeed, R. Nathan's ideas are reminiscent of the Leap of Faith described in Søren Kierkegaard's writings on religious existentialism. But a careful reading of Bratslavic writings reveals a more complex picture. In a string of studies in recent decades it was shown that in Bratslavic writings, as well as in other early hasidic writings, faith is not contrasted with mystical conceptions, as argued by Gershom Scholem and his student Yosef Weiss.[133] R. Nahman of Bratslav's existentialist view of

---

[131] Literally to-and-fro, *ratzo vashov* denotes the circularity of existence manifest in the undulation of the soul between worldly necessities and spiritual fulfillment; a notion derived from Ezekiel 1:14: "And the living creatures darted to and fro."

[132] R. Natan Sternherz, *Likutey Halakhot* (Jerusalem: Braslav Publishing House, 1985), Orah Haim, part II, Hilkhot Massa uMatan 4, section 17, p.13. See also ibid., Orah Haim, part III, Hilkhot Pesach 7, section 23, p.308:

For this is the nature of narrow minds. For he who has a broad mind knows and understands and grasps truly that it is impossible to understand God's ways, and accepts true faith. But due to their narrowness of mind, others cling to the husks [*kelipot*] that are in fact heresies; by that they think that they are wise and embark on studies until they reach great perplexity [...]. And the miracle of the tearing apart of the Red Sea was possible mainly thanks to the fact that the [Israelites] were able to empty their minds completely and only call at God and draw strength from faith alone, and jumped into the sea based on faith alone, and thanks to that they shook off the grip of the husks which are heresies.

[133] Green, *Tormented Master*, 285-336; Mendel Piekarz, "A. Green, *Tormented Master: A Life of Rabbi Nahman of Bratslav*, 1979," *Tarbitz* 51 (1982): 149-162; Abraham Yitzhak Green, "On Piekarz's Review of my Book, 'Tormented Master,'" *Tarbitz* 51 (1982): 508-509 (Hebrew); Ada Rapaport-Albert, "'Ktanot,'

faith does not rule out the possibility of mental *devekut* in the spirit of the Besht, R. Nahman's great-grandfather. R. Nahman was equally committed to the maxim "prayer is faith."[134] The importance of faith lies in the fact that it may serve as a solid foundation for one's ascension to spiritual degrees that are higher than faith—the degree of *Hokhma* (wisdom), and yet higher to the degree of *Ratson* (will).[135] According to R. Nahman, it is possible to experience *devekut* during prayer, whereby the worshipper becomes immersed in the divine will through complete self-negation:

> And we see, that sometimes a man becomes so enthusiastic during prayer and says a few words with great enthusiasm; this [happens] through God's compassion for [that man], as the light of *Ein*

'Pshitot' ve 'Eini Yode'a' shel R. Nahman me Breslav," in *Studies in Jewish Religious and Intellectual History Presented to Alexander Altmann on the Occasion of his Seventieth Birthday*, ed. Siegfried Stein and Raphael Loewe (London, Alabama: University of Alabama Press, 1979), 7-33; Margolin, *Religion and its Denial in Braslav Hassidic Thought*, 133-134; 152-185; Shaul Magid, "Through the Void: The Absence of God in R. Nahman of Bratzlav's Likutei Moharan," *Harvard Theological Review* 88 (1995): 495-519; Mark, *Mysticism and Madness*. On the Kabbalistic aspect of the question of faith and heresy in the teachings of R. Nahman see Mordechai Pachter, "Faith and Heresy in the Doctrine of Rabbi Nahman of Bratslav," *Daat* 45 (2000): 105-134.

[134] And faith is prayer, as [Onkelos] translates [Exodus 17:12] *"prishan be tzilo."* For prayer alters Nature, and the knowledge and investigations that follow the ways of Nature are cancelled [in prayer's wake]. And this is our main end, that prayer be included in His unity, blessed be He, as [Scripture says] "He is your praise and He is your God" (Deuteronomy 10:21), for prayer and the blessed God are one, so to speak, and this is the kernel of our true purpose. (*Likutei Moharan, Tanina,* 19).

[135] And when one follows innocently faith alone, without any doubts, he may be fortunate to have the blessed God help him attain the measure of will (*ratson*), which is superior to wisdom (*hokhmah*). For in truth, holy wisdom is superior to faith, but still we must refrain from treading the paths of knowledge and doubts, and follow faith alone, for faith is very powerful. And then, when one follows innocently faith alone, without doubts and knowledge, then one is fortunate to attain the measure of will which is even superior to wisdom, that is, that he may be fortunate enough to have a great and mighty will to reach Him, may He be blessed, pining vigorously to the point where he would not know what to do with himself out of sheer pining. (*Sihot HaRan*, conversation 32)

Sof has opened up before him and shone down on him. And when one sees this splendor, "although he does not see [it] literally, he sees it clairvoyantly" (TB Megilla 3a), his soul becomes instantly excited [in its wish to] intensify its *dvekut*, to cleave unto the light of *Ein Sof*, and to the *she'ur* [measure] the revelation of *Ein Sof* reveals Himself, [a measure determined] according to the number of words that had opened up and sparkled [before that man], he utters all of these words with great *dvekut*, investing his soul and emptying his self. And when he empties his self before *Ein Sof*, then he embodies [the verse] "no man knew" (Deuteronomy 34:6), as even he himself does not know [anything about] himself.

But this [ecstatic] mode must be practiced *ratzo vashov*, in order to sustain his being. It has been found that when he returns [from the ecstatic state], he must reveal [the experiences acquired through *dvekut*] before his mind. Because initially, when practicing *dvekut* his mind is emptied, as it is written: "no man knew"; and when he returns [from the ecstatic state], he reunites with his being, and returns to his mind, he knows the unity of *Ein Sof* and His kindness. And then there is no divide between [the divine entities] *Adonai* and *Elohim*, between *Middat Ha-Din* [divine measure of judgment] and *Middat Ha-Rahamim* [divine measure of mercy]. For in *Ein Sof* there is no, Heaven forbid, change of will. Because the changes take place in the images only [i.e.. sensory impressions of worldly reality], but through man's *dvekut* in *Ein Sof*, [he comes to a place] where there is no change of will. It is because the [divine] will is simple [i.e., unitary], and only a *reshimo* [an impression] of this [divine] unity remains in him [in his inwardness]. And then he returns, and the *reshimo* instructs his mind to acknowledge that His entire being is good and His entire being is one.[136]

A person who has been through the experience of cleaving to the infinite divine essence (*Einsof*), has united his internality with the supreme will, and the impression he retained after returning to his normal state is the source of his knowledge, and his acknowledgment of the existence of this divine will. In light of the above passage, and in light of R. Nahman's notion of "*makif*" (the hidden divine truths surrounding us in this world) and "*penimi*" (the truths of the *makif* that one is able to internalize),[137] *devekut*, human mystical knowledge, remains

---

[136] *Likutey Moharan*, part I, torah 4, section 9.
[137] Ibid., torah 21.

forever partial and temporary. The belief in a world created according to a divine scheme may serve from an internal-experiential perspective as the foundation for mystical knowledge, attained by a select few in fleeting moments of grace. Faith in the *tsaddik* who has attained the highest degree of religious knowledge, understood as "the object of unknowable knowledge," protects the Hasid from his spiritual pride. In Bratslav, like in all hasidic schools, life's purpose lies in another world, the World to Come, which exists not only after death, but also hides behind the exterior existence of this world:

> For we must protect memory very carefully, lest we fall into oblivion, which is tantamount to having the heart cease from beating. And most important in relation to memory is to always remember the world to come, that this world is not the only world in existence. And by cleaving with our mind unto the world to come, divine *yihud* takes place. [138]

The Bratslavic conception is unique in its emphasis of the fact that attainment of this objective is far from simple, as suggested in other early hasidic homilies. Mystical consciousness is paradoxical in essence, because its attainment depends on the emptying of self-consciousness, and yet it is attainable. In the same way, R. Nathan maintains that one should accept the paradox of faith which is based on the incapacity to attain comprehension and knowledge of the divine, because "in truth the core of faith lies in that which the mind cannot comprehend." Only those who accept the paradox of faith derived from "no-knowledge" in its profoundest sense can attain a higher degree of knowledge that depends on the emptying of conventional consciousness. It therefore emerges that even Bratslav Hasidism is in fact a "Hasidism of mysticism and faith."[139]

Following the death of the Besht, a slow and gradual decline of the experiential conception of *devekut* as possessing prophetic or revelatory features began. While in early Hasidism this conception was reflected

---

[138] Ibid., torah 54, section 1.
[139] In *Mysticism and Madness*, Zvi Mark expands this claim and argues for the existence of a mysticism of faith in the writings of R. Nahman that conceives of a single scale of experiences in which prophecy and faith appear on the same sequence. See chapters 5 and 6.

in the synonymy of faith with *devekut*, it was replaced with conceptions of faith that are not identified with this form of *devekut*. As the direct struggles with doubts and apostasy, the earliest occurrence of which we find in the story of R. Pinhas of Korets and the Besht, became more prevalent, the Hassidic preoccupation with the notion of faith became more central. This was particularly conspicuous in the school of R. Simha Bunem of Pryzucha (1765–1827), which shifted its focus from the unmediated and experiential encounter with divine presence to a form of faith that is not founded on these experiences. The following conversation is a symbolic expression of this shift:

> One of the *tzadikim* once sent [a message] to the Saraf [nickname for R. Menachem Mendel of Kotsk]: "I see in my *sukka* (of the Feast of Booths) the seven *ushpizin* (Welcoming Guests) do come to see me and I'll show them to you." The Saraf replied: "I am better than you. I believe in the appearance of the *ushpizin* in my *sukka*, and faith supersedes the eyesight."[140]

The homily of R. Isaac Meir of Gur (1799–1866) on the verse "and the people of Israel believed in the Lord and his servant Moses" (Exodus 14:31) serves as a clear example for this shift:

> The Rabbi of Ger was asked: "It is written: 'and Israel saw the Great Hand,' and further on it is written: 'and they believed in the Lord and in his servant Moses' (Exodus 14:31). Why is this said? The question as to whether or not one believes can only be put while one does not as yet see." [The Rabbi of Ger] answered: "You are mistaken. It is only then that the true question can be put. Seeing the great hand does not mean that faith can be dispensed with. It is only after seeing that we feel how much we are in need of it. Seeing the great hand is the beginning of belief in that which we cannot see." [141]

---

[140] Levin, *Beit Kotzk*, Hasaraf, 85. Appears in abbreviated form in Buber, *Tales of Hasidim*, 274 according to Yoetz Kim Kadish of Preshitik, *Siach Sarfey Kodesh* (New York: Jerusalem Publishing House, 1954), part I, p.71.

[141] Buber, *Tales of Hasidim*, 308, quoted in Avraham Isaskhar Binyamin Eliyahu Alter, *Me'ir Einey ha Golah* (Warsaw: A.M. Alter, 1928-1932).

Similarly to R. Nahman of Bretslav, who praised the experience of *devekut* while also emphasizing the dichotomy of "faith" and "knowledge," R. Menachem Mendel of Kotsk (1787–1859) refined this distinction further: "I would not worship a God that my small brain could grasp and comprehend."[142] In *Si'ach Serafei Kodesh* it is told of the rabbi of Kotsk:

> Once the holy rabbi asked the great [rabbis] of his time, as follows: "Where does the blessed Holy One reside?" And they laughed at him, because the whole earth is filled with His glory, and the holy [Rabbi of Kotsk] replied to them as follows: "The blessed God lives where he is let in."[143]

R. Menahem Mendel of Kotsk does not repeat the well-known hasidic maxim about God's all-permeating presence. Surrounded by apostasy, the faith of man antecedes the ability to sense the all-permeating divine presence. From the two key principles that the Besht had posited at the heart of his teachings, "No place is void of Him," and "One is where one's thoughts are," the rabbi of Kotzk chose to emphasize the latter, after reshaping it: God is in the mind of the person who thinks about Him. Faith is the human struggle for a reason to live a meaningful life. Martin Buber included in his *Tales of the Hasidim* a series of aphorisms and teachings of nineteenth-century *tsaddikim* that attest to the existential nature of their faith:

> A hasid came to the Rabbi of Kotsk.
> "Rabbi," he complained, "I keep brooding and brooding, and don't seem to be able to stop."
> "What do you brood about?" asked the Rabbi.
> "I keep brooding about whether there really is a judgment and a judge."
> "What does it matter to you!"
> "Rabbi! If there is no judgment and there is no Judge, then what does all creation mean!"
> "What does that matter to you!"
> "Rabbi! If there is no judgment and no judge, then what do the words of the Torah mean!"
> "What does that matter to you?"

---

[142] Levin, *Beit Kotzk*.
[143] Yoetz Kim Kadish, *Siach Sarfey Kodesh*. Appears also in Buber, *Tales of Hasidim*, 277.

"Rabbi! 'What does it matter to me?' What does the rabbi think? What else could matter to me?"

"Well, if it matters to you as much as all that," said the rabbi of Kotsk, "then you are a good Jew after all—and it is quite all right for a good Jew to brood: nothing can go wrong with him."[144]

The measure by which R. Menahem Mendel of Kotsk evaluates the nature of the doubts of faith is one's degree of care for questions of faith. A person for whom the question of the existence of God is personal, subjective and crucial demonstrates that he is not indifferent to the question concerning God's reality and the purpose of creation.[145] Similar ideas are found in passages brought in the name of R. Noah of Lekuvitch:

> Once when Rabbi Noah of Lekhovitz was in his room, he heard how one of his disciples began to recite the Principles of Faith in the House of Study next door, but stopping immediately after the words "I believe with perfect faith" whispered to himself: "I do not understand that," and again, "I do not understand that." The *tzadik* left his room and went to the House of Study.
> "What is it you do not understand?" he asked.
> "I do not understand what it's all about," said the man. "I say: 'I believe'. If I really believe, why am I telling lies?"
> "It means" answered the Rabbi, "that the words 'I believe' are a prayer, meaning 'oh, that I may believe!'" Then the hasid was suffused with a glow from within. "That is right!" he cried. "That is right! Oh, that I may believe, Lord of the world, oh, that I may believe!" [146]

Faith requires us to struggle for it, because it is faith that infuses human life with meaning and purpose, whereas doubts and apostasy mean a life of despair, cynicism, and doubting the reason to exist. Said R. Hirsch of Zhidachov to R. Moses Teitelbaum:

> I stake my whole self for everyone, even the most unfaithful, and probe down to the root of his apostasy where wickedness can be recognized as need and lust. And if I get that far, I can pull him

---

[144] Buber, ibid., 280, quoting A.M. Haberman.
[145] Schechter, *Readings in the Thought of our Times*, 100.
[146] Buber, *Tales of Hasidim*, 158. A Hebrew translation of the Yiddish tale appears in *Or Yesharim*, collected by Moshe Haim Kleinman (Jerusalem: 1967), 42.

out all right! What do you say: shall we give all those souls up as lost? For wouldn't they be lost if the Messiah came today? [147]

R. Hirsch of Zhidachov (d. 1831) does not address the views of the heretics, but rather the existential-psychological source of their heresy. He claims that heresy is caused by distress and destructive desires, and hence should be dealt with by the appropriate measures—exposing these negative psychological causes. Therefore faith requires from us to struggle for it, because it is a device for infusing existence with meaning and purpose.

Conclusion

> Once [Rabbi David Moshe of Chortkov] spoke about [God's] concealment today, and then said: "Nowadays [God's] concealment is so great that even the *tzadik* cannot learn anything. And this is what is meant by the verse "the righteous [*tzadik*] shall live by his faith" (Habakkuk 2:4)," that even the *tzadik* himself does not witness any revelation but only lives with wholehearted faith in the Eternal God.[148]

The words of R. David Moses of Chortkov (d.1903) make clear the nature of the gap between the Hasidism of his day and that of the Besht, in which the distinctions between faith, *devekut* and knowledge were blurred. R. David Moses, who lived under the reign of the Austro-Hungarian Empire in the second half of the nineteenth century, confesses: "Even the *tzadik* himself does not see any revelation, he only lives with wholehearted faith." Doubtless, this statement was made in an era of intensifying materialistic heresy, and in the wake of the rise of scientific determinism in Western thought. The proliferation of faith as a central motif in Polish Hasidism, evident in the writings of the disciples of R. Simha Bunem of Pryzucha, resembles the process that R. David Moses of Chortkov describes. Like R. Nahman of Bretslav before him, R. David Moses drew on the Lurianic doctrine of *tsimtsum* (contraction) more than the Besht and many of his disciples, who were profoundly taken by R. Moses Cordovero's kabbalistic approach, which focuses on divine presence on earth.

---

[147] Ibid., 218, quoting Dov Baer Arman, *Pe'er ve Kavod* (Munkatz: 1912).
[148] Berger, *Esser Orot*, 148.

From a phenomenological perspective, the rise in popularity of a faith with existential overtones in Hasidism resembles the rise of Søren Kierkegaard's religious existentialism. Clearly, the latter's philosophical roots, and his direct response to the thought of G.W.F. Hegel, were not shared by nineteenth-century hasidic *tsaddikim*. Yet it would not be too far-fetched to argue that they shared with the fledgling existentialist thought the challenge posed by materialistic thought and scientific determinism, which had by then also seeped into the Hassidic world. R. Nahman's relations with the Jewish intellectuals in Uman in the late eighteenth century foresaw a process that intensified in the nineteenth century across the Jewish diaspora of central and Eastern Europe. R. Simha Bunem of Pryzucha made a living as a pharmacist; members of R. David Moses of Chortkov's circle had also received general educations and were immersed in Austrian social and financial life; some of them even left the Jewish fold before going back.

I began this discussion with the struggle against apostasy in early Hasidism, and with R. Pinhas of Korets overcoming his religious doubts by the power of the Besht's prayer and his encounter with his unique personality. The numerous textual sources presented in this article expose a process within Hasidism of contending with doubts of faith, which intensified since its beginnings in the mid-eighteenth century through to the lifetime of R. Menahem Mendel of Kotsk, R. David Moses of Chortkov, and others in the second half of the nineteenth century. Unlike R. Nahman of Bratslav's teachings, comprised of many varied spiritual approaches, including existentialism and *devekut*, the thought of the rabbi of Kotsk and the rabbi of Chortkov is defined by the supremacy of a notion of faith with existentialist overtones. I believe that this fact implies a position accepting of the deterministic thought which proliferated in nineteenth-century Europe.

I find the prevalent view of Hasidism in Jewish thought departments in Israeli universities, which sees is as an integral part of the medieval kabbalistic world, to be quite misleading. This position owes much to the decisive influence of Gershom Scholem's *Major Trends in Jewish Mysticism*, whose concluding chapter discusses Hasidism.[149] The movement, which Scholem himself perceived as characterized by a focus on

---

[149] Gershom Scholem, *Major Trends in Jewish Mysticism* (New York: Schocken Books, 1961).

the individual's mental life, reflects a complex process of struggle with the doubts of faith that slowly began to seep into East European Jewry following the rise of the new science, technology, industrialization, and philosophical materialism. This struggle began with the ecstatic and prophetic approach of the Besht, which directs religious attention to divine presence in the world by means of the mental-experiential *dveekut* that is founded on the maxim "One is where one's thoughts are." This path had led to the development of the institution of the *tsaddik*.

Alongside the incredible prosperity of *tsaddikim* and the abundance of hasidic courts (some of them led by *tsaddikim*) in the nineteenth century, the essence of this institution suffered from growing vulgarization. This occurred, among other reasons, due to the emergence of hasidic dynasties that immersed themselves in struggles over status and power, and the crowning of *tsaddikim* unworthy of the title. Concurrently, hasidic rabbis engaged in a serious attempt to address the threat of apostasy, by engaging with the question of personal faith and positing it as the locus of their life's work. The writings of these *tsaddikim* display considerable sobriety as they transform the individual's struggle over religious faith into an existential battle over the meaning of life. In seeking to gain an understanding of these processes in Hasidism, one must also consider the historical-intellectual context of the movement. In *Tradition and Crisis*,[150] Jacob Katz argued from the perspective of a sociologist of history that Hasidism reflects an attempt to deal with the crisis of the weakening of traditional social frameworks in Eastern Europe of the late eighteenth century. This chapter seeks to add the aspect missing from Katz's book: the hasidic engagement with religious doubts and the crisis of faith within European life in the eighteenth and nineteenth centuries.

Beginning in the late nineteenth century, it is possible to identify the overt personal interest of modern Jewish intellectuals in Hasidism, coming from different backgrounds of Jewish education: writers such as Y.L Perez, S.Y. Agnon, and Pinhas Sade; Jewish studies scholars such as Eliezer Zvi Zweifel, Simon Dubnov and Schneor Zalman Schechter; and thinkers such as Hillel Zeitlin, Martin Buber, Abraham Joshua Heschel, Joseph Schechter, and Arthur Green, among many others. hasidic

---

[150] Jacob Katz, *Tradition and Crisis: Jewish Society at the End of the Middle Ages* (New York: New York University Press, 1993).

engagement with questions of faith was a key factor in the attraction of these intellectuals to the hasidic world.

Moreover, the experiential and intellectual world of the Besht and his disciples inspires awe and amazement even today. Focusing faith on divine presence in the world, as opposed to the medieval tradition of a purely transcendent God, seems at first glance to contradict entirely post-Kantian thought. And yet, at second glance, it is clear that this conception, which bears the clear mark of R. Moses Cordovero's thought, somewhat narrows the gap between God and the world; a gap that any transcendental conception opens up, raising devastating doubts about the purpose and value of religious life in general and prayer in particular. The Besht's teachings on faith attract much scholarly interest today, thanks to the substitution of God with the notions of divinity and *Einsof*, and liberation from the labyrinthine kabbalistic theosophy by referring, for example, to the *Shekhinah* (the lowest *sefirah* in kabbalistic tradition) as "divinity that inheres in man." The conception of divinity as vitality, and the definition of religious faith as the belief in spiritual presence in the corporeal world, infuses religious life, as well as everyday life, with a spiritual meaning of which they were robbed by the monumental conceptions of divine transcendence.

Despite the charm and allure of hasidic faith, the modern intellectual seeking a path into Judaism would still find the conception of *hamshakhah* at the heart of the hasidic doctrine of the *tsaddik* as foreign as it was to the early followers of *Haskalah* some two hundred years ago. The doctrine of the *tsaddik* already faced harsh criticism by the second half of the nineteenth century. Unlike the Hasidism founded on the conception of the *tsaddik*, hasidic faith with existentialist overtones retains its vitality in the eyes of many, as attested by the great interest in the lives and teachings of R. Nahman of Bratslav and R. Menahem Mendel of Kotsk.[151]

---

[151] The fierce opposition to the existentialist aspect of hasidism due to the problematic subjectivity it entails was typical of Gershom Scholem and some of his disciples. It arose mainly from a personal preference for a Kantian, transcendental viewpoint. Scholem personally opposed any existential philosophy that attempted to face up to the challenge that this viewpoint posed to religious thought. In this context, his rejection of Martin Buber's thought is particularly conspicuous. Buber aspired to convert the mystical thought that had fascinated the young Scholem with a dialogical-existential approach.

The processes of counteracting doubt of faith undergone by the hasidic masters may serve as a key to understanding Martin Buber's evolution from a thinker preoccupied with mysticism to a scholar of Hasidism, and on to a man who formulated his dialogical philosophy. The clear identification of the older Buber with the school of R. Simha Bunem of Pryzucha, though centered on the question of messianism,[152] indicates that the process that the current chapter describes may reflect the general drift of Buber's intellectual-religious transformation in writing *I and Thou*,[153] and in his later interest in the Bible.[154]

The relevance of hasidic thought and faith is manifest also in its similarities to contemporary Jewish theological thought. An interesting example close to my heart is the theological thought of Hans Jonas (1903-1993), a scholar of Gnosis, who was an important philosopher of biology and technology and a student and critic of Martin Heidegger. A German Jew who fought against the Nazis in the Second World War with the Jewish Brigade, in his theological work Hans Jonas took on the major challenges Jewish thought faces in wake of the Holocaust. From within the transcendentalism that underlies deterministic nature, Jonas sought to find an opening through which the existence of divine immanence in the world may be acknowledged. Jonas pointed out the resemblance between the Heideggerian existentialism and dualist Gnostic doctrines of early Christianity. In light of this semblance, he tried to rectify the serious ethical distortion that he recognized in the philosophy of his teacher, who had erred grimly by attaching himself to the Nazi regime. For Jonas, after the Holocaust, Jewish belief in divine providence in history became either impossible or unethical. Like R. Nahman of Bratslav and R. David Moses of Chortkov, Jonas resorted to the Lurianic doctrine of *tsimtsum*:

> In order that the world might be, and be for itself, God renounced his being, divesting himself of his deity—to receive it back from

---

[152] Martin Buber, *Tikva le Sha'ah Zo* (Tel Aviv: Am Oved, 1992), 138.
[153] Martin Buber, *I and Thou*, trans. Walter Kaufman (New York: Touchstone, 1996).
[154] Similar claims can be made in relation to the influence of Hasidism in general, and the teachings of R. Menahem Mendel of Kotsk in particular, on the thought of A.J. Heschel. This consideration of the contribution of Hasidic learning to the formation of major trends in modern Jewish thought supports my claim that Hasidism should be considered part of modern Jewish thought no less than certain elements of medieval Kabbalistic thought.

the odyssey of time weighted with the chance harvest of unforeseeable temporal experience: transfigured or possibly even disfigured by it.[155]

Like R. Menahem Mendel of Kotsk and others, as an existentialist Jonas also refused to dismiss the dimension of faith as part of human life, despite his much keener awareness of the impossibility of metaphysical certainty after Kant. His faith relies on the understanding that the world of matter, which seemingly operates according to an internal regularity, inhabits the spiritual potential of interiority, culminating in the human consciousness of free will. In his article "Matter, Spirit and Creation,"[156] he explains that his solution to the relation of matter and spirit is founded on introducing a new meaning for the term "matter," one which is not exhausted by measurable physical units; for him matter is more than the sum of that the properties physicists ascribe to it in their speculation about the Big Bang. R. David Moses of Chortkov argued that nature is contained in the vessel of the belief in the divine spirit that inheres in the world and antecedes it. In his answer to the question "Who gave matter the possibility of the latent existence of internality"—i.e. the mentality and consciousness that evolve in the organic world from the single-celled microorganisms to the human—Hans Jonas replied that something which is less than spirit cannot be the cause of spirit. Outright belief in "No place is void of Him" is inadmissible for Jonas, but its devotional principle is retained, even if only partially, in his conception of matter.

---

[155] Hans Jonas, "The Concept of God after Auschwitz: A Jewish Voice," in *Mortality and Morality: A Search for the Good after Auschwitz*, ed. Lawrence Vogel (Evanston: Northwestern University Press, 1996), 134.

[156] Hans Jonas, "Matter, Mind and Creation: Cosmological Evidence and Cosmogonic Speculation," in his *Mortality and Morality*, 172-177.

"Beyond Reason"
On Faith in the Philosophy of Chabad*

Dov Schwartz

Chabad's reference to faith as *raza de mehemanuta* (the mystery of faith) points to a conceptual crossroads of several traditions.[1] Like many Jewish philosophers in the Middle Ages and in the early modern period, Chabad rabbis dealt with at least three aspects of faith:

(1) *A psychological and anthropological aspect.* Faith as an experience and as a spiritual state.

(2) *An epistemological aspect.* Faith as relating to a particular type of positive or negative knowledge, meaning realms not amenable to knowledge that might also be related to the definition of faith (for instance, the negation of attributes).

(3) *A national aspect.* Faith as a special characteristic of the Jewish people.

Another aspect that has also affected the Chabad conception of faith is Kabbalah, thus introducing:

(4) *A mystical aspect.* Faith as reflecting a specific theosophical dimension.[2]

---

* Thanks to Batya Stein, who translated this article from Hebrew.
[1] Conceptions of faith in Jewish thought is a topic that has been widely explored. See, for instance, Eliana Amado Levi-Valensy and Shmuel Safrai, eds., *Ways to Faith in Judaism* (Jerusalem: Ministry of Education, 1981) (Hebrew).
[2] In kabbalistic literature, faith is generally viewed as reflecting the *sefirah* of malkhut. For a discussion of faith in Kabbalah and in Hasidism, see, for instance, Yoram Jacobson, "Truth and Faith in Gur Hasidic Thought," in *Studies in Jewish Mysticism, Philosophy, and Ethical Literature: Presented to Isaiah Tishby on His Seventy-Fifth Birthday*, ed. J. Dan and J. Hacker (Jerusalem: Magnes Press, 1986) (Hebrew); Mordechai Pachter, "The Root of Faith is the Root of Heresy in the Teaching of R. Azriel of Gerona," *Kabbalah* 4 (1999): 315-341 (Hebrew); idem, "Faith and Heresy in the Doctrine of Rabbi Nahman of Bratslav,' *Daat* 45 (2000): 105-134 (Hebrew).

This chapter will focus on the second aspect, which ties faith to kabbalistic and rational contents, but will at times also briefly consider others. The discussion that follows will thus essentially deal with Chabad doctrines of theology and creation,[3] since faith for Chabad rabbis revolved mainly on issues tied to creation and the origin of the cosmos.

R. Shneur Zalman of Lyadi clearly determined that the definition of faith cannot be detached from the special contents related to it. The mystery of faith is also the mystery of the divine essence or, more precisely, the infinite light or *Einsof*, which stands alone but also powers the vessels of the *sefirot* in the various worlds and is present in them after the refraction of *tsimtsum*. Some Chabad rabbis stressed that faith refers to the divine presence in the vessels of the world of emanation and, as such, cannot be apprehended rationally. Some texts of R. Shneur Zalman applied faith to *sovev kol olmin* ("surrounds all worlds") or to *mekif kol olmin* ("encompasses all worlds"), whereas other texts applied it to the divine dimension that is even higher than the rungs exposed through inquiry into the origin of the cosmos. Both constituted faith on a paradoxical dialectic that simultaneously endorses negation and affirmation. Ascribing faith to the higher rungs of the divine world is an extremely significant step and, in this chapter, I consider its implications.

In the following discussion, I briefly examine R. Shneur Zalman of Lyadi's conception of faith and its connection to the divine presence and to negative theology in his thought.

---

[3] See, for instance, Rivka Schatz, "Anti-Spiritualism in Hasidism: Reflections on the Thought of Shneur Zalman of Liadi," *Molad* 20 (1963): 515-520 (Hebrew); Yitzhak Tishby and Yosef Dan, "Hasidism," in *Encyclopaedia Hebraica*, vol. 17, 777 (Hebrew); Joseph G. Weiss, "Hasidism of Mysticism and Hasidism of Faith," in *Studies in Bratslav Hasidism* (Jerusalem: Bialik Institute, 1974), 89 (Hebrew); Yoram Jacobson, "The Doctrine of Creation in the Thought of R. Shneur Zalman of Liadi," *Eshel Beer Sheva: Studies in Jewish Thought* 1 (1976): 308, 326-327 (Hebrew); Moshe Hallamish, *The Theoretical System of R. Shneur Zalman of Liadi* (Ph.D. Dissertation: Hebrew University of Jerusalem, 1976), 58-59 (Hebrew); Tamar Ross, "Rav Hayyim of Volozhin and Rav Shneur Zalman of Liadi: Two Interpretations of the Doctrine of Tsimtsum," *Jerusalem Studies in Jewish Thought* 1:2 (1981): 153-169 (Hebrew); Rachel Elior, *The Paradoxical Ascent to God: The Kabbalistic Theosophy of Habad Hasidism*, trans. Jeffrey M. Green (Albany, NY: SUNY Press, 1993), 49-57.

Faith and Knowledge

R. Shneur Zalman's conception of faith is not clear-cut and, like his doctrine in general, is marked by signs of diversity and dialectics. In his teachings, he ascribes different meanings to the concept of *faith*, and his approach has been the subject of extensive scholarly inquiry.[4] In this chapter, I emphasize several motifs that were elaborated on in the writings of later Chabad rabbis. Three characteristics are fundamental to R. Shneur Zalman's approach in particular and to Chabad philosophy in general:

(1) *Knowledge*. Faith is not rational apprehension.
(2) *Contents*. Faith applies to different aspects of paradoxical dialectic.[5]
(3) *Value*. Faith is not the supreme rank vis-à-vis the divine.

---

[4] For a comprehensive discussion of R. Shneur Zalman's conception of faith, see Hallamish, *Theoretical System*, 200-209. On faith from a specific conceptual perspective, see Shimon Gershon Rosenberg, "Faith and Language According to ha-Admor ha-Zaken of Chabad: A View from Wittgenstein's Philosophy of Language," in *On Faith: Studies in the Concept of Faith and its History in Jewish Tradition*, ed. Moshe Halbertal, David Kurzweil, and Avi Sagi (Jerusalem: Keter, 2005), 365-387 (Hebrew). On the controversy between R. Shneur Zalman and R. Abraham of Kalisk on this question, see Raaya Haran, *Inter-Hasidic Ideological Controversies in the Late Eighteenth and the Beginning of the Nineteenth Centuries* (Ph. D. Dissertation: Hebrew University of Jerusalem, 1993) (Hebrew). See also Binyamin Brown, "The Return of 'Simple Faith': The Conception of Haredi Faith and its Growth in the Nineteenth Century," in *On Faith: Studies in the Concept of Faith and its History in Jewish Tradition*, ed. Moshe Halbertal, David Kurzweil, and Avi Sagi (Jerusalem: Keter, 2005), 418-423 (Hebrew). The sources of the "contradiction" pointed out in this article are not only in the character of R. Shneur Zalman's thought, as noted below, but also in his appeal to different groups.

[5] I define paradoxical dialectic in contrast to relative dialectic, as follows:
(a) Relative dialectic. The concern of this dialectic is to look at the object from several complementary perspectives. Instances of relative dialectic are the object *per se* and the object vis-à-vis its causes; the realist dimension of the object and its epistemic dimension; a partial grasp of an object as opposed to its complete grasp. Relative dialectic acknowledges a true and well-grounded statement that, from another perspective, is perceived differently or in contrary ways. The pole of the object's reality is factual truth; the pole of the different epistemic dimension reflects the (usually limited) character of the observer and the knower. The (complete) divine grasp is factual truth versus

These three characteristics are three aspects of the same approach: since reality is dual in that it is built on coexisting opposites, it cannot be apprehended by rational means. And since Chabad philosophy attaches value to rational apprehension, perfect understanding of the divine, insofar as it is possible, is to be left to the messianic era.

As is true of his conception of creation, R. Shneur Zalman's conception of faith was neither conceptually nor epistemologically consistent. For instance, faith is sometimes perceived as inferior to rational apprehension and at times as equal to it. Chabad's conception of faith should thus also be viewed as a series of conceptual intuitions and as an expression of the special experience and ethos that developed within this hasidic group. The following analysis presents several sources that attest to the unfolding of the conception of faith in the writings of R. Shneur Zalman.

Faith as Paradox

I open with a detailed formulation of R. Shneur Zalman's conception of faith. In *Shaʿar ha-Yihud ve-ha-Emunah*, he ties faith to the Maimonidean view on the unity of knowledge, as follows:

> Just as it is impossible for any creature in this world to apprehend the essence and the substance of the Creator, so is it impossible

---

the (partial) human truth that reflects a subjective angle. Relative dialectic is a harmony of opposites, that is, the contradictions are reconciled within one system.

(b) Paradoxical dialectic. This dialectic does not allow the reconciliation of contradictions by means of different compatible angles and claims that both poles are factually true. Paradoxical dialectic is not solely acosmic, just as it is not solely panentheistic. This view supports both outlooks simultaneously, and could be viewed as a radical conception of constant creation in the sense that the disappearance and appearance of the world are simultaneous. This tension cannot be settled except by claiming that a paradox is impossible according to rational order but is possible according to divine order. Paradoxical dialectic is ultimately irreconcilable. The opposites remain as they are. Unity is not homogeneous but correlative, that is, a unity of opposites. For discussions of Chabad dialectic, see Hallamish, *Theoretical System*; Jacobson, "Truth and Faith," and Elior, *Paradoxical Ascent*. I intend to discuss this issue further elsewhere.

to grasp the essence of his knowledge. We can only believe with a faith that is beyond reason and knowledge[6] that the Holy One is unique and special and he and his knowledge are indeed one. By knowing himself, he knows all that are found above and below, from the small worm on the surface of the sea and up to a small fly in the navel of the earth. Nothing escapes him, and this knowledge adds nothing to his multiplicity and complexity, since it is only knowledge of himself, and his essence and his knowledge are one.[7]

I have already shown that R. Shneur Zalman used the notion of the unity of knowledge (knowledge, knower, and known—"He and his knowledge are indeed one") to enable this paradoxical dialectic.[8] The notion of coexisting polar opposites is impossible in human perception but is possible in the divine world, since the divine world is ruled by an order we cannot apprehend. The mystery of this knowledge is indeed the unified perception of multiplicity (without "multiplicity and complexity").

R. Shneur Zalman's definition of the term *faith* and of its connection with a (Jewish or Gentile) believer remains ambiguous. His basic assumption is that human beings apprehend some realms through reason (the immanent dimension of divinity), whereas some realms are beyond reason (the transcendent dimension of divinity and the paradoxical dialectic of existence). He presents two models of faith. According to the first, *faith* means immediate and intuitive knowledge without any need for rational verification, even in realms where reason applies ("and it is

---

[6] In his homilies, R. Shneur Zalman resorted to the same style regarding paradoxical dialectic: "That is why His attributes, may He be blessed, have been called *raza de-mehemanuta*, since they are beyond reason and knowledge. Just as the measure of his grace and greatness is inapprehensible, when boundless vitality flows from him to create *ex nihilo*, so is the measure of his *gevurah*, when he conceals his light of *Ein Sof* so that the creature will be a defined, existing, and separate object" (*Likkutei Torah, Balak* [Vilnius: 1904; Brooklyn and Kefar Chabad: 1979], 68d).

[7] *Sha'ar ha-Yihud ve-ha-Emunah*, ch. 7, 83a. R. Shneur Zalman's formulations in this passage rely on *The Code of Maimonides*, "Laws on the Foundations of the Torah" 2:9; *Guide of the Perplexed* 3:17. See also M. Teitelboim, *The Rabbi of Liadi and Chabad*, vol. 2 (Warsaw: Tushiyah, 1913), 7 (Hebrew).

[8] See Dov Schwartz, *Chabad Thought: From Beginning to End* (in preparation) (Hebrew). See also Yaakov Gottlieb, *Chabad's Harmonistic Approach to Maimonides* (Ph. D. Dissertation: Bar-Ilan University, 2003) (Hebrew).

called faith due to the impression it left in the roots of their souls").[9] In this definition, faith applies to creation and to both the immanent and the transcendent dimensions of the divinity. Only aspects related to the beginning of creation ("his being and essence"), are beyond human consciousness. According to this view, faith characterizes only the apprehension of the Jew; it is rooted in and impressed upon his soul, whereas the Gentile requires learning and contemplation.

According to the second model, *faith* means admittance and (gradual) acknowledgement of supra-rational realms. It relates, above all, to the transcendent dimensions of the divinity (from the rung of "surrounds all worlds" up to the essence of the *Einsof*). By contrast, the immanent dimensions of the divinity are rational and are not included in faith at all. The apprehension of these dimensions is common to both Jews and Gentiles. Specifically: these understandings are impressed upon the soul of the Jew from its very creation and are no less certain than rational certainty, but the pious Gentile also shares in them.[10]

The second model is the dominant one in the thought of R. Shneur Zalman, who pointed to three supra-natural realms of knowledge to which faith applies:

(1) *Transcendence*. The concealed dimension of the divinity, as noted.

(2) *Psychology*: The paradoxical state of the divine soul in its material manifestation:

> Since the divine soul dresses up in the sack of *kelipath Nogah*, which is bodily matter, mortals need to the see the transformation of nihility into being so as to remove blindness from their

---

[9] *Maa'marei Admor ha-Zaken*, vol. 1 (1803), 176. Faith relates directly to "the matter of creation *ex nihilo*, as if one were actually to see with the eye of reason the nihility emanating and creating heaven, earth and all existent creatures emerging as objects, and the nullification of the object vis-à-vis its divine source" (ibid.).

[10] "Indeed, this matter does not only concern creation *ex nihilo*, since the divine soul did not come down to the material world only for that, which even the pious of other nations will recognize, as we have been told 'To thee it was shown, that thou mightest know that the Lord he is God' [Deuteronomy 4:35], and that is faith. Not so when power [is seen to] work on an object—that cannot be called faith, because any mortal can immediately see that" (*Siddur Admor ha-Zaken*, 284c).

eyes. They mistake the trivial for the core and do not apprehend the nullification of being vis-à-vis nihility, which is the crux—every created material being is nullified vis-à-vis the divine spiritual power that gives it life and creates it *ex nihilo*.[11]

(3) *Magic*. The commandments bring down the divine emanation ("*hamshakhat elokut*").[12] This bringing down is entirely spiritual and abstract, and takes place through a material act. The paradoxical association between spirit and material action is "beyond reason, solely faith." R. Shneur Zalman therefore concludes "that all the commandments are a preparation for faith."[13]

We can now formulate the definition of faith according to R. Shneur Zalman as referring to the supra-rational realm as follows:

(1) Faith applies to the dialectic integration of opposites (being and nihility, substance and vessels, substance and *sefirot*, multiplicity and unity).

(2) Reason does not grasp this integration (the Maimonidean construct).

Hence:

(3) Faith applies to the realm inapprehensible through reason.

Faith, therefore, refers to *Einsof*, to the light of *Einsof*, and to other terms that describe the divine present in the vessels of the world of emanation (*kav, reshimu*). The realms that these terms point to cannot be apprehended rationally and are therefore part of faith. R. Shneur Zalman claimed that knowledge deals with the immanent aspect of the divinity ("fills all worlds"—*memale kol olmin*), whereas faith relates to its transcendent aspect ("surrounds all worlds").[14] The reason is that the

---

[11] Ibid.
[12] See Moshe Idel, *Hasidism: Between Ecstasy and Magic* (Albany: SUNY Press, 1995).
[13] *Ma'amarei Admor ha-Zaken ha-Ketsarim* (Brooklyn: 1986), 178.
[14] Hallamish, *Theoretical System*, 202-203. Because of its psychological structure and its symbolic adaptation, faith belongs to the "encompassing" aspect: the psychology of faith is above reason and, symbolically, reflects the *sefirah* of *malkhut* according to, for instance, *Zohar* literature. See *Torah Or* (Zhitomir: 1862; Kefar Chabad and Brooklyn: 1978), *Mishpatim* 75a.

immanent dimension: 1) Is grasped immediately and intuitively; 2) Is amenable to rational proof.

The presentation of the immanent dimension as rational tends to rely on three arguments:

(1) *Microcosm.* This argument deals with an analogy between the human body, whose actions cannot be explained without the soul present within it, and the world.[15]

(2) *Creation.* This argument relies on the cosmological evidence of the existence of God, whereby from the reality of a created world we infer the existence of the Creator.[16]

(3) *Logic.* This argument points to the unquestionable existence of a divine vitality that powers the world so that the determination of its existence is a statement whose refutation is necessarily false.[17]

Faith, therefore, deals with the realm of "surrounds," "encompasses," and the "esoteric (lit. covered)";[18] that is, the realm that "is neither seen nor apprehended and to which no fear is pertinent—only faith."[19]

---

[15] See, for instance, Alexander Altmann, *Studies in Religious Philosophy and Mysticism* (London: Routledge and Kegan Paul, 1969), 1-40.

[16] See, for instance, Harry A. Wolfson, *Studies in the History of Philosophy and Religion*, vol. 1, ed. Isadore Twersky and George H. Williams (Cambridge, MA: Harvard University Press, 1973), 571-582.

[17] "Simply because a statement is not refuted, we cannot say it is a matter of belief. For instance, we say the soul lives inside the body and, although no one has ever seen its essence, it is impossible to say that we believe we live because of the soul, since we see the movements of the limbs" (*Ma'amarei Admor ha-Zaken ha-Ketsarim*, 444).

[18] *Torah Or, Tetsaveh*, 84c. But at the opening of *Iggeret ha-Koddesh*, R. Shneur Zalman claimed that "true faith" is faith "in the one God, *Ein Sof*, who fills all worlds and surrounds all worlds and no place is empty of Him ... as well as the time [lit. year—*shanah*] and the soul [*nefesh*]." For the reference to *shanah ve-nefesh*, see ch. 1, 102a, according to *Sefer Yetsirah* 6:1, printed in Ithamar Gruenwald, ed., "Preliminary Critical Edition of *Sefer Yezira*," *Israel Oriental Studies* 1 (1971).

[19] *Torah Or, bi-Shlah*, 62a.

Faith and the Transcendent

An important discussion about faith appears in the *Likkutei Torah* commentaries on *Parashat va-Ethannan* (Deuteronomy 3:23-7:11). This discussion enables clarification of two important questions:

(1) Why is the divinity's transcendent dimension not self-evident?

(2) Is it possible, and if so how, to trace the parameters of the esoteric realm to which faith applies, even though faith is by definition inapprehensible?

Again, the answer lies in the paradoxical dialectic typical of Chabad thought. R. Shneur Zalman emphasized that the "surrounds" aspect is never really transcendent. A topographic division is implausible: we cannot claim that the borders of the "surrounding" aspect mark the scope of the material world, and the "filling" aspect is within the cosmos. The transcendent divinity is present within the cosmos as well. "The meaning of 'surrounds all worlds' is not that He is above the worlds; rather, He is also within all worlds, and still 'surrounds' all worlds."[20] Hence, the divinity within the world is simultaneously immanent and transcendent. Reality is complex: every immanent divine aspect includes a transcendent dimension and vice-versa, every esoteric aspect includes a dimension of revelation. The inability to discern the transcendent aspect, and indeed discern dialectical and paradoxical existence, is ascribed to original sin. Since original sin, human beings can sense only the immanent dimension of the divine, and the transcendent dimension will only be exposed in the messianic era.[21] We can now answer the two questions asked above:

(1) Human knowledge is limited and, therefore, precludes the understanding of the transcendent.

(2) The transcendent dimension is merely the divine presence when concealed and hidden, whereas the immanent dimension is that presence when revealed.

Faith, then, applies to the realm of the "surrounding." R. Shneur Zalman clarified in the article he wrote for the Sabbath of *Parashat*

---

[20] *Likkutei Torah, va-Ethannan*, 4b. And in a similar formulation, 8a.
[21] Ibid., 4c.

Shekalim (Exodus 30:11-16) that the "surrounding" aspect does not fully include the transcendent dimension of the divinity. When relating to the infinite substance, he writes: "Yet, what is beyond 'surrounding' and 'filling' is beyond the matter of faith."[22] Elsewhere, however, R. Shneur Zalman presented an epistemological structure that ascribes faith to the supreme stage that is beyond the "surrounding" aspect; that is, to the primeval dimension beyond the transcendent dimension of the divine.

R. Shneur Zalman predicated the notion that faith relates to the realm above "surrounding" on an epistemological construction based on the division between essence and reality:[23]

> There are three rungs in man. One is the dimension of sight and the apprehension of the essence. The second is that of knowledge,[24] meaning the knowledge and the feeling of reality rather than the apprehension of the essence. The third is the dimension of faith, when man believes in the truth with all his heart, even though this is not knowledge and feeling in him.[25]

From R. Shneur Zalman's discussion of these stages and their application to the theosophical realm, the structure of knowledge can be described as follows:

Type of knowledge	*Symbol of knowledge*	*Content of knowledge*	*Reference to the theosophical level*
Intuitive certainty	Sight	Essence	Wisdom
Knowledge	Affection and feeling (*da'at*)	Reality	"Surrounding all worlds": The outside rung of *keter* as the source of wisdom.
Faith	Heart	The esoteric	Beyond "surrounding all worlds": The inner rung of *keter* (*malkhut de-Einsof*).[26]

---

[22] *Ma'amarei Admor ha-Zaken*, 563 (1), 176.

[23] On the sources of this division in Jewish thought, see, for instance, Altmann, *Studies in Religious Philosophy and Mysticism*, 108-127.

[24] In his articles, R. Shneur Zalman noted that "knowledge," contrary to "knowledge of the known only," relates to "this intellectual concern [with Creation] constantly and incessantly spreading" (*Ma'amarei Admor ha-Zaken*, 568, 443).

[25] *Likkutei Torah*, *va-Ethannan*, 7b.

[26] A higher aspect, higher than "surrounds all worlds."

Two notes on this scheme are in place:

(1) The link between each type of knowledge and its theosophical contents is formulated according to the partial, fragmented present. In the messianic era, when the limits of apprehension will expand, certainty will extend to realms that are now part of knowledge or faith. So far, faith relates to the supreme rungs of the divinity evident at the beginning of creation.

(2) Even in the present, the borders of apprehension can be expanded through the study of Torah and through compliance with the commandments. Although this study is practical in its orientation (Halakhah) and this action is material and concrete, they ensure certitude in the apprehension of the divine essence because the essence "assumes form" in the material performance and can be apprehended through it.[27]

Hence, regardless of whether faith applied to the "surrounding" or to the realm beyond it, R. Shneur Zalman clearly sought to ascribe it to the transcendent dimensions of the divinity, that is, the dimensions characterized by existential fluctuation.

Faith applies both to fluctuations typical of the divine realm and to the fluctuations typical of knowledge. R. Shneur Zalman also conveyed the paradoxical dialectic entailed by the symbolic conception of faith. The knowledge aspect of the world of emanation is "upper unity" [*yihud elyon*], whereas the *malkhut* aspect is "lower unity" [*yihud tahton*]. *Malkhut* is a paradoxical rung: the upper unity nullifies all that is under it. By contrast, the lower unity is concerned with being, given that *malkhut* is the source of the worlds of creation, creativity, and action. Bringing down knowledge in *malkhut* is thus a fusion of being and nihility. *Malkhut* symbolizes faith, and it is therefore clear that faith itself is the recognition of the existential paradox.[28]

To some extent, rational and intuitive knowledge relates mainly to the realm of being, whereas faith relates mainly to the realm of nihility

---

[27] *Likkutei Torah, va-Ethannan*, 7c. In the "summary" [*kitsur*] that appears after the discussion, the following clear formulation appears: "In the Torah, there is also an apprehension of the essence and knowledge of the reality" (7d). On the identification of faith with the aspect of *malkhut*, see, for instance, *Ma'amarei Admor ha-Zaken ha-Ketsarim*, 74. See also *supra* note 1.

[28] *Likkutei Torah, va-Ethannan*, 7c.

(the nullifying divine substance). R. Shneur Zalman limited knowledge to the field of existence above the world of emanation. He also emphasized and explained the definition of the realms that become known through faith.

The Rational Connection and Intuitive Certainty

Faith, then, applies to dialectic realms that reason is incapable of knowing. In his homilies, however, R. Shneur Zalman qualified this categorical statement. He claimed that the beginning of creation (meaning the primary revelation of the light of the *Einsof* that powered the vessels of the world of emanation belonging to the "surrounding" realm) is connected to apprehension, and particularly to negative apprehension. Though this is not apprehension of the essence, negative knowledge is still a specific type of knowledge. R. Shneur Zalman writes:

> The light of *Ein Sof* in the supreme *sefirah* of *keter* cannot be drawn down and revealed through actual understanding and apprehension. And yet, it is brought down and revealed through the union of *hokhmah* and *binah*,[29] except that this revelation is not really a form of apprehension but rather its dismissal. And no parallel can be found for it in the nether world except though the matter of negative knowledge, which is actually revelation and knowledge through actual apprehension because, through it, we come closer to our goal.[30]

R. Shneur Zalman therefore supports the critics of Maimonides' negative theology, such as Thomas Aquinas, who claim that negative knowledge still entails some kind of affirmation. When commenting on the verse "Know therefore this day, and consider it in thy heart" (Deuteronomy 4:39), R. Shneur Zalman drew a distinction between "fills all worlds" and "surrounds all worlds." Whereas the immanent aspect is apprehended through intellectual contemplation, the transcendent one is apprehended through a divine command. R. Shneur Zalman refers to knowledge of the transcendent dimension as *emunah ve-da'at* (faith

---

[29] On the Maimonidean principle of the unity of knowledge in the understanding of the *sefirah* of *Hokhmah*, see *Likkutei Torah*, *Pekkudei*, 3d.

[30] *Likkutei Torah*, *Pekkudei*, 6c.

and knowledge).[31] Referring to the commandment to read the *Shema*, he states: "*Shema* means contemplation."[32]

R. Shneur Zalman, then, refused to ban reason even from the dimension that is beyond reason. This dimension is also included in the term *knowledge*, which is contrary to the *Sha'ar ha-Yihud ve-ha-Emunah*, in which he had claimed that faith is absolutely beyond reason. Possibly, the character of *Sha'ar ha-Yihud ve-ha-Emunah* as a work meant for a wider public dictated the non-rational conception of faith. In any event, R. Shneur Zalman recognized faith both as a feature of the divine soul that draws no distinctions between various rungs and circumstances and as a product of intellectual contemplation. In this contemplation, primacy is obviously granted to the esoteric, but Maimonidean philosophical traditions also play a significant role.

Faith is perceived as an epistemic and experiential dimension, below direct certainty but above rational discourse. This cognitive statement has value implications as well. R. Shneur Zalman distinguished between truth and faith as follows:

> Truth is the drawing down from *Ein Sof*, meaning that one can actually contemplate the real Unity with one's own reason without any alien thoughts, and this is called "truth." And when one is confused by alien thoughts and by one's own innerness, this is called "faith," meaning that we are genuine believers, but we cannot actually contemplate with the eyes of reason, since Unity is emanations and flows from *Ein Sof*, and this is the meaning of "*ehad be-ehad…*" ["one is so near to another… "].[33]

This passage attaches positive value to faith. R. Shneur Zalman had so far claimed that faith does not allow for rational apprehension because the realms to which it applies are sublime. Now he clarifies that the human condition does not allow for clear rational apprehension at present

---

[31] Ibid., *va-Ethannan*, 4d. The connection between faith and knowledge has a psychological aspect. Pure faith, without the expansion and the depth provided by knowledge, is a "point in the heart" [*nekudat ha-lev*] and "minor" [*ketanot*] (*Torah Or*, *Tetsaveh*, 84a-b). In the current discussion, as noted, my focus is on the "intellectual," meaning on the knowledge dimension of faith.

[32] *Likkutei Torah*, *be-Ha'alotkha*, 36c.

[33] See Job 41:8, *Zohar* 2, 135a; *Ma'amarei Admor ha-Zaken ha-Ketsarim*, 78. I will deal elsewhere at length with the metaphor of the sun.

because, in the absence of absolute nullification, full contemplation is impossible. Faith, as noted, applies to the paradoxical realms. Due to sin and to the flawed human condition "we have nothing but faith and faithfully believe that all is as nullified before Him, may He be blessed as, for instance, in the light of the sun, against whose powerful light all is nullified, and the sun stands for God."[34] The metaphor of the sun again locates faith in the realm of existential paradox, and creates an essential link between faith and contents related to the beginning of creation.

Summary

R. Shneur Zalman's conception of faith is open in the sense that it includes diverse and contradictory elements:

(1) Contemplation vs. experience.

(2) Elitism vs. mass inclusion.

(3) Rationality vs. supra-rationality.

(4) Philosophical sources vs. kabbalistic sources.

R. Shneur Zalman determined the uniqueness of Chabad thought through his very support for the first pole in these antitheses. He set to faith the ideal of drawing down knowledge.[35] The initial meaning of this ideal is the attachment to faith and its absorption in the soul, reflecting the unique Chabad ethos dependent on knowledge. But this meaning does not exclude the contemplative and intellectual dimension of knowledge; indeed, quite the contrary—it compels a solid philosophical foundation. Intellectual and experiential contemplation are both essential components of faith, and relative toleration of abstract rational study was a prominent characteristic of Chabad rabbis.[36] In this sense, even rabbis inclined to support the opposite pole in the antitheses mentioned above did not change the intellectual landscape in Chabad but, instead, adapted experience to the disposition of rational and mystical knowledge. Henceforth, faith focused on the dialectic of existence and

---

[34] Ibid., 79.
[35] Hallamish, *Theoretical System*, 201-202.
[36] Under the leadership of R. Menachem Mendel Schneerson, the last Chabad rabbi, this approach was evident in his attempts to influence the academic community.

its components and contents (such as, for instance, negation and affirmation in R. Shneur Zalman's negative theology) also express a fundamental fluctuation.

As is true of other topics in Chabad philosophy, R. Shneur Zalman's discussions of faith served as a constitutive text that Chabad rabbis took as a starting point for their own views. By way of summary, I will point to several landmarks in the approach of his successors when developing this idea.

Following R. Shneur Zalman, Chabad rabbis connected the intellectual dimension of faith to the question of creation, which is founded on the doctrine of divine attributes. The distinction between creation (lit. radiation *he'arah*) and emanation (*hishtalshelut*) became essential when shaping the knowledge dimension of faith. The dialectic that characterizes the beginning of creation and the approaches to existence that follow from it are the crux of faith.

In his concern with faith, R. Dov Ber (*ha-admor ha-emtzai*) stressed its experiential character, laying particular emphasis on the reason and the legitimacy of identifying the value of simple faith as opposed to mature and critical faith. This identification had already featured in the thought of R. Shneur Zalman, and R. Dov Ber exposed the depth aspect of intuitive faith. The experiential character of mature faith, however, is not only intuitive, and R. Dov Ber noted that the acquisition of extensive kabbalistic knowledge is a popular demand, that is, ecstasy occurs against a backdrop of broad mystical knowledge.

R. Menahem Mendel (the Tsemah Tseddek) stressed the structural and epistemic disposition of faith. His intellectual curiosity and his philosophical leanings added a special quality to the link between faith as a psychic act and the contents of the faith. The division between the theoretical and the practical (activity, magic, and so forth) dimensions of faith became a significant feature of his thought. He conducted abstract discussions on the concept of faith, ignoring the practical dimension almost entirely. Though he did not adopt this approach in some of his arguments, he did show that faith can be a subject of intellectual discussion (within philosophical or kabbalistic parameters).

R. Shmuel Schneerson returned to the more innovative approach toward philosophy and argued that faith is only an expression of the divine soul in the Jewish people. R. Shmuel endorsed the explanation of Jewish history according to a faith criterion, no longer accepting the conceptual distinction between the theoretical and the practical dimensions of faith. By contrast, R. Shalom Dov Ber Schneerson and R. Yosef Yitzhak Schneerson deepened the connection between rationality and Chabad contents. Obviously, I am not referring here to rationality in the sense of logical validity or scientific knowledge, but in the sense of enlisting order and systematization for the purpose of mystical discussions. The general orientation emphasized by R. Shalom Dov Ber and by R. Yosef Yitzhak is formally similar to the model of "dual truth," marking a coalescence of revelation and rationality. In fact, however, it points to the superiority of Kabbalah, which already includes rationality within it when perfectly coordinated with the kabbalistic interest. The remnant that is inappropriate to the revelatory content is perceived as a product of "alien wisdoms" or imperfect "research." R. Yosef Yitzhak drew closer to the Tsemah Tseddek, tending to a discourse using theoretical and philosophical tools, but he did not rely on rationalist sources.

Yosef Weiss defined Bratslav Hasidism as one of faith, as opposed to Chabad, which he defined as a Hasidism of mysticism, and Hallamish has already criticized this distinction on the matter of faith.[37] Weiss wrote:

> The abysmal gap between the believer and the object of his faith is manifest in Bratslav in the paradoxical character of faith. The abyss between the divine realm and the human realm emerges not only in God's ontological transcendence (God is not "within" the world) but also in his logical transcendence (he is "inconceivable").[38]

In a formal sense, this distinction is inaccurate. Faith in Chabad Hasidism applies to the realm beyond reason, and its concern is precisely the transcendent dimension of the divinity. Phenomenologically, however, Weiss was certainly right. Although faith is a depth experience in Chabad thought, it is always tied to contents, to order, and to the

---

[37] See Hallamish, *Theoretical System*, 205. See also Abraham Green, *Tormented Master: A Life of Rabbi Nahman of Bratslav* (Alabama: University of Alabama Press, 1979), 289-290.

[38] Yosef Weiss, *Studies in Bratslav Hasidism*, ed. Mendel Piekartz (Jerusalem: Bialik Institute, 1974), 92 (Hebrew).

system. The transcendent realm is always amenable to mapping and to constructive assumptions. The aspect of "surrounding all worlds" and its connection to the *Einsof* is an essential topic in Chabad discourse.

The trends that appeared in the thought of R. Shneur Zalman are detailed and emphasized in the teachings of the rabbinic leaders that followed him. Each one, however, highlighted a different aspect of R. Shneur Zalman's writings, emphasizing aspects that had not always been stressed in the founder's writings. One prominent example is the network of associations between faith, the *tsaddik*, and redemption articulated in the writings of R. Menachem Mendel Schneerson, the last Chabad leader. The issue of faith thus emerges as an instance of a dynamic conceptual development.

Faith and Song in the Poetry of Zelda: On the Mystical Elements in Zelda's Ars Poetica and their Hasidic Origins

Zvi Mark

The connection between faith and poetry is significant in the poetry of Zelda. An examination of this tie could shed light on several paths in her spiritual world, and reveal an additional layer in her ars poetica. Zelda's understanding of "faith" leads to a new interpretation of the elements that validate belief and of the challenges and trials faced by the believer when his faith is put to the test. Our discussion is not as straightforward as it would be in an examination of prose; as is the way of poetry, it entwines the poetical and the thematic in her works.[1]

The belief at the center of the poem "With My Grandfather" can serve as a convenient starting point for our discussion:[2]

> *With My Grandfather*
> Like our father Abraham
> who counted stars at night,
> who called out to his Creator
> from the furnace,
> who bound his son
> on the altar—
> so was my grandfather.

---

[1] The most comprehensive study of Zelda's poetry to date is by Hamutal Bar-Yosef, *On Zelda's Poetry* (Tel Aviv: Hakibutz hameuhad, 1988) (Hebrew), which served as a basis for the current article. Most translations of Zelda's poems printed here are based on the translations by Marcia Falk, *The Spectacular Difference: Selected Poems of Zelda* (Cincinnati: Hebrew Union College Press, 2004); the rest follow the Hebrew collection: *Poetry of Zelda* (Tel Aviv: Pnai, 1985).

[2] On the poem "With My Grandfather," see Bar-Yosef, *On Zelda's Poetry*, 119; *A New Song: Studies and Teaching Methods for the State Religious School*, no. 3: *Zelda* (experimental edition: Hebrew; Jerusalem: Ministry of Education, 1976), 8-12. The booklet was composed by Shulamit Yinon, Devorah Bergman, Hamutal Bar-Yosef, Aryeh Sivan, Yaffa Kamar, and Bilhah Rubinstein.

> The same perfect faith
> in the midst of the flames, the same dewy gaze
> and soft-curling beard.
> Outside, it snowed;
> outside, they roared:
> *"There is no justice,
> no judge."*
> And in his cracked, shattered room,
> cherubs sang
> of the Heavenly Jerusalem.

The analogy between the grandfather and the patriarch Abraham serves as the structure of the poem. The main arena in which the comparison is conducted is the realm of faith, "the same perfect faith" shared by both.

The poem is constructed of four sentences, which we will call "stanzas." The first stanza already presents the comparison: "Like our father Abraham [...] so was my grandfather." Adding the traditional title "our father" to Abraham creates a sense of family closeness between the grandfather and the father. The description of Abraham mentions three of the ten trials that he was made to undergo,[3] by increasing order of difficulty: in the first, God asked Abraham to go outside, to look at the countless stars, and promised him (Genesis 15:5): "So shall your offspring be." Although the assurance of offspring requires nothing from Abraham, containing no demand of self-sacrifice while providing hope for the future, his faith in his destiny and in the eventual realization of the promise is recognized as the withstanding of a test, as is implied by the concluding biblical verse (v. 6): "He reckoned it to his merit." The second trial mentioned in the poem is based on a rabbinic midrash that relates the story of Nimrod casting Abraham into the fiery furnace because of his faith in God and as punishment for the smashing of his father's idols;[4] this test reveals Abraham's willingness to give his life for his faith. The third trial demands of Abraham the most difficult thing of all: the sacrifice of his son. The Binding of Isaac turned Abraham

---

[3] The rabbis list ten trials experienced by Abraham, "and in all of them he was found steadfast" (*Avot de-Rabbi Natan*, Version A: *The Fathers according to Rabbi Nathan*, trans. Judah Goldin (New Haven: Yale University Press, 1956), 132.

[4] *Gen. Rabbah*, ed. Theodor-Albeck (Jerusalem: 1965) 38:28, pp. 361-64.

into the "prince of faith"[5] and the ultimate symbol of the willingness to sacrifice on the altar of faith what is most precious.

The second stanza states explicitly what is implicit in the first. "The same perfect faith" characteristic of Abraham, who unwaveringly withstands all the trials, is also typical of the grandfather. "The flames" in which faith prevails is linked to the fiery furnace of Abraham, thus implying that fiery furnaces also threatened the grandfather's faith, alluding to the crematoria in Europe into which Abraham's descendants were cast, and to the harsh test of faith they posed, the "climax" of the continuing binding-sacrifice. The "faith in the midst of the flames" can also be understood as a reference to all the suffering, the pogroms, and the flames that engulfed the grandfather and his contemporaries everywhere; in Eastern and Western Europe, Russia, the Land of Israel, and the Arab lands, without suggesting any specific event.[6] Whatever the case, the flame is perceived in this context as something negative and threatening that the believer must overcome, girded with strength, in order to maintain his faith, even within the fire. Below we will see the possibility of another reading, in which the flame arouses positive connotations.

The physical description of the facial features of the grandfather and of Abraham, "the same dewy gaze and soft-curling beard," alleviates the harsh depiction of the believers who are seemingly inured to life and death. The softness of their dewy gaze (the glitter of their pupils is compared to dewdrops) and the round and curly softness of their beards coexist with force and decisiveness.

While the first stanza is devoted mainly to the faith of Abraham (and by extension, to that of the grandfather), the second stanza depicts what is shared by both, as the physical description of the known and tangible grandfather is extended to the presumed character of Abraham. The third and fourth stanzas, proceeding with a description of the events in the grandfather's world, extend beyond a portrayal of the grandfather

---

[5] As is argued by the Christian existentialist Søren Kierkegaard, *Fear and Trembling*, ed. C. Stephen Evans and Sylvia Walsh, trans. Sylvia Walsh (Cambridge and New York: Cambridge University Press, 2006); and numerous other editions. The book centres on Abraham's faith, as embodied in the Binding of Isaac.

[6] Zelda personally experienced pogroms in her childhood, and her uncle, R. Solomon Menahem Mendel Hen, was murdered in a pogrom. See Bar-Yosef, *On Zelda's Poetry*, 14.

himself and go outside, to describe his surroundings ("Outside [...] outside"), while leading us back inside: from the snow outside, through the shambles of his room, to the grandfather's inner world.

The anaphora "Outside [...] outside" emphasizes the contrasting analogy between outside and inside. Outside, the heretical cries of "There is no justice, no judge" are heard, while "the same perfect faith" endures within; outside, "they roar," while inside, they sing; "Outside, it snowed," cold and alienated, while inside there is "the same perfect faith in the midst of the flames."

The shouts of "There is no justice, no judge," burst forth from the harsh external reality, from the crematoria and the outcry of the burned. This is not the voice of an individual or even a society, but of the reality that prevails without justice, and consequently without a judge.

The heretical voices that threaten faith slowly work their way in from outside. While the beginning of the poem portrays the inner world as one of "perfect faith," the last stanza reveals the cracks in this perfect world. First, the grandfather's room is "cracked"; then, we learn of the increasing gravity of the situation when his room is "shattered." The grandfather is left defenceless, with no barrier between him and the roaring and menacing outside. This could be interpreted as relating to a concrete, physical attack on the grandfather's house, as well as to a spiritual threat by the sacrilegious world on his home and life. His spiritual world does not remain impervious to all: the voices of heresy penetrate into the surrounding society, possibly even into his home and family, and perhaps even into his very thoughts. The events in the poem can be seen as a struggle between different voices: the voices of faith; the prayer of Abraham "who called out to his Creator" and the singing of the cherubs; and the heretical roars that spring forth from outside and threaten the inner world.[7]

The equating of the force of the grandfather's faith with that of our father Abraham is inherent in the first part of the poem, and its last two lines teach us of the nature of the test undergone by the grandfather,

---

[7] Zelda carefully and delicately crafts the tone of the poem in accordance with its thematic progression. The struggle is between the voices: "who called out," "they roared," and "[cherubs] sang"; and also between the external snow (**shel**eg) and the internal flames (**shal**hevet). See *A New Song*; Bar-Yosef, *On Zelda's Poetry*, 119.

which parallels the intensity of Abraham's tests of faith, such as the fiery furnace and the Binding of Isaac. The intriguing insight that emerges is that the grandfather's ability to hear the singing of the angels within the cacophony of the roar and the pandemonium of destruction is his withstanding of the test of faith. Within the cracked and shattered walls he succeeds in maintaining an independent inner space that enables him to hear the cherub's song of the heavenly Jerusalem.

According to this understanding, contemporary tests of faith are unlike Abraham's classic tests. A person will not be cast into the fiery furnace if he declares that he believes in the Creator, nor will God be revealed to him and tell him, "Take your son, your only son, whom you love, and offer him as a burnt offering." The arena in which tests of faith occur today is completely different; the current struggle for faith is the battle over the ability to hear poetry; and the challenge is to contend with the aggressive, vocal, and threatening outside. The home can no longer provide shelter from the voices of heresy that threaten to enter. The ability to listen to the poetic voices of the Heavenly Jerusalem within a world estranged from faith, where the cries of "There is no justice, no judge" constantly burst forth, is the modern test of faith.

The transformation of the tests of faith does not reflect a change in the intensity of faith, nor does it diminish the stature of its champions. While hearing poetry does not entail jumping into the fire or offering one's son, Zelda argues that this is "the same perfect faith" as that of Abraham.

Hearing and reading poetry, and certainly poetry that comes from the heavenly realms, requires quiet, clarity of thought, and deliberation. Only one whose inner world is unfaltering, with a degree of inner harmony, can create an enclave of sanctity, an island of faith and poetry, within the encircling tumult and chaos.

A study of other poems by Zelda demonstrates that her fashioning of faith as the ability to hear poetry is not a random choice, but rather reflects a complete worldview that touches upon the essence of poetry and faith. Before listing the additional lyrical expressions of this philosophy, I would like to expand on the faith-poetry connection, drawing on the sources of her inspiration from Hasidism and the world of R. Abraham Yitzhak Kook.

Zelda, who was raised in a hasidic family, attested of herself that not only was she brought up on hasidic values, "I remained close to its ideas my entire life."[8] Our examination of her poems will confirm that Hasidism was one of the foundations underlying the conceptual system and worldview reflected in her work.[9] Zelda also studied the writings of R. Kook, whose personality and scholarship she profoundly esteemed.[10] My proposed reading of her hasidic sources does not presume to exhaust the possibilities of textual and conceptual analysis, but rather to highlight the directions of mind and mood in Zelda's poetry.

> On the Sabbath of Song when the song sung beside the Red Sea was read, the rabbi of Sadagora said:
> "It is not written that they sang the song immediately after they crossed the sea. First they had to reach the rung of perfect faith, as it is written: ... 'and they believed in the Lord, and in his servant Moses.' Only after that come the words: 'Then sang Moses and the children of Israel ....' Only he who believes can sing the song."[11]

R. Abraham Jacob of Sadagora saw the connection between faith and poetry (or song) as greatly exceeding this specific biblical occurrence, and he presents it as a broad and general insight: "Only he who believes can sing the song." The assertion of a link between faith and the ability to sing the song/recite poetry, might indicate that it is the belief in the existence of the spiritual in the world and in man that makes poetry possible. Poetry, even if engaged with the secular, characteristically tends to view the festive in the reality, and to identify the refined and the illuminated within mundane events. Poetry, it would seem, is founded on the inherent belief that the external reality and the human reality are usually greater than their physical, or even psychological, sum total, and they contain something beyond that poetry aspires to express. The tendency to impart spiritual meaning to a flower, a vista, or the weather is revealed more clearly and forcibly in the world of poetry than in prose discussions.

---

[8] From an interview with the poet conducted by Rahel Hollander-Steingart, "Zelda-Poetry-Encounter," *Zehut* 3 (1983): 232 (Hebrew).

[9] See Hillel Barzel, "Zelda: Between the Revealed and the Eulogy," in *Poets in Their Greatness: Scholarly Essays on Hebrew Poets* (Tel Aviv: Yahdav, 1979), 404-26, and esp. 404-5 (Hebrew); see Bar-Yosef, *On Zelda's Poetry*, 9-13, 33-34, 135, and 146-59.

[10] Bar-Yosef, *On Zelda's Poetry*, 19, 135.

[11] As retold by Martin Buber, *Tales of the Hasidim: The Later Masters* (New York: Shocken Books, 1948), 71.

The following statement by R. Kook will further clarify this conception, and provide an additional backdrop to Zelda's poetry:

> Faith as a whole includes the poetry of life, the poetry of all existence. Poetry is the emotion that penetrates the deepest within, into the depths of the essence of a concept, into its inner content, which cannot be attained by prose. Consequently, the true looking glass to life is to be found within the poetry of life, and not in the mundane life that is expressed by prose. Woe to the one who wants life to lose the majesty of its song; it would forfeit all of life's content and all its truth. Prose gains its entire value from being based on the poetry of life. [...]
>
> There is no poetry in the world in which the sacred glimmerings of faith do not shine forth, and when sanctity is manifest in the poetical spirit in its purest and most whole form, then it is truly holy poetry, that will be sung only by the holy angels and the angels of God.[12]

Poetry, for R. Kook, is embraced within faith; it is not merely a vehicle for expression, but a certain manner of perceiving and sensing reality. In contrast with the approaches that detach poetry from reality, and argue that it cannot faithfully reflect the latter, Rabbi Kook argues to the contrary: it is poetry that more profoundly sees life's essence. Prose's strength lies in its ability to describe the outer strata of reality, but it is not there that we find the plane of meaning that imparts purpose and value. It is specifically the poetical perception that uncovers the essential inner stratum and reflects, in the most fitting manner, the value-centeredness and significance inherent in life. Every action in the plane of outer reality, in the realism of prose, science, medicine, technology, and industry, draws meaning and value from the great worthiness that we ascribe to life, to man, and to the reality that surrounds him. If they are of no worth, the importance of all the fields meant to advance human activity simply collapses.

This, then, is the power and uniqueness of poetry.[13] The disparity between the lexicographical or botanical description of a tree and

---

[12] R. Abraham Isaac ha-Kohen Kook, *The Lights of Faith* (Jerusalem: Mosad Harav Kook, 1985), 40 (Hebrew).

[13] I do not intend to make sweeping generalizations; obviously, some works of prose have clearly poetical qualities, and vice versa. I refer to the "dominant

its lyrical portrayal is in the intention to confront the reader with an additional layer of that tree—the layer of meaning. The poem brings us face-to-face with life's festivity, refinement, and beauty, with the centrality of values to life, and the attitude they will likely engender in man. This highly charged confrontation with reality must infuse it with meaning and value.

A person who encounters only the prose stratum of life meets an empty and hollow reality. Likewise the meeting of one person with another: if it does not transcend the meeting of so many pounds of flesh and blood with another physical mechanism of parallel height and weight and with similar metabolism, or even that of an encounter with a creature of a certain psychological profile, the engagement will be empty and meaningless. Only poetical vision and perception (even if written in a story or in prose) uncovers the added layer of such an encounter, by waxing poetic of love or hate, thereby injecting it with some sense.

This approach regards the ability to engage in poetry as faith-based. This is not the concrete belief in a God who is depicted as a grandfatherly type with a white beard who resides in Heaven, or in the divine origin of the Bible, but rather the belief that reality also includes layers of meaning that exceed its physical sum total, and that man and his life possess worth beyond being a living creature with a psychological profile. This is the belief in something—sanctity, spirituality, or by any other name—a connection with which brings out the value and beauty in life and in man.

According to this understanding, loss of faith eliminates the basis for and possibility of poetry, for without faith, poetry is merely empty verbiage that attempts to wrap the hollow reality within a stream of words and images.

The talent to sing is therefore the ability to make contact with these strata of reality and of life itself. The test of faith is to succeed in acquiring the requisite attentiveness, deliberation, and mental clarity needed to hear poetry, in order to sense reality's spiritual stratum. The grandfather's ability to hear the angels' song of the heavenly Jerusalem, beyond

---

functions" that characterize poetry, as opposed to prose, following the tendencies in Hasidism and the writings of Rabbi Kook that provide the conceptual basis and background for Zelda's ars poetica.

the emptiness and void, is the great and meaningful test of faith that the grandfather withstands.

In the poem "I Am a Dead Bird," as well, singing expresses the presence of God:[14]

> I am a dead bird,
> one bird that has died.
> A bird cloaked in a gray coat.
> A scoffer mocks me as I walk.
>
> Suddenly Your silence envelops me,
> O Ever-living One.
> In a teeming market, a dead fowl sings:
> "Only You exist."
> In a teeming market, a bird hobbles
> with a hidden song.[15]

The poem opens with the harsh sensation of living death. The apathy and mockery encountered by the speaker teach of the insignificance of death and of life. Death is portrayed as the death of a bird, thus ridding it of the importance attributed to a person's life and death. The bird has no name, nor are we told the type of bird, just "one bird that has died." The alienated word "one," that lacks any identification, replaces the personal and charged "I" of the preceding verse, and thereby reinforces the alienation and inexplicability of death in the poem.

The living-dead bird that is "cloaked in a gray coat" is grounded, heavy, and choked in the grayness that envelops it and its life. To all this the end of the stanza ("A scoffer mocks me as I walk") adds the scorn heaped on her as she walks in the street, which is also derision at her death, for "as I walk" could also be understood as "departed."

In contrast with the death and finality of the first stanza, the second stanza is one of resurrection. This change appears in the guise of an unanticipated revelation: "Suddenly Your silence envelops me." The speaker, who was just wrapped and weighed down by a gray coat, now finds herself enveloped in the silence of the Ever-living One. "*Hai Olamim*" is an appellation for God that has its source in three blessings: "(He) who creates

---

[14] See Bar-Yosef, *On Zelda's Poetry*, 53-54.
[15] Falk, *The Spectacular Difference*, 36-37.

souls" (recited after eating some foods),[16] and the blessings preceding and following the *Pesukei de-Zimrah* (Verses of Song) section of the morning *Shaharit* service. This appellation means that God revives the world, or that He is the vitality of the world. When the "Ever-living One" envelops the speaker, she is wrapped in the force that revives and sustains all the worlds, which is the force that revives and sustains her as well.

As the poem continues, the speaker walks about in a bustling and noisy marketplace, but in an abrupt shift from life's hustle and bustle, characteristic of the market, she feels dead. At this stage, the speaker does not even compare herself to a bird, but to "a dead fowl." In the market context, "fowl" represents meat for sale, either fresh or frozen, in contrast with a "chicken" or "bird," that are purchased while still alive. Notwithstanding this, and specifically because of this, the dead fowl sings: "Only You exist." This is a song of existence, and not of death; on the edge of oblivion, the song is one of clinging to God, who alone exists. This contrast is reminiscent of the second half of the *piyyut* (liturgical hymn) *U-Netanah Tokef*, which is recited on Rosh Hashanah and Yom Kippur and compares man, whose existence is tenuous and fleeting, "like a wind that blows and a dream that passes," with God, "for You are King, the God who lives and exists."

The powerful presence of the Ever-living One's silence and the song of the absolute Existence have revived the speaker, who was "one bird that has died." The dead fowl comes back to life and once again becomes a hobbling bird that moves, lives, and remains alive. A sort of resurrection of the dead occurs in the poem, one that ensues from the presence of God, the Ever-living One who alone exists.[17]

---

[16] The *borei nefashot* ("who creates souls") blessing (recited after eating some foods) concludes: "for all that You have created, with which to sustain the life of every living creature. Blessed is the One who lives forever."

[17] Zelda writes of the vivifying force of poetry in additional poems as well, such as: "A very ancient song / wakened me to life [...] A song of a generation that went silent / ages and ages ago / awakened me to life" ("Ancient Song," Falk, *The Spectacular Difference*, 206-7). The perception of poetry and melody as possessing vivifying qualities is rooted in Hasidism. R. Nahman of Bratslav advised his followers: "It is a good practice for a person to be able to vivify himself with some melody" (*Sihot ha-Ran* [Jerusalem: Hasidei Breslov, 1985], para. 273, p. 169). At the end of the tale "The Seven Beggars," the dying king's daughter is revived by ten types of melody (*Rabbi Nachman's Stories*, trans. Aryeh Kaplan [Jerusalem: Breslov Research Institute, 1985], 433-34).

What is the nature of the song with which the bird hobbles in the end? The division of the verses parallels the "hidden" with the "Ever-living One" and with "Only You exist." Concealment is one of God's traits and among His appellations. The prophet Isaiah calls God "a God who conceals Himself,"[18] and Zelda frequently addresses Him as "the veiled and hidden God."[19] The poem is concerned with the concealed God, but "hidden" is also the attribute of the poem itself, and not only a descriptive of God. His presence is tangible, even though this is the presence of silence, and His song exists and is sung, even though He and His song are unseen.

In this poem, as well, the sense of God's presence is depicted as poetry. The tension between this and the portrayal of the Divine Presence as silence is somewhat moderated, since the poetry is hidden and does not disturb the divine repose. The divine silence that envelops man is given the quality of a presence felt as poetry that can be sensed and heard.

Hearing the concealed poetry, like hearing the song of the cherubs in the grandfather's room, reveals the Divine Presence in the world, and puts the listener in contact with the heavenly sphere. Just as the grandfather, against all the odds, in the midst of the tumult of the snow, the roars of heresy, and the outside's growing threat to destroy and shatter his inner world, succeeds in hearing the concealed poetry and in connecting with the heavenly Jerusalem, here too, in striking contrast to the place, the time, and the situation, in the heart of the teeming and clamorous marketplace, when the outside is alienated and deprecates her life and death, in the minute after the last, when death already has her in its grasp, the speaker is enveloped by the silence of the Ever-living One, which successfully revives her with the power of the song; this is the hidden song that reveals the presence of the hiding God who gives life to every living creature.[20]

---

[18] Isaiah 45:15.

[19] "At This Thoughtful Hour" (*Poetry of Zelda*, 140); "The Fine Sand, the Terrible Sand" (Falk, *The Spectacular Difference*, 128-31).

[20] The connection between the sense of divine presence and vitality [*hiyyut*] is an important element in Hasidic thought. "This [*hiyyut*] is a crucial concept in Hasidism [...] *Hiyyut* stands [...] for the Divine Presence in the world" (Moshe Idel, *Hasidism: Between Ecstasy and Magic* [Albany: State University of New York Press, 1995], 237; see also 235-38).

As we shall see below, the underlying poetic conception is that every poem is from the world of concealment. Poetry belongs to the hidden stratum of reality: it does not describe the visible layer that is the domain of prose. Poetry, the language of the concealed, is meant to raise above ground the gentleness, the festivity, and the sanctity that sometimes, while generating fierce tension in the process, oppose the pandemonium of the marketplace and the roar of the outside that can distract our attention.

In the religious-hasidic semantic field that is an essential component in the lyrical vocabulary of Zelda's poetry,[21] the term "hidden" is laden with a contextual system that brings into sharp focus the meaning of the wording "hidden song." The Jewish esoteric teachings, also called *"torat ha-nistar"* (literally, the teaching of the concealed), are concerned with the unseen stratum that lies beyond the visible layer of the Torah and which is deemed the more spiritual and innermost stratum of the Torah and the reality to which it relates. Mysticism, for Hasidism, does not relate to the study of secret texts or esoteric bits of knowledge transmitted from teacher to pupil. Rather, it is the pursuit of the inner and refined strata, for which speech is difficult, which can be tasted and sensed but can hardly be expressed. Love and fear of God means immersion in the concealed, for a person cannot transmit to his fellow the love of God that he feels in his heart.

> The wisdom that is called concealed means what is called concealed is what a person cannot perceive, such as the taste of a food: for a person who has never tasted this taste, it is impossible to explain in speech what this is, and how it is called. And similarly, the entire matter of the love of the Creator and His fear, may He be blessed: a person cannot explain to his fellow what is the love in his heart, and this is called "hidden." But what is called hidden, the wisdom of the Kabbalah, how is it hidden? For if anyone wishes to learn, the book lies before him. If he does not comprehend, then he is an ignoramus, and for such a person, the Talmud and *Tosafot*, too, would be regarded as hidden. Rather, the question of being concealed in all the *Zohar* and the writings of R. Isaac Luria, of blessed memory, all is built on adherence [*devekut*] to the divine.[22]

---

[21] Examples of this are to be found throughout Bar-Yosef's book; see esp. 144-59.
[22] *Keter Shem Tov* (Brooklyn: Otsar ha-Hasidim, 1987) fol. 31a, end of para. 240; see also Idel, *Hasidism*, 173-75.

Poetry in Zelda's world is the preoccupation with life's concealed and inner stratum. It uncovers the vitality, spirituality, refinement, and sanctity that are present in reality and vivify it. This is the hidden song of the Ever-loving One.

In this context as well, we can see Zelda's work as the development of the nuclei of thought and poetry in Rabbi Kook's writings. The following citation relates to the ending of the blessing that concludes *Pesukei de-Zimrah*: "who chooses musical songs, King, the Life of the worlds [*Hei ha-olamim*]." Rabbi Kook identifies two descriptions of God in this wording: "who chooses musical songs" and "King, the Life of the worlds," which perceive poetry and song as leading to contact with God as "the Life of the worlds":

> "Who chooses musical songs"—[...] our perceptive ability is too limited to describe the musical, poetical value of all that exists in His exalted singularity. Through, however, our ascent by means of the freedom of divine poetical songs [...] we see the good of the light of the Life of the worlds [...] and we recite the blessing with the joy of the worlds: "Blessed is the One who chooses musical songs, King, the Life of the worlds."[23]

Inherent in "all that exists" is the value-centered poetical quality that cannot be described or exhausted; nonetheless, the poetry that we declaim, despite its limited nature, leads to spiritual elevation that reveals the goodness and light of the Life of the worlds that is present in all existence. Poetry arouses joy from our very existence, and therefore man blesses and praises God as the One who chooses musical songs and as the Life of the worlds.

Hearing poetry and song is the manifestation of the life-force and connection to it, while not hearing the melody and the song constitutes severance from the Source of vitality. This in turn causes *hester panim*, the "hiding" of the Divine countenance, where the concealed abides in its concealment.

> *The Hiding of Your Soul*
> You hid Your soul from me
> and within me there no longer is the sound of the full river,
> that overflows its banks.

---

[23] R. Abraham Isaac ha-Kohen Kook, *Arpelei Tohar* (Clouds of Purity) (Jerusalem: The Rav Kook Institute, 1983), 117.

> My life has been severed from song
> and I shall stand in the cleft, confounded,
> without sun
> without moon
> and without candle.
>
> You have hidden Your soul from me
> and the bread on the table is dry
> and has grown stale.[24]

The concealment of the (divine) countenance and soul results in detachment from the song, from the source of water and life, and creates drought and decay.[25] Life without song is life without illumination, "without sun, without moon, and without candle." Poetry and song are manifestations of the concealed world, the inner place of the soul, while the bustling and clamorous external world constitutes the central threat to the existence of poetry and the ability to connect with the inner world, and with the heavenly sphere.

Echoes of the hidden poetry that reveals God's presence and existence also resound in this next poem:

> *From the Poetry of the Hidden*
> A restless one from the band of the learned
> whispered: "There are constrictions in the earth and in the oceans."
> I left his whisper in the void of the house
> and I went outside to gaze upon the world
> facing the tremendous skies
> and a branched pine that I loved as a forest.
>
> Within the freedom of the night the hymn enveloped me
> (it was from the hidden song of the celestial signs)
> and, after all,
> the Awesome one Himself shall reign.
> The earthly element in me trembled
> for my soul is stuck
> deep deep
> in the blinking of an eye that is my life.

---

[24] *Poetry of Zelda*, 53.
[25] On this poem, see Ora Yaniv, "The Religious Experience in Zelda's Poetry" (Master's thesis, Bar-Ilan University, Ramat Gan, 1990), 70-71 (Hebrew).

> When will I be worthy
> to sing like the hills,
> like the rivers:
> **"The Lord is for me, I shall not fear."**[26]

As in "I Am a Dead Bird," our speaker finds herself enwrapped in the divine presence; and here, too, she feels this presence as a poem, as the hymn of the universe that is called the "hidden song." Here, as well, in order to hear the hidden song of the hills, the rivers, the stars, and the astrological signs, she must overcome the talking and language of the "band of the learned," whose interest is confined to the laws of the material and its events. She must defeat the individual's immobility in the personal component of the universe, in order to hear the hidden song that says that, "after all," when everything will erode and pass away, then only God will remain, when "the Awesome one Himself shall reign." The hidden song, as well, declares: "Only You exist." Hearing the song causes the speaker to tremble, for her soul is still tied to the earthly element whose existence is ephemeral and passing as the blinking of an eye. Facing death, which consumes all that exists, causes the speaker to tremble, but she hopes to be among the hymn singers in whom listening to the hidden song aroused confidence and tranquillity, and not fear and trembling; and then she will be able to sing: "The Lord is for me, I shall not fear."

Zelda's conception of poetry as the arena of the revelation of the divine and the holy is a refreshing development and representation of hasidic thought, especially that of R. Nahman of Bratslav. Zelda speaks with admiration of the latter, identifying with him, and going so far as to declare: "I feel very close to him."[27] Not only did she feel an affinity with R. Nahman as a storyteller, but the place of melody and song in Bratslav thought and worship served as a point of departure for her and the foundation for the mystical strata in her poetic conception.

---

[26] *Poetry of Zelda*, 180; emphasis in the original.
[27] From the interview with Zelda (Hollander-Steingart, "Zelda-Poetry-Encounter," 235). Zelda then finds further support in the writings of R. Nahman of Bratslav (p. 236). See also Dov Sadan, *Hebrew Literature Borrows and Absorbs* (Tel Aviv: Tel Aviv University Press, 1969), 155-56 (Hebrew); Aryeh Weinman, "Echoes of Bratslav Hasidism in the Poetry of Zelda," *Shdemot* 65 (1978): 57-61 (Hebrew); Bar-Yosef, *On Zelda's Poetry*, 33, 135, and 155.

R. Nahman urges man to heed the song of the grasses and their melody, and even to join them in their singing. Seclusion, which is one of the outstanding and famous Bratslav modes of behavior, is closely linked with R. Nahman's call to leave the city for the fields and attempt to hear the song of the grasses.

> A person from Zlatopol [Ukraine] told me that when our master [R. Nahman], of blessed memory, was residing in Zlatopol, one time in the summer our master prayed early in the morning. Afterwards he sent his daughter, the girl Sarah, may she live long, to summon him to our master. Our master told him: "Come with me for a walk." He went with him outside the city, and they walked among the grasses. Our master told him: "If only you would merit hearing the sound of the songs and praises of the grasses, how each and every grass proclaims song to the Lord, may He be blessed, without partiality and without any foreign thoughts, and without the expectation of any recompense. How beautiful and fine it is to hear their song, and it is very good in their eyes to serve the Lord with awe."[28]

The grasses sing to the Lord, but their song and praise is not revealed, and not everyone is so fortunate as to hear it. "How beautiful and fine it is to hear their song"—which leads their audience to join their song and worship the Lord with them. Man's worship of the Lord, his melody and song, is influenced by the song of the grasses that he hears:

> Know that every shepherd has his own special melody, according to the grasses and according to the place where he tends his flocks [...] and according to the grasses and the place where he grazes his flocks, he has a melody of the aspect of *Perek Shirah* [nature's hymn to the Creator], and the shepherd's melody is made from the song of the grasses [...] for melody is made by the grasses growing in the land.[29]

---

[28] *Shivhei ha-Ran*, para. 163: "His Labor and Occupation in the Service of the Lord."
[29] R. Nahman of Bratslav, *Likkutei Moharan, Tanina*, para. 63.

R. Nahman understands melody and song as instruments, the media through which the divine element in the world is revealed; and this is the element of vitality that sustains the world:

> For by melody [...] that is of the aspect of what is capable of understanding all the allusions in every thing in the world, which are of the aspect of divine vitality, the aspect of the holy footings that are enwrapped in all these things in the world, which is the meaning of [Proverbs 30:4] "who has established all the extremities of the earth," who elevates and sustains, the aspect of the holy footings in which the world is clothed.[30]

The "holy footings" are the lowest part of the holiness in the world, which are revealed through melody and song. The divine sanctity and vitality are hidden in and clothed by every thing in the world, but the allusion must be understood and the song and melody must be heard in order to sense them. This is the source of the "song of the grasses" to which Zelda refers when she writes:

> A light, sudden bird
> prepared my soul for the song of the grasses.[31]

In these and other sources R. Nahman uses melody and song as proximate and equivalent terms, since melody, like song, expresses an additional layer of reality that can hardly be expressed in prose.[32]

---

[30] Idem, *Kamma*, para. 54.
[31] "New Fruit in the Season of Childhood" (Falk, *The Spectacular Difference*, 86-89). R. Nahman's song of the grasses might be playing in the background when Zelda writes: "The grasses sang of the rejoicing of the soul" (*Poetry of Zelda*, 83-84).
[32] Thus, for example, in *Likkutei Moharan, Tanina*, para. 31: "It is evident by the melody whether a person accepted the yoke of the Torah, the sign of which is [Numbers 7:9]: 'they bore them on their shoulders,' and the Rabbis, of blessed memory, expounded [TB Arakhin 11a]: 'They bore them [*yis'u*] means song, as it is said [Psalms 81:3]: "Take up [*se'u*] the song, sound the timbrel."' This scriptural passage speaks of the sons of Kehat, who bore the Ark on their shoulders, which is the aspect of the yoke of the Torah." This exposition is possible only if we assume that *niggun* (melody), *shirah* (hymn), and *zemer* (loud song) are synonymous. In this source as well, the *shirah* and *niggun* teach more about a person than the content of his speech, since melody reflects an inner stratum which reveals the concealed essence that is not manifested in words.

At times, things are given their vitality by their melody, which, stated differently, reveals their existing significance. Words or statements that are uttered without inflection or music can sound dry, meagre, and lifeless. It is the melody that vivifies them, and gives them force and the power to persuade. The melody is an important component of the pathos of what is said, and has the ability to transform a series of disassociated words and sentences that do not speak to a person's heart into a statement of conative capability, with driving force and pregnant with meaning.[33]

Many of Zelda's poems reflect the notion that not only does reality contain layers of spiritual meaning; it is charged with divine allusions and messages of more concrete meaning. Coming, as they do, from the upper orb, it is poetry that is the fitting language and medium to absorb and signify them. We will examine several poems that portray the processes of listening to the different voices that issue forth from the song of the grasses and of the internalization of these voices.

---

[33] A well-known Hasidic parable cited in the name of the Ba'al Shem-Tov, the founder of Hasidism, exemplifies the power of *niggun*: "'All the people saw the sounds, etc.' (Exodus 20:15)—this is to be interpreted in accordance with a parable that I heard from my grandfather, may the memory of the righteous be for a blessing, of a person who played very finely, sweetly and pleasantly, on a musical instrument. Those who heard him could not restrain themselves, because the sweetness and pleasure were so great, so that they danced almost to the ceiling, for the pleasure, delight and sweetness were so overpowering. Anyone who was closer, and who would draw himself closer to hear the instrument, had the greatest delight and would dance to excess. Amidst all this, a deaf person came, one who could not hear the pleasing sound of the musical instruments, but only saw people dancing to excess, and he thought of them as mad. He said to himself [Ecclesiastes 2:2] 'Of merriment [I said], "What good is that?"' In truth, if he were wise and knowledgeable, and were to understand that this was caused by the greatness of the pleasure and delight in the sound of the musical instruments, then he, too, would dance there, and the moral is self-understood" (R. Ephraim of Sidilkov, *Degel Mahaneh Ephraim* [Jerusalem: 1994], *Yitro*, s.v. "*Ve-Khol*," 101). The deaf person sees the dancing as a series of strange and baffling actions, lacking rhyme or reason. Song does not "explain," in a formalistic sense, nor does it infuse the movements of the hands and feet with purpose or logic. Nonetheless, it is this melody that gives meaning to the puzzling behavior of the dancers, and is the force that vitalizes and drives the dance.

> There was something startling
> in the blue of the sky.
> I was amazed that the treetops
> swayed gently
> with no shadow of fear.
> I wanted to flee from the white sky
> but the small garden showed me signs
> that His mercy had not ceased.[34]

The religious significance of the process described by Zelda is revealed only upon the conclusion of the poem.[35] First, we follow the undefined feeling of anxiety that seizes the startled speaker at the sight of the hue of the sky that prompts her to flee. At this point, the emotional process is still not charged with any religious significance. Only in the next phase, when a certain lull sets in, and after the small garden "showed me signs that His mercy had not ceased," we understand that a sort of implied conversation about God, of whom the book of Lamentations avers, "His mercies are not spent,"[36] has actually been conducted all the while. At this juncture, the feeling of being startled and anxious, as well, is given a new meaning, as something of a revelation of the menacing countenance of God.

The poem is the intriguing end result of attentiveness to the melody of the grasses and the garden that begins with fear and culminates in mercy. The hidden melody of the grasses that speaks in the language of signs teaches of what is possibly the most important and common distinction between the two components of the religious sentiment: fear and love. The kabbalistic-hasidic conceptualization of *"dehilu u-rehimu"* (fear and mercy, or fear and love) is more fitting for the poem. This expression, which usually appears as a set phrase, expresses the demand that man worship the Lord with both *dehilu u-rehimu*.[37] The process that begins with sensitivity to the landscape, the color of the sky, the

---

[34] Falk, *The Spectacular Difference*. 204-5.
[35] On this structure as characteristic of many of Zelda's poems, see Bar-Yosef, *On Zelda's Poetry*, 135-39.
[36] "But this do I call to mind, therefore I have hope: The kindness of the Lord has not ended, His mercies are not spent" (Lamentations 3:21-22).
[37] "The main thing is Torah for its own sake, that is, that one's occupation with the Torah should be with *dehilu u-rehimu*" (R. Ephraim of Sidilkov, *Degel Mahaneh Ephraim*, Vayetze, s.v. "Oh," 39).

movement of the treetops, and the small garden, is fashioned in the end as a religious experience of the divine presence that is so startling and fearful that it motivates the speaker to flee, on the one hand, and to feel pity and mercy, on the other.

In this context, the language of signs is a proximate continuation of the language of the melody and song. Signs express a meaning that is only hinted at, a primordial, meaningful statement that cannot be transmitted by concrete speech or defined content. Attentiveness to the signs in the garden or the treetops, like listening to the song of the grasses and the hidden poem, prepares a person for the experience of a concealed and implied conversation with the Creator. Zelda uses "signs" in additional places to depict subtle allusions sent from above. Plants are not their exclusive domain, and they are also to be found in living creatures:

> The butterfly from the flower's
> days in paradise [...]
> with heavenly letters
> in its orange wings,
> signs of God.[38]

The signs in the butterfly's wings and in the small garden are the letters of the heavenly language, and the handprint of God that the poet so frequently reveals and depicts in her poetry.

The Bratslav use of "signs" to describe the hidden conversation with the Creator is close to the more frequent Bratslav use of the word "*remazim* [hints, allusions]."[39] As we will see below, Zelda adopts this appellation as well when she writes of "clues [*remazim*] from heaven."[40] Behind these terms is the kabbalistic conception that views this world as a reflection of the supernal worlds:

> As is generally understood and explained in the books of *tikkunim* and the holy *Zohar* (and the words of R. Isaac Luria, of blessed

---

[38] "The Fine Light of My Peace" (Falk, *The Spectacular Difference*, 188-89).

[39] On the proximity between signs and allusions in Bratslav terminology and "signs that are of the aspect of allusions," see R. Nathan of Rymanow, *Likkutei Halakhot, Orah Hayyim*, "Laws of Washing the Hands for a Meal," halakhah 6:89.

[40] In the poem "The Sun Lit a Wet Branch" (Falk, *The Spectacular Difference*, 100-101). We will discuss this song below.

memory, who explains them), that the earth and all that is on it, to the smallest detail [...] are present and marked [*mesumanim*] in the smallest details of the heavenly host (the spiritual and the intellectual, from the divine attributes and the letters of the Torah) in the supernal world above it, that devolved from Him, in His creation and providence, from the beginning to the end. They likewise will be deemed as signs and allusions of the details of the spiritual and intellectual host in the firmament of heaven and the most supernal world.[41]

For Bratslav Hasidism, signs and allusions are not only a reflection of the structure of the supernal worlds; they are also a divine message that can bring the individual closer to God:

For (Isaiah 6:3) "His presence fills all the earth"—this holy knowledge is mainly to be acquired by the aspect of allusions, for no thought can at all conceive this. Rather, (Proverbs 31:23): "Her husband is known in the gates"—for everyone, as he imagines, which is of the aspect of allusions. For everyone must direct his mind to understand the allusions, until he draws down to himself the Godhead, may He be blessed, everywhere, and understands that His presence fills all the earth. This is of the aspect of every creature will understand that You are his activator, etc. It is impossible to speak of this at length, and a word to the wise will suffice.[42]

R. Nahman of Tcherin, one of the leading disciples of R. Nahman of Bratslav, writes that the man on a high spiritual level "sets times every day to seek and search for the signs of holiness."[43]

---

[41] R. Abraham ben Nahman, *Sefer Biur ha-Likkutim* (Jerusalem: Meshekh Hanakhal, 2003), "R. S[imeon] Commenced," 60:4. R. Abraham explains R. Nahman's exposition of the importance of tales as part of his broader attempt to understand the essence of the symbolism in the tales.

[42] R. Nathan of Rymanow, *Alim le-Terufah* (Jerusalem: Hasidei Breslov, 1981), *Mikhtav* 394, p. 344.

[43] R. Nahman of Tcherin, "The Allusions in the Tales," Tale 10, p. 15, in R. Nahman of Bratslav, *The Vocalized Tales* (Jerusalem: Meshekh Hanakhal, 1985) (Hebrew). For an extensive discussion of the place of the allusion and the melody in R. Nahman's thought, see Zvi Mark, "Union with God: Allusion, Spark, and *Niggun*—On the Bratslav Worship of God," in *Mysticism and Madness in the Work of R. Nahman of Bratslav* (Tel Aviv: Am Oved, 2003), 175-224 (Hebrew).

Thus, the hidden is revealed in allusions, in signs, in the song of the grasses and the singing of the cherubs. Man is to be attentive to them, and thereby to sense the presence of the holy and the divine in the world, and receive their inherent messages, both those reflective of the attribute of strict judgment and those that teach "that His mercy had not ceased."

The following poems provide additional examples of the processes in which the letters, the signs, the allusions, and the melody that come from the supernal world are revealed to the reader:[44]

> *In the Kingdom of Sunset*
> In the kingdom of sunset
> even a thorn shines.
>
> Suddenly crowns melt away
> and the thorn becomes a thorn again
> and the mount returns to its shapelessness,
> the attribute of strict judgment is revealed
> and the skeleton of the Universe breaks through.
>
> But we do not die of fear
> for the mercy of the night arrives
> and the soul ascends to a new awareness
> of the Creator.[45]

In this poem as well, the religious meaning of the experience it describes emerges only at the conclusion. It begins as a nature poem depicting the appearance of thorns and hills by the light of the setting sun, and describing the mood of the speaker who gazes upon this scene. The attribute of strict judgment (*din*) mentioned in the continuation of the poem represents inflexibility and insistence upon rules and laws, outside of the traditional Jewish contexts of the concept. Only at the end of the poem do we learn that this entire psychological process leads to "a new awareness of the Creator," with the wording "a new awareness" raising the possibility that what it replaced was also an awareness of

---

[44] The following discussion is based on the analysis proposed by Bar-Yosef, *On Zelda's Poetry*, 136-37 and 42.
[45] *Poetry of Zelda*, 202.

the Creator. A rereading of the poem reveals a system of anticipatory preludes that hint of the divine dimensions that infuse the poem: terms such as *malkhut* ("kingdom"), *nogah* "(shines"), *keter* ("crown[s]"), *midat ha-din* ("the attribute of strict judgment"), *pahad* ("fear"), and *hesed* ("mercy") now are heard as kabbalistic and hasidic concepts that describe the supernal world, that of the Godhead.[46] Our rereading draws our attention to a series of terms each of which could be understood divorced from its kabbalistic context, but when taken together as a dense and concentrated assemblage teach of a meaningful group of terms from the kabbalistic-hasidic semantic field.

In the world of Kabbalah, the terms *Keter*, *Malkhut*, *Din*, and *Hesed* are positioned within the symbolic structure of ten *sefirot* that serves as a meta-symbol and meta-model to describe the world of the Godhead. The kabbalistic discussion of the *sefirot* and of the dynamics and processes related to them refers mainly to this divine realm. "*Nogah*" or "*Kelipat Nogah*" is an appellation for one of the four husks (*kelipot*) that encircle the world of sanctity, and that constitute part of the internal structure of evil; *Kelipat Nogah* has a special status, as an interim phase between good and evil.[47]

Hasidism moves the center of interest from the world of the Godhead to the human sphere. Hasidic writings frequently use kabbalistic terms and structures to conceptualize and give meaning to what happens in the human sphere. The system of kabbalistic concepts and models in the hasidic discussion is concerned mainly with the states of the soul, the structure of the human personality, and the characterization of the forces at work upon man.[48]

Zelda continues this hasidic direction and weaves this cluster of kabbalistic terms into her poetry to give voice to the manner in which man experiences the divine world that is revealed to him in the sunset and

---

[46] On the roots in Habad Hasidism of Zelda's use of the term *malkhut*, see Bar-Yosef, *On Zelda's Poetry*, 31-42.

[47] The term "*nogah*" appears again in Zelda's poetry, in proximity to "*kelipah*," in the poem "Their Soul Appealed" (*Poetry of Zelda*, 82). See also Bar-Yosef, *On Zelda's Poetry*, 146.

[48] See Yoram Jacobson, *Hasidic Thought*, trans. J. Chipman (Tel Aviv: Ministry of Defence Press, 1998), 16-17; Idel, *Hasidism*, Appendix A: "Psychologization of Theosophy in Kabbalah and Hasidism," 227-38.

descending night, and not in order to depict or conceptualize the world of the Godhead itself. The natural world is the world of the *sefirot*, and through it man experiences the attributes of strict justice and of mercy, the *sefirah* of *Malkhut*, and the husk of *Nogah*. This world of the Godhead is not revealed in a nocturnal vision or a waking prophecy, but as the experiential culmination of the sensitive and charged communion with nature. The contact with the divine world is diverse and constantly changing, and matches the unceasing transformation of nature, even that of inanimate objects such as hills and thorns. The light of sunset, the darkness that descends, and night all lead us to differently sense nature and the God that it reveals, thus opening the way for a new understanding of the Creator.

Zelda's perception—her poetry—includes the same terms and strata in the world of the Godhead with which the kabbalists and Hasidim portrayed their spiritual perceptions. Zelda experienced these cognitions as the "hidden song" of creation, and she documents and expresses them in the same poetic medium.

The mental process depicted in the poem corresponds with that of its reading: the process begins with natural vistas and concludes with an encounter with the divine that retroactively refashions the meeting with nature as engagement with the divine. The poem's set of anticipatory gestures parallels the system of divine allusions and signs present in nature that are uncovered only when the primal, pre-religious encounter with nature has been experienced to the full, and as a second stage of this meeting. In this manner Zelda leads the reader on a path similar to the experience of "reading" nature.

The next poem describes in greater detail the journey of the psyche that begins by standing breathless before this bit of nature and ends with a religious experience that includes a dimension of revelation:

> *The Sun Lit a Wet Branch*
> The sun lit a wet branch
> and gold leaves captured my eyes.
> The gold leaves that coursed
> night and day
> through my heart's blood
> changed their configuration.

> And when they reached the soul,
> its solitude,
> they became distant signs
> of light,
> clues from heaven,
> ancient wonders.[49]

The poem opens with an aesthetic experience of nature: the wet leaves glitter in the sunlight like pieces of gold that capture the speaker's eyes. This experience undergoes a process of protracted internalization, and the sights become part of the blood's circulation and the heart's beating, "night and day." During the phases of this internalization, the sights undergo a gradual change, at the end of which, when they reach "the soul, its solitude," they become "distant signs / of light / clues from heaven / ancient wonders." The light and the sights are no longer an enchanting aesthetic experience; they are signs and allusions sent from the supernal world, from heaven.

This poem describes in greater detail the process we observed in the previous poems. An event that starts as an admiring gaze upon a plant, a hill, or a sunset, evolves, undergoes a refashioning, and is deciphered as a conversation and as the transmission of an implicit message from heaven.

The transition from aesthetic to religious experience is neither swift nor simple. The voyage from the aesthetic to the religious, with its seeming revelation of "clues from heaven," reaches its destination only after a lengthy process of internalization, in the course of which the vista becomes an integral part of man himself, of his circulatory system; and only after the passage of days and nights is this sight fully realized, when it reaches the individual's innermost point.

The speaker incorporates, in her description of the views that she saw as signs and allusions from heaven, the terms "*otot*" ("signs") and "*moftim*" ("wonders"), whose biblical meanings are sign and proof.[50] These words are still used in contemporary Hebrew to denote a definite proof. God's signs and wonders are the miracles that exceed the bounds of nature, thereby confirming the existence of God and His authority and

---

[49] Falk, *The Spectacular Difference*, 100-101.
[50] E.g., "If there appears among you a prophet or dream-diviner and he gives you a sign or a portent [*mofet*], even if the sign or portent that he named to you comes true" (Deuteronomy 13:2-3). See also Deuteronomy 28:46 and Isaiah 8:18.

power.⁵¹ The prophets needed signs and wonders in order to prove their agency from God and the veracity of their prophecy. Divine revelation is effected by signs and wonders, teaching of His ability to change nature and do as He wills. In the medieval period, when some philosophers rejected miraculous acts as a method of proof, the term *ot u-mofet* acquired an additional meaning: intellectual and logical proof.⁵² During this time, a "logical proof [*mofet hegyoni*]" or an "intellectual proof [*mofet sikhli*]" was mobilized to prove the existence of God.⁵³ Zelda adds another layer of meaning to these words. She too maintains that signs and wonders are the way to reach faith in God and to sense His contact with mortals, but in her poetry they are not linked with miracles that exceed the way of nature, nor with intellectual proofs and scholarly exercises in logic. For her, the sight of a wet leaf on a sunny day is a sign that has come from afar, the ancient wonder that reaches the most secluded and intimate levels of the human soul, and the "hidden song" that awakens upon seeing external beauty and undergoes a lengthy process of digestion and internalization before becoming a part of man and his soul: this is the sign and wonder that validates faith. As in "With My Grandfather," the test of faith in Zelda's world is the ability to hear poetry: the song of the grasses and the song of the cherubs. Anyone capable of hearing and absorbing the singing receives from heaven a sign and wonder for the existence of the Ever-living One.⁵⁴ Consequently, the poet's task is to aid

---

[51] As in the wording of the blessing following the evening recitation of the *Shema* ("Hear, O Israel"): "Who performed miracles for us, [took] vengeance on Pharaoh, [and performed] signs and wonders on the land of the offspring of Ham."

[52] See, e.g., Judah Halevi, *The Kuzari*, trans. Hartwig Hirschfeld (New York: Shocken Books, 1971), Part I, paras. 13, 15 and 65-67. Another example appears in the writings of Maimonides: seemingly non applicable fields of study "may have as their purpose the sharpening of the intellect and the [training in the] use of proofs so that a person will acquire the methods of logical proof. In this manner, one will come to the true knowledge of the existence of God," Maimonides, *Shemonah Perakim: A Treatise on the Soul,* trans. and comm. L. S. Kravitz and K. M. Olitzky (New York: UAHC Press, 1999), 63-64.

[53] *The Kuzari*, Part I, paras. 66 and 67.

[54] Zelda portrays crisis and the concealment of the divine countenance as a lack of signs and the inability to decipher the wonders: "I had no shield / besides God / whose wonders are unfathomable [...] I shall be supported by God / in the bitterness of my soul—/ but when there is no sign [...]" ("Go, Charms of Childhood," in *Poetry of Zelda*, 185).

in hearing the melody, in the process of infusing the sights and senses with meaning as "clues from heaven" and as "signs of God."[55]

Finally, we will examine the poem "The Good Smell of Distances," one of the most clearly ars poetica poems in all of Zelda's work:[56]

> *The Good Smell of Distances*
> Something within me
> took his head from the sea,
> longing for existence in words.
> I stand like that beggar
> and on the tablet of my heart a song
> that tells every passerby,
> every runner,
> of the hidden regions of the heart—
> what madness,
> what shame,
> to lead strangers there.
> The song, too, begs for death,
> for trees and stones touched ungently
> the melody.
> The song on the tablet of my heart
> makes signs to me
> for the sunset flung it
> a drop of gold
> so that I would rejoice once again
> rejoice once again
> for the rain that falls on a sunny day.
> The song whispers to my soul:
> "Do not flee,"
> I hear my friend's steps.
> From one end of the world to the other
> rove the songs
> of every people and language.
> Parables and signs come;
> the good smell of distances
> emanates from them
> if on their way they did not touch
> the stench of standing water
> or blood.

---

[55] A similar voyage of the soul is depicted in the poem "The Rose of Sharon," which begins by longing for the flower's fragrance and blooming, and then develops into the certainty that the world "is surely holy" (*Poetry of Zelda*, 58).

[56] On this poem, see Bar-Yosef, *On Zelda's Poetry*, 138.

> But the finest of all the songs
> is the white curtain
> in which is embroidered with a white thread:
> "Silence is Your praise."[57]

The song focuses on the question of exposure and concealment in poetry, in which all the regions of the soul that are "hidden in the heart" are revealed. The poem opens a window to the hidden, the secret, and the intimate in the poet's world, and it consequently conveys the distress and confusion caused by the public nature of the poem and its exposure to all. What madness it is to open to all what is closed in the heart; how shameful to tell every chance reader of those private regions. The poem, by its very nature, needs a refined and intimate reading. It could die by a strange and ungentle touching of its melody.

Like the Hasidim, Zelda views the poem's melody as the source of its vitality. Without the right melody, the poem becomes lifeless, loses its very essence as poetry, and is liable to become a dry and meaningless text lacking inspiration.

The aversion to writing poetry and the distress caused by its exposure are tempered by the voices that burst forth from the poem itself. The whisper to the poet's soul hints of the concealed and concealing qualities of the poem itself. The poem speaks in the language of "signs" and "parables," all of which it murmurs, and does not speak aloud. It soothes the writer, and tells her "I hear my friend's steps." The friends that are heard are other poems that come from afar, but they are also the readers. Not only is the writing of poetry in need of friendship and refinement; its reading also demands such attentiveness and tenderness. The hidden regions that are laid bare in the poem are spoken in a whisper and concealed in the language of signs and parables, the key to which is the refined reading of friendship.

The poem's closing stanza appears as a separate unit, independent of the rest of the poem, which is written without interruption, apparently as an addition to the poem whose main course has been exhausted. The body of the poem explores the reasons for writing, the dilemma of exposure and concealment, and the purpose that poetry gives to writing and reading. The last stanza appears to address a different topic, the

---

[57] *Poetry of Zelda*, 200-201.

white curtain and its beauty. The conjunction of contrast "but," seems to object somewhat to what was previously said; "the finest of all the songs" is apparently unappreciative of poetry and is little moved by the beauty of poems. But the white curtain, so it appears, is not set forth in contrast to poetry; rather, it too is embroidered with words and is the most beautiful of all poems. This understanding is strengthened by the verse that is embroidered on the curtain, which is borrowed from the poetry of King David in Psalms: "For the leader. A psalm of David. A song. Silence is Your praise."[58] The ars poetica poem ends by demarcating both the summit and limitations of poetry.

In this poem, as in many of Zelda's works, God appears only at its conclusion.[59] And as in the poems discussed above, the culmination of the process that is depicted in the poem (in this case, the climax of the poem itself) leads to God. As is usual for Zelda, God is hardly ever directly addressed, nor is he mentioned by any of his specific names. Instead, Zelda uses the less common appellations and adjectival descriptions from the prayers and the *piyyutim* that describe God's action in the world.[60] In this poem, the religious context is introduced by the *parokhet*—the curtain that covers the Torah Ark in the synagogue, and that, in its biblical use as a "screen," divides the Holy from the Holy of Holies. This context is reinforced by the content of the embroidered verse and its implicit message that the poem, like it, relates directly to God: "Praise befits You, O God." Zelda thus chooses to conclude the discussion of the place and role of prayer by presenting the poem to God as the apex of poetry, as "the finest of all the songs."

Although the song to God is kept apart, and appears only in the last stanza, this stanza also continues the poem's preoccupation with poetry as an activity that, on the one hand, reveals the secret and the hidden,

---

[58] Psalms 65:2, which is included in the *Nishmat* prayer that concludes the Sabbath morning *Pesukei de-Zimrah* section.

[59] Dan Levi argues that this phenomenon attests that faith is not an integral part of the poem, but rather an artificial and nonessential addition (D. Levi, "Facing the Tremendous Skies," *Maariv*, November 13, 1984, literary section, pp. 4-5 [Hebrew]). Hamutal Bar-Yosef, however, clearly proves, in detail, the extent to which the religious stratum that is revealed in the poem endings is the basic key to understanding the meaning of the poem as a whole (Bar-Yosef, *On Zelda's Poetry*, 135-39).

[60] See Bar-Yosef, *On Zelda's Poetry*, 140.

while, on the other, is capable of existing as a covert statement that borders on silence. For Zelda, the most exalted writing is white on white: neither complete silence, nor a blank page on which nothing is written. This is a minimalist, modest, and hidden statement, unseen within a fine combination of the visual image of the white threads on the white curtain together with the exalted words "*dumiyah*" (with the two meanings of "befitting" and "silence") and *tehillah* (praise) that adorn it. It is meant to be both a gate to the holy and a covering, a "screen," that conceals what is innermost.[61] The curtain symbolizes the epitome of poetry—an entrance and a covering, a statement and a concealment. It should be noted that in the esoteric writings, the curtain (*pargod*, in Aramaic) is a multifaceted symbol for the revelation of the divine glory and for its concealment (its two different, yet intertwined aspects),[62] for "It is the glory of God to conceal a matter" (Proverbs 25:2). Accordingly, the unique quality of poetry as writing and statement that contains both revelation and concealment finds its most exalted expression in poetry that relates to God. The "finest of all the songs" is the poem concealed from all poems, the subject of which is God, whose revelation is his concealment.

An interesting precedent that may have inspired Zelda's image of the white thread embroidered on the white curtain appears in the writings of R. Hayyim Vital, the disciple of R. Isaac Luria. In his book *Sha'arei Kedushah* (The Gates of Holiness), Vital prescribes various techniques for attaining divine inspiration. One of these consists of a process that begins with the purification of one's traits and thoughts, upon the conclusion of which the individual imagines that he ascends from one firmament to the next, until he reaches the seventh firmament, which is called "*Aravot*." There "he shall visualize that above the

---

[61] "So that the curtain shall serve you as a partition between the Holy and the Holy of Holies" (Exodus 26:33); "Then he put up the curtain for screening, and screened off the Ark of the Covenant" (Exodus 40:21).

[62] See Haviva Pedaya, "The Glory and the Curtain," in *Vision and Speech: Models of Revelatory Experience in Jewish Mysticism* (Los Angeles: Cherub Press, 2002), 237-55 (Hebrew); esp. see "The Curtain: Partition and Revelation," 248-49. For an extensive discussion of the complex nature of the secret about to be revealed, see also Moshe Halbertal, *Concealment and Revelation: The Secret and its Boundaries in Medieval Jewish Tradition*, Yeriot 2 (Jerusalem: Orna Hess Books, 2001) (Hebrew).

firmament of *Aravot* there is a very great white curtain, upon which the Tetragrammaton is inscribed in [color] white as snow, in Assyrian writing in a certain color."[63]

Thus, at the highest rung, the name of God is written with white thread on a white cloth, in the most supernal firmament, the one called *Aravot*, where a person in his mind has passed through all the screens and firmaments that separate him from his Maker. Here as well, it seems that the culmination of all thought and speech about God leads to the silence, portrayed as a mental statement and as writing: white on white.

The choice of white as the color in which God's praise is silence has an intriguing source in the hasidic literature. R. Levi Isaac of Berdichev explains the wearing of white garments by the High Priest on the only day in the year in which he enters beyond the curtain into the Holy of Holies:[64]

> This will enable you to understand why the High Priest would wear white garments on Yom Kippurim: because the appearance of white is completely colorless, and only afterwards can receive all colors. Now, the Lord, may He be blessed, has, as it were, no coloration, for He has no image or countenance.[65]

In her poem "As a Blossom of the Valleys,"[66] Zelda also describes the highest perception as "a colorless gate."

Interestingly, the "white on white" motif is also represented in the visual arts at the opposite poles of Western culture, and is used to describe the indescribable divine sublime. Thus, for example, the work of Kazimir Malevich, an early twentieth-century Russian artist who produced a series of white-on-white paintings, the color white

---

[63] Following the manuscript version in Moshe Idel, *Kabbalah: New Perspectives* (New Haven and London: Yale University Press, 1988), 110. Slight variations appear in other versions, but the principle of writing white on white remains. See *Sha'arei Kedushah*, Book 4, in *Katavim Hadashim le-Rabbenu Hayyim Vital z"l* (New Writings by Our Master Hayyim Vital, of Blessed Memory) (Jerusalem: Yeshivat Yehuda Press, 1988), 6-7 (Hebrew).

[64] M Yoma 3:6.

[65] R. Levi Isaac of Berdichev, *Sefer Kedushat Levi ha-Shalem*, vol. 1 (Jerusalem: 1993), 209; see also 195, where R. Levi Isaac discusses this "*Ayin* that is called 'white,' since it has no color or configuration."

[66] *Poetry of Zelda*, 56.

symbolizing the infinite and the eternal.[67] In his 1918 oil-painting entitled *Suprematist Composition: White on White* we see an inclined white square on a similarly colored white background. Naomi Werman wrote of this painting: "Malevich is concerned here with the infinite, but this is not a mathematical infinity, but rather a mystical one, that is symbolized by color."[68] After producing several white on white variations, Malevich felt that he had reached the apex of painting and had exhausted this field of creative endeavor, which he then abandoned totally. He began to teach painting and art, and engaged in architecture, which seemed to realize his aesthetic and spiritual vision in this world.[69]

On another continent, the Jewish-American painter Barnett Newman was one of the innovators of "fields of color" painting. He called one of his paintings the exalted *The Name II* (oil, 1950), a title that is a precise rendering of the Hebrew *Hashem*, the substitute for the divine Name that may not be uttered. The painting is composed of three contiguous areas, all in white. Ruth Apter wrote: "This painting is the way in which Newman expresses the concept of divinity: blinding light, a pure white that cannot be described and that has no expression [...] He chose to describe the indescribable essence, since its infinity cannot be contained within a limiting form. In his attempt to present this infinite essence with a white on white portrayal, Newman produced the succinct summation of the minimalist treatment of the sublime."[70]

The ars poetica conception in "The Good Smell of Distances" is an additional layer in Zelda's view of poetry as it has been set forth above. Poetry is the proper medium in which to expose and express the concealed presence of God; conversely, poetry, at its best, remains concealed and covert, even after it is exposed to the light of day. This is true for the most secret recesses of the heart, and even more so regarding the concealed song of the Ever-living One. The covert conversation that is spoken in allusions and that borders on silence, that characterizes man's conversation with his God, is present both in the hidden poem that is

---

[67] Naomi Werman, *Art in the Technological Era*, Unit 4 (Tel Aviv: Open University Press, 1981), 13 (Hebrew).
[68] Ibid., 15.
[69] Ibid., 15-17.
[70] Ruth Apter, *Art in the Technological Era*, Unit 11 (Tel Aviv: Open University Press, 1983), 88 (Hebrew).

the divine stratum that plays music throughout all Creation, and in man's modest and silent poetry when he sings His praises.

I know of no parallels in hasidic thought and literature with such a concrete and refined development and actualization of hasidic values, such as attentiveness to the song of the grasses, and to the "clues" and "signs" of God that are scattered in reality, as appears in Zelda's poetry. This unfolding, which marks a new stage in hasidic thought,[71] provides a firm infrastructure for the poetic conceptions reflected in her work. These conceptions give meaning to her poems, placing them in a broader context. Zelda's crafting of these early concepts also makes an important and relevant statement on the meaning of faith in the modern world.

---

[71] This issue is a component of a broad philosophical view, woven into Zelda's poetry, that profoundly resembles and continues Hasidic thought, only a small amount of which has been uncovered and explained in this article. A number of central issues in Zelda's poetry that should be explored within this context: the ecstatic experience, the inner point, the concepts of "sacred" and "mundane," religious freedom, and the attitude to death.

3
PERSONS AND IDEAS

"My desire for the living God hath constrained me": Belief as Unfulfilled Desire in the Writings of Rabbi Judah Halevi

Dorit Lemberger

"I *am* only to the extent that I know myself.[1] This reconciliation happens in the ideal world, in the world of the spirit into which men take flight when the earthly world satisfies them no longer."

—Hegel, *Introduction to the Lectures on the History of Philosophy*[2]

"My heart is in the east, and I in the uttermost west—
How can I find savour in food? How shall it be sweet to me?
How shall I render my vows and my bonds, while yet
Zion lieth beneath the fetter of Edom, and I in Arab chains?
A light thing would it seem to me to leave all the good things of Spain—
Seeing how precious in mine eyes to behold the dust of the desolate sanctuary."

—Rabbi Judah Halevi,
"My Heart is in the East"[3]

Preface

This article suggests a reading of the later religious poetry of R. Judah Halevi (1075-1141) as a poetry that presents a reflective and dialectical disposition of belief, while concomitantly examining the disposition of

---

[1] G. W. F. Hegel, *Introduction to the Lectures on the History of Philosophy*, trans. M. Knox & A. Miller (Oxford: Clarendon Press, 1985), 112.
[2] Ibid. 113.
[3] *Selected Poems of Jehudah ha-Levi*, ed. H. Brody, trans. Nina Salaman (Philadelphia: Jewish Publication Society of America, 1946), 2.

belief as set forth in the *Kuzari*.[4] In Halevi's poetry we find, alongside the poetic and aesthetic qualities, a recurring description of self-examination; a description of the speaker's doubt over his way of life and his ability to fully realize his religious belief; and, above all, the sweeping self-criticism of a speaker whom "the earthly world satisfies ... no longer." A major paradox in much of Halevi's poetry is the speaker's desire to perform God's will (the ultimate expression of which is immigration to the Holy Land) versus his surrender, time and again, to worldly temptations in various aspects of life. The poem *My Heart is in the East*, for example, embodies this paradox in a striking way, pitting the realization of God's will and commandments ("my vows and my bonds") against the creature-comforts of Spain, in which the speaker feels himself "sinking." The speaker wonders how he will be able to enjoy life when he is so far from Zion ("How can I find savour ... how shall it be sweet"), and, even more important, how he will ever fulfill his religious obligations ('How shall I render my vows and bonds?"). Then he declares the ease with which he could leave Spain and all of Spain's charms, and puts this on the same level of importance as seeing "the dust of the desolate sanctuary" with his own eyes, using a word-play (*yeqal / yeqar*) that emphasizes the similarity between the two actions and also the essential difference between them. This triadic process raises the obvious question: if the speaker's religious priorities are so clear-cut and decisive, why in the world does he tarry?

The literary and historical scholarship has answered this question up until now in a dual manner: scholars of literature see Halevi as an important writer who was wonderfully adept in applying the poetic conventions of medieval Arabic poetry, one of which is the use of paired oppositions to create conflict at every level of the poem—grammatical, metaphorical, ideological—and it is in this framework that *My Heart is in the East* should be read, along with many other poems founded on

---

[4] The term "later poetry" refers to poems classified by Schirmann in *Ha-shirah ha-ivrit bi-sefarad u-vi-provans* (Jerusalem: Mossad Bialik, 1960) (Hebrew) and others as belonging to the final years of Halevi's life, the year before he immigrated to the Holy Land and the year he spent in Egypt (1040-1041). An English translation of Halevi's sea poems has been published in a separate volume edited by Gabriel Levin, *On the Sea* (Jerusalem: Ibis Editions, 1997).

paired oppositions.[5] The literary-historical scholarship is represented by a series of articles dealing with the historical evidence for Halevi's intended immigration to the Holy Land. The focus on the technical aspects of the journey, using the evidence to answer questions of a biographical nature, neglects the existential level.[6] What this article suggests, then, is a new way of interpreting the dialectic in Halevi's writing, one which sees it as a Hegelian process of Subject-constitution.[7] I do not mean to argue that pitting belief against these obstacles constitutes an Abraham-style "leap of faith," but to show that the poetry of Judah Halevi represents a dialectical development of repeated negations of an existing state that both preserves and advances this state from level to level until it reaches the religious "telos": immigration to the Holy Land. Such a reading of Halevi's poetry shows his disposition of belief as being optimistic and even idealistic, and singularly consonant with the process suggested by Hegel in *The Phenomenology of Mind*, and in an

---

[5] A description of this kind can be found in the studies of D. Pagis, *Hidush u-masoret be-shirat ha-hol: sefarad ve-italia* (Jerusalem: Keter, 1976) (Hebrew); Yosef Yahalom, "Ganzei leningrad ve-heqer shirat hayav shel rabbi yehuda ha-levi," *Pe'amim* 46-47, (1990): 55-74; Y. Danna, *Ha-poeticah shel shirat ha-qodesh ha-sefaradit bi-yemei ha-beinayim* (Haifa: Center for Comparative Studies, 1999) (Hebrew); E. Hazan, *Torat ha-shir be-piyyut ha-sefaradi le'or shirat rabbi yehuda halevi* (Jerusalem: Magnes, 1986) (Hebrew); Schirmann and Fleischer, *Toldot ha-shirah ha-'ivrit bi-sefarad ha-muslamit* (Jerusalem: Magnes, 1996), 148-150, 443-444 (Hebrew).

[6] See for example S.D. Goitein, "Ha-im higia' rabbi yehuda halevi el hof eretz yisrael?," *Tarbitz* 46 (1977): 245-250 (Hebrew); "Ha-bibliografiah shel yehuda halevi le'or kitvei ha-geniza," in *Yehuda Halevi: mivhar ma'amarim al yetzirato*, ed. Haya Schwartz (Jerusalem: Misrad ha-hinukh ve-ha-tarbut, 1988), 57-71 (Hebrew); Yosef Yahalom, "Ganzei leningrad 1990, Aliyato shel rabbi yehuda halevi le-eretz yisrael" (in Hebrew), *Shalem* 7 (2001): 33-46.

[7] Hegel (1770-1831) defined self-consciousness as the final stage of a process that advances dialectically in which the Subject reaches Absolute Knowledge. Eventually, all subjective consciousnesses find its fulfillment in an overall objective spirit, the absolute truth. This idealistic and harmonic philosophical view is described in his major work, *The Phenomenology of Mind*, trans. J. B. Baillie (New York: Dover Publications, 2003). Hegel presents the dialectic process by which the spirit advances towards its fulfillment as a timeless truth while the final stage that preserves and transcends all negations is called "Aufhebung" (sublation).

intriguing relationship with the Jewish dialectic as portrayed by Rabbi Joseph Soloveitchik.[8]

I wish to argue that an historical-Hegelian reading of Halevi's expressions of belief in various poems can help clarify the difficulty noted above, both biographical and poetic. This problematic issue becomes greater when we realize that even according to the most optimistic interpretation of the historical evidence, Halevi did not live in the Holy Land (i.e., did not realize his concept of belief) for more than two months. I argue that if we look at Halevi's disposition of faith in light of Hegel's interpretation of Catholic religiosity in the Middle Ages, we will be able to describe the latter in terms of Hegel's "unhappy consciousness."[9]

---

[8] "Man is a dialectical being; an inner schism runs through his personality at every level ... man is a great and creative being because he is torn by conflict and is always in a state of ontological tenseness and perplexity" (J. Soloveitchik, "Majesty and Humility," *Tradition* 17:2 [1978]: 25). Soloveitchik's description, which focuses on the figure of the modern believer that is the opposite of Hegel, shows how Halevi's disposition of belief reflects (nevertheless) modern elements: "Judaic dialectic, unlike the Hegelian, is irreconcilable and hence interminable. Judaism accepted a dialectic, consisting only of thesis and antithesis. The third Hegelian stage, that of reconciliation, is missing. The conflict is final, almost absolute. Only God knows how to reconcile.... To Hegel, man and his history were just abstract ideas; in the world of abstractions synthesis is conceivable. For Judaism, man has always been and still is a living reality, or may I say, a tragic living reality. In the world of realities, the harmony of opposites is impossible" (ibid).

We need to give a meticulous reading to Soloveitchik's position towards Halevi, and say that although the course of Halevi's life indeed reinforces his position, Halevi's religious disposition leans toward Hegel and not Soloveitchik.

[9] "Consciousness, by giving the enemy a fixedness of being and of meaning, instead of getting rid of him, really never gets away from him and finds itself constantly defiled. And since, at the same time, this object of its exertions, instead of being something essential, in the very meanest, instead of being a universal, is the merest particular—we have here before us merely a personality confined within its narrow self and its petty activity, a personality brooding over itself, as unfortunate as it is pitiably destitute. But all the same both of these, both the feeling of its misfortune and the poverty of its own action, are points of connection to which to attach the consciousness of its unity with the unchangeable. For the attempted immediate destruction of its actual existence is affected through the thought of the unchangeable and takes place in this relation to the unchangeable. The mediate relation constitutes the essence of the negative process, in which this consciousness directs itself against its particularity of being." (Hegel, *Phenomenology of Mind*, 127-128).

The unhappy consciousness, according to Hegel, is the stage in which the consciousness becomes aware of the existence of the "Absolute Spirit" and feels itself to be remote from it, as well as anxious to attain it.

This experience creates a sense of being torn in two, of alienation, and, in particular, of failure and degradation in relation to existence in the present, culminating in a feeling of unhappiness. But this experience, according to Hegel, also conceals a latent optimism.[10] In contrast to the other two options for recognizing the existence of the absolute (skepticism, on the one hand, and a stoic equilibrium of spirit, on the other), the unhappy consciousness may lead, eventually, to negating the existence in the present and destroying it, in order to leave it for the "Absolute Spirit." Looking in this way at the paradoxical disposition of belief in Halevi's poems may help us to understand them better, and show it to be a personal expression of "the spirit of the times," similar to the disposition of medieval Catholicism which Hegel critiqued.[11]

In the poems analyzed below, the poetic speaker looks at the schism in his life deriving from the conflict between the desire to realize his belief, both in daily life and by immigrating to the Holy Land, and the various obstacles that stand in his way. The speaker in these poems deals with a variety of obstacles that face him, ranging from his "sorrows" to un-named other people, and it is interesting to correlate the sincere confessions of the speaker with the biographical facts of the poet's life—all the while wondering over his ability to create all this in poetic forms so strict in their conventions of rhyme, meter, and verbal imagery. The disposition of belief in the poems is different from that which takes

---

[10] As can be seen immediately afterwards in the following sub-section of Chapter 4 of *Phenomenology of the Mind*.

[11] "The essential category is unity, the inner connection of all these different manifestations. Here we must keep hold of the fact that it is only *one* spirit, *one* principle, which is stamped on the political situation and manifested in religion, art, moral and social life, trade, and industry, so that all these different forms are but branches of one main trunk.... The spirit is *one* and one only; there is one spirit as the substance of an era ... but it is shaped and manifested in various ways.... However manifold all these different things are, there is no contradiction between them. Not one of them contains anything different in kind from their basis.... There is only *one* spirit; its development is a single progress—one principle, one character expressed in the most verified formations. This is what we call the spirit of an age (Zeitgeist)" (Hegel, *Introduction to the Lectures on the History of Philosophy*, 109-110; emphasis in the original).

shape in Halevi's "formal" work of philosophy, the *Kuzari*, but it poses a fascinating existential alternative that can be better understood using the philosophy of Hegel, especially in light of Hegel's concept of history, as found in his writings. The points of intersection between Halevi and Hegel illuminate questions dealing with the nature of history in human thought in general, and, in particular, with the formation of the Subject's consciousness.

Over the course of this article I will try to show the paradox of the disposition that finds expression in the poem "My Heart is in the East" and in his many other poems where worldly desires stand in immanent conflict with the desire to realize belief.

The centrality of Judah Halevi's thought and writings in the Jewish consciousness are a matter of consensus and have been amply discussed in articles and books for scholars and laymen alike.[12] His writings and his life have been the subject of repeated scholarly discussion over the years. Of particular interest is the question of whether Halevi did or did not reach the Holy Land, given the fact that our last piece of evidence describes Halevi as having set sail from Egypt, but not as having reached

---

[12] A representative example of Halevi's centrality can be seen in Fleischer's dramatic and picturesque opening to his article "Tamtzit artzenu u-mashma'uto: Le-diyuqano shel rabbi yehuda halevi 'al-pi mimtzei ha-geniza," *Fe'amim* 68 (1996): 4 (Hebrew): "Of all the abundant light thrown on various figures of the past, thanks to the findings of the Cairo Geniza, the figure of Yehuda Halevi—the greatest Hebrew poet of the Middle Ages—has come in for more than its share. Yehuda Halevi stirred the imagination of his contemporaries, sparking off waves of excitement wherever he set foot: of all the great Jewish figures of the past, it seems that none was more loved and revered by the people of his time. His genius as a poet dawned—and received recognition—in his earliest youth ... but his contemporaries were as charmed and fascinated by his personality as they were by his poems." Fleischer stressed that the Geniza findings included anonymous texts that spoke about Judah Halevi as well as more mundane documents written by Halevi himself, thereby revealing more substantial aspects of his personality and the extent of his importance: "We knew that Yehuda Halevi was a great and highly revered poet, and we knew that he was involved in the local scene, but by no means did we know that he was the recognized leader of Spanish Jewry or that the Jewish grandees of Spain regarded him as the 'essence of their land and its meaning, its strongest fortress and its leader.' ... The Jewish grandees and the educated circles saw him as the ultimate embodiment, perfect and complete, of their cultural values; their spiritual aspirations in concentrated form." (Fleischer, "Tamtzit artzenu," 7).

the Holy Land.¹³ No less interesting is to see how Halevi's personal story was transformed into a myth embodying the Jewish aspiration over the centuries to immigrate to the Holy Land.¹⁴ Nevertheless, the characteristics and processes of both his philosophical writings and his poems have been discussed only in general terms, and to date there is no comprehensive comparative study to show what these two bodies of work have in common, and in what they differ.¹⁵ Judah Halevi, as a man of many

---

13 An example of the mythic function of Halevi's immigration in Jewish consciousness can be seen in David Hartman, *Moreshet bi-mahloqet* (Tel Aviv: Schocken, 2002), 40-41: "Like his proto-type in the *Kuzari*, Halevi also demonstrated his belief in the redemptive power of God by leaving the Diaspora and setting out for the Promised Land. This bold action expressed Halevi's profound confidence in the divine providence of the Holy One, blessed be He. He was not deterred by the political reality of his day, which pushed the Jews into a corner, or by the struggle for power in the Holy Land between two great powers—the Crusaders and the Muslims. Above and beyond practical considerations and political realism, Halevi believed that Jewish history could not be understood in the same empirical terms of cause and effect that apply to other nations."

14 The most important discovery concerning the question of whether or not he reached the Holy Land is that Halevi's ship set sail on the second day of Pentecost, 1141, headed for the Holy Land. Goitein published this discovery in his article of 1977. Goitein's findings did not prove that Halevi reached the Holy Land, but only that his boat left in this direction. Yosef Yahalom, "Ganzei leningrad" and "Ganzei leningrad 1990," and Fleischer, "Tamtzit artzenu" accepted this position without reservation and concluded that Halevi reached the Holy Land a few days later, in the middle of June, 1141. Since we have evidence for Halevi's death in August, it would seem that he managed to live in the Holy Land for approximately two months. The tendency of these three important scholars to believe that Halevi reached the Holy Land, despite the lack of evidence confirming it, illustrates the power of the myth concerning Halevi's arrival to the Holy Land. It is also interesting to see the continuing scholarly interest in this issue as new discoveries continued apace: the findings in the Cambridge Geniza (in 1975) and in Leningrad (discovered in 1949 but published only intermittently over the years, and discussed at length only by Yahalom's "Ganzei Leningrad"), revealed letters by, and about, Judah Halevi that confirm his struggle over the question of immigrating to the Holy Land, as well as the expectations of his contemporaries that he would do so.

15 We need to distinguish between arguing about the connection between Halevi's philosophical writings and his poetry, and making comparisons between them. For a survey of the pros and cons in the issue, see E. Hazan, "Ha'hasid hamoshel le'or shirat Yehuda ha-Levi," *Ma'im Midalyo* (1990): 236 (Hebrew).

talents—physician and public figure, philosopher and poet—gave rich expression to various aspects of his life, especially in his poetry, with the motif of desire serving as a fundamental axis for his disposition of belief. The main argument is that Halevi's poems can be read as the expression of a continuing spiritual struggle, over the course of which the subject of the poem establishes his disposition of belief while dealing with the philosophical and aesthetic conventions of the period. This struggle constitutes a reflection of Halevi's own life, which oscillated between the ideological belief embodied in the *Kuzari* and the sense of being swept up in the currents of daily life in Spanish culture and society. Because of the "constant motion," in his poems as in his life, Halevi was unable to realize his belief to the fullest, since even if we accept the scholarly position which believes that Halevi reached the Holy Land, he could not have lived there more than two months.[16] The goal of this discussion is not to exhaust every manifestation of Halevi's belief, but to argue that it is his poetry, with its wider range of genres and subject matter, rather than the more formal exposition of faith in the *Kuzari*, that expresses in greater depth and complexity Halevi's disposition of belief. Whereas the *Kuzari* suggests a course that is ostensibly coherent, the poetic corpus presents a series of unresolved conflicts expressing the belief of a torn and divided Subject who restlessly oscillates between the poles of his life. Following the description of the unhappy consciousness in Hegel, I suggest that the idealistic belief not only leaves the conflicts unresolved but indeed magnifies them into a feeling of sin and degradation that feeds the constant need to do penance, as well as the springs of poetic creativity. Halevi often used metaphors of sleep and waking as synecdoches of the soul and the spirit in order to describe his sense of guilt over the delay in fully realizing his belief.[17]

Reading these poems also helps us to understand in retrospect the sense of guilt which the "Rabbi" in the *Kuzari* feels, in particular because he has not immigrated to the Holy Land, and, more generally, because of the gap between the disposition of belief formally laid out in the book

---

[16] Y. Yahalom, "Aliyato shel rabbi yehuda halevi le-eretz yisrael," *Shalem* 7 (2001): 34 (Hebrew).

[17] See for example "Asleep in the Lap of Childhood; Sleeper with Heart Awake; A Servant of God" (in Y. Halevi, *Sefer ha-Kuzari*, trans. from the Arabic by Yehuda ibn Shmuel [Jerusalem: Dvir, 1973]).

and the failure of the Jewish people as a whole to give their religious belief an ultimate expression.[18]

We can divide the poems representing this complex position into three categories. **The first category** includes poems in which the speaker addresses God and asks for His help in resolving his internal struggle; these poems come under the heading of personal poetry.[19] The very fact of writing in this genre was problematic for Halevi, as he himself was to testify.[20] **The second category** consists of poems in which the speaker

---

[18] Halevi showed the highly problematic "Janus-face" of creativity and personality in a famous passage in the *Kuzari* in which the rabbi responds to the king's question of why he does not realize the ideal and immigrate to the Holy Land: "The Rabbi: This is a severe reproach, O king of the Khazars. It is the sin which kept the divine promise with regard to the second temple ... from being fulfilled.... If we say: "Worship his holy hill—worship at his footstool—He who restoreth His glory to Zion" and other words, this is but as the chattering of the starling and the nightingale. We do not realize what we say by this sentence, nor others, as thou rightly observest, O Prince of the Khazaras." The English translations in this article are quoted from *The Kuzari*, trans. Hartwig Hirschfeld (New York: Schocken, 1964), ch. 2, sec. 24.

[19] For a discussion of the problematics in classifying certain *piyyutim* as religious poems due to the difficulty of ascertaining their liturgical character and their role in the prayer service, see Hazan, *Torat ha-shir*, 21-23. Because of these problems, Hazan suggests dividing religious poetry into three categories: the first, of *piyyut*, includes religious poems included in the prayer service; the second, of "personal religious poems," includes religious poems on personal subjects; and the third, of religious poems not meant for the prayer service, such as the "table songs" (*zemirot shabbat*) traditionally sung during or immediately after the Sabbath meals (ibid., 23). Halevi's most widely analyzed and translated poem is "O Lord, before Thee is My Whole Desire". For a detailed analysis of the dialectical nature of this poem, see my article "The Dialectic Nature of Desire in Halevi's Poem: 'O Lord, before Thee is My Whole Desire'" in *Rabbi Yehuda Halevi Book* (Ramat-Gan: Bar-Ilan University, forthcoming).

[20] The general *piyyut* focuses on traditional Jewish content and has a clear liturgical role, thereby continuing a long tradition going back to the *piyyutim* of Yanai in the Land of Israel, but the personal *piyyut* inaugurated a new tradition under Arabic influence, creating a private, individual speaker and a finely-honed poetic form. Yehuda Halevi, as a major poet, apparently regarded such *piyyutim* as a challenge to his poetic virtuosity, but because of the problems noted above he made do with a single *piyyut* in this style. The problematics of Halevi's attitude to poetry are particularly striking in view of his unmatched artistry in using the poetic conventions of the period, and the fact of his having composed poems

addresses himself, or his soul, in an attempt to take the desired religious path. **The third category** consists of poems in which the speaker addresses "the other," that is, a person or persons representing society as a whole, and "responds" to the question of why he is taking so long to realize his religious goal. I suggest reading these poems as a poetic and aesthetic expression of a process that has its beginning in the poetic formation of Subject, its continuation in the speaker's own historical circumstances within a general history (that of the Jewish people in the Middle Ages in particular, and in Spanish culture in general), and its conclusion in the attempt, apparently successful, albeit short-lived, to realize his belief by immigrating to the Holy Land.

"I Believe": Constitution of the Subject as a Starting Point for Religious Faith

> If only I could be/ a slave to God who made me;
> Though others drive me away/ He always draws me near!...
> My heart within me yearns/ to have you draw it near,
> But all my cares just drive it/ further from you still...
> If I, within my youth/ am slow to bring you pleasure,
> What then in decline/ could I expect or hope for?...
> Incline my heart to offer/ in service of your kingdom...
> Redeem me once again/ and tell me: *Here I am.*[21]

---

in all the accepted genres. Schirmann eloquently describes the inner contradiction between Halevi's attitude to poetry in general and the conventions of Spanish poetry in particular: "His opinions on the subject of poetry are rather amazing ... already in a poem composed in his youth, Yehuda Halevi claimed that wisdom can be compared to a great sea, whereas poetry is nothing but the foam on the water's surface. To us, there seems to be an internal contradiction in this definition. Yehuda Halevi wrote more than a few poems with his very heart's blood, and the truth is that it is hard to believe he regarded his poems as mere trifles. Another contradiction, no less sharp, emerges as well in Halevi's attitude to Arabic forms in Hebrew poetry; forms that he himself handled with the most perfect mastery till the end of his days ... in defining the actions of Hebrew poets who scan their poems using Arabic meters, [Halevi] only grumbled against the use of foreign forms: "Behold," he says, "writing *piyyutim* gave us lots of room for maneuvering, since *piyyut* does not spoil the language." (Schirmann-Fleischer, *Toldot ha-shirah ha-'ivrit*, 443-444 [Hebrew].)

[21] Yehuda Y., in P. Cole, *The Dream of the Poem* (Princeton, NJ: Princeton University Press, 2007), 160-161.

In this poem the speaker addresses God, at first asking His assistance in general and then, toward the end of the poem, requesting God to "incline" his heart, with the poem ending in a plea for divine revelation itself. This poem therefore belongs to the first category suggested above, in which the speaker addresses God in order to draw closer to Him and realize his belief. But the speaker in this poem in fact makes a heartfelt confession of his weaknesses: sorrows that draw him away from God; the lack of strength to do what his belief tells him is right, and not only in temptation-filled youth but even in old age. At the end of the poem, the speaker even asks God to "purchase" or "acquire" him all over again, using the Hebrew word *qeniah*. The first such "purchase," according to Jefim Schirmann, consisted of the exodus from Egypt. This "wholesale" purchase, so to speak, does not satisfy the speaker, or at least does not stand the test of his subjective determination. This argument contradicts the claim repeatedly found in other poems (see, for example, the poem "My Thoughts Awaken Me," analyzed below); as well as the opening argument of the "Rabbi" in the *Kuzari*, which presents the exodus and the giving of the Torah as being both personal experience and the experience of the Jewish people as a whole. Hence it seems that the speaker's distress arises from his need to be "purchased" by God in a personal-subjective way, with an emphasis on divine revelation in the first person, heightened by the allusions to Abraham. The speaker beseeches God to appear before him, just as he appeared before Abraham, but this can also be interpreted as an expression of the speaker's need for a private revelation, Abraham's experience in the Binding of Isaac being the ultimate example of such revelation. But along with the allusion testifying to his readiness to make the supreme sacrifice, the speaker describes obstacles of a humbler kind, such as "sorrows" and growing turpitude of will. Thus the poem embodies the root of Halevi's belief: belief is a function of inner conviction in the Subject's soul, from whence his external actions spring. This inner conviction occurs not only at the cognitive level of the speaker's soul, but at all levels of the Subject's personality. The poem reflects a dialectical position of self-consciousness that, as will be shown, can be better understood with the help of Hegel's description of Subject-formation.

One of Hegel's most important innovations is his redefinition of the Absolute truth as resulting from the development of the "Subject."[22]

---

[22] "The truth is the whole. The whole, however, is merely the essential nature reaching its completeness through the process of *its own development*. Of the

Unlike Descartes, who identified the Subject with the thinking self-consciousness, or Kant, who defined it as the logical condition of experience, Hegel saw the Subject as the logical structure of both the personal and the general (the "Absolute Spirit"). Hence the Subject is not only substance, but also a dynamic entity, "a circle which presupposes its end and its purpose ... it becomes concrete and actual only by being carried out and by the end it involves."[23] Such development is concomitant with the negation of both the self and the "other."[24] We can see the beginning of the *Kuzari* as the formation of the Subject of the King of the Khazars, who begins by negating his own actions ("Thy way of thinking is indeed pleasing to God, but not thy way of acting") and from there goes on to negate the replies of the three "others": the philosopher, the Christian, and the Muslim.[25] But the *Kuzari* is mainly interested in presenting the rabbi's concept of belief, which can be seen as the personal position of Judah Halevi himself.

Absolute it must be said that *it is essentially a result* that only at the end is it what it is in very truth, and just in that *consists its nature, which is to be actual, subject*, or self-becoming, self-development" (Hegel, *Phenomenology of Mind*, 11, emphasis mine).

[23] Hegel, *Phenomenology of Mind*, 10. Hegel described the course by which consciousness rises to the stage of constituting the Phenomenology of Mind as "Concrete substantiality implicates and involves the universal or the immediacy of knowledge itself, as well as that immediacy which is being" (ibid., 9).

[24] "The living substance ... is that being which is truly subject, or, what is the same thing, is truly realized and actual (wirklich) solely in the process of positing itself, or in mediating with its own self its transitions from one state or position to the opposite. As subject it is pure and simple negativity ... True reality is merely this process of reinstating self-identity, of reflecting into its own self in and from its other, and is not an original and primal unity as such, not an immediate unity as such" (Hegel, *Phenomenology of Mind*, 10).

[25] The process of self-negation ostensibly begins with revelation, but it seems that "revelation" can be understood as an internal experience that is caused, to use Hegel's terminology, by the desire in relation to an "Other," and not necessarily a revelation of a concrete kind. In the framework of Subject-formation in Hegel, the Subject forms its personal world beginning "from the standpoint of the non-philosophical individual—certainty of the senses, of perception, of the sexual urge, of the familiar world—and is meant to rise with it, step after step, stage after stage, to Absolute Knowledge. The development, in this respect, is the development of a personal, subjective consciousness whose dialectical contradictions wake up inside of it and become its personal problem; while it itself is pushed forward, beyond them (Y. Yovel introduction in *Haqdamah la-fenomenologia shel ha-ruah, tirgum u-vi-ur* [Jerusalem: Magnes, 2001], 13-46 [Hebrew]).

If we examine the starting point of the Rabbi's words in the *Kuzari*, we find that it simply indicates the "I" as the initial source of religious certainty, and only afterwards presents its historical anchorage and reinforcement. In contrast to Maimonides' general starting point in his introduction to *Sefer Mada*, the Rabbi chooses to justify his belief as a matter of individual choice; one that is historically justified, to be sure, but empirical in nature and not based on fact.[26] From this point forward in the *Kuzari*, the rabbi gives two parallel arguments on the rhetorical plane: the general, universal level, and the personal, individual level. Sometimes there is a conflict between the two levels, and sometimes they run on parallel tracks, but the more important of the two levels—the one from which belief finally emerges—is that of the personal, as the poems considered in this article all show. On the personal level, the rabbi, the paradigmatic believer, deals with internal and external factors challenging his philosophical system, but in dealing with them he also creates his consciousness. Here, the dialogic framework helps to move the process forward, since the questions of the Khazar King represent the same factors, internal and external, with which the rabbi himself must contend. Hegel's description of Subject-formation may also throw light on the genesis of the believer's self-consciousness in the *Kuzari*.

The first stage in the Hegelian process is the constitution of Subject, in whose framework self-consciousness is created as a basis for consciousness of every kind. Self-consciousness must recognize itself in relation to three major factors: nature, other self-consciousnesses, and the context of collective life, such as a state or society. The "result" which Hegel hoped to achieve was that self-consciousness would be perceived only when certainty in relation to reality had been reached, including self-certainty. The first stage of self-certainty, in relation to nature, is embodied by desire, instinct, impulses, and so on. This is the non-mediating stage of the self-consciousness, the earliest and most direct. It is less satisfying and complete than the other stages, but at the same time, it shows the way to the next stage—the stage of self-consciousness in relation to other consciousnesses.[27] Reaching self-consciousness is ac-

---

[26] "The basic principle of all basic principles and the pillar of all sciences is to realize that there is a First Being who brought every existing thing into being." Maimonides, *Mishneh Torah* (Jerusalem: Boys Town Jerusalem Pub., 1962), ch. 1, sec. 1.

[27] For an explication of the goal of self-formation in the *Phenomenology of the Spirit*, see Baillie's introduction to Hegel (Hegel, *Phenomenology of Mind*, 98-104).

complished through becoming aware of other consciousnesses, so that in contrast to the Kantian position, the formation of self-consciousness is contingent. Hegel rejects the notion of the Platonic and Romantic "ideal form" and describes the process of Subject-formation as a process that begins in relation to an Object, recognizes its dissatisfaction with it, and hence feels the need to examine the formation of consciousness in relation to another Subject. At this point, another fundamental idea of Hegel finds expression, and that is "negation," meaning the negation of the given situation that pushes the Subject forward and causes it to burst through its partial and unmediated identity. The first stage in being a Subject is therefore to become a negating force in relation to one's self and others, with the movement of negation and affirmation repeating itself in unending motion, from the Subject's point of view. It may, to be sure, come to a momentary rest, but not to a lasting one, since the substance of the Subject's essence contains the negating force.

At the end of the process the self-identity of the spirit, which has the character of a Subject, is formed through division and opposition. And the Subject itself is formed through the general spirit. However, this same negating force is not derived only from the Subject itself in relation to itself and others, for there are other forces abroad in the world that act in their own right and impact the Subject. For example, the socio-cultural system in which the Subject lives exerts its power both openly and in more subtle ways, and influences the formation of the self-consciousness.[28]

---

[28] The process of self-consciousness constitution does not end with the triumph of one force on another, but continues in a never-ending process of repeated negation. At this juncture it is worth noting an important point in Hegel's dialectical process, derived from the idea of sublation: the force or the negated essence does not disappear; remainders of it are preserved and become a part of the consciousness. In this way, the triumph of one force does not mean that the other force is abolished but rather that memory is "rescued" and internalized inside the stronger force. Hegel compared this to the bud of a flower: it changes form and ostensibly becomes unidentifiable with its source, yet is nevertheless preserved in some fashion. The guiding principle of Hegel's position is that the spirit advances teleologically, and this development is circular and terminal at one and the same time (i.e., returning at the end of the process to its point of departure), as it realizes its self-principle and identifies itself as a self-consciousness.

This description may help to clarify the dialectic in Halevi's disposition of belief; in particular that which is openly represented in his poems, but also that which comes more obliquely in the *Kuzari*. The speaker in the poems deals with the three factors listed by Hegel: the natural impulses of his personality, other consciousnesses (as embodied by other speakers, as well as metaphorical figures such as the spirit and the soul), and also with social and historical circumstances. Ranged against all these is a clear confidence in the rightness of a belief based on the personal experience of having spoken with God, and on the personal identification with formative events in Jewish historical memory, such as the Giving of the Torah and the Exodus from Egypt. And here it is worth emphasizing an important way in which the poetry differs from the *Kuzari*. Halevi's poetry focuses on the creation of the speaker's subjective disposition of belief as a Jew, whereas the *Kuzari* describes a universal position in whose framework the individual (such as the rabbi or the king) forges his belief. Hence we can say that in the poetry, more room is given to the characteristics of the individual-spiritual position, whereas the *Kuzari* creates an historical position of first importance.

Servants of Time and "A Servant of God:" Personal versus General History

> Philosophy is identical with the spirit of the age in which it appears; It does not rise above its time.... Neither does an individual transcend his time; He is a son of it; Its substance is his own essence, and he only manifests it in a particular form.
>
> —Hegel, *Introduction to the Lectures on the History of Philosophy*[29]

> Servants of time are servants of servants;
> Only God's Servant alone is free.
> That is why when for his portion everyone prays,
> My heart, it says: God Himself, my portion may he be![30]

---

[29] Hegel, *Introduction to the Lectures*, 111-112
[30] Barbara A. Galli, *Franz Rosenzweig and Jehuda Halevi: Translating, Translations, Translators* (Montreal: McGill-Queen's University Press, 1995), 88.

> My thoughts awaken me with Thy name
> And set Thy mercies before me
> They teach me of the soul Thou hast formed,
> Bound up within me; - it is wonderful in mine eyes!
> And my heart seeth Thee and hath faith in Thee
> As though it had stood by at Sinai.
> —Rabbi Judah Halevi, "Servants of Time"[31]

The poem "Servants of Time" ostensibly expresses Judah Halevi's theological basis: true freedom is only given to those who free themselves from all temporal considerations and devote their lives to God's service. With wonderful conciseness, this short poem contains the essence of Halevi's religious disposition: considerations of the here-and-now mean bondage; belief in God means freedom. In effect, what we have here is an indirect but highly significant statement regarding belief, namely that man's main goal is to be free, and that God's service, or, more precisely, servitude to God, is the only way to achieve it. Inverting the meaning of the root עב״ד (abd) could of course be explained away as a literary device, but we may also suggest that the poem offers a ratiocination of Halevi's religious paradox: man is reluctant or unwilling to serve God since this is tantamount to "servitude." In contrast to the portrayal of longing and desire, here is a more realistic description of the path of belief, whose meaning is synonymous with the "yoke of commandments." The commandments are first and foremost an encumbrance, and hence it is understandable that man naturally prefers to be a servant to the worldly vanities that are so much more pleasurable, at least in the more immediate sense. This natural inclination causes a sinking into a turpitude from which the speaker is aroused, as in the second poem quoted above. The speaker is in need of an external factor to wake him up, to show him its loving-kindness, and to cause his heart to believe in, and feel part of, a general historical experience. The historical link thus removes the speaker from his private, temporal world and connects him to the shared historical memory, and to belief.

Halevi deals with history in three ways in his writings: the first is to discuss the condition of the Jews in Spain and in his own period, the twelfth century, as a whole. The second way is to interpret history as a

---

[31] Yehuda Halevi, Brody edition, 1946, 138. These lines are part of a longer religious poem, of a kind known as *"reshut."*

teleological process due to end in universal recognition of the Kingdom of God by all the peoples of the world. The third way is the biographical story that oscillates between the two paths described above. On one hand, Halevi dealt with the degradation of Jewish existence and its deterioration in his own lifetime in the wake of the Christian conquest of Spain; on the other, he dealt with his own sense of commitment towards Jewish culture and religious belief.[32] These introductory remarks are important in describing the disposition of belief in Halevi's writings, since they not only lay the foundations for his system as a whole, but also expose the root of its complexity: a position based on three parallel historical trends (biographical, national, and general) necessarily contains two characteristics of the Subject according to Hegel, and these are the development in relation to an "other" through repeated negation, and progress towards the realization of historical destiny. On this issue, it may be interesting to read Halevi's poetry in parallel with his philosophical writings, to see how the spiritual and emotional nuances arising from such a reading help illuminate the complexity of the belief founded on these three planes.[33]

The subtitle of the *Kuzari* itself bears witness to the main goal of the book: "The Book of Refutations and Proofs of the Despised Faith by

---

[32] A significant example of Halevi's historical consciousness vis-à-vis his commitment to Jewish culture can be seen in his attitude towards Arabic poetry. On the first plane described above, Halevi regarded the use of Arabic conventions in Hebrew poetry as worthless imitation, expressive of cultural decline and inimical to the rules of the Hebrew language: "I see, however, that you Jews long for a prosody, in imitation of other peoples, in order to force the Hebrew language into their meters" (Halevi, *The Kuzari*, part 2, sec. 73). However, the great majority of his poems were composed in the most complete and perfect harmony with Arabic conventions. Halevi had a mastery of written Arabic, in addition of course, to Hebrew, but his uniqueness lies primarily in his success in expressing his personal position, and in creating an impressive variety of original idioms in Hebrew—while preserving the poetic Arabic conventions. The poems quoted throughout this article all exhibit this verbal and cultural complexity.

[33] Y. Silman, *Bein filosof le-navi* (Ramat Gan: Bar-Ilan University, 1985), 124-129 (Hebrew), emphasized the gaps in Halevi's theological attitude resulting from his historical awareness. Silman pinpointed several contradictions between religious ideals and certain needs deriving from the historical conditions while the most striking contradiction is the avoidance of immigration to the Land of Israel.

Judah Halevi." Here already we see a major component in Halevi's concept of belief, one that will inform the dialogue over the course of the entire book: the believer has a collective responsibility and obligation to justify the religious path in which he believes.[34] This might be interpreted as undermining the value of the individual Subject, but it can also be interpreted from another perspective, from which it appears that the individual cannot be satisfied with a belief that only serves his personal needs, since his personal belief is based on a collective historical consciousness and when this collective is imperiled, it directly impacts his own personal condition. If the opening of the book reflects the individual's responsibility toward religion in a time of imperiled existence, the reason for this responsibility becomes abundantly clear at the beginning of the rabbi's speech: individual belief is based on personal experience and inner conviction of the reality of historical consciousness: "I believe in the God of Abraham, Isaac and Israel, who led the children of Israel out of Egypt with signs and miracles ... who sent Moses with his law ... our belief is comprised in the Torah—a very large domain."[35] The rabbi begins by positing a subjective and empirical starting point, devoid of rationalizations, and, most important of all, based on the historical narrative of a specific group. At this stage the narrative does not have a universal dimension; indeed the reverse is true, for it stresses God's commitment to the Jewish people alone, and the belief of the Jewish people in the Law sent "to it" by "its prophet," Moses. This rhetoric, so rich in possessive inflections, reinforces the subjectivity of the belief, especially if we compare it with the rhetoric employed by Maimonides in portraying the basis of belief:

> All existing things, whether celestial, terrestrial, or belonging to an intermediate class, exist only through His true Existence. If it could be supposed that all other beings were non-existent, He alone would still exist.... For all beings are in need of Him; But He, blessed be He, is not in need of them nor of any of them.[36]

---

[34] In this matter the *Kuzari* reflects a popular genre in twelfth- and thirteenth-century Spain, namely the inter-faith disputation, in both verbal and written form. The most famous disputation is of course that in which Nahmanides took part in Barcelona in 1263.
[35] Halevi, *Kuzari*, part I, sec. 11.
[36] Maimonides, *Mishneh Torah*, ch. 1, sec. 1-2.

Maimonides chose to begin his great legal work, which is ostensibly addressed to believing Jews alone, with a universal, timeless starting point, with no connection to history and a given people, or to criteria of human experience and understanding.[37] David Hartman represents the approaches of Maimonides and Halevi as being dichotomous, in the sense that Maimonides bases belief on a universal, a-historical reality as the source of certainty, without any need of divine revelation or redemption to prove the existence of God.[38] In contrast, Halevi bases belief on "the life of the Jewish people in history" and emphasizes, moreover, that "the history of the Jewish people is that which allows human beings access to the Divine Influence. The reality of the living God is proved by His deeds during the Exodus from Egypt, and by the miracles that He openly performed in the desert."[39] Such a representation of dichotomies would seem to preclude any possibility of an intellectual understanding of history as a basis for belief, and Hartman stresses this point further: "According to Halevi, adherence to God cannot be understood by means of human intellect, 'since in the worship of God there is no room for conjectures or rational deductions or logical considerations.'"[40] But interpreting Halevi this way runs into difficulty already at the beginning

---

[37] In view of the significant difference between the starting points of belief in Maimonides and Halevi, it is important to note that both of them stated in the most unequivocal fashion that there could be no contradiction between the intellect and the Torah. Thus the rabbi claims in the *Kuzari*: "Heaven forbid that there should be anything in the Bible to contradict that which is manifest or proved!" (Halevi, *The Kuzari*, part I, sec. 67). Maimonides devotes the beginning of his *Guide of the Perplexed* to an explanation of possible reasons for contradictions between the words of the Torah and the intellect, and takes upon himself the task of resolving them all (ibid., p. 4).

[38] Hartman, *Moreshet be-mahloqet*, 41.

[39] Ibid., 42.

[40] Ibid., 43-44. Hartman subsequently quotes the "parable of the medicines" as proof that in serving God, there is no place for subjective thinking but only for action consonant with the directions given by revelation. But this parable in fact illustrates the universal intellect in the rabbi's rhetoric, since in every society people turn to the person possessing the relevant knowledge in order to solve problems in a given field. The parable of the medicines ostensibly places the physician on a parallel with God, and his medical knowledge on a parallel with revelation, but the parable can also be seen as reinforcing the ability of the person possessing knowledge to prescribe a path for others.

of the *Kuzari*, since the King did, in fact, experience a divine revelation, even if this revelation did not include being shown the desired practical path. On the contrary: the revelation not only failed to "reveal" the correct path to the King, but it put the task of finding it on his own powers of intellect.[41] Moreover, Halevi's criticism of "rabbis" who refrain from innovating with tradition and who "look for a fortress where they can entrench themselves" can be seen as criticizing slothful thinking and lack of creativity, and not as encouragement to adhere to the safe and narrow path when serving God.[42] We must, therefore, consider the rhetorical complexity of the book: on one hand, it begins with a clearly defined quest that gives personal responsibility to the King of Khazar himself. On the other hand, the rabbi seems to give consistently clear and decisive replies to questions relating to the basic principles of Jewish belief. This complexity reaches its climax in defining "the root of belief" as "the root of unbelief."

> Al Khazari: How is the root of belief also the root of unbelief?
> The Rabbi: These conditions which render man fit to receive this divine influence do not lie within him. It is impossible for him to gauge their quantity or quality, and even if their essence were known yet neither their time, place and connexion, nor suitability could be discovered. For this, inspired and detailed instruction is necessary.[43] He who has been thus inspired, and obeys the teach-

---

[41] Silman interpreted the unexplained dream as one circumstantial component among others in the king's life, driving him to search for the suitable religious way for him. Silman concludes that Halevi presented a humanistic attitude in which circumstances, form of life, and historical horizons play an important role in determining one's self-fulfillment (Silman, *Bein filosof le-navi*, 236-238).

[42] Yehuda Halevi, the *Kuzari*, chap. 3, sec. 37. Hartman sees Halevi's criticism of the "Rabbanites" as the rabbi's legitimizing the "luxury of obeying the commandments in perfect tranquility" (Hartman, *Moreshet be-mahloqet* 52), but it seems that in the same way, it could also be interpreted as sharp criticism.

[43] "The Rabbi: I told thee that there is no comparison to be made between our intelligence and the Divine Influence, and it is proper that we leave the cause of these important things unexamined" (*The Kuzari*, chap. 2, sec. 60); "Do not believe him who considers himself wise in thinking that he is so far advanced that he is able to grasp all metaphysical problems with the abstract intellect alone, without the support of anything that can be received or seen, such as words, writing, or any visible or imaginary forms" (*The Kuzari*, chap. 4, sec. 5). We can see in these words the Kantian position on the intellect as

ing in every respect with a pure mind, is a believer. Whosoever strives by speculation and deduction to prepare the conditions for the reception of this inspiration, or by divining, as is found in the writing of astrologers, trying to call down supernatural beings, or manufacturing talismans, such a man is an unbeliever[44]

The root of belief and apostasy is one and the same according to Halevi, and this definition bears a striking resemblance to Hegel, who, as we saw above, attributed the schisms of the human spirit to a single origin. Both kinds of people described by Halevi strive "to receive Divine Inspiration [*ha-'inyan ha-elohi*]," and this is their common origin. But while the former recognizes the limits of his intellect and receives Divine Inspiration, the latter strives to attain it through human means and intelligence. Going about things in this way ultimately leads to aspostasy, since human beings do not have the power to bridge the gap between

---

well as the origin of Hegel's criticism of it. Kant began his *Critique of Pure Reason* with the pronouncement that "Experience is without doubt the first product that understanding brings forth as it works on the raw material of sensible sensations" (E. Kant, *Critique of Pure Reason*, eds. & trans. P. Guyer & A. Wood [Cambridge: Cambridge University Press, 1998], 127). But subsequently, he describes the epistemological process of the intellect as based on objective and transcendental components. It is one thing to indicate the existence of "a thing-in-itself," and another to describe human recognition as being based, from the start, on absolute notions; and the tension between them created the two different branches in a sweeping criticism of Kant's system. One branch is that of Hegel, who developed the trend of thought that regards human recognition as working teleologically towards realization in the framework of the "Absolute Spirit"; the other branch is that of the analytical trend, which is based on realistic, empirical experience. Halevi's words represent the Hegelian branch, according to which the human spirit is drawn to divine wisdom, and may, with the help of its guidance (and not by relying on human intellect alone), reach it in the end. Another point of resemblance is that man requires every plane of his recognition and experience in order to reach divine wisdom. In Kant, to be sure, the intellect includes various planes of life (e.g., recognition, morality, and aesthetic judgment), but the experiential-subjective aspect is minimized and pushed to the margins. Hegel carries this aspect into the center of his discussion, and Halevi, in the framework of his debate with Mutazilite rationalism *á la* Saadiah Gaon, also brings the subjective-individual experience into the center of his own philosophical discussion.

[44] Yehuda Halevi, the *Kuzari*, chap. 1, sec. 79.

the Subject and divine knowledge. Hegel formulates his claim as a major principle in the way that the Subject forms its self-consciousness: according to Hegel, the self-consciousness cannot take form by itself but must relate to something that is external to it; to another consciousness. Of course, in Hegel the process begins with an inner longing for the "other" and is not the result of an external factor that awakens the self-consciousness, and here we ostensibly find a difference in the way the process is described in the *Kuzari*. Yet it should be noted that the process in the *Kuzari* begins with revelation, and this can also be interpreted as a manifestation of inner longing.

Another interpretational approach is formulated by Shalom Rosenberg, according to which the path of intellect and the path of prophecy do not express two different paths to religious certainty. Instead, the path of knowledge is "limited" and does not lead to a total certainty of belief, whereas the path of prophecy is based on inner certainty and is therefore absolute.[45] History and prophecy, according to Rosenberg, are "a bridge to philosophy," and tradition is the historical proof of the truth of the Torah. Hence it is only natural for Rosenberg to end his discussion by showing the problematics which rise in particular from the position of the Jewish people during the period in which the *Kuzari* was written; and with an unavoidable conclusion concerning the problematics of the historical testimony in general. I would argue that the two approaches set forth above, both that which sees Halevi's concept of belief as being inimical to the intellect and that which sees tradition-based belief as a more advanced stage in the believer's path, are part of a wider position in the *Kuzari*, in which ostensible contradictions (nature/history; the Jewish people/other nations; body/soul/intellect) merge into a single whole.

Inspired by Hegel's concept of history, Halevi's disposition of belief can be seen as a disposition that is based on the certainty of teleology in general history, in whose framework the Jewish people exist, too. One can make a parallel between Halevi's "Divine Inspiration" and Hegel's "Absolute Spirit," and see in knowledge, as in a particular historical tradition, different branches in the historical spirit of mankind as a whole:

---

[45] S. Rosenberg, *Be-'iqvot ha-kuzari* (Jerusalem: Ma'aleh, 1991), 54-56 (Hebrew).

> God has a secret and wise design concerning us, which should be compared to the wisdom hidden in the seed which falls into the ground, where it undergoes an external transformation into earth, water and dirt, without leaving a trace for him who looks down upon it. It is, however, the seed itself which transforms earth and water into its own substance, carries it from one degree to another, until it refines the elements and transfers them into something like itself, casting off husks, leaves, etc. and allowing the pure core to appear, capable of bearing the Divine Influence. The original seed produced the tree bearing fruit resembling that from which it had been produced. In the same manner the Law of Moses transforms each one who honestly follows it, though it may externally repel him.... Then, if they acknowledge Him [the Messiah, D.L.], they will become one tree.[46]

This optimistic position, according to which the existence of the Jewish people in the diaspora can be explained using human logic, does not correspond to the difficulty that Halevi expressed regarding the historical reality or to his sense of deep commitment towards the community. Historian Isaac Baer based himself on Hegel's concept of the community in describing the Jewish community of the Middle Ages.[47] He illustrated the importance of the "community" by giving examples of the sacred

---

[46] Yehuda Halevi, the *Kuzari*, chap. 4, sec. 23. The similar quotation in Hegel: "The bud disappears when the blossom breaks through, and we might say that the former is refuted by the latter; in the same way when the fruit comes, the blossom may be explained to be false form of the plant's existence, for the fruit appears as its true nature in place of the blossom. These stages are not merely differentiated; they supplant one another as being incompatible with one another. But the ceaseless activity of their own inherent nature makes them at the same time moments of an organic unity, where they not merely do not contradict one another, but where one is as necessary as the other; and this equal necessity of all moments constitutes alone and thereby the life of the whole" (Hegel, *Phenomenology of Mind*, 2).

[47] Y. Baer, "Ha-yesodot va-ha-hathalot shel irgun ha-kehilah ha-yehudit bi-yemei ha-beinayim," in *Mehqarim u-masot be-toldot 'am yisrael* (Jerusalem: The Israeli Historical Society, 1986), 60-100 [originally published in *Zion* 15 (1950)] (Hebrew). A central trend in the application of Hegel's notion of dialectic comes in the description of the reciprocal dialectical relations between man and historical reality. Although Hegel described universal historical process and not a concrete one, Baer refers the reader to the Hegelian term *Gemmeinde* (p. 60, note 1) in distinguishing between the "community" and "society."

epithets often applied to it,[48] and claimed that the community was a "double" link, both between members of the local [Jewish] population and between the members of different Jewish communities.[49] The medieval Jewish community, in Halevi's period, is described by Baer as being exceptionally cohesive:

> The Jewish community now appears [i.e., in relation to two earlier periods in medieval times, D.L.] as a living organism uniting every member of the community in equality and in every branch of public life, both religious and "secular," insofar as there is room for making such divisions. This "holy community" ... united in self-defense and in martyrdom during persecutions ... was united in all other matters as well, both personal and public.... The community passed laws and promulgated ordinances in religious, political, administrative and economic matters, and exerted its authority by means of fines and excommunications ... the local community was granted the privileges of a virtual Sanhedrin."[50]

Basing himself on Baer's description, Menahem ben-Sasson describes the "sources of authority and the elements of social stratification."[51] The "Messianic idea," which occupies a central place in the poetry and thought of Judah Halevi, is described as being a major ideological element in the Jewish community of his period:

> The desire to live a Jewish life apart from other peoples and in conformity with Divine Law was bound up with a vision of the

---

[48] "The term 'holy community' hasn't been formed in the Middle Ages. It is already found in Antiquity, though not in the realm of official rabbinic literature ... there are grounds for thinking that already in the time of the Apostle Paul, Jews tended to describe their local community in terms of sanctity ... similar terms have been found in letters from the Cairo Geniza dating to the tenth and eleventh centuries." (Baer, "Ha-yesodot," 68).

[49] Baer exemplifies this with an inscription from a synagogue in Jericho, and argues that the inscription "expresses the metaphysical feeling of the local Jewish community, which united all the members of the place large and small, and linked the local community to the Jewish people as a whole." (Ibid., 69).

[50] Ibid., 88-89.

[51] M. Ben-Sasson, "Ha-hanhagah ha-'atzmit shel ha-yehudim bi-artzot ha-islam bi-me'ot ha-7 'ad ha-12," in: *Qahal yisrael: ha-shilton ha-'atzmi ha-yehudi bi-yemei ha-beinayim ve-ha-'et ha-hadashah ha-muqdemet*, ed. Avraham Grossman and Yosef Kaplan (Jerusalem: Zalman Shazar Institute, 2004), 11-55, esp. 17 (Hebrew).

> return of the Jewish people to normalcy: **a return to the Land of Israel**, with Jerusalem as its capital; to the Holy Temple standing proud in a central place; **to the worship of God in the manner He taught**, in the place He chose ... **the anomaly of Jewish life was perceived as being bound up with life in the Diaspora**. The Diaspora was not only the physical dispersion of the Jewish people but a spiritual, mental and religious condition. The Diaspora was perceived as being the expression of the people's rejection by God, as punishment for their failures. The continuing existence of the Diaspora testifies more than a hundred witnesses could do, that although the Jews are a Chosen People—they are now rejected by God, and it is incumbent upon them to find a way of appeasing God and fulfilling His precepts in order to rehabilitate their relations with Him. **Keeping the commandments is meant to rehabilitate these relations**.[52]

Ben-Sasson's words reflect the fact that Halevi's thought was integrally related to the "spirit of the times," expressing a common trend in matters of spirituality and faith.[53] The similarity between the ideological traits of the community noted by Ben-Sasson and the characteristics of Halevi's thought may help clarify the background of the poem "My Desire for the Living God," in which the speaker, through rhetorical means, finds his anxiety to reach the Holy Land urging him to take action:

> My desire for the living God hath constrained me
> To seek the place of the throne of mine anointed
> Even so that it hath not suffered me to kiss
> The children of my house, my friends, and my brethren;
> And that I weep not for the orchard which I planted
> And watered, and my green shoots that prospered;
> And that I remember not Jehuda and Azriel,
> My two beautiful choice flowers;
> And Issac, whom I counted as my child...
> And that I have all but forgotten the house of prayer
> In whose place of learning was my rest...
> And I have given my glory unto others,
> And forsaken my praise unto graven images...

---

[52] Ibid., 19-20. The emphasis is mine, and refers to the thematic layer of the poem "My Desire for the Living God."
[53] As phrased by Hegel, respectively (see remark 29 above).

And I have ceased to walk with my face bending to the ground
But I have set my paths in the heart of the seas—
To the end that I may find the footstool of my God,
And there pour out my soul with my thoughts,
And stand at the threshold of His holy mount and set open
Towards the doors of Heaven's gates, my doors....[54]

Many poems express the idea of longing for Zion, but only this poem represents it as a desire that acts on the speaker's soul exactly as *ta'avah* ("lust," or "desire") acts on his soul in the poem: "O Lord, before Thee is My Whole Desire;" that is, in ostensibly negative fashion.[55]

Just as *ta'avah* in the poem "O Lord, before Thee is My Whole Desire" caused the speaker to forget his service to God and his religion, in the poem "My Desire for the Living God," desire (*teshuqah*) for "the living God" causes him to forget the pleasures of the Jewish holidays and to be

---

[54] Yehuda Halevi, Brody edition, 1946, 226-27.

[55] O Lord, before Thee is my whole desire
/ Yea, though I cannot bring it to my lips...
When far from Thee, I die while yet in life
/ But if I cling to Thee I live, though I should die;
Only I know not how to come before Thee
/ Nor what should be my service nor my law...
My youth, until to-day, hath done its pleasure
/ But when shall I do good for mine own soul?
The world which Thou hast set within my heart
/ Hath held me back from seeking out mine end;
And how then shall I serve my Maker, while
/ A captive to my lust, a slave to my desire?;
What can I say? Temptation doth pursue me
/ As doth an enemy, from youth to age...

Halevi, *Selected Poems of Jehudah ha-Levi*, 87-89. The desire (*ta'avah*) in this poem "O Lord, before Thee is My Whole Desire" is the speaker's "Pandora's Box," harboring inside of it the factors that prevent him from serving God, to the point where he forgets "his service and his religion." The speaker "accuses" the "world" in his heart that keeps him from taking the desired path, in a synecdoche that alludes to Ecclesiastes 3: 11: "[God] has placed the world in their heart." Ibn Ezra comments here that "their heart" means a "desire for the world" (*ta'avat 'olam*), to use the language of the sages, and Halevi uses the verse in a similar meaning: desire for the world prevents him from seeking a worthy end. For a detailed analysis of the poem, see my article "The Dialectic Nature of Desire in Halevi's Poem: 'O Lord, before thee is My Whole Desire'" (forthcoming).

in such a rush that he does not even find time to give a parting kiss to his family, students, and friends. As in the poem analyzed above, here, too, desire becomes the "master" that enslaves or subordinates every facet of reality to a single idea. But by mentioning the "forgotten" things in the poem—the holidays, the house of prayer, a parting kiss—so that, indeed, most of the poem is devoted precisely to these details and not to a description of the overpowering desire, the poem creates a dialectical process here, too, in the following way: in the poem, desire is represented as a spiritual factor that dominates every aspect of the speaker's character and life, and focuses his entire being on one single goal: that of reaching the Holy Temple in Jerusalem. For this purpose the speaker adopts the language of hyperbole whose purpose is to emphasize the speaker's determination to reach Jerusalem. The language of hyperbole functions at the level of both content and literary device: the speaker does not have time to kiss his family and friends before setting out, does not have time to regret the parting from his students, almost forgets the House of Prayer, and does forget the pleasures of the Sabbath and holidays. The words testifying to the speaker's anxiety are emphasized by a triple negative ("hath not suffered me to kiss;" "I weep not;" "I remember not"), a triple mention of his students' names (Judah, Azrael, Isaac); a triple reference to the holy days ("my Sabbaths;" "my feast-days;" "my Passovers"), and of course an intensive use of the running end-rhyme (-ai) that creates internal rhyme in the opening, the transition, and the closing line. But the multiplicity of literary devices essentially deconstructs the plain meaning of the words: instead of convincing the reader of the speaker's urgency of purpose, the language of exaggeration creates a sense of self-contradiction and unreliability. The reader has no need of biographical information concerning Halevi in order to understand that the conflict between the desires of the body and the desire of the soul expresses, in fact, the discrepancy between the desire for religious realization and the desire to enjoy the pleasures of life in Spain. [56]

---

[56] A comparative analysis of different poems shows that in most cases, Yehuda Halevi uses the root א.ו.ה when speaking in a pejorative sense; it is ta'avah ("desire") that keeps him from doing the right thing (as in the poems: "Will Thou yet Pursue Youth or Zion," "Wilt Thou Not Ask"). This can be attributed to the fact that in the Bible, too, the root א.ו.ה is always used in negative contexts, whereas the root ח.ש.ק (also expressing lust or desire) is sometimes used in a favorable sense. The word תאוותי ("my desire") appears in this way once in the Bible, in Psalms

But there was another side to the community's power of influence, one that also had a considerable impact on Halevi's life and in this way created the dialectical process. This "other side" finds expression in the norms concerning Jewish involvement in Muslim culture:

> In the aristocratic courts of Muslim rulers and dignitaries, [Jews] who were associated with the ruling elite encountered a unique cultural, social and economic reality considerably different from that which was known in Jewish society, **and whose scale of values was different from that of Jewish society. Amongst the outer trappings of this reality were material splendor, the**

38:10 (though the context clearly refers to the sins of the Children of Israel regarding the קברות התאוה , that is, the "graves of desire" in Numbers 11:4-35). There the verb תאוה appears in Proverbs 21, in the context of evil: "The soul of the wicked desires [אותה] evil" (verse 10); and also "The desire [תאות] of the lazy man kills him; for his hands refuse to do labor; he covets greedily [התאוה תאוה] all the day long, but the righteous gives and spares not" (verses 25-26). The literal meaning of the verse shows that תאוה brings about death, with the Gaon of Vilna explaining that the desire of the wicked person is not satisfied, and that when he fails to obtain the object of his desire, his desire causes his death. The language of desire, תשוקה, appears only twice in the Bible, but in two highly important settings: the sin of the Tree of Knowledge, and the sin of Cain. One part of the woman's punishment is in becoming subservient to man: "and thy desire [תשוקתך] shall be to thy husband, and he shall rule over thee" (Genesis 3:16). It is interesting that, along with the explanations we might reasonably expect for the woman's desire, such as a strong wish or longing, or some such neutral word as found in *Da'at Mikra*, Saadiah Gaon explains תשוקה as "discipline and concern for making a livelihood" (ibid.). In the context of Cain, desire, תשוקה, appears in a negative way, in the sense of actually *wanting* to sin: "If thou doest well, shalt thou not be accepted? and if thou doest not well, sin crouches at the door, and to thee shall be his desire[תשוקתו]" (Genesis 4:7). In later rabbinic homilies the word תשוקה is synonymous with the word תאוה (for example, in *Pesiqta Zutra* on Genesis 3, from the eleventh-twelfth centuries). The verb חשק appears in the Bible in two primary meanings: (1) God's desire or חשק for the Children of Israel in the sense of election: "The Lord did not set his love [חשק] upon you, or choose you, because you were more in number than any people" (Deuteronomy 7: 7); "Only the Lord took delight [חשק] in thy fathers to love them, and he chose their seed" (Deuteronomy 10: 15); "Because he has set his delight [חשק] upon me, therefore will I deliver him" (Psalms 91: 14). (2) חשק in the sense of wanting or wishing. For example, in the contexts of Solomon's deeds (the expression "Solomon's desire," ואת חשק שלמה, appears three times in II Kings), as well as in Isaiah 21: 4: "the night of my pleasure [חשקי] has he turned into terror for me."

> **importation and cultivation of cultural values, a concern for the security of one's subjects and friends** [as described in lines 2-5 of Halevi's "My Desire for the Living God," D.L]. and a radical expression of the political and economic power ... in addition to involving them in events outside Jewish society, they gave rise to a new phenomenon in Jewish history; [certain circles] sought to imitate the life of the Muslim court in the Jewish setting, and to introduce Jewish content into their courts. These circles did so because **they acknowledged the prestige of some of the Muslim courtly values** ... [Ben-Sasson mentions the panegyrics and the use of poetic norms founded on Islamic culture as prominent examples of this, D.L.] ... Arab patronage and aesthetics therefore merged with the world of Torah, and this "merger" created a foundation of basic values in the life of Jewish society.[57]

The historical description reflects a complex ideational background, one that expresses the involvement of Jews in Muslim culture despite a particularist consciousness and a culture of their own, together with a willingness to imbibe from Muslim culture and take part in its life, out of an acknowledgment that certain principles in this culture were of value. But the historical description does not deal with the philosophical complexity or, more particularly, with the conflicts arising from this complexity in the realms of both praxis and consciousness.

To conclude the discussion of Halevi's personal history within the framework of the period's history in general, let us bring examples from a group of poems written by Halevi towards the end of his life, during his sojourn in Egypt. In the group of poems known as his "sea-poems," the speaker describes his fears in the most palpable way, and in order to cope with these fears he pictures to himself scenes of one kind or another showing the realization of his belief. At the same time, these poems underscore the clash between present sufferings and eternal faith, as an authentic reflection of the reality he portrays. In the poem "I Cry to God with a Melting Heart," the speaker describes the spiritual difficulties he faced while in a storm at sea, during one of his failed attempts to sail from Egypt to the Holy Land.[58] The enjambments in three of the poem's four lines emphasize his sense of helplessness and fear of the unknown. The speaker dwells on the terrors before him ("a melting

---

[57] Ben-Sasson "Ha-hanhagah ha-'atzmit," 54-55.
[58] For a detailed discussion of these attempts, see Yahalom "Ganzei Leningrad."

heart;" "knees that smite;" "anguish;" "astounded at the deep;" "find not their hands;" "am dancing and tossed about"), thereby showing that the problematics of immigration to Zion did not end with the decision to do so, but indeed continued to plague him, technically and spiritually, during the course of the journey itself:

> I cry to God with a melting heart and knees that smite together,
> While anguish is in all loins,
> On a day when the oarsmen are astounded at the deep,
> When even the pilots find not their hands,
> How shall I be otherwise, since I, on a ship's deck,
> Suspended between waters and heavens,
> Am dancing and tossed about?—But this is but a light thing,
> If I may but hold the festal dance in the midst of thee, O Jerusalem![59]

Along with the speaker's sense of terror in a reality where even the sailors, old hands at sea, are powerless to act, the speaker ends his poem by simulating his celebrations in Jerusalem in order to overcome his anxiety.

In another poem, the speaker uses the language of double metaphor in order to show the direct impact of reality (the storm at sea) on his soul, using the word "heart" as both a metaphor ("heart of the seas") and a metonym ("a quaking heart"). Here, the speaker adopts a different poetic technique in order to ward off his fears of the storm: by means of synecdoche he in effect separates his heart from his body so that, on the one hand, the heart still represents the turmoil in his soul, while, on the other, he can address it as though it were a separate entity, to persuade it to believe in the Lord's salvation, and that He who created the sea would be sure to subdue it now and keep it within limits. Keeping fear at bay through the language of metaphor is parallel to the therapeutic effect inherent in the act of writing the poem itself:

> I tell the heart in the heart of the seas
>   / as the pounding waves bring on its fear:
> If your faith is firm in the Lord who made
>   / the sea—whose name endures for eternity
> The deep won't frighten you with its swells
>   / for He who sets its bound is near![60]

---

[59] Yehuda Halevi, Brody edition, 1928, 29.
[60] Yehuda Halevi, Cole edition, 2007, 168.

To conclude the discussion of Halevi's biography within the historical framework of his period, we can clearly see his writings as a vibrant reflection of the "spirit of the times," his attitudes to messianism and the Holy Land included. But even more striking is the uniqueness of Judah Halevi as an "individual poet." The speaker in the poems seen here is unwaveringly faithful to his ideal belief, keeping it constantly before his eyes even when it clashes with his life in the present, and resolving to realize his belief as fully as possible in spite of the difficulties in his path, technical and spiritual. It is important to stress that the speaker does not for a single moment allow doubt to creep into his desire to realize his belief, or attempt to minimize it. The problematics and the schisms emerge time and again in different forms, but they are unable to undermine Halevi's belief, both as a poet and individual (as we learn from his biography), that, as a Jew, his belief can only be realized by reaching Jerusalem. But in light of the fact that he realizes his belief only at the end of his life, we must raise the possibility that we have before us a model in which belief is founded on "unfulfilled desire," in the spirit of Hegel's unhappy consciousness, and in the spirit of the modern believer as portrayed in the writings of R Joseph B. Soloveitchik.

"My Desire for the Living God": The Motif of Belief as Unfulfilled Desire

Belief as unfulfilled desire is one of the most frequent motifs in the religious and secular poetry of Judah Halevi. The discrepancy between the will and the way, or between desire and fulfillment, was a common motif in various genres of poetry in Moslem Spain, especially in love poems, wine poems, and gnostic poetry. But Halevi used this motif to create a vehicle that was unique, thematically and linguistically, for the Hebrew language and for Jewish history.[61] One potential reply to the paradox of objecting to poetic conventions while at the same time using them himself can be found in looking at the dialectical reality in which Halevi lived.

---

[61] Ann Brener shows how Yehuda Halevi wove motifs of Arabic poetry into wine and love poems, along with biblical verses and references to Jewish history. See A. Brener, *Judah Halevi and his Circle of Hebrew Poets in Granada* (Leiden: Brill, 2005), 73-91. This article focuses on Halevi's religious poems and the *Kuzari*, since space does not permit us to exemplify this motif in the secular poetry as well.

On one hand, he was well-entrenched in the culture of his period and highly influential in both Jewish and Muslim public life.[62] On the other hand, his thought and poetry accord a central role to particularist ideas, such as the uniqueness of the Jewish people and the Hebrew language, and the personal mission of the individual believer. As demonstrated at the beginning of this chapter, the poems portraying belief as unfulfilled desired can be classified as poems designated for three different interlocutors: God, the speaker himself (or his soul or spirit), and another person or persons. Below we shall illustrate each of these categories.

Amongst Halevi's religious poems are poems in which the speaker addresses God and reproaches Him for "hiding His face" from the Jewish people, and for the plight of the Jewish people under foreign rule. The speaker adopts a language of metaphor inspired by the Song of Songs in which God is the "lover" and the Jewish people are the female, whence comes the justification for complaining that the Lord has abandoned His people.

> My love, hast Thou forgotten Thy resting between my breasts?
> And wherefore hast Thou sold me for ever to them that enslave me?
> Have I not followed Thee of old through a land not sown?
> Lo, Seir and Mount Paran and Sinai and Sin are my witnesses!
> And my love was Thine, and Thy favour upon me,
> And how now hast Thou apportioned my glory away from me?[63]

This poem shows a problematics of faith in sharp contrast to the kind of justification offered in the *Kuzari* for the plight of the Jewish people in the diaspora, as we saw earlier. If we take poems of this kind and compare them with the *Kuzari*'s justification of the course of history, these religious poems can be seen as an expression of the "unhappy consciousness," for they represent a position of unwilling alienation from the

---

[62] "Yehuda Halevi—perhaps more than other poets—was a highly popular and renowned public figure, and due to his easy-going personality he also had no inhibitions about writing, even in an unfamiliar social setting." (Yahalom, "Ganzei leningrad," 79). On the subject of verifying Halevi's status in Spain in light of the Geniza documents, see Goitein, "Ha-bibliografiah shel yehuda halevi Le'or Hagniza," in *Yehuda Halevi: Selected Aricles*, ed. Chaya Swartz (Jerusalem: Ministry of Education, 1978), 57-71 (Hebrew).

[63] Yehuda Halevi, *Selected Poems*, 1946, 96.

Absolute Spirit and this engenders a temporary sense of desperation. Unlike the *Kuzari's* justification of a teleological course in history, the religious poetry exhibits a disposition of belief that neither identifies with the course of history nor pretends to understand it. Jefim Schirmann and Ezra Fleischer both emphasize Halevi's sense of personal identification with the sufferings of his people in the wake of the Reconquista, and suggest that it is more conspicuous in Halevi than in other poets of the period, apparently because of his central role in society.[64] The inability to fulfill the desires of belief in poems of this kind derive from the distance between the believer and God.

In the second kind of poem, the non-realization of belief derives from the speaker's soul, or, in our own language, from the clash between worldly desires and the demands of faith. The speaker addresses his soul, captive in the pleasures of youth whose time has long passed:

> Long in the lap of childhood didst thou sleep,
> Think how thy youth like chaff did disappear;
> Shall life's sweet Spring forever last? Look up,
> Old age approaches ominously near…
> Soar upward, seek redemption from thy guilt
> And from the earthly dross that round thee clings.
> Draw near to God, His holy angels know,
>   For whom His bounteous streams of mercy flow[65]

Personifying the soul makes it possible to relate to it as a separate entity and to adopt, over and over, the language of command in order bring home the need to act according to the desired path of belief. In the poem, two obstacles in serving God join forces: personal problematics ("thy guilt") and the pitfalls of time ("old age"). Dealing with these obstacles does not testify to any obscurity in the path of belief or doubts about the subject itself, but rather to the incompatibility between ideal belief and the speaker's heart, or in other words, to the clash between two kinds of desire: the desire of the speaker as a private individual, and his desire as a believing Jew.

The poem "I Run Towards the Fountain of True Life" does not, to be sure, show the speaker directly addressing his soul, but in effect it pins

---

[64] Schirmann—Fleischer, *Toldot ha-shirah ha-'ivrit*, 443-444.
[65] Yehuda Halevi, Lazarus edition, 1888.

the non-realization of belief on the difficulty of internalizing belief, so that the epistemological level corresponds with emotional identification ("within my heart"). The speaker certainly recognizes "the fountain of true life" but at the stage of writing the poem he is still captive to a life that is "false and empty," which the poem encourages him to abandon.

> I run towards the fountain of true life
> / and loathe the false and empty
> My one concern is to see my Sovereign
> / he whom I fear; if only to see
> Him in my dream, I'd sleep an eternity
> / and never wake. If I could only behold
> His face within my heart, my eyes
> / would no longer seek to gaze abroad[66]

The speaker contends that if he is granted a personal revelation he will be satisfied with this and prepared to renounce worldly pleasures for the sake of eternal sleep ("if only to see Him in my dream / I'd sleep an eternity"). This bit of hyperbole is of course the opposite of the rabbi's position in the *Kuzari*, according to which the individual feels the revelation at Mount Sinai as though he himself had been there. We could, perhaps, attribute the poem's hyperbole to the language of exaggeration common to poetry in Moslem Spain, but it can also be interpreted as a discrepancy between the affinity to historical memory and the need for personal revelation.

A last example of poems expressing the dialectic of belief is a group of poems addressing external "hecklers," as it were, or people who try to dissuade the speaker from carrying out his resolve. This group reflects public criticism towards Halevi and, no less than that, his sense of obligation to answer such criticism. Unlike the personal poems in which the speaker "beats his breast," so to speak, the following poem reveals an intriguing factor that does not find expression in poems from the first two categories: the condition of the Holy Land in his day. In view of its present sorry state, the interlocutor thinks that Halevi should not immigrate.[67] The Arabic rubric to the poem notes that it is

---

[66] Yehuda Halevi, Levin edition, 2002, 81.
[67] In contrast to this, Yahalom, "Ganzei leningrad," showed evidence from the Geniza that during Halevi's sojourn in Egypt, which lasted about a year, people began criticizing his delay in immigrating to the Holy Land.

"the poet's reply to a person who wrote him, rebuking his desire to go to the Holy Land":

> Thy words are compounded of sweet-smelling myrrh
> And gathered from the rock of the mountains of spice...
> Thou comest to meet me with sweet speeches,
> But within them lie men in wait bearing swords—
> Words wherein stinging bees lurk
> A honeycomb prickly with thorns.
> If the peace of Jerusalem is not to be sought
> While yet with the blind and the halt she is filled[68]

The speaker expresses his appreciation for his addressee's words, notwithstanding the fact that, in addition to being true, they are as sharp as a bee's sting. The speaker bridles at the request not to ask after the "peace of Jerusalem," since Jerusalem is in ruins and over-run with "the blind and the halting," though at the same time he acknowledges the truth of these claims. To conclude this section, Halevi's poems can be seen as demonstrating a diverse means of coping with the problems involved in realizing his belief: beginning with a sense of being far from God due to the plight of the Jewish people in his own period of history; continuing with the personal obstacles of not having experienced his own personal revelation and the lingering desires of youth; and culminating in the technical problems involved in the journey and the sorry plight of Jerusalem. Despite all this, this episode in Halevi's life and poetry ends in his realizing his belief by making the decision to immigrate to the Land of Israel, and apparently in accomplishing his goal, too.

Judah Halevi as a "Prisoner of Desire": The Journey to the Holy Land

> Zion, won't you ask after your captives
>   / who seek your welfare, remnant of your flock?
> From west to east, north and south, peace
>   / from the far and the near, from all sides accept
> Greetings from desire's captive who offer tears like the dew
>   / of Hermon, and longs for them to streak your slopes.

---

[68] Yehuda Halevi, Brody edition, 1928, 14.

> I howl like a jackal at your afflictions, but dreaming
> / the return of your captivity I'm a lute for your songs[69]

"Zion, Will You Not Ask" is one of the most beautiful and best-known poems expressing the desire for Zion in Hebrew poetry of all time, and makes an appropriate starting point from which to conclude our discussion of Halevi's disposition of belief, which culminates in his immigration to the Holy Land.[70] This poem has become the classic expression of the yearning to reach the Holy Land and the sense of being a "prisoner" in the diaspora, as well as the speaker's answer (albeit temporary) to his dilemma, by making himself a "lute for your songs," or, in other words, into a medium for expressing the unfulfilled yearnings of a "prisoner of desire." The "imprisonment" of course has a double meaning: actual imprisonment in the sense of being chained to a concrete reality that prevents the speaker from immigrating to the Holy Land; and the imprisonment of the soul to its desire to reach the Holy Land and to dream about the "return of your captivity."[71]

It was only towards the end of his life, with the development of a palpable anxiety and the certainty of approaching death, that the speaker decided to "extricate" himself from the conflict and to determine his course in what he perceives as being the "metaphysics of the Absolute." Another and final expression in this article to the gap between epistemological belief and the speaker's desire is found in a poem composed by Halevi towards the end of his life, in which we find a clear sense of

---

[69] Yehuda Halevi, Levin edition, 2002, 100.

[70] The category of "poems of desire for Zion" was devised by Chaim Schirmann in *Ha-shirah ha-ʿivrit*. The poem became one of the laments for the Ninth of Av in the Ashkenazi rite, and was translated more than sixty times into various languages (Schirmann, *Ha-shirah ha-ʿivrit*, 485).

[71] It is important to note that Halevi made a change in the verse that he quotes from Zechariah: "Return to the stronghold, you prisoners of hope; even today will I restore to thee a double portion" (ibid., 9:12). Whereas the prophet Zechariah describes the End of Days and called to those who hope to return to Zion since they will have a leader there, Halevi reverses the meaning in order to describe the permanence of the Diaspora, a "prison" that prevents people from immigrating to the Holy Land and keeps them virtually "prisoners of desire." In other words, Zechariah's "prisoners of hope" (*asirei tiqvah*) become Halevi's "prisoner of desire" (*asir taʾavah*). The surrender to *taʾavah*, "desire," is a recurring motif of Halevi, as we have already seen.

guilt over the difficulty of renouncing worldly desires in favor of realizing his belief:[72]

> Wilt thou yet pursue youth after twoscore years and ten
> / since thy days are equipped for flight?
> And wilt thou flee from the service of God
> / and long for the service of men?...
> And art thou too slothful to take provision for thy way
> / and wilt thou sell thy portion for a mess of pottage?
> Saith not thy soul yet unto thee, "Enough,"
> / But reneweth her desire month by month?
> Incline from her counsel to the counsel of God
> / And turn aside from the five senses;
> And make thyself acceptable to thy Creator for the rest
> / Of thy days which press on and hasten;
> And seek not with a double heart for his favour
> / And go not to meet good omens...
> And let not Thine heart be shaken in the heart of the seas
> / When thou beholdest mountains move and totter.[73]

The poem presents a series of binary oppositions that graphically illustrate the speaker's conflict: youth versus approaching death; serving God versus serving people (running away from the ideal because of a yearning for human desires); divine guidance, as opposed to being led by the senses; the hope of salvation in exchange for a "mess of pottage." Another literary device is that of rhetorical questions through which the speaker emphasizes the obvious: the need to take the path of belief. Yet it is precisely this which heightens our sense of puzzlement: if God's path is so obviously the preferable one, why did our addressee find it so hard throughout his life? The antitheses, rhetorical questions, imperatives ("Enough!"; "make thyself acceptable") and negations (the triple repetition of the negative "*al*") unequivocally clarify the desirable path at the first stage; but at the second stage we start to wonder, why should taking this path be so problematic?

Another poem written during this same period, and which is represented as a continuation of our poem, represents in a different way

---

[72] Yehuda Halevi, Brody edition, 1928, 10.
[73] The Arabic rubric above this poem is "And he also said about the sea;" Schirmann, *Ha-shirah ha-'ivrit*, classified this poem as a poem that preceded Halevi's journey (ibid., 494).

another aspect of the complexity. The poem "Can Lifeless Bodies" shows the problem of immigrating to the Holy Land as stemming from three factors: the speaker's fear and anxiety at leaving the charms of Spain, and the travails of the journey itself, along with the social pressure to remain in al-Andalus. The Arabic rubric before the poem reads: "And he said when they persisted in asking him to stay in al-Andalus."[74] But further on in the poem, the speaker dwells on his own trepidations:

> Can lifeless bodies/ be chambers
> For hearts lashed/ to eagle wings –
> A man at the end of his tether,/ whose only desire
> Is to rub his cheeks/ in chosen dust?
> He shivers with fear/ and tears well up
> As he casts Spain behind him/ and roams beyond,
> First by ship, then foot/ across parched lands…
>   Rebuking his friends/ he's fixed on wandering[75]

The speaker "replies" to those who try to dissuade him from going that after death the body can no longer serve as a "dwelling-place" for a heart that yearns to soar on "eagles' wings" to the Promised Land. The synecdoche of the heart often represents unfulfilled desire in Halevi's poetry, sometimes, as in this poem, in contradictory ways.[76] In "Can Lifeless Bodies," the heart is the source of the yearnings to reach "the chosen dust," the dust of the Holy Land, but it has two problems to deal with: the first one a problem on the "home-front," so to speak, in other words the fear and anxiety of leaving the good life in Spain; and the second, the need to reply to those who argue against his going. Because these people are termed *"dodim"* in the poem, things become even more problematic, for in the Song of Songs and elsewhere in the Bible, the word *dodim* is a highly favorable epithet for lovers, whether divine or human. It is harder, therefore, to take a stand against *dodim*, especially when their words correspond to the speaker's own fears and troubles in leaving Spain.

To sum up, Halevi's writings exhibit a disposition of belief in which there exists a dialectic for dealing with external and internal problems. Halevi gave powerful expression to the clash between epistemological

---

[74] Schirmann, *Ha-shirah ha-'ivrit*, 497.
[75] Yehuda Halevi, Levin edition, 2002, 104.
[76] See, for example, "Sleeper with Heart Awake" and "My Heart is in the East."

claims and the desires for important aspects of human life, such as family and friends, community and culture, and the physical pleasures of the body. Hegel's position on Subject-formation offers a fruitful direction of interpretation in regarding such clashes as a natural process in the framework of which the Subject forms its consciousness, since it is essentially impossible to form self-consciousness at the epistemological level alone. Thus Halevi's writings express a dialectical procedure, and not a "defect" of the mind or turpitude of the soul. The biography of Judah Halevi, which culminates in his immigration to the Holy Land, complements the Hegelian process according to which unification takes place, in the end, with the "Absolute Spirit."

Yehuda Amichai's poem, "Yehuda Ha-Levi," gives eloquent expression to the contradictions in Halevi's personality: the soft hair versus the curly one; "The white fist of his brain" (rational knowledge) versus "The black seeds of his happy childhood" (his joyful youth); and most of all, the unceasing attempt "to carry the soul inside his body to Jerusalem" despite all hindrances. But above and beyond all this is the clear knowledge that in the end, "when he reaches the beloved, bone-dry land—he will sow."

Yehuda Ha-Levi

The soft hairs on the back of his neck
Are the roots of his eyes.

His curly hair is
The sequel to his dreams.

His forehead: a sail; his arms; oars
To carry the soul inside his body to Jerusalem.

But in the white fist of his brain
He holds the black seeds of his happy childhood.

When he reaches the beloved, bone-dry land—
He will sow.[77]

---

[77] Y. Amichai, *The Selected Poetry of Yehuda Amichai,* ed. & trans. Chana Bloch & Stephen Mitchell (New-York: Harper & Row, 1986) (originally published in Hebrew, 1955), 5.

The Strengthening of Faith in Orthodox Discourse: A Reevaluation of Models of Faith

Isaac Hershkowitz

1. Introduction

There have been very few studies regarding Jewish Orthodox models of faith prior to the second half of the twentieth century. Moreover, whatever relevant research was done tended to focus on prominent figures such as R. Abraham Yitzhak Kook, other hasidic leaders and thinkers, and theorists of the Musar movement. Little work has been done in connection with grassroots efforts to confront the crises in faith owing to exposure to modernity—modern lifestyle and norms—which led to a weakening of the traditional hierarchy in Jewish communities.

Benjamin Brown illustrated a shift in the concept of faith within Orthodoxy, according to which the Kabbalah, as well as other, more rationalistic argumentations of theistic faith, lost their place as the most influential sources of ideas and inspiration to a very simple fideistic model.[1] He distinguishes between two types of believers: the simple (*tamim*) believer, "who inherits his belief from tradition, and does not wish to develop it, to refine it or to elevate it," and the theological believer, who "is not satisfied with the simple faith, but wishes to establish his faith and to enhance it by using a coherent and systematic philosophy."[2] According to Brown, in this new fideistic model, there is a prohibition against, or perhaps an annulment of, theological inquiry. Instead of belief resulting from knowledge and investigation, or a belief in a complex cosmogonist structure that expresses God's epiphanic creation of the

---

[1] Benjamin Brown, "The Return of 'The Simple Faith': The Concept of Haredi Faith, and Its Growth in the Nineteenth Century," in *On Faith*, ed. Moshe Halbertal, David Kurzweil, and Avi Sagi (Jerusalem: Keter, 2005), 403–443 (Hebrew). I translated the extracts from this paper.
[2] Ibid., 403.

world, this model is based on a fiducial trust in God, his existence, the fact that he created the world, and the fact that he has Providence on the world and specifically on his nation, the People of Israel. The trust and belief in an inexplicable relationship between God and the world led to a lifestyle wherein an individual was encouraged to concentrate on moral deeds and his own spiritual development and to be humble and accepting of the religious hierarchies.

Brown contends that ever since the nineteenth century the major model of faith in Haredi (ultra-Orthodox) circles is a simple one, dictated by the forefathers of the Haredi lifestyle, which has very little room for questioning and original criticism. Such a model of faith may include a major element of venture, since the believer withdraws from any attempt to understand the world and God. Yet, since Haredi societies have solid hierarchical structures, there is room to believe that the venture does not affect daily life; indeed, in most cases the believer is not even aware of it because the solidity of a homogeneous collective faith induces a feeling of warrant.

Brown's contention was based on a limited number of sources from various geographical and communal regions of Eastern European Jewry. In contrast, I believe one can trace some sophisticated models of faith within these regions. In what follows, I show that there were propositional discussions and endeavors to fortify the weakened Jewish faith throughout the decades prior to World War II. These initial efforts to justify religious faith by means of rationalistic argumentation produced new models of faith that differ significantly from the fideistic outlook I have just described. In order to demonstrate this notion I cite Orthodox works from various geographical regions, from Lithuania in the east to Hungary in central Europe, as well as several works from the United States and Palestine.[3] The period I researched begins in the final years of the nineteenth century, but my major focus is on a Slovakian-Hungarian treatise published in 1926 which illustrates several prominent meditations on advanced models of faith.

---

[3] Two additional works that deal with the obligation of the believer to reason his faith and justify it that I do not refer to in this discussion are Hayyim Yehudah Schlesinger, *Kuntres Yeshu'ah uNehamah* (A Pamphlet on Salvation and Consolation) (Budapest: 1938) and Aharon Arye Meirovitz, *Lev ha'Arye* (The Heart of the Lion) (Riga: 1929).

2. Fideistic Faith and the "Special Knowledge Model" in Orthodox Thought

Alvin Plantinga defined faith as a special knowledge of truths that was not acquired by the believer but rather was inherited from a divine source in an act of revelation. These truths cannot be subject to cognitive inquiry on the part of every believer, since their logical foundations are beyond human grasp, but this faith is warranted. This model of faith (known as the A/C model, as it was much inspired by Aquinas and Calvin), suggests that faith must be reasonable, yet the believer must learn to live without supporting arguments to defend it. Plantinga uses Calvin's *Sensus Divinitatis*[4] in order to explain the cognitive faculties that humans use in order to establish their faith in an externalist epistemic way. He sees Calvin's ideas as a development of Aquinas' claim: "To know in a general and confused way that God exists is implanted in us by nature."[5] Faith, according to Plantinga, is basically evident, a disposition. It cannot be proved logically:[6]

> According to the A/C model, this natural knowledge of God is not arrived at by inference or argument (for example, the famous theistic proofs of natural theology) but in a much more immediate way. The deliverances of the *sensus divinitatis* are not quick and *sotto voce* inferences from the circumstances that trigger its operation [...]
>
> It is rather that, upon the perception of the night sky or the mountain vista or the tiny flower, these beliefs just arise within us. They are occasioned by the circumstances; they are not conclusions from them.

Despite the fact that Plantinga's version of the A/C model can be considered a moderate fideistic one,[7] since it does not accept clear argumenta-

---

[4] Jean Calvin, *Institutes of the Christian Religion*, ed. John T. McNeill, trans. Ford Lewis Battles, Library of Christian Classics (London: S.C.M. Press, 1961), I, iii, 3.

[5] *Summa Theologica*, trans. Fathers of the English Dominican Province (New York: Benziger Bros., 1947), I, ii, 1.

[6] Alvin Plantinga, *Warranted Christian Belief* (New York/Oxford: Oxford University Press, 2000), 146. For an important review on this treatise, see Richard Swinburne, "Plantinga on Warrant," *Religious Studies* 37 (2001): 203–214.

[7] See Terence Penelhum, *God and Skepticism: A Study in Skepticism and Fideism*, Philosophical Studies Series in Philosophy, Vol. 28 (Dordrecht: D. Reidel, 1983), 146–158; Alvin Plantinga, "Reason and Belief in God," in *Faith and Rationality:*

tion as a tool to sustain it and is not radical, in the sense that it does not see faith as contrary to reason,[8] Plantinga's model does not alienate reason; it merely insists that reason is an external cognitive faculty, which allows humans to believe with great confidence.[9] Moreover, Plantinga himself called for the reasoning of basic religious truths, especially in his work on the ontological argument.[10] He holds that faith is not merely the act of "believing in" something, but rather an act of knowing or, more precisely, the stance of knowing. Thus, the religious truths must be clearly evident and understandable. They cannot be paradoxical.[11]

As I show hereinafter, the model of faith alienating reason, as Brown introduced it, does not suit many Orthodox thinkers, as their models are made up of unyielding reasonable truths. Moreover, they see the accusations that religious faith is non-reasonable as harmful to Orthodox faith

---

Reason and Belief in God, ed. Alvin Plantinga and Nicholas Wolterstorff (Notre Dame, IN: University of Notre Dame Press, 1983), 87–91. Also see Richard Askew, "On Fideism and Alvin Plantinga," *Philosophy of Religion* 23 (1988): 3–16.

[8] On another form of moderate fideism, see John Bishop, "How a Modest Fideism may Constrain Theistic Commitments: Exploring an Alternative to Classical Theism," *Philosophia* 35 (2007): 387–402. Inspired by William James, Bishop attempts to offer a limitation of the doxastic venture of theistic faith by creating a "modest, moral coherentist, fideism," which requires "positive ethical evaluation of both the motivation and content of religious doxastic." This work, similar in its ambitions to Plantinga's model, differs substantially from the model I present hereinafter. Both this work and Plantinga's do not leave room for the essential idea that faith can be reasoned by human comprehension, which is the core of the model presented in this paper.

[9] Ibid., 148:
> On the A/C model, then, theistic belief as produced by the *sensus divinitatis* is basic. It is also *properly basic*, and that in at least two senses. On the one hand, a belief can be properly basic for a person in the sense that it is indeed basic for him (he does not accept it on the evidential basis of other propositions) and, furthermore, he is *justified* in holding it in the basic way: he is within his epistemic rights, is not irresponsible, is violating no epistemic or other duties in holding that belief in that way.

[10] See Alvin Plantinga, *The Nature of Necessity* (New York: Oxford University Press, 1974), 197–221 and throughout the book.

[11] For some critique on the A/C model, see James P. Moreland and William Lane Craig, *Philosophical Foundations for a Christian Worldview* (Downers Grove, IL: InterVarsity Press, 2003): 166–168; Michael L. Czapkay Sudduth, "Plantinga's Revision of the Reformed Tradition: Rethinking our Natural Knowledge of God," *Philosophical Books* 42:2 (2002): 83–84.

and society. There is no need to say that, in their eyes, the common belief that it is a religious merit to conceive faith as non-reasonable is harmful.

In order to prove my contention I cite R. Yissakhar Shlomo Teichtal's work, *Tov Yig'al* (He Will Liberate in Goodness), which he wrote in order to strengthen Jewish faith.[12] Although not a systematic treatise, *Tov Yig'al* does include several important notions concerning Orthodox faith that are consonant with some basic criteria of the "special knowledge model" of faith.

When Calvin spoke of special knowledge, he referred specifically to the words of the Holy Spirit, as they are manifested in the Gospel. Despite the evident differences between Judaism and Christianity in this regard, Teichtal's exposition of the origins of faith adopts similar concepts[13]:

> We are like donkeys and lack human wisdom compared to the wisdom of the older generations, but we have their books of wisdom. Moreover, those who came after them have set us a table full of delicacies for the soul, something that those earlier generations did not have, which stands as a replacement for their additional wisdom, in a sense that all generations are equally liable when they appear before God. The early generations are liable by virtue of their wisdom and the later generations by virtue of the wisdom they inherited from their forefathers, as manifested in their books.[14]

---

[12] *Tov Yig'al* (Bardiov, 1926) [Hebrew]. On the cover page Teichtal wrote: This book consists of sermons [...] destined to strengthen the Torah and the faith. It is a necessity in our epoch, since, owing to our many sins, the sickness of heresy and rebelliousness against the Torah and *mitzvot* has grown, and this is the source of all our distress [...] Every Jew [...] will find himself reinforced in faith as a pillar that cannot be moved after reading this book.
Teichtal (1885–1945) was rabbi of Piestany, Slovakia, and was killed in Auschwitz during the Holocaust. On *Tov Yig'al*, see Isaac Hershkowitz, "The Vision of Redemption in Rabbi Yissakhar Shlomo Teichtal's Writings: Changes in His Messianic Approach during the Holocaust" (Ph.D. Diss., Bar-Ilan University, 2009), 51–64. All of the rabbinic sources cited in this paper were originally written in Hebrew. The English texts are my translations.

[13] Ibid., 10.

[14] It should be noted that Aquinas himself found a substitution for the natural sense of God in empirical impressions of His presence in the world (see *Summa Theologiae*, I, ii, 2). However, as opposed to Teichtal's model, this does not stand as a cognitive systematical action.

The concept of spiritual heritage as a tool for allowing the spiritual quest of later generations to begin at a higher level repeats itself in Teichtal's treatise,[15] and I call it the "special cognitive heritage model" of faith. There is a major difference between the "special knowledge model" and the "special cognitive heritage model," inasmuch as the latter requires that some concrete cognitive actions be taken, whether by the believer or by one of his spiritual forefathers. Here, some actual person had to do the logical deduction to reach a firm conclusion, factual knowledge, to be transmitted later to future generations, whereas the "special knowledge model" does not require that there be actual human reasoning. The knowledge is affirmed by an external, non-human, faculty. There is room to question whether there was actual reasoning involved in coming to the special knowledge, ontologically separate from the truth itself in a reflective mode, or whether the knowledge is inherently reasonable, a self-evident divine truth. However, when speaking of the Special Cognitive Heritage model, the actual reasoning is a necessary condition. Thus, it is clear that when one attempts to evaluate the place of that model compared to that of the Special Knowledge model in a fideistic spectrum, the latter represents a less rational form, but both are far from pure irrationality.

In the following discussion, I show that the "special cognitive heritage model" is itself more of a range of various forms, all containing two major factors: (1) the existence of actual cognitive reasoning; and

---

[15] See p. 9, where Teichtal explains the impact Moses had on his people such that the mere sight of him would strengthen one's faith. This statement is given in the context of rabbinic preachers that wander around and enlighten people with their sermons. Teichtal explains that inasmuch as "modern" preachers have better rhetorical abilities, their internal power of truth is weak, and therefore they cannot be successful in their preaching as "authentic" preachers are. Also see p. 11, where Teichtal asserts that it is a "great element" of religious practice in his days to:

> Seek the truth by our weak wisdom in the books, especially in our generation [...] and to diligently study our holy literature, which originates from a fountain of spring water, our wise and godly rabbis, whereas all the gates of concealed, revealed, and natural wisdoms were open to them widely, and their words are pure, clear, and without doubt true. Albeit their conclusions might be far from our minds, we shall attribute the shortcoming to our lack of consciousness and the weakness of our mind, not to defame their words, God forbid.

Also see throughout the preface.

(2) the acceptance of the cognitive truths arrived at by others in earlier generations, but in the light of preceding reasoning. In other words, the "special cognitive heritage model" is a propositional model of faith based on the existence of cognitive reasoning. As it aims to reduce the unreasoned elements of faith, we can say that it is designed to reduce the venturous facet of faith.[16]

3. The "Meta-Trust Special Cognitive Heritage Model"

Despite the fact that many Orthodox writers illustrate their concepts of faith in the light of the "special cognitive heritage model," they differ in their use of its variants. The major issue on which they diverge relates to the importance of the cognitive efforts of the individual believer. Those who nullify the need for personal verification of the accepted knowledge see faith as an act of commitment to and trust in the cognitive endeavors of earlier generations to prove the truths of faith. Or, to rephrase it, theistic faith, from their point of view, is an act of trust in humans, which could be considered as meta-trust in God.

> R. Moshe Katan, in his work *Beit Yisrael* (Israel's House) notes:[17]
> Our Torah and the books of the prophets are written in profound eloquence, but sometimes in a form so abbreviated that their meaning cannot always be clearly discerned. This results from the (divine) need to teach sublime and prominent ideas, known only to the sages of the Torah, transmitted from person to person [...] there is no possibility of obtaining this knowledge without a tradition, person to person, and with the help of God [...] because the secrets of the Torah and the powers of the soul (*hanefesh ve-ha-neshama*) cannot be grasped by the human mind, even in its wisdom. They can be acquired only by righteousness and purity and divine aid.[18]

---

[16] See Moshe Halbertal, "On Believers and Faith," in *On Faith*, 17–22, on the dispute between William James and Bernard Williams. Also see John Bishop, "Faith as Doxastic Venture," *Religious Studies* 38 (2002): 471–487; idem, "On the Possibility of Doxastic Venture: A Reply to Buckareff," *Religious Studies* 41 (2005): 447–451.

[17] Moshe Katan, *Beit Yisrael* (Vilnius: 1908), VIII. This excerpt is part of a paper entitled *Reishit Hokhmah* (Beginnings of Wisdom). The paper is meant to "establish the true faith derived from logic."

[18] Also see *Lev ha'Arye*, 7–11.

This alignment is basically rooted in the personalities of the Jewish sages and the public respect for their spiritual merit.[19] As noted above, the act of "believing in" is shifted here to the acknowledgment of the value of the sages, since their spiritual and cognitive levels, despite their profundity, are within one's grasp. They act as mediators between humanity and God, and one should trust their abilities and the cognitive conclusions they reached.

R. Yehonatan Shteif, who introduced what can be identified as a meta-trust model,[20] wrote a treatise dealing with the details of the commandment of faith, *Mitzvot Hashem* (God's Commandments). In his preface he explains why he does not include the logical inquiries many of the sages used in order to affirm Jewish faith:[21]

> Apart from the fact that I am not used to dealing with such ideas, and that many holy books have been written on the veracity of faith [...] I did so because in my opinion the basic truth of faith should be implanted in the heart of every Jew because of the tradition we inherited from the prophets of the Bible and the words of our sages in the Talmud and Midrash literature [...], and

---

[19] See ibid., X, where Katan states:
> We are obliged to listen to the words and testimonies of our sages [...] the testimonies of Maimonides, Nahmanides, and the Vilnius Gaon are sufficient, since they are not so far from our generation, and we know they were wise and knowledgeable of every science and wisdom [...] and they said our Torah is Godly, full of secrets and true wonders [...] We should believe them wholeheartedly, since if they would not have seen and comprehended all this in clear evidence and unambiguous grasp they would have not written these things down, and would have not bequeathed lies to us and to their offspring, God forbid.

In a sense, this excerpt is even more radical than my conclusion stated above, since it is not the trust in the sages' spiritual level that allows the believer to depend on them with regard to faith, but rather the trust in them as adherents of the sages before them, who were even more superior. This chain of trust is not considered a weak spot in Katan's view. It is the only possibility by which to bridge the cognitive gap between man and God and among humans at various cognitive levels.

[20] Rabbi Shteif (1877–1958) served as rabbi and *Dayan* in several congregations in Hungary before World War II, after which he lived in the United States.

[21] Yehonatan Shteif, *Mitzvot Hashem*, vol. 1 (Pioterkov: 1931), 6.

behold the words of *Rivash*[22] [...] who completely prohibited any inquiry [...].

Shteif went on to explain that whereas he did refer to the widespread philosophical literature on faith in his book, he did not use its argumentation, but only the logical conclusions, the fruits of the inquiries that led to clear-cut truthful dictums of faith. These dictums, when properly studied, allow the individual to acquire firm and solid perceptions of the principles of faith without confusing him with the complicated and perplexing process of reaching the desired outcome of the logical inquiries.[23] He repeatedly declared the need for a clear mind, without the confusion engendered by philosophical treatises, yet he does not decry the crucial need for the existence of such inquiries. The gap between those "allowed" to conduct philosophical research and those who must inherit the fruits of the knowledge so acquired is an extreme exemplar of the "meta-trust model." Shteif did not wish to bridge this gap, and he accepted every word that Judaism's philosophical forefathers ever wrote down as a solid and unquestionable truth.

Applying an epistemological point of view to the relationship between God and humans elucidated here reveals another layer of meta-trust, in a somewhat circular argument on faith. According to the "meta-trust model," faith is based on the reliance of the believer on the cognitive achievements of precedent figures. Shteif believed that these earlier thinkers delivered a solid set of truths that he could believe in and thus worship God in a pure and proper manner, without the need for a cognitive critique. However, it is a common convention among those who offer this model that (having) faith is a fulfillment of a divine commandment. Since we define a divine commandment

---

[22] Rabbi Yitzchak bar Sheshet (1326–1408) was one of the most important responsa authors of medieval times. He is famous for his objection to both Kabbalah and other non-rabbinic disciplines, especially philosophy (see his responsa, sections 45, 157). See Avi Sagi, "The Controversy about Secular Studies in the Responsa Literature," in *Studies in Memory of Professor Ze'ev Falk*, ed. Michael Corinaldi, Moshe David Herr, Rivka Horowitz, and Yohanan Silman (Jerusalem: Mesharim Press, 2005), 231–253 (Hebrew), and Menachem Kellner, "Rabbi Isaac Bar Sheshet's Responsum Concerning the Study of Jewish Philosophy," *Tradition* 15 (1975): 110–118.

[23] *Mitzvot Hashem*.

as an act meant to be performed owing to a trust in human cognitive achievements, it is inevitable to conclude that these human cognitive achievements are, in fact, an act of God, inasmuch as they play a crucial role in His commandment.

A similar circular argument can be found in the sanctification of the rulings of the *Beit Din haGadol* (the Supreme Judicial tribunal) as the exclusive and official commentary on the divine commandments manifested in the Torah (see Maimonides' *Hilkhot Mamrim* 1:1). Yet there is a difference between these two cases, as the sanctification of the rulings of the high tribunal are needed in order to create a homogeneous religious praxis in which only one group of sages, an official religious forum, has the power to guide the Jewish nation. Thus, even if not revealing the words of God, allegedly explaining "His side" of the interpretation of the Torah, the tribunal's rules have as much power as God's. Yet we do not know of an institutional sanctification of a set of beliefs or truths given to us by a specific sage or prophet. Can there actually be plural and different "truths" about God, his existence, his relationship with Creation and with the Jewish nation, the giving of the Torah, and so on, all of which God ordered us to believe in?

Another aspect of the problem of God's involvement in the act of faith, as he also commands humans to have faith, is suggested by Teichtal, who defiantly asks:[24]

> I have pondered myself striving to understand why God sent us such a challenge, to fight such a terrible war. Do we have the power of rocks to endure all of this? We have no more strength left to bear the burden of exile from the outside, and why should we suffer from inner exile?

Teichtal believes these complexities are meant to refine and clarify the faith of the true believers and to bestir them to take responsibility for other Jews. Yet the question itself reveals a multi-layered perspective regarding faith both as a Godly act and as a human challenge and responsibility.

Returning to the "meta-trust model," Teichtal expresses a more moderate mode, glorifying Maimonides and amplifying his complete

---

[24] *Tov Yig'al*, 6.

knowledge in every discipline in order to overrule all of the "academic" and modern attempts to weaken Jewish religiosity[25]:

> Behold how we are obliged, in our feeble brains, to trace the truth in the books [...] since we have two shortcomings: we are mentally weak, and as Abaye says: They are more numerous than we are and they surround us like a fence around a field.[26] [...] Now, my dear son, shall your heart not fail when you see these words of deceit [...] of these professors and university scholars [...] against the giant scope of our master, Maimonides! Know, my son, a clear undoubted knowledge, that all their words are acts of blindness and madness!

I believe this is not an extreme mode of the "meta-trust model," for we will soon see that Teichtal did explain that every Jew has a significant role, even if not an intellectual one, in establishing his faith. He saw the role of *tsaddikim* and rabbinic leaders as kindling a fire in the heart of every Jew, a glowing ember of faith. Every Jew, according to Teichtal, has a spark of faith within him, and he has no need for knowledge from without, that is, knowledge that comes from an external faculty, to be given to him (in some kind of resemblance to the A/C model). Thus, it would be inaccurate to consider Teichtal's conception as simply a "meta-trust special cognitive heritage model."

4. The "Temporary Special Cognitive Heritage Model"

Other thinkers who wrote about the "special cognitive heritage model" did not create a dichotomous differentiation between contemporary and past believers. They believed that the great sages of the past had a higher level of cognizance, but that every human should attempt to achieve a high level of cognizance as well. That being the case, the preceding cognitive effort merely supports a cognitive belief, enhancing it

---

[25] Ibid., 11–13.
[26] Teichtal is referring to the Babylonian Talmud, Tractate Berakhot 3a. Abaye speaks there of the numerous boors crowding the *Beit Midrash*, who are unintelligent and have bad manners. Their presence impedes the *talmidei hakhamim*, the serious students in the *Beit Midrash*, from achieving high levels of Torah scholarship.

by means of granting guidance and advice. According to this variant, theistic faith means knowing God's truths oneself, not just trusting others who do, and here it would be more accurate to talk about a temporary special cognitive heritage model.' By using the word "temporary," I am not implying that in this model heritage cannot be long-lasting, but rather indicating that one who does not use such heritage as a ladder to elevate himself to a higher level of cognizance regarding God's truths does not fulfill his mandate as a believer. Let us begin the description of this model with the words of R. Shmuel Moshe Hilf, in his book, *Gan Hayyim* (The Garden of Life):[27]

> This is why our sages included faith as part of the commandments, though one could ask how it is possible to command humans to believe if they do not believe in the first place. Yet it is obvious that this commandment is intended to counter all self-interest and to encourage clear-minded inquiry into the truth.

Hilf admits that the fundamental bemusement that the command to have faith engenders is indeed legitimate, if not natural. Thus he abjures the Orthodox notion emphasized by Brown that one should believe because one is ordered to do so, but rather considers the commandment an obligation to conduct an objective and open-minded inquiry in order to reach a firm and reasoned set of true beliefs. Faith, or the commandment of faith, according to Hilf, is in fact not believing, but rather studying and sorting truths from fallacies.[28] He does not speak of an external source for knowledge of God but relies solely on an individual's effort to reason his faith. In this sense, Hilf is exceptional in terms of thinkers who concur with the "special cognitive heritage model," but his call for acts that will justify faith are not at all unusual.

R. Mordekhai Arye Nissenbaum's ideas are a better fit to this model. Author of *Mossadot haEmunah* (The Institutions, or Foundations, of

---

[27] Moshe Shmuel Hilf, *Gan Hayyim* (Warsaw: 1914), 9a. On the title page of the book Hilf declares that the book is intended "to remove all of the questions, minor and grave, until the faith is clear-cut, with lucid evidence."

[28] This notion in itself is not unique to Hilf, and has deep roots in Jewish philosophy, e.g., Rav Saadia Gaon's preface of *Emunot veDe'ot*, but it is still important to point it out when it is expressed in the twentieth century by an Orthodox rabbi.

Faith),[29] Nissenbaum called for a re-establishing of the logical foundations of the Jewish faith in light of modernity, and specifically owing to the desertion of the Jewish religious community by many young people. He lamented the transformation of Judaism from a reasoned religious movement which gave Jews the power to withstand many challenges during the medieval period to a religion that can no longer attract or hold its youth, due to its archaic nature and lack of logical validation.[30] He called for revisiting the elements of Jewish faith, arranging them according to three principles, which can apply to a range of models of faith: (1) Faith should be based only on sensual impressions, since "faith is the fruit of reality"; (2) Faith should then be justified by logical arguments; (3) No logical argument can contradict sensual conclusions, since the human mind is "very weak."[31] It is clear that Nissenbaum was convinced that humans have the intellectual resources needed to establish their own faith (he even speaks of an institutional establishment of faith principles, a revised composition of the Jewish faith to be presented to Jewish youth).

Despite the skeptical tone of Nissenbaum's words regarding the powers of human cognition, I believe he can still be included in the "special cognitive heritage model," since he does require reasoning, but he primarily bases his faith on sensual impressions. On the other hand, seeking to base Jewish faith on sensual impressions creates a serious problem, as the constitutive events of Judaism occurred thousands of years ago, and no person still alive witnessed them. Nissenbaum uses the "cognitive heritage model" here as a "sense heritage":[32]

> The concept of divine Torah from heaven is not based on philosophical arguments, that is, logical arguments, but on the sense-impressions of six hundred thousand people, who witnessed the greatness of the miracles of Egypt, the Exodus, the giving of our Torah [...] because all of these facts should not be doubted, considering the multiplicity of the events and of the witnesses.

---

[29] Mordekhai Arye Nissenbaum, *Mossadot haEmunah* (New York: 1924). Rabbi Nissenbaum was *rosh yeshivah* of several yeshivot in Lithuania and then in New York.
[30] Ibid., 9–10.
[31] Ibid.
[32] Ibid., 14.

Here Nissenbaum uses a classical argument presented in R. Saadia Gaon's *Emunot veDe'ot* and in R. Judah Halevi's *Kuzari*, inasmuch as they see Judaism's historical heritage as a substitute for personal witnessing.[33] Rav Sa'adia emphasizes the vast number of witnesses to the giving of the Torah as a substitute for the personal validation of the contents given in the Torah. According to his unique argument, the wide-scaled revelation should act as a stimulant for personal validation of the truths of faith. Nissenbaum, on the other hand, does not call for an active argumentation of faith resulting from revelation. Thus, historical revelation as substitution for argumentation is not equal in the two texts: whereas R. Saadia sees it as a shortcut incorporating concrete cognitive efforts, Nissenbaum sees it as an infra-structure of faith, merely allowing cognitive efforts.

Yet, following his disposition manifested throughout the book, it is clear that Nissenbaum claims to require reasoning and does not base his faith solely on an historiosophical notion.[34] This is why I believe that his concept fits the "temporary special cognitive heritage model," since the historical impressions help to light a one-time spark, but one that cannot replace the individual's efforts to believe according to his own feelings and sensual impressions.

A more distinct representative of the temporary model is R. Eliyahu Feldman.[35] In his treatise *Yihhus haYahadut vehaYehudim laHayyim haEnoshiyyim* (The Attitude of Judaism and Jews to Human Life), Feldman tries to explain the process of faith.[36] He begins by illustrating the difference between *tsaddikim* and ordinary believers. *Tsaddikim* (the righteous), owing to their constant occupation with Torah and *mitzvot*, achieve a clear, powerful, and solid faith. As a result they are bound to God's virtue and their souls are purified. Ordinary people, according to

---

[33] See *Emunot veDe'ot*, Preface, sections 5-6.

[34] Nissenbaum continues to explain why the Torah is Godly, in light of the scientific knowledge it contains, knowledge Moses could not have achieved by himself. He calls this a logical argument (ignoring other ways of dealing with the question), and is not satisfied with the historical heritage.

[35] Feldman, born in 1875, was a Ukrainian rabbi. He served at Halmiazev, in the Platova district, near Kiev, beginning in 1900. See Rabbi Nathan Zvi Friedman, *Otzar haRabannim* (Tel-Aviv: Agudat Otzar haRabannim, 1975), 47.

[36] Eliyahu Feldman, *Yihus haYahadut vehaYehudim laHayyim haEnoshiyyim* (Berdichev: 1907), 2a-b.

Feldman, receive aid from God in the shape of a strong disposition for faith, which exists in every human being at all times. This disposition nests in every individual from childhood and, like every other human characteristic, should be continually developed. Feldman explains the difference between *tsaddikim* and others:[37]

> The sense of faith atrophies in people who do not develop it as grownups, unlike the *zadikim*, who were so educated as to become fully conversant with the Torah and the *mitzvot*, and therefore they are always elevated in the development of their true sense of faith. Yet, in order to prevent persuasion in degraded beliefs by the sense of faith, God imbued human nature with skepticism and objection to faith.
>
> The *zadikim*, who, by their virtues and feelings, mend the world, believe in God and in our holy Torah, and in all that is customary in the Jewish nation, and protest against false faiths, which do not accord to the holy Torah.

One can be a *tsaddik* only by continuing to nurture his inner disposition of faith. If he has not yet done so, he has to scrutinize his own beliefs, since he cannot rely on his primitive sense. The *tsaddik*, after a lifetime of spiritual endeavor, can safely rely on his beliefs, knowing that they are true and coherent with Judaism's demands. Although Feldman does not develop the relationship between the *tsaddik* and ordinary people, I believe we can assume the connection to the *tsaddik* is crucial if misleading beliefs are to be overruled and pure and knowledgeable beliefs, which are the estate of those who have purified their minds, are to be perpetuated.[38]

R. Moshe Salmon had a more radical notion of bridging the gap between individuals with unique powers of faith and those who were not granted, or did not achieve, such powers.[39] In his treatise *Netiv Moshe* (Moshe's Path), he cites the Talmudic rule by which prophets are not

---

[37] Ibid.

[38] I must note that elsewhere in his book (see p. 6a-b, in example) Feldman virtually rules out any logical attempt to reason faith.

[39] Rabbi of Turdossin, Slovakia; Born in 1835 and apparently passed away at the beginning of the twentieth century. About him and his writings see Yitzchok Yosef Cohen, *Sages of Hungary* (Jerusalem: Machon Yerushalayim, 1995), 405 (Hebrew).

allowed to initiate any decree by virtue of their prophetic status, unless it is to answer a temporary need, and even then it is to be by virtue of their wisdom, not their prophecy.[40] Yet he broadens this rule and applies it to questions of faith as well.[41] Despite an intuitive attitude that might question the necessity and reason for this limitation, in light of the many sources I cite in this paper that emphasize the status of Judaism's spiritual forefathers, Salmon is decisive in his innovation:[42]

> This rule was essential in its time, and ever since, because if it would not have closed the gate on prophetic innovations, the religion and faith would have been like a breached city without a wall, under the influence of every prophesying individual and spiritualist. They would create faulty laws and verdicts our fathers never even heard of in the name of God [...]. Yet our earlier sages handed another rule down to us, and it is as great in my eyes as the previous one I mentioned: that we should not trust the rule [...].

Salmon, despite his undeniable admiration for Judaism's prophets and sages, calls for a critical attitude toward any innovation related to faith, especially if it is not based on lucid sources in the authorized Judaic texts. His notion is not destructive to the existence of tradition; it only calls for an honest dialogue within the Jewish nation regarding every trend in faith. This point is clear from his ironic addendum, which clarifies exactly the major place he gives to the sages. There should be a balance between innovativeness and conservatism, between the ruling of a charismatic, wise, and spiritual leader and the common sense and knowledge of the community of believers. Salmon's insight can also be interpreted as a fear of tradition as a temptation, the beginning of a falling into a substitute for an authentic and meaningful faith.[43] By temptation I mean that the fear of confronting the challenges of faith, of standing on one's own two feet and personally creating the

---

[40] See Babylonian Talmud, tractates Yoma 80a, Megillah 2b, Temurah 16a.
[41] Moshe Salmon, *Netiv Moshe: Ma'amar Mehkari 'al Koah haHakhamim* (Budapest: 1898), 5–6.
[42] Ibid., 6–9.
[43] See Avi Sagi, "Faith as Temptation," in *On Faith*, 58–60, where he discusses the preference for religious ritual over living with authentic faith as a temptation.

foundations of a solid and reasonable faith, can lead to the convenient use of the ideas of the prophets and the sages without any venture. This is the first of four stages of falling into in-authenticity, according to Martin Heidegger.[44]

R. Shlomo Fruchter's ideas fall somewhere between the temporary model and the meta-trust model.[45] In his book *Divrei Shlomo* (Shlomo's Words), he dedicated several sermons to "the obligation of faith,"[46] and in one of them he deals with the question of faith and reason:[47]

> If your faith would originate from logic you will be able to walk in all of His paths, even to love Him [...]. But that is the level only of true fearers of God, who know themselves well enough to understand that whatever they will not achieve in their limited minds is because of the profundity of the object and the inaccessibility of the subject, and they are loyal to the true tradition and faith.

Fruchter continued by explaining that God's enlightening benevolence is the same for all humankind, yet not everyone is capable of comprehending it correctly and using it in a constructive way. Again, we see wisdom, scholarship, and critical reasoning as important elements of Jewish faith, and we see the distinction between those who can and those who cannot achieve individual reasoning regarding their faith as relative development in terms of religious virtue and not as a matter of essential differences among people. There are no institutional definitions or objective standards one can adhere to in order to be allowed to deal with these sensitive issues and materials. Whoever sees himself as religiously apt is invited to delve into reasoning.

Perhaps the most lucid source for the temporary model that is written from an epistemic point of view is R. Arye Leib Gordon's *Hazon*

---

[44] See Martin Heidegger, *Being and Time*, trans. John Macquarrie & Edward Robinson (Oxford: Blackwell Publishing, 1967), 179.
[45] R. Shlomo Fruchter, a son of the Ruzin hasidic dynasty, was a rabbi in Transylvania. Years after publishing this book he immigrated to Palestine, where he composed some moral and religious notes as well as his family tree for his relatives in the United States. See *Iggeret Shlomo* (Jerusalem: 1960).
[46] Shlomo Fruchter, *Divrei Shlomo* (Romania: Vişăul-de-Sus, 1927).
[47] Ibid., 15–16.

haEmunah vehaHashgaha (The Vision of Faith and Providence).[48] In his preface Gordon expresses a very honest and manifest statement regarding the limitations of human comprehension, on one hand, and the need for faith's reasoning on the other[49]:

> I do not have geometrical proofs to show you the justification of faith, just as I do not have such proofs to justify my love of my parents. Faith and love originate from the heart's feelings, and the heart does its job even without logical proof.
>
> But there are ample reasonable proofs and, as you surely know, hypotheses are the principles of science, and wise people are accustomed to trust them as if they were geometrical proofs.
>
> Criticism was founded on three profound principles [...] (1) Man's mind is limited [...]. (2) Self-esteem: a man should always remember that there were wiser and smarter people before him [...]. (3) Following the majority [...].
>
> These three principles show me clearly the God in which I believe in full faith, without doubt. I have not seen this God and have not understood his essence; my mind is limited [...] so how could I have been shown Him clearly? When I realize the limitations of my mind and brain, in a sense I cannot trust them to overrule what they do not understand, and since I know there have been wonderful wiser people [...] and they believed in the supreme God and trusted His salvation, and when I see that at every time and in every place, the majority of humanity, from the wisest of the wise to the most primitive of savages, believes in the existence of a leader of the world, which is beyond human comprehension [...] it is as if a *Bat Kol* comes out of the "hall" of reasonable hypotheses declaring: He is in front of you!

Despite the similarity of this argument to Plantinga's model, we can see the important factor of the precedent wise individuals, who apparently understood what normal human beings cannot comprehend—the logical arguments for the existence of God and for the religious belief in Him. However, I do not think Gordon should be understood as a

---

[48] Arye Leib Gordon, *Hazon haEmunah vehaHashgaha* (Jerusalem: 1899). Gordon (1845–1913) was an enthusiastic Zionist and a *talmid hakham*, with a professional knowledge of chemistry and engineering. See his entry in David Tidhar, *Encyclopedia of the Founders and Builders of Israel*, vol. 1 (Tel-Aviv: Rishonim Library, 1947), 228–229 (Hebrew).

[49] Ibid., 3–4.

meta-trust thinker, as he does not present an impassable barrier to humans. He does not even identify these mysterious wise people necessarily as part of the Jewish collective. There were wise individuals in the past, and presumably the future will look at our generation as a source of some wise people as well. It is tradition that convinces Gordon in a reasonable warrant that his belief is true and that tradition continues to renew itself.

5. The Spark of Faith and Cognitive Models of Faith

Despite the emphasis many of the works cited above placed on cognitive elements of faith, as opposed to the extreme fideistic characteristics attributed to Orthodox thought in some studies, I cannot conclude this paper without commenting on a common element in these works—the kindling of a "spark of faith" that lies, even if dormant, in every Jew. The clearest source dealing with this element is, again, *Tov Yig'al*, in a note extending over five pages of the book.[50] Teichtal's illustration of this matter derives from a citation of one of his mentors, R. Shmuel Rosenberg of Unsdorf:[51]

> The belief in God is an autonomous natural act, which resides in the heart of every Jew, without any external action. The souls of Jews are a Godly revelation from above (חלק אלוה ממעל), carved from His Throne, and since every part is an extension of its root, the root from which it has been carved, every Jewish soul knows and feels for itself its Creator and acknowledges its Lord, since it sees and feels how it is attached to Blessed be He without undertaking any action at all. That is to say, faith comes from itself, as a force of nature from the Creator Blessed be He, like any other force of nature that operates in and of itself.

This illustration allows Rosenberg to negate the need for philosophical inquiries, since human cognizance is not where faith resides. It is only a congenital natural element responsible for faith. Thus, his model of

---

[50] *Tov Yig'al*, 20–24.
[51] *Tov Yig'al*, 20. Rabbi Unsdorf (1842–1919) was known as one of Hungarian Orthodoxy's greatest halakhic leaders and educators. See Yitzchok Yosef Cohen, *Sages of Hungary*, 400–401.

faith is not propositional *per se*. Yet we have seen that Teichtal himself believes that faith should be strengthened and is thus not simply a natural human power! Even here, with quite a loose and non-explanatory commentary to Rosenberg's exposition, Teichtal demands a personal endeavor for faith.

I believe Teichtal's answer to this dissonance could be implemented in an attempt to resolve the gap between the sages' impact on faith and the approach of normal believers in the "temporary model," especially when applying it not only to normative acts but also to beliefs, as Teichtal does himself. He insists that the role of every believer is not to "invent" faith within himself, as such faith was not there in the first place. Rather, the role of the believer is to shed his sins, as those sins separate him from God.[52] As faith resides within a person, this separation is internal. Thus, the call for strengthening faith is, in fact, a call for self-harmonization of the soul.

As we have seen, both the "temporary special cognitive heritage model" and the "meta-trust special cognitive model" call for the use of external faculties of cognitive knowledge concerning the truths of faith, yet both emphasize the importance of an inner effort, whether cognitive or not, on the part of the believer, who cannot remain passive in the act of faith. Teichtal himself defined faith elsewhere in propositional characteristics, and perhaps the self-harmonization he talks about can include such a mental process. Thus there is no contradiction between the "spark of faith" and the various efforts demanded of the believer.

6. Conclusion

In this paper I have tried to challenge the assertion that Jewish Orthodoxy concurs with an extreme fideistic model of faith by citing Orthodox thinkers who wrote freely and naturally on the need to strengthen faith through cognitive reasoning. The fact that these authors represent grassroots trends is even more important, since it proves that even if calls for an extreme fideistic model of faith existed, they had no effect on popular literature within circles throughout Orthodox societies. Instead of the extreme fideistic model I presented one inspired by but not

---

[52] *Tov Yig'al*, 20–21.

indebted to Plantinga's "A/C special cognitive model" of faith—the "special cognitive heritage model" of faith. According to the latter, Jewish faith is established with the aid of a cognitive heritage by virtue of the power of Jewish tradition. However, this external faculty of knowledge does not replace individual effort to self-implement the truths of belief. The faith is understood as a commandment and not merely as a mental mode. It is to be reasoned, and no one who is totally ignorant can be regarded as a believer.

The Special Cognitive Heritage model is divided into two major typological variants, the meta-trust model and the temporary model. According to the first, the actual cognitive effort is the estate of precedent sages, and the individual is called upon to trust and believe in them in order to be counted as a believer in God. To do so he must learn and assimilate their truths, even if the process by which they were deduced is not fully comprehended.

The latter model does not set a dichotomous gap between the sages and every believer; thus the responsibility to fully comprehend the truths of faith lies on the shoulders of every individual. However, owing to relative differences between the cognitive or spiritual levels of the sages and the ordinary believer, one should imbibe from the works of the sages. The traditional heritage is utilized not as a tool for trusting God and believing in him, but as a tool to elevate the individual's spiritual and cognitive level so he can reason and justify his faith, standing alone in the face of God.

Hillel Zeitlin in Search of God: An Analysis of Zeitlin's Meditation "The Thirst"[1]

Shraga Bar-On

A Religious Life of Question Marks

Faith is not a binary characteristic. This seems obvious when considering the semantic field of this term, which includes multifarious accounts of varied occurrences of faith. Phrases like "complete faith," "master of faith," "faith concerns," "simple faith," etc. reflect its varied manifestations and degrees. The vast corpus of religious literature presents heroes of faith who are put to spiritual trials, face temptations and undergo trials of faith. The concept of a "trial" and the complete or partial success of the heroes who withstood them, such as Abraham, Job, Jesus, R. Akiva, Paul, Saint John of the Cross, the Ashkenazi Hasidim, and many others of all generations, not only testifies to their own degree of faith, but also brings to light the existence of other degrees of faith—those of the audience of such literature—of the believers of such myths. Each of these "masters of faith" represents an extreme degree of faith, manifested under extreme circumstances. The readers who are raised within this tradition aim for the same degree of faith which the great and experienced ones had, and place themselves at a lower degree, for if it were otherwise these tales of faith would become meaningless. Still, many philosophical discussions over the terminology of faith tend to regard the person as either a "believer" or an "infidel." These discussions often presume that faith is a defining feature of life. Others define faith as the approach to a fundamental truth or a defended truth-claim,[2] some see in it a personality trait or a personal inclination, and others see in it a complete disposition, so that once a person takes it he is no longer

---

[1] Translated from Hebrew by Jonathan Howard and Liat Lavi.
[2] See, for instance, Ludwig Wittgenstein, *Philosophical Investigations* (Oxford: Blackwell Publishers, 2001), 153ᵉ-154ᵉ §§584-587.

subject to the doubt, questions, contemplation, or scepticism that may sprout from the encounter with the world or with alternative metaphysical doctrines; other discussions strive to present faith as a total achievement that derives from a one-time decision. The most famous of these last opinions is Pascal's Wager.[3] However, in life, perhaps unlike in speculative philosophy, "A throw of the dice will never abolish chance," as Mallarme's critique brilliantly points out.[4]

Upon the wide spectrum that lies between faithlessness and faith is a central religious phenomenon which could be termed a "Quest for God." The Quest for God is a faith-characteristic of "Godseekers." The religious drama of the Godseekers is the product of an existential gap. Godseekers live in a constant state of discrepancy between the world of experience, which could be phrased as their "internal faith," and the fashion in which they themselves perceive external evidence. The starting point of this description is introspection. The Godseekers discover a given in their soul: they assume that God exists either because they can feel His presence or because they find themselves thrown into a tradition that planted God in their hearts. Still, and in spite of this initial certainty, they experience a disparity between the assumption of God's existence and the external evidence supporting it. Following M.J. Berdyczewski I shall refer to this state as a "rent in the soul": "we feel that God exists, but, despite our longing, He does not come in touch with us and we do not know Him." God, who is experienced in such a clear fashion, remains an enigma. This problem which pesters the mind of this group of believers sets them on at least three different paths: the eternal search after God and trying to identify His presence in the world; various attempts of defining the span of God's action and His relationship with humanity; and a redefinition of His being. When a Godseeker has found his God or denied Him, he has bridged the gap and therefore no longer falls into this group of believers; when he returns to admitting a gap between what is in his soul and reality, he positions himself again in the realm of search—in the state of faith of a Godseeker.

The Quest for God is a central phenomenon that has many manifestations in religious literature. However, it never conquered a true place

---

[3] Blaise Pascal, *Penseés*, §§184-241, esp. §233.
[4] Stéphane Mallarmé, *Collected Poems*, trans. & commentary by H. Weinfield (Berkeley: University of California Press, 1994), 266.

in the Jewish religious and philosophical literature.[5] It appears that the main reason for this is that this state of faith (God-seeking) does not belong within the traditional framework of philosophical-speculative thought. The traditional scholarship normally deals with statements about reality and perception whose pretension is to provide answers to religious problems and to validate or negate religious statements, whereas the phenomenon of Godseekers is in its entirety a problem, a temporary state rather than an absolute or desired solution. A philosophical or religious essay seeks normally to end with exclamation marks, whereas religious life as it is expressed in the state of faith of Godseekers is a life of question marks. A Godseeker may sit down to write a contemplative essay once he overcomes the "rent" in some way or another, but by that stage, by definition, he is no longer a Godseeker.

Another main reason for the absence of descriptions of this state of faith in Jewish thought is a problem I wish to describe as the "lack of honesty" or "lack of personal touch" of religious philosophical literature. The majority of writers of both general and Jewish philosophical books were either community leaders or those who saw themselves as such. The self-image of a person of such stature carries with it a sense of responsibility. Rabbis bear the responsibility for the education and behaviour of their literary audience. The scholarly literature therefore strove to play a sociological role in modeling religious life and identity, and thus was required to provide answers rather than ask questions. The rabbis normally functioned as the members of society who answer and decree, and as such they normally avoided revealing themselves and their own concerns. Instead, they chose to serve the public and wished to lay the foundations for the beliefs they perceived as desirable. As the agents of this socialisation process, their writing is impersonal, and even where personal testimonies were brought, it was in the name of a greater social purpose and not for the sake of putting down on paper the actual experiences of the writer. It's no wonder then, that descriptions of faith-concerns and the Quest for God would appear instead in

---

[5] Abraham Joshua Heschel, *God in Search of Man* (New York: Farrar, Straus and Giroux, 1976); idem, *Man's Quest for God* (Santa-Fe: Aurora Press, 1998); Arthur Green, *Seek My Face, Speak My Name* (Northvale: Jewish Lights, 1992); Joseph B. Soloveitchik, *And From There You Shall Seek*, trans. N. Bloom (Jersey City: Ktav Publishing, 2008).

non-normative literature (i.e., non-halakhic and non-scholarly literature) some of whose peaks were expressed either by a secondary elite that did not serve as community rabbis or in the writings of central figures whose writings were not intended to be published, and were published either unauthorised or edited.

Despite the aforementioned, a person who thoroughly studies thoroughly these writings (as well as the canonical books) will discover many expressions of the Quest for God. However, the literary frameworks in which this state of faith is expressed do not belong, normally, to philosophical literature but rather to confessional literature and to the poetic and mytho-poetic expressions abundant in religious literature, and in miscellaneous expressive media such as music, dancing, and fine arts. In contrast to philosophical writing, expressive discourse is more personal in its essence and style; the mytho-poetic language mostly offers descriptions of situations rather than ontological claims. These frameworks—of poetry, fiction, and confessions, music, dancing, and painting—are better suited for expressing the state of faith of Godseekers. They are more flexible and varied in structure and are judged by different criteria than those by which philosophical literature is judged. While philosophical literature is judged by the validity of its claims or its effect upon the intellectual atmosphere of their time, the expressive discourse is also judged by aesthetic criteria and its emotional effect upon its recipients.

The Quest for God during the Hebrew Renaissance[6] Period

The late nineteenth century and the early twentieth, a period of Hebraic renaissance in various fields—including the late literary works of the enlightenment period, the literature of the *Hibbat Zion* movement, and the literature of that renaissance generation, as well as the developments in the fine arts—is sometimes perceived as a period of creation stemming from a revolt, as an expression of a rapture, a crisis facing tradition and the faith of the people of Israel of all generations. This conception,

---

[6] In translating the Hebrew term "תְּחִיָּה" I followed Harshav's choice of "renaissance" rather than "revival" due to the connotation of the Italian Renaissance of the fourteenth century. See Benjamin Harshav, *The Polyphony of Jewish Culture* (Stanford: Stanford University Press, 2007), 11 ff.

which has long been a matter of controversy, is only partially true. As Avidav Lipsker beautifully summed it up in the form of an oxymoron, we are faced with a "tradition of a revolution" and not necessarily with genuine revolts. This assertion is reinforced when historically analysing the changes of faiths, beliefs, and lifestyles in Jewish tradition. It seems that a more accurate description of the modern shift in Jewish literature is enabled by using Avi Sagi's distinction between "tradition" and "traditionality."[7] The self-image of Jewish and Hebrew literature as "new literature" turns its back to the ethos of "traditionality"—i.e., relies upon tradition for later innovations, but does not necessarily detach from the "tradition" itself in regards to the inspiration it draws from it. Beside expressions of revolt against tradition and the detachment from the traditional system of faiths and beliefs, and beside expressions of revolt against the parental tradition and the appearances of out-and-out faithlessness, at the heart of this wide-spanned creation stands the conscious Quest for God. Many of the artists of this period saw themselves as Godseekers and expressed this state of faith in various forms. As a counterview to Kurzweil's critical statement, which characterised Modern Hebrew literature as anti-religious and secular, it appears that a significant portion of this Hebrew creation can be classified as "literature of the Quest for God." One can easily identify within Hebrew literature "faithful-yet-secular" voices who called for the adoption of expressions of faith and/or elements of faith from the past in order to serve the renaissance. I shall refer here only to two of the more famous and influential writers in this group, Asher Ginsberg, otherwise known as Ahad Ha'am, and Aaron David Gordon. Ahad Ha'am highlighted the vital element of faith in God for Israeli national identity:

> Any thing whose action in life is evident, even if in itself it is naught but an imaginary illustration, is indeed a real "being" in the historic sense. Hence, even he who does not believe in the existence of God taken in itself, cannot deny His existence as a real force in history; and the national Jew, even if he be an infidel, cannot say: 'I have no part in the God of Israel,' in that force in history that resurrected our people and affected its spiritual charectaristics and its way of life for millennia. He who really does not

---

[7] Avi Sagi, *The Challenge of Returning to Tradition* (Jerusalem: Shalom Hartman Institute, 2003), 15-29 (Hebrew).

have a part in the God of Israel, he who does not sense in his heart any connection to that "higher realm," in which our forefathers gave the best of their heart and mind throughout history and from which they drew their moral strength—can be an acceptable person, but a national Jew he is not, even if he "lives in the land of Israel and speaks the holy tongue."[8]

Ahad Ha'am admits his denial of a realistic existence of God, but he nevertheless wishes to accept the conceptual idea of a god due toh historic effect upon the Jewish way of life, and wishes to clarify and refine the national implications of this idea. Very different from him is A.D. Gordon, who in *Our Dealings with Ourselves* engages in a personal-collective debate with the relation of faith, and as in all his writings rediscovers in his heart a strong religious passion in new apparel:

> The religious approach is an existing, perpetual thing in man's soul. It is the deeper relation in his soul.... Wherever there is a deep spirit and a deep relation to life, that is, first of all to the life of nature without mediation, there we find a religious approach, whether there is in it a faith in God, or even where this faith is missing, and even where it includes a denying of life itself.... Man, as his soul becomes bare and freed from all that is common and accepted, from all that is intellectual and sophisticated, from all the meaningless drivel of men, at the hour when he sees nature in its bareness, and life uncloaked—why then he necessarily relates to all in a religious manner. This religious fashion, why, it is itself the bare and free relation, freed from all that separates man's soul from the soul of the world, a complete unity.... But the highest degree is reached by the religious stance at the time when the entire nation arrives at such a state. This is, in fact, that same national spiritual state that, in the spirit of the ancient generations, that were closer to nature with regard to their spirit, but not close enough with regards to knowledge and awareness, took on the form of the discovery of God. And in that there is truth, but a spiritual truth that is not to be translated to the language of consciousness in a fixed manner, but rather in an ever-renewed language in accordance with the renewal of that language.... And from here you see ... how far we still are from the path, that man (if indeed there is a man, as we wish and can depict to ourselves)

---

[8] Achad Ha'am, *Complete Writings* (Jerusalem and Tel-Aviv: Dvir, 1965), 408 (Hebrew).

should have walked ... researching or arguing about the being of God, if there is a God, or there is none, and we see that God, the true God, the evasive Mind, is not a matter of consciousness, but rather a matter of spiritual approach. The deep spiritual approach, the profound—this is the realisation that man has of God.... He cannot realise more, and whatever more he reaches—that is not God.[9]

However, though Ahad Ha'am and A.D. Gordon differ in their spiritual relation to "Godliness," they both provide a positive statement of faith. They both believe that they understand the function of a religious approach in human life and harness God, according to their understanding, to the personal and national project of redemption. Ahad Ha'am and Gordon do not adopt the traditional illustrations of God, but rather give new content to the concept of God, content that in their eyes may outline the path to a new Hebrew nationality. In that sense, these two great thinkers excluded themselves from the group of Godseekers. Thus, despite the great importance of these opinions, I wish to exclude them from our analysis of the Godseekers phenomenon, a phenomenon which has at its core a problem of faith rather than its solution; a ponder rather than a programme.

While some of the writers of the Hebrew Renaissance rejected faith as such, others were influenced by the upsurge of spirituality brought about by the neo-romantic atmosphere in philosophy and poetry, the focus on the expression and power of the individual, the legitimacy to stray from communal norms of behaviour and expression, the emerging youth culture with its ambivalent view of its parent community, the personal and collective self-examination with regards to tradition, and the expansion of cultural boundaries and those of identity. This rise of the spiritual often expressed the Godseekers' state of faith. This state does not adopt religious dogmas or treat the religious conventions of the past as obvious, yet it could not be farther from heresy. Many of the artists of the renaissance period aimed, even further, at offering a new interpretation of the Jewish tradition. A significant portion of its important literary output deals with the faith difficulties of young Jews. Thus, for instance, Y.L. Perez defined the renaissance in his essay "Paths

---

[9] Aaron David Gordon, *Writings*, I (Tel-Aviv: Hapoel Hatzair, 1925-1929), 351-352 (Hebrew).

of Alienation from Judaism", dealing with the process of secularisation and assimilation amongst young Jews:

> "Renaissance," a single, small word, and without any additions, without conditions of time and place.... A small word that is a seed, from which an entire world shall sprout, a Jewish world.... And great and proud is this word, nor is it new; why, it is the old word of the prophets! The word of the Messiah!"[10]

Y.L. Perez sees in the renaissance the Jewish answer for the "murderers of God and religion":[11]

> If I seek for my Judaism, I search for it for my own self, I search for it in the future, based on past composition....[12]

Later authors offered a comparison between the spirit of the Godseekers to that of cultural heroes of past generations. Ancient heroes of the distant past, community-members in the diaspora, including the parents of the first pioneers, and literary heroes, both those of the Enlightenment period such as J.L. Gordon and Mendele Mocher-Sforim and those of the early settlements who became legendary within a single generation—all became the objects of modern Hebrew composition. Religious icons, such as the ancient synagogues, traditional prayers, religious requisites, and needless to say the entire corpus and extent of Jewish literature, became the backbone of the new and emerging Hebrew literature. In the process of linking the founders of the renaissance period with traditional literature, a new idealisation of the religious state of the Godseeker began to be marked. Thus, it was possible to see in the renaissance of the Quest for God in modern Hebrew literature a religious renaissance of literature itself and a new interpretative approach towards past writings and heroes, now understood not as "masters of faith" but rather as "masters of the Quest for God."

This phenomenon surpasses the common dichotomised schemes, which strictly differentiate between the "religious" and the "secular," "believers" and "infidels," and even between "Jews" and "Gentiles." This

---

[10] Isaac Leib Peretz, *Writings*, VIII (Tel-Aviv: Dvir, 1966), 305 (Hebrew).
[11] Ibid., 296.
[12] Ibid., 310.

phenomenon of Godseeking can be understood neither by questioning the fulfillment of the divine commandments nor by certain sociological characteristics. Rather, the Quest for God in the renaissance period should be understood as a focal point around which certain literary circles and literary composition developed, and to which the standard stereotypes (including those laid down in academic literature) often cannot be properly attributed. Among the Godseekers we can name characters of all political and literary-political archetypes, such as Y.L. Perez, M.J. Berdyczewski, H.N. Bialik, R. Abraham Yitzhak Kook, A.Z. Rabinowitz, R. Binyamin (J. Redler-Feldman), A. Shlonsky, U.Z. Grinberg, J.Z. Rimon, the Meiri, B. Katznelson and others—all gave vigorous expression to the state of Godseeking.

The Thirst: Hillel Zeitlin

It appears that Hillel Zeitlin was the Jewish thinker who placed this state of faith—the Quest for God—in the centre of his literary output and expressed it in the most acute fashion. The Quest for God recurs in Zeitlin's literature through all the biographical changes and shifts of thought he underwent. Following Zeitlin's short autobiographical listing, different scholars tended to develop a linear model to describe his life, starting with his growing up in a hasidic home, followed by a period of secularity, then a quest for a path towards faith, and finally, his arrival at a new state of faith characterised as a "second innocence." However, upon a careful inspection of Zeitlin's writings, it appears that his religious approach was characterised throughout by the Quest for God rather than by His presence. Thus I believe that a developmental, spiral model is better suited with regard to his writing: a spiral model revolving around the axis of the Quest. Zeitlin's strong biographical shifts and the different foci of his public activity should be examined as different expressions of the same basic state of faith, which stands at the heart of his varied literary output.

It was M.J. Berdyczewski who captured the tension in Zeitlin's works: "Divine presence at the feet of this thinking, emotional author; surround with divine presence, and angels of wrath standing before him and blocking his way ... his spirit and heart are never at peace."[13] Zeitlin

---

[13] Micha Josef Berdyczewski, *Articles* (Tel-Aviv: Dvir, 1960), 225 (Hebrew).

phrased the Quest for God in different ways and also tried to ease it or even break out of it at various times. In a relatively short meditation called *The Thirst* which was published in 1910, we can find a very accurate manifestation of the *Godseeker*. In this meditation Zeitlin uses concise and tightly-knit language in short sentences, and does not refer much to the Jewish bookshelf. Therefore it is fit that the sources that are in fact implied in this meditation should be carefully considered. As Zeitlin himself testified, this meditation is a "special merging of thought and poetry," and it is recited in a personal and confessional tone. As aforementioned, these confessional and mytho-poetic characteristics are particularly appropriate for describing the Quest for God. Following Lev Shestov and William James, Zeitlin attributed great value to confessions and regarded them as the very core of religious experience (as well as literature and philosophy):

> The artists ... do not mean to write confessions. But intention and truth of life are apart. The confessions peek out from every single page ... thus too the great philosophers soundly examine ... philosophical doctrines, and in truth all these doctrines reveal ... personal confessions of their composers ... for that which is religious can be learned only from true confessions, particularly from human confusions, which are grievous and sweeping, smitten and answered with tremendous suffering of body and soul.[14]

These words are particularly true in regard to Zeitlin's own work, and it is through their prism that we should understand the meditation before us as an expression of his philosophical and religious doubts in the form of a personal confession.

Between the Titles

A title and two subtitles were given to the meditation when first published in David Frischman's collection *The Literature*. Between these titles the aforementioned rent in Zeitlin's soul between old and new, conformity with Jewish tradition and his dwelling in the literary and philosophical movements of his time, is noticeable. In its title – *The*

---

[14] Hillel Zeitlin, "Depths of Doubt and Despair," *Hatkoffa* 20 (1923): 442-443 (Hebrew).

Thirst – is the clear reference to Psalms 42:3: "My soul thirsts for God, for the living God." As we shall later see, one can easily see the entire meditation as an exegesis of the two famous verses from this psalm that have accompanied Zeitlin in his various writings for years.

The first subtitle which appeared in the body of the meditation—*A Vision of the Heart*—is characteristic of the meditation's genre and its style of writing. Zeitlin's thoughts are expressed here in the first person. He translates in a literary way the speculative philosophy of faith which he has become acquainted with, and responds to it poetically. In the course of the vision, Zeitlin meets various characters who manifest different cultural opinions about God and faith in Him. This personification of the different speculative answers puts a face and body on the philosophical approaches, and formulates the discourse over faith and divinity as a live discourse between believers and infidels. The personification of speculative philosophy and its incorporation into a vision move the discussion from a speculative and supposedly objective plane to a personal one.

Furthermore, the combination "a vision of the heart" places the work within the traditional and ancient heritage of visions and prophecy, yet at the same time binds it with personal introspection. This move plants Zeitlin deep within both worlds—the traditional world, in the company of prophets, on the one hand, but also in the modern world among "those who feel." Indeed, this position does not highlight the gap between the modern and classical prophets. Zeitlin conceives of the phenomenon of classical prophecy through the horizon of the present and brings the two together, not as a meeting with a heteronomic God, but rather as an inner religious experience, which he identifies with a transgression of the boundaries of the regular world. This state is called a "vision of the heart."

Another subtitle (which did not appear in his compiled works) appears in the table of contents of *Hasifrut: Mikitvei Achad Hato'im* (*The Literature: from the Writings of One of the Wanderers*), without being part of the title of the volume elsewhere. This title refers quite boldly to one of the foundational novels of the Enlightenment, *Hato'e Bedarchei Hachayim* (*A Wanderer on the Paths of Life*) by Perez Smolenskin. In the choice of both subtitles, which outline the tension between the Psalter and the well-known Enlightenment author, Zeitlin exposes his dialectical worldview. In all his writings Zeitlin claims the identity of contradictions as expressed in the image of faith and faithlessness. In *Kitzur Toldotai (My Brief Biography)*, Zeitlin mentions that he came to acknowledging God specifically through the writings of Schopenhauer, Hartman, and Nietzsche, "supposedly, the utter and complete infidels." Using the second subtitle, Zeitlin identifies himself as a wanderer amongst other protagonists who rather earned their name as infidels and as the catalysts of faithlessness and secularity in Jewish society. If at first Zeitlin's paternalistic move in relation to these infidels seems apologetic, why then his self-identification as "a lost one" places him and them elsewhere altogether. In Zeitlin's view, faithlessness is not a methodological move on the way to acknowledging God, but an inseparable part of the phenomenology of contemporary faith, the faith of a Godseeker, a wanderer on his way.

Zeitlin constructs an entire framework of wandering for his meditation. He opens the meditation with a confession made by the Godseeker:

> I lost my way. I sought my God.[15]

But he does not reach his destination even at the very end of the composition. The meditation's end reflects its beginning—the state of being lost does not end by arriving at the destination or finding an answer:

> And I was lost in a great plain and sunk into profound thought,
> and I conversed with my soul.
> "What is the name of your God that you seek?"
> "…I know no name for my God. I know not his boundaries…"
> "And what did the mountains declare to you?"
> "Only that which I seek."
> "And what seek you?"
> "I know not its name yet."
> "And what do men call it?"
> "Wonder."
> […]
> "And what are the ways of your 'wonderment' and what is
>   the path to it?"
> "I know not yet. Let me seek."

This state of wandering, as described by Zeitlin, is not unique in Hebrew renaissance literature. Both the Enlightenment and the neo-romantic

---

[15] Benjamin Harshav, *Hebrew Renaissance Poetry: A Historical-Critical Anthology*, II (Jerusalem: The Bialik Institute, 2000), xx-xxvi (Hebrew).

authors intensified the state of wandering—a state of tragic heroes. Although late Enlightenment literature is concerned with tragic characters who are kicked about at the fault of a corrupt and alienating society, Hebrew renaissance literature can be characterised as being mainly interested in the dilemmas of the individual and especially in the psychological dynamicity stemming from his biographical experiences. The lonely protagonist undergoes journeys of identity and apprenticeship while pondering over his internal conflicts. Zeitlin's meditation draws from both movements as if they were one. He describes in the first person his own state of wandering—a personal state of someone subject to doubts of faith. However, in the centre of discussion stands not personal psychology nor biographical events, but rather a dealing with speculative thought seeking time and again to provide a basis for faith, and time and again remaining unfulfilled and rejected.

The Rejection

The journey of the Godseeker passes through several stages where he meets representatives of various solutions for the problem of faith. It appears that Zeitlin begins his journey with a contemporary and attractive opinion of his time—the *death of God*. The first two characters he meets suggest to him that he acknowledge his God's death. The first, "A black-eyed youth with golden curls, and around him bright flowers and fair maidens," announces to him the death of all Gods. This youth can be identified with Dionysus and his announcement with the explicit Nietzschian influence upon Zeitlin. Yet Zeitlin does not follow here the Dionysian that Nietzsche developed, but rather uses it as a representative of a young movement developing in the early twentieth century in Europe; a hedonistic movement, where the death of God serves as a tool for breaking down the weight of the painful past, and focusing on the present. Its opposite is the second opinion, that of the scientist arguing God's death alongside all metaphysics in the name of positivist science. This character is expressed as "an old and bald man, sitting in a chair and around him skeletons, bones, sinews." This old man knows to direct Zeitlin to the *tombstone* under which God is buried, yet with a murky shadow hovering over it, and "poets wandering amongst the trees and picking up the flowers and mystics speaking to the shadow." Magic and mysticism also acknowledge, in effect, the death of God and carry out their business in front of the shadow on his grave. It is possible, again under Nietzsche's influence, for the old, bald man to be seen as the admired and ridiculed character of old Kant. Heinrich Heine famously saw in Kant the catalyst of God's death. However, the old man whom Zeitlin meets in his vision announces also the death of the remains of metaphysics which Kant left after him, including the grave of the *thing in itself* (*das Ding in sich*) and even of Neo-Kantian doctrines. It is easy to imagine this bald scientist sitting in a chair and surrounded by skeletons, bones, and sinews as an angel of death bringing God and *every spirit* to a shameful burial.

The next character Zeitlin meets is the poet. The poet states that man is God. This romantic view identifies God not as an entity in itself but as a creation of man's genius. The poet advises Zeitlin to adopt this view and rid himself of the pointless voyage in search for God: "hew for yourself a god of your spirit, and if it shall come to be that you shall rage at him—you may shatter him. And if you are troubled or bitter, you may hew of your spirit another god, twice as beautiful as the first one." This suggestion brings to mind the cynical view of religion associated in Jewish tradition with Aristotle and expressed in the *Kuzari* as the philosopher's creed: "invent a religion." A single thread connects this view with the modern criticism of religion such as that of Marx or Feuerbach. According to these views, religion is nothing but a pragmatic human invention, often manipulative, and designed to serve human interests. However, while the modern criticism of religion focuses on political interests served by the invention of God and religion; the poet whom Zeitlin meets describes God as a poetic creation, who serves aesthetic interests in order to achieve inner tranquillity. Leaders invent God in order to control the public, the poets create God in their bitterness of soul, in order to fill their lives with grace and consolation. Both create God and in effect hew a molten calf in their own image. The poet presents the neo-romantic option of returning to God, God as constructed by man, who can be worshipped and destroyed at will—this God serves the "aesthetic"—to use Kierkegaard's typology. We should take note of this proposal and its rejection by Zeitlin. Some interpreters have suggested that his early writing be understood as having a neo-romantic character that he supposedly withdrew from at later stages of his writing. In light of Zeitlin's rejection of this option in *The Thirst*, it is clear that there is no basis for this reading.

The fourth character attempts to persuade Zeitlin to relinquish his quest in the name of pantheistic arguments cloaked in romantic apparel: "Why do you seek God outside you? For he is within you, in the flow of your blood [...] in every movement, in every slight emotion, every shock [...] in every star, every flower [...] in the eternal mountains and grain of sand [...] you shall see your God in all, and he is—all."

Later on, Zeitlin meets the representatives of the three monotheistic religions. The old Jew, "cloaked in his prayer-shawl and crowned in his phylacteries and around him numerous books," advises him to give up on the quest for the God of the present and choose the God of the past as embodied in the scriptures. The Christian monk, on the other hand, "as innocent as a dove on the outside, yet wicked as a snake from within," advises him to put his faith in the Son of God and be saved. On exiting to the street, he meets the masses of these three religions and they advise him to turn to the religious institutions of their priests, where God dwells.

Zeitlin rejects all these various suggestions in the name of what he considers an authentic experience of a wanderer. All those who have tried to show him a path to faith, "have not yet known the depths nor have they yet beheld the nether-world [...] they know a God of methods and religions and things; but they know not a God to Whom one cries when all has been lost...."

> And I had lost all. And I heard a voice calling me from the depths of eternity: Seek me, please!

The Godseeker refuses to accept the death of his God. On the contrary, he hears a voice rising from the depths, urging him to seek. Nevertheless, he rejects the speculative solutions, seeking to resurrect a dead God. From his response we notice a quest for a living God who is in contact with man and world: "my soul thirsts for God, the living, knowing, loving and omniscient God!" The revelation of this God emerging from the *depths of eternity* appears in the form of a single dictum—an imperative commanding the rejection of the institutional and speculative answers that culture offers the individual. He remains lost and seeking while rejecting those lifestyles: atheist, alienated and philosophised, neo-romantic, simplistic and religious-institutionalised—alike.

The Soul's Thirst

Following the rejection, Zeitlin departs from men's company in the vision and turns to the desert. The scene depicting the Godseeker in the desert is in fact a commentary to Psalms 42:2: "As a deer pants for the water brooks, so pants my soul for You, O God." In the verse, the thirst is a metaphor for the poet's thirst for God during crisis. In Zeitlin's interpretation, the metaphor becomes a metonymy: "lo, my soul thirsts for God." In much later writing, Zeitlin returns to clarify his metonymic reference to these verses: "We use illustrations taken from sense and sensation ... a longing for God—'my soul thirsts for God' ... these expressions are not—as others think—imagery and symbolism, but rather accurate illustrations copied off the external senses to the mental and inner ones."

Using the thirst motif, Zeitlin meticulously analyses the phenomenology of the Godseeker:

> Lo, my soul thirsts for God. I am going to seek him. But even before I shall find him—I know him. I know what I lack, I know *that for which my soul yearns*....
>
> Even before I taste the waters before me, even before I know its nature—I well know that I am thirsty for them.
>
> And even if the creek dries out, and even if all the springs and creeks dry out—my thirst will not be quenched.
>
> And even if I imagine to myself that water is but an empty utterance, that the vision of the water is a mere mirage, even then my thirst shall not be quenched.
>
> Whether there be water in the world, or not—my thirst is certain.
>
> The thirst does not know "is" and "is not," it knows only what is missing and it shall go forth seeking it.
>
> Even if I listen to the babbling of mortals saying "there is no God"—my thirst for Him shall not be quenched. If there is no God outside of me, why then He does exist—in my thirst.
>
> And yet the thirst is always for that which is missing, for that which is external. And so even if God dwells within me and not outside me, I shall always crave Him as something dearer to me than my very soul, and as something external to it, at an infinite distance from me, and so I must go towards Him, and to seek Him all the days of my life.

Zeitlin breaks down the biblical metaphor, replacing it with the metonymy of the thirst for God. The state of thirst functions as an analogy of the state of faith. Faith is revealed to the believer as a propositional state. The identification of faith with a propositional statement leads to the rejection of the faith answers offered by the poet, the pantheist, and the vitalist. Faith thus presents itself as referring to the God external to man. However, at the core of the analysis of the thirst is the recognition of absence. Man thirsts for a meeting with a missing God, a God whom he has not met yet. In general, the metonymy of thirst causes the discourse to veer from God's actual being to the existential state of the believer. It does so without losing the predicate of faith and falling into psychological solipsism. Just as he who thirsts for water senses its absence, so he who thirsts for God senses his absence.

As mentioned, the starting point for this journey Zeitlin undergoes is Nietzsche's death of God. An analysis of the state of faith based upon the phenomenon of thirst is an attempt to deal with the Nietzschean challenge. It is easy to notice that Zeitlin's thirsty Godseeker directs his words directly at Nietzsche's strict criticism of religion:

> How many there are who still conclude: 'life could not be endured if there were no God!'[...]—therefore there *must* be a God! [...] The truth, however, is merely that he who is accustomed to these notions does not desire a life without them: that these notions may therefore be necessary to him and for his preservation—but what presumption it is to decree that whatever is necessary for my preservation must actually *exist*!...[16]

Zeitlin avoids deriving knowledge concerning God's existence from his own state. He analyses introspection itself and the assumptions it contains regarding God. The introspection makes the statements regarding God's death irrelevant. Zeitlin does not deny the option that the statement of faith may be countered; on the contrary, he does not even state a positive *claim* of faith! The believer does not have confidence in a real existence of the faith's object; on the contrary, the analysis of the believer's consciousness reveals the state of faith as almost absurd: depicting

---

[16] Friedrich W. Nietzsche, *The Daybreak: Thoughts on the Prejudices of Morality*, trans. R.J. Hollingdale (Cambridge: Cambridge University Press, 1982), 52, §90.

the believer's pining for his god, while at the same time facing His absence. The drama of faith is its dissatisfaction. This lack requires it be filled and motivates the seeker for an action, an action which is a lifelong task—the Quest for God.

The Vision of Souls in the Hall of Truth

At the very centre of the meditation is a dream within a dream, a vision within a vision. Zeitlin highlights this scene and thus implies a reference to the cultural tradition of heavenly journeys designed to unravel secrets and the literary convention of prophetic dreams. The wanderer falls asleep in the desert and dreams of the rise of lost souls and their visiting the heavenly Hall of Truth. It is difficult not to tie this image of the souls swirling around the heavenly Hall of truth to the famous Platonic myth in *Phaedrus*.[17] Plato describes the striving of the souls toward the truth located in the heavens. A soul which has arrived at the ability to grasp the entire truth shall know no more sorrow, yet the souls who only caught a glimpse of it lose their ability to fly and are destined to a human fate, fitting the memory of truth implanted in them. Human suffering is the result of the souls' severed wings. Yet, human experiences that hold a share of the truth awaken the souls and bring their wings to life, wings that begin to grow under the inspiration of memories, and thus the souls turn their faces towards the truth, and soar up high. Zeitlin's seer falls asleep and gets to see types of *Merkava*, yet his use of Platonic myth is ironic. Zeitlin reverses the traditional aim of the visionary genre. While traditionally the prophetic vision in general and the guided vision in particular provide secret information which explains the secrets of reality, as in the Platonic myth, in Zeitlin's vision the souls swirl around the Hall of Truth and are unable to attain any new information or reach the truth. Zeitlin focuses the frame on the souls nearest to the truth; and here we find that it is specifically the various infidels who are described as closest to the truth. That which earned them this attribute is their being Godseekers. Their souls are souls of believers whose uncompromising

---

[17] Stephanus, 245-252; *The Dialogues of Plato*, III, trans. Benjamin Jowett (Oxford: Clarendon Press, 1953), 133-189.

and unattainable quest for truth brought them to various types of faithlessness:

> They sought truth, yet they did not wish to seek and wander. They were too afraid of being lost. And from their weakness and fear they took the first "certainty" and dressed it up in holy clothing, the clothing of God.

The argument contained within this dream, which holds the centre of the meditation, is that the human believer must be a Godseeker in his life and probably also after his death. He is unable, even in a dream or a vision, to achieve a state of faith that will fulfill his Quest. The Godseeker suffers on earth not because of his detachment from the source of truth, but because he is able to reach the deepest truth—the inability to attain it. The common believers do not believe, in fact, in God, but in the gods of their hearts' invention. Of all mortals, the closest to faith were the infidels. The intuition of faithlessness of those rejecting conventional faith is a proper intuition which went astray. The infidels' sin was that they were hasty in accepting a solution for fear of remaining in the vacuum of uncertainty and wanderment. In the world of truth, in the Hall of Truth, their faith shall be refined and cleansed. This process that the souls are bound to undergo is ambivalent—full of joy and full of suffering. On the one hand, it is full of the bliss that is to arrive when reaching the truth; on the other hand, it is filled with guilt for the mistakes and faithlessness which were part of these souls throughout their life. Nevertheless, it should be noted that even in this setting of the vision the souls will never reach complete truth. Their ability to keep individuality is conditioned on their entering the *outer* hall only, and not the *inner* one, for in the inner one they shall be annihilated.

Ascending the Mountain, and Descending It

The Godseeker's journey is not yet over. The vision is no longer. Contrary to the literary convention where a vision completely overhauls knowledge or character, in this meditation the vision is nothing but another part of the journey, and *not* a distinct answer of faith. The lost one's quest, seeking his God, does not come to a rest with the angelic revelation that man cannot reach God in his life, that no mortal can face truth.

Even the visions of the heart are part of the varied consciousness of faith rather than an answer to mental and emotional doubts.

After waking up, the lost one continues his journey. The alternative that yet remains is the advice common in East Asian religions of annihilating consciousness and human will, which in this meditation is borrowed from Schopenhauer's pessimistic philosophy of the "will." Yet even this fails. The protagonist climbs the mountain using a dangerous path that nobody knows and discovers there that he cannot reach nirvana. This sobering up from the climb is similar to the sense attested to by Nietzsche:

> This mountain makes the whole district which it dominates charming in every way, and full of significance. After we have said this to ourselves for the hundredth time, we are so irrationally and so gratefully disposed towards it, as the giver of this charm, that we fancy it must itself be the most charming thing in the district and so we climb it, and are undeceived. All of a sudden, both it and the landscape around us and under us, are as it were disenchanted; we had forgotten that many a greatness, like many a goodness, wants only to be seen at a certain distance, and entirely from below, not from above, it is thus only that it operates.[18]

Having been disappointed by the ascent of the mountain, he descends. This descent, a paraphrase on Zarathustra's descent from the mountain, does not entail an announcement of the death of God as in Nietzsche's writings. The protagonist descends the mountain with the spirit of an announcement beating in his chest, yet this is not a positive announcement of faith but rather a call for Godseeking, as can be inferred from the very end of the meditation, quoted earlier: "I know not yet, let me seek.'"

Death of the Tutor, or the Rejection of Godseeking

There were those who refused to accept Zeitlin's descent from the mountain without the discovery of God and his word to mankind. Thus,

---

[18] Oscar Levy, ed., *The Complete Works of Friedrich Nietzsche: The First Complete and Authorised English Translation*, X, *The Joyful Wisdom* ("*La Gaya Scienza*"), trans. T. Common (New York: The Macmillan Company, 1924), 54.

in his student Simcha Bonim Urbach's rephrasing, the meditation has an entirely different ending:

> And out of his terrible loneliness in the mountains, out of the fear of darkness, out of the shivering of terrible heights, Zeitlin heard the Living Voice of God, the God of goodness and mercy, the God bequeathing life, blessings and mercy to all the dwellers of the world. Out of the great fracture in his wounded soul, out of his great sorrow, Zeitlin found the truth of the heights and depths alike, the synthesis of Heaven and Hell, of the profundity of pessimism and the profundity of faith; he found his way to the great Wonder, transcendent to all human will, desire and longing ... and with these great and worldly forces of the mountains he seeks to descend with them; to water, to affect, to saturate ... his new fire he seeks to carry to his brethren standing at the foot of the mountain.
> Then did Zeitlin descend the mountain and the two tablets of the covenant in his hand....[19]

The image of a loved and influential teacher is subject to his followers, sons, students, commentators, and interpreters. This is especially true in the case of an emotional thinker with a poetic style such as Zeitlin. In many senses his son Aaron Zeitlin and his student Simcha Bonim tried to preserve his memory as one who had in his thought more exclamation marks than question marks. Based on the short (and rather vague in this context) autobiographical listing, *Kitzur Toldotai* they described his thought as developing in a linear fashion. Following them, it is common to distinguish four different periods in Zeitlin's thought: the innocent years of youth at a hasidic-Chabadic house; years of adolescence characterised by faithlessness (during this time Zeitlin was known as an "atheist with phylacteries"); years of "lostness" and spiritual questioning that began following the Kishinev pogrom in 1903 and intensified after the 1905 riots, continuing all the way to World War I; and finally a shift of heart apparently earning him a second innocence and bringing him back to Jewish tradition under the influence of the horrors of World War I. This period continued until his murder in 1942. In weaving this linear axis, Simcha Bonim rewrote the end of the meditation, and

---

[19] Simha-Bonim Auerbach, *History of One Soul: Zeitlin, the Man and His Teachings* (Jerusalem: Shem ve-Yefet, 1953), 75 (Hebrew).

Aaron Zeitlin edited his father's writings extensively so as to moderate views that appeared too radical or doubtful. Yet a thorough study of Zeitlin's writings will reveal that the linear description is inaccurate. Indeed, Zeitlin and his acquaintances testify a strengthening of views of faithlessness and faith during the years of his vast writing and public activity. Yet the comparison of the content of his literary output does not reveal a chronological development, but rather the expressions of different foci in the Godseeker's unresolved Quest for God. The developmental model of Zeitlin's spiritual biography, a model intensified after his murder, described his return to tradition in the rubric of his ecstatic childhood as expressed in *My Brief Biography*. However, with the coming of Hitler to power, Zeitlin gave one more testimony of his childhood, which can shed light on his autobiographical listing:

> And I was yet a mere child of ten years or so, and I chose an hour where my father was absent and there were no strangers at home, and I opened up the Book of Psalms and I read and shed tears reading Psalms 22, 38, and others.
> I felt a sense of relief after much crying, reading those psalms.
> I read "*My God, my God, why hast Thou forsaken me*" and cried.
> I read "*A Prayer of the afflicted, when he is overwhelmed*" and wept....
> I do not know any more what is the quality of a man feeling deserted by God ... and I do not know any more what it is being chased for no wrongdoing, and tortured by wicked people, and I—my heart is torn at the misery of all these things.[20]

This late testimony clarifies the content of the ecstatic experience Zeitlin had in his youth. It reveals that already at the core of his childhood's piety stood the absence, the detachment, the quest for closeness that remained unfulfilled. Long before he knew the taste of persecution, his heart was already torn. Thus it is to be said: Zeitlin's biographical and spiritual development rotated all his life around the axis of Godseeking. It took on many forms, but remained what it is: a faith of question marks and a constant dictum—*let me seek!*

Requiescat in pace.

---

[20] The poem was translated from Yiddish to Hebrew by Shraga Bar-Sela for *Between Storm and Silence: The Life and Teachings of Hillel Zeitlin* (Tel-Aviv: Hakibbutz Hameuchad, 1999), 285 (Hebrew).

A Metamorphosis in the Perception of God in Bialik's Poetry

Tzahi Weiss

I.

The tension between religious and secular attitudes expressed by Bialik in his oeuvre has been a popular subject of Modern Hebrew literature scholarship since the first quarter of the twentieth century. Most of the studies addressing this issue have presented an analytic scheme which defines a dichotomized conflict between the religious and the secular worlds, compounded by an antithetic affective attitude toward the former. This discord is expressed on the one hand as a longing and attraction toward the religious world and on the other hand as repulsion from that very same world.[1] The prevalent scholarly approach locates Bialik in between the religious and secular worlds, and delineates both based on monochromatic principal characteristics which in effect neglect the complexity of images and depictions of the religious and the secular worlds implied in his oeuvre. It should be stressed that while the main question posed and examined in previous studies was whether a study of Bialik's oeuvre uncovers basic support or rejection of the religious world, one rarely encounters a scholarly discussion concerning the various images and different depictions of the nature of the religious life and of God which abound in Bialik's writing. The main purpose of this study will be to maintain that Bialik did not, in fact, possess a set conception of religion or of God and religiosity, as such, and that a close and in-depth scrutiny of his poetry reveals a metamorphosis in his perception of God and in his mythical attitude toward religion.

This article was written with the support of the Shalem Center in Jerusalem.

[1] For a survey of the different attitudes toward this subject, see Shoshana Zimmerman, *From Thee to Thee; The Underlying Principle in Ch. N. Bialik's Poetry* (Tel-Aviv: Tag, 1998), 68-72 (Hebrew).

II.

An examination of a letter written by Bialik from Volozhin Yeshiva at age 18 will serve as an introduction to the unfolding of the metamorphosis he underwent in his theological life journey. In this letter, which was written to his friend Eliyahu Friedman, Bialik discusses, among other issues, the essential difference between the way in which his grandfather read Song of Songs every Friday night at the synagogue between the prayers and the way in which he himself read the very same book.[2]

> He [his grandfather] believes in his heart with a pure, simple and clear belief, without any shadow of doubt, that here, in *Song of Songs*, the *Shekhinah* and *Kneset-Israel* are spoken of with honor. He would not be willing under any circumstances to believe that our king in the sanctuary would sing of love and lust whose legend is founded on earth and its essence derived from dust.... He, like any other Jew, is required to raise from the dust the *Shekhinah*, to return her to her abode and to release her from her exile.... He lived according to the *Drash* (allegory) and he could not understand life according to the *Pshat* (literal meaning). He lived the life of the world to come, where there are the radiance of the *Shekhinah*, unveiled souls, and the *Ten Sefirot* ... and on these, on these, his eye wept...
> On this you had justly wept, poor old man! On this shall I too weep, and both of us shall weep.... I would just make one minor change in the first verse and instead of "*Song of Songs*" I would say "*Lamentation of Lamentations*".... I truly believe that even our king in the sanctuary sang of love.[3]

Bialik notes that the difference between the two ways of reading is comparable to the difference between Song of Songs and the book of Lamentations, and that the chasm between his world and that of his grandfather is designated by the gap between a literal reading (*peshat*) and a symbolic one (*drash*). To Bialik's mind, the picturesque natural landscape outside the synagogue, like the romantic depictions to be found in *Song of Songs,* is an affirmation of a vital and thriving world.

---

[2] H.N. Bialik, *Letters*, ed. F. Lachower, vol. 1 (Tel-Aviv: Dvir, 1939), 29-30 (Hebrew).
[3] Ibid, 30-31.

This, his own stated position, he contrasts to the tenaciously held mythic and symbolic perspective of the older generation, of which his grandfather is an example, wherein physical reality as well as literary realities represented by his grandfather's descriptions were believed to be no more than a reflection of the tragedy of the heavenly realm: the exile of the *Shekhinah*. The clear distinction outlined by the 18-year-old Bialik between his world and that of his grandfather, as well as the rejection of his grandfather's narrative and its mythical dimensions, will be discussed in this paper. It will be demonstrated that contrary to the reductive and perhaps simplistic attitude which was expressed in the letter written as a youth, Bialik in fact had a complex attitude toward the mythical perception and interpretation held by his grandfather.[4] The mythical narrative of theurgical nature, which perceives the *Shekhinah* as an impaired divine figure and allots the observant Jew the responsibility for her rehabilitation, served as an important source for Bialik's writing for many years. It will be attested that the poem "Alone" (לבדי), a prominent milestone in Bialik's poetic oeuvre, reflects, through the depiction of a metamorphosis that takes place in the speaker over the course of the poem, a psychological maturation Bialik himself underwent in the transition from the first to the second decade of his writing.

III.

The poem "If You Want to Know" (אם יש את נפשך לדעת), which conveys an image of the desolate *Beit-Midrash* as revealed to Bialik on his return from Volozhin to Zhitomir in 1892 and from which one can gather a definite image of the *Shekhinah* as possessing a motherly and protective character, reads in part:

---

[4] On the tension between the rejection of the world of his childhood in his early letters and the attraction to the same world later on, see Dan Miron, *Come, Night: Hebrew Literature between the Rational and the Irrational at the Turn of the Twentieth Century* (Tel Aviv: Dvir, 1987), 86-124 (Hebrew).

If you would know the mother merciful,	אִם-תֹּאבֶה דַעַת אֶת-הָאֵם הָרַחֲמָנִיָּה,
The aged matron, loving to the last,	הָאֵם הַזְּקֵנָה, הָאֹהֶבֶת, הַנֶּאֱמָנָה,
Who gathered of her wandering child the tears,	שֶׁבְּרַחֲמִים רַבִּים אָסְפָה דִמְעוֹת בְּנָהּ הָאֹבֵד,
With great compassion tended all his heart;	וּבְחֶמְלָה גְדוֹלָה כּוֹנְנָה כָל-אֲשׁוּרָיו,
And when the outcast came again and faint	וּמִדֵּי שׁוּבוֹ נִכְלָם, עָיֵף וְיָגֵעַ
She wiped away his tears, and 'neath her roof	אֶל-תַּחַת צֵל קוֹרָתָהּ תִּמַּח אֶת-דְּמָעָתוֹ,
Gave him wing'd shade and lullèd him to sleep...	תְּכַסֵּהוּ בְּצֵל כְּנָפֶיהָ, תְּיַשְּׁנֵהוּ עַל-בִּרְכֶּיהָ –
Ah! Chastened brother, if you know not these,	הוֹי, אָח נַעֲנֶה! אִם לֹא-תֵדַע לְךָ כָּל-אֵלֶּה –
Turn to the *Biet Hamidrash*, antic, old...[5]	אֶל - בֵּ י ת הַ מִּ דְ רָ שׁ סוּר, הַיָּשָׁן וְהַבּוֹשָׁן,...[6]

The feminine divinity portrayed in this stanza is a stable and strong mother totally preoccupied with the consolation of her weary sons— seemingly a conventional depiction of the *Shekhinah* as she was before the destruction of *Beit-Midrash*. However, such a depiction is not as common in Jewish sources as it may seem to be at first glance, and it certainly does not accord the relationship between the *Shekhinah* and the Jewish people the full complexity which is warranted. Contrary to the description in Bialik's poem, the commonly held relationship between the *Shekhinah* and the Jewish people as depicted from the end of the twelfth century onwards is of a reciprocal nature. In other words, in addition to the depiction of the comforting and the shepherding role of the *Shekhinah* who accompanies her sons to exile and stands by them in their times of misery, a reciprocal responsibility for her fate is ascribed to her sons when she is captured in exile between the evil powers. In folklore tales, piyyutim, and kabbalistic sources, the *Shekhinah* is described as a weak divine figure in constant need of her sons' favors. It is evident that in the poem "If You Want to Know" the description of the *Shekhinah* in the *Beit-Midrash* is lacking an important element with which many Jews, including Bialik's grandfather, as manifested in the aforementioned letter, were engaged—the Jew's commitment to elevating the *Shekhinah* and rebuilding her throne in the world.

---

[5] *Chaim Nachman Bialik: Poems*, ed. and trans. L.V. Snowman (London: Hasefer, 1924), 49-50.

[6] H.N. Bialik: *Poems*, ed. and notes by Avner Holtzman (Tel-Aviv: Dvir, 2004), 141 (Hebrew).

In another poem, "On an Autumn Day" (ביום סתיו), written about half a year prior to "If You Would Know", an analogous anthropocentric description of the *Shekhinah* can be found: In this allegorical poem, the speaker's mother is described as a lyrical muse, as a mother of the nation, and as a feminine divine presence. This fusion between the various feminine figures, earthly and divine alike, is not rare in Bialik's poems, and in this case it seems that the portrait of the earthly mother is similar to the description of the mother in the poem "If You Want to Know."[7] In this poem, like in the one previously discussed, the cause of the mother's tears is not her own sorry state as a young widow but the orphaned state of her son:

On an autumn day in a dark doleful corner I found her	בְּיוֹם סְתָו בְּקֶרֶן חֲשֵׁכָה נוּגָה מְצָאתִיהָ,
And widowly dressed she revealed herself to me in a vision	וּלְבוּשַׁת אַלְמָנוּת אֵלַי בַּמַּרְאָה הִתְוַדָּעָה,
And with much compassion she eyed me, and silently	וּבְחֶמְלָה רַבָּה שָׂמָה בִּי עֵינֶיהָ, וּבְדוּמִיָּה
Her caressing hand faintly trembled on my head	עַל-רֹאשִׁי יָדָהּ הַמִּתְרַפֶּקֶת חֶרֶשׁ הִזְדַּעְזָעָה –
'My Orphan' – she whispered to me – "my orphan! Forgotten in the darkness	"יְתוֹמִי" – לָחֲשָׁה לִי – "יְתוֹמִי! נִשְׁכָּח בַּעֲלָטָה,
As a budding sapling in the frost, you suffer in your youthful sorrow;	כְּצֶמַח רַךְ בַּקֹּר, בְּדָמֵי יְגוֹנְךָ תִּתְיַגַּע;
But know, that an imprisoned tear shall burn to the lowest hell	אַךְ דַּע-לְךָ, כִּי דִמְעָה כְלוּאָה תִּיקַד עַד-שְׁאוֹל מָטָּה,
And a restrained weeping rises and penetrates the sky.	וּבְכִי מִתְאַפֵּק עַד-שָׁמַיִם עוֹלֶה וּבֹקֵעַ".[8]

In these lines the mother is described as trying to console her son in his agony, her own tribulations in fact serving him as a stable fountain of sustenance. Her words of lament, which allot the restrained crying prayer the power to open the gates of heaven, as well as the description

---

[7] On points of similarity between the depictions of the "mother" in "An Autumn Day" and "Alone," see Adi Zemach, *The Hidden Lion* (Jerusalem: Kiriat Sefer, 1969), 175 (Hebrew).

[8] Bialik, *Poems*, 97.

of the confined tear, which penetrates the netherworld, can be inferred to derive from her own life experience. Notwithstanding this implication in the poem, from which it can be safely surmised that the mother's words have germinated due to her own journey, in this description of her encounter with her son she is nevertheless portrayed as lacking any independent characteristics and personal attributes. Moreover, the relationship between the widowed mother and the son, like that in the previous poem, is not reciprocal. The speaker admits later on in the poem that the mother's tears are only for himself and his own misery:

'How do I pity you, poor child!' – and silently	'מָה רַחֵם אֲרַחֲמְךָ, יֶלֶד אֻמְלָל!' – וּבִדְמָמָה
Two burning fire-kindled tear-slivers dropped on my mouth.	שְׁנֵי רְסִיסֵי דִמְעָה רֹתְחִים קֹדְחֵי-אֵשׁ עַל-פִּי נָפָלוּ.
She did not weep, did not raise her voice—as a dumb sheep	לֹא בָכְתָה, לֹא הֵרִימָה קוֹל – כְּרָחֵל נֶאֱלָמָה
She stood, as if it was for me that her many mercies were directed.	נִצָּבָה, כְּמוֹ עָלַי הֲמוֹן רַחֲמֶיהָ הִתְגַּלְגָּלוּ

As some critics have noted, the mother's figure is not drawn in a realistic manner but is more of a lyrical reflection of a mother who serves as the speaker's inspiration in the creation of his oeuvre.[9] This aspect is relevant to the subject of this paper on two counts: first, in this poem, the mother does possess a mythical character and it is therefore difficult to sever the earthly from the heavenly figure.[10] Second, the mother's weeping, which is described as stemming from the son's sadness and troubles, is the source of his creativity in the poetic present. It should be stressed that the mother's figure is presented as impersonal, insofar as her sorrow solely reflects the orphanhood of her son and his

---

[9] On this, see for example Miron, *Come, Night*, 113.

[10] The heavenly mother can be identified as the *Shekhinah* in reference to the Zoharic and later kabbalistic interpretations of the biblical expression "*as a sheep before her shearers is dumb* (Isaiah 57:3). Those words were interpreted in the Zohar (Zohar 2:29b) as referring to the Shekhinah (רחל). On the image of the Shekhinah in this poem, see Hillel Zeitlin, "On Bialik the Poet of Clarity," *HaTekufah* 17 (1923): 432-433 (Hebrew).

wretchedness, and the speaker gives us no indication of her own feelings as a widow and as a poor and lonely person. This designation of the mother defines a complete cycle of egocentric signification: her grief and tears stem from her son's state in the past and serve as a source of inspiration for his creativity in the present and in the future. Moreover, the mother's silent crying enables the speaker to give his egocentric interpretation to her misery, as he writes: "She did not weep, did not raise her voice—as a dumb sheep/ She stood, as if it was for me that her many mercies were directed." The understanding that the mother's crying stems from his own suffering is explicitly indicated in the poem as the speaker's own interpretation, by the words "as if it was." It seems therefore that the prescription of forbearance and suppression expressed by the mother does not only refer to her silence but is also perhaps a convenient cloak over her silencing: speechless, she can be interpreted with greater ease.

The poem "My Song" (שירתי), written about four years later, is commonly held to be a mirror image of the poem "On an Autumn Day." While in both the suffering figure of the mother is considered a source of inspiration for the speaker's poetic sadness and for his sorrow, in the later poem, there is a significant reversal such that the suffering which is at the crux of the poem is that of the mother. Instead of the self pity expressed by the speaker in "On an Autumn Day," one finds identification, full of guilt, with the mother's figure as an other.

...	...
Do you know where I got my sighs?	וְאִי מִזֶּה תָבֹא אַנְחָתִי יָדַעְתָּ?
My widowed mother, with her orphaned mites	אִמִּי נִתְאַלְמָנָה, בָּנֶיהָ נִתְיַתְּמוּ;
was left without the means of sustenance.	עַד-קָמָה מֵאֶבְלָהּ הַדְּאָגָה קִדְּמַתָּה
Before her mourning ended, worry struck.	נִסְתַּתְּמוּ כָּל-מְקוֹרֵי פַרְנָסָה, נִסְתַּתְּמוּ.
She looked about her at an empty world—	הִבִּיטָה מִסְּבִיבָהּ: נִתְרוֹקֵן עוֹלָמָהּ,
Widowhood, orphanhood, filling all its space.	וְאַלְמֹן וִיתֹם בַּאֲשֶׁר עֵינָהּ נִבָּטָה.
Even the ticking clock was muffled now	גַּם-קוֹל הָאָרְלוֹגִין כְּמוֹ הֻמַּךְ מֵעַתָּה,
even the walls of rooms wept silently,	גַּם-כָּתְלֵי הַבַּיִת כְּמוֹ בוֹכִים בִּדְמָמָה,
each corner hushed in pity and in rage.	וּבְזַעַף וּבְחֶמְלָה כָּל-זָוִית הֶחֱרִישָׁה.
"Lord of the world," the woman softly sighed,	"רִבּוֹנוֹ שֶׁל-עוֹלָם! – נֶאֶנְחָה הָאִשָּׁה –
"support me lest I fall, a widow alone.	סָמְכֵנִי בַּל-אֶפֹּל, אַלְמָנָה אָנֹכִי;
Feed my chicks, poor worms: what is my strength?"	פַּרְנֵס-נָא אֶפְרֹחַי כְּתוֹלָעִים – מַה-כֹּחִי?"

She went to market, blood and marrow spent,	אָז תּוֹצִיא הַשּׁוּקָה אֶת-חֶלְבָּהּ וְדָמָהּ.
returned at evening crushed to her last breath,	בָּעֶרֶב הִיא שָׁבָה כָּל-עוֹד בָּהּ נְשָׁמָה,
each curséd penny gained vexatiously	כָּל-פְּרוּטָה הֲבִיאָה נָאֲרָה בִּמְאֵרָה,
made moist with her heart's blood and soaked in gall ...	רְקוּקָה בְדַם-לִבָּהּ וּטְבוּלָה בִמְרֵרָה,...,
and dumbly sighing out her aching heart.	וְדוּמָם מִתַּמְצִית מַכְאוֹבָהּ נֶאֱנָחָה.
Each motion of the hand or nod of head	וּלְכָל-מְנוֹד רֹאשָׁהּ וּלְכָל-תְּנוּעַת יָדָהּ
stirred the dim candle light as if, concerned,	שַׁלְהֶבֶת הַנֵּר הִזְדַּעֲזָעָה, חָרְדָה,
it said "Ah me. Poor thing.	כְּמוֹ נָדָה לָהּ: צַר-לִי עָלַיִךְ, אֻמְלָלָה!
That a mother's heart should wither	חֲבָל עַל לֵב אֵם אֲשֶׁר-יִמַּק בְּקִצְפָּה,
and waste away in beggary."	עַל-חֹם הֶבֶל פִּיהָ שֶׁיִּנָּדֵף בִּקְלָלָה.
When she lays down to rest her rickety cot	וּבְשָׁכְבָהּ – זְמַן רַב תַּחַת גּוּפָהּ הָרָפֶה
would creak and groan beneath her fragile weight	נֶאֶנְחָה, נֶאֶנְקָה מִטָּתָהּ הַפְּרוּקָה,
as if adversity might buckle it.	כְּמוֹ חֶשְׁבָה הֲרָמוֹטֵט מִנֵּטֶל הַמְּצוּקָה –
Her whispered, anguished "hear oh Israel, hear"	וּלְחִישָׁהּ שֶׁל קְרִיאַת שְׁמַע בַּאֲנָחוֹת טְרוּפָה
continued long to echo in my mind.	זְמַן רַב עוֹד הִגִּיעָה אֵלַי עַל-מִשְׁכָּבִי.
I heard her body's every aching joint	שָׁמַעְתִּי כָל-שֶׁבֶר כָּל-פֶּרֶק מְגוּפָהּ,
and in my heart of hearts I felt a scorpion's sting.[12]	וַיְהִי כַּעֲקִיצַת עַקְרַבִּים לִלְבָבִי[11]

The reader is led, in this detailed and vivid description of her daily horrific misery, to identify with the suffering of the mother, who is no longer portrayed as an allegorical mysterious feminine figure as in "On an Autumn Day" but rather as a figure quite human, suffering the harshness of life.

IV.

The shift from the egocentric description of the mother in "On an Autumn Day" to the empathic one in "My Song" is exemplified within the flow of the poem "Alone," which begins with a description of the speaker's loneliness and ends with a description of the mother's loneliness. The course of the poem delineates a psychological-theological process of maturation, in which the speaker succeeds, towards the end,

---

[11] Bialik, *Poems*, 191-192.
[12] *Chaim Nachman Bialik: Selected Poems—Bilingual Edition*, ed. and trans. Ruth Nevo (Jerusalem: Dvir, 1981), 16-18.

in acknowledging the feelings of the *Shekhinah* herself and hearing the silent crying emerging from her throat.

It is well known that loneliness is one of the most important themes developed in Bialik's poetry, and that "Alone" is one of the most studied poems in his corpus. The following discussion, like the discussion of the previous poems, does not pretend to offer a full analysis but rather to highlight and investigate what is relevant to my research proposition. In this vein I would like to dwell first on a detail in the poem—the moment in which everyone has abandoned the *Beit-Midrash*, leaving the speaker alone, though not for long, with the lonely *Shekhinah*. An extra-literary investigation of this crucial moment calls into question the position held by the majority of scholarly opinion, which grants loneliness, whether of the speaker or of the *Shekhinah*, a negative signification. In the famous autobiographical letter written by Bialik to Joseph Klausner about a year after this poem was written, in which Bialik describes the biographical background of the poem, one learns that the evacuation of the *Beit-Midrash* described in the poem is not only a negative experience, but also a basic condition for an intimate encounter with the Godhead, and in this respect it is positive. In Bialik's words:

> This lonesome sitting in the *Beit-Midrash* became one of the more important channels of influence on my state of mind and internal world. Alone with my old and new thoughts, with my doubts and reflections pent up in my heart, I would sit there many days by the bookshelves ... at times it seemed to me that I am an only son to God and a child of delight to his *Shekhinah*.... And behold, she too is here with me, spreading her wings over me and guarding me as the apple of her eye.[13]

The loneliness which stands at the core of the poem "Alone" is painful, and it is indubitably a result of the abandonment of the *Beit-Midrash*, but at the same time, it also serves as a fertile soil for attaining mystical experiences of intimacy between the speaker and the Godhead that could not have been achieved otherwise. Moreover, in Bialik's memoirs he defines the cause for the abandonment of the *Beit-Midrash* as possessing no dramatic circumstance or significance, such as an attraction

---

[13] Bialik, *Letters*, 164.

to the world of Enlightment, but rather as due to banal motives such as daily bothers and a lack of interest in the world of the *Beit-Midrash*:

> In those days our country was becalmed from the wars of "fathers and sons," "light and darkness", "ignorance and enlightenment." These expressions, integrated here, were already degraded and crushed. In sum, the pioneers and heroes of Enlightenment had already descended from the stage, since education for its own sake was considered stupidity, and simple education was no longer considered heroic, but rather a simple and common matter, and so the noise ceased ... at that time *Batei Midrash* were being forgone, being deserted, day by day. Their sons, their students, left them one by one to wherever the wind carried them ... and at that time I was the sole learner in the "rich" *Beit-Midrash*.[14]

In light of the above passage, it seems an exaggeration at the least to present, as did most critics of this poem, the crux of Bialik's *Alone* as the dichotomous conflict between the Enlightenment and the traditional world. Such an interpretation does not take into account other dimensions that can be found in this poem, one of which I would like to examine in the following lines.

The ironic dimension to be found in "Alone" is not confined solely to its title, which does not distinguish between feminine and masculine and therefore refers both to the speaker and to the *Shekhinah*. In the words "My heart knew her heart," an ironical twist is created, insofar as an expectation is induced in the reader's mind that the innermost feelings of the *Shekhinah* are to be revealed, whereas in actuality the reader is confronted with an almost anticlimactic understanding that nothing of the *Shekhinah* will be imparted, aside from the fact that the source of the *Shekhinah*'s anxiety is not her own feelings but the misery of her son, the speaker: "She feared for me her son, her only one." I suggest that this ironic dimension serves to accentuate the dramatic metamorphosis that can be found in the poem's second half. In the first part of the poem the speaker begins an odyssey which will enable him at the end to see traces of the misery of the *Shekhinah*, to hear the echo of her crying, and to comprehend that they are separate, "two" beings involved in a complex and reciprocal relationship.

---

[14] H.N. Bialik, *Unpublished Writings* (Tel-Aviv: Dvir, 1971), 209-210 (Hebrew).

Silently she wept on me and clung	חֶרֶשׁ בָּכְתָה עָלַי וַתִּתְרַפֵּק עָלַי,
at though enclosing with her broken wing:	וּכְמוֹ שָׂכָה בִּכְנָפָהּ הַשְּׁבוּרָה בַּעֲדִי:
"all gone with the wind, all flown away	"כֻּלָּם נָשָׂא הָרוּחַ, כֻּלָּם פָּרְחוּ לָהֶם,
and I remain alone, alone...."	וָאִוָּתֵר לְבַדִּי, לְבַדִּי..."
And like the end of an ancient lament	וּכְעֵין סִיּוּם שֶׁל־קִינָה עַתִּיקָה מְאֹד,
and like a prayer, a plea and a tear	וּכְעֵין תְּפִלָּה, בַּקָּשָׁה וַחֲרָדָה כְּאַחַת,
my ear heard that quite wept	שָׁמְעָה אָזְנִי בַּבְּכִיָּה הַחֲרִישִׁית הַהִיא
that boiling tear[16].	וּבַדִּמְעָה הַהִיא הָרוֹתַחַת.[15]

The metamorphosis manifested in *Alone* and the conversion of the poem's title from the speaker to the *Shekhinah* break the speaker's solipsistic circle, and it is only at that point that he is able to listen to the *Shekhinah*'s own crying and feel empathy with Her loneliness. The inevitable movement of the speaker toward the "light," outside the *Beit-Midrash*, does not, as I have already stressed, indicate the abandonment of the *Shekhinah*, but rather outlines a normative physical and psychological maturation process of a young person who feels that he does not have enough space under the wings of his mother. It is this distancing by the speaker which allows him to perceive her, the *Shekhinah*, as *an other*, and which enables him to feel her distress, to see her broken wing.

The depiction of the lonely, abandoned, and wounded *Shekhinah*, yearning for the worship of her sons, the people of Israel, is well known and well accepted in Jewish textual traditions since at least the twelfth century. This mythical depiction is similar to the way in which Bialik's grandfather read Song of Songs as a call to prayer in order to strengthen the *Shekhinah*. This similarity between the conclusion of Bialik's poem and the theurgical belief of his grandfather may shed light on an important question in the scholarship of this poem: what is the role of its last verse, which appears, as Adi Tsemach argued, to be an unnecessary appendix, since the main metamorphosis is achieved in the poem: the transition of the subject of the word Lonely from the speaker to the *Shekhinah* has already been completed in the fourth verse.[17]

---

[15] Bialik, *Poems*, 228.

[16] *Songs From Bialik: Selected Poems of Haim Nahman Bialik*, ed. & trans. Atar Hadari (New York: Syracuse University Press, 2000), 23.

[17] Zemach, *The Hidden Lion*, 165.

In the last verse of "Alone," we learn that the silent crying of the *Shekhinah* and her burning tears arouse in the heart of the speaker the memory of the end of the ancient lament, a prayer of "a plea and a tear." Many scholars who interpret this poem perceive this as an allusion to Lamentations, and argue that the abandonment of the *Shekhinah* and *Beit-Midrash* serves as a metonymy for the destruction of the traditional Jewish world in Eastern Europe, and is therefore described using words taken from the biblical book that tells of the destruction of the temple. I suggest that the lament in question does not refer to the destruction evoked in Lamentations, but rather that the quality of entreaty and trepidation of the prayers refers to the theurgical way in which Bialik's grandfather read Song of Songs every Friday night. It should be recalled that the young Bialik, in the letter he wrote to his friend, said that according to the traditional way in which his grandfather read Song of Songs it should be called The Lamentation of Lamentations. It follows that the lament does not refer to the description of the abandonment of the *Shekhinah*, nor to the crises of the so called "traditional Jewish world," but rather it is the sad theurgical melody in which one can hear the silent cry of the *Shekhinah*. This ancient lament is the way in which Jewish people heard the broken and weeping voice of the *Shekhinah* and tried to help her find her place in the world in their daily ritual. According to this understanding, the concluding verse should be considered an important key in the interpretation of the poem. The revulsion expressed by the eighteen-year-old Bialik in the letter to his friend in relation to the theurgical reading of Song of Songs might be considered an attempt of a young person who does not want to listen to the mythical voice of his ancestors, much like he avoids the silent sobs of the *Shekhinah*.

Evidence of the inner struggle Bialik had with these voices can be found in a note he wrote around the year 1900, which was published only after his death. In this note Bialik confessed that although he disparaged the lament of his fathers, the tune of the lament accompanied him throughout his life:

> Since my youth and up until I became a man they sang to me their mournful songs and lamented in my ears their sad and bitter lamentation. And their song took hold of my heart and embroidered and enfolded me with thousands of thin threads, which I knew

and did not know. And they planted in my heart, blood and marrow longings, love and respect to that which I later hated in them and to that which days later I despised with my mouth[18].

V.

The academic scholarship of the poem "Alone" tends to describe it as referring to the rupture in the image of the *Shekhinah* as a consequence of the transition from a "religious" to a "secular" world. This interpretation is based on a basically static and binary point of view inherent in this research which leads to a neglect of, and does not allow for an appreciation for, the different images of God that can be found in Bialik's poetry. Moreover, it follows that such a research attitude cannot comprehend the mythical metamorphosis expressed in Bialik's poetry between the first and the second decade of his writing. In "Alone" the *Shekhinah* is perceived and presented as a weak element in the divine system and as a figure constantly in need of her son's care. Depictions of the *Shekhinah* as a weak part of the Godhead are common in Jewish sources, and it seems that Bialik's depiction of the weak *Shekhinah* confronted him with the mythical origins from which he tried to escape in his youth. This personal journey of the author is likewise reflected in the maturational spiritual process which his literary heroes undergo, and is expressed in the transformed description of the mother in the poem "My Song" as compared with the earlier poem "On an Autumn Day." But perhaps the most poignant expression of this process is achieved within the poem "Alone," in which the whole gamut of the passage from the self-centered attitude of youth to the compassion which makes place for the other is laid out.

---

[18] Bialik, *Unpublished Writings*, 213.

Dialogue and Faith:
*The Lonely Man of Faith**

Dov Schwartz

The Lonely Man of Faith,[1] based on a lecture that R. Joseph B. Soloveitchik delivered at the National Institute of Mental Health at Yeshiva University, is founded on his conception of faith. The main focus in my current discussion, dealing mostly with this conception, will draw a comparison between the "early" and "middle" periods in R. Soloveitchik's work, presenting his discussion of faith in light of his sources through a phenomenological-religious and philosophical-existentialist analysis.

I will first trace the development of R. Soloveitchik's thought on faith from *And from There You Shall Seek*[2] to *The Lonely Man of Faith*. My claim is that this development is reflected in several conceptual and stylistic characteristics:

(1) In *And from There You Shall Seek*, written during the 1940s, faith records the constant and ongoing dialectical situation of humanity. Faith is the choice of a dialectical way of life and provides the motivation to contend with it. *And from There You Shall Seek* reflects a view of faith as encapsulating a consciousness of polarities. *Halakhic Man*,[3] being a description of the Brisk dynasty scholars rather than of R. Soloveitchik himself, does not enter into a deep discussion of faith because the scholars' consciousness is described according to Hermann Cohen's epistemological idealism. In this approach, non-epistemic factors such as feelings and existential states lack any philosophical meaning. By contrast, in articles written in the 1950s and 1960s, some of them

---

* Thanks to Batya Stein, who translated this article from Hebrew.
[1] Joseph B. Soloveitchik, *The Lonely Man of Faith* (Northvale, NJ: Aronson, 1997).
[2] Joseph B. Soloveitchik, *And From There You Shall Seek*, trans. Naomi Goldblum (Jersey City, NJ: Ktav and Toras HoRav Foundation, 2007).
[3] Joseph B. Soloveitchik, *Halakhic Man*, trans. Lawrence Kaplan (Philadelphia: Jewish Publication Society of America, 1983).

included in *Out of the Whirlwind*,[4] faith no longer fully reflects the dialectic situation but rather the pole opposed to success and self-affirmation. Faith reflects the unresponsiveness of nature and of society to the lonely man, an experience that reflects loneliness, alienation, and suffering.

(2) In *And from There You Shall Seek*, faith is an entirely individual experience. True, R. Soloveitchik never blurred the communal-social nature of Halakhah, but faith as such is regarded here as a feature of human intimacy. In his early works, the need to discuss the "other" had never surfaced. By contrast, in *The Lonely Man of Faith*, the other, the society, and the community play an essential role in the experience of faith, concerning both its definitions and its therapeutic role.

(3) Another feature characterizing the development of R. Soloveitchik's thought touches on his sources. In his early thought, the neo-Kantian philosophy of Hermann Cohen that had concerned R. Soloveitchik in his dissertation (later published as a book) is a constant partner to the dialogue, to which R. Soloveitchik then added the conventionalist philosophy of science. This addition explains the phenomenon of *hiddush* since, according to Cohen, there is only one absolute scientific truth. Even when R. Soloveitchik shifts to the use of a different terminology and other sources of influence, Cohen's epistemological idealism still serves as a key intellectual frame of reference. Henceforth, R. Soloveitchik gradually abandons this frame and his starting assumptions change. Epistemic idealism, however, is still a latent element shaping R. Soloveitchik's thought at all times, both positively and negatively.

(4) Finally, a consideration that is no less important touches on the character of the discussion. In *And from There You Shall Seek*, the discussion of faith is conceptual. R. Soloveitchik offered a speculative clarification on the status and the place of faith in the life of the believer. Factual-experiential occurrences are also described

---

[4] Joseph B. Soloveitchik, *Out of the Whirlwind: Essays on Mourning, Suffering and the Human Condition*, ed. David Shatz, Joel B. Wolowelsky, and Reuven Ziegler (New York: Toras HoRav Foundation and Ktav, 2003).

with phenomenological-systematic tools. By contrast, the most penetrating explication of faith in *The Lonely Man of Faith* resorts to ideal types, particularly to "the man of faith" himself, and to a personal and revealing writing style. The analytic approach is replaced by a descriptive-biographical one.

The changes in the status of Halakhah in R. Soloveitchik's various works, and particularly in *Halakhic Man* as opposed to *The Lonely Man of Faith*, have been extensively discussed in the growing scholarly literature of recent years. By contrast, the discussion that follows deals at length with the distinction between the conception of faith in *And from There You Shall Seek* and in *The Lonely Man of Faith*.

Let me emphasize again that the publication of *The Lonely Man of Faith* marks a change in R. Soloveitchik's approach to faith, which is reflected in several of its characteristics. The central one is that in *And from There You Shall Seek* he posits a connection to the other and to the community, which intensifies in the mid-1950s in "Kol Dodi Dofek," where it is expanded to the national sphere.[5] This connection, however, is not an essential component of his phenomenological discussion of faith. At this time, the concept of faith is explored and clarified as a constitutive component of the individual, the personal believer. The projection of the personal tension onto the collective, and questions about the possibility of a community whose members are believing men of faith, are almost entirely absent from R. Soloveitchik's writings up to this point. In sum, the intimate tense connection between the individual and God is the dominant one in R. Soloveitchik's early thought. By contrast, in *The Lonely Man of Faith*, the connection of faith to the "other" and to the community of believers plays an essential role. The possibility of communication between believing subjects and between them and the absolute subject, God, is at the center of his discussion on faith. An important reason for the difference between these two works

---

[5] Joseph B. Soloveitchik, "*Kol Dodi Dofek*: It Is the Voice of My Beloved that Knocketh," in *Theological and Halakhic Reflections on the Holocaust*, ed. Bernhard Rosenberg (New York: Ktav, 1992), 57-117. See also Dov Schwartz, "On Preachers and Preaching in the Religious-Zionist Movement," in *A Hundred Years of Religious Zionism*, ed. Avi Sagi and Dov Schwartz (Ramat-Gan: Bar-Ilan University Press, 2003), 357-392 (Hebrew).

is their variant methodology—that is, the phenomenological discussion of religious consciousness in *And from There You Shall Seek* and the existential autobiographical-therapeutic discussion in *The Lonely Man of Faith* are themselves quite different. In a sense, phenomenological discussion is still part of the inclusive methods, where the individual as such does not play a decisive role. Loneliness is not a subject for the phenomenologist's discussion. This philosophical course, shifting from an inclusive philosophical method to a personal-existential style of writing, is quite widespread among twentieth-century Jewish thinkers. R. Soloveitchik is among those for whom

> philosophic inquiry became a reorientation mechanism facilitating exploration and self-discovery.... Idealistic philosophy afforded him [the Jew] a means of transcending his personal biography, linking it instead to the history of his culture. And existentialism ... placed the actual experiences of individuals searching for their way as the proper point of departure for coming to terms with the "problem of man."[6] All this conformed to the self-understanding of a Jew who felt that the course of contemporary history was totally expressed in the individual's search for self, and in the return from collective history to its biographical underpinnings.[7]

Faith: A Flexible Concept

Characteristically, already at the opening of *The Lonely Man of Faith*, R. Soloveitchik essentially narrows the concept of faith until it sheds off all its traditional realms of discourse. How? R. Soloveitchik opens with a personal tone, using which he directly presents himself as a typological model of "a man of faith" (5).[8] Faith, then, will be dealt in an "autobiographic" mode, and writing will be a therapeutic activity. R. Soloveitchik

---

[6] The link leading from idealism to existentialism, at least concerning its religious dimension (Gabriel Marcel, Jacques Maritain, and others), appears to be the phenomenology of religion.

[7] Eliezer Schweid, *Jewish Thought in the Twentieth Century: An Introduction*, trans. Amnon Hadary (Atlanta, GA: Scholars Press, 1992), 352-353.

[8] Henceforth, all references in parentheses in the text are to pages in *The Lonely Man of Faith* (Northvale, NJ: Jason Aronson, 1965).

draws away from an abstract analysis of the concept of faith, and his writing turns to the inner world and to his concrete personality.[9] Henceforth, he will suggest the range of problems that concern him, exposing their negative aspects:

> I have never been seriously troubled by the problem of the Biblical doctrine of creation vis-à-vis the scientific story of evolution at both the cosmic and the organic levels, nor have I been perturbed by the confrontation of the mechanistic interpretation of the human mind with the Biblical spiritual concept of man. I have not been perplexed by the impossibility of fitting the mystery of revelation into the framework of historical empiricism. Moreover, I have not even been troubled by the theories of Biblical criticism which contradict the very foundations upon which the sanctity and integrity of the Scriptures rest.(7) [10]

This passage recognizes various meanings of *faith* at various times, since R. Soloveitchik was well aware that, in the nineteenth century for instance, biblical criticism had been viewed by many Jewish thinkers as a threat to the belief in revelation and in the holiness of the text. Nevertheless, in his view the modern person's faith is not at all troubled by this matter, just as the implications of Darwin's theory of evolution are not a matter for serious discussion. R. Soloveitchik, then, does not delude himself: what had concerned R. Samson Raphael Hirsch and R. David Zvi Hoffman, for instance, does not concern him. Many issues that had troubled religious-Zionist thinkers are, in his view, no longer relevant.[11] R. Soloveitchik, then, clearly excludes traditional contents and problems from the modern meaning of *faith*. As he rejects any of the traditional approaches to the problem of evil in "*Kol Dodi Dofek*," he does the same here concerning the concept of faith, and notes: "The cultural message of faith changes, indeed, constantly, with the flow of time, the

---

[9] See Avi Sagi, *Tradition vs. Traditionalism: Contemporary Perspectives in Jewish Thought*, trans. Batya Stein (Amsterdam-New York: Rodopi, 2008), 119-121.

[10] This passage has evoked great scholarly interest. See, for example, Lawrence Kaplan, "Models of the Ideal Religious Man in Rabbi Soloveitchik's Thought," *Jerusalem Studies in Jewish Thought* 4 (1984): 327-329 (Hebrew).

[11] See Dov Schwartz, *Faith at the Crossroads: A Theological Profile of Religious-Zionism*, trans. Batya Stein (Leiden: Brill, 2002), ch. 1. The discussion here is partly based on this chapter.

shifting of the spiritual climate" (105). If we wish to understand the meaning of faith in our generation, we must turn to its meaning in the conceptual web that R. Soloveitchik weaves in his essay. In this sense, R. Soloveitchik persisted in his rejection of metaphysics in general and of the methods that had guided Jewish thought throughout the ages, particularly concerning such questions as the human-divine connection, a rejection that had already featured clearly in *And from There You Shall Seek*.

But the difference between the concepts of faith adopted in *And from There You Shall Seek* and in *The Lonely Man of Faith* is also significant. In *And from There You Shall Seek*, the concept of faith assumes absolute meaning, to the point that R. Soloveitchik uses it to distinguish Judaism from other religions in general and from Christianity in particular. R. Soloveitchik was quite determined when he stated the positions of "Judaism" and "Halakhah" in shaping the status and role of faith. Not so in *The Lonely Man of Faith*, where he clearly retreats from the certainty of the mid-1940s. "Whatever I am about to say," writes R. Soloveitchik, "is to be seen only as a modest attempt on the part of a man of faith to interpret his spiritual perceptions and emotions in modern theological and philosophical categories. My interpretive gesture is completely subjective and lays no claim to representing a definitive Halakhic philosophy" (9).

Faith as a Dialectic Pole

In *And from There You Shall Seek*, faith is perceived in its basic Kierkegaardian sense as a recognition and a recording of existential tension. More precisely, faith is a tool that enables us to live with the tension and even encourages dialectical tensions of this type. Faith emerges in *And from There You Shall Seek* as an element that helps us to accept the tension revealed between the two poles: the dynamism of nature vs. its imperviousness, and affirmation vs. lowliness. Faith is the confrontation with scientific-intellectual success, together with the failure to penetrate nature; equally, faith is the confrontation with the heroic human stand before God, together with the disappearance of God and the attending pain. The consciousness of faith is dialectic. In *The Lonely Man of Faith*, faith reflects *one* of the poles. As noted, it emerges with the pole of recognition of nature's imperviousness and the pole of suffering, which reflects the believer's persistent dialectical-Sisyphean process. Rather than a balancing and therapeutic element or a source of motivation for living with the tension, faith explicitly represents the pole of lowliness, as R. Soloveitchik notes:

> The genuine and central cause of the feeling of loneliness from which I cannot free myself is to be found in a different dimension, namely, in the experience of faith itself. I am lonely because, in my humble, inadequate way, I am a man of faith for whom to be means to believe, and who substituted "credo" for "cogitc" in the time-honored Cartesian maxim. Apparently, in this role, as a man of faith, I must experience a sense of loneliness which is of a compound nature. (4-5)

Between the lines, R. Soloveitchik endorses the critique of Descartes' thought as a classic model of subjective rationalism, in the model of Heidegger in "Letter on Humanism"[12] and of Gabriel Marcel's claim that the only certainty provided by the *cogito* relates solely to the epistemological subject.[13] This type of subjective epistemic certainty does not touch on questions characteristic of concrete existence but, according to R. Soloveitchik, is the starting point for such questions. Faith in *The Lonely Man of Faith* has thus lost its essential connection to the pole of affirmation and to the finding of divine traces in natural laws, in philosophy, and in the contemplation of nature. Faith is entirely detached from any connection with affirmation. R. Soloveitchik would henceforth be concerned with the "passional experience of contemporary man of faith" (6) and with the meaning of being a "tormented soul" (22).[14] To be a believer is to experience the confrontation with a meaningless natural

---

[12] Martin Heidegger, "Letter on Humanism," in *The Existentialist Reader: An Anthology of Key Texts*, ed. Paul S. MacDonald (Edinburgh: Edinburgh University Press, 2000), 236-269.

[13] Gabriel Marcel, "On the Ontological Mystery," in *The Philosophy of Existentialism*, trans. Manya Harari (New York: Citadel Press, 1971), 16. See also Marjorie Grene, *Introduction to Existentialism* (Chicago: University of Chicago Press, 1959), 128.

[14] See Pinhas Peli, "On Man in the Philosophy of Rabbi Joseph B. Solcveitchik," *Daat* 12 (1984): 103-105 (Hebrew).

and human reality and thus to experience the torment. So where has the pole of affirmation gone?

This perception of faith requires fundamental changes in the set of anthropological-typological definitions. Making faith a characteristic of the *homo religiosus*, as he did in *And from There You Shall Seek*, no longer fits its true meaning. In *The Lonely Man of Faith*, therefore, R. Soloveitchik sets up two types: Adam the first, who represents majestic man, and Adam the second, who represents the man of faith. An examination of the man of faith's various characteristics, then, will reveal the concern as well as the contents of faith. The typological description that R. Soloveitchik chose to employ in *The Lonely Man of Faith* conveys the idea that rational analysis cannot provide a full description of existence, whereas the description of events, situations, and feelings successfully reveals the existence of faith. Following, then, is an attempt to describe the characteristics of existence through these types and their reactions.

Majestic man seeks to subjugate reality and place its powers at his service ("and subdue it"). Henceforth, the pole of self-affirmation undergoes a process of "personification" and differentiation' that is, it is embodied in a distinct and unique figure, majestic man. At the same time, the pole of lowliness is personified by a specific type, the man of faith.[15] Majestic man is characterized by an active consciousness that has already been defined by Kierkegaard as one that always focuses on elements outside consciousness and, in this case, on the concrete world through the mathematical sphere.[16] His consciousness is not directed to his own existence, as conveyed by the commandment to "be fruitful and multiply." In order to subdue reality, majestic man creates a series

---

[15] On the various characteristics of this type, see Aryei Fishman, *Judaism and Collective Life: Self and Community in the Religious Kibbutz* (London: Routledge, 2002), 10-20. In phenomenological-religious thought, these types converge into the divine entity and, as such, they represent two aspects of the divinity. Karl Barth claimed that on the one hand God reflects majesty, and on the other God is a person or subject. See Karl Barth, *The Knowledge of God and the Service of God According to the Teaching of the Reformation: Gifford Lectures 1937-1938*, trans. J. M. Haire and Ian Henderson (New York: AMS Press, 1979 [1939]), 33-34.

[16] See Ralph Henry Johnson, *The Concept of Existence in the Concluding Unscientific Postscript* (The Hague: Martinus Nijhoff, 1972), 77-78.

of ideal systems—mathematical and physical—that imitate reality and with their help subdues concrete reality to his needs. Again, the pivot is the conventionalist philosophy of science:

> The most characteristic representative of Adam the first is the mathematical scientist[17] who whisks us away from the array of tangible things, from color and sound, from heat, touch, and smell which are the only phenomena accessible to our senses, into a formal relational world of thought constructs, the product of his "arbitrary" postulating and spontaneous positing and deducing. This world, woven out of human thought processes, functions with amazing precision and runs parallel to the workings of the real multifarious world of our senses. The modern scientist does not try to explain nature. He only duplicates it. In his full resplendent glory as a creative agent of God,[18] he constructs his own world and in mysterious fashion succeeds in controlling his environment through manipulating his own mathematical constructs and creations. (18)

R. Soloveitchik presents a radical version of the conventionalist approach whereby the scientific theory is *arbitrary*, "subjective arbitrariness" in Reichenbach's terms.[19] Arbitrariness strengthens the image of majestic man as a creative and entirely independent figure.[20] He does not even depend on rational considerations of "thrifty" or convenient (but not "true") explanations in the creation of a scientific theory, as several conventionalist approaches note; there is no limitation to the "duplication" and control of nature. In this sense, there is no difference between *And from There You Shall Seek* and *Halakhic Man* on the one hand

---

[17] He usually means the Newtonian scientist, who deals with the mathematical natural sciences (*Naturwissenschaften*).

[18] R. Soloveitchik emphasized that the existence of majestic man is not inferior in its standing before God to that of the man of faith. Both types of existence are deliberate divine creations and, as such, both please God. R. Soloveitchik appears to have transposed the Heideggerian principle stating that inauthentic existence is no less real than authentic existence for existential-religious thought.

[19] Hans Reichenbach, *The Philosophy of Space and Time* (New York: Dover, 1958), 36-37. Reichenbach questioned the absoluteness of this statement.

[20] See Joseph Dov Soloveitchik, *The Halakhic Mind: An Essay on Jewish Tradition and Modern Thought* (New York: Seth Press, 1986), 25.

and *The Lonely Man of Faith* on the other: the creation of mathematical-physical theories is the product of reason's absolute freedom.[21] Majestic man is the antithesis of the feeling of dependence on the absolute, through which Friedrich Schleiermacher and Rudolf Otto describe the religious experience.

Majestic man creates his ideal models and as such does not need to seek divine traces in his creation; he himself—according to Cohen's epistemic idealism[22]—creates worlds! This statement emphasizes majestic man's absolute freedom and control, but without implying that he denies the reality or the power of God. Indeed, quite the opposite: he feels himself a "creative agent," God's emissary.[23] Since he realizes his creative ability, which is granted by God, he does not need to "follow the traces." Nor does the experience of facing a threatening nature that reflects the divine presence, an experience to which majestic man is a partner,[24] change the picture. The experience is described as follows:

> Majestic man, even when he belongs to the group of *homines religiosi* and feels a distinct need for transcendental experiences, is gratified by his encounter with God within the framework of the cosmic drama. Since majestic man is incapable of breaking out of the cosmic cycle, he cannot interpret his transcendental adventure in anything but cosmic categories. (50)

---

[21] On other distinctions in the conception of science, see David Schatz, "Science and Religious Consciousness in the Thought of R. Soloveitchik," in *Faith in Changing Times: On the Teachings of R. Joseph Dov Soloveitchik*, ed. Avi Sagi (Jerusalem: WZO, 1996), 325-332 (Hebrew). These important distinctions touch more on the social status of science and on its application than on the philosophy of science that concerns me here.

[22] The connection of majestic man to Cohen's thought has already been noted by Lawrence Kaplan. See Lawrence Kaplan, "The Religious Philosophy of Rabbi Joseph Soloveitchik," *Tradition* 14:2 (1973): 44.

[23] R. Soloveitchik emphasized that Adam the first, or majestic man, is a legitimate representation of God's servant, although this analysis differs from his analysis of Adam's story in "Confrontation," *Tradition* 6:2 (1964): 5-9.

[24] Lawrence Kaplan, "Maimonides and Soloveitchik on the Knowledge and Imitation of God," in *Moses Maimonides (1138-1204): His Religious, Scientific, and Philosophical Wirkungsgeschichte in Different Cultural Contexts*, ed. Gorge Hasselhof and Otfried Fraisse (Würzburg: Ergon, 2004), 516-517. Kaplan's article offers important insights, but our approaches appear to differ, and R. Soloveitchik's teachings are open to many interpretations.

The description of majestic man's "cosmic experience" indirectly relies, once again, on Hermann Cohen's interpretation of Kant. According to both Kant and Cohen, scientific laws are reached by applying thought categories to the "given" (*das Gegebene*), which transcends knowledge as a "preliminary assumption of the sense and the image."[25] Cohen, however, restricted "the given" to a minimum, going so far as to categorize as a mistake the thesis that something that has not emerged from thought can be assigned to it.[26] Hence, although majestic man ostensibly has a transcendent experience, no element in his conceptual world transcends knowledge and his experience is therefore not truly transcendent. Majestic man's ritual and image needs dictate the use of the term *transcendent* in reference to this experience. Yet this is a cosmic-immanent experience and, more precisely, an epistemological experience given a transcendent interpretation. Not so the man of faith. Both majestic man and the man of faith are in a quest for the element beyond the qualitative world. For majestic man, however, this element is knowledge and its models, while for the man of faith it is the divine presence. As R. Soloveitchik writes:

> While Adam the first is dynamic and creative, transforming sensory data into thought constructs, Adam the second is receptive and beholds the world in its original dimensions. He looks for the image of God not in the mathematical formula or the natural relational law but in every beam of light, in every bud and blossom, in the morning breeze and the stillness of a starlit evening.[27] In a word, Adam the second explores not the scientific abstract universe but the irresistibly fascinating qualitative world where he establishes an intimate relation with God. (23)

The dichotomy between majestic man and the man of faith is thus maximal: the philosopher-scientist (the Marburgian neo-Kantian

---

[25] Hermann Cohen, *System der Philosophie*, Bd 1, *Logik der reinen Erkenntnis*, dritte auflage (Berlin: Bruno Cassirer Verlag, 1922), 587.
[26] Ibid., 81. On this question, see the captivating description of Hans Georg Gadamer, "A New Epoch in the History of the World Begins Here and Now," in *The Philosophy of Immanuel Kant*, ed. Richard Kennington (Washington, DC: Catholic University of America Press, 1985), 7-11.
[27] In *And from There You Shall Seek*, the blessing is what encourages the quest for God in "cosmic phenomena."

and the conventionalist) shows no interest in the teeming qualitative world, while the man of faith is indifferent to the ideal models that knowledge creates. His subjective consciousness is not directed to the mathematical representation of the objects but to their real existence. The man of faith is focused on his private existence and on the dialogic relations with God. As such, then, he is alone, and the command that expresses his existence is "to till it and to keep it." The term "Hebrew man of faith" appears in William Barrett's *Irrational Man*, one of the first significant works on existentialist philosophy. Barrett contrasted the "Hebrew man of faith" with the "Greek man of reason" in the context of a confrontation he created between Hebraism and Hellenism. The quest of the Hebrew man of faith is for a concrete existence. Barrett writes:

> The man of faith is the concrete man in his wholeness. Hebraism does not raise its eyes to the universal and abstract; its vision is always the concrete, particular, individual man. The Greeks, on the other hand, were the first thinkers in history; they discovered the universal, the abstract and timeless essences, forms, and Ideas...
>
> The Hebraic emphasis is on *commitment*, the passionate involvement of man with his own mortal being (at once flesh and spirit), with his offspring, family, tribe, and God; a man abstracted from such involvements would be, to Hebraic thought, but a pale shade of the actual existing human person.[28]

In place of Barrett's Hellenism, R. Soloveitchik posits Cohen's epistemological idealism. But R. Soloveitchik adopted faith as an existential characteristic of the quest for reality and even as a problem of connection and communication, as shown below. More precisely, in *And from There You Shall Seek*, faith records the tension between scientific-philosophical majesty on the one hand, and the quest for teeming qualitative nature on the other, whereas in *The Lonely Man of Faith*, faith reflects only the quest for reality. In *And from There You Shall Seek*, the discursive proofs of God's existence, which is the channeling and balance of the religious experience, played an important role. In *The Lonely Man of Faith*, the

---

[28] William Barrett, *Irrational Man: A Study in Existential Philosophy* (Garden City, NY: Doubleday, 1962), 77-78.

opposite direction prevails: the decay of religious experience leads to rational proofs.[29]

For R. Soloveitchik, then, faith is closely connected to the foundations of concrete existence (extracting it from epistemological idealism) and, as he notes, it is an "existential experience." Knowledge of the qualitative-concrete and finite world becomes an existential experience. Indeed, faith reflects the attempt to penetrate reality and expose the "image of God" that is within it.

The approach opposed to this reality on the one hand, and to epistemological idealism and scientific conventionalism on the other, reveals the deep difference between the two types regarding their motives as well. Majestic man strives to manipulate nature. By contrast, the man of faith strives for "another mode of existence through which man can find his own self, namely, the redemptive" (25). The approach to reality as a hidden divine demand is only one aspect; the man of faith seeks to decode the meaning of personal existence and thereby to attain the redemption he longs for. This redemption is merely a palliative to suffering, loneliness, and pain. A preliminary formulation would be that redemption is related to the possibility of communication between the man of faith and others whose existence is distinctively subjective (another man of faith and God).

Unquestionably, presenting the man of faith as a figure whose interests are in radical conflict with those of majestic man prevents a true dialogue between the two ideal types, the subjective and the objective, and I address this issue below. What merits attention here is that the model of loneliness and pain as a primary and fundamental datum of existence had already emerged in R. Soloveitchik's essays on family life,[30] published in *Family Redeemed*. The need for a personal redemption that is tied to the intersubjective connection while anchored in the objective dimension of existence is also considered in great detail in these essays. Yet, channeling the models and concepts that appear in these essays into the issue of faith requires a more general elaboration, different from questions of coupledom and parenthood.

---

[29] "The cosmic experience was transformed into a cosmological proof, the ontic experience into an ontological proof, etcetera" (*The Lonely Man of Faith*, 51, note).

[30] Joseph B. Soloveitchik, *Family Redeemed: Essays on Family Relationships*, ed. David Shatz and Joel B. Wolowelsky (New York: Toras HoRav Foundation, 2000).

A Life of Faith

R. Soloveitchik does not clarify precisely the meaning of the term *faith*, and often uses it as an a priori datum. Furthermore, faith appears as a typical characteristic of the figure and the action of the man of faith. Conceptual clarification cannot exhaust the term *faith*, since such a clarification is still an abstract reflection. The meaning of this term, then, can be discussed in connection with an existence of faith or a life of faith. Here too, a distinction prevails between *And from There You Shall Seek* and *The Lonely Man of Faith*. Whereas in the earlier work the reader becomes acquainted with the conceptual-phenomenological explication, at the center of the later one is the concrete figure. In the earlier work, R. Soloveitchik tried to define the phenomenological state of faith through the conceptualization and articulation of a dialectical process. In *The Lonely Man of Faith*, the speculative concept is replaced by a description of real life. When phenomenological writing is replaced by biographic and therapeutic writing, faith is revealed as the pole of rift and pain.

According to this caveat, one might assume that faith according to *The Lonely Man of Faith* reflects a constitutive foundation or an element directing to a specific type of concrete existence that is characterized by a sense of challenge and mission (actually redemption). The fundamental and original characteristic of an existence of this kind, as noted, is pain and imperviousness. But what are the roots of the pain and the imperviousness? Suffering and pain are an "external" emotional expression of an "internal" real-existential situation.

The foundations of this type of existence, "a life of faith," should therefore be properly defined. Generally, the existence of majestic man can be characterized as objective, and that of the man of faith as subjective.[31] The three general elements that build up the experience of faith-subjective existence are:

(1) Existential loneliness.
(2) Renunciation and sacrifice
(3) Time and eternity.

---

[31] See Abraham Schweitzer (Sagi), "The Loneliness of the Man of Faith in the Philosophy of Soloveitchik," *Daat* 2:3 (1978-1979): 251-255 (Hebrew). R. Soloveitchik describes objective and subjective existence in connection with Halakhah in *Kol Dodi Dofek*.

I will now define the three elements that constitute faith and their possible sources.

(1) Existential Loneliness

The man of faith is aware that he is not only "alone," he is also lonely. "Aloneness" is a "practical surface experience," which immediately disappears when we join a group of other people. By contrast, "loneliness is nothing but the act of questioning one's own ontological legitimacy" (31). R. Soloveitchik again differentiates between a "surface" feeling and a "deep" situation (for instance, fear vs. anxiety, facing death vs. finitude) The man of faith is lonely because he is not understood. The redemption he strives for, which is concerned with a life of value and meaning, is incomprehensible to the surrounding society, that is, the society of majestic men. Loneliness is an existential component of the human figure. Kierkegaard had already clarified that "'the knight of faith'[32] is assigned solely to himself; he feels the pain of being unable to make himself understandable to others, but he has no vain desire to instruct others."[33] Heidegger argued that the subject is "thrown" against his will into a world of objects wherein he is to realize himself; thus, he is lonely.[34] Rollo May presented loneliness as an expression of existential anxiety.[35] From the start, subjective existence confronts meaningless objects.

This loneliness has a distinct social meaning: the man of faith operates in a social world ("a natural community") of indifference to and alienation from his values. According to R. Soloveitchik, the natural community is a manipulative association of rational creatures, majestic men who are prevented from "realizing the metaphysical dilemma and

---

[32] R. Soloveitchik too resorts to this expression in reference to Abraham. See *The Lonely Man of Faith*, 50. See also David Singer and Moshe Sokcl, "Joseph Soloveitchik: Lonely Man of Faith," *Modern Judaism* 2 (1982): 244-245.

[33] Søren Kierkegaard, *Fear and Trembling: Repetition*, trans. Howard V. Hong and Edna H. Hong (Princeton, NJ: Princeton University Press, 1990), 80. On the impossibility of speech and communication in Kierkegaard's thought, see Alastair Hannay, *Kierkegaard* (London: Routledge and Kegan Paul, 1982), 84-89.

[34] Martin Heidegger, *Being and Time*, trans. John Macquarrie and Edward Robinson (New York: Harper and Row, 1962), 236-237.

[35] Rollo May, *Man's Search for Himself* (New York: W.W. Norton, 1953), 27.

existential paradoxicality, indeed absurdity, embedded in the human 'I' awareness" (30).[36] The kind of connection that might redeem the man of faith from his existential loneliness is meaningless in such a community. Unawareness of the problem precludes any understanding of cathartic personal redemption and of the very need for it. R. Soloveitchik relied on Heidegger, who had viewed communication as the discourse typical of authentic existence. This kind of discourse exposes human-concrete existence in the world, the being here (*Dasein*). Authentic discourse is contrasted with artificial discourse.[37] But R. Soloveitchik seems to have made authentic discourse between subjects, insofar as it depends on them, impossible:

> And defeated must Adam the second feel the very instant he scores his great success: the discovery of his humanity, his "I" identity. The "I" awareness which he attains as the result of his untiring search for a redeemed, secure existence brings its own antithesis to the fore: the awareness of his exclusiveness and ontological incompatibility with any other being. Adam the second suddenly finds out that he is alone, that he has alienated himself from the world of the brute and the instinctual mechanical state of an outward existence, while he has failed to ally himself with the intelligent, purposive inward beings who inhabit the new

---

[36] See Gili Zivan, "The Religious Experience According to R. Soloveitchik," in *Faith in Changing Times: On the Teachings of R. Joseph Dov Soloveitchik*, ed. Avi Sagi (Jerusalem: WZO, 1996), 221 (Hebrew); Benjamin Ish-Shalom, "Language as a Religious Category in the Works of R. Joseph Ber Soloveitchik," in *Rabbi Mordechai Breuer Festschrift: Collected Papers in Jewish Studies*, ed. Moshe Bar-Asher, vol. 2 (Jerusalem: Academon, 1992), 799-821 (Hebrew).

[37] Heidegger, *Being and Time*, 204. See also Harrison Hall, "Intentionality and World: Division I of *Being and Time*," in *The Cambridge Companion to Heidegger*, ed. Charles Gignon (Cambridge: Cambridge University Press, 1993), 138-139. The intersubjective connection as a problem was emphasized in phenomenological and existentialist psychological writings. Carl Rogers, for instance, would write that "interpersonal communication is almost never achieved except in part" (*Freedom to Learn: A View of What Education Might Become* [Colombus, OH: C. E. Merrill, 1969], 222). On language and revelation in the work of R. Soloveitchik, see also Ish Shalom, "Language as a Religious Category." On the distinction between genuine and technical or formal dialogue in Martin Buber's thought, which also reflects the thought pattern of R. Soloveitchik here, see Paul E. Pfuetze, *Self, Society, Existence: Human Nature and Dialogue in the Thought of George Herbert Mead and Martin Buber* (New York: Harper and Row, 1954), 170.

world into which he has entered. Each great redemptive step forward in man's quest for humanity entails the ever-growing tragic awareness of his aloneness and only-ness[38] and consequently of his loneliness and insecurity. (37)

When the characteristics of faith are formulated according to the man of faith type, we find that faith is related to an existential situation of alienation[39] and the confrontation with it (or, more precisely, the attempt to alleviate it). Lack of communication with the natural community exposes the rootedness of loneliness, which is not confined to the social-communitarian aspect. According to R. Soloveitchik, the social dimension of loneliness rests on its natural-cosmic dimension. Loneliness has a cosmic meaning as well, then, which R. Soloveitchik had already discussed at length in *And from There You Shall Seek*: reality does not reveal itself to the man of faith but hides and vanishes when confronted with the sincere and desperate attempt to understand its essence and its purpose (the imperviousness of the nature pole). Added to these two dimensions is a distinctly religious-theological and metaphysical aspect: even God eludes the (rational and experiential) human yearning to know Him. Alienation, then, is also evident in God. Loneliness is thus a three-stage process: (1) natural-cosmic; (2) social; (3) divine. But the social-communal aspect of loneliness, that is, the impossibility of communication as a characteristic of faith, is the essential innovation of *The Lonely Man of Faith*. Man cannot, by definition, expose his deep existential structure to the other. He is unique, and his existential basis is intransitive.

Hence the failure that comes with success. When the man of faith finally succeeds in discovering the nature of his existence, he finds that it cannot be explained in rational or emotional terms. Like Abraham,

---

[38] R. Soloveitchik hints here at an idea he develops below, in the second characteristic typical of the man of faith: the more the man of faith understands the meaning of redemption as interpersonal (or more precisely, intersubjective) communication, the more he understands that such communication is impossible. This is a latent meaning of the failure (the ability to connect) which arrives at the height of success (understanding the idea of redemption). Only God's intervention will enable the connection. See below.

[39] See Avi Sagi, *Albert Camus and the Philosophy of the Absurd*, trans. Batya Stein (Amsterdam-New York: Rodopi, 2002), ch. 1.

the "knight of faith" according to Kierkegaard, the man of faith comes to learn that he is, by definition, incomprehensible to those surrounding him. "'To be' means to be the only one, singular and different, and consequently lonely" (40-41). Adam the second, therefore, "has no companion with whom to communicate" (38). Making the pole of suffering and imperviousness the starting point of faith sheds light on the distance from rationality and feeling typical of the pole antithetical to faith, thereby precluding genuine communication. The split between majestic man and the man of faith compels a starting point of loneliness and lack of communication, and the conception of faith is shaped accordingly.

(2) Renunciation and Sacrifice

The man of faith knows that redemption from loneliness is attained through self-retreat and sacrifice. R. Soloveitchik presented a paradoxical model: when the man of faith succeeds (by discovering his identity and his existence), he fails (the state of loneliness and renunciation); in his failure (loneliness and sacrifice) he attains success (redemption through communication with "the other"). "The medium of attaining full redemption is, again, defeat. This new companionship [with a special and unique friend like the man of faith] is not attained through conquest, but through surrender and retreat" (39). Faith, then, is linked to renunciation and sacrifice. Here too, R. Soloveitchik relies on Kierkegaard, who wrote: "Infinite resignation is the last stage before faith, so that anyone who has not made this movement does not have faith, for only in infinite resignation do I become conscious of my eternal validity, and only then can one speak of grasping existence by virtue of faith."[40]

The renunciation of the "knight of faith" that Kierkegaard describes in the context of the binding of Isaac hinges mainly on morality, but also involves another important dimension. Samuel Hugo Bergman, whose articles influenced R. Soloveitchik's thought and style, described the "movement" typical of Abraham: "The renunciation of the world. The renouncing man detaches himself from his ties to the world. Through this detachment from the outside, he turns these ties into something

---

[40] Kierkegaard, *Fear and Trembling*, 46. See also Reidar Thomte, *Kierkegaard's Philosophy of Religion* (Westport, CO: Greenwood, 1948), 56-57.

internal, ideal."⁴¹ What he renounces is the realization of the loving ties between the binding father and the bound son in the exterior world. But in R. Soloveitchik's discussion, the man of faith renounces initiative and "subduing" the other, since what must be clarified is:

(1) How will the lonely man find his friend? Majestic man and the man of faith coexist in one society and, ostensibly, do not look different from other society members. The experience of an existence pervaded by suffering and indifference touches the innermost layers of the "self." How, then, will what R. Soloveitchik called "existential companionship" be sustained? This problem was clearly formulated by Jacques Maritain: "I am known to other men. They know me as object, not as subject. They are unaware of my subjectivity as such."⁴² How, then, will one man of faith living a subjective existence find his companion, who lives a similar existence?

(2) In the previous questions, we assumed that the man of faith seeks to connect with another subject but is unable to find him. A deeper question is, how will the man of faith be aware of the actual need for communication with the other and of the concomitant cathartic experience? The man of faith is, by definition, a lone, introverted subject. How will he know that his redemption lies in exposure to the other?

The answer lies in renunciation and sacrifice: God reveals to man the secret of communication, in a manifestation of divine grace. The redemptive experience percolates into the believer's consciousness through divine revelation. The man of faith then finds that an exterior mediator is required, a "He." Faith implies a recognition of limitations, a gathering inward, and a dependence on the absolute subject—God. The man of faith a priori renounces any initiative and manipulation of the other. Dependence on the absolute assumes a social face: "Adam the first met the female all by himself, while Adam the second was introduced to Eve

---

[41] Samuel Hugo Bergman, "Søren Kierkegaard and the Binding of Isaac," in *Thinkers and Believers* (Tel Aviv: Dvir, 1959), 125 (Hebrew).

[42] Will Herberg, *Four Existentialist Theologians: A Reader from the Works of Jacques Maritain, Nicolas Berdyaev, Martin Buber, and Paul Tillich* (Garden City, NY: Doubleday, 1958), 48.

by God, who summoned Adam to join Eve in an existential community molded by sacrificial action and suffering, and who Himself became a partner in this community" (43-44).

This is how a "community of faith" or "covenantal community" is built, where the "I" and the "thou"—two lonely men of faith—are exposed to one another by virtue of the presence and participation of God ("He") in the community of faith. The perception of God as the initiator, mediator, and enabler of the connection with the other is clearly articulated in Karl Barth's analysis of the creation story. Barth writes:

> God Himself brings her to him. God Himself brings and gives her to him.[43] Without this link, everything which precedes and follows is unthinkable. It is God's relationship to man, His mercy toward him, which brings about this completion of his creation, giving meaning to the existence of woman and disclosing her secret. Naturally the completion of man's creation in the relationship of I and Thou, of male and female, in the mutual encounter and duality of the two, is the work of God.... He creates not only the I and Though, man and woman, but also their mutual relationship.[44]

It is God that enables the encounter between Adam and Eve, and exposes the dialectic of their intersubjective relationship.[45] R. Soloveitchik applied Barth's approach to the terminology and the existential problematic he presented in *The Lonely Man of Faith*. This approach recurs in the model offered by Buber, whereby the existence of God enables the dialogical connection, and is indeed a guarantee of its existence.[46]

---

[43] According to Genesis 2:22: "and brought her to the man."

[44] Karl Barth, *Church Dogmatics*, vol. 3, *The Doctrine of Creation*, part I (Edinburgh: T. and T. Clark, 1958), 298.

[45] Sagi, *Tradition vs. Traditionalism*, 33-34.

[46] See Rivka Horowitz, *Discoveries Bearing on the Germination of Martin Buber's I and Thou: Proceedings of the Israel Academy of Sciences and Humanities* (Hebrew series) 5:8 (1975): 185. Cf. Zvi Kolitz, *Confrontation: The Existential Thought of Rabbi J.B. Soloveitchik* (Hoboken, NJ: Ktav, 1993), 45; David Hartman, *Love and Terror in the God Encounter: The Theological Legacy of Rabbi Joseph B. Soloveitchik* (Woodstock, VT: Jewish Lights, 2001), 168; Ephraim Meir, *Jewish Existential Philosophers in Dialogue* (Jerusalem: Magnes Press, 2004), 67 (in Hebrew). Note, however, the difference between R. Soloveitchik and Buber. Buber makes connection a foundation of life and, in many ways, higher than the individual's personal existence. The dialogical association is certainly more interesting than individual existence.

The pole of suffering and imperviousness that is mentioned in *And from There You Shall Seek* assumes a distinctly social-communal aspect. Reliance on God's mediation is, as noted, the renunciation of the man of faith: "If God had not joined the community of Adam and Eve, they would have never been able and would have never cared to make the paradoxical leap over the gap, indeed abyss, separating two individuals whose personal experiential messages are written in a private code undecipherable by anyone else" (68).

Since the two men of faith are characterized by introversion, the relationship between them is a paradox. Going out of the self toward the "other" is intrinsically contradictory, since the meaning of the subjectivity characterizing the existence of the man of faith is a non-transferable uniqueness. Only God's intervention enables men of faith to bridge the gap between them. Unlike for Buber, for instance, who assumes that the finite I-Thou precedes the eternal I-Thou,[47] for the man of faith the eternal I-Thou precedes and conditions the connection between man and other.[48] Furthermore, unlike Buber, who holds that man confronts God with his independence and his autonomy in the context of their dialogue, and contrary to André Neher, who went even further and claimed that God needs the covenant more than man,[49] R. Soloveitchik

---

See, for instance, Pfuetze, *Self, Society, Existence*, 140. For R. Soloveitchik, by contrast, individual existence is fundamental and no less interesting than the existence of relations. Furthermore, R. Soloveitchik presented at the time extensive discussions about individual existence without resorting to question of dialogue; at times, the existential characteristic is not social.

[47] See Avi Sagi (Schweitzer), "The Relationship between 'I-Thou' and 'I-Eternal Thou' in the Philosophy of M. Buber," *Daat* 7 (1981): 151-152 (Hebrew); Yehoyada Amir, "Buber: The Finite Thou and the Eternal Thou," in *Martin Buber: On the Centenary of His Birth*, ed. Yohanan Bloch, Hayyim Gordon, and Menachem Dorman (Tel Aviv: Hakibbutz Hameuchad, 1982), 89 (Hebrew); Maurice Friedman, *Martin Buber's Life and Work: The Early Years, 1878-1923* (New York: Dutton, 1981), 354-371. See also Ish Shalom, "Language as a Religious Category," 819.

[48] R. Soloveitchik did not renounce the dialectic here either, and the integration of the prophecy and prayer communities leads to the wavering between divine and human initiative. See, for instance, *The Lonely Man of Faith*, 56-58.

[49] André Neher, *The Prophetic Existence*, trans. William Wolf (South Brunswick, NJ: Barnes, 1969), 120-121. This book was first published about ten years before *The Lonely Man of Faith*.

did not abandon the phenomenological model that speaks of a "creature-feeling" as a human characteristic, in the style of Schleiermacher and Otto.[50] R. Soloveitchik views man as absolutely dependent on God for his redemption through the covenant. In sum, the encounter and the dialogue with the other depend on the presence of the divine element. In this sense, R. Soloveitchik's teachings fit the approach of Jacques Maritain, who stated: "Religion is essentially that which no philosophy can be: a relation of person to person with all the risk, the mystery, the dread, the confidence, the delight, and the torment that lie in such a relationship."[51] God is revealed, above all, as allowing the paradoxical connection between two men of faith, and this connection is tied to renunciation and to a sense of worthlessness given the divine power and the *mysterium tremendum* that defines it.

Renouncing initiative is added to another basic renunciation. The state of faith, as noted, is related to suffering. The man of faith does not seek redemption in order to eradicate suffering, which is not possible. "Only the covenantal community consisting of all three grammatical *personae*—I, thou, and He—can and does alleviate the passional experience of Adam the second [the man of faith]" (53). Recognizing pain as the basic datum of existence that can be alleviated but not avoided is the renunciation of the man of faith who, a priori, renounces a theodicy that could blur and deny suffering. The man of faith acknowledges suffering and seeks to share the existential experience of pain with another subject in the covenantal community. The goal, in his view, is communication. "The loneliness of the man of faith is an integral part of his destiny from which he can never be completely liberated" (79-80).

In the essays on family life, which are largely a preface to *The Lonely Man of Faith*, renunciation for the sake of communication is epitomized by sexual fidelity. The partners give up sexual experiences with others (adultery) and take upon themselves other halakhic limitations. By contrast, faith requires us to renounce initiative and power. Only God can

---

[50] See Friedman, *Martin Buber's Life and Work*, 433; Robert Gibbs, "Teaching Rosenzweig as a Philosopher and Lévinas as a Jewish Thinker," in *Paradigms in Jewish Philosophy*, ed. Raphael Jospe (Madison, WI: Fairleigh Dickinson University Press, 1997), 222.

[51] Herberg, *Four Existentialist Theologians*, 45-46. Maritain clarified that he deals with the intersubjective relationship.

enable the dialogue. Another difference between these works concerns the alleviation of tension and pain. The tension and the pain that characterize faith and the existence of faith cannot be entirely resolved, and therefore one must learn to live with them. By contrast, the intersubjective relationship of marital partners, which unfolds within defined objective limitations, is a teleological relationship (to bring forth and educate children) that, to some extent, enables tension release. In any event, the model of renunciation as the foundation of the connection emerges in the discussions about family life, and is developed in detail in *The Lonely Man of Faith*.

(3) Time and Eternity

A significant feature of the man of faith is his attitude to the "experience of time" (71). R. Soloveitchik's earlier writings offer different time perceptions:

(1) In *The Halakhic Mind*, objective time for *homo religiosus* is in a mid-position between quantitative and qualitative time, as clarified below.

(2) In "Sacred and Profane,"[52] the dominant element in the experience of time of *homo religiosus* is the qualitative element.

(3) In *Halakhic Man*, the pure halakhic type leans in a quantitative direction.

The time perception of majestic man, according to his definition, is consistent with the quantitative-mathematical perception of halakhic man: "The time with which he works and which he knows is quantified, spatialized, and measured, belonging to a cosmic coordinate system" (70). On the time perception of the man of faith, R. Soloveitchik writes as follows:

> In retrospect, covenantal man re-experiences the rendezvous with God in which the covenant, as a promise, hope, and vision, originated. In prospect, he beholds the full eschatological realization of his covenant, its promise, hope, and vision. Let us

---

[52] Joseph B. Soloveitchik, "Sacred and Profane, Kodesh and Hol in World Perspectives," *Gesher* 2:1 (1966).

not forget that the covenantal community includes the "He" who addresses Himself to man not only from the "now" dimension but also from the supposedly already vanished past ... as well as from the as-yet-unborn future, for all boundaries establishing "before," "now," and "after" disappear when God the Eternal speaks. (71)

The starting point in a faith existence is, once again, tragedy and paradox, and the experience of time is included in such an existence. Action in the present, then, is paradoxical, since the present is abstract and lacks essence, missing either past or future. On the one hand, man is a historical creature, and on the other, he is supra-historical.[53] Initially, the man of faith confronts an unstable temporal existence. Such an existence is one of the expressions of loneliness. Only the appearance of God (in the covenantal community) gives meaning to paradoxical time and makes the man of faith responsible for both past and future.

Until the appearance of God, the man of faith had been subject to quantitative time, which for him is meaningless; through God's revelation, he becomes aware of the qualitativeness of time. Note that halakhic man too is a partner in the past and the future insofar as the continuing tradition of Torah innovations is concerned; and the tradition has a supra-temporal and supra-local dimension.[54] The difference between halakhic man and the man of faith, besides the tendency of halakhic man toward quantitative time, is the following: for halakhic

---

[53] The version of the paradox intended by R. Soloveitchik is not clear. Several versions have been considered in existentialist thought. Sartre, for instance, related the paradox of temporality to the other as well: "I myself am historical to the extent that others also make history and make me, but I am a transhistorical absolute by virtue of what I make of what they make of me, have made of me and will make of me in the future." Jean-Paul Sartre, *Between Existentialism and Marxism*, trans. John Mathews (New York: Pantheon, 1974), 161. See also, for instance, Hanoch Tennen, *The Conception of an Existential Ethics in Karl Jaspers' Philosophy* (Ramat-Gan: Massada, 1977), 60-61 (Hebrew), and Dov Schwartz, "On Finitude and its Existentialist Sources in David Hartman's Thought," in *Renewing Jewish Commitment: The Work and Thought of David Hartman*, vol. 1, ed. Avi Sagi and Zvi Zohar (Jerusalem and Tel Aviv: Shalom Hartman Institute and Hakibbutz Hameuchad, 2001), 495 (Hebrew).

[54] See Max Scheler, *Man's Place in Nature*, trans. Hans Meyerhoff (Boston: Beacon Press, 1961), 26-27.

man, the supra-temporal element is reflected in the scholarly tradition, whereas for the man of faith, what turns an unsubstantial and paradoxical temporal existence into a meaningful and qualitative one is God's revelation.

Faith and the "Other"

Having clarified that the starting point of faith is the pole of suffering and imperviousness, we can define the functionality of faith in the concrete existence whose characteristics were described above. Faith relates directly to the encounter and the connection with the other. This tie between faith and the possibility of dialogue has been discussed at length in the philosophy of Buber, who specifically states: "I said he believes, but that really means *he meets*."[55] R. Soloveitchik articulates this approach as follows:

> In the existential community ... one hears not only the rhythmic sound of the production line, but also the rhythmic beat of hearts starved for existential companionship, and all-embracing sympathy and experiencing the grandeur of the faith commitment; there, one lonely soul finds another soul tormented by loneliness and solitude yet unqualifiedly committed. (41-42)[56]

In other words, faith does not help a man leading a lonely existence, an existence that cannot be imitated, to reveal himself to the other and create a community. The "other" is, on the one hand, another man of faith, and on the other, God Himself. Faith, then, fulfills a distinctively redemptive role, which allows man to create a dialogue with another man and thus establish a social and communal existence. Without faith, extricating oneself from the fetters of existential loneliness, or even understanding it in the proper light, would be impossible. Furthermore, creating a teleological community is impossible without faith. Faith is the element that grants man the strength and the power to overcome constraints in the relationships between God and the world, individual and society, time and eternity. Paul Tillich recurrently emphasized in his

---

[55] Martin Buber, *I and Thou*, trans. Ronald Gregor Smith (London: Continuum, 2004), 49 (emphasis in original).
[56] See Kaplan, "Models of the Ideal Religious Man," 331-332.

writings the *community of faith* concept. He claimed that, as a structured part of the personality, faith requires its own language, the language of faith, and therefore, "only in a community of language can man actualize his faith."[57] By contrast, R. Soloveitchik saw faith as a pre-communal state, though he did agree that the most effective way of coping with this situation and its problems is in the context of a community—"the covenantal faith community" (79).

In 1950, Marcel published a work entitled *The Mystery of Being*,[58] in which he posited the existence of various types of thought. Primary thought rests on the "objective" method of the empirical sciences. By contrast, the second type of thought is transcendent, with consciousness perceiving itself as a unity beyond "objective" categories. Subjective consciousness continues with its characteristic transcendence, turning to the "other" as an immediate partner in the being and essence that the "self" takes part in,[59] including a quest for the divine. Subjective consciousness, then, is inter-subjective in the most basic "ontological" sense of the concept (in Marcel's terminology). Formally, Marcel's thought models resembles the structure of consciousness in *And from There You Shall Seek* and, to some extent, the division between majestic man, who relies on scientific thought, and the man of faith, whose existence is subjective and who is interested in transcendent existence. Marcel, however, views the turn to the other as a characteristic of the second type of thought. Acknowledging the other's existence is an immediate and direct expression of transcendent consciousness. The issue of the "other" does indeed fulfill an important role in his theological-existential thought. Marcel's philosophy is an interesting cultural link enabling us to understand the change recorded in R. Soloveitchik's thought from *And from There You Shall Seek*, in which the other does not play an essential role, to *The Lonely Man of Faith*, in which communication with the other is a significant component.

---

[57] Paul Tillich, *Dynamics of Faith* (New York: Harper and Row, 1957), 24.

[58] Gabriel Marcel, *The Mystery of Being*, trans. G. S. Fraser (Chicago: H. Regnery, 1950).

[59] As Moshe Schwartz showed, this is a fundamental move that transcends Buber's dialogical philosophy. See Moshe Scwarcz, *Jewish Thought and General Culture* (Tel Aviv: Schocken, 1976), 130-144 (Hebrew).

Faith in *The Lonely Man of Faith*, which enables a dialogue with the other and with God, is rationally and factually irreducible. "Only peripheral elements of the act of faith can be projected on a cognitive, pragmatic background" (101). Faith, then, has a deep existential meaning that is not exhausted through explanation nor amenable to conceptual-rational translation, since faith is the very core of subjectivity, hence the difficult and perhaps hopeless role of a message of faith to a modern generation that finds the existential experience of cathartic redemption and genuine dialogue entirely alien. The message of the modern world directs us to an extra-conscious object and its conquest, whereas the message of faith directs consciousness to a lonely existence and, in its light, to intersubjective communication. Acknowledgement of the other does not mean his recognition as an object, but acknowledgement of his being a subject with a personal existence. This philosophical-existential claim is the precise aim of R. Soloveitchik's biographical-therapeutic writing in *The Lonely Man of Faith*.

Turnabout

One conclusion of *The Lonely Man of Faith* is that these two types—the man of faith and majestic man—build the human being. The oscillation and the rift between them is what characterizes personality:

> Adam the first, majestic man of dominion and success, and Adam the second, the lonely man of faith, obedience, and defeat, are not two different people locked in an external confrontation as an "I" opposite a "thou," but one person who is involved in self-confrontation. "I," Adam the first, confronts the "I," Adam the second. In every one of us abide two *personae*—the creative, majestic Adam the first, and the submissive, humble Adam the second. As we portrayed them typologically, their views are not commensurate; their methods are different, their modes of thinking, distinct, the categories in which they interpret themselves and their environment, incongruous. (84-85)

R. Soloveitchik created an existential structure that is both subjective and objective. He thereby endorsed a widespread existential philosophical model that rejected pure subjective existence on various grounds, both ethical and concrete. Heidegger, for instance, presented human existence as a combination of the authentic and inauthentic or as an oscillation between them, and negated exclusive authenticity.[60] This model extends also to the associations between man and other (Adam and Eve), which also becomes dual and combined. This appears to be the way that R. Soloveitchik interpreted the dual relationship in Buber's thought. In *I and Thou* Buber was already laying the foundation for the existential leap between the "I-Thou" and the "I-He" relationships. Natural and human reality do not allow for purely subjective relationships:

> The world of It (*Eswelt*) ... offers him [man] all manner of incitements and excitements, activity and knowledge. In this chronicle of solid benefits the moments of the Thou appear as strange lyric and dramatic episodes, seductive and magical but tearing us away to dangerous extremes, loosening the well-tried context, leaving more questions than satisfaction behind them, shattering security—in short, uncanny moments we can well dispense with.[61]

Human existence is based on the presence of these two types and these two sets of relationships between the individual and the other.

The oscillation between majestic man and the man of faith turns into a rift when majestic man seeks to take over the experience of faith and translate it into his own terms. The rift emerges because the experience of faith is untranslatable. As a unique experience, it is intransitive. The man of faith is once more thrown into existential loneliness, and the dialectic becomes a recurrent crisis.

Faith, then, relates directly to the perception of an inner oscillation between various types of existence, product of a deliberate divine plan. Faith expresses a hope of balance between the extreme poles in the present or at the end of days.[62] The other, then, enables the reflection of personal consciousness, and the problem of dialogue and relationship leads to the problem of the religious person's conscious dialectic when confronting the modern world.

---

[60] See, for instance, William B. Macomber, *The Anatomy of Disillusion: Martin Heidegger's Notion of Truth* (Evanston, IL: Northwestern University Press, 1967), 89-90.

[61] Buber, *I and Thou*, 32. See Abraham Shapira, *Between Spirit and Reality: Dual Structures in the Thought of M. M. Buber* (Jerusalem: Bialik Institute, 1994), 153-154 (Hebrew).

[62] See Schwartz, *Faith at the Crossroads*, 193-210.

The concept of faith thus assumes new meaning in R. Soloveitchik's thought as formulated in *The Lonely Man of Faith*, different in two essential aspects from its previous articulations and, to some extent, also from *And from There You Shall Seek*:

(1) Reality. Faith turns, above all, to the existential situation of the concrete person, and the man of faith is defined and shaped accordingly. Faith, then, is not the psychological characterization of a particular ability or an epistemic characterization of one or another abstract truth, nor is it exhausted by a phenomenological discussion of religious consciousness.

(2) Redemption and relationship. The second element is no less important: faith becomes a necessary or even exclusive component in the process of personal and purifying redemption. Personal redemption at this point is essentially rooted in the question of the other, that is, in the ability to discover the other, in mutual exposure, and in the possibility of dialogue. Through faith, the person manages to find a companion, to establish a community, and even to discover the concealed God.

"Faith" in R. Soloveitchik's version is such an elementary characteristic that at times, one finds it needs no explanation whatsoever. Faith is not a way of approaching life, but rather life itself.

From *And from There You Shall Seek* to *The Lonely Man of Faith*

We can now re-examine the development of R. Soloveitchik's conception of faith in light of his sources and his times. This development is evident both in "external" characteristics, stylistic and formal, and in the essential features of the method.

And from There You Shall Seek takes rational and emotional achievements as its starting points, and the distortion of the quest for God as its opposite pole; faith can then reconcile and balance the tense process. R. Soloveitchik may have been directly influenced by the work of Barrett, who claimed that theodicy presents God as a metaphysical object amenable to logical thought. This approach was meant to give security in a world where human beings feel homeless. "But reason cannot give that security; if it could, faith would be neither necessary nor so difficult."[63] Faith, then, is the element that emerges in response to the collapse of trust in reason. In *And from There You Shall Seek*, faith grants us power to contend with the collapse of reason brought about by an elusive God and impervious nature. In this work, neo-Kantian philosophy and the conventionalist approach to science lead to absolute distrust in the power of reason. The negation of attributes plays a central role in the process of reason's collapse. R. Soloveitchik thereby adopted Schleiermacher's model: the inability to describe God focuses the philosopher's attention on the believer and, more precisely, on the feeling of faith.[64] *And from There You Shall Seek* definitely describes a philosopher-scientist who longs for God and discovers the pole of disappointment and indifference, when faith is what helps him to live with this tension.

Not so in *The Lonely Man of Faith*. This work describes a suffering man who, above all, seeks to understand his existence. Suffering and indifference as a *starting point* a priori rule out any chance of a perfect balance. Furthermore, pouring rational characteristics into the figure of majestic man precludes a view of faith as a dialectical record of the tension between philosophy and actual experience. The man of faith does not know the experience of nature's responsiveness on the one hand and its indifference on the other; he also gives up on nature as a source of knowledge about God.[65] Contrary to *And from There You Shall Seek*, faith itself does not ensure the man of faith's motivation or healing. In *The Lonely Man of Faith*, faith is not a balancing element. Quite the contrary, faith records the pole of suffering and imperviousness and expresses the hopeless quest for redemption through the encounter with the other and through self-sacrifice: "Only when he met God on earth as Father, Brother, and Friend—not only along the uncharted astral routes—did he feel redeemed" (50).

The perception of faith changes according to its function: in *And from There You Shall Seek*, faith appears in the tension between the open and the concealed, whereas in *The Lonely Man of Faith*, faith appears in the situation of concealment. In *And from There You Shall Seek*, faith *helps* the

---

[63] Barrett, *Irrational Man*, 97.
[64] See, for instance, Friedrich Schleiermacher, *On Religion: Speeches to its Cultured Despisers*, trans. John Oman (New York: Harper and Row, 1958), 94.
[65] This experience is described at length in *The Lonely Man of Faith*, 47-52.

individual to live a life of tense process, whereas in *The Lonely Man of Faith*, faith *describes and expresses* the "pessimistic" pole of the tension.[66] In *And from There You Shall Seek*, faith itself is, in many regards, a kind of (individual) redemption, whereas in *The Lonely Man of Faith*, faith is a situation (a kind of existence) that drives the believer to seek redemption.

The Lonely Man of Faith, which appeared several years after *And from There You Shall Seek*, precedes it in its description of the existence of faith. The man of faith becomes acquainted with the type of experiences presented in the work from the early period, but from a different starting point: the pole of indifference and suffering. Hence the different status of faith in each one of these works: in *And from There You Shall Seek* it is a functional status, which helps to cope with a life of tension and persist in it, whereas in *The Lonely Man of Faith*, faith plays a descriptive role (a kind of existence), and only from this perspective is its functional status ultimately exposed. The cause appears to be rooted in the style of writing, which attests to the realm of discussion. In *And from There You Shall Seek*, the writing is phenomenological-religious. R. Soloveitchik seeks to describe the life characterized by a dialectical experience. By contrast, in *The Lonely Man of Faith*, the writing is biographical-therapeutic. That is, R. Soloveitchik describes the kind of existence compelled by faith out of his own experience, on the assumption that such writing would inspire other men of faith to create a covenantal community. One may view *And from There You Shall Seek* and *The Lonely Man of Faith* as complementary or choose to emphasize the differences between them, but they clearly mark a process of development in R. Soloveitchik's approach to faith..

Background and Sources

We have followed the development of R. Soloveitchik's conception of faith, emphasizing his philosophical sources and the cultural climate of their emergence as well as his own consciousness of innovation vis-à-vis traditional Jewish thought.[67] Unquestionably, R. Soloveitchik devel-

---

[66] Again, the therapeutic role of faith is present in *The Lonely Man of Faith*. R. Soloveitchik refers to the ties between men of faith as a "faith commitment" (42). Faith, however, reflects above all a state (the pole of suffering and imperviousness).

[67] This consciousness emerges in *Kol Dodi Dofek*.

oped his ideas in the course of a theoretical dialogue with philosophical, religious, and existential conceptions, and many scholars have already pointed to the incorporation of Kierkegaardian ideas in his thought. In many regards, his thoughts on faith may be viewed as a "Jewish version" of various religious-existential motifs raised in modern Protestant philosophy from Schleiermacher and up to Niebuhr and Tillich, as well as in non-religious existential thought. R. Soloveitchik also engaged in a substantive and critical dialogue with Jewish sources. Besides his knowledge of phenomenological-religious sources, R. Soloveitchik was largely a religious-Zionist thinker.

Religious-Zionist thought tried to understand the order of the world and the plans of Divine Providence; in this regard, it was no different from traditional Jewish thought.[68] The guiding of history and the examination of its standing in light of the idea of redemption had been a concern of Jewish thought for centuries. But religious-Zionist philosophy is unique in that many thinkers considered it their role not only to describe the theological background of the period but also to inquire into the character of the person active at the time of redemption. The new religious type, the messianic anthropological model, concerns religious-Zionist thought no less than the cosmic and human aspects. The figure, the personality, and the consciousness of the believer are no less important than the concept of faith itself. R. Soloveitchik's philosophy is an indication of the extreme "human" and anthropological shift in religious-Zionist thought. The development of his conception of faith was affected by religious-Zionism, be it directly under its influence or formed as a counter-reaction and a sobering response.

---

[68] See, for instance, Schwartz, *Faith at the Crossroads*; idem, *The Land of Israel in Religious-Zionist Thought* (Tel Aviv: Am Oved, 1997) (Hebrew); idem, *Religious-Zionism between Logic and Messianism* (Tel Aviv: Am Oved, 1999) (Hebrew); idem, *Challenge and Crisis in Rabbi Kook's Circle* (Tel Aviv: Am Oved, 2001) (Hebrew).

Unity and Fragmentation of the Self in Leibowitz's Idea of Faith and their Repercussions:
A Critical Perspective

Ronny Miron

1. Introduction

This article deals with the issue of the self in relation to Yeshayahu Leibowitz's idea of faith and the characterization of the believer it drives. This issue does not appear in his writings as a distinct theme, although the very being of the self is not denied there explicitly. Elucidating and extricating this issue from the depths of Leibowitz's discussion of religious faith, which will be the focus of discussion in this article, can also serve as an essential basis for understanding some fundamental components of his thought, including: the origin of religious faith, the engatement in religious life, the status of God, and the significance and status of the individual personality in the religious way of life. My central argument is that Leibowitz's thought contains two concepts of self, which can be related, generally speaking, to the modernist ethos and the postmodernist ethos.

The modernist self appears as a symbolic project whose center is the search for identity, interpretation, reflection about the self and the surroundings, and, in general, an ongoing effort to obtain meaning in existence. One of the central challenges this perception of self faces is in clarifying the relation between the internal world, perceived as a unity, and the external reality, distributed into a multiplicity of contexts and relations. The dialectic weaving of the external and internal dimensions together reveals the human experience as a unity enfolding multiplicity within itself. In this context, the self's unity does not just denote the existence of a mutual reference between the self's various experiences, but also the affirmation of the self's recurrence in its various experiences. In fact, the repeated presence of the self is what connects these experiences with each other, thus affirming the identity of the self participating in them. The term "presence" therefore describes not only the embodiments of the modernist self, but also the recognition that the self is a real entity not identical to any of its particular experiences, but denoting the entirety of these experiences and, in some cases, transcending it. Some important aspects of the modernist perception of self[1] are outlined by Charles Taylor:

> We are selves only in that certain issues matter for us. What I am as a self, my identity, is essentially defined by the way things have significance for me.... These things have significance for me, and the issue of my identity is worked out, only through a language of interpretation which I have come to accept as a valid articulation of these issues. To ask what a person is, in abstraction from his or her self-interpretations, is to ask a fundamentally misguided question, one to which there couldn't in principle be an answer.
>
> So one crucial fact about a self or person that emerges from all this is that it is not like an object in the usually understood sense. We are not selves in the way that we are organisms... We are living beings with these organs quite independently of our self-understandings or -interpretations, or the meanings things have for us. But we are only selves insofar as we move in a certain space of questions....[2]

In contrast, the concept of self typical of the postmodernist ethos appears as an object, one of several composing the human sphere, which does not possess the establishing status or authority determining the

---

[1] For a detailed discussion of the modernist dimensions embodied in Leibowitz's thought, showing the connections I revealed with Husserl, see Ronny Miron, "Phenomenology of the Believer's Self: The Case of Yeshayahu Leibowitz's Thinking," in *On Faith: Studies on the Idea of Faith*, ed. Moshe Halbertal, David Kurzweil, and Avi Sagi (Jerusalem: Keter, 2005), 124–189. 597–604 (Hebrew). For an analysis of the centrality of personal autonomy in modern religion, see Peter Berger, *The Homeless Mind* (New York: Random House, 1974), 196; David Berger, *The Heretical Imperative* (New York: Anchor Press, 1979), 1–31; and Moshe Sokol, "Religious and Personal Autonomy," in *Rabbinic Authority and Personal Autonomy*, ed. Moshe Sokol (New Jersey: Jason Aronson, 1992), 169–216.

[2] Charles Taylor, *Sources of the Self: The Making of the Modern Identity* (Cambridge: Cambridge University Press, 1992), 34. On the history of the perception of the subject in modern times, see Anthony J. Cascardi, *The Subject of Modernity* (Cambridge: Cambridge University Press, 1992), 56–71.

meaning of the individual's action in the various experiential contexts. These determine the personality each time according to the individual's performance within the boundaries of the single experience. One of the most notable features characteristic of the postmodernist discourse regarding the self is that it marginalizes the category of identity in favor of the category of self.³ The approaches assuming this perception of self repeatedly argue the argument that the self cannot be expressed beyond its practices.⁴ A recurring emphasis in this approach is the inability to grant rational or other meaning to the components of the multiplicity, as they do not combine into one organic body. Unlike the modernist perception of the self, the one anchored in the postmodernist ethos also rejects the possibility of achieving unity, including dialectical unity, from this multiplicity. As a result, the self appears as a "flexible, fractured, fragmented, decentered and brittle" entity.⁵

Indeed, the element of multiplicity also appears in the modernist idea of self, but the postmodern understanding of self denies the existence of the self-referential mechanisms that could enable individuals to examine the relations between the various experiences in which they participate. In any case, it rejects the possibility of forming a unity from them. Instead, the multiplicity is enhanced, creating a split that delimits each single experience within its own boundaries and even denying the self's very existence beyond its appearances in the different experiences. Many of the fundamental elements described here appear in the approach of Erving Goffman, considered one of the precursors of the postmodernist theory of self.⁶ In his words:

> [The Self] does not derive from its possessor, but from the whole scene of his action, being generated by that attribute of local events which renders them interpretable by witnesses. A correctly staged and performed scene leads the audience to impute a

---

³ On the early philosophical roots of this process, see Sydney Shoemaker, *Self-Knowledge and Self-Identity* (Ithaca and London: Cornell University Press, 1963). See also Seyla Benhabib, *Situating the Self: Gender, Community, and Postmodernism in Contemporary Ethics* (Cambridge: Cornwall University Press, 1992).

⁴ In this context, see Anthony Elliott, *Concepts of the Self* (Malden, MA: Polity and Blackwell, 2001), 12–16.

⁵ Ibid., 2.

⁶ Ibid., 36.

self to the performed character, but this imputation—this self—is a *product* of a scene that comes off, and is not a *cause* of it. The self, then, as a performed character, is not an organic thing that has a specific location, whose fundamental fate is to be born, to mature, and to die; it is a dramatic effect arising diffusely from a scene that is presented, and the characteristic issue, the crucial concern, is whether it will be credited or discredited.[7]

The two perceptions of self presented here are based on the assumption that people act within the possible multiplicity of contexts of experience and life. However, these are anchored in different ontological understandings of human experience and of the reality in which human beings live and act. The assumption of the modernist ethos perceives people as sovereign entities with the power to influence the contexts of their activities and to design the relations between them. Furthermore, the self is perceived as an arena in which the various experiences are assimilated, and where they crystallize into one unity constituting the individual's identity. In contrast, the perception of self related to the postmodernist ethos, particularly in its more extreme forms, usually does not acknowledge the existence of a relation between different contexts of activity. Accordingly, the various contexts of human activity are split, appearing as separate realms that cannot be identified with a particular self.

The traces of both ethoses of self, modernist as well as postmodernist, are apparent in Leibowitz's idea of faith, but their status within it is not equivalent. On the immediate level, the modernist self plays a role in the act of choosing to believe, at the basis of which lies an experience of self that bears an identity and strives for personal expression. However, once the choice has been made, within the experience of religious practice, the modernist self gives way to a fragmentary self, divided between different life contexts. The connection of the self that fulfils the religious experience to the postmodernist ethos is apparent in its fragmentation. It refers to the distributed human experience within the multiplicity of contexts and relations, and its expressions are explicitly particular. However, on the deeper level, even within the field that is distributed and split into different contexts, of which religious experience is only

---

[7] Erving Goffman, *The Goffman Reader*, ed. C. Lemert and A. Branaman (Oxford: Blackwell, 1997), 23–24.

one, the traces of the modernist idea of self are still apparent in the effort to realize control that would reinforce the separation between them and give the split itself a religious significance. The aim of this paper will thus be to expose Leibowitz's complex dialog with these two ideas of self that are present in his thought, and to discover the implications for the formation of the character of the believer within his thought.

2. The Spheres of Human Activity

Three different spheres of human activity can be inferred from Leibowitz's thinking, each with its own characteristics. First, there is the individual world of the believer as a person, to which access is blocked off from any kind of reflection or rationality. Second, there is the world of religious experience, which is ruled by Divine commandments that cover all the religious praxis as well as the instructions for its fulfillment. Finally, there is the natural world that can be accessed by every means developed by human civilization. True, the sphere in which religious life takes place is that of the natural world, "in the world as it is." Moreover, Jewish commandments appear to be a program that governs daily life,[8] which suggests rules and norms that dictate one's eating, mourning, celebrating, and so on. Nonetheless, the split between the three spheres is not violated by this fact, for these rules are considered God-given. Furthermore, as will become clear later on, Leibowitz saw the commandments as conflicting with human nature. In any event, Leibowitz's thinking is directed exclusively to the sphere of religious experience. He used to say that he never discussed "religion" or "religiosity," but rather Judaism, which is a particular way of obedience to the Divine commandments.[9]

The understanding of the arena of human activity as composed of multiplicity can be reconciled with both the modernist conception of self and the postmodernist conception of self. Only understanding the contents filling each of these conceptions and the relations between them reveals the connection to each ethos. To a large extent, the issue of the self and its complex connection to these ethoses is only treated

---

[8] Yeshayahu Leibowitz, *Judaism, Human Values, and the Jewish State*, trans. E. Goldman, Y. Navon, et al. (Cambridge, MA: Harvard University Press, 1992), 5.
[9] Ibid., 64.

in regards to the first sphere, while the other two do not receive special reference. Leibowitz does not propose a new idea of the actual reality in which human beings, believers and non-believers, regularly participate. Nor does he usually discuss the specific religious rituals related to the believer's daily life. Instead, he assumed the context of religious law as formulated by the halachic authorities.[10] However, the duality typical of the first sphere, fed simultaneously by the modernist and the postmodernist ethoses of self, trickles into the other two spheres in the form of a radical split, which Leibowitz perceives as having religious value.

One of the surprising things about Leibowitz's thought is that even regarding the sphere of individuality, at the focus of the current discussion, Leibowitz says little. The main information concerning the believer in Leibowitz's writings depicts a person who out of free will has decided to accept the whole framework of God's commandments—a decision that can be taken by a secular person or, in the case of one who was educated religiously, by an adult. Leibowitz describes the decision to believe as unrelated to any factual state of affairs, and as such it cannot be imposed by any facts or rational reasoning. In any event, the decision to believe is an indispensable condition for the very constitution of the religious way of life in which God's commandments will be realized. Allegedly, Leibowitz's argument that the decision to believe stems from one's individuality may enable using the study of that act as a key to the understanding of the believer's individual personality.

Yet this stance requires justification, for it is quite obvious that not every act of will can be considered as a means to access one's personality. Therefore, what is demanded in the first place is a clear distinction between the will to believe, which is a free will for it represents "an obligation that one imposes upon oneself,"[11] to other wills. For the present, Harry Frankfurt's distinction between two kinds of wills—"First-order desires" and "Second-order desires"—can be of value for understanding how people's free will can testify about their personality. Whereas the former relate to human beings' motives, which are common also

---

[10] Leibowitz's famous references are to the mitzvah of Tefilin and the Shema prayer, but even here he did not refer to their practical aspects but used them as an example of his abstract principles. Leibowitz, *Faith, History, and Values* (Jerusalem: Akademon, 1982), 11–19 (Hebrew).

[11] Ibid., 11.

to "members of certain other species" and are basically designed to satisfy biological needs, the latter are "particularly characteristic of humans."[12] "Someone has a desire of second order when he wants simply to have a certain desire or when he wants a certain desire to be his will." In other words, desires of the second order take place whenever one wants a certain desire "to be effective—that is to provide the motive in what he actually does."[13] Logically, the fact that human beings may experience desires of the second order shows that "they are capable of wanting to be different ... from what they are."[14] To conclude, people's ability to identify themselves with a certain will, and the fact that such a will may generate changes in their personality and life, which underlies Frankfurt's idea of desire of the second order, provides substance for elucidating the subjectivity of religious people out of their will to believe.[15] The introduction of the split between the two types of self and the believer's sphere of individuality starts with Leibowitz's argument, whereby a severance between the will to believe and the realization of God's commandments will void the will to believe of any meaning. According to him "Faith in Judaism, is the religion of Mitzvoth [commandments], and apart from this religion Jewish faith does not exist."[16]

One of the tangible expressions of this split is apparent in the statement that not only is it impossible to trace back the roots of the decision

---

[12] Harry G. Frankfurt, "Freedom of the Will and the Concept of a Person," *The Journal of Philosophy* 68:1 (1971): 6.

[13] Ibid., 10.

[14] Ibid., 7.

[15] Nonetheless, Frankfurt's analysis of the free will cannot be adopted completely for the present discussion, for it does not include the demand to realize the practical implementations that emerge from a desire of the second order. Frankfurt terms such a case as "wanton," and clarifies that by such a position one does not turn out to be an animal that has only "First-order desires." Ibid., 11.

[16] Leibowitz, *Judaism, Human Values, and the Jewish State*, 38. Though Leibowitz shared with Frankfurt the idea of free will which cannot be imposed by any facts or rational reasoning, for Leibowitz freedom does not refer to the practical implementations of that will, but ends exactly once the decision has been made. However, this reservation does abolish the relevance of Frankfurt's understanding of desires of the second order as characterizing persons to the analysis of Leibowitz's idea of faith. For an analysis of the centrality of personal autonomy in modern religion, see Berger, *The Homeless Mind*, 196; Berger, *The Heretical Imperative*, 1–31; and Sokol, "Religious and Personal Autonomy."

to believe, but it is also impossible to influence the believer's decision. Leibowitz states that "Even if one could be absolutely certain that the world was created by the will of God, and that He liberated our forefathers from Egypt, and that He reveals Himself to them on Mount Sinai ... one may still refuse to serve God."[17] That is to say that even when the proof of religious faith seems certain, an individual can still reject it or at least overlook the practical norms that come out of it—two options that for Leibowitz mean one and the same thing. It transpires, then, that since the decision to believe is not an outcome of external circumstances, but is embedded in the depths of the individual's internality, it is not predictable and not predicable. George Herbert Mead's distinction between two concepts of self, "me" and "I," may help emphasize the radical nature of the idea of self at the basis of Leibowitz's approach. The first constitutes the product of socialization processes, while the latter denotes a dimension not assimilated into the social framework enabling diversity among individuals. As Mead put it:

> To have self-consciousness one must have the attitude of the other in one's own organism as controlling the thing he is going to do. What appears in the immediate experience of one's self in taking that attitude is what we term the "**me**." [...] Over against the "me" is the "**I**." The individual ... is not only a citizen, a member of the community, but he is one who reacts to this community and in his reaction to it [...] changes it.[18]; [...] The attitudes involved are gathered from the group, but the individual in whom they are organized has the opportunity of giving them an expression which perhaps has never taken place before.[19]

In Mead's terms, we can say that in the context of faith, Leibowitz stresses the "I," and creates a radical contrast between it and whatever can be contained within the boundaries of the "me." However, unlike Mead, Leibowitz does not recognize the power of social and collective processes to influence the self, and eventually his idea of self significantly pushes aside any social dimension in the way the believer is understood. Moreover, while for Mead the "I" is a dimension in the phenomenon

---

[17] Leibowitz, *Judaism, Human Values, and the Jewish State*, 75.
[18] George Herbert Mead, *Mind, Self, and Society from the Standpoint of a Social Behaviorist* (Chicago: University of Chicago Press, 1967), 196.
[19] Ibid., 198. My emphases.

of self, for Leibowitz it has acquired separate reality, not related to the "me" in any way. Anthony Elliott rightly notes:

> [...] this conceptual move also allows Mead to avoid the charge that his theory of the self is deterministic—that is, that the self is a mere reflection of the attitudes of general society, or an internalization of social structure.... Mead's distinction between "me" and "I" thus introduces a level of contingency and ambivalence to each social encounter: the "I" reacts to the "me" in a social context, but we cannot be sure exactly how that 'I' will react.[20]

It appears that the dimension of the "I," which in Mead is intended to protect from a severe idea of self limited to the symbolic meanings formed within a social context, operates almost the opposite way for Leibowitz, who refuses to grant the religious action a symbolic meaning that would connect it to the world of human concepts. Instead, he seeks to understand religious life as aimed at a transcendent entity, even at the cost of losing the meaning of the religious actions. This choice undoubtedly contributes significantly to the severity typical of Leibowitz's idea of faith, which, without the ability to contain it, forms a deep divide within the being of the self. Thus, while the act of deciding to believe shows the modernist ethos of the self as a unity, and as a presence that forms it, these dissipate immediately after the decision stage thus separated from the sphere of religious law in which the self, at least the self as a crystallizing element, is absent. Eventually, the duality of the concepts of self permeates the believer's sphere of individuality, where the features of the fragmented and split postmodern self are apparent. More accurately, the split is not only within the sphere of individuality, but also between it and the other two spheres of human activity: that of religious practice and that of the secular life.[21]

---

[20] Elliott, *Concepts of the Self*, 28.

[21] Here we can also note a surprising link between Leibowitz's idea of self and that of the early Jean-Paul Sartre. See Jean-Paul Sartre, *The Transcendence of the Ego*, trans. R. Kirkpatrick and F. Williams (New York: Noonday, 1957), and Jean Paul Sartre, *Being and Nothingness* (New York: Philosophical Library, 1956). Sartre, too, rejected the possibility of identifying the presence of one's self in the range of experiences of consciousness, and characterized it as transcendent in relation to the realm of consciousness. Like Leibowitz, Sartre worked ceaselessly to fortify the separateness of the self from consciousness, and in fact from all

The far-reaching implications of this idea of self apparent in Leibowitz's approach to the believer will serve to broaden the discussion later on. First, to the extent that belief is based on the individual's decision to believe, the decision itself does not say anything about this believer as an individual, and its implications for shaping the believer's life do not bear the person's individual stamp, but are rather pre-determined by religious laws. Moreover, it is impossible to come to terms with the connection between the actuality by which the believer is surrounded and the believer's decision to believe. Actually, the possibility that such a connection does not exist at all was not explicitly dismissed by Leibowitz, who constantly employs restricted language about faith:

> I know no ways to faith other than faith itself.... I do not regard religious faith as a conclusion. It is rather an *evaluative decision* that one makes, and, like all evaluations, it does not result from any information one has acquired, but is *a commitment to which one binds himself*....
>
> No method can guide him in this. Nothing he could experience would lead him to faith if faith did not spring from his own decision and resolve.... It is not nature or history that give origin to religious faith. In that case, faith could have no meaningful value. It would impose itself on man even as the findings of science impose themselves on any mind that understands them, leaving no room for choice, deliberation, and decision.[22]

The argument that the individual background is shut from any observation remains valid also in the case of people who can express the considerations they took into account before deciding to accept God's commandments, for these can be meaningful only for their owner. Those same considerations will have a different meaning for another believer,

---

other contexts of human activity. He saw this as defending the individual's freedom. For a comprehensive discussion of Sartre's concepts of self, see Hugh Silverman, "Sartre's Words on the Self," in *Existentialist Ontology and Human Consciousness*, ed. William L. McBride (New York: Garland, 1997), 181–200. The surprise in this comparison is because Leibowitz's move was intended to enable religious faith as he understood it and to fortify the transcendent reality (of God), while Sartre's was part of a quite radically atheist approach that relied on an anti-substantive perception of self. On this issue, see James Collins, *The Existentialists: A Critical Study* (Chicago: Henry Regency, 1952), 40–87.

[22] Leibowitz, *Judaism, Human Values, and the Jewish State*, 37–38.

or even at a different period in the lifetime of the same believer. This is the inescapable nature of a decision that does not stem from objective data and hence cannot be explicated.

In Leibowitz's writings one can find two kinds of reasoning for his extreme understanding of the individuality. The first refers to biblical history, claiming that even though the Bible is full of miraculous proofs of the existence of God, as well as attempts to persuade people to believe, those attempts failed completely.

> Scriptural historiography teaches us that events in which "the finger of God" is incontestably manifest do not inevitably lead to faith and service of God. The generations that witnessed wonders and miracles in Egypt … did not believe. Forty days after the revelation at Sinai they made the golden calf. The prophets who rose in Israel and delivered the word of God did not succeed in influencing even one person to repent. On the other hand, during many periods in Jewish history multitudes of men and women adhered to God and His Torah, and sacrificed their lives even though God was never revealed to them, no prophets rose among them, and miracles were never performed for them … still they believed. There is no correlation between what occurs in nature or in history … and man's faith in God and his willingness to serve him.[23]

Leibowitz does not intend to deny either the occurrence of what he terms "religious facts" (such as the creation of the world, the revelation at Mount Sinai, etc.), or the important role they played in the collective consciousness of the Jewish people throughout history. Though Leibowitz refers especially to historical facts, this is also true for other facts of any kind (natural, psychological, etc.). Like Spinoza in *Tractatus*, Leibowitz rejects the theological interpretation of such facts, claiming that it inescapably rests upon human understanding and hence cannot argue for religious validity. In his words: "Historical facts … per se, are religiously indifferent. No historical event assumes religious meaning unless it is an expression of religious consciousness … of the participants in the event."[24] Religious meaning can be conferred upon a historical fact solely when there is a commandment that attributes such

---

[23] Ibid., 75.
[24] Leibowitz, *Judaism, the Jewish People, and Israel* (Jerusalem and Tel Aviv: Schocken, 1976), 92 (Hebrew).

meaning to it. To be more precise, only a commandment can indicate that a religious meaning was bestowed upon a certain fact. Hence facts as such cannot speak by themselves of religious meaning.[25]

The pronounced distrust of the possible contribution of facts to faith clearly represents Leibowitz's effort to protect the independence of religious faith from external reality—namely the secular sphere.

Yet, it seems that more profound support for Leibowitz's concept of faith can be elicited from his strong dualistic worldview, which he proclaims in another context. According to Leibowitz:

> [...] there is no logical correlation [...] between our concepts which refer to things or events of the psychic reality and those which relate to the same in the physical reality ... nothing can be changed in the physical world because of the psychic reality. On the other hand, my psychic reality, which I know by a direct acquaintance, is totally independent of any physical reality, in any event of logical necessity;... we do not discover any functional association between these two worlds.[26]

In the same context, Leibowitz states that one's wills are composed of "the intimate realm of one's consciousness." In contrast to what can be observed and recognized by everyone, one's wills and the like (wishes, thinking, feelings, etc.) cannot be estimated or evaluated. These are known only to their owner, who is familiar with them and does not need any method or guidance in order to know them.[27] That is to say that people's consciousness concerns their intimate realm, and as such it cannot be communicated with other individuals.

---

[25] For a detailed discussion of the meaning of "facts" in Leibowitz's thinking, with a comparison to Wittgenstein's concept of language, see Avi Sagi, "Yeshayahu Leibowitz: A Breakthrough in Jewish Philosophy: Religion without Metaphysics," *Religious Studies* 33 (1997): 207. The understanding of meaning as a human product, and the struggle to maintain the separation of it from any divine matter, appears in Leibowitz's thinking as the supreme principle in the Jewish fight against idolatry. Leibowitz emphasized this issue in his interpretation of Maimonides. See Moses Maimonides, *The Guide of the Perplexed*, trans. Shlomo Pines (Chicago: University of Chicago Press, 1963), 95 ff.

[26] Leibowitz, *Between Science and Philosophy* (Jerusalem: Akademon, 2002), 211 (Hebrew).

[27] Ibid., 210–212.

The connection to the postmodernist ethos of self largely explains Leibowitz's argument whereby the will to believe cannot be subjected to any objectification or reasoning.[28] Furthermore, it seems that the case of the will to believe in particular uncovers the dualism characteristic to the human being as a psycho-physical entity that participates at the same time in two different worlds: internal and external. The religious belief belongs to the first world and is blocked from the second.[29] What distinguishes between believers of the same religion is not the religious praxis that is regulated by the religious authority and leaders and is applied equally to each member, but rather their concealed individuality, out of which their initiated will to believe stems. Believers differ, then, from each other on the basis of their internal world, i.e., the same basis that separates between human beings as such—be they believers or non-believers. While the modernist ethos is apparent in Leibowitz in the understanding whereby one's individuality is the indispensable origin of religious belief, the postmodernist ethos of self is expressed in his argument that believers cannot be defined by their beliefs. However, whatever the individual differences between believers, these cannot have any religious validity.

The blocking of the will to believe to any external observation is supported, then, by an ontological theory that differentiates and separates between the two realms of being in which human beings participate. For Leibowitz considers human beings' individuality as incapable of communicating itself understandably to other people, and since the will to believe appears in his thinking as stemming exactly from this realm, it transpires that it is impossible to come to terms with the origin of faith.[30] In other words, though the entire individuality is involved in one's decision to believe, that decision cannot bear witness to the individual's personality. Hence, the individuality that is responsible for choosing a life ruled by religious commandments does not become transparent because of that choice. At most, one can speak of it in a negative way, i.e.,

---

[28] Leibowitz, *Faith, History, and Values*, 62–63.
[29] In this context, Leibowitz's idea of self can be compared to Sartre's "womb of the in-itself." See Sartre, *Being and Nothingness*, 3–7; Sartre, *The Transcendence of the Ego*, 83–84; Collins, *The Existentialists: A Critical Study*, 62; James M. Edie "The Question of the Transcendental Ego: Sartre's Critique of Husserl," *Journal of the British Society for Phenomenology*, 24:2 (1993): 112.
[30] Leibowitz, *Judaism, Human Values, and the Jewish State*, 74.

as not observable, not communicative, etc. Thus, in Leibowitz's mind, even a religion like Judaism, whose commandments demand so much involvement and co-operation with other practitioners, cannot get in touch with the believer's personality, which finally remains unaffected and separated from the religious experience.

The double explanation of the blocking of the will to believe to rational discourse is evidence of the feebleness of rationality and objectivity when they are faced with the phenomenon of religious faith. Indeed, these features are very much responsible for the link between Leibowitz's idea of faith and the postmodernist ethos of self. Such feebleness cannot be repaired or overcome by new findings about faith or with the help of newly discovered methods. Yet the elimination of the individual being from the explication of faith does not make the will to believe irrational or capricious. Harry Frankfurt rightly contends that one is not allowed to deduce from the equation of the personality with the will that the individual personality is deprived of reason and rationality. For him, "it is having second-order volitions, and not having second-order desires generally, that ... [is] essential to being a person."[31] Therefore the very structure of personality presupposes the person's rationality.

Furthermore, it is exactly the absence of any correlation between two of the contexts of human activity denoted in Leibowitz's approach, i.e., the internal one of individuality and the external one of the secular sphere, and the blocking of the first from the second, that left him no choice but to identify religious belief with the praxis of God's commandments. So, he states, "Faith and worship are born of the resolve and decision of man to serve God, which is the whole of Judaism."[32] Finally, the will to believe that led to the acceptance of God's commandments as a whole reveals the decision that the believer has taken as sharp and clear-cut in its very nature. The meaning of this is twofold: firstly, that decision creates a dramatic change in the believer's life from the normative aspect. From that point on, religious experience is entirely

---

[31] Harry G. Frankfurt, "Freedom of the Will and the Concept of a Person," *The Journal of Philosophy* 67:1 (1971): 10. Frankfurt's approach to free will presupposes the important distinction between rationalism and rationality. For a fine discussion of the differences between the two concepts, see Avi Sagi, *Albert Camus and the Philosophy of the Absurd* (Amsterdam and New York: Rodopi, 2002), 59–65.

[32] Leibowitz, *Judaism, Human Values, and the Jewish State*, 75.

ruled by Divine commandments. In addition, it blurs or even casts aside the individual's background which preceded it. Therefore, though the decision to believe is anchored in the believer's individuality, this individuality does not endure in active religious experience. Hence, the reason there is no use in discussing ways to religious belief stems not only from the fact that once he has taken that decision, no remnant of the original individuality is left, but also from the specific nature of the individuality of the believer. This sphere transpires as an arena where a struggle takes place between the two ethoses of self—the modernist one aiming at unity, and the postmodernist one that denies the very possibility of unity. Even if we assume that Leibowitz was not completely aware of the internal split within the concept of self on which his idea of faith was based, several penetrating questions arise: what were the considerations that supported this extreme conception of the believer in Leibowitz's thinking that created such a sharp separation between individuals' subjectivity and their faith? Is it accurate to say that once the decision has been taken, the believer as an individual personality no longer has any impact on his or her religious experience? Can it be really possible that within the religious praxis no remnant will be left to the being and personality that preceded the decision to believe? Which kind of philosophical problems arise from such a conception? The following section will be dedicated to uncovering the reasoning for the stance of the believer within the religious praxis in Leibowitz's thinking.

C. The Strategy of the Split

The understanding of religious faith as identical with the praxis of God's commandments was designated by Leibowitz both to promote a specific idea of the Jewish religion, which is free of subjectivization and naturalization that would turn it into a human matter, and to defend believers' right to remain individuals despite their total commitment to an authority external to themselves.

The first goal is based on the modernist ethos of self, aiming to maintain the general character of its objects and to prevent the assimilation of private criteria into their evaluation. In contrast, the second goal is anchored in the postmodernist ethos of self, aiming to protect it from fixation and to thwart any attempt to understand it using external criteria—objective, cultural, and social. In regard to these goals, this strategy, which will be exposed as follows, seems to find its preliminary justification. Logically, if one does not want religion to be subjective and subjectivity to be religious, one must separate between the religious faith and the individuality of the believer. Religion and subjectivity speak different languages, express themselves in dissimilar behavior, and demand unalike capabilities. Therefore, mixing up religiosity with one's subjectivity confuses things that cannot get along.[33] The *first function* of the split is the definition of the limits of the realms of discourse according to the spheres of human experience. Concerning the goals toward which the strategy of the split is aiming, guarding the boundaries of each sphere of being appears to be an indispensable condition. This is no more than a formal or necessary condition, but not a sufficient one, for it does little directly to promote the specific meaning of religion and subjectivity to which Leibowitz's thinking was aiming.

The *second function* of the splitting strategy is narrowing and limiting the scope of religious life solely to what is defined by the religious commandments. It is true that in the case of Judaism these cover a vast amount of details. Nevertheless, Leibowitz stresses that outside these borders, believers are free to conduct themselves just like everybody else, namely, like non-believers. Accordingly, the figure of the believer is disclosed as bearing a resemblance to that of the non-believer, except for the part of the believer's life that is ruled by defined commandments. That is to say that the phenomenology of the believer in Leibowitz's thinking is not identical with his general conception of anthropology. As a matter of fact, according to Leibowitz, aspects in the individual's personality that appear in the phenomenon of religious belief do not come into view in a person's religious experience as a believer. Leibowitz exemplifies the differences between the believer and the non-believer in regard to their attitude towards seeing themselves as natural beings; whereas a non-believer can live in peace with the very fact of being a

---

[33] Leibowitz did not point in the present context to an abstract problem of violation of imagined borders, but to the inescapable influence of one of the main characteristics of modernity, i.e. the split within the human being, on the religious experience. For a general view of the split within modernity, see Karl Jaspers's analysis of the "impossibility of steadfast life-order," Karl Jaspers, *Die geistige Situation der Zeit* (Tübingen: Max Niemeyer, 1931), 46–48. For a discussion of this feature in regard to religion, see Berger, *The Homeless Mind*, 36 ff.

natural and finite being, believers struggle with the same fact and strive to get in touch with infinity. In Leibowitz's words:

> The religious person is different from the one who did not accept the authority of heaven or freed himself from that authority, in that he [the religious person] did reconcile himself with the fact that he is part of the natural reality which he cannot transcend. His belief ... is not in accord with the objective reality in which he already finds himself and with which he will never be in accord.[34]

The present function relates more directly to the content that fills the religious sphere, guarding it from spreading to spheres that might distort the essence of the religious existence as referring to the transcendent entity. Without doubt, to achieve this goal, the modernist idea of self may suffice, as it realizes control of the spheres of life, and in any case may prevent leakage from one sphere of human activity to another. But this does not exhaust the purpose of the second function of Leibowitz's strategy of split, relating more radically to the sphere of individuality where his idea of faith is anchored. In this context, Leibowitz appears to be wishing to fortify the understanding whereby a religious person is nonetheless a natural being, and hence is doomed to carry out an unending struggle in order to realize a religious faith. By narrowing and limiting the scope of religion in one's life, Leibowitz not only takes into account the fact that believers unavoidably remain natural beings. An approach that strives to separate between people's individuality and their faith may also decrease the conflict between the two by making room also for non-religious aspects and activities that concern the natural existence.[35] Consequently, a religion that covers a delimited sphere appears to be a single dimension among others, none of which claim superiority, let alone exclusivity. The limited concept of religion appears as respecting the individuality of the believer and defending it from the possible invasion of elements that belong to the religious sphere.

---

[34] Leibowitz, *Faith, History, and Values*, 57. Other differences between the two are discussed also in Leibowitz, *Judaism, Human Values, and the Jewish State*, 142.

[35] The understanding of Judaism as a religion that does not close its believers from the non-religious aspect of life is emphasized in David Hartman's studies of Maimonides and in Soloveitchik. See David Hartman, *Israelis and the Jewish Tradition* (New Haven: Yale University Press, 2000), x-xii; Hartman, *Love and Terror in the God Encounter* (Woodstock: Jewish Lights, 2001).

On the face of it, one can argue that Leibowitz thus leaves open the possibility of accepting the modernist ethos or the postmodernist ethos. On the one hand, his approach nurtures the split between the realms of human activity, expressing a modernist understanding of human existence. On the other hand, the significance of the split is not contained within the religious sphere but in the realm of the individual, and this, as we have seen, appears for him to be a dark area that cannot be objectified. At this point, the dominance of the postmodernist ethos in Leibowitz's idea of faith becomes clearly apparent, and is more suitable than the modernist ethos. From a modernist perspective, we seem to have a paradox, since what may enable religion, which is based on accepting authority, is the individual's control in acting to fortify the boundaries surrounding it. But from the viewpoint of the postmodernist ethos, this paradox disappears, since religion appears as one more of the contexts in which the person participates, and it does not have a special status among them. Moreover, concerning the split mind suggested by postmodernity, one can tell that only a narrowed version of religion can have any chance at all of communicating with people who are not willing anymore to commit themselves to any total authority. Therefore, Leibowitz's concept of religious faith can justly be considered as supportive of religion and not as enfeebling it.

The third function of the splitting strategy is compartmentalization of the aforementioned three spheres, which appear, then, as not only distinguished but also as detached from each other by an unbridgeable gap.[36] The idea of compartmentalization in this context is that though the decision to believe originated in one's individuality, the commandments themselves were not designed to fulfill any individual need. This

---

[36] The theory of compartmentalization became common in the current interpretations of the phenomenon of Orthodoxy. See Charles Liebman, *Deceptive Images* (New Jersey: Transaction Books, 1988), 54–59. It should be noted that Leibowitz's original position did not adopt a narrowed version of Judaism but spoke for a model that was more akin to Catholicism. See "Jewish Education in a Modern Society" (article from 1954), in Leibowitz, *Judaism, the Jewish People, and Israel*, 37–45. Leibowitz himself did not fully admit a change in his thinking, but presented it more as a shift of emphasis (he referred to it in a note, see Leibowitz, *Judaism, the Jewish People, and Israel*, 45). Nevertheless, the understanding that a real change occurred in Leibowitz's thinking is common among his commentators.

is exactly the meaning of religious belief as a transcendental act—it directs believers to what lies beyond themselves and not towards their internal personalities or concrete needs. Consequently, the believer in Leibowitz's thinking is one who functions in two different spheres: natural and religious. The natural sphere contains everything that is connected to the existence and the culture of the believer as a human being. The religious sphere includes everything ruled by the religious imperatives. Leibowitz considers the religious sphere to be not only external to the natural one, but also inaccessible to it. True, the acknowledgment of the opposition between the religious sphere and the natural one is not an innovation in the religious discourse; what is unique about Leibowitz in this context is that he did not look for bridges or connecting points between the two spheres, but made great efforts to strengthen the split between them in order to defend religious belief from the invasion of any natural or human elements.[37]

Nonetheless, the compartmentalization is not evidence that there are no interrelations between the different spheres that were separated. On the contrary, the compartmentalization is actually defining the framework in which the relations between the different spheres can be elucidated; namely these are crystallized around the principles of the heteronomy of God's commandments and the idea of absolute transcendence. According to Leibowitz, only complete detachment of the Divine from the human can ensure the total devotion of the believer to the work of God. In order to illustrate his approach, he suggests distinguishing between two types of religions: granting and demanding. The "granting religion" appears to be a means of fulfilling believers' needs, whereas the "demanding religion" imposes upon them obligations without promising them anything in return.[38] For Leibowitz, as long as one's faith is based on what religion grants to human beings it should be seen as idolatry.[39] Therefore, only the "demanding religion" is a genuine religion, and vice versa: only when belief is detached from worldly experience and reality and has no function in one's life is it really belief.

---

[37] For a sketch of typical Jewish responses to modernity, see Eliezer Goldman, "Responses to Modernity in Jewish Thought," *Studies in Contemporary Jewry* 2 (1956): 52–73; Liebman, *Deceptive Images*, 43–59.
[38] Leibowitz, *Judaism, Human Values, and the Jewish State*, 13–14.
[39] Ibid., 64.

At the present point, the distinction between religions is further developed by Leibowitz, in regard to two principles taken from the Jewish classics, which he employs in order to support his concept of Judaism: "belief for its own sake" and "belief not for its own sake."[40] What distinguishes between these two is the motivation behind them and not the praxis of religious commandments. "Belief not for its own sake" is actually an instrument for fulfilling one's needs, or it appears as a conclusion that one reaches out of his worldly experience. It is clear that this kind of belief is dependent on believers achieving their goals. "Belief for its own sake" that lacks any external purpose and does not actually give the believer any kind of benefit or satisfaction is different. According to Leibowitz, only this kind of belief is genuine, precisely because a believer is not expected to feel "happiness," "perfection," or "morality."[41] For all these, Leibowitz determines, one does not need religious belief; one can get them from even better agents. The only satisfaction that "belief for its own sake" can wish to have is the contentment from fulfilling the divine obligation.[42] However, a genuine belief must be independent even of this satisfaction. Finally, as long as one's belief bears witness to the believer's needs or motivation, this can be considered as evidence of its falseness.

The link to the two ethoses that have accompanied the discussion so far—the modernist and the postmodernist—may explain Leibowitz's choice of the "demanding religion" and of "belief for its own sake" over a "giving religion" and "belief not for its own sake." What the "giving religion" and "belief not for its own sake" have in common is their being directed at the believer. The "giving religion" gives the believer something—a giving that makes the believer's faith become "not for its own sake." Furthermore, the "giving religion" affirms the self's desires and needs, and this reveals the self to be the center of the faith. The solid and crystallized sense of self that the believer acquires in this approach clearly links it to the modernist ethos of self. But, as noted, Leibowitz rejects this approach in favor of the one he characterizes using the

---

[40] This classical distinction has appeared in many contexts. For instance, see TB Ta'anith 7a. Leibowitz wrote a series of articles on the topic of "Lishmah and Not-Lishmah" ("for its own sake and not for its own sake"). The one that was translated into English appears in Leibowitz, *Judaism, Human Values, and the Jewish State*, 61–78.
[41] Ibid., 63.
[42] Ibid., 37–42.

concepts "demanding religion" and "faith for its own sake." Beyond all the meanings these concepts may be granted, one thing is utterly clear about them—the denial of the believer's self as the center point and anchor of the experience of faith. The demand from the believer is aimed from the person outwards, but it does not encounter any inside or any center. Quite the opposite, the self is scattered among the multiplicity of experiences, of which faith is just one. This believer's faith is "for its own sake," since among other things it has no center to absorb the benefit that the religion could have granted the believer. The believer is distributed among the range of experiences, and presumably what is beneficial in one place does not necessarily have the same influence elsewhere. The clear link between Leibowitz's idea of faith and the postmodernist ethos of the self thus receives further support from his choice of the concepts of the "demanding religion" and the "faith for its own sake."

D. Disharmony, Conflict, and Gap

Having said all that, it should not be surprising that not harmony but rather an experience of crisis and conflict appears as a permanent component in the daily routine of the believer. The frustration that accompanies this experience has many reasons whose examination may elucidate and establish the link between Leibowitz's idea of faith and the postmodernist ethos of self.

First, it is due to the existence of an extremely large gap between the autonomy that is granted to believers at the constitutive stage of their decision to believe and the unreserved heteronomy to which they must commit themselves within the religious experience. In a way, the concept of compartmentalization mentioned above can be regarded as a supreme expression of the understanding of this gap as unbridgeable. Furthermore, the understanding of the religious experience as governed by compartmentalization regulates the moments of crisis. As a result of that, these do not appear as stemming from one's caprice or emotional condition but as a substantial component of the religious belief without an anchor or center point, but constituting one experience out of a range of experiences that do not join together.

Secondly, the experience of crisis is a result of the demand to severely split between the religious faith and the believer's personal life, so much so that what is demanded from believers is relinquishing some of the values that they hold as natural beings. Leibowitz regards the biblical story of Abraham, who was commanded by God to sacrifice his beloved son Isaac and to reject the supreme value of fatherhood of defending one's child, as a paradigm of the conflict between the human and the divine.[43] Out of the study of this biblical story, Leibowitz concludes the following:

> Sacrifice is a very religious crisis … in the sacrifice God demanded of Abraham all he had … relinquishing human and collective values … all the elements of human consciousness—those concerning the individual and those relating to all human problems—everything was rejected. There is no crisis as big as the one between the reality of the human being, including his material and emotional reality, and the status of man when he stands in front of God.[44]

---

[43] The understanding of the Binding of Isaac (Akedah) as a paradigm of religious experience, in which the believer is required to abandon his humanity, has appeared in both Jewish and Christian sources. See Maimonides, *The Guide of the Perplexed* III:24, 497 ff; and *Neues Testament*, Römer, chap. 4 ("Das Beispiel Abrahams"). Yet among the Jewish thinkers a different approach appears, according to which Judaism and humanity can meet each other. See Erich Fromm, *Psychoanalysis and Religion* (New Haven: Yale University Press, 1950), 34–55. Fromm also suggested a comparative view of the understanding of God in Judaism and Christianity. Erich Fromm, *Das jüdische Gesetz, zur Soziologie des Diaspora-Judentums* (dissertation from 1922, Heidelberg, Basel and Weinheim: Beltz Verlag, 1989), 57–65. David Hartman, who was acquainted with Fromm's thinking, criticized Leibowitz's understanding of the binding of Isaac and suggested an alternative model of "Covenant" to the relations between God and his believers. Hartman, *A Living Covenant: The Innovative Spirit in Traditional Judaism* (New York: Free Press, 1985), 42–59; and Hartman, *A Heart of Many Rooms* (Woodstock: Jewish Lights, 1999), 11 ff. Hartman also referred to Leibowitz's concept of Judaism, see ibid., 267–296. These two polar models of Judaism appeared in Joseph Soloveitchik's thinking and were explored as two indispensable components of the religious experience. For a comparison between Leibowitz's view of God's commandments and that of Soloveitchik, see Avi Sagi, "Contending with Modernity: Scripture in the Thought of Yeshayahu Leibowitz and Joseph Soloveitchik," *The Journal of Religion* 77 (1997): 421–441. See also Sokol, "How do Modern Jewish Thinkers Interpret Religious Texts?," *Modern Judaism* 13:1 (1993): 25–48.

[44] Leibowitz, *Faith, History, and Values*, 58. For a comprehensive commentary of the biblical story of the Binding of Isaac (in Hebrew, *Akedah*), see Avi Sagi, "The Meaning of the *Akedah* in Israeli Culture and Jewish Tradition," *Israel Studies* 3:1 (1998): 45–60. See also Louis Jacobs, "The Problem of Akedah in Jewish Thought," in *Kierkegaard's Fear and Trembling*, ed. Robert L. Perkins (Tuscaloosa, AL: University of Alabama Press, 1981), 1–9.

Against this background one can accurately understand the meaning of Leibowitz's objection to the idea of "Jewish morality," where he contended that a person who acts as a moral agent cannot be acting as a religious agent. In other words, a religious action cannot be simultaneously a moral action. Whereas the morality of an action is determined by one's intentions and desires—which in the modernist approach are identified with the center of the person's being and selfhood as an individual—the religious appropriateness of an act is determined by one's commitment to follow God's commandments. This match, like the postmodernist ethos of self, does not refer to the self, which does not constitute an anchor or a center, but rather is directed outwards, outside everything within the realm of the individual's constitution and control. In Leibowitz's words:

> Being moral, from the standpoint of a secular ethic, can have only either of two meanings; directing man's will in accordance with man's knowledge of reality ... or directing man's will in accordance with man's recognition of his duty.... The Torah does not recognize moral imperatives stemming from knowledge of natural reality or from awareness of man's duty to his fellow man. All it recognizes are Mitzvoth, divine imperatives. The Torah and the prophets never appeal to the human conscience, which harbors idolatrous tendencies. No equivalent of term "conscience" appears in the scripture.[45]
>
> [Therefore] Morality can be neither Jewish nor non-Jewish, neither religious nor irreligious.... [It] is an atheistic category which differs radically from religious consciousness or religious feeling. From the standpoint of Judaism man as such has no intrinsic value. He is an "image of god," and only as such does he possess special significance. That is why Judaism did not produce an ethical theory of its own, was never embodied in a moral system, and made no pretenses of representing a specific moral point of view.[46]

In Leibowitz's idea of faith two opposed aspects meet: the negative one eliminates the "utilitarian Justification, whether it be for the good

---

[45] Leibowitz, *Judaism, Human Values, and the Jewish State*, 18.
[46] Ibid., 6–7. The words "is an atheistic category which" were mistakenly dropped from the English translation, and were added above according to the Hebrew original.

of individuals, of society, or of the nation,"[47] which usually plays an important role in ethics. The positive aspect refers to the emphasis on the performance of the religious imperatives. That is to say that as a result of the principle of compartmentalization the believer does not appear in the religious experience as a complete being but solely as a non-personal performer of the commandments of God.[48]

Yet, the reduction of the believer's being in Leibowitz's thinking, which actually amounts to a reduction of any human aspect of faith, does not imply that the believer is not crucial for the actualization of the compartmentalization itself. Whereas the two above-discussed reasons for the believer's experience of crisis—the gap between the believer's initiative autonomy and the demand to commit oneself to Divine commandments; and the demand to severely separate between religious faith and the believer's personal life—actually originated in Leibowitz's specific understanding of the Jewish faith, a supplementary one refers to the disposition of the believer himself. Leibowitz depicts the believer as, "One who cannot live in peace with natural reality, even though he himself is part of this reality which he cannot transcend, no matter whether he is a believer or a non-believer, whether he accepts divine authority or not."[49] The reduction is then all about the specific position, which the believer is required to shape, that conditions genuine faith as such.

However, the difference between the ontological split in human beings as such, and not necessarily as believers, and the split suggested by Leibowitz must be marked in order to achieve an accurate understanding of the function of the compartmentalization in his thinking. Actually, the split that concerns religious experience, which

---

[47] Ibid., 19.

[48] For a general discussion of the relationships between religion and morality, see Avi Sagi and Daniel Statman, *Religion and Morality* (Amsterdam and Atlanta: Rodopi, 1995); and Michael J. Harris, *Divine, Command, Ethics* (London: Routledge, 2003). For a more specific critique of Leibowitz's position, see Sagi and Statman, *Religion and Morality*, 155–164. For a further perspective into this topic in Judaism, see Sagi, "Punishment of Amalek in Jewish Tradition—Coping with the Moral Problem," *Harvard Theological Review* 87:3 (1996): 323–346; Sagi, "'He slew the Egyptian and he hid him in the sand': Jewish Tradition and the Moral Element," *HUCA* 67 (1994): 55–76.

[49] Leibowitz, *Faith, History, and Values*, 57.

is suggested by Leibowitz, adds a further and unnecessary section to the more basic one that concerns one's psychophysical being. Choosing this way, Leibowitz not only strengthens the individual's coping with it but also radicalizes the initial split. It is important to note that since the psychophysical split is part of one's given factuality, it does not necessarily have any religious value. It is only the carrying out of an unnecessary split that can be of value, for it transcends one's given factuality. The religious value is granted to faith precisely because it involves carrying out a voluntary compartmentalization and facing the challenges that accompany it. In other words, though the believer is acquainted with the feeling of split, to the believer such a feeling cannot be helpful, and hence the compartmentalization remains a religious mission to fulfill.

It is exactly Leibowitz's respectful attitude toward the human condition that removes him from the attempt to suggest any solution or relief either to the human wish to transcend natural reality or to the situation of the split. Instead, he speaks for an adoption of the split itself and for a routine of constant contact with the difficulties and frustrations that come out of this very choice. Actually, what is suffering in the disposition of the believer is not only the very fact that it can change nothing in the human condition, but that the religious praxis does not shape the individual's personality from inside and hence cannot really become a habit. The believer will always remain a natural being, whereas religious imperatives are divine. Therefore, no comfort but endless crisis and battles appear as the daily portion of the believer. Even though the believer becomes acquainted with these, it is impossible to develop better tools to deal with them, for they stem from the very fact of the individual's natural being. Believers are doomed to find themselves daily at the beginning of the path with no sense of achievement from the previous day's battle. Every day they start at the very same point.

> Performance of the Divine Mitzvoth [commandments] is man's path to God, an infinite path, the end of which is never attained and is, in effect, unattainable. A man is bound to know that this path never terminates. One follows it without advancing beyond the point of departure. Recognition that the religious function imposed upon man is finite and never ending is the faith, which finds expression in the regularity, constancy and perseverance in

the performance of the Divine Mitzvoth [commandments]. The circle of the religious praxis rotates constantly about its center. "Every day they will appear to you as new," for after each act the position of man remains as it was before. The aim of proximity to god is unattainable. It is infinitely distant, "for God is in heaven and you on the earth" (Ecclesiastes 5:1). What then is the substance and import of performance of the Divine Mitzvoth [commandments]? It is the man's striving to attain the religious goal.[50]

Clearly, Leibowitz strives to maintain the dichotomy between the human and the divine; in his thinking, the demand to overcome one's own human nature becomes the core of the religious praxis, without promising believers any payment or compensation for their struggling and suffering. In fact, the clear link to the postmodernist ethos thwarts this possibility, since compensation assumes a uniform and integrated being to assimilate the compensation within it. As noted, in Leibowitz's approach, the believer is not such a being. This is why the initial decision of the believer, the one from which everything started, is never safe and stable. It needs constant care and maintenance. The experience of the believer transpires to be a Sisyphean one—all the efforts that believers put into obeying the religious imperatives cannot prevent them from conceding to their natural beings. Living this way demands the ability to withstand daily frustrations, which appear as a constant component in one's religious experience.

E. The Paradox of the Believer's Subjectivity

The three functions of the splitting strategy discussed above—defining the spheres of human experience, narrowing the scope of religious life, and compartmentalization—point clearly to an increasing process of pressing the believer's individuality outside the religious experience. Though by the founding decision the believer attributes an indispensable transcendental condition to the realization of the religious belief, the splitting strategy has finally set the believer aside from the religious experience or even outside of it. As we have seen, in the decision stage that preceded the implementation of the splitting, the believer enjoyed

---

[50] Leibowitz, *Judaism, Human Values, and the Jewish State*, 15–16.

the status of an establisher of the religious experience, so that without him or her, such experience could not come into being. This was the crucial infrastructure of religious life. In fact, this is the main part where the traces of the modernist ethos are apparent in Leibowitz's idea of self, and accordingly the believer appears there as a coherent personality and as a source of its own action. However, later the uniform fabric of selfhood seems to disintegrate. This disintegration is expressed in two ways: first, the believer does not serve as a resource to the self becoming more intelligible. Second, believers do not become more comprehensible in light of their decision. It transpires, then, that we are dealing here with a double cut. The believer as an individual does not bear witness to the religious belief, and the belief itself cannot provide evidence about the believer. Yet, the dismissal of the believer from religious experience was an unavoidable consequence of the splitting strategy. This dismissal is actually uncovered as a necessary condition for the bestowal of a transcendental and divine meaning to religious life. Therefore, the individuality of the believer—whether permeated by the modernist ethos that forms it into a unity, or split into a multiplicity of experiences, of which the religious is just one—has become irrelevant to such a meaning of religious life. The self of the believer does not blend into the religious experience, but remains outside of it.

One can regard the selfhood of the believer also as transcendental, but this is a different kind of transcendentalism from the one that can be attributed to God. Whereas the transcendentalism of the believer is immanent, that of God is transcendent. Nonetheless, God's transcendentalism is accessible by his commandments, which in the religious experience are perceived as the core of his reality, but that of the believer remains closed, and any attempt to approach it encounters its disintegration into a multiplicity of experiences.

Finally, the figure of the believer is elucidated neither in the immanent sphere—for the very decision to become a believer transcends the borders of immanence—nor in the transcendent sphere—for the individuality of the believer finds no expression in the religious praxis. As a result of that, the believer in Leibowitz's thinking remains an enigma as long as one tries to access it from the viewpoint of the sphere of religious experience. Surely, the believer can still be open to rational reflection—that is to say, the believer is not deprived of the possibility of achieving self-understanding—but Leibowitz says that such an understanding has no religious meaning or value and hence cannot have any impact on religious experience. That means that the split is not only between the natural sphere and the religious one, but also in the very being of the believer who functions in two different and unbridgeable contexts. The radicalism that characterizes Leibowitz's thinking is that even the believer, who is the establisher of the religious experience, cannot bridge the gap between the natural experience and the religious one, for the believer is eliminated from it together with every natural component of the human life.

Believers as practitioners can be depicted, then, as atomistic beings, detached from any realistic context, closed off from themselves as well as from the external world. They function in the religious praxis, devoid of any particularity and individuality. Being purified of any essential components, believers cannot become an object for investigation. In other words, believers must appear in the religious experience in order to bring it to reality; they are the subjects who establish the religious experience. Yet once the decision to believe has been made, the self of the believer seems to disintegrate and scatter into experience in general, which is divided into a multiplicity of contexts, with religion occupying only one of them. In the absence of a core of self in which a typical attitude of the believer towards the various religious commandments can formulate, the commandments appear to the believer to be equivalent in their importance and value. In other words, there is no basis to talk about a particular closeness or connection of the believer to any particular commandment. All are equally foreign to the believer, and thus require a uniform attitude.

In fact, there is no reason why believers should not treat the different commandments of religion equally, since according to Leibowitz the different religious imperatives are contrasted in equal measure to their natural and individual being precisely because they are God-given. This contrast and the elimination of all individual elements from the sphere of faith are exactly what guarantees the unity of the religious experience and defends it from subjectivitisation and particularization. Therefore, one should be reserved about describing believers unilaterally, for they are supposed to appear just the same along their praxis; their ideal being is exactly the reason why it is possible to reach an adequate understanding of them. The separation between the praxis and the believers' individuality transpires then to be extremely crucial for

Leibowitz's thinking, for it maintains the deep contrast between the religious experience and the natural one. Of course, believers do not cease to be immanent beings, but they function, or better, are expected to function, as ideal beings detached from any individuality. Only as such can they not damage the transcendental character of the religious experience.

Only at the present point may we understand Leibowitz's contention, according to which the essence of the religious belief is not one of cognition but one of endeavor. In other words, the religious belief is not linked with the attempt to achieve certain knowledge about religion or faith, but rather with the effort to execute the practical implementations of it.[51] While the demand to understand the commandments would have maintained the believer as the center of their treatment, the removal of understanding from the religious experience in Leibowitz's approach, in favor of performing the commandments in practice, places the commandments themselves at the center—although they do not occupy the whole of the experience, but only one segment of it. This does not mean necessarily that believers do not understand what they practice, but only that their faith is independent of such understanding. Finally, believers' disposition locates them at a middle point—they functions as non-empiric and ideal beings in the religious experience, but at the same time they are separated from the idealistic frame of consciousness, for they are not required or expected to achieve understanding concerning religious faith, but to practice the religious imperatives. This is the way they are about to take, or better, they are obliged to face religious commandments: cleared of their own individuality, no matter what its meaning might be, but, thanks to the early establishing decision, not ceasing to be individuals. In other words, religious experience does not destroy believers' individuality, but rather eliminates it.

However, the proposed understanding of the location of the believer may only regulate the gap between the two ideas of the self in which Leibowitz's thinking is imbued, ideas arranged in two stages of the religious experience. The modernist idea of the self is located in the empirical and constituting stage where the decision to believe takes place, while the postmodernist one occupies the arena of practical religious experience guided by the commandments, whose origin is abstract and

---

[51] Leibowitz, *Judaism, Human Values, and the Jewish State*, 15.

transcendent. However, spreading the religious experience over two stages—the volitional decision stage and the practical stage of following the commandments—does not solve the fundamental paradox of subjectivity in Leibowitz's thinking.[52] This paradox has two dimensions: first, the believer, as the one who takes that decision, is transcendent to any rational explanation and reasoning, though as we have seen, the traces of the modernist ethos of the self, granting the believer's being a formed and uniform nature, are apparent. At least historically, this stage is linked to an attempt at self-understanding. Yet, once believers put themselves into the religious experience, they are expected to transcend their empiric being and to function as ideal beings, meaning people equally devoted to the various religious commandments as a whole. In any case, what transpires is that behind this devotion there was not one self, as a formed pole of reference to the commandments, as giving them meaning, or as achieving self-understanding through them. Quite the opposite: even if we assume according to the influence of the link to the modernist ethos that the decision to believe is taken by one cohesive self, it disintegrates within the religious experience into a multiplicity of experiences behind which there is no unifying self. Therefore we can expect that one's original individuality leaves no impact on the believer's religious experience. Believers in Leibowitz's thinking are deflected from their initial status of "establishers of faith" by their volitional act and transferred to the status of compliance, so much so that their individuality is eliminated from the religious experience.

Clearly, Leibowitz by no means understood the above-depicted changes, which occur to the believer as reflecting loss of freedom. On contrary, for him, "None but he who busies himself with the Scripture (Torah) is free—he is free from the bondage of nature because he lives a life which is contrary to nature."[53] In other words, as long as we are natural beings, we cannot claim the status of establishers, for we are subjected to forces over which we have no control. Only when we make a decision that we are not compelled to make—and the decision to believe

---

[52] For a phenomenological perspective, that underlies my discussion, see: Robert Sokolowski, *Introduction to Phenomenology* (Cambridge: Cambridge University Press, 2000), 112–129; David Carr, *The Paradox of Subjectivity* (New York and Oxford: Oxford University Press, 1999), 67–97.

[53] Leibowitz, *Judaism, Human Values, and the Jewish State*, 22.

is of this kind—can we justly enjoy the status of establishers, and hence be really free beings. Leibowitz reverses, then, in a Spinozistic way, the ordinary thinking according to which freedom means not being subordinated to external factors. According to him, as natural beings we are subordinated anyway, but we can have a touch of freedom once we subordinate ourselves to something that we can avoid: the religious praxis. However, only in the sphere into which we entered by our decision to believe are we free beings; outside that sphere we helplessly remain subordinate beings due to our human nature. Freedom is, therefore, accepting limitations that one can avoid.

Finally, believers appear to be those who have their own personal way of being, so one can never really know what is happening in their hearts. It is impossible to understand them, or to be more precise, to understand the specific will to accept God's commandments, and hence to become believers. Actually, the stage of the decision is the only moment in which one can find accordance between the individual and his or her activity—an accordance which ceases to appear in the sphere of practical deeds or in the cognitive sphere where individuals can separate themselves from what they do or think. In other words, only where unity may appear should one search for the accord between parts, or at least a system of relations between them. In contrast, they have no place in an arena ruled by multiplicity and dispersion, such as the one where the postmodernist self dwells.

F. The Ongoing Need for a Modernist Self

Leibowitz's defense of religion from subjectivitization and particularization, as we have seen previously, rests upon an extreme individualistic idea of subjectivity, which transpires to be marked with traces of the postmodernist ethos of self. In light of the two main goals of Leibowitz's thinking, i.e., guarding religion from being subjective and guarding subjectivity from becoming religious, the implemented splitting strategy is undoubtedly revealed as a useful means. However, this choice transpires to have a price in terms of the believer, and could also have wider implications for the religious experience. In the present section I shall contend that the dominant postmodernist characteristics of Leibowitz's idea of self, which largely led to the removal of the subject from religious experience, are seriously problematic from the viewpoint of Leibowitz's idea of faith itself. My central argument here is that the presence of the believer within the religious experience, including the practical experience, is indispensable, and therefore the believer should not be eliminated from it. Moreover, it is the subject, as a being striving for meaning and significance in trying to connect the various experiences in which the subject participates, including the religious experience, that is essential for realizing the idea of faith as Leibowitz himself perceived it, without which it lacks meaning. In other words, I argue that it is the modernist self, perceived in terms of unity and even substantivism, that is essential for realizing religious experience the way Leibowitz understood it, as directed towards a transcendent reality.

In order to come to terms with the suggested criticism, one must go back to the very basic assumptions of Leibowitz, not necessarily in order to refute them, but in order to illuminate their problematic nature. The *first assumption* to be scrutinized is the one that regards **the status of the believer in religious praxis.** As we have seen before, Leibowitz treated the involvement of the believer's life and personality as a threat to the sacredness of the religious experience. The wish to defend religious experience from subjectivization and naturalization led Leibowitz to eliminate the believer from it. As a result of the implementation of the splitting strategy, not only the empirical factors that concern the believer's life, but also his or her personal consciousness, are doomed to be excluded from the religious experience. It is precisely the exclusion of one's consciousness that finally led to the identification of the religious experience with its praxis. It seems, then, that in the context of his discussion of faith, Leibowitz treats human beings' consciousness essentially as an expression of their individuality or even as identified with it, but not as having also general aspects. Certainly, lacking the factor of consciousness, one cannot even regard the religious praxis as experience. In a deep sense, the removal of consciousness from the realm of religious experience is even more radical than pushing aside the dimension of identity from the believer's understanding. While the category of identity denotes a wide integration of the individual and a formation of a complex of the person's expressions and experiences into one unity, the removal of consciousness can in principle also refer to the individual context or to an individual act within this context. Leibowitz not only pushes aside the category of identity from religious praxis, but further, in the absence of a dimension of consciousness, the practitioner is denied the possibility of saying: "I follow God's commandments."

The following questions now emerge: Cannot personal consciousness be influential in other ways than subjectivizing and naturalizing? Do people's intentions not come from their consciousness and therefore represent at least a mode of their presence at the same time? Why assume that every meaning inevitably makes the intended object subjective, i.e., charges it with an individualistic significance? Leibowitz's writings provide no answers to these questions. Undoubtedly, consciousness is essential to the practical realization of the religious experience, which is based on an abstract intention; only thanks to this intention is a link created between the human action and God. Thus, the "I" is crucial not only as the performer of the divine commandments, but also as a person of consciousness who can bestow upon praxis a religious meaning.[54]

Moreover, especially regarding Leibowitz's idea of unconditioned religious praxis, the elimination of the individuality of believers and the reduction of their being to that of practitioners is problematic. The meaning of these things is that the link between religious praxis and the postmodernist ethos of the self is problematic, and that the category of identity in religious experience, originating in the modernist ethos of self, is not only possible but worthwhile. Believers as whole, uniform beings are needed not only for taking the initial decision to believe and hence as constitutive subjects for faith, they are also necessary precisely for Leibowitz's idea of unconditioned religious praxis. As said above, what differentiates between "belief for its own sake" and "belief not for its own sake" is the intention behind them and not the mere praxis of religious imperatives, which are in any case carried out according to identical criteria not subject to the believer's own opinion.

But it is not just the link between the perception of the practical religious experience and the postmodernist ethos of self that is problematic. The relation between practical religious experience and the modernist ethos of self, i.e., the stage of the decision to believe, is also

---

[54] For further discussion in this context, see my review article about similar flaws in Arendt's idea of self, with similar central characteristics of the postmodernist ethos: Ronny Miron, "The Self in the Realms of Ontology: A Critical View of Hannah Arendt's Conception of the Human Condition," *The International Journal of the Humanities* 6:11 (2009): 41–52.

not without difficulties. This becomes apparent when studying the *second assumption* regarding **the link between freedom and individuality**, in which Leibowitz's idea of freedom is anchored. Here we reveal a contrast, and even a paradox, in what Leibowitz considers expressions of freedom. On the one hand, he sees the decision originating in believers' individual being as an expression of their free will, which cannot be reduced to aspects related to the facts or circumstances surrounding them. The constituting status of the volitional decision to believe in Leibowitz's thought seems to be the last stronghold of the individual being in Leibowitz's idea of faith. On the other hand, Leibowitz argues that religious experience is free precisely due to its being liberated from subjectivization and neutralization. In other words, what makes religious experience free is that it is full of limitations conducted by practitioners who can avoid them, limitations that are not necessitated by the practitioners' nature as subjects and natural entities. While the first expression of freedom places the individual at its center, the second expression distances this individual in favor of the decisive dominance of the practical activities entailed in it. We are once more seeing the split typical of Leibowitz's thought between the stage of deciding to believe and the practical religious experience, or between the arena dominated by the modernist ethos of self and the one where the postmodernist ethos leaves its mark.

Leibowitz's approach to the issue of freedom, which also restored and revealed the presence of these two modes of self, raises the following serious question: does Leibowitz provide sufficient protection for individuality when he states the independence of individuality, of which he considers the volitional decision to believe to be the highest expression, in the circumstances and context in which it is contained? Contemporary critiques, such as those of Foucault, Lacan, Bordieu, and others in the spectrum between Freudianism and Feminism to post-structuralism and Post-modernism, reject this possibility. These critiques argue that the total being of the individual, and even the individual's self-perception, are subject to the dramatic influence of historical and social forces. The understanding at the basis of these approaches is important here, since it considers a sharp separation, like the one arising from Leibowitz's approach, between the internal and the external in the being of the self to be impossible. Moreover, such a separation undermines the believer's ability to form an identity within the religious experience, and thus it is unlikely to hurt the individuality that is vital to realizing Leibowitz's idea of faith. It is no coincidence that in a period when the self shattered and fragmented into the splinters of its experiences, awareness of the power of total ideologies to enslave individuals increased. Without doubt, such ideologies can play this destructive role, particularly for a broken and fragmented self. In contrast, people's chance of defending themselves from the power of these approaches starts in recognizing that they have an internality, an identity, and even a unique substantive dimension that distinguishes them from other individuals, and at the same time enables them to encounter them and to experience similarity with them.

The *third assumption* refers to **God's mode of presence in the religious experience**, which was perceived by Leibowitz as absolutely transcendent. Leibowitz states that not only does God's being leave no traces in the world, but in fact the path the believers are about to take, or better, the religious imperatives they are obliged to face, must be independent of the immanent reality in which the religious praxis takes place. In his words: "the position in front of god is not mirrored in the objective reality; it is above that reality and beyond it."[55] This aspect may either indirectly explain the logic behind depriving consciousness of any role in the religious praxis itself or complete it. Simply put, God is transcendent—to human consciousness and to the world. Therefore, the attempt to understand him or the way he relates to the world is in vain. However, it seems to me that the more profound idea that supported these two theses— concerning God and concerning the believer—is Leibowitz's wish to support independent relationships between immanence and transcendence; in other words, between the worldly reality, including that of human beings, and God's entity. God's independence of his believers and of the immanent reality rests on the very fact of his absolute transcendence: "God's divinity is entirely intrinsic to Him and does not consist in his relation to the world, whose contingent existence adds nothing to God's divinity.... Clearly, his kingship is essential to Him. God is a king even in the absence of a world in which He reigns."[56] In God's transcendence is embodied, then, not only God's entity but also the meaning of it to the religious praxis.

---

[55] Leibowitz, *Faith, History, and Values*, 59.
[56] Leibowitz, *Judaism, Human Values, and the Jewish State*, 74.

Yet, what are problematic in the above exposed argumentation are not necessarily Leibowitz's assumptions but the conclusions he deduces from them. In the first place, an independent relationship does not rule out, at least not by definition, the very possibility of having an affinity—both from God's side and from that of the believer. One can have contact with something and remain independent of it. Presumably, Leibowitz's radical way of thinking did not enable him to discern the possibility of gradation. Therefore, for him any kind of touch or contact ends up, sooner or later, in total absorption. Moreover, in my opinion this logical deficiency is not the main problem in Leibowitz's present concept; rather, the fact that the ideal of total transcendence unavoidably excludes God from the religious experience as a whole is. Consequently, God "appears" in the religious praxis in an analogical mode, by following his commandments, but his very entity, i.e., exactly the core of his meaning according to Leibowitz, is absent there. Leibowitz himself admitted this, saying that "in reflecting and speaking about man's standing before God, the believer tries to refer minimally to God, who has no image at all, and makes effort to direct his religious consciousness to himself as recognizing his duty to his God."[57]

The question is, then, if God's vanishing presence within the religious praxis and metaphysics is not acknowledged as a legitimate means to give expression to God's entity or to the way he relates to his believers, what meaning can one bestow upon God? Does Leibowitz's unreserved emphasis on God's transcendence, as a being as well as an object of consciousness, not finally leave unanswered the question of why at all one should believe? Leibowitz would have replied, "Because I want to." Yet, in his thinking, Leibowitz supplies no means to maintain that will or to defend it from opposition. In other words, my contention is that an extreme conception of absolute transcendence damages the very possibility of constituting a real relationship to God as the subject of religion. Mere acknowledgment of God's transcendent being, which does not receive constant confirmation in the believer's consciousness and within his praxis, cannot support the religious praxis as directed to God. The vanishing of God and that of the believer add up to a meaningless religious praxis, for it has neither subject nor object.

---

[57] Ibid., 76.

A possible explanation for the double elimination that occurs in Leibowitz's idea of faith can be that he preferred expressing His being to its meaning for the believer, or else that he preferred ontology to epistemology. Yet one wonders why he assumes the need to choose between the two? Moreover, what sense can ontology have when it is not accompanied by an epistemology or at least by a rational account of the being to which that ontology refers? In other words, an ontology that does not include within itself the means to validate the being it strives to represent remains denuded and may end up as a groundless idea. Therefore, in order to give support to his ontology, i.e., his concept of God as absolutely transcendent, Leibowitz should have suggested the means to understand it. Clearly, there must be "someone" seeking such an understanding. This is in fact the self-understanding that is part of the human experience in the world, of which religious praxis is a part. Just as the possibility of obtaining such understanding does not detract from the transcendence of God, it also does not provide complete understanding of the self, though such an understanding does not have to be complete or rooted in coherent epistemology. Elliott described this well in the following words: "To stress that self-interpretation and practical understanding is crucial to the formation and maintenance of the self is not, however, to argue that we can have complete access to our inner worlds and sense of identity."[58]

> Furthermore, perhaps the individual's experience of the inexhaustibility of self-understanding can serve as a basis for experiencing God's transcendence. This means that the obvious human need to refer to the contexts in which we participate and to understand ourselves can serve as a basis for the religious experience, despite it being directed at a heteronymous and transcendent object. Whatever the nature of self-understanding, such understanding not only cannot damage the specific idea of Leibowitz's faith, but may support the very possibility of it. In other words, not only does religious experience as directed at a transcendent being not benefit from pushing the believer out of it, but moreover the believer is essential to confirm the directedness of this experience to God or transcendence.

---

[58] Elliott, *Concepts of the Self*, 5.

G. Summary

Leibowitz's attempt to establish religious faith solely on praxis rejected the widespread traditional approaches that usually regard metaphysics as theoretical justification or as a mental infrastructure to the religious praxis. Instead, he contends that there is no such difference between belief and religion, for "belief is but the religion of divine commandments, outside of which the religious belief does not exist at all."[59] This means, then, that all we know about believers is a depiction of the religious imperatives that rule their lives; we know nothing about their individuality and the subjectivity from which their initial decision to believe stemmed. Consequently, their decision to believe and their entire individual world are excluded from the realm of the religious experience, and the differences between them and non-believers are narrowed to the sphere of praxis.

Yet the suggested commentary to Leibowitz's idea of faith strove to point also to its deficiencies. I argue that Leibowitz's endeavor to free the religious experience of subjective elements, personal as well as mental, was dependent precisely on the subjectivity of the believer—not only for the performance of the religious praxis, but also in order to have the right intention within the act. As a matter of a fact, without the presence of the believer as an agent of thinking and truth, an approach largely responding to the modernist ethos of self, God himself would be dismissed from the religious praxis. Needless to say, the idea of a religious faith devoid of believers and of God is meaningless.

Seeking the total independence of religious praxis, Leibowitz failed to differentiate between different kinds of conditionality. Whereas the conditionality that refers to factual reality is contingent by its very nature, the conditionality that relates to the believer is crucial to faith itself, to the extent that without the believer no faith or praxis can exist at all. Hence it is exactly the demand to achieve the total independence of transcendence from immanence which was addressed to the believers as conscious beings that made Leibowitz's idea of faith impossible to implement. However, anchoring religious conception in immanence entails more than necessarily relinquishing the idea of transcendence or the experience in God's presence. On the contrary, a conception that

---

[59] Leibowitz, *Judaism, Human Values, and the Jewish State*, 38.

assumes that God is absolutely transcendent of the religious experience should facilitate and even demand the involvement of immanent consciousness that will speak for the being of God, and by that confirm its presence in the religious experience. Admitting the essentiality of the believer's subjectivity to the praxis by no means implies that faith turned out to be a subjective matter. Yet the fact that religious faith cannot but be realized as human experience indicates that subjective beings are incessantly involved in it. Therefore, in my opinion the presence in religious experience of believers as united beings that strive to achieve meaning for their experience and to connect its different parts should be defended.

Index

A
Aaron 27-8, 38
Abigail 69
Abrabanel 51
Abraham 30, 46-54, 56, 58-9, 63, 97, 114-15, 117, 131, 166, 312, 343, 369, 385-8, 428, 435, 478, 529-30, 566
Abraham Jacob of Sadagora 389
Absolute Spirit 422, 429, 438-9, 450, 456
Abulafia, Avraham 323-4
Achituv, Yoske 245
Adam 108, 215, 520-3, 528, 530-4, 539-40
Ahab 69-70
Ahad Ha'am 482-4
Aher, Elisha 293-4, 296, 301
Akiva 294, 296, 301, 322, 478
al Qaeda 150, 157, 182
Alfasi, Yitzhak (RYF) 76
Alston, William 202
Alter, Judah Aryeh Leib 75, 77-8
Altmann, Alexander 355
Amalek 214, 304, 307, 568
Amichai, Yehuda 456
 "Yehuda Ha-Levi" 456
Apter, Ruth 415
Aquinas, Thomas 378, 459, 461
Aristotle 125, 128, 491
Asher, Bahya b. 116
atheism 126, 137-8, 143, 150, 156, 159, 161, 176-7, 246, 267, 492, 554n21, 567
authentic 17, 33, 57, 133, 163, 266, 446, 462n15, 472-3, 492, 528, 540
Avihu 27-8
Avraham, R. 22-3
Azriel of Gerona 278-80, 282-3, 285-301, 442
 Derekh ha-Emunah ve-Derekh ha-Kefirah 278-9, 282, 287, 299-301
 Sha'ar ha-Sho'el 278-9, 282, 285, 287, 299, 301

B
Ba'al Shem-Tov 20-2, 35, 37, 313, 345, 401; *see also* Besht
Bacon, Francis 202
Baer, Isaac 440-1
Bar Yohai, Simeon 214
Bar-Yosef, Hamutal 384, 412
Barr, James 219
Barrett, William 524, 541
 Irrational Man 524
Barth, Karl 520
Beit-Midrash
 in Bialik 502-3, 508-11
belief 9, 107, 120, 137, 143-53, 169-73, 181-6, 194-5, 204, 282, 285, 299, 384, 418-30, 432-9, 448-55, 466, 471, 482, 582
 false 138, 154-7, 162, 178
 for its own sake 564, 577
 not for its own sake 564, 577
 religious 176, 188-91, 197-200, 206-210, 215-22, 228, 230-40, 332, 351, 557-65, 570-3
ben Dosa, Hanina 349-50
Ben-Sasson 442, 446
Ber, Dov 81, 302, 314, 319n49, 320, 326, 330-1, 333, 335, 342, 345, 352, 381
 Maggid Devarav Le Ya'akov 320
Berdyczewski, M. J. 479, 486
Berger, David 166, 172, 187

Index

Bergman, Samuel Hugo 47, 56, 85, 98-100, 123, 125, 133, 530
Berkeley, George (Bishop) 92
Berlin, Isaiah 243, 246
Berlin, Naftali Zvi Yehuda 28-31, 40-1, 307
Besht 302-9, 311-16, 318-22, 324-31, 333-5, 337, 340-2, 345-7, 350, 355, 357-9, 361, 363-4
   "Epistle of the Ascent of the Soul" 315
   Tsava'at ha-Ribash 19, 27
Besht's disciples 319, 327
Bezalel 311
Bialik, Haim Nachman 486, 500-12
   "Alone" 502, 507-12
   "If You Want to Know" 502-4
   "My Song" 506-7, 512
   "On an Autumn Day" 504, 506-7, 512
Binding of Isaac (Akedah) 46, 54, 385, 388, 428, 530, 566
Bishop, John 460
Blau, Yitzchak 139
Blustein, Jeffrey 180-2
Bonim, Simcha 498
Book of Job 259, 270
Book of Psalms 499
Bordieu 578
Borowitz, Eugene, 223
Bratslav 239, 299, 357, 382, 403
Brener, Ann 448
Brown, Benjamin 457-8
Buber, Martin 12, 48, 52, 54-6, 60, 304, 359, 363-5, 532-3, 537, 540
   I and Thou 365, 540
   Tales of the Hasidim 359

C

Cain 445
Cairo Geniza 423, 441
Calvin, John 459, 461
   Sensus Divinitatis 459
Cambridge Geniza 424
Camus, Albert 14, 16, 79, 250
Carmy, Shalom 179, 187
certainty 51, 83, 106, 135, 156, 162, 221, 225, 228, 325, 329-30, 366, 372, 377-9, 430, 436, 439, 453, 518-19
   uncertainty 37, 50-1, 56-9, 135, 272, 496
Chabad 329, 367-70, 375, 380-3, 498
Christ 18, 79, 151
Christianity 19, 34, 79, 107, 115, 125, 129, 137, 164-8, 173, 223, 365, 461, 518
   Catholicism 125, 139, 421-2
   Protestant 32, 37-8, 63, 139, 209, 269-70, 544
Clifford, William Kingdon 139, 145-6
   "Ethics of Belief, The" 145
cognitive heritage 462-3, 467-70, 476-7
cognitive models of faith 475-7
Cohen, Hermann 513-14, 522-4
commandments 19-20, 25-30, 35-6, 40-2, 98, 117-8, 131-4, 255, 264-5, 269-71, 373, 419, 442, 486, 549-64, 567-8, 571-5, 582
   acceptance of 39-40, 130, 257, 433, 554, 575
   obeying/following 343, 377, 437n42, 549, 577, 580
   of faith 464-8, 477
communion 35-6, 407
community of believers 188, 207, 210-3, 228, 472, 515
compartmentalization 562-3, 565, 568-70
concealed God 394, 541
consciousness 14, 16, 73, 85, 89, 91-5, 105-10, 122, 125, 184, 231, 268, 366, 372, 497, 518, 531, 538
   critical 18

false 20-2, 27, 45, 68
   historical 435
   of revelation 531
   religious 26, 41, 55, 84, 111, 130-1, 260, 516, 541, 555, 567, 580
   split 530, 551, 553, 559-60, 562, 569
   unhappy (Hegel) 421-2, 425, 448-9
Confucius 165
constructivism 196, 215, 220-2, 230
contemplation 123, 244, 279, 283, 286, 299-300, 372, 378-80, 479, 519
context 14-5, 41, 71, 121, 127, 182, 199, 201-6, 209, 219, 221, 230, 282, 291, 395, 405, 416, 545, 547-8, 558, 562, 572, 581
contingency 77, 93-6, 127-8, 131, 231, 237, 431, 553, 579, 582
conventionalism 514, 521, 524-5, 542
Cordovero, Moses 361, 364
Crescas, Hasdai 312-13
   Or Hashem 312
cultural-linguistic approach 203, 205, 208-12, 214, 222, 240

D

Dan, Joseph 298
David 26, 66-9, 336, 345, 349-50, 412
Dawkins, Richard 143, 150-1, 156, 176, 185
   "New Atheism, The" 150
deconstructionism 230, 240
demonic 52-5, 61, 65, 68-9, 78, 80, 82-7, 102, 104, 320
Descartes 202, 283, 429, 519
desires 82, 221-2, 361, 423, 444, 450-6, 564, 567
   first order 550
   second order 550-1, 558
   unfulfilled 448-9, 453, 455
Dessler, Eliyahu 175, 234-5
determinism 305, 307, 337, 361-2, 365, 553

dialogue 9, 71, 91, 140, 166-70, 275, 435, 472, 514, 525, 534-5, 537, 539-41, 544
Din 311, 406
divine providence 107, 145n, 351, 274, 303, 332, 334, 338, 346, 365, 544
divine revelation 59, 64, 96, 409, 428, 436-7, 531
Dostoevsky 18
dvekut 308, 310, 312, 322, 325, 327, 356
Dvir-Goldberg, Rivka 120

E

ecstatic 356, 363, 381, 499
   experience 416n, 499
   state 356
effort 20, 112, 118, 121, 137-40, 156-7, 217, 220, 240, 327, 463, 467-8, 470, 476-7, 545, 580
ego 14, 22, 506-7
Egypt 131, 211, 309, 347, 419, 423, 428, 432, 435-6, 446, 469, 552, 555
Eidels, Shmuel 68
Einsof/Eyn Sof 231, 233, 279, 282-8, 293, 299, 301, 313, 332-4, 356, 364, 368, 372-3, 378-9, 383; *see also* infinity
Eleazar, R. 67
Elimelech of Lyzhansk 346
   Noam Elimelech 346
Elisha 294
Elliott, Anthony 553, 581
end of days 173, 254, 453n71, 540
Engel, Yosef 76
Ephraim, Moses 326, 329
error 23-4, 46, 55, 74, 89, 161; *see also* mistake
ethics 106, 127, 141-2, 150, 187, 249, 274, 568
Eve 215, 531-3, 540

evil 87, 102-4, 114, 123, 241, 246-57, 268, 273-4, 296, 320, 406
  problem/question of 172, 189, 244, 248, 250, 252, 256, 270, 517
  reality/existence of 104, 247, 249-50, 253, 257
  triumph of 253n32, 334
evil inclination 13, 22-7, 30, 55, 80-2, 85, 354
  temptation of 12, 19-20, 22, 24, 35-8, 41, 45-6, 48, 50, 53, 57, 67-8, 78, 88-9, 122
existentialism 9, 47, 51, 60, 188, 193, 195-6, 198, 229, 250, 331, 353-4, 362-6, 513, 516, 524-33, 538-40
  existential experience 192, 225, 268, 525, 534, 539
  existential paradox 377, 380, 528
experience 8-9, 71, 105-6, 119, 192-3, 196, 199, 212, 220, 225-8, 236, 244-50, 327, 367, 380, 428-9, 435-7, 479, 514
  mystical 508
  religious 18, 30-1, 36, 54, 82-4, 91, 93, 96, 107, 121, 132, 264, 269, 345, 403, 407-8, 487-8, 522-5, 547-9, 558-60, 565, 568-83
experientialism 105, 125, 192-3, 224, 228, 310-1, 325, 330, 357, 358, 363-4, 379-81, 407, 514, 529, 533, 547
expressivism 192-3, 196, 198, 202, 204, 206
Ezekiel 69, 71, 354
Ezra of Gerona 295-8

F

faith 50-65, 77-85, 88-91, 95-7, 100-11, 135, 170-2, 197, 218, 265-76, 278-95, 297-315, 317-25, 329-33, 335-55, 358-92, 458-84, 488-90, 514-27, 529-35, 537-47
  as paradox 17, 131-2, 357, 368, 370-3, 536
  as temptation 12-19, 22-27, 30-8, 41, 45-9, 52-6, 60, 71-4, 78, 80-2, 87, 93, 101-4, 113, 122
  choosing 74, 87, 103, 257, 276, 280, 303, 513
  complete 314, 332, 339, 354, 478
  concept of 8-9, 109-10, 130, 261, 266, 289, 346, 369, 381, 457, 515-8, 541, 544, 556, 562
  for its own sake 258-9, 565
  in Hasidism 302-3, 309, 318-9, 331, 345, 348, 364
  natural 114-5
  non-illusory 130
  not for its own sake 258
  of the Sages 71-2, 112, 256, 293, 296, 301, 346, 463-4, 467-8, 472-3, 476-7
  of the tsaddik 114, 311-3, 342, 345-52, 364, 467, 470
  simple 105, 110, 114-5
  strengthening of 257, 457, 461-2, 476, 499
  the knight of 56, 58-9
  types of 275, 299, 529
feeling 14, 31, 44-5, 176, 218, 376, 470-1, 474, 508-9, 513, 520, 527, 556
guilt 67, 188, 425, 454, 496, 506
happiness 15, 85-6, 146-7, 149, 178, 184, 186, 242, 564
loneliness 148, 498, 507-8, 510, 514, 516, 519, 525-30, 534-7, 540
religious 44-5, 55, 268, 567
shame 32, 410-1
Feivel 339
Feldman, Eliyahu 470-1
feminine 503-4, 507, 509
Feuerbach, Ludwig 491
Finkelman, Yoel 140, 187

Fishbane, Michael 300
  Sacred Attunement 300
Fleischer, Ezra 423-4, 450
Foucault, Michel 578
Frankfurt, Harry 18, 551, 558
Frei, Hans 203, 209
  Eclipse of Biblical Narrative, The 209
Freud, Sigmund 15-16, 104
Friedman, Eliyahu 501
Frischman, David 487
  Literature, The 487
Fromm, Erich 566
Fruchter, Shlomo 473
  Divrei Shlomo 473

G
Gandhi 274
Gaon, Nissim 71, 133
Gaon, Seder Olam 84
Gaon of Vilna 32, 84, 233, 235, 350, 445n
Geertz, Clifford 16, 204, 243-4
Genesis 114-15
George Herbert Mead 552
Gershon, Levi 66
Gershon of Kutow 315
Gide, André 21, 61
  Counterfeiters, The 61
Ginsberg, Asher 482
God 19-20, 32-4, 40, 46, 53, 60-75, 86-8, 90-103, 114-7, 209-10, 226-9, 231-4, 241-8, 250-9, 264-72, 308-14, 335-42, 348-51, 390-8, 412-16, 424-9, 432-6, 457-66, 470-7
  belief in 14, 18, 179, 202, 255, 259-60, 308-9, 337, 343, 347, 433, 475
  commands of 29, 47-52, 55-9, 269, 343, 550-1, 554, 558-9, 563, 567, 575
  communion with 22-3, 27, 35-6
  fear of 27-31, 41, 51, 55, 83, 102-3, 105, 258, 350, 395, 473
  image of 80, 90, 212, 267, 523, 525, 567
  love of 16, 28, 30, 62, 219, 269, 272
  quest for 479-82, 485-7, 492, 495, 499, 541
  search of 479; *see* quest for
  word of 29, 47-52, 56, 59-60, 70-1, 73-4, 83, 94, 96, 211, 251, 313, 324, 555
  worship of 17, 23, 30-1, 38, 41, 79, 81, 100, 112-3, 118, 124, 131-2, 134, 228, 326, 399, 436, 442, 465, 491
Godseeking/godseekers 479-82, 484-7, 489-90, 492-9
Goffman, Erving 547
Goitein, S. D. 424
Goldman, Eliezer 96, 224, 227-30, 246-7, 256, 260-5, 273
  "Religious Statements and Scientific Statements" 263
Gordon, Aaron David 482-4
  Our Dealings with Ourselves 483
Gordon, Arye Leib 473-5
  Hazon haEmunah vehaHashgaha 474n48
Gordon, J. L. 485
Green, Arthur 74, 363
Grinberg, U. Z. 486

H
Habakkuk 130
Hacohen, David 83
Hacohen, Jacob Joseph 308-12, 315-16, 319-20, 326-8, 334, 346
  Ben Porat Yosef 316
  Toldot Ya'akov Yosef 309
Halakha(h) 29, 31-2, 37-8, 42, 44-5, 72-5, 96-8, 128, 131, 134-6, 144, 188, 226, 233, 242, 262, 264, 274, 377, 403, 514-15, 518
  literalism 189, 213, 225
  thematic 249, 253-4
  topical 249, 251

Halakhic discourse 72
Halakhic norms 29, 31, 40, 82, 95
Halbertal, Moshe 143-4, 149, 153, 169, 179, 184, 285
Halevi, Judah 143, 279-82, 285, 287, 418-21, 423-9, 433-8, 440-4, 446, 448-56, 470
  "Can Lifeless Bodies" 455
  "I Cry to God with a Melting Heart" 446-7
  "I Run Towards the Fountain of True Life" 450
  "My Desire for the Living God" 442-3, 446, 448
  "My Heart Is in the East" 418-9, 423
  "My Thoughts Awaken Me" 428, 433
  "O Lord, before Thee is My Whole Desire" 426, 443
  "Servants of Time" 432-3
  "Zion, Will You Not Ask" 453
Hame'agel, Honi 349-50
hamshakhah 342-7, 364
hasidism 31-2, 120, 317, 332, 337, 344-6, 352, 361-5, 388-9, 406
  Bershad 305
  Bratslav 352, 357, 382, 404
  hasidic movement 303-4, 346, 350, 362-3
  hasidic schools 302-4, 317, 331, 357
  Korets 306
  mystical 302-3, 317, 331, 352, 365, 382, 395
  of faith 302, 309, 331, 382
  Shomer Emunim 339-40
  See also Chabad
Hartman, David 85, 170, 224, 226-7, 243, 245-6, 254-7, 260-1, 265-8, 270, 273, 436, 489, 566
Hayyim, Abraham 81
Hayyim Haykl of Amdur 21-2
Hayyim of Volozhin 31, 35-7, 233, 236
Hebrew Renaissance 481-2, 484-6, 489-90
Hegel 105-6, 362, 420-3, 425, 428-32, 434, 438-40, 448, 456
  Phenomenology of Mind, The 420
Heidegger, Martin 201, 365, 473, 519, 527-8, 539
  "Letter on Humanism" 519
Heine, Heinrich 491
hell 48, 137, 160, 301, 498, 504
Hellenism 125, 189, 524
Henderson, Edward 228, 230
heresy 97, 110, 161, 175, 231, 278, 280, 282, 287-301, 352-3, 361, 387-8, 394, 484
  materialistic 361-2
heritage 462, 470, 488
  cognitive 462-3, 467-70, 476-7
  sense 469
Heschel, Abraham Joshua 14, 71, 87, 170, 365
Hesse, Herman 19
  Narcissus and Goldmund 19
hester panim (hiding the face) 251, 396
Hick, John 202
Hilf, Shmuel Moshe 468
  Gan Hayyim 468
Hirsch, Samson Raphael 166, 517
Hirsch of Zhidachov 360-1
history 78, 143, 163, 168, 175, 190, 209, 211, 226, 251, 254-6, 365, 381, 423, 427, 433, 436, 439, 449-50, 544, 554-5
  human 108, 123, 127, 151, 191, 220, 245, 271
  personal 424, 446, 452
  religious 85, 110
Hitchens, Christopher 150, 156
Hitler, Adolf 499
Hoffding, Harald 107
Holmes, Oliver Wendell 151
Holocaust 220, 251, 340, 365, 461
Holy Land 316, 419-25, 442, 446, 448, 451-6
honesty 107, 116, 130, 140, 247, 480

Index

Horowitz, Isaiah 346
  Shnei Luchot Habrit 346
Humanism 128, 178, 437n41
Hume, David 92, 234
Hungary 339, 458, 464
Husserl 92

I
ibn Gikitilla, Joseph 297
ibn Pakuda, Bahya 115-6
Idealism 125, 420, 425, 516, 573
  epistemic/epistemological 513-4, 522, 524-5
Idel, Moshe 296-8n, 342
identity, group 141, 169, 177-9, 181-6
idolatry 17, 38, 54-5, 79, 114, 226, 237, 328, 349, 563, 567
  molech worship/service 52, 54
incarnation 107, 269, 339
individualism 181, 249, 575, 577
infinity/infinite 85, 91, 119, 231, 233, 236-7, 269, 283, 290, 312-3, 334-5, 356, 368, 376, 415, 561; *see also* Einsof
innocence 21n22, 80, 215, 259, 486, 498
Isaac 46, 48, 50-1, 131, 312, 435, 444, 530
Isaac, Levi 346, 414
Isaiah 99, 445
Islam 210, 446
Israel 13, 29, 43, 52, 73, 82, 128, 138, 154, 212, 214, 220, 239, 316, 330, 340, 343, 345, 347-9, 351, 386, 441, 452, 482-3, 555
  children of 27, 67, 98, 389, 435
  people of 23, 30, 40, 62, 66, 69, 78, 312, 358, 458, 481, 510
  State of 251

J
Jacob 131, 274
  dream of 320

James, William 146, 197-8, 228, 236, 460, 487
  "Will to Believe, The" 146n23, 197
Jehoshafat 70
Jephtah 48, 58
Jerusalem 40, 339-40, 388, 391, 394, 442, 444, 447-8, 452, 456
Jesus 61, 79, 107, 137-8, 478
Job 132, 243, 259, 270, 478
Jonas, Hans 365-6
  "Matter, Spirit, and Creation" 366
Joshua 71-2
Judah 66, 444
Judah bar Pazi 43
Judaism 9, 62, 88, 96-8, 100, 111, 120, 124-6, 130, 136, 139, 144, 163-5, 173, 188-9, 231, 259, 364, 469-72, 518, 549, 557-8, 563, 567
  Conservative 174n109, 223
  Modern Orthodox 175n111, 185, 239
  Orthodox 75, 166, 185, 188n1, 223-4, 457-8, 460-1, 463, 468, 475-6
  ultra-Orthodox 175n111, 184-5, 339, 458
justice 97, 129, 195, 220, 241, 254-5, 260, 270-2, 387-8, 407
injustice 180, 219, 246, 270, 334

K
Kabbalah 143, 230, 238, 278, 288, 302, 308, 320, 331, 339, 342, 361, 367-8, 380-2, 395, 402-3, 457, 503
  combination of letters 311, 313-17
  prophetic 323-4
  ten *sefirot* 237, 240, 308, 321, 364, 378, 406-7, 501
  tsimtsum 231-2, 234-5, 237, 240, 335, 337, 351, 361, 365, 368
Kant, Immanuel 14, 49, 366, 429, 438, 491, 523

Critique of Pure Reason 438
Kantian 32, 127, 168-9, 216, 235, 258, 431
Neo-Kantianism 491, 514, 523, 542
Post-Kantianism 364
Katan, Moshe 463-4
Katz, Jacob 363
  Tradition and Crisis 363
Kempis, Thomas 86-7
Kierkegaard, Søren 16, 47, 56-60, 100-1, 106, 119, 229, 354, 362, 491, 520, 527, 530
  Fear and Trembling 47, 56, 58
King, Sallie B. 166
Klausner, Joseph 508
knowing 111, 210, 218n52, 265, 371, 460, 492
Kolitz, Tzvi 266
Kook, Abraham Yitzhak 9, 52-6, 60, 82-4, 114-5, 119, 146, 213, 235-9, 388-90, 396, 457, 486
  Orot ha-Koddesh 83
Korah 26, 29
Kornblith, Hilary 187
Kurzweil, David 33, 84, 100, 278, 299, 369, 457, 482, 546
Kuzari 279, 281-2, 287, 419, 423-6, 428-30, 432, 434-7, 439, 448-51, 491

L
Lacan 578
language 105-7, 125, 134, 192, 195, 199, 201, 208, 238-9, 314-5, 318, 323, 398, 444, 450-1, 481, 538, 554, 560
  language game 8, 200, 203, 216-7, 220-1, 230, 264-5
  religious 191, 205, 207, 211-2, 214-5, 220-1, 237, 261, 263-5, 273
  signs 401-3, 411
La Pérouse 21, 61
Lavater, Johann Kasper 165

law 43-5, 51, 55, 76-7, 79, 128-9, 173, 200, 213-4, 269, 272, 274, 333, 398, 405, 435, 441, 523, 550, 553-4
  natural 54-5, 262, 519
laws of nature 305, 337
leap of faith 198, 354, 420
Leibowitz, Yeshayahu 16, 31-2, 37-8, 89, 97, 123, 131-2, 225-7, 243-4, 246-7, 256-61, 266-7, 273, 545-82
Leikes, David 345, 347
Leiner, Mordechai Yosef 27-9, 31-2, 49-52, 58-9
Levi bar Hamma 22
Levinas, Emmanuel 91-3, 95, 246, 266-74
  "To Love the Torah More than God" 266
  "Yosl Rakover Talks to God" 266
Lewis, David 160-2
Licht, Jacob 13, 62
Lindbeck, George 190, 192, 203, 205
Lipsker, Avidav 482
Lithuania 307, 458
Loew, Judah 107-9
  Netivot Olam 107
Lubavitcher Rebbe; see Schneerson, Menachem Mendel
Luria, Isaac 317, 395, 403, 413
lust 79, 360, 443, 501
Luther, Martin 38, 100

M
Maggid of Mezeritch; see Ber, Dov
Maggid of Zlotshov; see Michal, Yehiel
MaHaRSHA ; see Eidels, Shmuel
Maimon, Shlomo 307
Maimoni, David b. Yehoshua 85
Maimonides 9, 63-4, 76-7, 108, 125, 128, 144, 191, 223, 245, 254, 256, 261, 263, 293-4, 296, 307-11, 378, 430, 435-6, 463-7

Guide of the Perplexed 9, 108, 125, 128, 133, 293, 307
Laws of the Foundations of the Torah 64, 309
Mishneh Torah 261, 309-10
"Yemen Letter, The" 245
majestic man 520-3, 525-6, 530-1, 535, 538-40, 542
Malcolm, Norman 229
Malevich, Kazimir 414-15
  Suprematist Composition: White on White 415
Manasseh 40
Mann, Thomas 102-4
  Doctor Faustus 102
Marburgian 523
Marcel, Gabriel 519, 538
  Mystery of Being, The 538
Margalit, Avishai 180
Marion, Jean-Luc 92, 94
Maritain, Jacques 531, 534
Mark, Zvi 357
Marty, Martin 150, 152, 163, 166, 169, 177
martyrdom (Kidush Ha-Shem) 30, 91, 163, 441
Marx, Groucho 162
Marx, Karl 344, 491
May, Rollo 527
Mead, George Herbert 552-3
Meir, Isaac 358
Meiri 486
Menahem Nahum of Chernobyl 319-20, 332-3
Mendelssohn, Moses 165, 307
Mercier, Hugo 148
metaphysics 8, 189-92, 195-202, 205-7, 220-32, 235-59, 264, 272-5, 289-95, 300, 366, 453, 479, 490-1, 518, 527, 541, 580, 582
Michal, Yehiel 343-4
Mill, John Stuart 148, 151, 153-4, 158, 160-2, 184

On Liberty 151, 184n
miracle 234, 305-7, 309, 312, 334-5, 337-8, 347, 408-9, 435-6, 469, 555
miracle workers 348-9
Mishnah 38-9, 42-3, 144
mistake 17, 49, 51-3, 68-9, 89, 111, 136, 267, 272, 373, 496; *see also* error
mitzva(h) 38, 213, 227-8, 237, 250, 256-7, 265, 269, 312, 330, 470-1, 551, 567, 569-70
Mocher-Sforim, Mendele 485
Modern Jewish Mysticism 229
Montefiore, Alan 160-1
morality 41, 49, 53, 55-9, 97-9, 114, 118-9, 126-9, 135, 148, 150, 155-7, 171, 186
Moses 24, 27, 29-30, 64, 73, 165, 307, 310, 312, 321, 323-4, 336, 347-8, 435, 462
Moses, David 335, 337-8, 350-1, 361-2, 365-6
Motl of Chernobyl 345
Mount Sinai 24, 64, 72, 107, 194, 215, 220, 257, 309-10, 451, 552, 555
Muslim 184, 429, 445-6, 449; *see also* Islam
Mysticism 232, 236, 238, 357, 365, 382, 395, 490
See also mystical Hassidism; Zelda's Poetry

N

Nadav 27-8
Naeh, Shlomo 322, 324
Nahman of Bratslav 27, 81-3, 110-14, 119, 121, 303, 352-5, 357, 364-5, 393, 398-400, 404
  Likutey Moharan 353
Nahman of Tcherin 404
Nahmanides 117, 311, 435, 464

Index

Nahshon 336-8
Nathan, R. 111, 352, 354, 357
   Likutey Halachot 353
narrative 69, 120, 190-2, 196, 198, 209, 211, 435, 502
   meta-narrative 245, 257, 272
Neher, André 533
Nehru 274
Neo-Wittgensteinian 216, 229
Newman, Barnett 415
   The Name II 415
Nietzsche, Friedrich 149, 182-3, 489-91, 494, 497
   Death of god 490, 494, 497
Nissenbaum, Mordekhai Arye 468-70
   Mossadot haEmunah 468
Nissim Gaon 71-2, 133
Noah 198, 319, 343-4
Non-foundationalism 198, 201-2, 216, 221-3, 225, 228-30, 232, 239
Novak, David 167

O

Okin 184
Otto, Rudolf 84, 270, 522, 534
Ouzziel 23-4, 79-80
oven of Akhnai 71

P

Pachter, Mordechai 278-83, 285, 288, 290-3, 295, 299, 301
pantheism 146, 238, 303, 317, 326, 492, 494
Pascal, Blaise 196-8
   Pascal's Wager 196-8, 479
Peikarz, Mendel 346
   Hassidic Leadership, The 346
Perez, Y. L. 363, 484-6
   "Paths of Alienation from Judaism" 484
perfection 53, 104, 108-9, 288, 293, 564
   divine 123, 284
   ethical and religious 75, 78, 115, 118
   human 110, 116
   of creation 65, 104
Perl, Yosef 350
   Megalle Temirin 350
persuasion 135, 138-43, 149-55, 158-63, 167-8, 172-79, 183-7, 197, 471
   ethics of, 141-2, 187
   pro-persuasion 153, 162
phenomenology 88, 93-4, 105, 489
   of faith as temptation 89-90, 95
   of self 526, 534
   of the believer's self 93-4, 493, 515, 560
   paradox of 92
Phillips 216-17, 229-31, 264
piety 26, 29, 103, 112, 227, 499
Pinhas of Korets 32-4, 42-3, 304-7, 317-18, 327, 341-2, 346, 349, 358, 362
Pinhas of Polotsk 32
   Rosh ha-Giv'ah 32
piyyut 393, 412, 426-7n, 503
Plantinga, Alvin 202, 459-60, 474, 477
Plato 103-4, 126, 144, 495
   Phaedrus 495
poetry 134, 312, 388-91, 397, 402-3, 411-3, 448, 481, 484, 487
   Arabic 419, 434, 448n
   of Bialik 500, 508, 512
   of Judah Halevi 418-21, 425, 432, 434, 441, 449, 452, 455
   of King David in Psalms 412
   of Zelda 384, 389-90, 394-6, 398, 406-9, 415
   religious 391, 419, 426n19, 450
positivism 125, 136, 490
   logical 193-5, 202, 234
   theological 196, 225
post-analytic philosophy 230

post-liberalism 202-7, 209-12, 219, 223, 225, 227, 232
postmodernism 162-3, 176, 199, 201, 223-4, 229-30, 238-40, 545-50, 557-9, 562, 564-5, 567, 570, 573, 575, 577-8
  religious belief in the age of 188
pragmatism 125, 128, 146-7, 149, 151, 196, 207, 218-21, 491, 539
  classical 196-7, 199, 202, 204, 211
  neo-pragmatism 198-201, 232
prayer 82-3, 87, 132-3, 215, 229, 297n, 305-8, 316-21, 328, 332, 341-2, 355, 364, 412, 444, 485, 501, 510-1
  as Dvekut 308-9, 311-5, 355
  of the lips 316, 322, 324
privacy 141, 169-77, 179, 183, 186
Promised Land 424, 455
prophecy 51, 64-5, 69, 71, 83-4, 136, 308, 323-4, 407, 409, 439, 472, 488
prophets 51, 62-6, 69-71, 83-4, 97, 117, 130, 136, 322-4, 394, 409, 435, 463-4, 466, 471-3, 488, 555, 567
proselytizing 137-41, 150-2, 156-7, 165-77
  preclusion of 161n69, 170, 172-3
  religious 140, 143, 152, 159, 164, 174, 186
Putnam, Hilary 216

R

Rabbi of Kotsk 359
Rabinovitz, Zadok Ha'cohen 209, 323
RaDaK (R. David Kimchi) 69-70
radical post-modernism 203, 209
radical traditionalism 204
radicalism 41, 572
Rakover, Yosl 266-8, 270-1
Raphael of Breshod 305, 349
Rashi 42, 70-1, 117, 322, 324, 344, 349

rationalism 8, 125-6, 189, 206, 219, 305, 307, 313, 352, 382, 457-8, 519
rationality 149, 152, 185, 208, 246, 380, 382, 530, 549, 558
  supra rationality 308, 372-3
Ratta, Aharon 339-41
realism 192, 199, 209, 216-8, 220, 247-9, 390, 433, 483, 505, 572
  mitnaggedic 234-5
  skeptical 221-2
reason 36, 65, 72, 104, 107, 112, 115, 162, 171, 217, 220, 281-2, 287, 301, 353, 371-3, 378-9, 459-63, 469-77, 522, 541-2, 550, 555, 557, 558
  human 125, 128, 197, 289, 462
  practical 127, 381-2
rebellion 79, 278-82, 285-7, 301
recognition 75, 93, 96, 100, 191, 232, 234-5, 257-8, 318, 377, 423, 434, 438, 518-9, 539
Red Sea 336, 347, 354, 389
  splitting of 219-20
redemption 12, 38, 55, 123-5, 129, 253, 383, 436, 450, 484, 525-31, 534, 539, 541-4
reflection 45, 56, 89-90, 105, 111-3, 115, 118-21, 230, 233, 289-90, 294, 403-4, 425, 446, 448, 502, 505, 526, 540, 545, 549, 571
Reichenbach, Hans 521
relativism 145, 162-3, 176, 190, 200-2, 226
religion 14-7, 56-7, 78, 85-8, 137-41, 150, 159-161, 164-79, 181-3, 193-204, 207-8, 216-8, 221, 244-5, 443, 491-4, 500, 534, 551, 557-62, 572-3, 575, 582
  demands 37, 75, 89-90, 93, 98, 105, 124, 227, 563-5
  for its own sake 258-9
  illusory 123-5, 127-30, 133-4, 273, 351

Index

not for its own sake 258
zealotry 42-5
religious
  devotion 25-7, 34, 37, 41, 47, 49, 51, 55, 65, 74, 202
  disposition 17-8, 22, 24, 29, 31-3, 37-8, 46, 51-3, 60-1, 65, 72-3, 80, 84, 89, 90, 93, 100-1, 433
  existentialism 9, 16, 195, 354, 359, 362, 544
  life 15-7, 36-7, 41, 52, 57, 72-4, 81, 87-8, 93-5, 103-5, 109-10, 113-4, 120-1, 208, 216, 228, 364, 480, 500, 545, 549, 553, 570-1
  paradigms 63, 208-9, 218, 260
  tradition 12, 18-9, 88, 169, 205-6, 210, 212, 219-21, 262
religious doubt 304-7, 313, 360, 362-5, 487, 490
religious intention 31-3, 36, 79, 90, 120, 132
religious praxis 192, 466
  in Leibowitz's thought 549, 557-9, 564, 569-77, 579-83
religious reductionism 200
religious Zionism 239, 517, 544
revelation 49, 60, 71, 83, 93, 95, 131, 134, 226, 261, 268-70, 323, 337, 361, 375, 382, 392, 407-8, 452, 459, 470, 496, 517
  at Mount Sinai 64, 107, 194, 309-10, 451, 555
  consciousness of 531
  divine 59, 64, 96, 409, 428, 436-7, 531
  of God 46, 50, 237, 356, 378, 398, 402, 413, 475, 492, 536-7
righteousness 30n45, 41, 97, 165, 241-2, 244, 255, 311, 320, 338, 343, 463, 470
Rilke, Rainer Maria 34
Rimon, J. Z. 486
ritual 25, 38-40, 52, 86, 131, 167, 207-8, 226, 342, 511, 523, 550

Rizhiner 350
Rogers, Carl 528
Rorty, Richard 216, 230
Rosenberg, Shalom 439
Rosenberg, Shimon Gerson 239-40
  Kelim Shevurim 239
Rosenberg, Shmuel 475-6
Rozen-Tzvi, Ariel 274-6
Rozen-Tzvi, Yishai 274
Rynhold, Daniel 174, 187

S

Saadia Gaon 9, 438, 445, 470
  Book of Beliefs and Opinions, The 9
Sade, Pinhas 363
Safrin, Isaac Judah 318
  Zohar Hai 318
Sages, the 36, 43, 63, 71-2, 112, 136, 256, 293, 296, 301, 346, 463-4, 467-8, 472-3, 476-7
Sagi, Avi 192, 224, 250, 252, 265, 273
Salmon, Moshe 471-2
  Netiv Moshe 471
sanctity 194, 388, 390-1, 395-6, 400, 406, 517
Satan 46-8, 50, 66-9, 87, 100, 112-13, 118
Schechter, Joseph 329
Schechter, Solomon 326, 363
Schiller, Friedrich 119
Schimmel, Solomon 183-5
Schirmann, Jefim 427-8, 450
Schleiermacher, Friedrich 522, 534, 544
Schneerson, Menachem Mendel 121, 358-9, 383
Schneerson, Shalom Dov Ber 382
Schneerson, Shmuel 381
Schneerson, Yosef Yitzhak 382
Scholem, Gershom 297-8, 304, 309, 327, 331, 354, 362, 364
  Major Trends in Jewish Mysticism 362
Schopenhauer, Arthur 489, 497
Schweid, Eliezer 245

science 112, 134, 138, 140, 143, 161, 163, 172-4, 190, 194-6, 199, 209, 261, 353, 363, 390, 474, 490, 538, 554
  philosophy of 514, 521, 542
scientific determinism 307, 361-2
secularism 137, 159, 171, 177-8, 186, 213, 239
  radical 14
  secularization 227, 485
  Zionism as secular movement 78
Segal, Aaron 157, 176, 181, 187
self 8, 108, 121, 208, 237, 300, 332, 356, 429, 485, 516, 525, 531, 533, 538, 546-54, 557-61, 564-7, 571-83
  corporal 320
  fragmentation of 547-8, 553, 579
  modernist 545-6, 548, 575-6
  unity of 545, 553, 559
self consciousness 33, 121, 357, 428-31, 439, 456, 552
self-criticism 89, 112-4, 118-20, 419
self-knowledge 24, 182, 218-20, 356, 371
self-negation 94-8, 355, 429
self-preservation 152
self-restraint 29, 33
self-understanding 24, 516, 546, 571, 574, 581
sense 24, 106, 130-1, 193, 197, 202n25, 207, 211-2, 216, 219, 234, 249, 254, 375, 391, 405, 407, 409, 472, 483, 493, 523
  nonsense 195, 200, 234
Shagar; see Rosenberg, Shimon Gerson
Shakh 78
Shapira, Zvi Elimelech 25-7
Shaul Israeli 43
Shekhinah 30, 40, 237, 308, 314-15, 317-18, 320-4, 341-2, 364, 501-5, 508-12
Shichor, Rachel 264

Shlonsky, A. 486
Shoah 245-6, 251, 266
Shteif, Yehonatan 464-5
  Mitzvot Hashem 464-5
signs and wonders 64, 408-9
Simha Bunem of Pryzucha 358
sin 12-3, 27-9, 37, 40, 65-6, 69, 75-7, 102-4, 122-3, 242-3, 257, 263, 274-6, 304-7, 380, 425-6, 496
  of Adam 108-9
  of Korah 26
  original 375, 445
Sinai; see Mount Sinai
skepticism 110, 141, 145, 156, 161, 185, 334, 422, 471
Smolenskin, Perez 488
  Hato'e Bedarchei Hachayim 488
Sofer, Moshe 75-6
Solon 165
Soloveitchik, Joseph B. 9, 96, 146-7, 166, 170, 172-4, 224-5, 242, 246-55, 260, 262-3, 267-8, 273-4, 421, 448, 513-44
  And From There You Shall Seek 513-6, 518, 520-1, 524, 526, 529, 533, 538, 541-3
  "Confrontation" 173
  Family Redeemed 525
  Halakhic Man 96, 513, 515, 521, 535
  Halakhic Mind, The 147, 174, 535
  Kol Dodi Dofek 247, 251, 515, 517
  Lonely Man of Faith 513-20, 522, 524, 526, 529, 532, 534-5, 538-9, 541-3
  "On Mental Health" 242, 247-8, 251-2
  Out of the Whirlwind 514
  "Sacred and Profane" 535
song
  song of the grasses 399-401, 403, 405, 409, 416
  Song of Songs 321, 449, 455, 501, 510, 511

Verses of Song (Pesukei de-Zimrah) 393, 396
Spain 418-19, 423, 425, 427, 433-5, 444, 449, 455
Sperber, Dan 148
Spinoza, Benedict de 69-70, 245, 307, 555
  Tractatus Theologico-Politicus 307, 555
spiritual trial; *see* trial, spiritual
St. John of the Cross 33-4, 86
  Dark Night of the Soul, The 86
Stein, Batya 12
Sternherz, Nathan 352
Strauss, Leo 144
symbolism 16-7, 181, 190-1, 193-4, 205, 230, 289, 290, 319, 358, 377, 404n41, 493, 501-2, 545, 553

T

Talmud 13, 39, 42-3, 48, 67, 72, 143, 256, 276, 295, 297, 311-12, 325, 349, 395
Taylor, Charles 546
Teichtal, Yissakhar Shlomo 461-2, 466-7, 475-6
  Tov Yig'al 461
Teitelbaum, Moses 360
temptation 13-4, 20-1, 28, 34-8, 57-8, 84-7, 113, 472
  faith as 15-19, 22-27, 30-1, 38, 41, 45-9, 52-6, 60, 71-4, 78, 80-2, 87-90, 95, 101-4, 122
  God as tempter 60-3, 66-70, 75, 78, 93, 102, 113
  internal (inner urge) 38
  ritual as 38, 40
theology 74, 103, 126, 130, 210, 218, 221, 223, 227, 230, 238-9, 300, 331, 368
  contemporary 191, 199
  liberal 192, 209
  negative 222n57

Thiessen, Elmer 141-2, 152
Thou 534, 539
  I-Thou 132, 533, 540
Tillich, Paul 65, 84-5, 544
Torah study 22-3, 35-6, 134, 330, 332, 339, 342, 467
torat ha-nistar 395
Transcendental Ego 557
trial 62-3, 86-7, 242, 385-6
  of faith 60, 217, 384
  spiritual 57-8, 478
trial of Abraham 59
tsaddik 83, 113-4, 311-3, 321-2, 324, 337, 342, 345-52, 357, 359, 362-4, 467, 470-1
Tsemach, Adi 510

U

Uffenheimer, Rivka Shatz 21
Uncle Tom's Cabin 175
Unger, Abraham 162
United Nations 251
Urbach, Simcha Bonim 498
utopia 128

V

Valabregue-Perry, Sandra 279-80, 286, 293, 298
Van Orman Quine, Willard 160
Vidas, Elijah, 346
  Reshit Hokhmah 346, 348
Vilnius Gaon 464
visions 71, 124, 221, 236, 238, 324, 330, 391, 407, 415, 488, 491, 493, 495-7, 524, 535
Vital, Hayyim 413
  Sha'arei Kedushah 413
Volozhin 37, 501-2

W

Waltersdorff, Nicholas 202
Weil, Simone 34, 81-2
Weinberg, Yaakov Yehiel 96

Weiss, Joseph G. 302-3, 317, 326, 330-1, 352-3, 382
Weiss, Yosef 110, 302, 326, 352, 354, 382
"*Qushiyah* in Rabbi Nachman's Teachings, The" 353
Werman, Naomi 415
will
  freedom of 102-5, 235, 263, 366, 550, 575, 578
  of God 29-30, 50, 59-60, 96, 101, 113, 243, 255, 274, 419, 552
  to believe 197-8, 228, 550-1, 557-8
Wittgenstein, Ludwig 162, 194-5, 199-200, 203
Wurzburger, Walter 181

Y

Yerushalmi, Yosef Hayyim 180
  Zakhor 180
Yisrael Friedman of Ruzhin *see* Rizhiner
Yitzhak Arama 63
Yosef Yahalom 424
  Ganzei Leningrad 424n14, 451
Yosl Rakover 266-7, 270-1

Z

Zalman, Shneur 233, 313, 329-30, 346, 368-73, 375-81, 383
  Sha'ar ha-Yihud ve-ha-Emunah 370, 379
Zechariah 453
Zeitlin, Aaron 499
Zeitlin, Hillel 363, 486-95, 497-9
  Kitzur Toldotai 489, 498
  Thirst, The 487, 491
Zelda 384, 387-91, 393-6, 398, 400-3, 406-7, 409, 411-16
  ars poetica 384, 391, 410, 412, 415
  "Good Smell of Distances, The" 410, 415
  hasidic roots in poetry of 388-9, 393n17, 395, 398, 406-7, 411
  "I Am a Dead Bird" 392, 398
  mystical elements 395, 398
  "With My Grandfather" 384, 409
Zion 419, 426, 443, 447, 452-3
Zionism 78; *see also* religious Zionism
Zivan, Gili 224
Zondel, Hanokh 68
  Ets Yosef 68
Zweifel, Eliezer Zvi 326, 363

www.ingramcontent.com/pod-product-compliance
Lightning Source LLC
Chambersburg PA
CBHW070744020526
44116CB00032B/1921